1001 ESCAPES
TO EXPERIENCE BEFORE YOU DIE

GENERAL EDITOR **HELEN ARNOLD**

PREFACE BY **CATHERINE FAIRWEATHER**
TRAVEL EDITOR, *HARPER'S BAZAAR*

← *Enjoy a relaxing trip down the Nile by felucca and soak up the atmospheric landscape.*

A Quint**essence** Book

First published in Great Britain in 2009 by Cassell Illustrated
A division of Octopus Publishing Group Limited
2–4 Heron Quays, London E14 4JP
An Hachette Livre UK company
www.octopusbooks.co.uk

ISBN: 978-1-84403-675-2
QSS.ESCA

2009 2010 2011 / 10 9 8 7 6 5 4 3 2 1

This book was designed and produced by
Quint**essence**
226 City Road
London EC1V 2TT
www.1001beforeyoudie.com

Project Editor	Chrissy Williams
Editors	Philip Contos, Rob Dimery, Becky Gee,
	Lucinda Hawksley, Fiona Ploughman
Editorial Assistant	David Hutter
Art Director	Akihiro Nakayama
Designer	Rod Teasdale, Dean Martin
Editorial Director	Jane Laing
Publisher	Tristan de Lancey

Colour reproduction by Pica Digital Pte Ltd., Singapore.
Printed in China by SNP Leefung Printers Ltd.

Contents

Preface

By Catherine Fairweather

You're high up in a tree house attempting mediation techniques in a jungle canopy where, later, the parrots will roost and howler monkeys rest. This particular eyrie, looking out across seven sacred hills in the forgotten heart of Sri Lanka, is Ulpotha. It is an untouched landscape, a prelapsarian paradise beyond the reach of cellphone reception, and miles away from the constant "white noise" of urban life. There is no electricity and no hot water, but you can shower beneath waterfalls, swim in a lake through lotus blossom and butterflies, and go to bed with the glow of the oil lamps and fireflies. An hour passes in the bat of an eye. The scent of citronella and queen of the night fills the air. The peace and quiet is so complete you can hear the blood pumping in your ear and the pulsating of your own heart. When were you last offered such a chance to do nothing, to chew the cud, to simply "be?" When did you last let your guard down enough to lose yourself, reconnect with yourself, or become someone different altogether? With only a banana leaf for shelter, ants for entertainment, and a string of cowrie shells for worry beads, you have managed to pare down the physical and emotion clutter of your life to this.

The allure of places like Ulpotha and many of the other escapes in this book is, precisely, that they offer this kind liberating respite from routine, a break from the sometimes humdrum familiarity of everyday life. They cast a spell which lingers long after the smell of incense or suntan oil has been washed out of the sarong, offering the perfect antidote to the frenzied pace and pressure of modern life.

For many of us, the notion of escape entails shifting down a gear and savoring the art of "slow." The perfect example is a gentle kayak on the Yukon River, and getting the hang of the repetitive, meditative rhythm of the paddle and settling into the mellow pace of pottering around the network of sheltered coves and inlets. Imagine yourself under full moon, setting a course across a phosphorescent sea, when you spot a stag swimming in your wake, antlers proudly aloft, or an orca beneath your boat, breaking the treacly surface of the water in a graceful pirouette. Such moments offer glimpses of the eternal, all the more precious in our increasingly, spiritually-impoverished lives.

The very sedate pace of many of the journeys in the book encourages you to take stock, to pause, reflect, and make a reconnection with the spiritual and natural world. To spend time on a felucca languidly drifting down the Nile, to chug gently on a train through the Australian outback or to punt slowly through the flood plains of the Okavango in a dug-out canoe or mekoro allows you space and time to really get under the skin of a place and a culture. The only thing to happen swiftly is the metamorphosis from stressed out to blissed out.

But whether your notion of escape embraces a reconnection with your inner self or a total departure from it, this book also celebrates the vital element of fantasy, which sets so many of these journeys, hotels, and retreats apart. I am as inspired by the excessive flights of fancy that go into creating the architectural folly that is the gilded Burj Al Arab in Dubai, as I am by the driftwood creativity of an Evason Hideaway or the fairy tale allure of sleeping in a yurt. They are all escapes that awaken the senses, kick-start the jaded palate, and represent the antithesis of home.

The temptations are all here in the pages of this book. We have long moved on from the notion that "getting away from it all" means a piña colada, a beach, and a T-shirt to prove you were there, but with time being an increasingly precious commodity, it is more important now than ever to make those breaks resonate and ring true.

This collection of toothsome images and descriptions of undulating dunes, rippling shorelines, and flirting palms is certainly nectar for the soul, but on a lighter note is also a diverting indulgence which is perfect to dip into at bedtime or bath time, or as a distraction on the commuter train. We all need to dream. So even if you never make it to the mythical portals of the Gazelle D'Or, or fail to embark on that hike you promised yourself up the Vikos Gorge, sometimes just knowing that places like this still exist in the world is reassurance and wish-fulfilment enough.

Catherine Fairweather

Catherine Fairweather, London

Introduction

By Helen Arnold, General Editor

Key to Symbols

 Tented

 Lodge/Small Hotel

 Rental Property

 Hotel

 Spa/Meditation

 Journey

 Mountain

 Water

 Island

 Beach

 Parkland/Garden

 City

 Outstanding Food

Natural Beauty

Cultural Interest

❶	Free
⑤	£1–60
⑤⑤	£61–300
⑤⑤⑤	£301–700
⑤⑤⑤⑤	Over £700

The dizzying pace of twenty-first-century life and state-of-the-art technology means that you are never more than a phone call or email away from the office, making it increasingly difficult to escape from the pressures of the modern world. However hard you try to get away, your cell phone rings and everyone wants a piece of your time. It's hardly surprising, then, that sometimes we just want to escape from it all.

In this book we've decided to focus on the decidedly relaxing. From a yogi retreat in the Himalayas to a remote Scottish hideaway, a tranquil garden in the middle of a bustling city to the cool and calm of a church in the heat of summer, we've concentrated on escapes that are contemplative, tranquil, relaxing, meditative, or spiritual. We've left out the adrenaline-busting, nerve-shredding, thrill-a-minute type of escapes for another time. However, that's not to say that the escapes we've included in this book are dull and pedestrian—far from it. There is plenty of variety in these escapes to provide a calming respite from reality. What could be more chilled out than snorkeling in the crystalline waters off the balmy coast of Belize, among the manta rays and marine turtles, or ambling on horseback through the perfumed orange and lemon groves in Andalucia?

Thirty or forty years ago it would have been financially impossible for the average person to visit remote destinations such as Bhutan or Bengal. However, the growth of discount airlines and the increased number of routes have opened up parts of the world that were formerly the preserve of the very rich or those with plenty of time on their hands—or both.

All the escapes selected for this book offer a chance to get away from the mundane, the everyday, and the routine, and provide an opportunity to relax and recharge your batteries in beautiful, unfamiliar surroundings and return home relaxed, rested, and with renewed vim and vigor.

Looking around the world, there's a huge variety of relaxing places to stay. Canada, for example, has some wonderfully remote lighthouses where you can hole up far away from the crowds. Check into Quirpon Lighthouse Inn on Quirpon Island, a tiny speck of land to the north of Newfoundland, which is completely deserted save for the two fully and lovingly restored lightkeeper residences. There are also some amazing hotels included in the book, from world class hotels with Michelin-starred restaurants such as Le Manoir in the depths of the English countryside, or the iconic Peninsula Hotel in Hong Kong, to simpler properties such as the homely Sonderho Kro in Denmark converted from former fishermen's cottages. We've also included rather less conventional accommodations, such as the stunning

Ice Hotel in Sweden, sculpted entirely out of ice, and a tree house at the appropriately named Tranquil Resort in Kerala, India. While they offer varying levels of comfort and luxury, rest assured they are all laid back and lovely and you simply won't want to leave.

France has an amazing selection of former chateaux that have been converted into hotels, enabling you to live out your Louis XIV fantasies to the fullest, from the imposing eighteenth-century Chateau Lasalle deep in rural Gascony to Chateau de Montriou in the Loire Valley, while Portugal has an equally impressive collection of *paradors*—former castles, palaces, fortresses, and monasteries now converted into stunning accommodations. The U.K. is bursting at the seams with ancient country-house hotels filled with faded chintz, labradors snoozing in front of crackling log fires, and butlers bearing the perfect gin and tonic. Marrakech in Morrocco is renowned for its beautiful *riads*, converted townhouses that provide a welcome oasis from the surrounding alleyways. Riad El Fenn is one of the most sumptuous, but there are hundreds of others to suit all budgets.

An increasing health-conscious world population and the growing recognition of the link between mind and body means that spa breaks have never been so popular. No longer the preserve of pampered princesses and bored housewives, spas are now attracting greater numbers than ever before. Few new hotels open nowadays without the requisite spa. But the health retreats described in this book are more than simply a whirlpool tub and a dingy treatment room tacked on to a new-build as an afterthought. These are sublime, relaxing refuges where you can succumb to the ministrations of experienced therapists and drift off into a state of blissful relaxation, or experience healing and invigorating treatments that target specific problem areas. For the ultimate in pampering, head for Chiva Som in Thailand, or Ananda in the foothills of the Himalayas. Those who prefer something a bit more puritanical to kick-start a healthy lifestyle might want to check into the Spartan, but brutally effective, Mayr & Mohr spa in Austria.

For the ecology-conscious there are also some great eco-lodges and environmentally friendly retreats to visit. Central America in particular seems to be blazing a trail in this area, offering a wide selection of eco-lodges. From Nitun Reserve, deep in the heart of the Guatamalan rain forest where you can take fascinating wildlife treks, to Morgan's Rock Hacienda and Eco-lodge in Nicaragua where you can saddle up one of the horses and ride along the Pacific, you're spoiled for choice. Costa Rica has countless eco-lodges, but those listed in this book are something special.

El Silencio, for example, boasts not only impeccable green credentials, but is also utterly luxurious, while La Cusinga Lodge doesn't simply pay lip service to environmental concerns; all of the lodge's cabins and furniture have been made using wood grown on site in a sustainable plantation.

However, not all of our escapes are sedentary. One of the best ways to get to know a place is by walking. While some of the stunning routes we've included are more taxing than others, there's no reason why you can't pick up a route midway, or pick and choose how much of a walk you do. From the famed pilgrims' route to Santiago Compostela in northern Spain, where you will be following in the well-trodden footsteps of pilgrims from centuries ago, to the wild and beautiful but decidedly unromantically named GR20 walk in Corsica, where you're unlikely to bump into another soul for days, a walk is the perfect way to clear your mind of worries and sink exhausted but happy into bed for a dreamless sleep. In fact, the great outdoors and nature offer a wide variety of different terrains and climates where you can escape from it all. Go camel riding in the shifting sands of the Dubai desert, snorkeling in the azure Caribbean Sea off Peter Island, or bicycling down Haleaka volcano in Hawaii; admire the surreal, stunning Perito Moreno Glacier in Argentina; gaze wonderingly at the dancing Northern Lights; or simply enjoy flopping, Robinson Crusoe-style, on a deserted beach on Bora Bora.

Africa is the place to head to if you like your wildlife raw and untamed. And banish any thoughts of camping boy-scout style. While you can choose to rough it, there is now a great selection of luxury camps where you can enjoy getting back to nature without having to sacrifice your creature comforts. Some of the best include the Selous Project in Tanzania, where you can escape the hordes of tourist-packed jeep convoys in a private nature reserve, or Singita Faru Faru Lodge in the heart of the Serengeti, a perfect location to view the epic annual migration of more than a million wildebeest. Chiawa in Zambia is an award-winning retreat that oozes luxury yet still manages to meld beautifully into the landscape, and it is particularly known for its canoeing safaris.

There's something undeniably soothing about the sound of water, be it the crashing of the waves on a beach or the gentle plop of an oar as you paddle your way along a waterway. Try out a floating hotel in Sweden, go canoeing along the Ardeche in France, go kayaking on the Yukon in Canada, or visit an underwater hotel in Florida where you need to don a scuba-diving kit to reach your room. Alternatively, enjoy the waters in Evian in France,

renowned for their health-giving properties, or in Bath in England, where for centuries aristocrats descended upon this beautiful town to benefit from the health-giving waters. Or, you can soak in one of Iceland's geothermal hot springs, where the warm water works wonders on aching muscles.

If you want to sit back and relax as the world passes effortlessly before your eyes, we've also included some of the world's most spectacular train rides, from the epic Trans-Siberian route in Russia to the Kuranda Railway in tropical Queensland, Australia. For a different perspective, try gently drifting over the rugged landscape of Cappadoccia in central Turkey in a hot-air balloon, seeing the Egyptian sights from the luxury of a Nile cruise, or take a leisurely drive through California's scenic Big Sur.

Whether you eat to live or live to eat, for many people eating and drinking is one of the central pleasures of visiting new places. France is still renowned as one of the world's gastronomic centers, which is why some of the French escapes focus on food and drink. Go wine tasting in the Loire, sample Armagnac in Gascony, sip champagne in the musty vaults at Reims, or enjoy a Michelin-starred dinner at the Oustau de Baumaniere in Provence. Gastronomes and vinophiles will find themselves transported to food heaven. But France is not the only country to offer food-related escapes. You can taste Madeira on the eponymous island where it is made; eat delicious organic food at Petersham Nurseries, a Bohemian garden center in London; and enjoy Michelin-starred cuisine at Le Quartier Français in the heart of South Africa's winelands.

If it's a temporary refuge from the hustle and bustle of city life you're looking for, where better to head than a leafy, verdant garden? The Jardin Majorelle in the heart of dusty Marrakech is an oasis of green, while the Plantem um Blumen garden in Hamburg, Germany, is a botanical bolthole, the perfect place to take some time out on a sunny day.

However, the ultimate escape has to be to outer space. Inhospitable, barren, and (as far as we know) uninhabited, it has to represent the absolute pinnacle in getting away from it all. Currently in its infancy, commercial space travel offers a very real escape from the world, for the brave—and for those with exceptionally deep pockets. With the price busting budgets of $200,000, who knows what will happen. Perhaps, in a few years' time, it may be as affordable as today's budget airlines.

I hope that this book manages to entertain, inspire, and encourage you to break away from the workday and the routine, and start planning your very own escape. Bon Voyage!

Index of Escapes

The variety of escapes available in North and South America is second to none. Whether it is an energizing dogsled trip across Canada, a pampered stay in a glamorous New York City hotel, a relaxing day on a remote Caribbean beach, a trip through the Amazonian rain forest, or an enlightening trip to an Argentinian vineyard, the Americas have it all.

The AMERICAS

← **Little Good Harbour, Barbados**

Canoe the Yukon River

Location Yukon, Canada **Website** www.touryukon.com;
www.naturetoursyukon.com **Price** 🌕🌕

Explore Dawson City

Location Yukon, Canada **Website** www.dawsoncity.ca
Price 🌓

You have just left the city of Whitehorse, but already you have the teal-green waters of the Yukon River to yourself. Above soars a pair of white-headed bald eagles. The only sound is the slosh and drip of your paddle as you glide along. You may even find yourself alone when you reach your campsite—save for the black and grizzly bears that inhabit the surrounding woods. Even in peak season, the Yukon River is a sparsely populated place.

It was not always so. As you pitch your tent, you will notice rusting artifacts from the Yukon's gold rush days, for this is Klondike country. The story goes that in the summer of 1896, a rich seam of gold was struck in the creeks of the Klondike River. The United States was in the grips of depression, and when miners carrying boxes of nuggets reached the outside world, they elicited a frenzied reaction. "GOLD! GOLD! GOLD! GOLD!" hollered the *Seattle Post Intelligencer* on July 17, 1897. "Sixty-eight Rich Men on the steamer Portland. Stacks of yellow metal." Around 100,000 dreamers headed north to seek their fortune. Many climbed over the Chilkoot Pass and White Pass, then built boats to paddle along these same waters, which bustled with stern-wheelers and wood camps until the 1950s, when the Klondike Highway was built. Today, you can still see the dilapidated ruins of one or two of those mighty boats, laid up on the shore.

As the world's cities have become ever more packed, this tiny corner of the globe has settled ever more blissfully into tranquility, a remote retreat ruled not by humans but by moose, wolves, and bears. **PE**

← *The fast-moving Yukon makes canoeing a joy. If you are feeling indolent, the river will do most of the work.*

Dawson is the town that sprang up in response to the Klondike gold rush of the late nineteenth century, and to this day it maintains an eccentric, Wild West vibe.

Hordes of hopefuls, including a young Jack London, abandoned the city slog and set off for the Klondike. Hardly any of them found their fortunes. Within a couple of years, the rush had moved on and Dawson's population began to decline. Nearly 40,000 people lived in Dawson in 1898; now there is a population of just 2,000. Somehow, though, it has retained its charm.

The buildings are in traditional style; raised wooden boardwalks line the roads. Tourists can hike and paddle the river, pan for gold in the creeks, or try their

---

"You can drink it fast, you can drink it slow. But the lips have gotta touch the toe."

Sourtoe Cocktail Club rule

---

luck at the casino, Diamond Tooth Gertie's. They tour the town, listening to its extraordinary stories, and chat with the colorful local characters. Brave souls can visit the Sourdough Saloon in the Downtown Hotel and order a "sourtoe cocktail"—a shot of whiskey garnished with a severed human toe (from a supply that have been dehydrated and preserved in salt). The first toe—the frostbitten digit of a man who smuggled bootleg booze over the border to Alaska during Prohibition—is sadly no longer. It had to be replaced after one over-enthusiastic drinker downed ten cocktails, fell backward off his bar stool, bumped his head, and swallowed the toe. **PE**

Stay at Inn on the Lake

Location Marsh Lake, Yukon, Canada **Website** www.exceptionalplaces.com **Price** 💲💲

On the shores of Marsh Lake, a little more than half an hour's drive from the Yukon's capital—Whitehorse—sits the log cabin retreat of Inn on the Lake. It's one of those places where your every whim seems to have been catered to before you'd even dreamed of it, and from the moment you step out onto the lodge's spacious deck (a glass of wine or a cold beer has already been pressed into your hand), you feel yourself sink into a deep relaxation.

Stretch out and soak up spectacular views over the snowcapped mountains, pristine forest, and crystal-clear lake, which freezes over in winter. If this seems insufficiently arduous, why not grab the binoculars and birding field guide that live on the windowsill and spot a loon or two while you sip a sundowner? In the evening, there is a four-course dinner, which guests eat together at a long table. During the summer there's fishing, kayaking, and canoeing on the lake, or hiking and mountain biking in the surrounding wilderness. Passes to the nearby golf course are included in the package. In winter, the Yukon days are crisp and skies are often blue. Guests can ski (cross-country, backcountry, and downhill are all on the menu), drive snowmobiles or dog teams, try their feet at snowshoeing—or their hands at ice fishing—and at night lie back in the hot tub and watch the northern lights dance green and red against black starry skies.

The lodge is open year-round, and accommodation is available both in the main house and in independent cabins. The biggest of the cabins comes complete with its own deck and hot tub, both of which face north, to guarantee the best views of the Aurora Borealis. Steal a few nights here during winter, and you can curl up for a romantic evening in the steamy waters while the northern lights fill the sky. **PE**

⬆ *A major attraction for visitors to the Inn on the Lake is the opportunity to see the magical northern lights.*

Dogsled Across the Yukon Territory

Location Yukon, Canada   **Website** www.muktuk.com; www.uncommonyukon.com; www.bluekennels.de   **Price** ⓈⓈ

It is silent out there, except for the rhythmic patter of husky paws on snow and the gentle creaking of the sled. Occasionally the dogs' heads pivot in unison to left or right—perhaps they have scented a flock of pure-white ptarmigan or a snowshoe hare amid the surrounding spruce trees. You may be able to spot a line of tiny wells in the powder, indicating that a wolf has walked this way before you. For you are traveling through one of the last remaining great wildernesses in the world. It is a territory larger than the state of California, yet one that only 31,000 humans call home. There are, however, 70,000 moose for company, along with considerable numbers of grizzly and black bears, caribou, wolverines, and Dall sheep.

You leave the forest trail and mush along the surface of a river. Evening is falling and a full moon rises high in the sky, casting a silvery light across this remote, bitterly beautiful land. Later, perhaps, the northern lights will dance across the starry night sky for you.

Afterward, you may find yourself under "The Spell of the Yukon," along with poet Robert Service: "Some say God was tired when He made it / Some say it's a fine land to shun; / Maybe; but there's some as would trade it / For no land on earth—And I'm one."

Visitors to the Yukon Territory can try their hand at dogsledding for anything from half a day to a week—or more. They can base themselves in comfortable accommodation at a kennel or can opt to camp with dogs along the extensive trails of the north. They can even, if they wish, watch how the experts do it and follow the course of the Yukon Quest, billed as "the toughest dogsledding race in the world." Inaugurated in 1984, it runs each February, when conditions are often at their harshest, for 1,000 miles (1,600 km) between Fairbanks, Alaska, and Whitehorse. **PE**

⬆ *Journey to the pristine heart of the Yukon wilderness with a loyal team of canine companions.*

Drive the Ice Road from Inuvik to Tuk

Location Northwest Territories, Canada   **Website** www.tuk.ca; www.inuvik.ca; www.explorenwt.com   **Price** 🟢🟢

Slowly, cautiously, you inch out of Inuvik and onto the winter road that is carved for 120 miles (193 km) into the ice of the Mackenzie River and then across the Beaufort Sea. It leads to the Inuvialuit settlement of Tuktoyaktuk, usually referred to simply as Tuk, which sits on the shores of the Arctic Ocean, at the most northerly limits of Canada.

The road is wide and smooth, like a skating rink. Contrary to your expectations, your surroundings are not all white. The sun reflects primrose yellow from the sheer ice. The snow, banked up to the sides, casts shadows of purplish blue. At first, weak little trees grow on the river's banks. Then they disappear and the landscape grows wide and flat.

In places, pingos push up from the earth. A little like giant molehills that stretch to more than 150 feet (45 m) in height, these formations were created when underground water was trapped, then frozen and subsequently expanded under the permafrost.

Finally, the river ends and you strike out across the ocean. Tiny spots of buildings appear in the distance. On and on you drive, through this vast expanse of frozen silence where perspective is thrown from all known proportions. You arrive on the main street of the village, where a schooner lies grounded—this boat once took local children to residential church schools. Farther along, the village cemetery's archway is inscribed, "Eternal rest grant to them, O Lord, and let perpetual light shine upon them." (Ironically, perpetual light at times shines on the living here, too, courtesy of the Midnight Sun, a feature of northernmost latitudes.) The light shines over a hodgepodge of crosses that looks across the muted pinks and purples of the Beaufort Sea. If one must perish, you consider, there can be few better spots to be buried than this. **PE**

⬆ *Plan your trip around the seasons: In summer, the road turns to river and there is no land access to Tuk at all.*

Unwind at King Pacific Lodge

Location Princess Royal Island, British Columbia, Canada **Website** www.kingpacificlodge.com **Price** ⊖⊖⊖

Canada's Great Bear Rainforest sweeps along British Columbia's Inside Passage and is more than twice the size of Yellowstone National Park. In the midst of all this unbroken, pristine wilderness, more than 150 miles (240 km) from the nearest paved road, is the King Pacific Lodge, a floating fishing lodge moored on the serene waters of Princess Royal Island's Barnard Harbor, home to black wolves, grizzlies, black bears, and a maximum of thirty pampered guests.

The flight there takes you over nothing but trees, lakes, and rivers, the lodge's isolation is genuine enough to lure A-listers such as actor Kevin Costner, who is a longtime devotee. Every spring this unique hotel is towed 100 miles (160 km) to the north, moved from its winter home in the coastal town of Prince Rupert to its summer surrounds on Princess Royal Island, where the lodge's seventeen rooms offer either wilderness or ocean views and access to everything that true wilderness is meant to be.

Humpback whales have been known to breach in the waters of Barnard Harbor just a few feet away from the lodge. Guests can kayak to uninhabited islands or take guided hikes to as-yet-unnamed peaks. If you're lucky, you may even be fortunate enough to see the rare Kermode "spirit bear"—a black bear with a recessive gene that gives it a white coat.

King Pacific Lodge sits on an old navy barge and was designed by a team of marine architects. A Toronto-based firm was responsible for the hotel's interior, which features furniture made from driftwood and unadorned wooden railings and overhead beams above Inuit tapestries hanging alongside paintings by local artists. Its hull contains freezers and coolers to store meat and fish, and vegetables are flown in weekly with the hotel's guests. **BS**

⬆ *The Great Bear rain forest behind King Pacific Lodge is a huge tract of undisturbed temperate wilderness.*

Relax at Knight Inlet Lodge

Location Glendale Cove, British Columbia, Canada
Website www.knightinletlodge.com **Price** ⊖⊖

Tucked away in picturesque Glendale Cove, 36 miles (60 km) from the mouth of Knight Inlet and accessible only by seaplane or boat, is Knight Inlet Lodge, a floating eco-lodge anchored beneath the glacier-fed waterfalls and temperate rain forests of the Coast Range, amid the largest concentration of grizzly bears in British Columbia. The lodge's twelve rooms are simple yet spacious and spread across a collection of buildings on the water's edge. They date from the 1940s; most rooms have either a king- or queen-size bed and a single bed, and all have private bathrooms. Meals in the large communal dining hall are first-rate and include Dungeness crab, salmon, and prime rib.

This is the place serious bear watchers come to see grizzlies and their newborn cubs in their natural habitats. Every April, the bears descend from their mountain dens into the streams and estuaries that empty into Knight Inlet to graze on the area's abundant berry crops and natural grasses. Viewing the bears takes different forms and varies from season to season, from standing offshore in lodge boats to venturing on land and using specially built tree stands; Knight Inlet Lodge works with hunters and the local community to restrict the practice of legal trophy hunting. The grizzly population depends on the yearly migration of Pacific salmon through the rivers, and the lodge also actively supports methods of sustaining the salmon population in the region's rivers.

The area is home to timber wolves, sea lions, otters, and bald eagles. Whale-watching tours featuring orcas, humpbacks, and minkes complete a smorgasbord of wildlife viewing that would satisfy the palate of even the most discriminating outdoor enthusiast. **BS**

Stay at Clayoquot Wilderness Resort

Location Vancouver Island, British Columbia, Canada
Website www.wildretreat.com **Price** ⊖⊖⊖⊖

Horseback riding, bear- and whale-watching trips, kayaking, trekking—these are just some of the activities available at Clayoquot Wilderness Resort, possibly North America's only luxury safari-style resort. This tented camp is surrounded by verdant rain forest; in 2000, the area, near British Columbia's Tofino, was designated by UNESCO as a Biosphere Reserve.

The twenty tents (twelve doubles and eight family-sized) offer lots of space and homey features, such as remote-controlled propane woodstoves, Adirondack furnishings, and an abundance of candles and kerosene lamps that muster up a wonderfully rustic

> *"Clayoquot Sound is a place of wonder, one whose beauty takes the breath away."*
>
> Jean Chrétien, former Canadian prime minister

atmosphere at night. The ranch cookhouse has a huge stone fireplace and an open kitchen where up to six diners can watch culinary maestros prepare the resort's famed delicacies. An area called The Healing Grounds boasts three cedarwood hot tubs, seawater baths, and four massage and treatment tents, plus a new spa building with two indoor treatment rooms for water therapies. Add in the exotic, untamed surroundings and wealth of wildlife and it's safe to say today's urban explorers have never had it so good. **PS**

➡ *Inspired by the late-nineteenth-century Great Camps, Clayoquot offers sophisticated comfort in the wild.*

Canoe at Poets Cove

Location Vancouver Island, British Columbia, Canada   **Website** www.poetscove.com   **Price** ⊖

The romantically named Poets Cove, southwest of Pender Island, is shielded from the ocean's swell by Canada's Vancouver Island, creating a calm and quiet inlet where time seems to stands still. With forty-six quaint yet modern vacation cottages, most of which feature hot tubs on the deck, it is an ideal place to get away from it all and breathe in nature. And as the majority of the local population is in North Pender, the southern part is almost uninhabited.

Take a ferry from the mainland across the Strait of Georgia—or even better, take a propeller seaplane. With around a hundred mooring rings, the marina at Bedwell Harbor has become famous among the wealthy Seattle-based yachting crowd. A hot destination for fishing, boating, and scuba diving, it is at its best in low season, when taking a canoe to the waters effectively means having the bay to yourself. Wrap up warmly in waterproof gear before venturing straight from the deck onto the bay, out onto the

glimmering water, lying as still and flat as an oil slick. The first paddle strokes send ripples out as far as the eye can see. It is so silent, it is almost eerie. Gathering speed very quickly, without having to struggle against any waves, it is difficult to believe you are on the Pacific. But you are, so be sure to keep an eye out for killer whales twice the size of your canoe.

Follow the coastline, gliding gracefully, and take in the panorama with its stunning wooden log cabins and giant designer houses. Carry on north toward the Pender Island Bridge, passing below to get to Mortimer Spit, a steep hill covered in dense forest. Paddling alone on the incredibly blue waters, moving past remote deserted beaches, and being utterly at one with nature offers a serene and almost magical way to see the really great outdoors. **RCA**

⬆ *Two canoeists glide gently into the twilight, the bay to themselves, on the calm waters of Poets Cove.*

Drive the Icefields Parkway

Location British Columbia, Canada   **Website** www.icefieldsparkway.ca   **Price** $

Nestled in the majestic Canadian Rocky Mountains, the south-to-north highway route linking Jasper to Lake Louise near Banff is an area of outstanding natural beauty. Dubbed the Icefields Parkway, it is just that: a route through the frozen landscape. Following the Continental Divide, it crosses the rugged landscape of the National Parks of Jasper and Banff and stretches 143 miles (230 km), offering an unbroken supply of breathtaking vistas.

Leaving the small ski town of Jasper behind, it soon becomes apparent that a four-by-four vehicle is crucial. With temperatures hovering around the -10°F (-25°C) mark, everything is covered in a blanket of fresh snow with a deliciously crisp and crunchy cool layer of ice. Said to be one of the world's most spectacular mountain highways, the Icefields Parkway was completed in 1940 and is open year-round, although in winter the few buildings along the route, including the solitary gas station, are shut.

Although the speed limit appears a little slow at 55 miles per hour (90 kph), the road is fraught with danger. Roads are snow-packed, covered in slush, and sometimes patched with ice, making for treacherous conditions. Prepare wisely before setting out: Fill up with gas, take supplies, get a national parks permit, and wear cozy thermal underwear.

Follow the Sunwapta and Athabasca rivers up to Tangle Ridge via the Montane Forest. Keep an eye out for bighorn sheep, elk, caribou, moose, or even grizzly and black bears that roam freely through the park's trees and dense snow. The all-white scenery is overwhelming, and the Columbia Icefields, Bow and Crowfoot glaciers, Athabasca Falls, and Peyto Lake are awesome. Locals boast about the 33 feet (10 m) of snowfall every season, and it is easy to believe. **RCA**

⬆ *The Icefields Parkway is your passport to a humbling world of breathtaking, sparkling landscapes.*

Visit Eagle's Eye Suites

Location Kicking Horse Mountain, British Columbia, Canada
Website www.kickinghorseresort.com **Price** 💲💲

The champagne powders of Kicking Horse Mountain in British Columbia cover more than 2,700 skiable acres (1,090 ha), with over one hundred ski runs and seventy inbound chutes. Presiding over it all at an altitude of 7,700 feet (2,345 m) above the town of Golden at the confluence of the Rocky, Purcell, and Selkirk mountains are the aptly named Eagle's Eye Suites. Winner of Ski Canada's Best Private Mountain Chalet award and Best On-Mountain dining in Canada's highest restaurant, Eagle's Eye is complemented by an oversized log fire, floor-to-ceiling windows, and a 360-degree view of the surrounding mountain peaks.

From Kicking Horse Resort a leather-lined VIP gondola complete with surround sound and a glass of wine will keep you warm as you ascend to your boutique hideaway. Exclusivity is the key ingredient at Eagle's Eye Suites. You are greeted by attentive hotel staff who will wrap you in fleecy blankets as they lead you to one of only two suites, aptly named Sunrise and Sunset, which beckon you with soaker tubs, private balconies, heated bathroom floors, and an around-the-clock personal valet service.

Waking up on the summit guarantees you can be the first to descend mountain slopes every bit as steep as those in Jackson Hole and Whistler, with endless route options once the sole preserve of heli-skiers. If you are not the skiing type, visit in the summer months and see the nearby Kicking Horse Mountain Grizzly Bear Refuge—the world's largest enclosed habitat. Hiking is popular, too, from twenty-minute jaunts to the six-hour haul via Dogtooth Ridge to the Gorman Lake area. **BS**

◀ *Be the first to welcome the sunrise—while relaxing in the lap of luxury—in mountaintop Eagle's Eye Suites.*

Go Ice Walking in Jasper

Location Jasper National Park, Alberta, Canada
Website www.pc.gc.ca/pn-np/ab/jasper **Price** 💲

In summer, the canyons of the Rocky Mountains are filled with foaming, rushing rivers that are deathly in their speed. However, in winter, these waters stop still. Waterfalls no longer tumble, but turn to white ice that drips like a vast candle frozen in time. Visitors can easily explore this winter wonderland on an ice walk.

Various companies offer guided ice walks within Jasper National Park; they provide rubber boots and ice cleats. One of the most popular treks is through Maligne Canyon. Here, the canyon's walls soar almost a hundred feet (30 m) above the floor and torrents of solid ice, created by an underground water system that seeps through the limestone walls of the canyon

---

"Each footstep can send sounds of crushing ice softly echoing off the walls above the group."

John Korobank, journalist

---

and freezes, plunging from rocky outcrops like enormous stalactites. Beneath them, rippling statues have formed in otherworldly shapes. Intricate alabaster curtains cover solitary grottoes; gleaming ice walls hide caverns and crannies. It is not all white: In places, the ice is turquoise, blue, or the palest jade green, and always, from hour to hour, it is changing.

The routes on ice walks tend to be around 2 miles (3.2 km) long and are even suitable for children, who particularly enjoy slithering down natural ice slides. Most operators require that participants be at least six or seven years old; some also offer evening tours where you walk by the light of a headlamp. **PE**

Stay at Fairmont Chateau

Location Lake Louise, Alberta, Canada
Website www.fairmont.com/lakelouise   **Price** $$

Conceived by the Canadian Pacific Railway (CPR) in the late nineteenth century, this impressive hotel on the shore of Lake Louise, two hours' drive west of Calgary in the Canadian Rocky Mountains, has one of the world's great mountain-and-lake vistas virtually all to itself.

Known to locals as the Diamond in the Wilderness, this pioneering hotel began as a humble log cabin in 1890, providing accommodation for fifty clients in its first twelve months. Some 120 years later, the emerald-green waters of Lake Louise and the majestic Victoria Glacier have not changed much, but the log cabin now has 552 sumptuous guest rooms and seven restaurants all styled with the past firmly in mind.

> *"As God is my judge, I never in all my explorations saw such a matchless scene."*

Thomas Wilson, CPR employee, 1882

Carved timbers and exquisite detailing echo the Arts and Crafts style, and historic photographs, antique chandeliers, and documents hark back to the days when British royalty treated it as a second home.

The Louise Lakeshore Trail, one of the most popular hikes in the Rockies, begins in front of the château and winds its way up the western shoreline of the lake. There are also kayaks available to sail Lake Louise's languid waters and affording views back across the lake to this iconic Canadian landmark. **TM**

← *Awe-inspiring views of the lake and surrounding mountains come with a room at Fairmont Chateau.*

Unwind in Log Cabins at Baker Creek Chalets

Location Canadian Rockies, Alberta, Canada
Website www.bakercreek.com   **Price** 💲💲

"The Rockies seem to double in size presenting incredible scenic vistas."

Proprietors, Baker Creek Chalets

For a real remote log-cabin experience, you can't beat the Canadian Rockies. Surrounded by the forest, heavy with fresh snow, there's something reassuringly safe about being holed up inside. Steer clear of the bigger resorts like Whistler and make a beeline for the stunning rocky peaks of Lake Louise in Banff National Park, Alberta. The resort, where the likes of Robbie Williams and Bruce Willis have whooshed through the powder, has a great choice of slopes for all and is known as the hiking capital of the Rockies.

With the season lasting from November to March, when the snow falls thick on the trails, the busiest times are around Christmas and New Year—although even then there isn't a line in sight. The ski season is considered low season, which means better rates and no crowds. Bright blue skies, crisp air, and very few people equal dream skiing conditions. Be warned, though: The temperatures can drop to -23.8°F (-31°C).

Keep warm in the family-run Baker Creek lodge, in a peaceful corner of a pine forest. The cozy trapper-style cabins are equipped with stone fireplaces, double whirpool tubs, and kitchens for total independence. If you don't want to cook, you can visit the Bistro restaurant, where gourmet game is the specialty.

Peeking out into the snow-covered forest every morning is like seeing a fairy-tale winter wonderland. Pine martens frolic, wapiti occasionally wander by, and unseen wolves roam. Get even closer to nature by trying your hand at dogsledding. Racing along the ice pulled by huskies is delightful, but even tucked under a blanket in the sled it's rather chilly. **RCA**

◪ *Enjoy a snowshoe walk in the woods or a hike around Lake Louise, then warm up in front of a cozy fire.*

Enjoy Cree Village

Location Moose Factory, Ontario, Canada
Website www.creevillage.com **Price** ⓢ

There is no easy way to reach the remote island of Moose Factory. No road mars the miles of sparkling rivers and pristine forest on the edge of the Arctic, just a single rail track that carries the Polar Bear Express from Cochrane to the frontier town of Moosonee. For the final short hop across the Moose River, take a river taxi that docks at the Cree Village Eco-lodge.

It is worth the effort. The first indigenous eco-lodge in the northern hemisphere, this is a twenty-first-century vision of a traditional Cree dwelling, made of pine and cedar with cathedral-like windows looking out over the Moose River. The environmental effect of every detail is carefully considered by the MoCreebec

---

"Join a sunset boat tour, watch the northern lights or spend time with a Cree elder."

Ode magazine

---

people, from natural-wool carpets and bedspreads to organic cotton sheets and biodegradable soap. This wilderness retreat feels like it is on the edge of the world. Take boat trips on the Moose River or across to the Tidewater Provincial Park to see eagles, ospreys, bears, and caribou. Head to James Bay to look for seals and beluga whales in season. Spend a day with members of the Cree tribe in this far-flung community to see how customs and traditions are being revitalized.

This is the ancestral land of the Cree, where previous generations danced and sang at powwows and the toughest men tracked moose on snowshoes for weeks on end in freezing temperatures. Who needs roads? **AD**

Experience Cap Jaseux

Location St. Fulgence, Québec, Canada
Website www.capjaseux.com **Price** ⓘ

The Saguenay Fjord, in southern Québec, is one of the world's longest and the only navigable fjord in North America; its near-vertical cliff faces boast an average elevation of almost 500 feet (150 m). One of Canada's great natural wonders, this is the dramatic backdrop for Parc Aventures Cap Jaseux, an outdoor world of rope bridges, organized aerial rope courses, kayaking, sailing, and rock climbing. At the end of a strenuous but fulfilling day, you can loosen your safety harness and retire to your own elevated tree house, furnished with bunk beds, a table and chairs, oil lamps, and panoramic views over the fjord and forest canopy.

Cap Jaseux is spread over a 450-acre (182-ha) forest of white birch, pine, and black spruce, near the town of St. Fulgence, and allows for extensive viewing of Saguenay Fjord's dramatic escarpments from an aerial vantage point. More than seventy elevated suspension bridges lead you through the forest canopy on a seemingly precarious but totally secure path from platform to platform, testing your skill and endurance, honing your ability to appreciate nature from a rare and unusual point of view—and always in the company of the park's experienced guides.

Metal ladders and fixed cables provide the basis of an exhilarating climbing route across the rock faces of the fjord. Less adventurous visitors can sail Saguenay's serene waters in a 25-foot (7.5-m) quillard. For a more strenuous activity, paddle a kayak over a three-hour course or take the daylong, 12-mile (20-km) route to the Cap au Leste lighthouse.

Many guests are content with Cap Jaseux's signature rope course, retiring to their tree house to await the nightly twilight excursion and reflect on the day's adventures in the glow of another Saguenay sunset. **BS**

Relax at the Hôtel de Glace

Location Sainte-Catherine-de-la-Jacques-Cartier, Québec, Canada   **Website** www.hoteldeglace-canada.com   **Price** 🟢🟢

"It's a cocoon that cuts you off from the rest of the world and its daily stresses."

Proprietors, Hôtel de Glace

⬆ *Sleeping overnight in a hotel room with a temperature of 23°F (-5°C) is a once-in-a-lifetime experience.*

➡ *Even a simple walkway in Canada's Hôtel de Glace glistens with sophisticated, icy beauty.*

Canada's Ice Hotel is playful and awe inspiring in equal measure—a genuine escape to a winter wonderland. Half an hour's drive west of Québec, the hotel is in the French-speaking province—hence Hôtel de Glace—and open for just three months a year, from January to the start of April. Given the way global warming is going, it is fair to say that your best bet is to be wary of the last couple of weeks of March.

The appearance of the hotel itself is immensely impressive, though its novelty chilliness might get to the more sensitive visitor. Thankfully, if your toes are not quite toasty enough, you can always decamp to the nearby Auberge Duchesny hotel. A visit here is not just about the hotel either. The surrounding area is a playground for those who like snow: dogsledding, snowmobiling, skiing, skating, and massages are all on offer, too. The hotel has been featured in *National Geographic*, on MTV, and in a number of glossy photo shoots, confirming that it is both an adventurous and fashionable choice.

The hotel is rebuilt every December to different specifications by a team of twenty builders using stainless steel molds. You can expect to see 4-foot-thick (1.2-m) walls and 2-foot-thick (0.6-m) ceilings—all the better to keep the cold out, apparently. Pelts cover ice chairs and ice beds, which are supplied with sleeping bags; rooms are carved with ice sculptures and filled with candles, and there is even a special ice chapel available for weddings.

In the Ice Bar, you can ask for shots in the rocks rather than on them—the glasses are made out of ice themselves—then you can dance the night away on the polished ice dance floor. Our fantasy playlist features Vanilla Ice, Ice-T, and Ice Cube, along with a whole host of chill-out classics. **LD**

Visit Cape D'Or Lighthouse

Location Cape D'Or, Nova Scotia, Canada
Website www.capedor.ca **Price** $

The view from the restaurant of Cape D'Or Lighthouse is, by any definition, a memorable one. Fifteen large glass windowpanes covering three walls of the restaurant look directly out over the Bay of Fundy, Cape Split, and Ile Haut with its 300-foot (90-m) cliffs, all the while watching the world's highest tides rise and fall and peregrine falcons in flight while dining on the freshest of fresh local seafood.

The first lighthouse on Cape D'Or was built in 1922, although the current concrete tower dates back to 1965. When the light was automated in 1989, the lightkeeper residence was converted into a bed-and-breakfast, which offers visitors the choice of staying in individual rooms or the option to take over the whole property.

The tower, lightkeeper residence, restaurant, and interpretive center preside over an ocean seemingly at war with itself. The rising and lowering of the tides here represents a movement of water comparable to the flow of all of Earth's rivers. To witness it is to see standing waves up to 10 feet (3 m) high churning in a frenzied tempest that has, over the eons, sculpted myriad rock shapes such as Hopewell Rocks in New Brunswick and the jagged beauty of Cape Split. Away from the coastline, soil rich in organic silt laid down by the formation of vast tidal flats is home to vineyards and apple orchards.

Talk to the locals and they will tell you it is the sunsets that gave this place its name. In French, Cape D'Or means "Cape of Gold," and every night as you gaze westward out across the frigid waters of the Bay of Fundy and run your eye across the peculiar hues the setting sun creates here, concerns evaporate, worry lines fade, and tranquility reigns. **BS**

Visit West Point Lighthouse

Location Prince Edward Island, Canada
Website www.westpointlighthouse.com **Price** $ $

West Point Lighthouse on the North Cape Coastal Drive, in the extreme southwestern tip of Prince Edward Island, was built in 1875 and is the tallest square lighthouse on the island. Designed in the style of the square, tapered, timber lighthouses that became popular along Canada's eastern seaboard in the late nineteenth century, it boasts distinctive broad, black striping and a gabled roof. It received a detailed and meticulous restoration by volunteers and began to offer overnight accommodation In 1984. Eight rooms, all with private baths, are now available in the old lightkeeper's inn, although the most popular room by far is on the second level of the lighthouse itself

"The lighthouse combines distinctive architecture, folklore, shipwrecks, and dramatic scenery."

Proprietors, West Point Lighthouse

with its high ceilings and windows that afford, as one would expect, unobstructed ocean views across the western entrance to Northumberland Strait.

A flight of stairs ascending the east wall allows visitors to climb to the top, where the distinctive red light continues to burn twenty-four hours a day. The Lighthouse Craft Guild next door operates a small gift shop and there is an on-site museum. On the third weekend of July each year, West Point Lighthouse hosts a lively lighthouse festival. **BS**

➡ *Originally built in 1875, an automated electric light was installed at West Point Lighthouse in 1963.*

Stay at Quirpon Lighthouse Inn

Location Quirpon Island, Newfoundland, Canada
Website www.linkumtours.com **Price** $ $

Quirpon Island, a tiny speck of land to the north of Newfoundland, is barely 2 miles (3.2 km) long. Peat bogs, spongy mosses, and tuckamore thickets cover the ground, while its cliffs rise to more than 200 feet (60 m) in height and cast long shadows over its coves and scattered, sandy beaches.

The island is now deserted, save for two fully restored lightkeeper residences turned inns, which can sleep up to twenty-five people in eleven rooms at the base of Quirpon Lighthouse. Handmade quilts adorn the walls, and there are no televisions or phones. It opens from May to September, coinciding with one of the world's great whale migrations.

The island is accessed via a forty-five-minute ferry ride from the fishing village of Quirpon on the Newfoundland coast across the narrow Strait of Belle Isle—a sort of nautical highway for any fish wanting to get from the Gulf of St. Lawrence to the North Atlantic. This wealth of whale food draws in minke, orca, and humpback whales that swim so near to the shoreline's deep waters that you can see them herding their feed toward the subterranean cliffs beneath you. Some guests have even reported being sprayed by the water from their spouts. The Strait of Belle Isle is also known as Iceberg Alley, part of a giant conveyer belt bringing icebergs from the glaciers of western Greenland.

When you have had your fill of dodging icebergs and being splashed by humpback whales, you can take the 3-mile (4.8-km) stroll past unexcavated Viking sod huts to the reconstructed Viking settlement at L'Anse aux Meadows—the first European community on North American soil, predating the arrival of Christopher Columbus by 500 years. **BS**

Stay at Cape Anguille Lighthouse Inn

Location Cape Anguille, Newfoundland, Canada
Website www.linkumtours.com **Price** $

Cape Anguille is a headland on the westerly tip of Newfoundland, overlooking the Gulf of St. Lawrence. It is a pristine world of ospreys and eagles, beluga and blue whales, and windswept meadows. The Cape Anguille Lighthouse and Light Keepers Residence is a forty-minute drive from the village of Port aux Basques. Construction on the inn and fog alarm buildings began in 1907, and on the tower the following year; in 1960, the tower and fog alarm building were replaced by the structures we see today. All three were listed as a Registered Heritage Structure in 2003. The residence is a split-level dwelling with a

> *"We … are certain that all hikers will find enjoyable terrain and spectacular views."*
>
> explorenewfoundland.com

combined kitchen, large pantry, and dining room downstairs, with four upstairs bedrooms that can be rented independently. Two rooms face the ocean and are only marginally more expensive than those facing the sheep-filled meadows out back.

The western shoreline of Newfoundland is a major north–south corridor for migrating birds, and sightings of a vast array of birdlife patrolling and nesting in the sea cliffs can be assured—including the endangered piping plover, of which fewer than 5,000 exist worldwide. For hikers, paths begin at the back gate and lead to the Starlite Trail that snakes its way up into the nearby Long Range Mountains. **BS**

Hike Along the Chilkoot Trail

Location Dyea, Alaska, U.S.A. to Bennett, British Columbia, Canada
Website www.nps.gov/klgo **Price** 🔵

Gold was discovered in the creeks of the Klondike River, near Dawson City in Canada's Yukon Territory, in August 1896. A few hopeful prospectors were already living in these parts; now they staked their claims and, cut off from the outside world by frozen rivers and icy wilderness, they worked all winter piling up the pay dirt. When, in May 1897, the ice on the Yukon River broke, some workers made their way to Seattle and San Francisco. The United States was in the depths of depression; the yellow nuggets carried by these grizzled miners set the public's imagination alight. Teachers left their classrooms; policemen walked off their beats. It is estimated that 100,000 men and women set out for the Klondike.

The most popular route was the Chilkoot Trail, a former Tlingit Indian trading route that ran from the Alaskan coast at Dyea to the lakes of Canada's British Columbia and Yukon Territory. It was tortuously steep and, fearful of a famine in Dawson, Canadian border regulations required that prospectors carried goods sufficient to last them a year. Those who could not afford porters spent months ferrying their supplies.

Today the trail falls within national park land, and hikers carry just one pack each. The trip takes between two and five days, and the scenery is extraordinary. The route starts in coastal rain forest, then ascends to the alpine, where glacial lakes glimmer turquoise and grizzly bears roam. Still today, rusting paraphernalia lies along the route—picks, shovels, and even collapsible boats discarded by desperate men more than a hundred years ago. The Chilkoot would be a remarkable hike if it were for the scenery alone. The history makes it a deeply poignant one, too. **PE**

Enjoy Afognak Wilderness Lodge

Location Kodiak Islands, Alaska, U.S.A.
Website www.afognaklodge.com **Price** 🔴🔴🔴

After a low flight across the Gulf of Alaska, over rocky coves and islets covered by spruce trees and small ponds, the tiny floatplane splashes into the calmness of Seal Bay, where the cluster of log cabins of Afognak Wilderness Lodge emerges into view. Surrounded by dense forest, streams, and fjords, the sheltered bay is protected from the worst of the Alaskan weather. The nearest neighbor is 15 miles (24 km) away.

Roy and Shannon Randall have created a self-sufficient wilderness paradise of considerable style and luxury on Afognak island. They generate hydro-electricity and grow their own vegetables, and their

> *"A State Park has been established to preserve this . . . stunningly beautiful 'enchanted' forest."*
>
> **Proprietors, Afognak Wilderness Lodge**

freezers are packed with local fish and game from which they produce wholesome, delicious meals. Each cabin is built from hand-hewn spruce logs, and is spacious, cozy, and furnished in elegant, rustic comfort. The views from the windows are mesmerizing, and can include pods of humpback or killer whales passing in the bay or even a brown bear on the doorstep.

The cabins are packed with creature comforts, but the creatures outside are invariably the main attraction. Wildlife watchers can expect to see a variety of animals including moose, wolves, brown bears, eagles, elk, deer, otters, porpoises, seals, and whales. Nature at its purest demands fitting appreciation. **ML**

Stay at the Inn at Langley

Location San Juan Islands, Washington, U.S.A.
Website www.innatlangley.com **Price** ⊖⊖

Just off the coast of Seattle, the San Juan Islands offer a calm haven where nature thrives. Located in the Puget Sound in the United States's unspoiled Pacific Northwest, the islands are a quick hop from Seattle or Vancouver, B.C. Each island has its own identity and charm. Whidbey Island is a popular whale-watching spot where the relaxed northwestern vibe rules: healthy living, the great outdoors, and taking it easy.

Prime time for whale watching is from May through September with both resident and visiting killer whales. The archipelago is also home to other wildlife such as eagles, Steller sea lions, and porpoises. This is a simple paradise for lovers of the great outdoors, with hiking, bicycling, fishing, boating, camping, and scuba diving on offer in a spectacular environment. Rest assured, unlike "rainy" Seattle, the islands have a "rain shadow" climate and benefit from around 250 days of sunshine a year.

Settle into the Inn at Langley, a charming twenty-six-room wooden inn overlooking the very scenic Saratoga Passage. With 180-degree views and cozy wooden outdoor porches on which to sit and ponder, the rooms also have a little indulgence: a hot tub with a view and an open fireplace. Food is also a priority, with the chef whipping up a six-course gourmet meal using fresh local ingredients on weekends; the muffins delivered to the room for breakfast are heavenly.

At sunrise, the waters are still, flat, and shimmering in the first rays of sunshine. It is at that moment that one understands the meaning of the word "silence." If a hard day's kayaking among the orcas is not for you, then relax at the Essencia Spa, or tuck in at the restaurant with its cozy double-sided river-rock fireplace and extensive wine cellar. **RCA**

Stay at Heceta Head

Location Heceta Head, Oregon, U.S.A.
Website www.hecetalighthouse.com **Price** ⊖⊖

For over a century, the lighthouse here has shone over the Pacific Ocean's notorious currents in the isolated area of Heceta Head. Now its solitude is the main reason for visiting: Surrounded by 40 miles (64 km) of Oregon dunes, it is a fine place to escape from it all.

Heceta Head is one of the last remaining lighthouse keeper's cottages on the Pacific coast. It was placed on the U.S. Registry of Historic Places in 1973. Since 1995, the Korgan family have been its innkeepers, looking after guests and the interior of this national treasure with equal care. As the waves break outside, best viewed from the Mariner I and Mariner II bedrooms, the sense of isolation is awe inspiring. With six queen bedrooms,

> *"Breakfast . . . proved to be splendid. There were seven courses in all, I believe—I lost count."*
>
> *New York Times*

the whole property can be rented, sleeping a total of fourteen guests in its cozy and historic interior. Sitting down for breakfast with one of the two lighthouse cats on your lap has to be the highlight of a stay here. Mike and Carol, who now run it, are both trained chefs and have created a breakfast that showcases the best of Oregon's ingredients. Expect artisanal cheeses, sausages, Carol's pastries, and freshly made frappés, served on Victorian-style sprigged plates and garnished with freshly picked herbs. **LD**

➡ *Heceta Head Lighthouse has been keeping ships off the rocks since 1894—and welcoming guests since 1973.*

Stay at Amangani

Location Jackson Hole, Wyoming, U.S.A.
Website www.amanresorts.com **Price** $$

High in the Rockies, on the doorstep of Yellowstone National Park, the jagged peaks of Wyoming's Teton range rise abruptly out of the valley. This is the bucolic idyll of Westerns. In winter, the valley is peppered with thousands of elk, which share their refuge with free-roaming bison, wolves, grizzlies, and mountain lions.

The inhabitants of Jackson Hole are pathologically outdoorsy. Winter's deep snows mean that if residents are not skiing or snowboarding, they are snowshoeing, mushing a dogsled, or ice skating. In summer, they join the hikers, bikers, kayakers, and fishers at nearby Yellowstone. Jackson Hole Mountain Resort has a cult skiing image, famed for its pristine conditions.

> *"For the mountain men, a 'hole' indicated a high valley that was surrounded by mountains."*
>
> **Jackson Hole Chamber of Commerce**

Amangani is the best place to savor this landscape. The view from here is so untouched it feels polar. In the early evening, the white world turns bluey-pink and the stark mountain peaks pierce the sunset; the perfect place to watch is in the chic lounge, or from the heated outdoor pool. The hotel is built from cedar and is designed to blend into its setting. High redwood ceilings are supported by vast Oklahoma sandstone columns that dip down to a lounge where skiers gather in the evening by the roaring fire. Each suite has views of snowy landscapes from a sunken bath. The 1970s retro minimalism of Amangani adds to the magic of this hidden valley. **LB**

Unwind at Home Ranch

Location Elk River Valley, Colorado, U.S.A.
Website www.homeranch.com **Price** $$$

Home Ranch is a passport back to the time of the American Wild West. Guests stay here to experience the traditional ranch vacation—no cell phones, no television, just pure 360-degree views of nature. The ranch is set in one of the United States' last alpine ranching valleys, the Elk River Valley, with 580 acres (235 ha) of aspen and evergreen forest, silver birch trees, wild deer, and soaring eagles, plus the wild Elk River running through it.

The luxury accommodation at the ranch consists of six comfortable rooms within the main house and eight private cabins, all of which have a hot tub in which to soothe your saddle-sore behind. Each day includes a variety of rides—some up into the wooded hillside for lunch, others working cattle in the pastures—as well as training in horsemanship and plenty of time to experience both the ranch and the natural delights of the Elk River Valley. As the sun sets, the campfire is stoked and cowboy nightlife is laid on for you. Afterward, you can curl up under your down comforter while the wood-burning stove rushes and keeps you warm all night.

Two things in particular make this place really special: the natural surroundings and the absolute lack of contact with the outside world. Simple pleasures, but oddly hard to come by today. It really does feel as though you have stepped back in time, into an era when being this close to Mother Nature was normal, and the modern scourges of cell phones and television were unknown and undreamed of. As you sit and watch the fire crackle in the evening, the sparks rise up to the starry sky just as they did a hundred years ago; when you sleep at night, all you will hear is the silence. Nature in the raw is a beautiful thing. **LD**

Relax at 63 Ranch

Location Elephant Head Mountain, Montana, U.S.A.
Website www.sixtythree.com   **Price** 🅢🅢

As you ride the trails above the ranch, a guide might tell you tales of wagon trains that followed trappers and prospectors through these hills 200 years ago. After one wagon train was attacked by Crow Indians, only one woman survived. Her mournful cries could be heard long after the battle. The Crow named the area "mountains where crazy woman lives." Today, they are still called the Crazy Mountains.

It may no longer be the Wild West in Montana, but the wooden corrals, lodges, and log cabins conjure images of the old days when the ranch was established, in 1863—hence the name. No wonder the old stories live on. The 63 Ranch has been owned by the same family since 1929 and has now been declared a National Historic Site. Today, it is a 2,000-acre (810-ha) working cattle ranch where guests can escape into a world of horseback adventure.

The air is clean and crisp 5,600 feet (1,707 m) up Elephant Head Mountain, straddling Mission Creek Canyon near Yellowstone National Park. It is a patch of hills covered with aspen, cottonwoods, sagebrush, and wildflowers with an inexhaustible range of trails. You stay in rustic cabins with log furniture and private bathrooms. Meals are hearty and social in the main lodge, where there are evening games and a roaring fire. In the mornings, guests take gentle rides through canyons to a hidden waterfall or a wind-in-your-face gallop over a mountain pass. The afternoon could involve another ride or a hike, fishing in mountain streams, learning to lasso, or collapsing in your cabin and simply gazing at the views until dinner. **SH**

↗ *Horses always outnumber the guests by more than two to one at Montana's 63 Ranch.*

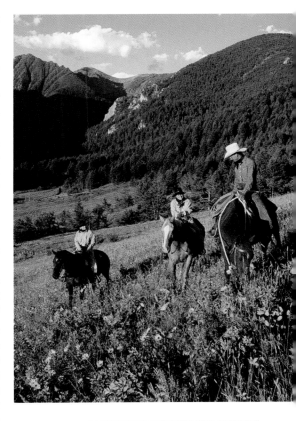

"With all of its history, visiting this Montana dude ranch is like going back in time."

Mark Bedor, *America's Horse* magazine

Stay at Sundance

Location Near Provo, Utah, U.S.A.
Website www.sundanceresort.com   **Price** ⊖⊖

A regular on "world's best hotel" lists, Robert Redford's rustic Sundance resort is unique. It sits in 6,000 acres (2,425 ha) of wilderness on the slopes of the 12,000-foot (3,660-m) Mount Timpanogos. Rivers burble and birds sing in summer; in winter, mugs of hot chocolate steam beside a crackling fire waiting for skiers to return. The cozy rooms feature American quilts and Native American wall hangings, and the food is superb, whether in The Foundry, praised by Zagat's for its luxury brunch, or the five-star restaurant.

Winter sports remain the key draw in this area. In January, you might find yourself sharing the slopes with luminaries of independent cinema, many of

> *"Our commitment to Sundance has always been to develop very little and preserve a great deal."*
>
> **Robert Redford, actor and director**

whom stay here during the annual Sundance Film Festival. Out of season, the lush pastures are great for hiking, mountain biking, and riding. A luxury spa draws on the Sioux idea of Hocoka, a sacred place in which body and spirit can be revived.

Long before eco was chic, Sundance was making a stand. And a passion for the environment is carried through from the Aveda products in the bathroom to the hybrid cars and regeneration projects the resort carries out on the surrounding hillsides. **LD**

◄ *Sundance offers a cozy, relaxing gourmand's paradise for the environmentally aware.*

Enjoy Circle S Ranch

Location Lawrence, Kansas, U.S.A.
Website www.circlesranch.com   **Price** $$

When visitors ask Jack Cronemeyer, proprietor of the Circle S Ranch, what there is to do around here, he replies, in a relaxed Kansas drawl, "Absolutely nothing." That is the joy of it.

There are things to do, of course, if you must. You can stroll along the Hawks Nest Trail, or laze on the hill under the apricot tree (planted by Mary Cronemeyer's grandmother) and dig into a picnic. You can hike through the tall-grass prairie, visit the bison, longhorns, Herefords, and Angus cattle, and then soak it all away in the eight-person hot tub. Or you can spend a carefree hour with the ranch's licensed massage therapists. Alternatively you could just plant yourself in a rocking chair on the porch and rock there for a good while.

The ranch has been in Mary's family for five generations; three of those were educated in the schoolhouse, which still stands. Her uncle Millard's sweat-stained cowboy hat decorates the lodge's Great Room. The lodge itself is new, though. Jack, a fifth-generation Kansas carpenter, built this 11,000-square-foot (1,022-sq-m) inn using many traditional building techniques, and the pair have fitted it out with every luxury. There are touches of the prairie—original western paintings by regional artist Ernst Ulmer, for example—alongside comforts such as thick bath towels, luxurious meals, and an ample bar.

Each of the twelve guest rooms has a unique decor. The cowboy room, for instance, features horns over the queen-size bed and a corrugated tin shower with a bucket for a shower head. If you really want to take it easy, many of the rooms also feature claw-foot baths, from which bathers can admire views over the ranch. And it's blissfully quiet. **PE**

Stay at The Point

Location Upper Saranac Lake, New York State, U.S.A.
Website www.thepointresort.com   **Price** $$$$

Often rated the number-one resort hotel in the United States, The Point is one of the nation's most exclusive hideaways. Built in the early 1930s in the style of the Great Camp Movement, and once home to William Avery Rockefeller, The Point is a pristine retreat spread over 10 acres (4 ha) along a small peninsula on the shores of Upper Saranac Lake, surrounded by the forests of the Adirondack Mountains.

Adirondack-style furniture adorns the eleven rooms, and cathedral ceilings combine with huge room sizes to give the impression of a grand lakeside home. There are four rooms in the Main Lodge, one of which, the Algonquin, was the property's original library. Eagles

> *"The Point [has a] unique combination of warm hospitality, grace, and rustic elegance."*
>
> **Proprietors, The Point**

Nest has three rooms, as does the Guest House, and there is one room in the converted boathouse over the water, which offers a large canopied bed and stunning panoramic views across the lake to the wilderness beyond.

Dinner is taken in the Main Hall or can be brought to your room. The menu changes every week and is fastidiously prepared by The Point's chefs and kitchen staff, who have been trained by renowned London-based, three Michelin–starred chef Albert Roux. **BS**

➡ *As might be expected of a former Rockefeller residence, The Point is the last word in rural luxury.*

See Saugerties Lighthouse

Location Esopus Creek, New York, U.S.A.
Website www.saugertieslighthouse.com   **Price** ⊖⊖

At one time there were sixteen lighthouses guiding ships along the commercially important Hudson River, but of the handful that survive today, only one invites visitors to stay the night. The beautifully restored Saugerties Lighthouse, built in 1869, sits in splendid isolation as a landmark beacon on the river, and its operational light tower offers panoramic views of the Hudson River with the Catskill Mountains to the west and Magdalen and Cruger islands to the south.

The lighthouse can be reached either by boat or by a half-mile walk through a nature trail. Breakfast is provided for overnight guests, and for dinner you can either dine at a local restaurant or carry food to the lighthouse and cook for yourself, either in the kitchen or on the outdoor barbecue; public tours and special events are also available.

Furnished as it may have looked in the early twentieth century, the building also contains a small museum, gift shop, parlor, kitchen, keeper's quarters, two guest bedrooms, and a shared first-floor bathroom. The toilet operates on a composting system because the lighthouse is too far to be linked up to the municipal sewage system, and instructions for its use are provided on arrival.

Saugerties Lighthouse is open year-round, though weekends are reserved well in advance and weekday stays are very popular between April and October. Once booked in, however, you are guaranteed one of the most relaxing couple of days possible this close to New York, with the sights and sounds of the Hudson River Valley literally all around you. The lighthouse is the perfect place to kick back and relax, although canoeing, kayaking, fishing, wading, and swimming are all there to be enjoyed as well. **HA**

Stay at 60 Thompson

Location New York, New York, U.S.A.
Website www.thompsonhotels.com   **Price** ⊖⊖

There is hip, there is achingly hip, and there is New York's 60 Thompson. This Soho hotel is fairly small but features one hundred rooms, each decorated in deep, beautiful hardwood. The interior offers a Zen-like calm that spreads like a massage from the lobby into the rooms, all of which are typical New York size (cozy rather than generous) and brim with aesthetic thrills. Walls are adorned with modern photos from a series of contemporary artists, including Laura Resen. The beds are sheer luxury, bedecked with superb coverings courtesy of Sferra. Bathrooms are marble-clad and feature glass shower-closets; minibars are stocked with exclusive drinks and snacks.

"A magnet for downtown celebs, 60 Thompson provides excellent people-watching opportunities."

New York Times

The dreamy sumptuousness of 60 Thompson is perhaps the reason why the hotel attracts such high-caliber guests: Gwyneth Paltrow, Jennifer Aniston, and Russell Crowe are just some of the celebrities who have called the hotel home, doubtless taking advantage of the larger suites, with designated living and working areas.

The hotel has some of the city's slickest amenities. In the restaurant, Kittichai, chef Ian Kittichai serves traditional Thai cuisine with an exciting contemporary twist; the Thom Bar is the place for quiet drinks. In the summer, 60 Thompson's A60 bar gives an unparalleled 360-degree view of the downtown area. **PS**

Unwind at The Mercer

Location New York, New York, U.S.A.
Website www.mercerhotel.com **Price** 🌑🌑🌑

Situated in a stylish neighborhood on one of the ultra-cool corners of retail heaven Soho, The Mercer's Romanesque revival style and location puts it high on the list for visiting movers and shakers. It also has the unique accolade of being New York's first-ever loft hotel, a phenomenon that was pioneered here in the sixties by artists who took one look at the multitude of abandoned warehouses and transformed the tumbledown ruins of a long-gone industry into havens of creativity and style.

The elegance of this seventy-five-room boutique hotel, spread over six floors, is manifested through the coolly exposed brickwork, huge windows, and iron column work, which give a sense both of space and permanence. The rooms themselves are large—huge by Manhattan standards, in fact—and feature high ceilings, walk-in closets, and furnishings designed by Christian Liagre, mostly in dark, African woods. Admire the pastel upholstery as you lie back on your generously proportioned bed and flick on your flat-screen television. You can also check out the comprehensive entertainment system, or slip from between your cozy Frette linens and cross the hardwood floors. Romantics may wish to inquire about the rooms with working fireplaces, leather banquettes, and marble tubs big enough for two.

World-class chef Jean-George Vongerichten is in charge of the delightful kitchen, and he also designed the exquisite twenty-four-hour room service menu. Greenwich Village is just around the corner; Times Square and Central Park are fifteen minutes away. In terms of both location and style, The Mercer does it better than most—which is doubtless why *Vogue* dubbed it "the hottest hotel in New York." **PS**

Stay at The Library Hotel

Location New York, New York, U.S.A.
Website www.libraryhotel.com **Price** 🌑🌑

For aspiring authors and would-be poets, New York's Library Hotel is the place to stay. As the name suggests, it is the perfect refuge for bibliophiles worldwide. Tucked away in a classic early-twentieth-century brownstone just around the corner from Grand Central Station, this classy and cultured boutique hotel mixes a love of all things bookish with a passion for contemporary design. The library theme is no gimmick, however: Each of the ten floors is dedicated to one of the ten major categories of the Dewey decimal system, and each of the sixty rooms is appointed with books and art that explore a topic within their floor category. The Library contains more

> "A refuge of calm ... from the glut of other boutique hotels that think they're nightclubs."
>
> *Independent*

than 6,000 carefully selected volumes—and if that is not enough, the New York Public Library and the Pierpont Morgan Library are a short stroll away.

Guests can request a room based on their personal interests, ranging from poetry and the classics to fairy tales and erotic literature. Although small, the rooms are comfortable, stylish, and come fully equipped. The three public lounges have the feel of a private members club, and there is also the Writers Den—a mahogany-paneled room with open fireplace—and the Poetry Garden, a lovely greenhouse. And when you have had enough of using your head, you will find New York literally at your feet. **PS**

Explore Wave Hill Gardens

Location New York, New York, U.S.A. **Website** www.wavehill.org **Price**

For a bucolic escape from the hustle and bustle of New York City, the Bronx might not be the first place that springs to mind. However, hidden away in this less than salubrious part of town is Wave Hill, 28 gorgeous acres (11 ha) of lush greenery that was bequeathed to the city for use as a public garden and cultural center, and is one of the most beautiful spots in New York.

Formerly a private estate, Wave Hill has at various times in its past been home to a British ambassador as well as to Theodore Roosevelt and Mark Twain. Nowadays, it is one of the city's best-kept secrets, a carefully cultivated oasis that offers spectacular views over the Hudson River and the Palisades below. For the very best views, head to the Pergola Overlook and the Elliptical Garden, where you can sit in quiet contemplation on a bench and enjoy the vista. They are particularly beautiful at sunset in the autumn.

Each season a riot of colorful plants transforms the pergola. Stroll along the wooded paths and visit the wild garden, where, as the name suggests, flowers and plants are allowed to grow freely; gaze at the limpid garden pool overgrown with water lilies and sprawling vines; and do not miss the Alpine Green House that houses high-altitude plants and flowers. These tiny, gemlike flowers are at their best in late winter and early spring. Hardy alpines planted within the cracks of a rustic stone wall create a vertical eye-level garden of flowers and foliage.

Breathe in the heady scents from the herb garden, where mint, rosemary, thyme, laurel, and a host of other plants that are grown for both medicinal and culinary purposes flourish. In the hot summer months, seek respite from the sun in the shade of an elm, beech, maple, or redwood tree. Wave Hill Gardens is horticultural heaven, indeed. **HA**

⬆ *The Flower Garden at Wave Hill uses both vintage and modern plants to create year-round color.*

Relax at Gramercy Park Hotel

Location New York, New York, U.S.A. **Website** www.gramercyparkhotel.com **Price** ❸❸❸

Gramercy Park Hotel is the latest notch in the boutique bedpost of Ian Schrager—the entrepreneur best known for setting up Morgans (the hotel that more or less invented the concept of the "design hotel"), Mondrian, Royalton, Paramount, and St. Martin's Lane in London, among others.

Like most of Schrager's other spots, the Gramercy puts an emphasis on the unique, the surprising, and the romantic. The lobby and public areas are particularly vivid, containing haphazard combinations of contemporary artworks, wild furnishings, and antiques that create a wholly memorable entrance.

The 185 guest rooms and luxury suites are equally idiosyncratic. Some are reminiscent of the Renaissance, with the requisite collections of furniture and objets d'art. Yet this kind of detailing might be balanced with photographs drawn from the hallowed Magnum photos archive—classic images by photographers such as Henri Cartier-Bresson, Robert Capa, Weegee,

and a host of other famous names—or with hand-woven rugs or contemporary mahogany furniture. The hotel's bars and restaurant are talking points of the town. The Wakiya, the Rose Bar, and the Jade Bar, plus the Private Roof Club & Garden, provide plenty of opportunities to unwind and enjoy terrific food and beverages amid the assortment of custom-designed furniture and twentieth-century art by artists including the likes of Andy Warhol, Cy Twombly, Julian Schnabel, and Damien Hirst. Music in the bars comes courtesy of playlists—not just any old playlists, of course, but custom-made lists from world-renowned DJs. You can find a state-of-the-art gym (Aerospace) on the second floor, and a spa (Aerospa) offers a vast array of treatments. Gramercy Park is simply a one-stop shop for all things in New York. **PS**

⬆ *Surreal interior design touches and a wealth of original art make the Gramercy a visual feast.*

Stay at the Waldorf-Astoria and Waldorf Towers

Location New York, New York, U.S.A.
Website www.waldorfastoria.hilton.com **Price** 💲💲

One of New York's oldest luxury hotels, the Waldorf-Astoria is also one of the city's art deco "crown jewels" (with the Chrysler Building and Rockefeller Center). The 1,300 guest rooms are situated in two different areas: The Waldorf-Astoria or Waldorf Towers, the latter of which has spacious suites for lease. Whether in the Towers or in the Astoria, however, the rooms are equally lavish. Work desks, fresh flowers, marble bathrooms, and triple-sheeted beds are common. All the accommodation is opulent, but the suites feature full kitchens, terraces, dressing and dining rooms, fast Internet access, and express checkout.

"Try … the Waldorf Towers, where most rooms are bigger than most New York City apartments."

New York Times

The Waldorf-Astoria's three bars are considered some of the best around. Sir Harry's Bar is ideal for a palate-waking cocktail, and the Bull and Bear's steak menu is renowned, as is its unique round mahogany bar. Oscar's is open for breakfast, lunch, and dinner, and so is Peacock Alley, off the enormous lobby—check out the signature clock! Inagiku completes the food options, serving up delicate and exquisite Japanese dishes. If it is traditional, top-class comfort you seek, the Walfdorf has it in abundance. **PS**

◀ *The formidable 47-story Waldorf building is an art deco landmark and is impeccably decorated.*

Meditate at Mayacama Mountaintop Retreat

Location Sonoma, California, U.S.A.
Website www.mayacamamountain.com **Price** 💲💲

In the heart of the wine district of Sonoma in California, the Mayacama Mountaintop Retreat is an idyllic hideaway for two. The small cottage, styled like a tree house with views across 5 acres (2 ha) of pristine countryside, is cozy, quiet, romantic, and peaceful, the perfect place to reconnect with what is important. Honeymooners love it for its seclusion; nature lovers walk the trails nearby, watching birds, butterflies, and rabbits, and stressed-out city dwellers find the peace and tranquility they need to unwind. The retreat has just one dwelling: Clair de Lune cottage, named after the dusk, sleeps two in a queen-size bed in its simple, clean interior, with wooden floors and Native American–style rugs.

There is nothing here to distract you from the process of relaxation. At the head of the waterfall trail, with fine views, an outdoor hot tub bubbles away; elsewhere the sun-dappled trees overlook a babbling creek. Make sure you walk the suspension bridge over the waterfall to the other side of the canyon and watch the sunset from Stargazer house, part of the retreat, with a glass of local organic wine. As the night falls, the stars begin to shine in the unpolluted sky.

The cottage is found between Kenwood and Santa Rosa, on the edge of Sugarloaf Ridge National Park and close enough to Sonoma for it to be a good spot for dinner. You can also try the town's mud baths and hot stone massage treatments, or book a massage at Clair de Lune cottage itself. You will be greeted with a basket of organic wine, gourmet coffee, and teas, as well as natural soaps and shampoos. Apart from that, there will be nothing to disturb you except the local wildlife and the deafening sound of silence. **LD**

Ride the *Coast Starlight* Train Through California

Location Seattle, Washington, U.S.A. to Los Angeles, California, U.S.A.
Website www.amtrak.com   **Price** $$

Is this one of the world's finest unsung railway trips? The *Coast Starlight* train links the great cities of the West Coast on a 1,400-mile (2,253-km), thirty-six-hour route starting in Seattle and ending in Los Angeles (or vice versa). Most travelers to this part of the world automatically drive along the highway and along the famed Big Sur. However, similar views are far more easily enjoyed from the comfort of a railway carriage. Every day the express train plows through the ever-changing mountain-, desert-, and cityscapes of the West Coast. It passes through fertile valleys, the snowy peaks of the Cascade Range, and the rugged shoreline of the Pacific Ocean. San Francisco, Sacramento, and Santa Barbara are also in its path.

Chronic underfunding recently threw the future of this wonderful train journey into doubt. However, Amtrak has at last invested in the *Coast Starlight*; the private sleeping cars and coaches have been upgraded, and the menu in the evocative dining car has been revamped to include fresh regional cuisine. Guests are seated together, presenting a golden opportunity to share traveling tales. An Arcade Room is set to entertain children, whereas overnight passengers can sample local wines, or have afternoon tea, in the refurbished Pacific Parlor Car.

The culturally curious will enjoy the Trails & Rails program—the result of an initiative between Amtrak and the National Park Service. Volunteers jump on board and offer a commentary of the scenic highlights as the train makes its way. **LC**

➡ *If relaxation is the order of the day, the views from the Coast Starlight provide a glorious backdrop.*

Stay at East Brother

Location San Francisco, California, U.S.A.
Website www.ebls.org **Price** 💲💲

East Brother Light Station is an impeccably restored Victorian lighthouse perched atop a tiny island in San Francisco Bay. You can stay and share the island with the seals, but beware: This is no ordinary luxury escape.

Although only a few minutes' boat ride from downtown San Francisco, arrival is an adventure. Guests are warned they will need: "The physical strength to climb from a bobbing boat up a vertical ladder 4–12 feet (1.2–3.6 m) in height, depending on tides." If in one of the five charming period rooms, you cannot use the shower unless staying for more than one night. (There is no freshwater other than what can be collected in the original rainwater cistern.)

> ## "One of the most peaceful bed and breakfast getaways on the West Coast."
>
> *San Francisco Chronicle*

So why escape there? Firstly, the light station is a unique experience, offering marvelous views of Mount Tamalpais, the San Francisco skyline, and the Marin coast. Moreover, although it is a nonprofit-making operation, you'll find your stay surprisingly indulgent: You are served champagne and hors d'oeuvres upon arrival, a multicourse dinner with wine in the evening, and a gourmet breakfast the next day. The most popular room is in the wood-paneled foghorn building, nestled close to the water's edge. **SH**

◄ *East Brother has been safeguarding shipping for more than 133 years and is still in operation today.*

Enjoy Yoga at Sivananda

Location Grass Valley, California, U.S.A.
Website www.yogafarm.org **Price** 💲

Party seekers beware: Tucked away in northern California's Sierra foothills, this ashram is a haven for those seeking a healthy break with a spiritual dimension. The Yoga Farm, as it is known, runs a year-round schedule of retreats for those in search of disciplined relaxation. You will be turfed out of bed at 5:30 A.M., to the sound of a chiming bell, for morning satsang—meditation, chanting, and a talk—and the days end at 10 P.M. In between, you will eat two generous, hearty vegetarian meals, outside in the lovely grounds, weather permitting, and have two yoga classes and some time off to sink into the beautiful setting and calming vibes.

The Sivananda yoga movement owns retreat centers worldwide, where both experienced yogis and beginners immerse themselves in the restful yoga lifestyle. This ashram sits in the foothills of the magnificent Sierra mountain range, among ancient oak trees. There is also a lake, where guests can swim in the long, hot summer months, or just sit, chill out, and reflect.

Wondrously, there is no cell phone reception, although there is a satellite wireless Internet connection, and the focus is on leaving busy lives far behind. Organized, themed retreats (a children's yoga camp and an ayurveda rejuvenation weekend, for example) run throughout the year, but guests can stay on an individual basis for as long as they desire to. Accommodation is in attractive, well-maintained cabins above the lake in the grounds, or in dormitories in the main building. Ashram living is not about luxury. It is about a nurturing, wholesome, and hugely rewarding experience for those with a passing interest (or more) in yoga and its accompanying lifestyle. **LC**

Bask in the Natural Spa at Calistoga Ranch

Location Napa Valley, California, U.S.A.   **Website** www.calistogaranch.com   **Price** ⊖⊖⊖

The first thing you notice when you hit Calistoga Ranch—situated just two hours from San Francisco—is just how incredibly big it all is. The size of the site is 157 acres (64 ha), but it is within a region so large you are guaranteed some extra visitors. Everything from deer to rattlesnakes can be spotted within the grounds, although the latter are thankfully confined to the farthest reaches of the region.

The forty-six rooms at the ranch nestle in Californian pines and boast peerless views of the surrounding terrain. The smallest dwellings offer some 6,460 square feet (600 sq m) of space and include outdoor showers, although the largest of them all is the Estate Lodge—a whopping 25,830 square feet (2,400 sq m) right on the gorgeous banks of Lake Lommel, with the forest at the rear. The Estate Lodge, with its two private bedrooms, indoor and outdoor living room, two half baths, two fireplaces, and an outdoor hot tub, is a natural choice for honeymooners.

There is a guests-only dining room, where chef Eric Webster impresses with simple, high-quality American cuisine. Wine buffs will also love it. Not only is nearby Napa Valley renowned for its wines (Calistoga's Old and New World vintages are exceptional), but the resort also has its own vineyard and offers wine-tasting classes and tours of the wine caves and vineyard.

Cars are not allowed on Calistoga Ranch, so transportation comes in the shape of golf carts. There is no chance of being disturbed by traffic noise when you are relaxing in the Bathhouse, Calistoga's natural spa, which draws water from local hot springs and promotes a variety of boutique treatments. The yoga deck and pool offer views onto the vineyard; both are wonderful ways to either start or end a day at one of the United States's classiest ranches. **PS**

⬆ *If you're traveling in Napa Valley, the richly appointed Calistoga Ranch is worth branching off for.*

Unwind at Spa Vitale

Location San Francisco, California, U.S.A.   **Website** www.hotelvitale.com/spavitale   **Price** ⑤

Wallowing naked in an outside tub in the bustling heart of San Francisco may sound like a fairly far-out activity. It's true there are not many places in the world where you can de-stress in this way in such an urban environment without the fear of Peeping Toms. Rest assured, though: There is no need to worry about such matters here. Hotel Vitale has created a wonderful bamboo roof garden to preserve your modesty. The tall, willowy trees provide a perfect barrier from prying eyes in nearby skyscrapers, and the city itself seems curiously removed from this small oasis.

Spa Vitale is the spa within Hotel Vitale and is in the penthouse. Offering three treatment rooms, it is small and intimate rather than flashy and commercialized like so many spas; the comparative intimacy ensures a friendly, attentive approach. The spa's most unique attraction is the rooftop bathing ritual, and it is a simple but striking concept. Two deep, set-apart bathing tubs nestle beneath a willowy line of bamboo

trees. An extra layer of trees divides each of the two tubs, so two friends can enjoy the ritual together while retaining their privacy. Other than this, only one tub is in use at a time—so on those occasions, you have the whole rooftop to yourself.

You will be handed a fluffy white bathrobe and towels and led to an invitingly full bath infused with seasonal bath products made exclusively for Spa Vitale by SumBody. An herbal drink and tray of bath products are placed by the tub, together with an exquisitely arranged plate of fresh fruit—and yet more fluffy white towels. There is nothing left to do but de-robe and climb in, placing the cucumber slices on your eyes as you sink back into the steam. Let the city sounds wash over you as you enjoy what has to be a truly unique urban experience. **LC**

⬆ *Bliss in the heart of the city: Spa Vitale's rooftop tubs offer a luxurious outdoor bathing experience.*

Drive Through Big Sur

Location Big Sur, California, U.S.A.
Website www.montereyinfo.org   **Price** ⊜

Big Sur Coast Highway is a stretch of Route 1 between Los Angeles and San Francisco where nature remains untouched. Some 200 miles (320 km) north of Los Angeles along Route 1 (the Pacific Coast Highway), the town of San Luis Obispo and the small fishing village of Morro Bay are the two alternative starting points of the Big Sur drive. This 144 miles (230 km) of highway is almost deserted, featuring just a handful of small towns and a couple of hotels, including the Post Ranch Inn, where celebrities like to take time out.

The wildlife protection area has recently seen California condors reintroduced. They swoop high over the precipices while, down below, local residents

> *"It was always a wild rocky coast, desolate and forbidding to the man of the pavements."*
>
> Henry Miller, writer

include sea otters and sea lions with the occasional migrating whale. Deer and foxes are often sighted, and the shy and elusive cougar is also at home here.

The narrow two-lane road snakes its way along the jagged cliff hugging the mountainside. Soak up the scenery as the road weaves along the sheer drops past Point Sur lighthouse before ending at picturesque Carmel, the heart of the West Coast's idyllic coastal country, best known for its fine beaches and movie-star resident (and onetime mayor) Clint Eastwood. **RCA**

➲ *After 1932, the remote coastal towns of Big Sur were finally connected by this striking coastal highway.*

Eat at Restaurant Nepenthe

Location Big Sur, California, U.S.A.
Website www.nepenthebigsur.com   **Price** $

It is not only tourists who rave about Restaurant Nepenthe and its superlative views. Locals will tell you that on no account should you miss this spot, credited with some of the best panoramas in Big Sur, perhaps on the whole west coast of America. Take in the breathtaking sea and mountain vistas from window seats and wide outside terraces adorned with bright Moroccan-style cushions.

Yet Nepenthe is no grand operation. The upstairs restaurant, downstairs Café Kevah, and enticing gift shop, Phoenix, all have a relaxed atmosphere, and are owned and run by the children and grandchildren of the original founders, Lolly and Bill Fassett.

> *"Perhaps the most stunning ocean view in the world? A Pacific romantic gateway."*

tripadvisor.com

Inside, the restaurant boasts panoramic vistas and comfy, cushioned seats; outside, on the roomy, stepped terrace, the views are just as spectacular. You may like to sample the signature Ambrosia Burger—a ground-steak sandwich on a French roll with a special sauce, described as the "quintessential California experience." The extensive wine list embraces some of California's most distinguished vintners, lovingly made with Gary Pisoni's Pinot Noir grapes.

Just below the restaurant, Café Kevah (open from March to the first week in January, weather permitting) boasts yet more terrace vistas. The menu homes in on fresh ingredients and gourmet coffees. **LC**

Unwind at Lucia Lodge

Location Big Sur, California, U.S.A.
Website www.lucialodge.com   **Price** $ $

It is possible to get totally unplugged within three hours' drive of the thriving hub that is San Francisco. Forget Silicon Valley and head out to one of the United States' most beautiful natural spots: Big Sur. Less than 170 miles (270 km) due south, following the coastline along Route 1, awaits an area of unparalleled wilderness and beauty, with more wildlife than humans per square mile. This is a tough but stunning natural environment that has not yet been tamed by man. Steep cliffs and rugged terrain follow the crashing Pacific Ocean in this raw locale that seems to have been forgotten by mankind.

This is no place for motels or city hotels, but rather cozy accommodation in tiny roadside hamlets such as Lucia. Where once there stood a gas station and a post office, now only the remote Lucia Lodge remains, built in the 1930s on the cliff's facade. Ten tiny blue-and-white beach-style cabins sit alone, looking lost in this unspoiled corner of California. It feels as if nothing has changed since this piece of land was found and settled by the Harlan family back in 1865.

The restaurant, with ocean views and award-winning fish-and-chips, is also steeped in history. The sepia faded prints on the walls are a reminder of generations gone by. In the bedrooms, whitewashed wooden walls, pine furniture, and a glowing fireplace set the scene. The grand bed, with its white linen overhang entwined with white cotton roses, is incredibly romantic. This lovely lodge, which is still run by the family's fifth generation, is all about rustic comfort the old-fashioned way.

With no televisions or phones, if ever there was a place to get cut off from the rest of the world on the California coast, this is it. **RCA**

Stay at Post Ranch Inn

Location Big Sur, California, U.S.A.
Website www.postranchinn.com **Price** $\bigcirc\bigcirc\bigcirc$

Take a mix of sensitive eco-consciousness and wild architectural creativity, and position it on one of the prime spots in California—what results is the Post Ranch Inn. This luxury modern resort is set on the cliffs of Big Sur just off Highway 1 which runs from Los Angeles to San Francisco.

Post Ranch has some of the world's most luxurious tree houses and wooden cabins, with views along the spectacular coastline and into the Ventana Mountains behind. The architecture is modern and dramatic—blending redwood, glass, and steel in sweeping curves, arches, and skylights. Interior design is all uncluttered simplicity with muted earthy colors, exposed wood, and plain fabrics. You may stay in a triangular room 10 feet (3 m) off the ground on wooden stilts or a house modeled on the shape of a butterfly, but all guests get a wood-burning stove, private spa tub and terrace, digital music system with forty-five channels, and free walking sticks. There are no televisions or alarm clocks.

Guests can have spa treatments in their rooms; a massage on the private deck overlooking the ocean is a big favorite among California's rich and famous. The inn's Sierra Mar restaurant is perched right on the cliff edge and is made mainly of glass to maximize the fantastic views from the tables. The gourmet Californian food is complemented by an award-winning wine list.

By day, visitors are free to simply relax by the pools or take hikes into the mountains. Some embrace the Californian spirit still further with daily yoga sessions, meditation, and stargazing talks. The less esoteric can take a short drive to the towns of Monterey and Carmel for shopping and sightseeing. **SH**

Stay at Kennedy Cottage

Location Near Santa Barbara, California, U.S.A.
Website www.sanysidroranch.com **Price** $\bigcirc\bigcirc\bigcirc$

Have you ever wondered where presidents and movie stars go on their honeymoons? The answer tends to be the private home of a celebrity or a remote island where the world's media cannot get within spitting distance. In the gardens of San Ysidro Ranch, in the exclusive Santa Barbara enclave of Montecito, Vivien Leigh and Sir Laurence Olivier exchanged vows one night in 1940, a moonlit minute after midnight. The legendary retreat, nestled between the Santa Ynez Mountains and the Pacific Ocean, is also where John and Jackie Kennedy celebrated their 1953 wedding. Today, guests can share in its myths and romance with a stay in the Kennedy Cottage. John and Jackie's

---

"The mountains, scored by deep canyons, rise up behind, for all the world like grand-opera scenery."

Winston Churchill, British statesman and writer

---

elegant haven has two master suites with king-size beds and a fireplace, an art- and antiques-filled living room, and an expansive ocean-view deck with an outdoor rain shower and large hot tub.

Idyllic days can be spent venturing on private wine-tasting tours in Santa Ynez, playing golf, and exploring 17 miles (27 km) of glorious hiking trails. You can contemplate your tempting dinner options for the evening while relaxing with an in-room spa treatment: the Stonehouse—in a nineteenth-century citrus packing house with creek-side views and an ocean-view deck—or the Plow & Angel—a cozy local favorite famous for its ribs and macaroni 'n' cheese. **LP**

Drive Through Death Valley

Location California/Nevada, U.S.A.
Website www.nps.gov/deva **Price** ❶

Like the moon's surface, the parched salt flats of Death Valley are devoid of human life, yet hauntingly beautiful. The national park that straddles California and Nevada across 140 miles (225 km) is one of Earth's least hospitable places: 3 million acres (1.2 million ha) of arid desert. It was given its name by a group of lost pioneers in the winter of 1849. Other spots in the vicinity share in the fatalism of that title, from Last Chance Canyon to Badwater and the Devil's Golf Course (an expanse of uneven, sharp clumps of rock salt said to be so jagged that "only the devil could play golf on such rough links").

Death Valley was born millions of years ago when an inland sea evaporated, leaving just salt behind. With most of the desert under sea level, it has record temperatures of 130°F (55°C). Amazingly, life does go on: More than 1,000 species of plants thrive here, including 50 species indigenous to the area and found nowhere else in the world. The animal kingdom, too, is alive and well with coyotes, rattlesnakes, scorpions, kangaroo rats (who can survive without water), black widow spiders, and even pupfish in Salt Creek.

Drive across the barren landscape and stop for a photo in the salt flats or take the 9-mile (14-km) loop around the volcanic hills dubbed "artist drive" because of their multicolored rocks. There is only one place to stay in Death Valley: Furnace Creek, home to the Inn and the Ranch motel. The motel is itself rather basic, but the Inn, dating back to 1927, is a historic landmark. With hostile terrain comes solitude, and Death Valley delivers plenty of that. **RCA**

← *A warm welcome to Death Valley—the hottest, driest, and lowest desert in the United States.*

See Zion National Park

Location Zion National Park, Utah, U.S.A.
Website www.zionmountainresort.com **Price** ❸❸

The oldest of Utah's parks, Zion was first brought to wider national attention by pioneering Mormon settlers in the 1860s who spoke of its glory; one of them, Isaac Behunin, gave the canyon its biblical name.

The walls of red-and-white Navajo sandstone that project parallel up to 2,000 feet (600 m) were carved by the relentless Virgin River, though this may seem quite unlikely today as the river meanders serenely along the canyon bed, creating an oasis of waterfalls and wild meadows. If you have the time, the park's 229 square miles (593 sq km) can cater for a wide range of engaging sports, including hiking, bicycling, riding, rock climbing, and rappelling.

"While it sits in the middle of nature, guests need only to step inside their cabin to feel pampered."

nationalparkreservations.com

The ideal base from which to launch into such a throng of activity—or simple meditation, if you wish—is a mere three-minute drive from the park's eastern entrance at the suitably rustic Zion Mountain Resort. Accommodation can be found in cozy wooden cabins for couples and spacious lodges for families and larger groups, all with glorious views across the mountains. Nearby are grazing buffalo, casually roaming the open plain as guests relax on private patios or unwind in a hot tub after the exertions of the day. The resort is also within comfortable driving distance of several other parks and monuments—notably Bryce Canyon and the north rim of the awe-inspiring Grand Canyon. **SG**

Stay at the Four Seasons

Location Las Vegas, Nevada, U.S.A.
Website www.fourseasons.com **Price** 💲💲

The infamous "City of Sin" in the Nevada Desert is just the way it looks on television: totally over the top. A jungle of casinos, neon, and hordes of people looking for a good time, the legendary Las Vegas Boulevard, better known as "The Strip," is where it all happens.

The only hotel "on Strip," as the locals say, without a hectic casino floor is the Four Seasons. Luxurious and exclusive, it takes up the top floors of the Mandalay Bay building and is the Strip's smallest hotel, with "only" 400 rooms. Curl up in a plush Strip-view suite to watch the Vegas craziness from above via the floor-to-ceiling windows. The glamorous rooms come with a 42-inch plasma screen, DVD player, and marble bathroom.

> *"There is only one true luxury resort… in town, located on the top five floors of Mandalay Bay."*
>
> *New York Times*

Guests can enjoy an alfresco breakfast at the Verandah restaurant. For dinner, the restaurant goes Italian with beef carpaccio and truffle gnocchi on the menu, or you can opt for surf 'n' turf at Charlie Palmer's. Here you'll find an elegant bar where the ambience is more low-volume jazz than the usual raucous Vegas pop. At the spa, try the very Vegas champagne mud wrap or the golden body treatment with passionflower oil. With pristine service and a wonderfully secluded pool the hotel is a real treat, despite the steep price tag. Meg Ryan, Reese Witherspoon, and even Michael Jackson have all found sanctuary in this relaxing refuge from the ultimate twenty-four-hour city. **RCA**

See the Grand Canyon

Location Arizona/Nevada, U.S.A.
Website www.nps.gov/grca **Price** 💲

It is more than a great chasm, more than the result of millennia of erosion, and more than one of the world's greatest views. The Grand Canyon is an experience that humbles every visitor. Whether you are driving, hiking, bicycling, riding, or white-water rafting, this is nature at its most raw and beautiful. It feels so huge and timeless that humans and their problems seem insignificant in comparison.

The sheer size of it is worth stressing: The canyon is 277 miles (445 km) long, 1 mile (1.6 km) deep, and up to 18 miles (29 km) wide. It was carved by the Colorado River and is mostly contained within Grand Canyon National Park—one of the first areas to be designated national park in the United States. It attracts five million visitors a year and has become one of the world's most popular natural attractions.

People come to stare at this gorge's intricate and colorful landscape of spires, rims, and cliffs. They watch the changing light and shadows on the rocks. (Sunrise and sunset are almost spiritual events here.) There is plenty of accommodation inside and outside Grand Canyon National Park and an array of activities to engage in. Some visitors wander along trails, watching ravens soaring above the rim and listening for the roar of the rapids far below. Others can ride mules. Perhaps the most memorable canyon experience is the glass-bottomed Skywalk, run by the Hualapai Indian tribe on their reservation. This horseshoe-shaped steel frame, with a glass floor and sides, projects 70 feet (21 m) into thin air from the canyon rim. It is not for the fainthearted. **SH**

➡ *The timeless grandeur of the Grand Canyon offers visitors a welcome tonic to the stresses of modern life.*

Explore Monument Valley

Location Utah/Arizona, U.S.A.
Website www.navajonationparks.org **Price** 🌓

This mesmerizing corner of the Arizona desert will be familiar to anyone who has ever watched a cowboy film, seen the surreal fantasies of painter Max Ernst, or read Paul Auster's 1989 novel *Moon Palace*. Like neon motel signs and roadside diners, we feel we have been there even before we see it for the first time. In the evocative Goulding's Lodge hotel—where director John Ford stayed—this is particularly so. Turn on the television and watch a film—Ford's *Stagecoach* (1939), perhaps, or *The Searchers* (1956)—from the hotel's extensive collection of Westerns. Let your eyes skip between the valley on the screen and the sun setting on the real thing beyond.

"If ever a place cast a spell, rooted you to the ground and refused to let you leave, this is it."

Los Angeles Times

It's worth taking time (perhaps in winter, after the main tourist season) to study the distinct forms: the much-filmed twin Mittens, the lofty Totem Pole, the arch of the Ear of the Wind. The buttes are stratified, their distinct rocks marking out the eons; the steeples and slender towers look fragile and weather worn.

Part of the Colorado plateau, Monument Valley acquires its deep sunset reds from the iron oxide in the Cutler Red siltstone, whereas manganese oxide shows up as blues, greens, and grays in the strata. The Grand Canyon is nearby and the Navajo Nation spreads all around—Monument Valley is a natural, and spiritual, magnet for any experience of the American West. **CM**

Discover Lake Powell

Location Utah/Arizona, U.S.A.
Website www.lakepowell.com **Price** 🌓

There was much hostility from environmentalists and anthropologists in the 1960s toward the controversial scheme to dam the Colorado River and flood Glen Canyon, creating Lake Powell—comparable to filling the Grand Canyon with water. Yet few could deny that the resulting artificial landscape is a staggering sight.

Crystal-clear turquoise waters reflect the towering rich-red canyon walls that ascend from the water, interspersed by wondrous arches, magnificent spires, and sandstone buttes, as well as countless inlets, and sandy beaches. The lake stretches for 186 miles (300 km) across southern Utah and northern Arizona, and comprises 2,000 miles (3,220 km) of coastline and ninety-six water-filled side canyons, many of which are accessible only by boat.

In fact, there is no finer way to appreciate what delights the lake has to offer than by houseboat. Rentals are available at Wahweap, Bullfrog, and Antelope Point marinas, and only a houseboat allows you the freedom to search out remote corners in which to dock. Boats range from the luxurious, complete with hot tub and wet bar for up to fourteen people, to those that feature only basic comforts. Water sports dominate the baking summer, though fishing is best enjoyed in the cooler months: April through June and October to November. The most popular mooring point lies near the spectacular Rainbow Bridge National Monument. At 290 feet (88 m) high and 275 feet (84 m) across, this breathtaking geological formation and deeply spiritual place is the world's largest natural bridge. **SG**

➡ *Named for explorer John Wesley Powell, Lake Powell has more coastline than the entire U.S. west coast.*

Stay at Dunton Hot Springs

Location San Juan Mountains, Colorado, U.S.A.
Website www.duntonhotsprings.com **Price** ⊖⊖

Tucked away in the San Juan Mountains, this romantic old mining town turned resort offers a refreshingly new tourist experience. Although the town where Butch Cassidy and the Sundance Kid are rumored to have hidden after robbing a bank in Telluride in 1889 may appear sleepy, nothing could be further from the truth. There is an abundance of activities to satisfy even the most hyper vacationer: Take a horse into the terrain to discover thunderous waterfalls and silent lakes, go desert hiking, heli-skiing, or snowmobiling in virgin powder, get your adrenaline pumping with river rafting, or enjoy a gentle afternoon's fly fishing on the Wet Dolores. Stay in finely

---

"Dunton Hot Springs ranks in our Top 10 favorite places on earth— a romantic, magical experience."

LuxuryTravelMagazine.com

---

furnished hand-hewn log cabins, dine on delicious local organic cuisine in an old saloon, enjoy reviving holistic Elemis treatments in a tepee. Plus, of course, you can soak in the town's natural, therapeutic hot springs, as the Ute Indians did thousands of years ago.

An array of fascinating sites lies just a short distance away, including haunting Monument Valley and Canyon de Chelly in the Navajo Reservation, and the town's own vineyard in McElmo Canyon. And how about having the whole town to yourself? Dunton Hot Springs can be reserved exclusively for private use for up to forty-two people, making it ideal for weddings and family celebrations. **LP**

Relax at Mii Amo

Location Sedona, Arizona, U.S.A.
Website www.miiamo.com **Price** ⊖⊖

Sedona is known throughout the United States for being the seat of strong spiritual energy, partly because of its powerful color combination of red-orange rocks, cornflower-blue sky, and evergreen vegetation. This part of Arizona is famed for its new-age spirituality, and there is definitely something special about these parts.

Super spa Mii amo is set within Boynton Canyon, overlooked by a wind-carved rock formation called Kachina Woman. It was voted the world's best spa in 2007 by *Travel + Leisure* magazine, and the staff, location, treatments, and facilities all score a perfect ten. There are sixteen casitas and suites on-site—the largest being the Mii amo suite—all with private courtyards and views of the Boynton Canyon. If you feel the need to take your soul on a journey, this is the place to do it. Create a link with your inner self in a soul-seeker session, restore your energy in the Crystal Grotto at the heart of the spa, or have a Mii amo signature massage with mineral crystals from Sedona. This is a place where magic happens.

The name *Mii amo* comes from the Native American word for "journey," and the spa offers a variety of ways to take your body and soul to a new level, whether by spending the day experiencing treatments from a traditional facial to an aura reading, or staying here for a three-, four-, or seven-day break. You can sign up for a straightforward spa package, a fitness package that includes hiking around Sedona, a new-age, Native American–influenced package, complete with sweat-lodge-style sessions, or a combination of all three. **LD**

➡ *The architectural style of Mii amo blends in almost seamlessly with the striking Arizona red-rock.*

Stay at Rancho de la Osa

Location Sonora Desert, Arizona, U.S.A.   **Website** www.ranchodelaosa.com   **Price** $$

Set in a traditional hacienda dating back to 1885, the Rancho de la Osa is just a mile away from Arizona's border with Mexico in the arid Sonora Desert. Miles away from U.S.-style civilization, its closest neighbor is the one-shop town of Sasabe.

Hip yet mellow, this is the ideal place to don a pair of cowboy boots and an old Stetson and head out on a ride across the dried-out riverbeds. It is the perfect place to indulge your inner cowboy. The electric pinks, yellows, and blues give the adobe-style buildings and Adirondack chairs a distinct modern Mexican vibe. In the cool cantina, with its giant sombreros and decorative piñatas, western-style saddle bar stools await, inviting. After a ride in the dusty heat through Geronimo's old stomping ground, ordering a fresh Corona (like John Wayne must have done when he stayed) is pure bliss. Aching and parched, it is the bona fide way of propping up the bar, listening to the lady wranglers' chat, the ranch hands' tall tales, and the

compulsory country soundtrack. For lazy days, there is the pool, the in-room massages, and the deliciously unavoidable siesta. For a little more action, try hiking, biking, and bird-watching, or possibly even watching a ranch hand hunt for rattlesnakes.

Meals are served in the hacienda or alfresco, with everyone tucking into gorgeous balsamic-glazed salmon or cookout-style steak at the grill. There is a real flavor of cowboy camping days—without any compromise on comfort.

At night, before retiring to the simple, uniquely styled rooms, there is an inescapable dreamer's ritual to attend to. The clear desert skies put on their nightly show, and it is impossible not to spend a while staring at the star-filled sky. Without a doubt, this is one of the most amazing views anywhere. **RCA**

⬆ *One of the last great haciendas, Rancho de la Osa is also rumored to be the oldest building in Arizona.*

Discover White Sands Desert

Location Tularosa Basin, New Mexico, U.S.A. **Website** www.nps.gov/whsa **Price** ◖

A U.S. military missile-testing range hardly sounds like an oasis of calm. Bizarrely, White Sands National Monument—a 275-square-mile (712-sq-km) desert of soft sands adjacent to the military base where the first atomic bomb was detonated in 1945—is one of the most serene places you will find, outside fire-testing hours. The paradox of finding such tranquility so near to destruction only underlines its beauty.

In the heat of the day, which regularly reaches 100°F (38°C) in summer, the whiteness of the wavelike dunes of sand threatens to dazzle you completely. When the sun slips behind the distant San Andreas Mountains, the land is bathed in a mysterious rosy light. At night, life is abundant, with 210 species of bird, 44 mammal species, and 26 different reptiles, as well as amphibians and insects coming out to play in the desert dunes. Lizards, oryx antelopes, turtles, lynx, and kangaroo rats scurry across the sand leaving a maze of traces in their wake, like the canvas of the previous night's activities.

Visit the museum set on Highway 70 to understand the area's fascinating history and geography. The desert is the world's largest gypsum dune field, 4,000 feet (1,200 m) high. Take the driving loop and stop for a walk into the pristine white dunes. The light is extraordinary and will guarantee some of your best photography; it is the ideal spot for a homemade photo shoot. As the sun begins to set, make sure you keep an eye out for Pavla Blanca, the ghost of Mañuela, a sixteenth-century beauty who is reputed to roam the dunes in search of her betrothed lover, the conquistador Hernando de Luna, who perished fighting the Apaches in the sand.

An extreme environment devoid of humans, White Sands has a dreamlike quality. These beautiful and immaculate dunes could be on a different planet. **RCA**

⬆ *Soft white dunes and deep silence make White Sands an eerily tranquil destination.*

Stay at Cibolo Creek Ranch

Location Near Presidio, Texas, U.S.A.
Website www.cibolocreekranch.com   **Price** ⑤⑤

This vast, 37,000-acre (14,975-ha) estate offers a total escape from the twenty-first century. A stay at the ranch, which is based around nineteenth-century cavalry forts, in mountains just north of the Mexican border is like stepping back into the old frontier days.

The adobe and cottonwood forts were originally built by a cattle baron as defenses against Apaches and Comanches. Now painstakingly restored, the luxurious rooms are crammed with antiques and local details such as baked saltillo tile floors, exposed beams, vintage lamps, Mexican blankets, and open fireplaces—but no televisions or phones. The forts are designated U.S. National Historic Monuments, so wander the ranch and you will find old wagons, stone walls, agricultural tools, and ancient artifacts.

Cibolo Creek is certainly of geographic interest, too: The vast estate is a very remote and private spot reaching as high as 6,000 feet (1,830 m) in the Chinati and Cienega mountains close to the canyons of Big Bend National Park. The area is full of wildlife, including mountain lions, antelopes, and deer, and scenery such as red granite peaks and cliffs, dusty deserts, and lush, spring-fed orchards. There is fine Mexican-inspired food here, as well as pools, a spa, and a gym. Yet this is certainly no fake tourist "dude ranch"—Cibolo remains a working farm, with longhorn cattle, horses, and buffalo.

Most guests find a perfect blend of peace and adventure here. There is a huge range of outdoor activities—including horseback riding, swimming, fishing, hiking, hunting, and off-road driving—but also the opportunity simply to relax quietly and anonymously on private terraces and under shady verandas, soaking up the spectacular scenery. **SH**

Enjoy Lajitas Resort and Spa

Location Texas Badlands, Texas, U.S.A.
Website www.lajitas.com   **Price** ⑤⑤

Arriving in Lajitas, having driven across the best part of Texas you will feel a million miles away from civilization. The onetime stomping ground of the Comanches and Pancho Villa, the outpost—set on the infamous Rio Grande at the Mexican border—is easily 300 miles (482 km) from the closest major U.S. city, although the resort has its own airfield to accommodate private jets.

Known as the Texan badlands, the barren terrain dotted with prickly pear and ocotillo cactus, and speckled with dried-out creeks is home to coyotes, mountain lions, and rattlesnakes: real cowboy country. The lost trading post village has now become

> *"Texas is a nation in every sense of the word. A Texan outside of Texas is a foreigner."*
>
> John Steinbeck, writer

a luxurious 25,000-acre (10,000-ha) playground complete with a plush spa offering desert scrubs, a gourmet restaurant with cowboy cuisine such as traditional Mexican dishes or rattlesnake cakes, and an "international" golf course. The 11A hole is optional: It allows you to tee off in the United States and aim for a "one par" across the Rio Grande into Mexico.

Go canoeing, riding western style, or action shooting with the local sheriff and you may be rewarded with a cowboy cookout breakfast at the Stargazer Mesa. Imbibe the atmosphere along the old boardwalk to the Thirsty Goat Saloon, named after Lajitas's four-legged mayor: Clay Henry, a beer-guzzling goat. **RCA**

Stay at Oak Alley Plantation

Location Near New Orleans, Louisiana, U.S.A.
Website www.oakalleyplantation.com **Price** 💲💲

Just 40 miles (65 km) from New Orleans lies plantation country, its grand, stately homes set in the vast Louisiana landscape where swamps, acres of sugarcane, and greenery cover the luxuriant banks of the Mississippi. Plantations set up in the late nineteenth century still function today, and tours to the oldest—Destrehan—or the largest—Nottaway—are almost compulsory. Visiting them, it is easy to become absorbed in the Southern grandeur of the past.

The stunning Oak Alley, which is still in working order, has been restored to its former glory and even offers accommodation. The white-pillared big house is straight out of a Southern belle's saga. Dating back to 1839, it has been named the "Grande Dame of the Great River Road." With its stunning grounds and numerous ghost stories, it was the perfect choice as a location for the movie *Interview with a Vampire*. At night, the grounds have a slightly eerie feel, and one can almost see the ghost of Scarlett O'Hara hovering through the mist down the ancient oak alleyway, although those skeptical of the supernatural are more likely to see one of the camera-shy armadillos.

Sleep in the tiny, cozy, wooden cottages with their wooden porches and swinging screen doors—once home to the workforce: It's a peaceful getaway, ideal for sipping mint juleps at sunset to a backdrop of gently buzzing critters in the air. The on-site restaurant is open for lunch, but finding dinner is a challenge. The rural communities are dotted with Baptist churches and little else. Local diners shut by 7 P.M. (And, yes, people do stop talking when you walk in.) Luckily, breakfast is easier, with Oak Alley's welcoming staff providing a hearty breakfast of bacon, eggs, and grits. Southern hospitality lives on. **RCA**

Unwind at Soniat House

Location New Orleans, Louisiana, U.S.A.
Website www.soniathouse.com **Price** 💲💲

Despite the tragic events of Hurricane Katrina, the city of New Orleans is still a must. Proud of its multicultural legacy—to which it owes its striking architecture, exotic Cajun food, voodoo folklore, and omnipresent jazz music—the "Big Easy" has oodles of character. However, the party town known for its wild Mardi Gras also has a quieter side: charming residential streets whose buildings are adorned with trademark beautiful balconies, as if wrapped in lace ironwork.

The French Quarter is a maze of antiques boutiques and shops selling everything from souvenirs to vintage jewelry or art, along with the odd voodoo store. The Soniat House on Chartres Street is set just far

> *"Soniat House exudes Old World elegance—and offers internet access."*
>
> *Time* magazine

enough away from the crowds but within easy walking distance of the town's attractions. The burned-orange facade is deceptive. Inside, a boutique hotel awaits, created by combining three historic Creole town houses dating back to the 1830s. Each room is unique. Canopied four-poster beds and antiques mixed with contemporary pieces give Soniat House a wonderfully atmospheric twist. The interior courtyard, with its ginger lilies, magnolias, and hibiscus, is a breath of fresh air—the flagstones and running water create a cooling oasis amid the muggy heat. The twinkling lights in the courtyard at night only add to the romantic ambience. **RCA**

Relax at The Setai

Location Miami, Florida, U.S.A. **Website** www.setai.com
Price ⊝⊝⊝⊝

Gray and black bricks from Shanghai line the walls, granite stones form a path across a watery floor, a Khmer statue brought over from Cambodia and a jade piece from a Chinese market are dotted here and there. It could be a sleek resort in Southeast Asia, but this is The Setai, right in the middle of Miami Beach.

There are many hot spots conducive to lounging and people-watching: maybe sipping a Chili Passion martini at the lobby cocktail bar; enjoying a bite of sushi next to the show kitchen of The Restaurant; or in a coveted pew at the beach bar by one of the three pools. The rooms spread throughout the building—originally created in the 1930s as the

> *"It has set new standards for sophistication and service in a city renowned for its world-class hotels."*
>
> *Condé Nast Traveler*

Dempsey Vanderbilt Hotel—are cocoons of comfort, with even "standard" Studio Suites coming with freestanding black granite tubs and rain showers, Lavazza espresso makers, and fine silk drapes. The larger suites in the forty-story tower are palatial, with hypnotic Atlantic Ocean views from private balconies. Needless to say, the penthouse is the last word in excess, with four bedrooms, a Lenny Kravitz–designed recording studio, a private wine cellar, and a gigantic party-friendly terrace with a lap pool. **LP**

⮕ *With a Zen-meets-art-deco style, The Setai is cool and calm—but busy South Beach is just a few steps away.*

Stay at The Sanctuary

Location Miami, Florida, U.S.A.
Website www.sanctuarysobe.com **Price** 💲💲

Miami's South Beach is known for many things, but tranquility has not traditionally been one of them. That was until the Sanctuary Hotel arrived: an ultra-luxury modern boutique hotel exuding Zen cool and a quietly Scandinavian designer edge that allows one to wallow in an exclusive milieu for a fraction of the price.

The hotel is centered around an open-air inner courtyard that comprises a multitude of small fountains wrapped in bamboo. The thirty-one rooms are modern but have a soothing ambience, and feature state-of-the-art Italian kitchens, flat-screen plasma televisions, and wireless Internet access, as well as whirlpool tubs, fully stocked in-room fridges, and—in

> *"Almost too cool for words . . . we think this hotel should be renamed the Swanktuary."*
>
> *New York Times*

selected rooms—steam showers. This being Miami, there is, of course, a modicum of hedonism. In the Sanctuary's case, this means a small roof bar that happens to be fairly lively at weekends and an infinity pool, which makes for a great hanging-out spot.

The hotel's Italian restaurant, Sugo, is a well-known local hot spot and sits in the middle of the stylish lobby. The Sanctuary Spa and Salon is the perfect place to give your body some deluxe attention. Guests can also avail themselves of various concierge services, including being picked up in a Bentley, procuring a jogging companion, and a G4 private aircraft for charter. Intimacy and indulgence, South Beach–style. **PS**

Relax at The Standard

Location Miami, Florida, U.S.A.
Website www.standardhotels.com **Price** 💲💲

There's one thing that you can guarantee from André Balazs's Standard hotels: a unique experience. Miami's version is in a surprisingly quiet neighborhood, the residential Belle Isle. The Scandinavian-style spa/hotel has tranquility as a byword. Music is banned from the pool—surely a first for a Miami Beach hotel.

As a place to unwind, it is both ultra-relaxing and unconventional, with a hydrotherapy area taking pride of place. There's a plunge pool, hot tub, and 12-foot-tall (3.6-m), three-inch-wide (7.6-cm) column of falling water to relax in; DJ-spun music plays through underwater speakers in the chlorine-free Sound Pool. There's also the hammam, Aroma Steam Room, Cedar Sauna, Roman Waterfall Hot Tub, and Mud Lounge—staying dry seems to be one of the biggest challenges here. Still a little tense? Then book a session with acupuncturist Lori Alexandra Bell.

Food is high on The Standard's menu, too. The Lido restaurant offers a fresh-fruit-and-organic-farm-egg breakfast; the Bayside grill aims for a healthful Mediterranean-inspired spread; another in-house eatery serves fish-based dishes dressed with home-grown herbs—all under the watchful eye of superchef Eric Ripert. Balazs's vision is everywhere: He's added his own touch to the existing white marble, terrazzo floors, and steel elevators with some seriously stylish touches such as Hans Wegner rocking chairs, vintage furniture from Denmark, Anne Jacobsen sconces, and Aalto tea trolleys. The rooms themselves are suitably hip and minimal, with light wood, crisp whites, sandy tones, and up-to-the-minute facilities.

The result is both delightful and dotty: wellness culture combined with left-field comfort—and all delivered with a raised eyebrow. **PS**

Discover Venetian Pool

Location Miami, Florida, U.S.A.
Website www.venetianpool.com **Price** $

The Venetian Pool is an incredible piece of living history (hence its place on the U.S. National Registry of Historic Places) and a beautiful escape in the heart of Miami. Step through the original wrought-iron gates and into another era—a time of whimsical architecture and romantic visions of how cities should be.

This was the quarry for the coral used in the model suburb of Coral Gables in the 1920s. Then, marvelously-named architect Phineas Paist and artistic adviser Denman Fink used it to create a pool inspired by the lagoons of Venice. With 820,000 gallons (3.1 million l) of spring water—and vivid imaginations—they created a Mediterranean-style oasis of tranquility.

"For a swimming hole like no other, don't miss the Venetian Pool in Coral Gables."

South Florida Sun-Sentinel

The swimming pool is surrounded by Spanish buildings, a tropical garden, and a grotto carved from the coral. There is a cave, a veranda full of parlor palms, and a rock diving platform. Wander among birds-of-paradise, fuchsias, and bougainvilleas; cross a Venetian-style bridge to discover the artificial island and its swaying coconut palms. Everywhere there are Latin arches and fountains amid ferns and flowers. After dark, the Venetian lanterns and underwater lights illuminate the scene in a flickering, romantic glow.

After a multimillion-dollar restoration program in 1989, visitors are now able to enjoy this Floridian fantasy world as it was originally intended. **SH**

Unwind at Little Palm

Location Little Torch, Florida, U.S.A.
Website www.littlepalmisland.com **Price** $ $

Florida has so much to offer, from the perpetual good weather that earned it that Sunshine State moniker to the beautiful Caribbean-style keys. For a really private hideaway, however, check into the ultra-exclusive Little Palm Island Resort in Little Torch. A million miles away from the rest of the world, the resort—accessible only by boat or seaplane—is a tranquil spot where elegance and casual cool rule. Even the staff look like they have stepped out of a fashion magazine.

The thatched cottage suites on stilts have a colonial feel, with their mosquito-netted beds, rich animal-print fabrics, and luxurious bathrooms. There is even an exterior shower for a spot of alfresco cleansing.

The vibe here is more Bali than Florida. Spend the day by the pool, on the palm-fringed beach, or swinging in a hammock. It may seem quiet, but there is plenty to do: You could try snorkeling, kayaking among the mangroves, or even taking out one of the hotel's Boston Whaler boats for a spin to explore neighboring islands.

It is all about romance at Little Palm. Take the welcome champagne hamper to the dock for the show: impossibly electric-pink sunsets followed by a candlelit dinner on the beach under the warm glow of the tiki torches. Delicious dishes include tuna tartare, rosemary lamb chops, and shrimp risotto. Breakfast is even better, with eggs Benedict, lobster, smoked salmon, and incredible pastries.

And if that is not enough to have you totally smitten, make sure you meet the miniature key deer. They amble through the property freely and, at night, even come to steal bread off your table. With their big eyes and wet noses, they are so lovely it is hard to resist the temptation to take one home. **RCA**

Visit Jules' Undersea Lodge

Location Key Largo, Florida, U.S.A.
Website www.jul.com **Price** 🌒🌒

Just think of it as a goldfish bowl in reverse. Here, you sit inside the world's only underwater hotel and look out as the fish swim by. Jules' Undersea Lodge was originally a research laboratory, created so that scientists could study the continental shelf off the Puerto Rican coast. Ocean experts Ian Koblick and Neil Monney decided to develop the facility—which sits at the bottom of the Emerald Lagoon in Florida's Key Largo Undersea Park—into a lodge. They named the venture after Jules Verne, author of *Twenty Thousand Leagues Under the Sea*—and managed to fit it out with hot showers, a DVD player, a microwave, and a fridge.

The lodge usually accommodates two couples, although six can stay here at a squeeze. The journey is not exactly straightforward. To reach the lodge, you must scuba dive down 21 feet (6 m), although you do not have to be a qualified diver to do this: In three hours, the Jules' staff can teach you all you need to know. Couples can even get married here—the notary public dives down for the service.

The bedding, admittedly, is not all that romantic. The duvets and pillowcases all have an underwater theme; cuddly fishes are available for those who left their teddy bears at home. Still, this underwater escape has attracted its fair share of notable guests, including former Canadian prime minister Pierre Trudeau, rock star Steve Tyler of Aerosmith, and Jon Fishman of the rather-too-aptly-named Phish.

The big attraction is the real fish, though. Wake up in the morning and you will see angelfish, parrotfish, barracuda, and snappers peering in at you through the windows. Are you watching them? Or are they, perhaps, making their own observations on the behavior of the strange humans inside? **PE**

Explore Islamorada

Location Islamorada, Florida Keys, U.S.A.
Website www.casamorada.com **Price** 🌒🌒

Pass the first of the Florida Keys—Key Largo, of Bogie and Bacall fame—and stop at Islamorada, the quiet and unpretentious "purple isle." Its most stylish hideout, Casa Morada, was set up by businessmen who decided to escape to the picturesque keys and create a boutique escape with a cool Caribbean feel. With reggae in the air, unfussy white decor, and tall palm trees, it is totally tropical. The bedroom is simple sophistication: an elegant wrought-iron bed swathed in white linens, a single dazzling orchid, and—of course—views over the intense blue waters. The hotel's tiny man-made island, covered in white sand, is home to a glorious pool and a cozy bar where guests gather

> *"Radiates serenity and style in an area where serenity is aplenty but style elusive."*
>
> *New York Times*

at night. At breakfast, fresh muffins, bagels, cake, and fruit make for a tasty start to the day before lying in a hammock, going bonefishing, or heading offshore for wahoo, tuna, or sailfish. After all, Islamorada is the "sport fishing capital of the world."

Another option might be to explore the reef that runs along the keys' entire 110 miles (177 km) or take a drive along the scenic road to Key West, the road itself a masterpiece of early 1900s construction with 43 bridges, including one 7 miles (11 km) long. **RCA**

➡ *The perfect end to a perfect day at Islamorada— enjoy the sunset with a cocktail in your hand.*

Discover Haleakala Volcano

Location Maui, Hawaii, U.S.A. **Website** www.nps.gov/hale
Price $

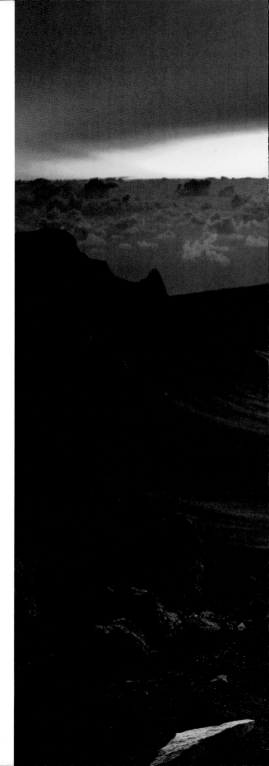

Maui needs no introduction. Synonymous with surfing paradise, this idyllic Hawaiian island has far more to offer—from helicopter tours to horseback riding or diving with turtles and sharks, to biking down a 10,000-foot-high (3,050-m) volcano. The Haleakala volcano, in a 28,655-acre (11,595-ha) park of the same name, earned its name from early Hawaiians who called the summit "house of the sun," believing it rose from behind the volcano's peak. For the best view, get up to the summit to take in the 2-mile- (3.2-km-) wide, nearly 2,600-foot- (800-m-) deep crater coated with fluffy white clouds. Some people cycle up the volcano (the record stands at less than three hours), but the fun

---

"Visually expansive, the summit eludes any attempt to understand its scale or dimensions."

U.S. National Park Service

---

part is bicycling the 28-mile (45-km) winding asphalt road down again. Early birds can join a sunrise expedition up to the top, definitely worth it if you can bear the early start around 2:30 A.M. To guarantee a little solitude at the top, you might try going alone on a Sunday—when tour companies are shut—and avoid the "honeymoon season" throughout spring and fall. After watching the stunning sunrise, it's time to whiz down, catching the incredible coastline views on the way: liberating and thrilling. **RCA**

→ *Maui's terrain is otherworldly—astronauts practiced moon walks here before the 1969 moon landing.*

Unwind at Hana

Location Maui, Hawaii, U.S.A.   **Website** www.slh.com/hanamaui   **Price** 💲💲

Surfing aside, the island of Maui has a wealth of attractions to offer. Part laid-back cool, part glamorous, part outdoorsy, there is something for everyone in this most famous of Hawaiian islands. To really escape from the crowds, however, head east to quiet, unspoiled Hana.

Hit the notorious 52-mile (84-km) "Road to Hana," twisting and turning along the cliff edge. With 600 curves and fifty-four bridges, the narrow route is not for the fainthearted. It is more than just scenic: Dramatic cliffs, lush tropical flowers, and aromas make for an exhilarating drive. The reward is Hana, a very, very quiet spot. It feels a million miles away from Maui's busier commercial side. Indeed, there is little here, aside from a few private villas, said to belong to the likes of Woody Harrelson and Oprah Winfrey, and the Hana-Maui resort, which is actually in the heart of the town, alongside the school, church, and library. Daytimes are spent surfing, swimming, and trekking through the dense tropical forest. At night, the bar and restaurant at the hotel are the only places to meet. Quaint Hawaiian cottages overlooking the wild Pacific coastline blend in with nature, making the most of the trade winds for natural air-conditioning. Rest assured, all other modern conveniences—including a luxurious sunken bathtub, a well-stocked minibar, delicious locally grown coffee, and cookies—are available. The resort has everything you could wish for to relax in style: from a luxurious heated wellness pool, to a fitness room with incomparable Pacific views, an outdoor lava-rock whirlpool, and the Honua Spa. The spa's philosophy is that true balance and health come from the gifts of the earth and nature—a perfect match for Hana, a place of nurturing and well-being among Hawaiian people. **RCA**

⬆ *Find true peace in the Pacific: Hana-Maui offers a wealth of wonders to soothe today's troubled brows.*

Walk Along Honopu Beach

Location Kauai, Hawaii, U.S.A.　**Website** www.kauai-hawaii.com　**Price** ❶

Landlubbers need not apply—the only official way of visiting Honopu beach is by swimming. Inaccessible by land and impossibly magical in its setting, this treasure trove of a beach has provided the scenery for many a film, among them *King Kong*, *Raiders of the Lost Ark*, and *South Pacific*. (Admittedly, the authorities may well have had to make an exception to the swimming-only rule for the film crews.)

Two deep, golden beaches flanked only by steep mountain rock and the enchanting azure waters of the South Pacific are connected by a colossal stone arch in the craggy rock face, before which a waterfall cascades like a shimmering curtain. Honopu, situated on the dense Na Pali coast, is nature's gift to the adventurer. Veering up the vertiginous cliffs, even more inhospitable terrain abounds—the last remaining track of the legendary jungle guarding Honopu beach was reclaimed a the hurricane in 1962. This thick, unnavigable wilderness is thought to be the final home of the native Mehuens, lending the Honopu jungle its alternative moniker: "Valley of the Lost Tribe." Honopu is among the best-kept secrets in the lush tropics of Kauai, the oldest of Hawaii's islands. A volcano formed Kauai's spectacular natural terrain, melding sheer cliff faces with dense jungle, lush waterfalls, emerald interiors, and theme-park-perfect rivulets and waterways. The cool temperatures of the mountains provide welcome respite from the balmy climate of the coast.

Honopu beach itself is steeped in legend, and is thought to be a sacred tribal burial site where nobility were laid to rest. Today it provides the perfect spot to explore the Pacific's finest sea life, luxuriating in splendid isolation as you bask in your thoughts and in the sheer wonder of nature. **VG**

⬆ *To really get away from it all, get those flippers on and head down to Honopu Beach.*

Relax at Baja Camp

Location Isla di Espiritu Santo, Mexico
Website www.bajacamp.com **Price** ⊙⊙

This luxurious tented eco-camp can be found on a remote beach on an unspoiled island in Mexico's Sea of Cortez, a one-hour boat ride away from La Paz. There are no high-rise hotels or noisy clubs, just the sound of gentle waves on the beach to lull you to sleep under a star-studded sky. Large ten-person tents house beds, soft linen, and warm showers. The biggest tent doubles as the dining area and lounge and has comfy chairs to sink into—an ideal spot from which to watch the sunset, margarita in hand.

Freshly caught fish and shellfish are a highlight of the Mediterranean and Mexican cuisine on offer. Spoil yourself with a huge selection of tropical fruit in the

---

"The area is so rich in marine life that Jacques Cousteau called it 'the world's aquarium.'"

Independent

---

morning; sample the choice of Chilean and Californian wines served with dinner. You can snorkel with sea lions, dive to see manta rays, sharks, and schools of darting, colorful fish, or take kayaks out to explore nearby coves. Go drift fishing on the camp boats, or try the thrill of sport fishing to catch marlin, tuna, wahoo, yellowtail, and mahimahi.

In fact, guests have only one complaint about Baja Camp: that they cannot stay longer. It is only open from June to September. **AD**

→ *The number of guests is limited at Baja Camp on this uninhabited dream island in the Sea of Cortez.*

Enjoy Esperanza Resort

Location Los Cabos, Mexico   **Website** www.esperanzaresort.com   **Price** $$

You know you have come to the right place when the hotel manager offers a complimentary head and neck massage as soon as you have checked in. Overlooking the glimmering Sea of Cortez and the Pacific Ocean in a breathtakingly natural setting, the Esperanza resort has fifty casitas (small villas) and six luxury suites spread across 17 acres (7 ha) of land.

From the outside, the resort resembles a Mexican village, with casitas connected to the resort's facilities via traditional stone footpaths. The interiors are decidedly elegant, decorated with original Mexican artworks, handcrafted furnishings, and fine Italian linens. Many have large outdoor terraces with views of the ocean, and the in-room amenities include fully stocked minibars and entertainment centers, plus roomy bathrooms with gorgeous complimentary products. The six luxury villas, some of which are situated on a secluded beach, boast larger dimensions as well as private pools and butler service.

You can dine alfresco at the Mediterranean-inspired restaurant at Esperanza, which is carved into the bluffs overlooking the Sea of Cortez and offers 180-degree views from each table. The bar serves appetizers and snacks together with an extensive tequila and cigar menu. With more than one hundred different kinds of tequila to choose from, a visit to the bar can be a little dangerous, although the abundance of activities on offer will soon cure any morning-after fatigue.

You can go whale watching and take a sea trip on a glass-bottom boat as well as fish, surf, dive, and windsurf. Not a water fan? Take a guided tour through the desert and along empty beaches, have a game of tennis, play golf, or ride a horse. Or there are always more of those luxurious massages available in the wonderful all-natural spa. **PS**

⬆ *For those in need of pampering, the idyllic spa offers therapeutic massages and revitalizing treatments.*

Stay at Las Ventanas Al Paraiso

Location Los Cabos, Mexico **Website** www.lasventanas.com **Price** $$$

A camera phone is recommended for a stay at Las Ventanas because no one back home will believe you when you reel off your "spotted" list. The air corridor from Los Angeles to Las Ventanas to Baja California's tip is thick with rock stars, fashion designers, and ex-presidents. Although privacy goes with the territory (there is no sign outside, so taxi drivers and chauffeurs must know where it is), there is no stopping the gushing from the celebs themselves. Jennifer Lopez told *Harper's Bazaar* that her favorite indulgence is "the Spa at Las Ventanas," whereas Jessica Simpson told *Rolling Stone* that the infinity pool is the best in the world. Why do they come? Well, 365 days of sunshine help, but with a fleet of Porsche Boxters for rent, twenty-four-hour butlers, and a palatial pool villa, Las Ventanas deals in only one currency—*la buena vida*.

Xeriscaping (the art of desert landscaping) finds a natural home in this exclusive corner of Mexico, where an eighteen-hole Robert Trent Jones II golf course winds its way around the resort and up the hilly desert landscape. The cacti-studded desert tableau is offset by a series of stunning infinity pools that lick the jewel-blue Sea of Cortez, and the resort's low-slung, whitewashed adobe villas straddle a generous swath of the Los Cabos coast. From the high-precision binoculars that thoughtfully dangle from the sea wall for use during the annual whale parade to the "hot type" unpublished novels that are made available to guests, they have thought of everything here. Romantics can even ride a white stallion for that ultimate beach proposal. Now, that is service.

Oh, and nobody really cares whether or not you have got a Lear jet parked nearby, which is just how it should be. What is good enough for Jennifer Lopez is good enough for the likes of us all. **TM**

⬆ *The Mexican-Mediterranean style of architecture reflects the desert location of this exceptional hotel.*

Hike the Copper Canyon

Location Chihuahua, Mexico
Website www.coppercanyonguide.com **Price** ❶

Mexico's Copper Canyon, in the Sierra Madre in the state of Chihuahua, is the largest canyon system in the world. Its maze of gorges comprises six interconnecting canyons that are even larger and deeper than the Grand Canyon; they provide awe-inspiring scenery of sheer rock walls, waterfalls, caves, and prime hiking territory. The name of the canyon comes from the copper-colored moss that grows around the canyon.

The canyon is home to the Tarahumara Indians, a seminomadic group who retreated there after the arrival of Spanish explorers in the sixteenth century. Over the years, Jesuit missionaries have also made the canyon their home, and Mennonites too have several settlements in the area. There are also more typical Mexican towns, some of which have a distinctive frontier feel to them, with plenty of cowboys.

To get to the start of your hike, take a train ride on one of the world's most exciting train tracks. From *El Fuerte*, the views are astounding as you pass over thirty-seven bridges, past towering canyon walls and cliffs, and then through eighty-six tunnels in total. There are many day hikes to take in the area, either around the rim of the canyon or down at the bottom, and plenty of guides willing to take you on week-long tours or longer. The rugged trails take you deep into the gorge, and, because many guides are well-acquainted with the local Tarahumara Indians, you might even get an insight into their lives. The hikes offer a chance to glimpse unspoiled wilderness and to enjoy the vast views of the huge canyon. **LD**

➔ *Mexico's Copper Canyon affords ample hiking and walking opportunities for all skill levels.*

Stay at One&Only Palmilla

Location Los Cabos, Mexico
Website www.oneandonlyresorts.com **Price** ⊝⊝⊝

There are not many places on the planet where you can wriggle your toes in powder-soft sand as you sip a perfect margarita, watching whales glide by in the distance from an infinity pool. One&Only Palmilla, sandwiched between San Jose del Cabo and Cabo San Lucas on the southernmost tip of the Baja Peninsula, is the quintessential chic beach resort—and much more besides. It is the hotel's stunning location, where the Pacific Ocean merges with the Sea of Cortez in the Los Cabos Corridor, that makes it utterly unique.

The ambience of the resort is conducive to serious relaxation. Surrounded by exotic blooms, rooms have terraces or balconies with daybeds overlooking the

> *"[One] of the region's most upscale resorts . . . complete with acres of vanishing pools."*
>
> *New York Times*

dramatic surf—ideal for siestas. You are also provided with a telescope for whale watching or stargazing. The Palmilla first opened in 1956 as a small, exclusive fishing lodge, popular with the likes of John Wayne and Bing Crosby. These days you are more likely to bump into Demi Moore or John Travolta. It is now a luxury beachside oasis complete with first-rate spa, beautifully manicured grounds, and a golf course, and there is still ample opportunity for world-class fishing. We are sure Bing would have approved. **LP**

⇇ *Palmilla's stone fountains, whitewashed walls, and wrought-iron doors hark back to old-world Mexico.*

Enjoy Hotelito Desconocido

Location Jalisco, Mexico
Website www.hotelito.com **Price** ⊝⊝⊝

If you are looking for the ultimate in eco-friendliness, this has to be it. The Hotelito Desconocido is a haven for nature lovers in the midst of a huge bird and turtle reserve in the wetlands, between the Sierra Madre Mountains and the Pacific Ocean. There is a touch of magic in the air as guests are rowed from the main hotel's lodge across the estuary to their beachside huts, where cacti poke out of the sand.

The colorful rooms are basic yet perfectly charming. Without electricity, the only amenities are a shower, sink, and toilet, as well as a mosquito-netted bed. You can lounge sleepily in shaded hammocks or on the pristine 40-mile (65-km) beach where, at dusk, turtle hatchlings dive into the sea under the gaze of a handful of relaxed guests. The food on offer here is fittingly simple, healthful, and delicious: calamari salad, seviche, and coconut cake.

After dark, signaling with a flashlight summons the boat for a pickup on the room side of the estuary to take you to the extraordinarily decorated El Cantarito restaurant for a candlelit evening meal. Sip a cold beer or a margarita and chat at the bar, or share a game of pool in the bar's dim twilight. Turn-down service involves dozens of tea lights twinkling in the dark, and in lieu of room service, you can hoist a flag up outside your window to indicate you would like a delivery of fresh Mexican coffee and cookies before breakfast. It is definitely different and really rather romantic.

It is quite impossible to remain in touch with the rest of the world here, but that is the entire point. With the closest village a few miles away, Hotelito makes sure you are in a world of your own: the sweetest seclusion. No wonder Madonna, Mick Jagger, and Quentin Tarantino have all hidden out here. **RCA**

Rent a Villa at Cuixmala

Location Jalisco, Mexico   **Website** www.cuixmala.com
Price 💲💲

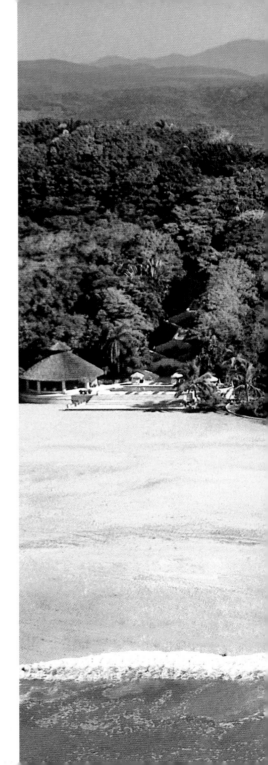

Modern-day fairy tales do not come much better than this. Cuixmala is a hot resort where luxurious villas are tucked away in a vast 25,000-acre (10,117-ha) ecological reserve fringed by golden beaches. This is a private sanctuary in more ways than one. Come here to rest your head, laze on deserted beaches, and get close to nature. Then discover the birds and animals that have made their home in this eco-reserve—from jaguars and sea turtles to exotic zebras and antelopes.

The top house is Casa La Loma with its distinctive blue and yellow striped dome. It looks like a castle and has a view out across the empty beach of Costa Alegre to the rolling Pacific surf. There are four other villas, fully staffed and decorated in sumptuous Mexican and European designs, as well as nine comfortable casitas (small villas) with a shared pool, clubhouse, and restaurant. Make yourself at home, then explore the organic farm on horseback, past mango and papaya trees, citrus orchards, and all those beaches. Some are perfect for snorkeling and kayaking; others have hammocks strung between coconut palms to escape the sun. Enjoy a picnic on a stretch of unspoiled beach, followed by a boat trip across the lagoon where you can watch the sunset as well as spot dolphins and whales. Finish the day with a cold margarita.

Celebrities adore this super-hip eco-resort. Food served in the gourmet dining room has been grown organically at the ranch or highland farm, and the two-tiered seating in the screening room has Indian pillow-topped settees the size of double beds. Perfect for weary A-listers. **AD**

➡ *The magnificent Casa La Loma was once the tropical hideaway of the late industrialist Sir James Goldsmith.*

Stay at Quinta Real

Location Zacatecas, Mexico
Website www.quintareal.com **Price** 💲💲

It has been thirty-four years since any bullfighting took place here, but Quinta Real offers an escape with a difference. Built in the oldest bullring in North America, San Pedro, the hotel sits alongside a sixteenth-century aqueduct. Before you think that its reputation is about gimmicks, think again. The Quinta Real hotel group is known for its attention to detail, and here it references high culture and Mexican traditions in a hotel that is renowned for its gourmet food and great service.

Inside, grand function rooms and colonial-style decor add to the sense of occasion. Original art hangs on the bedroom walls, with views over the courtyards outside. The hotel was garlanded with architectural

---

"They consistently deliver premier experiences, complete with superior personal service."

Tony Perrone, AAA regional manager, Mexico

---

awards when it opened, and it is easy to see why. The original bullring is now overlooked by the hotel's La Plaza restaurant, with shaded tables out on the terrace. Terra-cotta pots sit where spectators used to watch the bloody action from the steps, but the pièce de résistance is the bar. Once the stalls where the bulls waited before competing, El Botarel serves up the best South American wine in a hard-to-beat setting.

Zacatecas itself is said to have "the face of a quarry and a silver heart," in reference to its past as a silver-mining town. Gilded cathedrals and colonial buildings line the narrow cobbled streets. And the impeccable surroundings of Quinta Real have views of it all. **LD**

Relax at Dos Casas

Location San Miguel de Allende, Mexico
Website www.doscasas.com **Price** 💲💲

Sometimes leaving home feels like the only way to get a break. At Dos Casas you can relax feeling both at home and away. The charming boutique hotel is set in San Miguel de Allende, a picturesque little town in the mountainous "Bajío" center of Mexico. Dating back to 1542, San Miguel de Allende was at the heart of the Mexican war of independence and was renamed in honor of local General Ignacio Allende, one of the country's eternal heroes.

It is everything you would expect from a tranquil Mexican town: dazzling yellows and earthy-toned walls, grandiose villas, humble cantinas, and impressive doorways over cobblestone streets. The omnipresent dry heat and cooking aromas hang thick in the air, making for a mellow atmosphere. Dos Casas is tucked away, hidden from the imposing pink gothic church and milling tourists. A super-stylish hotel, it is exceptionally welcoming with a "mi casa, su casa" motto. With just five rooms, the designer retreat manages to blend chic and cozy, thanks to local colorful ceramics, dark exotic woods, neutral linens, and vases overflowing with fragrant orchids.

For breakfast sit on one of the patios, tiny but glorious havens with ironwork balconies and tumbling flowers. Sample huevos rancheros or homemade bread slathered with tomato jam. Escape the hottest hours by giving in to the local siesta tradition before heading out to browse for local arts and crafts.

At night, help yourself to a Corona beer from the communal fridge in the kitchen, or retire to La Terraza, the room with its own private terrace. Slip into the whirlpool tub and watch the sun set over the dusky city rooftops. Despite Dos Casas' exoticism, it becomes a home away from home almost instantly. **RCA**

Enjoy the Azulik Maya Spa

Location Yucatan Peninsula, Mexico
Website www.azulik.com   **Price** 💲💲

The Mayans were notoriously clever. The splendid ruins of their advanced civilization lie all around the luxury Tulum resort of Azulik, taking visitors back to a time when humans and their surroundings were in much closer harmony. Azulik's greatest asset is precisely this way of blending ancient feelings and wonders with a contemporary outlook. One of the major draws is the Maya Spa, which provides a large list of treatments that range from familiar Western techniques to ancient healing skills and relaxation treatments, including traditional Mayan massages. If they have been used for millennia, the wisdom goes, they must be pretty special—and they are.

This ocean-side resort is also well known for its fifteen wooden villas, each with its own thatched roof and authentic decoration. Located on a cliff top, the villas offer outstanding sea views, especially Numbers 1 and 12—both perfect for incurable romantics and honeymooners. Strolling along the white-sand beach, clad in as much or as little as you wish (the hotel is adults only, so nobody will mind if you strip off), is as memorable an experience as kayak trips around the coral reefs or hiking through tropical forest. You can also just relax in your villa (a concierge will discreetly pass by every half hour; place a red flag outside if you need something), enjoy the sea breeze on your own patio, or take a dip in your hand-carved bathtub.

There is no electricity at Azulik; come evening, candlelight provides an enchanting ambience as the Mexican night descends. It is a unique feeling to close one's eyes, listen to the nocturnal soundtrack of the jungle, and reflect that the Mayan spirit that left such a momentous cultural imprint seems to exist eternally in the very fabric of Azulik. **PS**

Trek the Sierra Norte

Location Oaxaca, Mexico
Website www.sierranorte.org.mx   **Price** ❶

The locals call them the "villages of the clouds" because of the beautiful veils of mist that frequently enshroud them. Others refer to them as the *pueblos mancomunados* (the "commonwealth villages"). Whatever appellation people give these settlements high in the hills of the Sierra Norte, all agree they are a blissful retreat from the urban rush.

There are eight villages in all, which perch some 10,000 feet (3,048 m) above sea level. The Zapotec people who live here have for centuries worked together, sharing the resources of their land and walking from village to village along the 60 miles (96 km) of paths that run between them. Still today,

> *"The landscape and flora are spectacular, and . . . it is always fresh and peaceful."*
>
> Graham Williams, journalist

the villagers use neither pesticides nor manipulated seed and so encourage their rich ecosystem to survive. It is a valuable resource: WWF has classified the Sierra Norte's mixed pine-oak forests as the richest and most varied on Earth.

Mindful of the threat being posed by modern agricultural methods and logging, a community-based ecotourism operation, Expediciones Sierra Norte, was established more than a decade ago to offer an alternative form of income to the villagers. Now it maintains the trails between the villages, supplies maps, and organizes accommodation in cabañas (huts) and meals in local homes. **PE**

Unwind at Hacienda Uayamon

Location Yucatan Peninsula, Mexico **Website** www.haciendasmexico.com **Price** §§

If one of the wealthiest men in Mexico, Roberto Hernández, decides to invest in a hotel, you imagine it would be a pretty luxurious affair. The Uayamon certainly does not disappoint. It is set in a grand seventeenth-century hacienda that once stood at the center of a sisal-growing plantation. The success of the crop's trade in the nineteenth century brought great wealth to the hacienda's owners, allowing them to expand their property to lavish proportions. However, a crash in the 1920s brought an end to the glory years; the plantation closed down and the hacienda was left to fall into picturesque decrepitude.

Today, thanks to Hernández's largesse, the Uayamon has been reborn as perhaps the peninsula's ultimate romantic getaway. Restored to its former grandeur, its elegant, high-ceilinged, rustic decor—all warm reds, dark yellows, and exposed brickwork—is highly evocative of the colonial era, but now comes accompanied by a host of modern conveniences.

There is a huge pool—with a phone so you can keep yourself plied up with cocktails—a highly respected restaurant serving local "Yucatecan" cuisine, and some charming, almost forestlike gardens.

Accommodation comes in the form of large suites in the main hacienda building plus a number of separate villas—all with huge beds, sumptuous bathrooms, and private terraces—many of which were the living quarters of the plantation's "elite" workers. Although it is the sort of place where you could spend your entire vacation without leaving its confines, the hotel's location also offers opportunities for exploring the region's history. It lies within easy reach of Edezná, the site of a Mayan ceremonial center of the sort that used to fill the peninsula's jungles from around 1500 B.C.E. to 1000 C.E. **JF**

↑ *Designed by Indonesian architect Jaya Ibrahim, the suites preserve the plantation style of the hacienda.*

Discover Isla Contoy National Park

Location Isla Contoy, Mexico   **Website** www.cancundays.com/islacontoy.php   **Price** 🕒

Located at the confluence of the Caribbean Sea and the Gulf of Mexico, Isla Contoy is the most important nesting place for seabirds in all of the Mexican Caribbean. This little island, just 5 miles (8.5 km) long, is a protected nature reserve and a well-known spot for an eco-adventure.

Just 200 visitors are allowed on its silky-sand shores every day, arriving in boats that run from Isla Mujeres or Cancun (approximately a two-hour trip). Here you can sit on the beach and watch the brown pelicans and double-crested cormorants on the water, or head inland to the Puerto Viejo lagoon, an important nesting site. The island is uninhabited, and a trip here is like being a castaway for the day. Climbing up the observation tower provides you with a great view of the whole island.

It is not just the birds that love to nest here. Isla Contoy is an important nesting site for four types of sea turtle, with secluded palm-fringed, white-sand beaches giving them the chance to bury their eggs undisturbed. The water around the island is crystal clear, so you can see from your boat what is going on under the sea: great manta rays swooping around and plenty of tropical fish against a backdrop of coral.

Boat trips to the island typically stop at the Ixlache reef so that visitors can go snorkeling. Giant stingray, primary-colored parrot fish, clown fish, barracuda, and angel fish are just some of the species you might see—not to mention the turtles. Every summer, visitors have the chance to see the world's largest living fish (the whale shark) pass by Cancun—a viewing trip may be incorporated on your watery safari. A trip to the island is certainly an adventurous addition to any journey to this part of the Mexican coast and is not to be missed. **LD**

⬆ *The uninhabited Isla Contoy provides an important habitat for birds and sea creatures in the Caribbean.*

Enjoy the Spa at Esencia

Location Yucatan Peninsula, Mexico
Website www.hotelesencia.com **Price** ❸❸❸

Along a 2-mile (3.2-km) empty stretch of one of Mexico's best beaches, you will find Esencia—a quiet, understated seaside escape on the Mayan Riviera. The hotel stands in a 50-acre (20-ha) private estate, with two swimming pools, a day spa, a gourmet restaurant, and a beguiling beachfront.

From the paths snaking through the lush gardens to the thatched cabins to shade guests lounging on the beach, this estate has a simple, relaxed style. The modern property and many of the buildings once served as the exclusive winter retreat of an Italian duchess. Esencia still benefits from her sense of taste. The hotel itself is a whitewashed low-rise stucco building with dark-wood shutters, terra-cotta-tiled roofs, and verandas. In front are lawns, decks, and sofas leading down to the white sands.

Esencia's circular spa is set in a quiet corner of the estate. It offers an array of treatments using indigenous fruits, plants, and herbs, many of which are grown in the garden. There are five treatment rooms, four whirlpool tubs, and two Mayan-style domed steam rooms. Treatments include massage, herbal saunas, and facials, all performed with traditional organic methods. Yoga and meditation classes are also available.

Bedrooms are simple and elegant, featuring native hardwood furnishings, white walls and floors, high ceilings, louvered doors, and windows with sea and garden views. A private chef is available, but most meals are eaten at the Sal Y Fuego Restaurant, which offers rustic Mexican cuisine, including fresh local ingredients and indigenous cooking methods. **SH**

➦ *The cool modern architectural style of the Esencia displays elegance, luxury, and impeccable taste.*

Relax at Chimino

Location Laguna Petexbatún, Guatemala
Website www.chiminosisland.com **Price** 🟢

The sudden screech of a rogue howler monkey may wake you in the middle of the night or you may be startled by a crocodile swimming past the window of your room, but that is all part of the appeal of staying at one of the world's top eco-archaeology escapes.

Chimino is a fortified island set in a huge lagoon deep in the Guatemalan jungle. Guests stay in one of five modern rustic houses built from local mahogany trees that had already fallen. Their roofs are draped with shaggy palm thatch. These houses, which sleep up to five, stand hundreds of feet from one another, overlooking the lagoon. Colorful toucans and parrots perch on branches outside, staring in, as interested in you as you are in them. The houses may look primitive, but inside they are equipped with simple beds, hot water, and bathrooms. You may feel up close and intimate with the jungle, but the owners assure guests that the bungalows are insect- and animal-proof.

A similar central building has a bar, restaurant, terrace, and hammocks. Down on the water, there is a floating wooden deck for sunbathing, swimming, canoeing, or fishing. The lodge cook prepares fresh fish from the lagoon for a traditional regional dinner.

The teeming wildlife is just part of the island's appeal. Many visitors come to see the overgrown tumbling stone ruins. Easy paths from the bungalows lead to the remains of an impressive Mayan citadel, including its defensive walls, ceremonial pyramids, and palaces. It is believed it was home to a branch of the Mayan royal family between 600 and 900 C.E., who barricaded themselves here as their civilization mysteriously declined. Even they found it a good place to relax: Deep in the jungle, archaeologists have unearthed a court for playing ball games. **SH**

Stay at La Lancha

Location Near Tikal, Guatemala
Website www.blancaneaux.com **Price** 🟢

Francis Ford Coppola's latest exotic jungle lodge recalls scenes from his epic *Apocalypse Now*. The movie mogul opened La Lancha on the shores of Lake Petén Itzá deep in the Guatemalan rain forest. However, you will not find Marlon Brando muttering "the horror, the horror" here. Coppola has created a desirable escape perched on a steep jungle hillside, with a two-tier swimming pool with its own waterfall, an open-sided restaurant overlooking the lake, and beautifully decorated Mayan-style casitas (small villas) to stay in.

The casitas have basic wooden decks and balconies with views through the trees and across the lake. Inside are simple whitewashed walls, tiled floors, high

> *"I loved the unspoiled area with howler monkeys living just outside the deck of my room."*

Francis Ford Coppola, director

wooden ceilings, and marble bathrooms. Color comes from Mayan wall hangings, rugs, cushions, and sofas. There is a restaurant, relaxed all-day bar, sun terrace with sofas and a fountain, and a small beach area on the lake. Guests can relax, take boat trips, go kayaking, fishing, or horseback riding, or take Spanish lessons. Farther afield, there are splendid Mayan ruins. The hotel arranges excursions to all of them, plus early morning bird-watching trips—watch out for toucans, parrots, kingfishers, hummingbirds, and vultures. **SH**

➡ *La Lancha has a thatched-roof restaurant open to the forest where local and Italian food is served.*

Unwind at Nitun Reserve

Location San Andrés, Guatemala **Website** www.nitun.com
Price 💲💲

Although not the most luxurious of escapes, there is something uniquely peaceful about curling up in a hammock at Nitun and watching the hummingbirds hover above you. Special feeders are hung around this eco-lodge so guests can see six different species of these tiny colorful birds perform their acrobatics.

Nitun was set up by a former coffee plantation owner in the rain forest alongside Lake Petén Itzá. It is an exciting place, with palm-thatched buildings built from rock and wood among the trees along the shoreline. The interior is as different from a corporate hotel as you can get—with rough stone and log floors and simple furniture. Nitun does not feel like a

---

"Once ensconced in this verdant beauty . . . the temptation is to find a hammock and never leave."

Lucas Vidgen, journalist

---

luxury intrusion into the forest, but a cozy part of the environment. However, there are still fans, fly screens, and private bathrooms with plenty of hot water.

The central lodge is a two-story house containing a restaurant, bar, and lounge. The food prepared in the open-plan kitchen has been acclaimed as some of the best in the country. Days are spent exploring the forest on wildlife treks and boat trips around the lake. The site is surrounded by a nature reserve, and the owners run things on strict ecological lines. **SH**

⬅ *The lodgings at Nitun Reserve are welcoming yet rustic, in keeping with its jungle surroundings.*

Enjoy Villa Sumaya

Location Lake Atitlan, Guatemala **Website** www.villasumaya.com
Price 💲💲

There is more to Guatemala than dense jungle, as this atmospheric retreat demonstrates perfectly. Villa Sumaya sits high in the mountains at 4,500 feet (1,370 m), on the shore of a beautiful lake, in lush orchid gardens facing the peaks of three conical volcanoes. The stunning landscape is at the heart of the Guatemalan highlands, and this picturesque and unpretentious hotel is a great place to stay to explore the surroundings.

Villa Sumaya stands on the edge of Lake Atitlan and was once the vacation home of a wealthy Guatemalan family. It has been converted into a hotel that is so peaceful and inspiring it has become renowned as a center for yoga and meditation breaks. Amid all this natural beauty, the hotel buildings have traditional thatched roofs and open sides to reveal the stunning panorama. There are stone paths winding through the terraces, where you will find sun loungers, a hot tub, saunas, and pergolas.

The cabanas are simple but comfortable. The color scheme is muted earthy brown and ocher, with handmade tiled floors, wicker chairs, candles, and hammocks. The decor consists of Mayan textiles and local folk art. You will spend most time on the spacious veranda, though, gazing at the view across the lake.

At the lakeside is the Blue Tiger Temple, the venue for all sorts of events and classes: yoga, dance, meditation, massage, aromatherapy, tai chi, Reiki, shamanistic ceremonies, impromptu drama, and family reunions. The pretty restaurant stands next to a fountain and serves a healthful blend of international and local food. The specialty is fresh fish from the lake, and it is hard to resist the smell of homemade bread and tortillas that drifts across the gardens daily. **SH**

Enjoy Parrot Nest Lodge

Location Cayo, Belize   **Website** www.parrot-nest.com
Price $

If your idea of a tropical getaway is spending a night in a thatched tree house at the top of a 100-foot (30-m) guanacaste tree in the depths of the Belize rain forest, then you need look no further than the splendid isolation of Parrot Nest Lodge.

Just a short drive from the tourist town of San Ignacio and enclosed on three sides by the Mopan River, Parrot Nest Lodge is an eclectic world of rustic yet comfortable living set amid lush, landscaped gardens. It provides an ideal base for exploring the many natural wonders of the surrounding Cayo district. The lodge offers full- and half-day trips that will take you into the depths of Belize's forests. A full-day excursion to the Rio Frio cave followed by a swim in the temperate waters of the cave's nearby rock pools is a must, as is a visit to Big Rock Falls and the recently discovered Mayan ruins at Caracol.

Half-day trips, for example, include horseback riding and dropping into a local Mennonite community at Barton Creek outpost. You can take a canoe through the Barton Creek caves with experienced guides from Parrot Nest Lodge, who will explain the formation of the cave and navigate its labyrinth of passages. Or why not just float downstream on the Mopan River on one of the lodge's giant inner tubes that will leisurely transport you past the spectacular Bullet Tree Falls. Along the way you can be guaranteed a sighting of the river's resident iguanas, and maybe even catch a glimpse of one of its giant otters.

The crystal clear waters of the Mopan River make it ideal for a long refreshing swim, and treks from the lodge that head along a series of so-called "medicinal trails" will take in some of the numerous examples of the region's rich medicinal flora. **BS**

Stay at Blancaneaux

Location San Ignacio, Belize   **Website** www.blancaneaux.com
Price $$

Nestled in the Mountain Pine Ridge Forest Reserve, close to the Maya Mountains, Blancaneaux was once a lodge for jaguar hunting. When film director Francis Ford Coppola fell for the area sometime after Belize's independence in 1981, he snapped up this property as a retreat for family and friends; after extensive renovations he opened Blancaneaux Lodge in 1993.

Today Blancaneaux boasts cabanas and villas overseeing the river, all with screened porches, showers, and Japanese baths. Luxury cabanas add a walled garden with outdoor shower to the equation, and the Enchanted Cottage also has a fireplace in the bathroom and a steam room. There are seven family-

> *"Beautifully decorated, the staff are terrific, the food is good, and the sense of escape complete."*
>
> *Daily Telegraph*

sized villas; you can even rent out Coppola's own, complete with art and personal memorabilia. One of the two restaurants, Montagna, reflects Coppola's love of southern Italian dishes, and you can sip fine wines from his own Californian estates in Napa and Sonoma.

As Blancaneaux boasts its own stables, horse treks into the forest are a must. There are a multitude of Mayan ruins in the reserve nearby; after a day of sightseeing, guests can unwind with a Thai massage in the spa—all this and not a jaguar in sight. **PS**

➡ *Subtle nighttime lighting at one of Blancaneaux's two swimming pools adds to the exotic atmosphere.*

Snorkel at Hol Chan Reserve

Location Hol Chan Reserve, Belize
Website www.holchanbelize.org   **Price** $

Just off the balmy tropical coast of Belize lies one of the world's greatest natural wonders—a 180-mile- (290-km-) long coral reef second only in extent to Australia's Great Barrier Reef. Although it may be smaller, Belize boasts one significant advantage over its antipodean rival: ease of access.

In places, the reef sits less than 1,000 feet (300 m) from the shore in calm, shallow, almost crystal-clear waters that make snorkeling the reef about as easy and laid-back an experience as you could wish for. The reef is a biologically intense environment, providing homes to a vast assortment of creatures—from brightly colored, almost fluorescent fish to giant manta rays and marine turtles—who weave in and out of the strange, undulating coral structures.

Renting a kayak and snorkeling gear to undertake your own coral exploration will set you back just a few Belizean dollars. For other rewarding wildlife-watching opportunities, take an organized tour, which will take you to some of the reef's more hard-to-reach spots. The most renowned is probably the Hol Chan Reserve, named after a narrow gap in the reef cut hundreds of years ago by local Maya tribes as an access passage for their boats. Today it acts as a bottleneck for marine animals traveling between the waters inside the reef and the open seas beyond. It is a particularly good place for spotting large fish, such as sharks, groupers, and barracuda, great numbers of which assemble both here and at the evocatively named Shark Ray Alley, where guides are allowed to bribe the fish with food to make an appearance. **JF**

➔ *The shallow, turquoise waters of the seas around Belize provide endless opportunity for snorkeling.*

Stay at Sabalos Jungle Lodge

Location Los Guatuzos Nature Reserve, Nicaragua
Website www.sabaloslodge.com **Price** 💲

From the frontier town of San Carlos, a two-hour panga ride on the coffee-colored waters of Nicaragua's Rio San Juan will bring you to the riverbank huts of Sabalos Lodge. Partially hidden by the dense greenery of Los Guatuzos Wildlife Refuge, the seven cabins offer wilderness accommodation at its most adventurous. Yaró Choiseul-Praslin owns the lodge, a silver-haired Sandinista who led the agricultural reforms of the 1980s. His tales of revolution regale the multinational visitors who venture into the jungle. Wooden walkways lead to an open-sided dining room and to the huts scattered among the jungle foliage. Sparse

---

"[I dined] to a background of oscillating crickets and the chirpy banter of frogs."

Joe Cawley, *Guardian*

---

on refinements, the huts offer soft mattresses, mosquito nets, private bathrooms with water, and electricity—at least until 9 P.M., when the generator is switched off and the lodge is plunged into darkness.

Lying in bed, listening to the soundtrack of jungle life, it is easy to imagine that this is virgin territory, uncharted by all but the most daring, but for centuries, pirates and buccaneers navigated this river. Downstream is El Castillo, a fortress laying testimony to those trying to thwart such attacks. Local excursions include wildlife walks and kayaking, although the true beauty of a stay at Sabalos Lodge need not extend far beyond the gentle sway of a hammock. **JC**

Relax at Morgan's Rock Hacienda and Eco-lodge

Location San Juan del Sur, Nicaragua
Website www.morgansrock.com **Price** 💲💲

It is said that good things come to those who wait. In the case of Morgan's Rock in Nicaragua it could not be more true. After an exciting journey in a tiny propeller plane to Granada's landing strip, there is a two-hour drive on bumpy roads. Past Lake Nicaragua, past scrawny dogs and barefoot children, past overcrowded buses and horse-drawn carts, it is a long way to the dirt track leading to this exclusive eco-resort hidden deep in the rain forest.

Arriving at the lodge is like stepping into the Garden of Eden: Giant butterflies flutter in the lush forest. The tempting pool enhances the picture-perfect view of the dazzling ocean below. With just fourteen cottages, the lodge offers high-end tourism with a taste of nature. Big on reforestation and sustainable development, as well as guest pampering, Morgan's Rock Lodge aims to become entirely self-sufficient.

Reaching the eco-designer cabins requires a mini Indiana Jones adventure: walking the solid hanging bridge suspended 72 feet (22 m) over the canopy. The cabins blend in perfectly with the environment: emerald tones, netting for walls, eucalyptus pillars, and decadent hanging daybeds.

The noise of the Pacific and its sonorous waves crashing onto the beach below is overwhelming, and the sounds of nature are all around. The 6 A.M. coffee delivery is surprisingly welcome, signaling time to join the turtle hatchlings fleeing into the surf. There is so much to do: surfing, kayaking, fishing, or even riding with Jesus, the weathered animal whisperer. **RCA**

➡ *Morgan's Rock has its own stables so that guests can ride through the ecosystems, ending up on the beach.*

Stay at El Silencio

Location Bajos del Toro, Costa Rica
Website www.elsilenciolodge.com   **Price** ⊖⊖⊖

Steeped in its own cloud forest reserve, El Silencio is a sophisticated retreat of just sixteen elegant villas. Each is poised on the jungle-clad hillside so that there are perfect views of mountain and forest through huge windows. The design is simple, using natural materials, and yet is utterly luxurious: Expanses of polished wood and woven bamboo sit well with bathrooms of polished stone with rain-head showers. Step out onto the private balcony and there is an open hot tub. Surely this is damaging the fragile ecosystem? Not a bit—the retreat is entirely carbon neutral. El Silencio is silent, too. Whereas Costa Rica's most famous cloud forest at Monteverde attracts hordes of visitors, El

> "In the country that invented eco-tourism, El Silencio sets a new standard for responsible luxury."

concierge.com

Silencio offers the same breathtakingly diverse wildlife, but without the crowds. Your dedicated eco-concierge will accompany you up magical trails through dense forest to three lovely waterfalls.

You could use El Silencio as a base to go rafting, visit coffee plantations, or see Poás volcano, with its steaming turquoise crater. But the magic of El Silencio lies in doing nothing—other than eating exquisite organic food created by chef Marco González, and yielding to pampering in the spa. **CD**

◄ *The simple wood and bamboo design of the villas works in harmony with the natural surroundings.*

Stay at La Cusinga Lodge

Location Parque Nacional Marino Ballena, Costa Rica
Website www.lacusingalodge.com   **Price** ⊖⊖

There are countless eco-lodges in Costa Rica. Few, however, live up to their environmental credentials as well as La Cusinga on the country's Pacific Coast. All of the lodge's cabins and furniture have been made using wood grown on-site in a sustainable plantation, electricity is provided by hydro and solar power, and the food served here is harvested locally or caught fresh from the ocean. Never fear, this is no Spartan back-to-basics hideaway. It may preach a green message, but it also offers a supreme level of comfort and cooking, allowing you to relax in a glorious natural setting without feeling too guilty about the environmental impact of your actions.

The lodge's greatest asset is its location, perched on a hill overlooking a bay where every year thousands of humpback whales arrive to breed. All around grows thick, lush rain forest where dazzling tropical birds (including the toucan, after which the lodge is named) feed on fruits, and white-faced capuchin monkeys scamper excitedly in the treetops.

The luxuries here are all organic. There are no hot tubs, but in the jungle you will find a crystal-clear pool where you can swim alongside iridescent fish. Sun loungers have no place on this beach, a stretch of chocolate-colored sand backed by a swaying border of palm trees, and entertainment comes courtesy of the startling sunsets, the rhythmic pulsing drone of a million cicadas, and the roars of howler monkeys.

The lodge is also well positioned for exploring some of Costa Rica's natural wonders. To the north is Cerro Chirripó, the country's tallest mountain, and to the south is the ecologically stunning Parque Nacional Corcovado, one of the largest swaths of virgin rain forest outside of the Amazon Basin. **JF**

Raft the Pacuare River

Location Pacuare River, Costa Rica   **Website** www.ticotravel.com
Price 💲

The Pacuare River stretches 18 miles (29 km) from San Martín to Siquirres and there are fifty-two rapids along the way, including those of the 5-mile (8-km) Pacuare River Gorge, which is considered to have some of the most exciting white water in South America. If you cannot imagine what battling white water in an inflatable raft might feel like, one of the gorge's rapids is named the "pinball." Yet the river, whose rapids range from class two to class four, is suitable for novices with a guide—just don't expect to stay dry.

There are peaceful stretches, too. After the adrenalin-pumping gorge, where you paddle for all you are worth across foaming eddies and through bottlenecks strewn with boulders, you will arrive at the tranquil Valle del Pacuare where the teal-green waters run smooth. The river borders the Talamanca mountain range, renowned for its wealth of wildlife, and here you will have the chance to catch your breath and admire the untouched wilderness through which you are floating. You will pass through virgin rain forest where vertiginous gorges are spotted with glittering waterfalls. Toucans and parrots soar above the canopy, watching monkeys who leap from branch to branch. You may also see ocelots and sloths while over the water and through the trees dancing morpho butterflies flash their vivid, metallic-blue wings.

Several guides offer the Pacuare River rafting trip; most work out of the town of Turrialba in Cartago province. The 18 miles (29 km) are usually completed in four hours, but some visitors opt to extend their rafting journey to two days. **PE**

➔ *A trip in a raft down the Pacuare River is a great way to immerse yourself in Costa Rica's stunning nature.*

Unwind at Pacuare Lodge

Location Siquirres, Costa Rica
Website www.junglelodgecostarica.com   **Price** 🅢🅢

As the raft enters the rapid and starts spinning, buffeted by an unseen force of water, there is no time to feel exhilaration or panic. Your guide is instructing you to paddle madly, and in another moment the raft goes soaring up, only to deliver you with one rushing surge, breathless and drenched, on the calm river again. Soon, this experience becomes nearly pleasurable.

Pausing at a waterfall to wallow in warm shallows, the surroundings are idyllic: Dense virgin rain forest rises up from the river, and tall trees sprouting orchids send long lianas trailing down into the flowing water. After another bout of rapids, it is a relief when the rafts come ashore at a clearing in the jungle. Here, as if miraculously, you'll see a beautiful wooden palenque and staff emerging with goblets of cold lemonade. This is Pacuare Lodge, hidden on a bend in the river in 25,000 acres (10,115 ha) of deep, protected forest. Accessed only by raft (although children may come by jeep and cross the river in a basket), the Pacuare experience starts with adventure, but ends with a deep sense of peace. Hundreds of species of birds can be seen in the beautiful gardens, and you will wake to the sound of howler monkeys calling through the forest.

Garden-view rooms are simple wooden palm-thatched cabins, open on all sides to the exotic gardens, but choose the much grander river-view cabins for their extensive space, verandas with hammocks, and stylish outdoor showers. As night falls, candles are lit, and guests gather in the palenque to sip caipirinhas before a superb three-course meal—carpaccio of fresh tuna, filet mignon, seared tilapia—served by local staff who are genuinely delighted to welcome you to their paradise. There can be no more romantic place to be marooned. **CD**

Relax at La Paloma Lodge

Location Drake Bay, Costa Rica
Website www.lapalomalodge.com   **Price** 🅢🅢

Many hotels in Costa Rica call themselves remote, but not all require a two-hour boat trip through mangrove swamps and out into the Pacific Ocean. Hidden high up in the jungle overlooking the beauty of Drake Bay (Sir Francis clearly enjoyed the view, too), on the southern tip of Costa Rica, La Paloma Lodge attracts mainly nature lovers who have come to discover the Parque National Corcovado and is both luxurious and designed in aesthetic harmony with the environment.

A twenty-minute boat ride takes visitors to the park office, from where multilingual guides lead parties into more than 100,000 acres (40,470 ha) of virgin and secondary rain forest. Other tours include kayaking,

> *"Corcovado—the most biologically intense place on earth."*
>
> *National Geographic*

horseback riding, bird-watching, and a particularly unforgettable and fascinating night-bug tour—not one for arachnophobes, certainly. Caño Island, 12 nautical miles (22.2 km) off the Osa Peninsula, as the whole area is known, is an archaeologist's dream. Perfectly round spheres, varying in size from a soccer ball to some 6.5 feet (2 m) high, were brought to the island by pre-Columbian indigenous groups. It still remains a historic puzzle.

For those who want more privacy, there are seven deluxe "Sunset Ranchos," two-story cabins perched on a cliff top, with only the melody of the jungle and the crashing of the Pacific to disturb the silence. **DN**

Enjoy Lapa Rios Eco-lodge

Location Osa Peninsula, Costa Rica
Website www.laparios.com **Price** 💲💲

Lapa Rios is tucked away in the Osa peninsula, one of the most biologically diverse regions in the world. Some 375,000 acres (152,000 ha) make it one of the largest existing wet forests on the Pacific Coast of Mesoamerica. It boasts the "who's who of endangered species," from puma to ocelot and tapir, and the rain forest is teeming with wildlife.

Set in 1,000 acres (405 ha) of private rain forest, the fourteen-bungalow lodge is all about sustainable development, supporting the environment and the local community—built to prove that "a forest left standing is worth more than one cut down." The main wooden lodge is thatched and furnished with wicker. Atop a wooden spiral staircase some 33 feet (10 m) above the dining room, the observation deck offers views from tropical rain forest to the Pacific coastline.

The local food is a revelation. Red snapper, burritos, or fajitas are served up in banana leaves. The smiling staff are jovial and eager to perfect their English. The fish seviche is tangy and fresh, tender pieces of fish blended with exotic fruit and lime juice, as well as sweet peppers and cilantro. Grilled jumbo shrimps taste surprisingly sweet on their olive linguine followed by sweet homemade brownies with macadamia nuts accompanied by glorious local coffee.

The bungalows are stunning, with wooden flooring, white and dark green linens, and romantic mosquito nets over the bed. Luxuries are kept to a bare minimum—with no televisions or phones, of course. Nip into the outside shower to hear the symphony from the jungle, or head to the cliff-top pool. Toucans, parrots, and scarlet macaws sit patiently while howler monkeys growl in the distance. The total immersion in nature is both invigorating and beguiling. **RCA**

Stay at Cambridge Beaches

Location Somerset, Bermuda
Website www.cambridgebeaches.com **Price** 💲💲

One look at Bermuda's famous pink-sand beaches and it is easy to see why Catherine Zeta-Jones and Michael Douglas call this subtropical paradise "home." Given their warm blush tones by particles of crushed coral, the pastel-colored sands literally glow alongside the clear turquoise waters.

Everywhere you turn in Bermuda, you see color. The azure waters of the ocean mirror the deep-blue sky. Wedged in between are candy-colored houses, in shades of green, pink, and yellow, nestled in lush green subtropical foliage. At the stunning Cambridge Beaches in Somerset, guests stay in luxury cottages painted in pastel pink. With four sandy beaches and

> *"For snob appeal, Cambridge Beaches is numero uno in Bermuda."*
>
> *New York Times*

coves lined with palm trees, it is a water lover's paradise. Dipping below the surface, snorkelers can admire the brightly colored tropical fish and exquisite coral sculptures. Divers can explore the skeletons of wrecked ships that rest on the sandy seabed. At night, guests fill the waterside alfresco restaurant Breezes.

Candlelit tables are set up on the powdery sand, and the Atlantic Ocean laps just a few feet away. For the ultimate romantic dining experience, staff will arrange dinner on a private island. Diners are escorted by speedboat to a sandy key, where a candlelit table awaits. After the meal, guests are returned to the resort, and the rising tides reclaim the island again. **JP**

Relax at Tiamo Resort

Location South Andros Island, The Bahamas
Website www.tiamoresorts.com **Price** ⊖⊖

The row of wooden cottages that dots the white-sand beach on Andros Island looks inconspicuous enough. Yet it makes up the resort of Tiamo, one of the most talked-about "luxe" resorts of recent times. Tiamo's eleven cottages are chic—huge beds, brightly tiled mirrors, and funky shower rooms give the place a stylish feel—though their greatest asset is the open porches offering panoramic views of forest and beach.

Possessing a fiercely eco-friendly philosophy, the resort has a vast solar-power system for electricity, runs solar-heated rainwater showers, uses a well for drinking water, and advocates the use of composting toilets. There are no televisions at Tiamo and no

---

"This is barefoot luxury at its most polished—as well as being kind to the environment."

Independent

---

phones in the rooms, and e-mail access is extremely limited. The menu is eco-friendly, too. You won't find endangered species such as conch, lobster, and grouper on the menu, but there are tasty alternatives.

The surrounding scenery is nothing short of breathtaking: Classic Caribbean white sand and sparkling turquoise seas greet you each day. Borrow some books from the well-stocked lodge, relax in your hammock, or simply enjoy the rays on the beach. Tiamo, after all, advocates pure relaxation. **PS**

← *In contrast to some of its more hedonistic Caribbean neighbors, Tiamo prides itself on its peace and intimacy.*

Stay at The Landing

Location Harbour Island, The Bahamas
Website www.harbourislandlanding.com **Price** 💲💲

The Landing, a seven-room boutique hotel on Harbour Island, was chosen by Ralph Lauren for one of his advertising campaigns. You can see why. The hotel is the epitome of easy luxury, occupying two converted houses, one dating from 1800 and the other from 1825, just a couple of steps from the beach.

Harbour Island is regularly rated as having one of the world's best beaches. The hotel's rooms hit the mark, too. Former Lauren model India Hicks—who lives on the island—is responsible for the traditional plantation-style rooms, with four-poster beds, dark polished wood floors, candlelit storm lanterns, and cool white furnishings. Beds are dressed in Ralph Lauren

> *"The outgoing tide creates soft herringbone patterns like Chanel's summer tweed."*
>
> *Condé Nast Traveler*

linen, with Indian cotton throws; a flash of hot-pink bougainvillea deviates from the classic color scheme. With no televisions or phones, The Landing is a real escape from reality; mellow light plays through the painted wooden shutters into the rooms. The real wow factor is the honeymoon suite in the eaves, however—it comes with a freestanding bath. Australian chef Ken Gomes serves up local seafood in the intimate restaurant in the evening. You can match it with fine wines from Toby's cellar, and finish with Cuban cigars and the finest Caribbean rum. Simple elegance can be one of the hardest things to pull off, but The Landing does it effortlessly. **LD**

Explore Kamalame Cay

Location Kamalame Cay, The Bahamas
Website www.kamalame.com **Price** 💲💲💲

The Bahamas archipelago, 60 miles (95 km) off the Florida coast, needs no introduction, but how to pick the right escape from a choice of 700 islands? Shy away from the crowds in Nassau and the busy mega-resorts like Atlantis in favor of the intimate and laid-back atmosphere of Kamalame Cay—a 96-acre (39-ha) private island oozing Caribbean cool just off the coast of Andros Island.

Simple yet sophisticated, this piece of paradise has a 3-mile (5-km) palm-fringed beach, gloriously turquoise waters, and pristine pastel Bahamian cottages nestling among the coconut palms, hibiscus, and bougainvillea. Inside, rustic meets colonial chic: Stone features, 20-foot-high (6-m) wood beam ceilings with gently whirring fans, Indonesian furniture, and huge baths all make for a plush yet exotic feel.

Kamalame Cay is a byword for indulgence and comfort with a casual attitude. Hit the 2,000-square-foot (185-sq-m) Balinese-style spa, take a nap in a hammock, or simply roam the beach in search of oversized conch shells. Go bonefishing, snorkeling, or kayaking in the mangroves, or diving along the third-longest barrier reef in the world's clearest waters, where colorful corals are teeming with tropical fish, turtles, nurse sharks, and spotted eagle rays. Venture out to the dramatic 6,000-foot (1,800-m) drop to the bottom dubbed the "Tongue of the Ocean," where tiny sea horses, rainbow-colored parrotfish, graceful manta rays, and others glide peacefully.

At sunset, settle down with a fresh Carib Beer or whiz down to the Great House in your own golf cart for a delicious homemade meal of Bahamian bread, lobster, and pastries. Leaving is tough, especially when the extraordinarily friendly staff shed a tear. **RCA**

Enjoy Musha Cay

Location Musha Cay, Southern Bahamas
Website www.mushacay.com **Price** ⊖⊖⊖⊖

Owned by world-famous illusionist David Copperfield, who purchased it at a cost of $50 million, Musha Cay is 150 acres (60 ha) of pampered seclusion, regarded by the chosen few who have stayed here as one of the world's most sought-after hideaways.

Opening its doors for the first time in 2001, this sliver of palm trees and powderlike beaches is surrounded by turquoise waters that are off-limits to outsiders: Copperfield bought the islands surrounding Musha Cay to ensure they remain uninhabited. This is privacy on an unheard-of scale. Beaches that have barely been walked on ring the island, and an adjoining sandbar, exposed briefly each day, permits an exhilarating 2-mile (3-km) stroll into the ocean to Musha Cay's nearest neighbor. There are five guesthouses, all in traditional English Tudor–style, including a grand manor house, each with their own private beach and attended by a year-round staff of thirty.

You will not find any dinner menus here. Instead, the island's internationally trained chef cooks freshly caught seafood each day according to the individual requirements and tastes of his guests.

Island activities center on The Landings, a group of buildings overlooking the island's dock and including a glassed-in dining room, an open-air thatched roof pavilion, a swimming pool, and even a library. Water sports include deep-sea fishing, sailing, and scuba diving. From tented dining on your own beach to sitting spellbound beneath an evening fireworks display, with Musha Cay it would seem that the master illusionist has created heaven on earth. **BS**

↗ *Virtually everything at Musha Cay could be described as beachfront—it's your own personal paradise.*

"*Musha Cay represents a . . . challenge for the title of ultimate private island retreat.*"

Town & Country magazine

Unwind at Parrot Cay

Location Providenciales, Turks and Caicos
Website www.parrotcay.como.bz   **Price** $$

Arriving at Parrot Cay by speedboat, only thirty-five minutes from Providenciales, the capital of Turks and Caicos, feels like you have just stepped into a James Bond movie. The 1,000-acre (405-ha) private Caribbean island complete with requisite powdery white beaches, azure sea, and swaying palm trees is a magnet for celebrity A-listers who adore the peace and privacy from the paparazzi.

The impeccable, discreet service whisks you quickly along the wooden boardwalk on a buggy to your accommodation. All bedrooms have private terraces, and the beachfront villas have private pools as well as fabulous open-air showers. Only a stone's throw from

> ## "Parrot Cay's beach is ridiculously spoiling, with picturesque dunes and impossibly soft sand."
>
> *Condé Nast Traveler*

the aquamarine Caribbean, the villas are the last word in understated elegance. A short walk along the sandy boardwalk brings you to the bar and restaurant area, overlooking a beautiful infinity pool, a library with Internet access, a gym, two tennis courts, and the Balinese-inspired Shambhala spa with a wide variety of treatments—all carried out in an atmosphere of Zen-like calm. The spa also has a special menu, a meditation garden, its own pool and sundeck, and separate yoga and Pilates pavilions. **HA**

➔ *For somewhere to unwind in the most glamorous of surroundings, Parrot Cay is second to none.*

Rent a Villa on Salt Cay

Location Salt Cay, Turks and Caicos
Website www.saltcay.org **Price** ⑤

Salt Cay calls itself "the island that time forgot," because since the salt trade dried up, it has stood still. All around it, Caribbean islands have soaked up the tourist traffic and grown luxury hotels; 2-mile-long (3.2-km) Salt Cay, however, has planted its feet in the past. Here, you can rent a villa that has no key—because you do not need one. Roosters wake you in the morning; there are few cars; cell phones have no reception.

The island is not just for those who wish to switch off and enjoy rum punch, sunsets, and grilled fish. Divers admire the pristine reefs, especially the 7,000-foot (2,134-m) Columbus Passage, a top drift-diving destination. Between 3,000 and 5,000 North Atlantic

---

"Buoyed by margaritas and somewhat sunburned, we ended the day very happy campers."

Guardian

---

humpback whales migrate around these islands every year, from December to mid-April, making it the world's largest humpback whale breeding grounds.

Only around eighty people live on Salt Cay. Tourism is still small scale, and you might find yourself one of the only non-natives here. You certainly will have a large part of the island's white-sand beaches to yourself for romantic strolls, beachcombing, and whatever it is we did with our time before technology and the modern world cluttered it up. **LD**

← *If you have ever thought, "Stop the world, I wanna get off," head back in time to Salt Cay.*

Discover Cayo Levisa

Location Archipiélago de los Colorados, Cuba
Website www.cubahotelbookings.com **Price** ❶

A two-hour road trip from Havana gets you to Palma Rubia, a one-horse town and jumping-off point for the Archipiélago de los Colorados, a cluster of tiny islands facing the Florida straits, enveloped by thick jungles of tropical mangrove and bordered by sugar-white, soft-sand beaches. Most idyllic among these is Cayo Levisa, where the virgin sands look across to the nearby black-coral reef and the daily grind has never been invented. There's nowhere to stay except twenty little bungalows, dotted among the pine trees, simply and rustically put together with local materials, and right on the beach.

The outdoor bar is the focal point in the evenings, and the friendly barmen keep the cocktails and the Cuban music flowing. Other than the bar and grill, there is one restaurant, and that is it. The only thing that could disturb you are the day-trippers who arrive mid-morning and leave late afternoon. There is abundant marine life, with snorkeling and diving on tap—this region is home to one of the largest coral reefs in the world, and there are about twenty-three identified dive sites within a forty-five-minute boat ride.

The joy of Cayo Levisa is that it is completely different from other Cuban resorts, which are, with the exception of a few places, almost all soulless all-inclusive vast "party" venues block-booked by cheap package vacation companies. This, by contrast, is practically your own private island; just 1.8 miles (3 km) of fabulous white sand washed by a warm clear aquamarine sea. The island is just several hundred yards wide at most points. The archipelago includes Cayo Paraíso, an even smaller little island reputed to be a favorite fishing haunt of Ernest Hemingway. All in all, a dreamy Caribbean paradise. **LB**

Explore the Viñales Valley

Location Pinar del Rio, Cuba
Website www.cubahotelbookings.com   **Price** 🌙

If you want to see a valley so magnificent that it gets you thinking about what the Garden of Eden might have looked like, travel to Cuba. Richly fertile, with endless tobacco, sugarcane, and coffee plantations, the western province of Pinar del Rio is blessed with a lush greenness, beautiful rivers, and natural springs. The pretty village of Viñales is tucked into the breathtaking Sierra de los Organos mountains, and the Viñales Valley is UNESCO-protected. A glance from the road down to the town will tell you why: Nothing can prepare you for your first view of the mogotes—tree-covered limestone knolls, molded by underground rivers, rising dramatically out of green landscape.

"We are only 150 kilometers from Havana, but millions of years away."

Reina María Rodríguez, Cuban poet and novelist

The eerily quiet, humid, countryside can be explored on foot, bike, or horse. The sleepy village of Viñales itself is a classic small Cuban country town, with a strip of colonial-style bungalows painted in various pastel shades overlooked by pines. Most of the houses are a good deal smarter and the owners more house proud than the average Cuban campesino. This is the best place to sample rural Cuban hospitality, too: The people are friendly, sweet, courteous, and helpful, more so than any streetwise Habanero. **LB**

➦ *With its distinctive round-topped hills, the valley is an outstanding example of natural beauty.*

Visit Royal Plantation

Location Ocho Ríos, Jamaica
Website www.royalplantation.com   **Price** ⑤⑤⑤

Push the boat out at the Royal Plantation in Jamaica's Ocho Ríos. With all the airs and graces of an old-style plantation house, the hotel is a glamorous mix of antiques and Caribbean artwork, fabrics, and furniture.

Lush tropical vegetation, the sea, and bougainvillea give the air a fragrant exoticism. With movie-set looks, it is hardly surprising the hotel was used in films such as *Prelude to a Kiss* and *License to Wed*. And you will be in good company: Winston Churchill, Ian Fleming, Noel Coward, Robin Williams, Alec Baldwin, and Meg Ryan have all enjoyed the "Royal" treatment.

The only thing on the agenda here is chilling out. Grab a hammock or hit one of the two beaches, complete with loungers, water sports, and a beach grill. Relax on the upper pool deck with its whirlpool tub and gorgeous view, and be sure not to miss a very civilized afternoon tea with fantastic scones.

For the ultimate relaxation, get pampered at the spa. Try the couples' special "scrub-a-dub-2 in the tub," which starts off with a salt and brown sugar scrub, followed by a whirlpool bath armed with a sweet fruit punch milk shake, and finishes with a deliciously relaxing and tropically fragrant massage.

Indulge yourself at the fine-dining French restaurant, Le Papillon, where you can sample lobster ravioli and giant tiger prawns sitting on updated Louis XIV–style chairs upholstered in eclectic mismatching fabrics. Want to be alone? Ask the staff to set up a romantic dinner on the jetty surrounded by the sea and the twinkling stars. If you love the food so much you want to know how it is prepared, enroll in a half-day cooking course with chef Owen Bain. Before you know it, you will be producing fantastic breadfruit soup and oven-baked lobster tails. **RCA**

Stay at Strawberry Hill

Location Blue Mountains, Jamaica
Website www.strawberryhillresort.com   **Price** ⑤⑤

Leap out of bed, throw open the shutters, and pinch yourself: No, you are not dreaming. That scent of an exotic tropical garden is real, carried in on the cool breeze coming off the Blue Mountains behind you.

Strawberry Hill is based around an eighteenth-century colonial plantation house perched high in the mountains. It belongs to Chris Blackwell, the record producer who discovered Bob Marley and founded Island Records. Now an elegant, exclusive boutique hotel, it is still a popular meeting place for famous musicians, models, and the international jet set. The Georgian-style ornate wooden cottages are scattered among the gardens with striking views of the city of

> *"The Great House looks out over velvety emerald peaks rearing and dipping in 360-degree views."*
>
> *Guardian*

Kingston 3,000 feet (915 m) below. French doors open onto spacious private verandas where hand-carved fretwork carefully re-creates nineteenth-century carpentry styles. Inside, the bedrooms are like showrooms for fine fabrics, crisp white linen, and polished mahogany furniture and floors. Of course, all rooms have a high-quality stereo system, with plenty of Island Records CDs available to enjoy.

At mealtimes, shuffle over to the open decks of the restaurant to enjoy its renowned "New Jamaican Cuisine," using local spices and sauces. Chef Kingsley McGregor has developed several trademark dishes that are said to exceed all expectations. **SH**

Walk in the Blue Mountains

Location Blue Mountains, Jamaica
Website www.great-adventures.com/destinations/jamaica/bluemo.html   **Price** 🌓

While snow might be the last thing to come to mind when you think of Jamaica, way up on the 7,400-foot-(2,256-m-) high Blue Mountain Peak, snow and frost have occasionally been seen.

The Blue Mountains is the largest mountain range in Jamaica, stretching 24 miles (38 km) long and, at its widest, 14 miles (22 km) across, in the eastern third of the island. From the rest of the island, the peaks appear shrouded in blue mist—hence their name—and have given that same name to a brand of coffee grown in the rich fertile slopes of the lower mountainsides. The mountains provided a refuge to slaves who ran to the hills when the Spanish left the plantations, and more than 500 species of flowering plant live there, half of which are found nowhere else in the world.

The classic hike to the top of Blue Mountain Peak is typically taken under the shadow of darkness. The three-to-four-hour walk takes you up a steep 3,000-foot (915-m) increase in altitude. By the time you reach the top, you should be able to watch the sunrise over the ocean, illuminating the north and south coast of Jamaica, and see as far as Cuba, 130 miles (209 km) away, on a clear day. On the walk down, you will experience the full glory of the canopy, cloud forest, and woodland slopes in daylight.

There is more than one hiking path in the mountains, of course—hundreds of trails connect the villages and are centuries old. Bird-watchers and botanists particularly recommend the Rio Grande Valley and Hardwar Gap for fantastic variety. **LD**

↗ *A waterfall and rushing stream add to the shroud of mist in the Blue Mountains, Jamaica.*

" . . . a landscape of coffee farms, rolling hills in many shades of green, and jagged peaks . . ."

Polly Rodger Brown, *Independent*

Stay at The Caves Resort

Location Negril, Jamaica   **Website** www.thecavesresort.com
Price ⑤⑤⑤

With its 10 acres (4 ha) of tropical jungle and seaside cliffs, stone walkways, and naturally formed grottos, Jamaica's Caves Resort is one of the island's most spectacular hideaways. Designed by Greer-Ann and Bertram Saulter, The Caves are ten handcrafted cottages ensconced in a lush garden near the ocean.

There is a cliff-side swimming pool, an open-air mini-spa (that looks out onto the sea), a couple of dining gazebos—each with a full bar—and additional swimming access and tanning areas. The seafront area, meanwhile, is awash with hidden nooks and crannies, including the eponymous "caves" themselves, which are notched into the cliffs.

"One of the most romantic getaways in the Caribbean . . . The Caves is a truly unique retreat."

Hilary magazine

Each cottage has been designed differently, with bright island colors and bamboo furniture. All are built from natural materials, mostly wood and stone with thatched roofs, and have a rustic-luxe ambience. The surrounding area is a marine wonderland, perfect for those who love swimming, snorkeling, and diving, and there is an abundance of dolphins, sea turtles, and fish around the nearby reef. The Caves can arrange scuba certification as well as motorcycle rentals, horseback riding, river tubing, and more. **PS**

➔ *The resort has a slew of great amenities and terrific sea views, and yet the island's nightlife is not far away.*

Relax at Saba Rock Bar

Location Virgin Gorda, British Virgin Islands
Website www.sabarock.com   **Price** 💲💲

"Remote" and "idyllic" are words that spring to mind when you come across the tiny island turned watering hole for passing yachts. Accessible by boat or seaplane, Saba Rock benefits from that "end of the world" feeling, probably because it appears to have been carelessly dropped into the Caribbean Sea. In the North Sound of Virgin Gorda in the British Virgin Islands, Saba Rock is wedged right between the Bitter End Yacht Club and the uninhabited national park of Prickly Pear Island. Just a stone's throw from the island is the renowned Eustatia Reef, a snorkeling heaven and home to yellow-head jaw fish, sail-fin blennies, angelfish, and sea horses, among others.

> ## "By far the Caribbean's least spoiled inhabited island, Saba is spectacular."
>
> *Condé Nast Traveler*

With a colorful history rich in pirate tales featuring everyone from Bluebeard to Captain Kidd, the rock is still one of the yachting crowd's favorite stops. Its relaxed Caribbean vibe is enhanced by the dark wooden decks, palm trees, crystal-clear waters, and local air-conditioning: overhead ceiling fans gently whirring with the sweetly scented trade winds.

Watch the world go by with a cool drink, or hit the hammock. At night, the bar and restaurant come alive with steel bands. If you don't want to get back below deck, check into one of their nine rooms and suites. There's no doubt that Saba Rock is one of the coolest bars on Earth—or rather, on sea. **RCA**

Visit Biras Creek

Location Virgin Gorda, British Virgin Islands
Website www.biras.com   **Price** 💲💲💲

The archipelago of the British Virgin Islands includes some sixty volcanic isles surging out of the sea with a jagged, rough coastline dotted with pristine white-sand beaches. None is more idyllic than Biras Creek, a low-key hideaway on the northeastern tip of Virgin Gorda. The island, first named the "Pregnant Virgin" by Christopher Columbus because of its rotund shape, was rechristened the "Fat Virgin" when the technical impossibility of its original name dawned on him.

Biras Creek, accessible only by boat, is in a unique setting, wedged between the peaceful Caribbean Sea and the Atlantic Ocean. The journey over the tempting waters is full of promises. From the arrival at the jetty, with its aquamarine waters amid the mangroves, to the smiling faces all around, guests and staff alike, the ambience is utterly enchanting. No matter which way you turn, you are surrounded by tones of brilliant blue.

Each view is reminiscent of glossy brochures selling paradise. They say that there are three different paces here: slow, slower, and full stop. Borrow a bike to explore, or a Boston Whaler dinghy to visit the nearby deserted beaches of Prickly Pear Island or watch the wildlife go by: Geckos and the grumpy iguanas wander around oblivious to their human neighbors. Spend a lazy day on the beach interrupted only by the tasty lunchtime grill, snorkel in the limpid sea, hit the gym or even the spa.

With recently revamped suites, an affiliation to the Relais & Chateaux group (synonymous with gourmet cuisine and top-end service), the 140-acre (57-ha) estate feels like a private tropical sanctuary. **RCA**

➡ *The view over the creek itself is always idyllic, whether in bright sunshine or the fading light of the evening.*

Enjoy Virgin Gorda's Baths

Location Virgin Gorda, British Virgin Islands
Website www.bvi.com **Price** Ⓢ

There is more to be seen in the Virgin Islands than deserted beaches lined with swaying palm trees tucked away among the many tiny coves and inlets.

On Virgin Gorda, the third-largest island, one of the hottest attractions is the natural miracle dubbed "The Baths." They are exotic pools and grottos formed by giant granite boulders that appeared approximately 70 million years ago when molten rock merged into the layers of lava on the Caribbean seabed. The magma slowly formed enormous pieces of granite made of feldspar and quartz. Some 50 million years later, a shift in the continental plates lifted the seabed and the granite was exposed.

> *"A bed of sand with massive granite boulders ... strewn in irregular piles along the coast"*
>
> *Condé Nast Traveler*

Arrive early to have the place to yourself, pay the $3 fee, and walk into the grottoes, a magical place where it is easy to lose your bearings. Hidden rooms with shafts of light and transparent shallow waters are almost surreal. Some pools are deep enough for snorkeling, but be careful of the north swell. Follow the trail to the white-sand beach, where boulders are scattered. One of the beaches below the Baths, the Crawl, even has its own lagoon, protected by the rocks with a reef busy with turtles, rays, and sea horses. **RCA**

↤ *Unspoiled and lush, the exotic British Virgin Islands offer a wealth of sea, sun, sand, and solitude.*

Snorkel at Peter Island

Location Peter Island, British Virgin Islands
Website www.peterisland.com **Price** Ⓢ

After a long flight, followed by a transfer on a tiny eight-seater propeller plane, hopping on board the launch to get to the private shores of Peter Island is a real thrill. On arrival in the all-inclusive tropical haven, a golf cart whizzes you to your plush room, where the Caribbean views stretch all around.

Although the resort has the requisite trimmings, from a huge spa to live music and luxurious rooms, the real attraction is in the crystal-clear waters. Head to Deadman's Beach, named after Blackbeard left fifteen pirates stranded across the water on Dead Chest with just one bottle of rum. One escaped and made it to the shore. The rest, as they say, is history.

Within yards of the sand, you will be immersed in snorkeling heaven, swimming among a rainbow of blue tangs, orange and yellow long-snout butterfly fish, and shimmering purple-hued Creole wrasses. Farther afield, toward the waters known as the "Indians," there is more prime underwater viewing with moray eel, sea turtles, trumpet fish, and bar jacks weaving through the brain corals. The area is dotted with protected dive sites such as Salt Island's 310-foot- (95-m-) deep wreck, which is recognized as one of the world's best. Hop onto the ferry to Jost Van Dyke Island, an unspoiled oasis with just 150 inhabitants. Explore the picture-postcard waters off Diamond Cay or the atoll of Sandy Spit, a tiny, pristine, palm-fringed islet and snorkeling favorite.

At the end of the day, reward yourself with a rum and coconut "Painkiller" cocktail at the Soggy Dollar Bar, which was once accessible only by swimming to shore, or join the yachting crowd at Foxy's, the beach shack where Foxy himself tells his dubious jokes between Calypso renditions. **RCA**

Go Diving in Little Cayman

Location Little Cayman, Cayman Islands
Website www.paradise-divers.com **Price** $

Little Cayman is said to be tiny—just 10 miles (16 km) long by 1 mile (1.6 km) wide, with a handful of permanent residents—but that only counts the part above water. The Cayman Islands make up an underwater mountain range whose peaks just poke their tips beyond the surface. Underneath, there are cliffs and drop-offs that create some of the most renowned diving sites in the world. Most famous are Bloody Bay and Jackson Blight, two distinct walls that both fall within Little Cayman's Bloody Bay Marine Park.

Bloody Bay's wall starts at just 20 feet (6 m) below the water's surface but it drops to 1,000 feet (305 m) or more—some claim the wall plunges a staggering 6,000 feet (1,829 m). The wall is covered in sponges and corals in extraordinary shades of red and yellow. Starfish undulate infinitely slowly, while moray eels dart their toothy heads in and out of the crevices. Gaudy angelfish, butterfly fish, and parrot fish show off their vibrant hues as they scoot alongside elongated trumpet fish with tubular snouts. Eagle rays and stingrays, sharks, barracudas, and groupers swim nearby, as do the turtles for whom the Cayman Islands were originally named—when Christopher Columbus arrived here in 1503 he named the islands "Las Tortugas." All this is set against the incredible azure waters of the Caribbean Sea.

Above the water, Little Cayman is a peaceful place. There is not a great deal to do other than dive, snorkel, and watch the wildlife. A small number of hotels and resorts invite you to lie back beneath the warm Caribbean sun and do nothing much at all. **PE**

→ *A diver hovers above the colorful reef of Little Cayman, which offers some of the world's best diving.*

Stay at Eden Rock

Location St. Barthélemy, French West Indies
Website www.edenrockhotel.com **Price** 🅢🅢🅢

Once upon a time, Eden Rock was a private house owned by Rémy de Haenen, the first mayor of the Island of St. Barts and friend of Greta Garbo, Howard Hughes, and Robert Mitchum. Today it is no less than the Caribbean's glitziest institution, a family-owned hotel that has been the height of glamor and sophistication for decades.

We are talking full-blown glamor here, from the thirty-four exquisite suites and villas, including Villa Rockstar, a 16,000-square-foot (1,485-sq-m) party pad complete with golf putting green and cinema, to the resort's 65-foot (20-m), fully crewed *Princess* yacht, which has a personal watercraft in the hull. An island

> *"Discover private moments of contact with the natural magnificence of the Caribbean."*
>
> *L.A. Confidential*

tour on the yacht may be pricey, but at least any passing boats (containing the likes of P. Diddy) should approve of your suitably swish mode of transport.

The chic island boasts pretty coves, rugged beaches, and marine reserves teeming with a rainbow of underwater life. Back on dry land, the sights are equally impressive—as previous guests Mick Jagger and Mariah Carey can attest. Romantics will love the Garbo Suite, oozing 1930s Hollywood charm, with a wood and white-leather bed and a Philippe Starck bathroom. James Bond wannabes might be seduced by the James Suite, sitting at the water's edge with a private pool, deck, and hot tub. **LP**

Unwind at La Samanna

Location St. Martin, French West Indies
Website www.lasamanna.com **Price** 🅢🅢

St. Martin is a unique island split between two nationalities: French and Dutch. A fascinating mix of cultures, its dual personality means food is a priority on the French side—excellent patisseries and restaurants abound; the Dutch half has casinos and a busy nightlife. Thankfully, there is more to it. Visit the two capital cities—Marigot and Philipsburg—with their distinctive charm and architecture, the 7-acre (3-ha) Eden Park, and the 1,400-foot (426-m) Paradise Peak for stunning island views, or disappear to La Samanna, a classy and elegant resort with an air of quiet grace.

This glamorous retreat is the epitome of Caribbean chic. The upper rooms have very private rooftop terraces where whitewashed walls sparkle against azure blue cushions, while below hammocks hang lazily in the gardens beyond the atmospheric terraces, pleasantly shielded by palm trees.

The resort's bijou Elysée spa, named after the "abode for the blessed" in Greek mythology, has eight soothing massage rooms and more space to relax in. The choice of treatments is extensive, with everything from shiatsu to reflexology, Thai massages, and hot stone therapy, as well as Pilates and yoga; there is even a personal trainer on hand for one-to-one training.

At sunset, the pool area comes alive with burning torches and live music for cocktail hour. The hotel's restaurant on the hillside has fantastic views over the Baie Longue, and offers a fusion menu blending European and Caribbean dishes. Lobster ravioli and delicious confit duck come with a flabbergasting wine list. It is an epicurean's dream come true. **RCA**

➡ *The unobstructed views from the beach at La Samanna are among the best in the Caribbean.*

Hike in the Morne Trois Pitons National Park

Location Morne Trois Pitons National Park, Dominica
Website whc.unesco.org/en/list/814   **Price** ◑

"Luxuriant natural tropical forest blends with scenic volcanic features of great scientific interest."

UNESCO World Heritage Committee

An Eden for the eco-conscious, Dominica's Morne Trois Pitons National Park offers some of the most spectacular hikes in the Caribbean, with more than 300 miles (483 km) of trails. A designated World Heritage site, the park sprawls over 16,980 acres (6,870 ha) of streams, waterfalls, unspoiled tropical rain forest, and mountains, not to mention five volcanoes, fifty fumaroles, and numerous hot springs. The park's star attraction, sitting beneath a thick vapor cloud, is Boiling Lake, the second largest lake of its kind in the world. It is a bubbling cauldron of unknown depth, whose milky-colored waters range in temperature from 180°F to 197°F (82°C to 92°C).

"Trois Pitons" refers to the triple-peaked mountains that top 4,672 feet (1,424 m) and are shrouded in mist. No mammals live in the park, but expect to see plenty of insects, birds, crustaceans, reptiles, and, if you are lucky, one of two endemic parrots. One of these, the Imperial, is Dominica's national bird.

Walkers normally head to the park's Valley of Desolation, a grueling seven- to eight-hour trek that involves scrambling over rocks and tackling wet and slippery steep ascents. Starting from the village of Laudat, hikers venture through lush rain forests teeming with rare exotic birds. The moss-covered and lichen-clad valley itself appears bleak, but it is a hotbed of geothermal activity, bubbling with hot springs, boiling mud pots, and mini geysers. For back-to-nature spa treatments, walkers can slather on mud masks and relieve their aches and pains by bathing in hot spring waterfalls or swimming in cool lakes. **JK**

◰ *Hikers make their way down a path in the Valley of Desolation in Morne Trois Pitons National Park.*

Stay at Zandoli Inn

Location Near Fond St. Jean, Dominica
Website www.zandoli.com **Price** 💲💲

Like the small native lizard it is named after, Zandoli Inn bathes in the sun by the rocks on the southeast coast of Dominica. It is a small hotel, rather like a villa, with five rooms and a plunge pool, surrounded by 6 acres (2.4 ha) of rain forest and whispers of the sea. As the sun goes down, the heavy scent of ylang-ylang wafts in through the gauzy curtains hanging between your open veranda and the simple yet stylish bedroom, and the scene is set for total relaxation.

The most rugged and mountainous of the Lesser Antilles, Dominica is sandwiched between Guadeloupe and Martinique, and its topography means that getting around is no easy feat. Zandoli Inn is just 13 miles (21 km) from Roseau on the island's southeast coast, but feels farther. With wonderful hiking trails in its grounds and beyond, it is easy to lose yourself in the forest among date palms, vanilla vines, nutmeg, and avocado trees, while watching tropical birds flit overhead, seeking hummingbird nests, or just enjoying the huge, brightly colored indigenous flowers. With only five rooms in the hotel, staying here is an intimate experience. The boulder shoreline is a popular meditation spot, and Zandoli is a popular honeymoon spot, too. Importantly, there are no televisions, radios, or telephones in the whole place.

Being green is another theme. There is a freshwater plunge pool to help you cool off, which is treated with chemicals that are kind to the environment (you can also snorkel off the boulders near the hotel), and water for the showers is heated by the sun. You can enjoy fresh local fruit as well as plenty of local specials in the evening, when a communal meal is served; cocktail hour heralds rum punch and Kubuli beer as the perfect accompaniment to the sunset. **LD**

Visit Carlisle Bay Resort

Location Carlisle Bay, Antigua
Website www.carlisle-bay.com **Price** 💲💲💲

Antigua has a beach for every day of the year; the island's 365 beaches and tempting waters are some of the Caribbean's finest. A hub in the Leeward Islands, Antigua has a real celebrity following: Oprah Winfrey, Denzel Washington, Morgan Freeman, and Eric Clapton all own villas here. For holidaying celebs such as Donatella Versace, the place to be is Carlisle Bay, a swish, luxurious haven to the south of the island.

Far from having the usual rough-around-the-edges Caribbean decor, the Carlisle has managed to blend regional style with urban, contemporary cool. The hotel's interior is sumptuous: an entrance pavilion with plantation-style shutters, oversized exotic floral

> *"This is a place that feels like a sanctuary, the perfect retreat in which to wind down."*
>
> *Daily Telegraph*

arrangements, and sleek dark furniture covered in crisp white fabrics. The elegant rooms decorated in subtle grays and lavenders have rich Jim Thompson raw-silk curtains, decadent daybeds, and enormous oval bathtubs for two. Gadgets include a snazzy espresso machine and fiber-optic bedside reading lights. Choose from two gourmet restaurants on the spot: Indigo On The Beach or the Asian fusion East.

Plus, there is the stunning swimming pool, slick spa, ultra-hip library, forty-five-seater, blue-leather screening room, and a poolside bar for sipping refreshing vodka, coconut rum, and pineapple Indigo Coolers. You simply will not want to leave. **RCA**

Enjoy Hermitage Bay

Location Hermitage Bay, Antigua
Website www.hermitagebay.com **Price** 🌀🌀🌀

Set high above a hidden bay that has been in private hands for more than a century and only a twenty-minute drive away from the capital, St. John's, the twenty-five Balinese-themed wooden cottages of Hermitage Bay tumble down a secluded hillside overlooking the azure waters of the Caribbean. Antigua has reserved one of its finest beaches for this exclusive hideaway, a world of mahogany floors, infinity plunge pools, and impeccable service.

Roomy cottages are adorned with the finest of linens, massive flat-screen televisions, iPod docking stations, and wireless broadband Internet connectivity. It could, therefore, be some time before you get

> *"The views from the hillside cottages are worth staying for alone."*
>
> *Daily Telegraph*

around to venturing beyond your wall of solid timber, bifolding doors onto the wraparound veranda, and the panoramic views to the bay and ocean beyond.

To emphasize Hermitage Bay's commitment to relaxation and well-being, motorized water sports are banned in favor of less intrusive, more leisurely pursuits such as sailing and windsurfing. If you would rather have a massage over the water on the end of a wooden pier beneath a purpose-built thatched roof than in the in-house spa, then that is what you can have. And the most noise you are likely to deal with once the sun goes down on this 10-acre (4-ha), all-suite resort is the lapping of the waves. **BS**

Stay at Jumby Bay Resort

Location Jumby Bay, Antigua
Website www.jumbybayresort.com **Price** 🌀🌀🌀🌀

Jumby Bay Resort, a 3,000-acre (1,215-ha) private island, has recently undergone a multimillion-dollar renovation that has freshened up the resort to high standards. The calming beige and cream color schemes of the rooms are astutely matched to British colonial furnishings, which include ample beds and ultra-roomy bathrooms (indoor soaking tub included). Nearly all Jumby Bay suites feature their own entrance and courtyard, large terraces with teak furnishings, and private plunge pools. There are bookable in-room treatments: The Beach Pavilion's massage therapists are adept in Eastern and Western techniques.

For naturalists, Jumby Bay is as exciting as it is relaxing, with wildlife such as White Egret and Blue Pelican (and sheep) roaming around. The crowning glory is Pasture Bay Beach, a protected nesting site for the endangered hawksbill turtle. Guests can sign up for the turtle-watch scheme and play an active role in helping out. For outdoors types, various water sports are available, including snorkeling (lessons can be arranged), sailing, windsurfing, kayaking, waterskiing, diving, boat rentals, and deep-sea fishing. Three tennis courts, bike tours, trail walking, and croquet are also all available. And let's not forget deluxe retail therapy at The Beach Pavilion, which also features a fitness center should you want a workout.

For sustenance, The Veranda is beautiful, breezy, and open for breakfast, lunch, and light dinner, whereas the Estate House, a 230-year-old colonial manor house, provides a more upmarket experience—just the thing after a hard day's sunbathing. **PS**

➡ *Jumby Bay is home to the endangered hawksbill turtle, which lays its eggs on Pasture Bay Beach.*

Relax at Rock Cottage Villa

Location Blue Waters, Antigua   **Website** www.bluewaters.net
Price ⊖⊖⊖

Perched on a rocky outcrop in the Caribbean, Rock Cottage is the kind of place where you can stay holed up for days and—happily—not see another soul. Located in Soldiers Bay on Antigua's north coast, this private property allegedly has ocean views of 270 degrees. Whether that figure is accurate or not, few can argue that this hideaway has a panoramic and spectacular vista over the vast, twinkling ocean.

A fusion of whitewashed walls, marble tiles, and wooden shutters set against the rich-blue sea and emerald-green foliage, Rock Cottage is everything the Caribbean should be. Along with a choice of sundecks and dining areas to suit the position of the sun, it also

---

"This was about as close to perfection as a Caribbean holiday could possibly get."

The Mail on Sunday

---

has a private whirlpool tub and five huge, airy bedrooms housing vast beds. Perhaps the pièce de résistance is the upstairs "his and hers" bathroom with its twin sinks set before shuttered windows, fringed by swaying palms, that open over the deep-blue water. Guests may be able to tear themselves away from those bathroom views, but there really is no need to leave the cottage, let alone the island—unless you want to play at being James Bond for a day and make use of the private motorboat moored below. **NS**

➔ *If you feel like losing track of time, in a beautiful and genuinely unusual location, Rock Cottage is for you.*

Relax at Jade Mountain

Location Anse Chastanet, St. Lucia
Website www.jademountainstlucia.com   **Price** 💲💲💲

The suites at Jade Mountain have one completely open wall staring straight at one of the world's greatest views: the twin peaks of the Piton Mountains on St. Lucia, a World Heritage site, and down onto the shimmering Caribbean Sea. Intruding halfway into the room is your own private infinity pool, measuring up to 900 square feet (84 sq m).

Ceilings are 15 feet (4.5 m) high, walls are of rock, concrete, and coral; there are few corners or straight lines, and the floors are made of tropical hardwoods. There are huge canopy beds, individually made pieces of eclectic furniture, and showers with a rain shower and six body sprays. Suites also feature a raised two-

---

"Architect Nick Troubetzkoy has created . . . spaces that seem to float out over the Caribbean."

Condé Nast Traveler

---

person "chromatherapy" hot whirlpool tub in which you can control the colored lights in the water for different effects while gazing at the view. Guests can also control the colored lighting in the infinity pools.

This exclusive resort of infinity pool suites high on the lush hills of St. Lucia is the creation of its wealthy and creative architect owner. There are luxury resort facilities available, including a beach, restaurant, pools, and a spa, but in truth you will find it hard to leave these extraordinary technology-free suites. **SH**

⬅ *Lie back in your own infinity pool at Jade Mountain and enjoy this stunning view of a World Heritage site.*

Stay at Jalousie Plantation

Location The Pitons, St. Lucia
Website www.thejalousieplantation.com   **Price** 💲💲💲

When the current owner of this former sugar plantation bought it, the place could be reached only by canoe. These days, you can take a taxi from the airport to tackle the steep and winding route to the hotel or charter a helicopter, flying close in to St. Lucia's stunning twin peaks, the Pitons. Nestled in the rain forest by St. Lucia's most stunning natural attractions, the location alone makes the hotel a hidden treat.

The Jalousie Plantation, in the Valley of the Pitons, has 192 acres (78 ha) of rain forest and 115 rooms, including first-class villas, suites, and rooms in the carefully restored eighteenth-century sugar mill. The accommodation is all decorated in modern Caribbean style—slightly chintzy, but very comfortable—with panoramic views of the mountains and the sea, as well as plunge pools and sundecks. The five-star hotel has stellar service for all, and if you want to do more than relax in the sun, the staff have plenty of ideas for you. The Rainforest Oasis spa can help you unwind, with the help of treatments inspired by the natural world. These include signature massages, body wraps, hot-stone treatments and facials, and body scrubs using water from the sulfur springs nearby, all with a view of the tropical rain forest.

On the beach, the sand shelves nearly as dramatically as the mountains peak, making the sea perfect for swimmers—and very calm. The hotel offers scuba lessons and one beginner or certified dive for free for every guest; just about every water sport under the sun is also on offer. If you want a vacation challenge, why not scale the Pitons? Guides are available to take you up there, as well as down to the sulfur springs, volcanoes, and waterfalls of St. Lucia. Relaxing under a tiki hut with a cocktail never felt so good. **LD**

Stay at Little Good Harbour

Location Shermans, Barbados
Website www.littlegoodharbourbarbados.com **Price** 🕄🕄

This boutique hotel is in the northwest of the island, in the small fishing community of Shermans. Small chalet-style guest cottages are arranged around a central pool and just off the beach, decorated in an elegant but not over-fussy way. The self-catering villas are colonial-style, with pink roofs and a laid-back, friendly feel, as well as sun terraces and a sea view.

Although there is no room service, the staff aim to make your stay as comfortable as possible, with the mantra "the hardest decision you should have to make is what to have to eat tonight." The hotel's Fish Pot restaurant mission is to make that decision as tricky as possible. It is a hidden secret among locals, a wooden-

> *"There are . . . waves breaking right beneath you. It's a classic Caribbean setting."*
>
> James Henderson, *Financial Times*

decked restaurant off the beaten track but close to the fish market, guaranteeing a spectacular catch of the day. Take your pick from grilled swordfish, baby clams in Creole sauce, and panfried lobster, but save space for the exceptional coconut crème brulée.

LGH is an escape within Barbados, and with its clear waters, sandy beach, and calm atmosphere, it is the ideal place to relax amid the hummingbirds, monkeys in the palm trees, and butterflies. Do: dress up—Little Good Harbour is on the books of luxury boutique hotel group Mr. and Mrs. Smith, and designer caftans are de rigueur. Do not: get too enthusiastic about the local rum and spoil the tranquility for everyone else. **LD**

Relax at Cotton House

Location Mustique, St. Vincent and the Grenadines
Website www.cottonhouseresort.com **Price** 🕄🕄🕄

From the tropical island location to the sense of total privacy, Cotton House checks all the right boxes. The verdant landscape, rich woodland, and dramatic cliffs that tower over the white-sand beaches and clear, deep blue ocean have attracted countless celebrity guests, from David Bowie to Tommy Hilfiger.

The eighteenth-century warehouse and sugar mill was restored by dazzling designer Oliver Messel, the uncle (by marriage) of Britain's late Princess Margaret. There are some 13 acres (5 ha) of pristine beachside garden, and guests stay in a choice of five fully restored Georgian houses, one of three cottages, a five-room beach house, or a block of two one-bedroom duplex suites with private plunge pools. Luxuriant Egyptian cotton sheets and net canopies adorn the king-size beds (some are wrought-iron four-posters). Modern touches include flat-screen televisions and DVD players, and each room has its own balcony or patio. "The Tower," on the upper floor of Coutinot House (the five-bedroom beach house), is a cut above the rest, but for true opulence the two-bedroom Cotton Hill is unsurpassable. A boot-shaped private swimming pool, complete with cool white surrounding flagstones and teak loungers, enables you to take a dip while idly contemplating the gardens and the sea beyond, and the bar in the original sugar mill provides colorful refreshments.

Health and beauty treatments are available in the fitness center, but with the Atlantic and the Caribbean both within reach, you may find yourself booking a sailing trip, going for a scuba dive or snorkel, or enjoying a motorboat excursion. Then again, just lounging supine on one of Mustique's protected coves or bays may well be exertion enough. **PS**

Hike La Soufrière Trail

Location La Soufrière, St. Vincent, St. Vincent and the Grenadines
Website www.state.gov/r/pa/ei/bgn/2345.htm   **Price** ❶❷

It might not seem the obvious thing to do on a Caribbean beach vacation, but climbing the 4,000-foot (1,210-m) active volcano on St. Vincent is one of the region's great adventures.

To make the most of your visit, join a tour party or get an independent guide. They will drive you along the coast road from the port, through banana, coconut, and arrowroot plantations to the start of the trail. Here you will be able to see the treeless peak above the tree tops. The path leads through bamboo and tree ferns of the rain forest, winding around giant roots, thick vines, and ancient lava flows. The forest eventually clears to a more alpine area on the slopes, and finally it is only dry scree stretches up to the rim of the crater. The total ascent takes about two or three hours, depending on conditions and physical fitness.

The view from the top takes away what remains of your breath. The crater floor is 700 feet (213 m) below the rim, and the island stretches away on the other side, right down to the ocean. Usually visitors sit and eat lunch at the top of the crater admiring the panorama. The descent is less tiring but more slippery; it usually takes between one and two hours.

At the top, some visitors have the energy to take an extra forty-five-minute hike to a lake in the crater for a dip. There is a mineral-rich mud bath there, too, but the route is quite challenging and uses a fixed rope to help climbers. If you have several hours to spare, hike right around the rim of the crater for views all around the island. La Soufrière last erupted in 1979, but experts say it could become active again at any time. **SH**

⤴ *The resting La Soufrière Volcano on St. Vincent is known for its beauty—and unpredictability.*

"St. Vincent is a nature enthusiast's dream with nature trails, tropical forest . . . and an active volcano."

Sophie Lam, *Independent*

Unwind at Raffles Canouan

Location Canouan Island, St. Vincent and the Grenadines
Website www.rafflescanouan.com **Price** 🟉🟉

Set in 300 acres (121 ha), with three white-sand beaches and one of the world's largest coral reefs, Raffles Canouan is so vast that you'll need the complimentary golf cart to get around—and even then you might see only a handful of other guests.

It's a great honeymoon destination; the seventeenth-century stone church has seen more than a few visitors tie the knot. The resort has been highly rated by *Brides*, *Condé Nast Traveler*, and *Elite Traveler*; its Trump International Golf Club has been commended as one of the best in the world, and its spa promises the secrets of eternal youth, as well as after-sun facials to maintain your golden glow for longer.

> *"The Caribbean has seen nothing on such a grand scale in some time."*
>
> *Condé Nast Traveler*

Canouan has the credentials to be one of the Caribbean's most elite retreats; what is special here goes beyond the superb service, perfectly appointed colonial-style rooms, and beachfront restaurants. Rent a boat and explore the nearby cays for a real taste of solitude, go snorkeling, or find out why Canouan means "Island of Turtles" by swimming with those majestic animals. In the evening, enjoy fresh seafood in the restaurant but remember the dress code. Dress elegantly after sundown: no jeans, no shorts. **LD**

➜ *You can swim, eat superbly, rejuvenate at a spa, play a round of golf, and even marry at Raffles Canouan.*

Visit Palm Island

Location Palm Island, St. Vincent and the Grenadines   **Website** www.palmislandresortgrenadines.com   **Price** ❸❸❸

Imagine having a Caribbean island as your plaything. Walk around the coast barefoot, paddling your way along the white-sand shoreline, or explore all 135 acres (55 ha), puttering along paths between palm trees and exotic shrubs, looking out for wildlife.

Palm Island is situated near the southern tip of St. Vincent and the Grenadines, an idyllic archipelago of thirty-two islands and cays known for its natural beauty and clear waters. The island resort has been kept carefully low-key. All forty-two low-rise guest lodgings blend with the vegetation on the shoreline— and provide a total break from the life you have left behind. There are no televisions or phones in the rooms, just great views of the beach and other islands.

Rooms have custom-made bamboo furniture, ceiling fans, woven rattan ceilings, exposed beams, and rich fabrics. You will also find the normal mainland hotel luxuries of marble bathrooms, air-conditioning, cotton bathrobes, mini-fridges, safes, hair dryers, and coffeemakers. Stays here are all-inclusive and guests are welcome to enjoy three fine meals a day in the two restaurants, plus afternoon tea, cocktails, and beach barbecues. It is all so very romantic: You can have lunch privately anywhere on the island and dine by lamplight at the water's edge. For those seeking activity beyond lounging on beach hammocks, the resort offers tennis, mini-golf, bike trails, and non-motorized water sports like windsurfing, snorkeling, kayaking, and catamarans. For quieter days, there is a spa, salon, swimming pool, gym, and library.

It is easy to explore beyond Palm Island with scuba-diving and excursions to nearby islands. Yet perhaps the most luxurious trip of all is an evening cruise aboard the resort's private boat *The Pink Lady*, sipping champagne as the sun sets over the Caribbean. **SH**

⬆ *Indulge your Robinson Crusoe fantasies to the hilt on your own private Caribbean resort—Palm Island.*

Rent L'Anse aux Epines

Location Prickley Bay, Grenada   **Website** www.lanceauxepineshouse.com   **Price** $$

From the sea, this small round tower looks like an old lighthouse or castle turret. As you land on the Caribbean island, though, you will find it is really an old stone sugar mill tower. The tower has been converted into a vacation home for those who need a very special escape indeed: a memorable hideaway for those who demand the very best. The location could not be bettered: on the side of a hill on the shores of Prickley Bay, Grenada, with wonderful views over the Atlantic Ocean and the Caribbean Sea.

The sugar mill tower belongs to the old nineteenth-century colonial estate house L'Anse aux Epines, which can be rented along with the tower to create a property for up to fourteen guests. The tower can be rented alone and sleeps up to four. You will find the sugar mill right on the water's edge in a private part of the lush 2-acre (0.8-ha) gardens of the main house. Inside the conical building are two bedrooms, a kitchen/bar and covered verandas, a small plunge pool, and access to a long, private swimming dock (shared only with the main house). The bedrooms have four-poster beds, flat-screen satellite televisions with DVD players, telephones, and Internet access. The gardens have private walkways, hideaways, and a 20-foot (6-m) waterfall. They lead down to the private beach and deepwater private dock. The infinity pool is 65 feet long (20 m): the biggest private pool in the Grenadines. There is also an "aqua gym" pool and a whirlpool hot tub.

Guests have the services of a staff of five: a cook/housekeeper, two domestic staff, and two groundsmen. A massage therapist and gourmet chef are available at extra cost and a sailing yacht is available for guests. If that is not enough, visitors can also use the property's powerboat, which comes with its own captain. **SH**

⬆ *A luxurious Caribbean retreat with a difference: a converted sugar mill complete with tower.*

Explore Carriacou Island

Location Carriacou, Grenada
Website www.carriacoupetitemartinique.com   **Price** ◗

Dotted with half a dozen swaying palms, Sandy Island is a mere 300 feet (90 m) long. Spread a towel, catch the sun, savor a picnic, or snorkel in some of the Caribbean's clearest, most fish-thronged waters—and you will likely have the place to yourself. When the sun starts to sink, meander the mile back to mainland Carriacou, the largest of the Grenadines, a necklace of island gems scattered between Grenada and St. Vincent, and discover a lively nightlife scene.

"Largest" is, of course, a relative term. Carriacou is 7 miles (11 km) long, by an average of 2 miles (3 km) wide, rising to a 956-foot (291-m) peak. Volcanic in origin, it was once covered in sugarcane and cotton fields, but tourism is now the key industry. Not that it has in any way damaged the laid-back ambience here. Yes, you can send e-mails to the outside world, but it is more important to relax over a thirst-quenching rum punch.

The only energetic pursuit for the locals seems to be boatbuilding, using skills bequeathed by the Scottish ancestors who gave so many of the islanders their surnames, after liaisons with West African slaves. Lively little Hillsborough is the island capital, where the high-speed ferry from the much larger sister island of Grenada docks. There is also a tiny landing strip, whose operation involves using part of the road and holding up the traffic so that the planes can land.

At the end of May, Belair Park hosts the Maroon Festival, whose high spot is the sprinkling of rum and water onto the ground as a blessing before the music and dance spectacle kicks off. If you are really lucky, you might stumble on to a local maroon celebration, where the community pools resources so that everyone can eat, drink, and have fun for free. **RsP**

Stay at Maca Bana Villas

Location St. George's, Grenada
Website www.macabana.com   **Price** ❺

A tiny Grenadian boutique resort in junglelike surroundings on a hillside above the idyllic Magazine Beach, Maca Bana is the ultimate place to play pampered Tarzan and Jane. Visitors stay in seven artistically designed "banas" dotted among tropical landscaped gardens, with an infinity pool overlooking the beach and a central waterfall feature.

It is a peaceful haven among coconut trees with strong eco credentials, and solar panels and water heaters supply energy. The intimate resort boasts an organic nursery, fruit tree orchard, and herb garden that supplement the local produce used in the Aquarium restaurant and the bar that sits right on

"Decorated by the artist owner, the villas are well equipped with … hot tubs and staggering views."

Observer

the beach. Each charming villa, set among babbling streams and ponds of koi, has a sleek, fully fitted kitchen, and guests can make their own meals or take advantage of the personal chef in the privacy of their sundeck.

Spa treatments can be arranged in the comfort of the villas or in the gentle breeze outside, and private yoga, tai chi, and meditation lessons add to the deep sense of soulful relaxation, as do the various art and cooking lessons on offer. The banas have outdoor hot tubs, spacious decks, and balconies, with plenty of loungers and love seats to make the most of the Caribbean vistas and dreamy sunsets. **LP**

Relax at Estate House

Location Mount Hartman Bay, Grenada
Website www.mounthartmanbay.com **Price** 💲💲💲

Mount Hartman Bay Estate, on a private peninsula on Grenada, is fit for the likes of James Bond. The Estate House, carved into the hillside with a grass and cactus roof and internal waterfalls, is spectacular. Locals call it the "Cave House" because when arriving from the private jetty or helipad, guests enter through a large door in the cliff.

Once inside, the fixtures and fittings are world class, recalling Le Corbusier and Gaudí. White columns drape to the floor, the polished wood bar is backed by a mossy waterfall, and an oversized dining table invites you to sit and enjoy the exclusive view. The thatched Beach House at the back of the property has a patio opening onto a secluded beach sheltered by coral reefs, and the library inside the house is stocked with must-read books: The owners ask guests to bring a copy of their favorite book to leave here.

Grenada was renowned as an island that sailors could smell before they could see it—the Spice Island's air is heavy with ginger, nutmeg, cloves, cinnamon, and cacao—and the estate's chef knows how to make the most of it. Roger Williams is an award-winning Grenadian chef and creates culinary heaven with the local ingredients.

If you are looking for the ultimate party house, for a maximum of twenty-four extremely well-heeled visitors, this is the place. Your every whim will be catered to—with everything from a 40-foot (12-m) yacht and its captain, to sea scooters and Mitsubishi Shoguns at your disposal. You can choose to picnic on a quiet, forgotten cay for lunch, snorkel on the coral reef in the afternoon, or explore the tropical rain forest all day with a guide. Or simply relax on the beach and let the world revolve around you. **LD**

Enjoy Mount Plaisir

Location Mount Plaisir, Trinidad
Website www.mtplaisir.com **Price** 💲

Mount Plaisir stands right alongside the largest nesting site for leatherback turtles in the western hemisphere. Every year these rare, endangered giant leatherbacks navigate the globe and return to this beach in their thousands. During the summer nesting season, these huge creatures lay their eggs in the sand in the night just outside the hotel rooms. Thousands of hatchlings complete the cycle by pushing out of the sand and rushing back into the sea.

The thirteen suites face the Caribbean Sea with the rain forest rising up the spectacular Mount Ju behind. The simple rooms are decorated with work by local craftspeople. There is a candlelit restaurant, and much

> *"Go on foot to the rain forest, where you'll see the pawi, a bird that lives here and nowhere else."*
>
> *Harper's Bazaar*

of the produce used in the kitchen is grown on the organic estate or caught off the beach. The sweetbreads, cakes, and coconut bread are renowned across the island.

Mount Plaisir is a relaxed base for wildlife trips into the forest, canoe trips along the Grande Riviere, or long beach walks. Trips into the forests with guides can end with a night spent sleeping high in a tree or climbing a hill to watch the sunset over neighboring Tobago. The local birdlife is particularly abundant, and some rare species live only in this area. Guests watch for the extraordinary daily return to their nests of the beautiful yellowtails in huge flocks. **SH**

Stay at Hotel Passion

Location Cartagena, Colombia
Website www.lapassionhotel.com   **Price** 💲💲

In the heart of the old walled city of Cartagena is La Passion—a small hotel created with all the emotion and romance that its name implies. Overlooking the Caribbean Sea, Cartagena de Indias is one of South America's most beautiful and vibrant cities, and this boutique hotel captures much of the Colombian city's spirit with its beguiling shabby-chic grandeur.

La Passion is too small to be a retreat for the glitterati. The ancient granite staircase rises to just eight high-ceilinged bedrooms. These traditional spaces combine eclectic antiques, ethnic fabrics, and modern conveniences. Expect to find murals, ancient floor-to-ceiling windows, wicker chests, old carved-

> *"The city, his city, stood unchanging on the edge of time."*
>
> Gabriel García Márquez, *Love in the Time of Cholera*

wood headboards, Persian and Colombian rugs, Moroccan ashtrays, and lamps from Seville. You may get a vast concrete bathtub, fashionably flaking plaster, or grand distressed French furniture. Amid all this period style there are still state-of-the-art features such as air-conditioning and plasma televisions.

La Passion is more than just style. There is substance, too, especially in the rooftop pool that is subtly lit at night and gives striking views of the city's monuments and the sea beyond. The hotel has its own speedboat that can whisk guests to nearby islands. There is even a small wooden fishing boat hung from the ceiling for guests to use as a swinging sofa. **SH**

Trek to Ciudad Perdida

Location Sierra Nevada, Colombia
Website www.hosteltrail.com/turcol   **Price** ⬤

Colombia's steamy, jungle-rich Caribbean coast is shrouded in mystery and intrigue, a landscape where guerrilla tribes roam and coca plantations thrive. It is also home to Ciudad Perdida, a stunning ancient city dating back to 800 A.D. Suitably remote, it takes three days of hard trekking to reach the foot of the mountain that marks the entrance to the archaeological site. Here 1,200 small, slippery, uneven steps rise up out of a river. Not as well-trampled as Machu Picchu and nowhere near as touristy, the city was discovered only in 1972 by treasure looters.

On reaching the top of the steps at the mountain's summit, the remains of the old city are spread out. Over a hundred stone terraces that once provided the base for huts are linked by a labyrinth of winding paths and steps. There is an eerily quiet feel to the place, especially when you think of how many thousands of people lived up here until it was abandoned during the Spanish Conquest. As so few tourists visit, it is easy to wander alone and feel like you are the first person to come and explore the weed-covered and palm-fringed ancient terraces studded with wildflowers. The place has the feel of discovering a secret garden.

The site's lofty position offers sweeping views of the lush jungle-covered mountains as well as revealing a sky rich with exotic birds and brightly colored butterflies. Local tribes, descendants of the Lost City inhabitants, live up here in thatched huts. The natives say they knew about the city for years before it was found in the 1970s, but unsurprisingly they wanted to keep this peaceful retreat to themselves. **JK**

➡ *A seemingly never-ending series of moss-covered steps, flanked by dense jungle, leads to the Lost City.*

Walk Along Tayrona Beach

Location Near Santa Marta, Colombia
Website wikitravel.org/en/El_Parque_Tayrona **Price** ❶

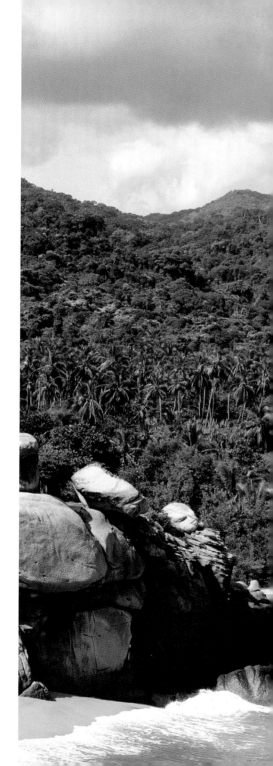

On the northern tip of Colombia's coast is Tayrona National Park, an area of 58 square miles (150 sq km) that is said to harbor some of the best beaches in South America. Here the foothills of the Sierra Nevada de Santa Marta—one of the highest coastal mountain ranges in the world—plummet toward stretches of powder-fine white sand and the lapping waves of the turquoise Caribbean Sea.

These beaches are not easy to get to, though. The nearest town is Santa Marta, from where most people take a bus or a taxi to the gates of the park at El Zaino. From there, a van can transport you to the beginning of the walking trails. Most people hike the rest of the way, although the footsore can rent a mule.

The beach at Arrecifes is about a forty-minute walk away. It is a wild and untamed spot where waves lash sea-sculpted boulders and swimming is off the menu due to dangerous riptides. However, a rocky path leads to the beaches at La Piscina or El Cabo where the waters are kinder. Hike for an hour or so up a steep trail from El Cabo and you will come to El Pueblito, an abandoned village from pre-conquest days. You may spot titi monkeys as you climb; you will certainly see some of the park's 200 bird species. Somewhere deep in the jungle, jaguars roam.

You can spend the night in an "ecohab"—a round, thatched cottage invoking the style of traditional Kogui homes—set into the cliffs at Cañaveral, a forty-five-minute walk from Arrecifes. Otherwise, just rent a hammock, hang it between two trees, and let the sounds of the Caribbean Sea lull you to sleep. **PE**

⮕ *The lush rain forest of Colombia's Tayrona National Park grows almost to the sea.*

Cruise the Galapagos

Location Galapagos, Ecuador **Website** www.celebrityxpeditions.com **Price** $$$$

> *"Met an immense turpin: took little notice of me. They well match the rugged lava."*

Charles Darwin, *Galapagos Notebook*

↑ *The Santa Fe land iguana is one of the unique species native to the Galapagos Islands.*

→ *Kicker Rock, the remains of a lava cone eroded by the sea, is a popular sight for cruise visitors to the islands.*

A trip to the Galapagos, nineteen small, rather scrubby islands 600 miles (965 km) off the coast of Ecuador in South America, is like a dream come true. It is a chance to get up close and personal to exotic creatures such as dancing booby birds, lumbering sea lions, and giant iguanas that have no fear of humans—a truly awesome and thrilling experience.

There are a couple of hotels on Santa Cruz, the island capital, but it is infinitely preferable to take a cruise, visiting two or more islands a day, to observe the animals that inspired Darwin's theory of evolution. As this is such a special place, it is worth paying for the best—and that means Celebrity Xpeditions' ninety-eight-passenger yacht. There are no casinos and no lavish evening production shows, but there are spacious cabins, great menus, and a cold towel and fruit juice to welcome you back on board after a few hours' trekking through the scrub.

As human visitors pose a genuine threat to the fearless animals, visitors to the Galapagos are kept on a tight rein. You can land only with a guide registered with the National Park, and once ashore (transfers are by inflatable boats), you must not stray from the beaten track. None of this is a great hardship though, because you learn so much: that the frigate birds have bloated red chests to attract passing females and that the booby dance is a mating ritual, for example. And did you know that marine iguanas in the Galapagos are black, except on Española, where they are red and green during the mating season? Guides will also find giant boulderlike tortoises in the highlands of Santa Cruz, creatures that were nearly driven to extinction by whalers in the nineteenth century. Alternatively, you may take a trip to the cliff from which, in summer, albatrosses launch themselves into the air. **JA**

Stay at Hacienda Aguasana

Location Paria, Venezuela
Website www.pixotomy.com **Price** $

Forget luxury spas in five-star glitzy hotels. Why not go back to nature for a heady dose of extreme pampering at Hacienda Aguasana, set in the lush Paria region of northeast Venezuela? Framed by rolling mountains and surrounded by grassy meadows where horses and buffalo graze, this remote and peaceful hacienda offers seventeen pond-sized geothermally heated pools, which vary in temperature. Some of the pools smell of sulfur, whereas others bubble with hot mud. There is a shallow well bursting with mud (said to work wonders for the skin), which can be slathered on from head to toe using a stick-long spatula. Let the mud dry under the hot sun before diving into one of the pools

> *"The word 'Aguasana' defines what this space offers: health and well being through water and mud."*

Proprietors, Hacienda Aguasana

to wash it off, revealing baby-soft skin. Also on offer are antistress massages and acupressure treatments. The hacienda has several simple but comfortable guest rooms and a swimming pool. The benefit of sleeping here means you can wallow in one of the hot pools while watching the sunset. Untamed, exotic jungle is just a short walk away and is worth exploring for its vibrant flowers and vegetation. Also nearby are the idyllic beaches of Playa Medina and Playa Puy Puy.

Hacienda Aguasana itself, however, is devoted entirely to relaxation. There is literally nothing to do but lie back and soak in the healing waters until your skin wrinkles up or it is time for bed. **JK**

Relax at Hacienda Bukare

Location Paria, Venezuela
Website www.bukare.com/inght/hacienda.html **Price** $$

Still as wild and exotic as when Christopher Columbus set foot here during his third voyage to the New World in 1498, Venezuela's northern Paria region is a chocoholic's heaven. At the balmy heart of what is known locally as the "chocolate coast" is Hacienda Bukare, a guesthouse and working cocoa plantation where handmade chocolates are produced.

There are four simple but spacious guest rooms overlooking a shady and perfectly manicured garden with hammocks and a small circular pool. Surrounding the garden are groves of cacao trees. Venezuela's answer to Willy Wonka is knowledgeable plantation owner Billy Esser, who runs hour-long tours where visitors can learn more about the harvesting and production of cocoa before the real treat: tasting the stuff. For a bittersweet buzz, try cacao nibs straight from the tree, the rawest form of chocolate, believed to have amazing health benefits thanks to its high antioxidant levels. It is also a source of serotonin, which promotes sleep and lessens depression.

That said, dieters should beware: This is no place for those watching their weight. Although the chocolate produced here is of the highest caliber—consisting of almost 90 percent cocoa solids—guests are treated to a daylong gluttonous feast beginning from the moment they wake up.

Breakfast consists of bread smothered in chocolate spread and washed down with a thick and creamy hot chocolate, whereas dinner options include succulent beef drenched in a rich chocolaty sauce.

Relax in a hammock and feast on a delicious array of Bukare's chocolate delights without feeling a single trace of guilt. After all, when the chocolate is this pure, it surely cannot be bad for you. **JK**

Ride the *Hiram Bingham* Train

Location Cusco to Machu Picchu, Peru
Website www.perurail.com   **Price** 💲💲

Traveling on the *Hiram Bingham* train from Cusco to Machu Picchu has to be one of the most spectacular ways of discovering the ancient land of the Incas. It is certainly a lot less arduous than the three-day trek undertaken by thousands of footsore visitors each year.

Named after the Yale historian who came across the ruins of the ancient citadel in 1911, the train departs six days a week at 9 A.M., giving a more leisurely start to the day than the traditional 6 A.M. departures of other services. After slowly making the steep ascent out of Cusco the train takes a stunning route through the ever-changing landscape of the Sacred Valley, which includes lush fields and colorful villages in the foothills of the Andes. Mimosas and brunch are served while travelers enjoy the scenery unfolding before them from the luxurious interior of the train. From fantastic mountain vistas to the beautiful Urumbamba River, there is plenty to keep passengers occupied during the three-and-a-half-hour journey.

The 12:30 P.M. arrival at Machu Picchu gives train passengers the advantage of entering the historic site at an hour when most visitors are already leaving for their journey back to Cusco. This gives passengers the chance to experience the site in relative solitude and for a longer period of time, as they return to the train only as the sun goes down. On arrival passengers are taken on a private guided tour followed by afternoon tea in the Machu Picchu Sanctuary Lodge before exploring the citadel at their leisure. Appropriately for this sophisticated brand of sightseeing, cocktails and dinner are served on the return journey. **HA**

↗ The Hiram Bingham, *with its distinctive blue and gold livery, winds its way through the mountains.*

"[Instead of] a punishing four-day trek … you can let the train take the strain."

Condé Nast Traveler

Stay at Casa Andina Private Collection

Location Isla Suasi, Peru   **Website** www.casa-andina.com
Price 💲💲💲

The private island of Isla Suasi, in the north of Lake Titicaca, is as high as the Andes, and the views are literally breathtaking. You can see the vast blue lake from every one of the twenty-four rooms in this small rustic hotel, not to mention alpaca and vicuna grazing on the hotel's garden out front. Stripy hammocks swing outside in the breeze as multitudes of birds catch fish in this, the deepest part of the lake. It is hard to believe here that stress exists.

The downside to this Peruvian paradise is how long it takes to get here; on the upside, this means the place is not going to be swarming with tourists. The island is about five hours from Puno, and you can access it by speedboat, stopping off at the Uros islands, where traditional communities live on artificial islands made of floating reeds.

Staying on Suasi Island feels like a real retreat. The Casa Andina Private Collection hotel might be built from traditional adobe and totora reed, but the wine cellar is well-stocked with Chilean and Argentine wine lying next to the Moët. If you desire more privacy, the Andean Cottage has two private rooms, a lakeside terrace, and private butler service. It is decked out with a sober cream and dark-wood interior and is designed with honeymooners in mind.

If you are looking for a genuine South American sanctuary, there is a traditional Andean sauna here, and you can also arrange sessions with a shaman, to make offerings to the Earth. Or you can take in the serenity of the lake with a canoe or wooden boat tour, hike up the flower-strewn hillsides, or watch the stars by telescope at night. The air is so clear and unpolluted here that you can see for miles. **LD**

Cruise the Amazon River

Location Amazon River   **Website** www.responsibletravel.com
Price 💲💲

There is a reason why the Amazon is high up on every adventurous traveler's wish list: The world's largest wilderness provides an escape back to the time when the world had not been circumnavigated. Despite the advance of technology, we still have not mastered this majestic rain forest, where much remains unexplored.

Passing through nine countries and stretching 2,890 miles (4,650 km) in length, the Amazon River asks more questions than it answers. Where to start is one, and many visitors choose a route from the port of Iquitos in Peru, which allows for a ten-day cruise upriver to Lima. Alternatively, a smaller boat lets you explore the

---

"A regal, ruling river there exists, unique, and vast, of loveliness unmatched."

Carlos German Amezaga, *Hymn to Brazil*

---

little-known tributaries, spotting monkeys, giant otters, and sloths. Along the bank, the giant water lily grows up to 6 feet (1.8 m) in diameter. Treks into the forest are available, with the chance to explore and visit local tribes. As night falls, you might have the chance to hunt for bats, black caimans, and poisonous tree frogs. It is truly an adventure of a lifetime, but be sure to book with a responsible company: The Amazon rain forest is being destroyed at an alarming rate, and we must do all we can to preserve it. **LD**

➡ *The snaking brown course of the majestic river contrasts with the lush green jungle vegetation.*

Relax at Hotel Monasterio

Location Cusco, Peru

Website www.monasterio.orient-express.com **Price** 💲💲

Gisele Bündchen and Leonardo DiCaprio have laid their A-list heads on the soft linen pillows. Jane Fonda, Ben Kingsley, and Goldie Hawn have all sampled the famous house cocktail, the pisco sour, at the chichi bar, and Colombian pop pixie Shakira has had her morning coffee in the shady courtyard. Where are we? Cusco's Hotel Monasterio, one of the luxury properties at the vanguard of South America's style revolution.

Converted from a sixteenth-century monastery and built around a cloistered courtyard, the Monasterio has an ambience of calm efficiency. Gregorian chants accompany the serene breakfast buffet, a private chapel is at your disposal, and the bath butler service offers a

---

"The five-star Hotel Monasterio is one of the grandest establishments in South America."

Independent

---

soak fit for an Andean princess. The heart of the hotel is a central courtyard with soft fountain and 300-year-old cedar tree surrounded by gardens and cloisters.

The hotel takes a very modern approach to the issue of altitude sickness (the thin air at high altitude deprives the body of up to 30 percent of usual oxygen levels). Fifty bedrooms here are enriched with oxygen gently pumped through filters to reduce atmospheric pressure and aid gentle slumbers. It is all part of life enjoying Cusco's finer side. **DA**

➔ *The chapel is adorned with seventeenth-century paintings—one of the delights at Monasterio.*

Enjoy Reserva Amazonica Lodge

Location Near Puerto Maldonado, Peru
Website www.inkaterra.com **Price** ⚅⚅

Gazing down on the Peruvian Amazon region with the aid of a satellite image, the town of Puerto Maldonado appears as a series of rough gray smudges in unending green, and a tawny river winds away through thick rain forest. Unlikely as it seems, an hour down the river and a short scramble up a rough clay riverbank is one of Peru's most enchanting and exciting hotels.

Inkaterra's Reserva Amazonica Lodge is part of a private 30,000-acre (12,140-ha) nature reserve. It is a haven of peace and quiet luxury in a wild natural setting: from screeching macaws in vivid primary colors to delicate pygmy marmosets; from single-minded columns of leafcutter ants to elaborate heliconia blossoms, spectacular in crimson. All of this is before you have even made it to your room.

Traditional constructions updated by the addition of tight-fitting mesh screens, the thirty chic cabanas are open to the elements so that on the hottest of nights, a faint breeze might float up from the river. A heavenly lack of phones, Internet, and even electricity (which is rationed) is complemented by thoughtful, luxurious touches and by discreet staff who know when to offer a cocktail, hand you an ice-cold washcloth, or light you to bed with glowing kerosene lamps.

If you are lucky enough to be in one of the two "suites Tambopata," their private plunge pools and terraces are the ideal spot to relax and cool down after an excursion into the jungle. Activities include trekking through the trees in thrall to one of the Reserva's knowledgeable guides; spotting the sentinel, flash-lit eyes of caimans on the riverbanks on a nighttime boat trip; or an electrifying canopy walk 100 feet (30 m) above the ground through whispering treetops. **CR**

Visit Machu Picchu Sanctuary Lodge

Location Cusco, Peru
Website www.machupicchu.orient-express.com **Price** ⚅⚅⚅

Despite increasing limits on the number of people trekking the Inca Trail to Machu Picchu, the iconic fifteenth-century Inca citadel, voted one of the new Seven Wonders of the World in July 2007, remains one of the world's most popular tourist attractions.

Machu Picchu attracts up to 700,000 visitors each year. In high season, you can see nothing but waterproof jackets clambering over the Sun Gate at dawn. The Machu Picchu Sanctuary Lodge is the ideal place to escape the hordes and get a feel for the spirituality of this UNESCO World Heritage site; the only hotel within the grounds, it has two suites and twenty-nine rooms.

> *"You can't help but think of the mysterious mountain gods whom the Andean people still venerate."*
>
> *Independent*

The views, obviously, are spectacular. It is well worth splashing out for a Mountain View room, or better still a Panoramic Room, which comes with its own balcony overlooking the ancient site. Equally impressive is the Tampu Restaurant Bar, where the gourmet dinner is served with views across the ancient ruins.

The hotel will arrange guided visits of the site with knowledgeable guides, but most of all this is a place to escape into another world and be alone. Get up early and walk around the citadel in the morning half-light to really appreciate the unique atmosphere. The crowds are already approaching the Sun Gate, but for a few precious moments you can enjoy perfect peace. **DA**

Walk Through the Andes on the "Other" Inca Trail

Location Ollantaytambo to Machu Picchu, via Choquequirao, Peru
Website www.peru.info; www.aito.co.uk **Price** 🌗

As wear and tear have impacted the traditional "Capaq Ñan" Inca Trail from Ollantaytambo to Machu Picchu, walkers have sought alternative ways of reaching the unmissable UNESCO World Heritage site. The 75-mile (120-km) route from Cachora is, if anything, more impressive—and more demanding—than the more established trail, and passes through the great, rarely visited citadel of Choquequirao, meaning "Cradle of Gold." You ford teeming rivers and hundreds of streams and pass through high Andean hamlets, swaths of sun-dappled forest, and idyllic wide-open valleys en route. The six- to eight-day walk involves Inca staircases that attack the slopes frontally, and less aggressive zigzags designed for mules, goats, and llamas. You are in one of Peru's most inaccessible corners—little wonder the Incas retreated up these valleys in the 1560s, after Spain took Cusco.

Orchids are as good a reason as any to stop and catch your breath, as are the perfumed scents of peppermint and *muña*, a wild oregano that keeps flies away. Peaches, Cape gooseberries, prickly pears, and blackcurrants can all be picked freely.

Choquequirao comes like a dream vision, sitting in a saddle at a natural high pass between two peaks. When the sun begins to set, you can grasp why the ancient tribes wanted to have their homes above the clouds—the cradle of gray ashlar stone glows gold. From here it is another three days to Machu Picchu. But you arrive knowing you have seen a far less famous but larger and probably more important Inca city. **CM**

↗ *A Choquequirao jaunt will take in irrigation channels, ruins, ceremonial chambers—and magical sunsets.*

"Choquequirao truly is the lost city of the Incas ... [it] does not appear in any of the chronicles of the age."

New York Times

Stay at Hacienda de Cayara

Location Near Potosi, Bolivia
Website www.cayara.com.bo   **Price** $

The pièce de résistance of Bolivia's heritage of colonial haciendas, Cayara is a gem. Set 15 miles (25 km) outside of Potosi in a rural village idyll, it remains one of the very few working haciendas still in Bolivia today.

The property, originally built in 1557 and home to Spanish nobility, has a living-museum feel, with cobweb-strewn passages leading to secret, hidden nooks and crannies. The 247-acre (100-ha) grounds are home to a working dairy farm, which makes about 75 gallons (350 l) of milk daily, used to make the delicious Cayara-brand dairy products served at meals. Although with private bathrooms, the twenty rooms are fairly basic, and when the mercury plunges at night, the lack of

---

"One of Bolivia's most endearing and eccentric hotels, Hacienda de Cayara."

Michael Jacobs, *Independent*

---

heating will certainly be character building. But it is worth it. By day, guests can explore the portrait-adorned dining hall or blow dust from the covers of ancient tomes in the library to really get the feel of stepping back in history. Then, how about a sunny stroll through the fields of the estate and a homemade Cayara ice cream? (The vanilla flavor is particularly good.)

Most of all, the quintessential Cayara experience is all about taking a post-lunch siesta in the sunny plant room, or curling up by the open fire after a hearty, three-course dinner with a drink and chewing the fat with your fellow guests. This place is living history at its most evocative. Do not miss. **DA**

Enjoy Chalalan Eco-lodge

Location Near Rurrenabaque, Bolivia
Website www.chalalan.com   **Price** $$

Deep in the remote Madidi National Park, in the Bolivian Amazon, a dream has become reality. In 1992, the community of San Jose de Uchupiamonas needed to create an economic alternative to cash crops and stop the migration of their children to big cities in search of work. With the help of a government grant, seventy local families began construction of Chalalan Eco-lodge, accessible only via a five-and-a-half-hour canoe trip along the Beni and Tuichi rivers. The lodge is hidden from the prying eyes of the twenty-first century in a lost world of chinchillas, monkeys, tapirs, alligators, and more than 350 species of bird.

The lodge sits on the shoreline of Chalalan Lagoon, a pristine body of water that doubles as Chalalan's private swimming pool. The twenty-eight traditionally styled cabanas share four standalone bathrooms, and running water is supplied via a solar-powered system. There are more than 15 miles (25 km) of hiking trails along which local guides point out the forest's fauna and its rich tapestry of medicinal and endemic plant life. Night hikes with headlamps are available to observe the surreal nocturnal habits of the Madidi's frogs, birds, black caimans, and other night dwellers. San Jose residents also hold informal cultural evenings in which they share their traditional stories on the origin of the forest and its many inhabitants with guests.

Known as one of the world's biodiversity hot spots, this pristine rain forest has more than 45,000 species of plants and, despite the difficulty in getting here, still provides indelible memories to more than 1,000 intrepid tourists a year, who come to learn about the fragility of the forest, and who in turn help the people of San Jose preserve this unique wilderness for the enjoyment of future generations. **BS**

Unwind at Hotel Rosario

Location La Paz, Bolivia
Website www.hotelrosario.com   **Price** $

La Paz can get to be a bit much. The sprawling market district behind San Francisco Cathedral is exhilarating but exhausting, so this charming little colonial-style hotel at the heart of the market provides a rare oasis of tranquility, with surprisingly high standards of accommodation in a budget category.

Adapted from a nineteenth-century hacienda and built in a typical Spanish style around a sunny courtyard, this is a really pleasant, airy place in which to escape the bustle of the nearby market, with plenty of quiet corners of the plant-dotted terrace to sit, read a book, and soak up the atmosphere of quiet refinement at your leisure. The rooms manage to be both comfortable and stylish, with ethnic woven blankets and bedspreads adding a homey feel to the decor. Many of these are available to buy downstairs in Anyi, a community arts shop that sells handicrafts created by a local artisan project.

The final touch to foster the boutique-hotel-meets-Andean-tradition ambience is the on-site Tambo Colonial restaurant, which serves up a huge mix of international favorite dishes in a buffet style. At weekends, the restaurant comes alive to the sound of panpipes and charangos, a traditional ukulele-style instrument, with live folk tunes supplied by poncho-wearing local musicians.

In the reception area downstairs there is a help-yourself supply of free *maté* (a coca-leaf tea good for altitude sickness), and snacks are also served here throughout the day, making this a perfect community area to swap experiences with other travelers. On the same level, the in-house agency, Turisbus, can arrange excursions to Lake Titicaca and onward transfers across the border into Peru. **DA**

Visit Hostal de Su Merced

Location Sucre, Bolivia
Website www.desumerced.com   **Price** $

Set in a beautifully restored colonial hacienda dating from the eighteenth century and boasting a fantastic panoramic view across Bolivia's so-called "White City" from its roof terrace, Hostal de Su Merced is a real find, offering a welcome retreat from the busy streets.

Opened as a hotel in 1997 for a major political summit, this place stands out both for its tasteful decor and for the fact that, unlike many other hotels in Sucre, it benefits from plenty of light and air, lending a sunny feel to the property. Whereas the rooftop is a haven for sun worshippers, the downstairs patio is cooler, splashed by a mosaic-decorated fountain, and a great place to read while sipping a cool drink.

"You can have a breathking view of the city, breathe the purest air, and enjoy the sun."

Proprietors, Hostal de Su Merced

The standard of the facilities makes this the natural choice for a place to stay in Sucre—the twenty-one rooms are spacious, with tasteful period fittings, and there is a good buffet breakfast (lots of muesli and yogurt) and free Internet access in the computer room. More crucially, however, Merced captures a step-back-in-time ambience that recalls the finesse of a former age. Meals are served in a genteel dining room, all starched tablecloths and immaculate service; it feels like stepping onto a film set as an extra. A pre-dinner drink in the bar epitomizes the colonial age with faded works of art on the wall, battered leather seats, and the delicate chink of ice in crystal glasses. **DA**

Explore Laguna Verde

Location Salar de Uyuni, Bolivia
Website www.enjoybolivia.com   **Price** 🌗

The Salar de Uyuni, the sprawling salt flats in Bolivia's remote southwest, nudging the Chilean border, is the country's greatest natural wonder. With a spectacular, snow-blind landscape and an array of exotic flora and fauna, the area is flatter than Holland and whiter than Mont Blanc, with temperatures that fluctuate from -22°F (-30°C) at night to 86°F (30°C) by day.

Local tour operators can arrange a three-day tour of the region by jeep. Starting out from the train hub at Uyuni, one of the highlights of this tour is a chance to visit Laguna Verde (green lake), which is set some 14,435 feet (4,400 m) above sea level. The water's elaborate colors reflect the high mineral content of the region: magnesium, calcium, lead, and arsenic. The lake sits at the foot of Volcan Licancabur, a towering volcano astride the Bolivia-Chile border. Laguna Verde and its sister lake, Laguna Colorada (colored lake), form part of a protected area: the "Eduardo Avaroa" National Andean Fauna Reserve. The surface of the landscape around the lakes is pure crystalized salt and masks a vast expanse of subterranean lakes, the water from which rises to the surface during the rainy season (December to March).

The lagunas perfectly encapsulate the serene natural beauty of the Salar. They also provide a harsh but evocative habitat for indigenous species. Andean flamingos are abundant and take on a delicate pink glow caused by the pink algae that is their main source of food. The animal population includes Andean foxes and rabbitlike viscacha, whereas the flora includes quinoa plants and the kenua bush. **DA**

➡ *The thermal waters of Laguna Verde are set in one of the world's last great wildernesses.*

Relax at La Posada del Inca

Location Lake Titicaca, Bolivia **Website** www.titicaca.com **Price** ⑤⑤

A visit to Lake Titicaca, a sacred place of worship and mysticism straddling the Peruvian–Bolivian border at an altitude of 12,530 feet (3,820 m) above sea level, is a true escape. The Isla del Sol, where La Posada del Inca nestles among rural villages, is—according to legend—the birthplace of the Inca civilization.

With that kind of pedigree, La Posada has a lot to live up to, which it does magnificently. This seventeen-room, terra-cotta-tiled, converted hacienda, built around a series of small, sunny courtyards in private grounds, feels perfectly in keeping with the mystical ambience of the Isla del Sol. The hacienda offers a very peaceful away-from-it-all experience of serene island life with great views across to both the Isla de la Luna and the spectacular mountains of the Andean Cordillera Real range.

Condors soar overhead, and the waters of the lake lap gently around you. The sense of perfect calm is everywhere. The accommodation has a comfortable yet rustic feel: Bedrooms are furnished with chunky wooden beds and handcrafted knickknacks. All rooms have private bathrooms, with solar-powered showers providing dribbles of hot water. As the late afternoon sun sets over the island, the guests gather on the sun loungers in the garden to chat, read, and soak up the prevailing chilled-out atmosphere.

After the sun goes down, meals are served in a modern, communal dining hall that feels a little like a school cafeteria. The food is generous (try the fresh trout, straight from the lake) but a little on the pricey side. Crillon Tours, a La Paz–based tour agency, which also runs a hydrofoil service across the lake, exclusively manages the property and offers packages only on a full-board and transport basis. So splash out: True hideaways like this are few and far between. **DA**

⬆ *The perfect chill-out retreat: Isla de Sol, in Lake Titicaca—there are few places more peaceful.*

Stay in a Treehouse at Ariau

Location Near Manaus, Brazil   **Website** www.amazontowers.com   **Price** 💲💲

Deep in the Amazon rain forest sits the Ariau Amazon Towers—the only hotel that is situated amid the forest canopy and also the largest treetop hotel in the world. It consists of seven accommodation towers and ten gravity-defying tree houses, and includes what must surely be one of the most extraordinary honeymoon suites ever built, at the apex of a 110-foot (30-m) mahogany tree.

Tower Five has rooms with 360-degree panoramic views of the surrounding forest and its resident fauna, which include red macaws, sloths, and spider monkeys among others. A restaurant in Tower Four cooks regional specialties such as freshwater pirarucu, and the restaurant walls proudly display the signatures of its ever-growing list of famous guests, whose number includes Kevin Costner, Jennifer Lopez, and former U.S. president Jimmy Carter. Do not be surprised if the place looks more than a little familiar either. Cinema and television have both employed the startling resort as a backdrop. It was used in the Hollywood movie *Anaconda*, and also served as the setting for the reality television show *Survivor*.

This vast assemblage of towers and tree houses, which was the brainchild of the famous French naturalist Jacques Cousteau, is interconnected by 5 miles (8 km) of catwalks and represents the gateway to one of the wildest and most biologically diverse regions on Earth. It is just downstream from the Anavilhanas archipelago, the largest concentration of freshwater islands on Earth and home to the rare pink dolphin; day trips can include piranha fishing on the hotel's private boat. If that seems too much of a risky pastime, take a refreshing swim at canopy level in the hotel pool and admire the unique perspectives afforded by this one-of-a-kind hotel. **BS**

⬆ *For a bird's-eye view of the rain forest, check yourself in at the Ariau Amazon Tower Hotel.*

Bird-watch at Fazenda Barranco Alto

Location Matto Grosso do Sul, Brazil
Website www.fazendabarrancoalto.com.br **Price** 💲💲

"The remoteness of the location and the limited number of rooms make for an intimate experience."

Tribes Travel

With room for a mere nine guests and accessible only by private plane, the Fazenda Barranco Alto is hidden away in a remote paradise and enjoyed by the privileged few. Set in the grassy savannas, forests, and lagoons of this vast Brazilian wilderness, this is a nature reserve like no other. It is an area that hums and moves with the incessant activity of the wildlife all around.

There are more than 450 species of birds that fly in after the rains stop in April. Jabiru, hyacinth macaw, and hummingbirds are as common as sparrows are in the United Kingdom, and in the morning you will be thrilled to see swirling flocks of waking birds. Guests soon become used to regular visits from howler monkeys, giant otters, and crab foxes, too, but it is the rare sighting of the jaguar that is most coveted. Patient devotees observe this majestic creature as it patrols its territory, and its paw prints pepper the clay of the marshlands just in case you miss the animal itself.

Guests can go on an open-vehicle Land Rover safari with the very knowledgeable owner, Lucas Leuzinger. Touring the grasslands and marshes, you will see herds of white-lipped peccaries and caimans basking in the sunshine on the shores of the Rio Grande. Or spend your days in the saddle, trailing a giant anteater or splashing through a flooded water meadow, and you will feel truly in the Pantanal habitat. Go canoeing or fishing, or take part in the cattle mustering: Barranco Alto is still a working ranch, so you can join in with the cowboys. At the end of the day, a delicious home-cooked meal, a campfire, and the brightest Milky Way you have ever seen will be all yours. **SWi**

◤ *The green-winged macaw* (Ara chloroptera) *is one of the many exotic birds to be seen in the Pantanal.*

Stay at Pousada Maravilha

Location Fernando de Noronha, Brazil
Website www.pousadamaravilha.com.br   **Price** ⊙⊙⊙

Fernando de Noronha is one of Earth's peerless places. It was a stop on Charles Darwin's famous 1839 *Beagle* expedition, became a UNESCO World Heritage site in 2001 (with nearby Rocas Atoll), and is one of Brazil's top scuba-diving spots, with spectacular flora and fauna. Its environmental fragility means it is monitored by Brazil's Environmental Protection Agency; visitors are limited to 700 a day, and Fernando de Noronha's sixteen beaches are kept immaculate, with clear waters giving visibility of up to 165 feet (50 m).

Pousada Maravilha has only eight exclusive rooms (five bungalows and three deluxe apartments), with huge beds, outdoor showers (and bamboo hammocks),

> *"Heaven is one word that immediately comes to mind …"*
>
> *Travel+Leisure* magazine

Japanese hot tubs, and furniture from top Brazilian designers Artefacto. Floor-to-ceiling windows help make the most of the spectacular bay views. The infinity pool is one of the few places you might actually see a fellow guest before having a dinner that has been lovingly prepared by chef Adriana Sala. You can also dine at the Brazilian/Italian restaurant bathed in a mixture of candlelight and the pool's luminescent glow. Organized activities include guided island tours, scuba diving, surfing, and the magical experience of watching baby Green Sea turtles hatch on the beach in the middle of a velvet night—just as Darwin did almost two hundred years before. **PS**

Unwind at Anima Hotel

Location Tinharé Island, Brazil
Website www.animahotel.com   **Price** ⊙⊙

Set in 15 acres (6 ha) of private rain forest on the island of Tinharé on Brazil's beautiful Bahia coast, Anima Hotel is a group of nine exquisite bungalows, just 8 miles (15 km) south of the town of Morro de San Paulo, and set on the pristine Encanto beach.

The bungalows are spread among the hotel's luxurious foliage; high ceilings, bamboo partitions, and private decks provide an overwhelming sense of privacy. Anima Hotel's restaurant serves a mix of local and international cuisine, and though the menu changes with the seasons, year-round favorites may include delicacies such as shrimp in fruit sauce with sweet chilies and banana flambé with rum, spices, and coconut sorbet served with wines from Anima Hotel's private cellar. Alternatively, if you happen to snare an octopus from the rock pools next to the hotel, the chef will happily cook it for you. Breakfasts are entirely homemade and include pastries, preserves, fresh breads, and local favorites such as tapioca crepes.

The atmosphere here is completely laid-back. Hammocks are slung above wooden balconies where you can laze away your time reading a book from the hotel's multilingual library. An outdoor lounge is set on a raised wooden platform open on all sides to permit cooling ocean breezes free rein; it also doubles as a conference center and exhibition space for the display of local arts and crafts as well as programs designed to make guests more aware of local customs, history, and traditions. Here you can also find binoculars for viewing the area's abundant birdlife, and board games to while away the hours.

You can reach Tinharé Island by boat from the historic town of Salvador in two hours, or via a twenty-minute flight from Salvador International Airport. **BS**

Relax at Etnia Pousada

Location Trancoso, Brazil   **Website** www.etniabrasil.com.br
Price 🅢🅢

Etnia Pousada is in Trancoso, the hippest and most cosmopolitan village in Bahia, which in turn is the coolest part of Brazil. It is an area of beautiful unspoiled beaches, rural charm, and a relaxed, bohemian way of life. You cannot help feeling like a model here, even if you are in a scruffy T-shirt and flip-flops. Etnia is a deliciously stylish boutique hotel, often used for photo shoots by fashion magazines.

You will find the hotel's eight eclectic rooms among the trees. Each has a different ethnic theme: There is an African bungalow with leopard-skin upholstery and tribal wood carvings, a Moroccan suite with Arabic arches and whitewashed stone steps, and a minimalist Japanese one, too. Others showcase Roma, rural, Mediterranean, Indian, or Brazilian styles.

Most rooms have elegant, modern four-poster beds with fine Italian linen and are draped with mosquito nets. The rooms also have polished concrete floors, walk-in showers, private verandas, and gardens. It is no surprise when you learn that the owners are from the world of Italian fashion.

The public rooms feature open-sided walls with pure white drapes fluttering in the breeze, matching white cushions on rattan armchairs, and low-level lighting after dark. There is a large open-air pool, small spa center for massages and yoga, and hammocks dotted around the palm, banana, and mango trees.

It is only a short stroll to Trancoso's grassy and traffic-free square, lined with impressive boutiques selling the latest hot fashion labels and handmade jewelry; the white colonial church and several laid-back restaurants are just around the corner. In the daytime, many hotel guests head to the nearby beaches—they are some of the best in Brazil. **SH**

Stay at Fazenda da Lagoa

Location Ilhéus, Brazil   **Website** www.fazendadalagoa.com.br
Price 🅢🅢🅢

Forget the throngs and thongs at Copacabana beach, Bahia is Brazil's new hot spot, and there is nowhere hotter than Fazenda da Lagoa. The owners fell in love with it at first sight, and it is easy to see why. It stands on a virgin white-sand beach, with rain forest and mangroves to the rear and a saltwater lagoon close by. The husband and wife team describe the place as a *planetinha* (little planet).

Each of the spacious fourteen bungalows has a deck, outdoor shower, television, CD and DVD players, hammocks, air-conditioning, and gauze-netted beds. The interior design is enough to put a smile on your face: pop-art style, bright and bold, designed by

> *"If you're not a morning person, you'll relish the breakfast protocol at this hotel."*

i-escape.com

architect Lia Siqueria and decorated by Carioca artist Mucka Skrowronski. However, this is not just a luxury wilderness retreat because it is also an eco-hotel. You will find biodegradable toiletries in the shower, and there are plenty of outdoor activities to enjoy, such as kayaking, surfing, and river trekking.

Location aside, it is the little unexpected things that make Fazenda da Lagoa so special. Sure, the infinity pool is impressive and very stylish, as is the spa, but better still is the fact that when you are ready for breakfast, you simply raise a flag outside your bungalow, and the kitchen is alerted to deliver your food basket to your private terrace. **LD**

Enjoy Corumbau

Location Corumbau, Brazil   **Website** www.corumbau.com.br
Price $$$

In the language of the indigenous Pataxos people, *Corumbau* means "distant place." So when you wake up in Corumbau that first morning after arriving at Fazenda São Francisco and decide it would be nice to walk the length of the private beach, you better make sure you take some water with you because this is no ordinary resort beach. It stretches for more than a mile along the Bahia coastline with another 5 miles (8 km) of uninhabited beaches on either side. There is a coral reef breaking just offshore, and you can dive its aquamarine waters and come face-to-face with a myriad of tropical fish and plant life.

Brazil's Bahia coast—also known as the "coconut" coast—is a 124-mile (200-km) stretch of beautiful beaches and coconut groves, and the *fazenda* (ranch) sits within one of these groves. Its six spacious bungalows are elegantly furnished in dark Brazilian timbers, and all have private terraces. There are also two suites in the main house, and both offer dramatic ocean views. Traditional, gourmet seafood dishes are included in the room rate and are prepared fresh each day.

A large outdoor pool is surrounded by a deck that leads to a square, sunken outdoor lounge area with stylistic references to the architecture of ancient Mayan temples. After your swim, take a stroll through the surrounding virgin mangrove swamp to a nearby Pataxos Indian village. The Pataxos people were the first South American tribe to make contact with Europeans when the Portuguese explorer Pedro Cabral sailed into Porto Seguro in 1500, and today you can buy handicrafts and works of art from their descendants.

You can get to Fazenda São Francisco from all major Brazilian cities via Porto Seguro and from there by seaplane, boat, schooner, car, or helicopter. **BS**

Unwind at Tauana

Location Corumbau, Brazil   **Website** www.tauana.com
Price $$$

There is an air of intimate luxury at Tauana, a new hotel on an unspoiled Bahia beachfront. Here you can relax listening to the slight noise of wind rustling leaves and the gentle lap of the waves, but otherwise it is silent.

Portuguese architect-owner Ana Catarina Ferreira da Silva designed everything herself in an ultra-cool blend of Brazilian and Danish design, with a hint of 1960s modernism. It conforms to many of her eco-principles, too. There are just nine bungalows, but she planted 30,000 trees on the huge estate. Building wood is from sustainable sources, and traditional Indian building methods were used. The gourmet restaurant uses ingredients from the hotel's own

> *"Brazil is to cool what China is to commerce. And Bahia is the country's beachside boom state."*
>
> New York Times

organic garden, and visitors move around at night with lanterns, keeping light pollution to a minimum.

The huge bungalows are so shaggily thatched that they look like something from a Gauguin painting; inside they are as minimalist as a modern art gallery. Wood floors are highly polished, flimsy white drapes flutter in the breeze, and slumped amid candles and low sofas, you stare through walls of glass at the beach beyond. It might feel like you are part of something from the pages of a glossy magazine. However, do not worry that you will look out of place in such a manicured photo set—spending time at Tauana will soon make you feel like one of the beautiful people. **SH**

Visit Convento do Carmo

Location Salvador do Bahia, Brazil
Website www.conventodocarmo.com.br   **Price** 💲💲

Located in the picturesque district of Pelourinho in pretty Salvador (in Brazil's Nordeste region), the Pestana Convento do Carmo Hotel is designated by UNESCO as a Cultural Patrimony of Mankind. The building itself dates from 1586, having been commissioned by the First Order of Carmelite Friars to be used by the Sisters of Carmelita. Over the years it has played a part in a host of historic acts, from the Dutch invasion to Bahia's independence. Today it is one of the most luxurious hotels in the country. The seventy-nine beautifully appointed rooms and suites come equipped with LCD television sets, a pillow menu, and luxurious Egyptian cotton linens. There is a

---

"Pestana Convento do Carmo is one of the best new hotels in the world."

Travel+Leisure magazine

---

spa, whirlpool tub, sauna, and pool to relax in; you can, of course, also spend time reading in the library or any of the public salons. History lovers will delight not only in the convent's past, but also in the museum next door, which houses more than 1,500 exhibits.

Right outside this peaceful paradise is Salvador, founded in 1549 and itself a UNESCO World Heritage site. Famous for its fabulous carnival and generally colorful, festive atmosphere, the city was Brazil's capital for two centuries, and remains a meeting point for African, Portuguese, and indigenous cultures. With its great architecture and quaint cobbled streets, it is a wonderful place to discover, too. **PS**

Relax at Txai Resort

Location Itacare, Brazil
Website www.txai.com.br   **Price** 💲💲

On an undeveloped stretch of Brazil's famous Cacoa Coast, set among 247 acres (100 ha) of rare Atlantic coastal rain forest, Txai Resort is a secluded enclave of guest rooms sprinkled throughout the grounds of a privately owned coconut plantation.

Ocean views are unavoidable in this eco-friendly hideaway with natural springs and waterfalls aplenty in the surrounding verdant hills. There are forty rooms, all with king-sized beds, mosquito nets, and wraparound sofas, including twenty-six bungalows with thatch and wood ceilings, color-washed exteriors, and private spa baths. Two even have their own private plunge pools. Most bungalows are found on the resort's lower levels within easy walking distance of the palatial swimming pool, but others are scattered along the hillside and offer a mix of floor plans that can cater to every need. One bungalow has a mezzanine, making it ideal for a family of four, whereas others can be booked to sleep up to eight people.

With breakfast, lunch, and dinner included in the room rate, most meals tend to be eaten in the resort's Bahian-style restaurant. Menus are changed daily and follow a largely Brazilian theme, ranging from traditional fish stews and shrimps served with black beans and manioc through to the humble pizza.

The resort's hilltop spa offers hydro-massage, hot stone treatments, yoga, and a range of facials and manicure treatments that may well be a requirement rather than just an excuse to relax after a heady day of exercise. Activities include kayaking or sailing in a traditional Bahian boat along the Rio de Contas, riding horses through the rain forest trails, or hiking the beach trail to the Camboinha outlook to gaze over the beaches of this unspoiled corner of Brazil. **BS**

Enjoy Villas de Trancoso

Location Trancoso, Brazil
Website www.mybrazilianbeach.com **Price** 🌓🌓

The Trancoso Villa complex is a timber and thatch, five-star enclave, nestled amid palm and acacia trees. It consists of five villas designed by the noted architect Ricardo Salem, with interiors by the São Paulo–based Sig Bergamen, and represents the epitome of privacy and luxury. Its pure tranquility is able to attract the most discerning of travelers.

The one- and two-bedroom Trancoso Villas have all been constructed using rare Brazilian timbers and are filled with native furnishings, mosquito nets, and hand-painted cushions. They are superbly located on a landscaped and terraced beach just 1 mile (1.6 km) south of the historic village of Trancoso, founded in 1586 and spread along a cliff top with views over miles of pure white-sand beaches. Over the past seven years, this sleepy fishing village has been reinvented as one of the most trendy destinations in South America and boasts such regular visitors as actor Leonardo DiCaprio, model Naomi Campbell, and the former vice president of the United States Al Gore.

The villas all come with an English-speaking staff of cleaners, cooks, and a concierge, and there are hammocks, a cabana, white marbled infinity pool and swim-up pool bar, and indulgent waterfall showers that will leave you feeling pampered and refreshed. Dinners can be eaten by torchlight under the stars and range from the exotic to a simple burger and fries.

The experience can also include horseback riding along pristine beaches, kayaking, and off-road bicycling, or you can play at Trancoso's Villa Golf, the newest addition to the Trancoso Villa complex. **BS**

↗ *Many of the villas have an open-plan design
that accentuates the quality of the craftmanship.*

*"It was wonderful in all respects
. . . a very precious thing in such
beautiful surroundings."*

John Danilovich, U.S. Ambassador to Brazil

Stay at Fasano Hotel
Rio de Janeiro

Location Rio de Janeiro, Brazil   **Website** www.fasano.com.br
Price ⑤⑤⑤

Depite opening relatively recently, the Fasano Hotel
Rio de Janeiro is already the leader of the pack in a city
blessed with fine hotels but, until now, lacking the
fresh, contemporary charm the Fasano brings to its
enviable spot on Ipanema beach. Infused with all the
effortless beauty and grace of the city around it, the
five-star Fasano is a hip hotel; there is no doubt about
that. It also boasts a highly personalized, seamless
level of service that puts many other hotels of its class
in the shade. It is the result of cheerful hard work on
the part of the staff, but most of all, it is a tribute to its
owner and auteur, Rogério Fasano, whose good taste
and high production values are evident at every turn.

This is a dream hotel, from the acclaimed seafood
restaurant Fasano al Mare at its base to the tip of its
chic rooftop pool—a breathtakingly lovely spot in this,
the most heartbreaking of beautiful cities. It is the
kind of hotel in which it is all too easy to linger, with
stunning views wherever you glance, whether up by
the pool or lounging in a sumptuous, polished
wooden chair on your balcony. Splash out on a high-
up room with an ocean view and you will never regret
it; the view along Ipanema beach is simply astonishing.
Enhanced and remixed thanks to a bit of Philippe
Starck mirror trickery on the balconies, the view is one
of the hotel's most outstanding features.

Sip a cocktail by the pool after a day in Rio, and
watch as sea and sky turn molten under the faraway
gaze of Christ the Redeemer statue; then hit Bar
Londra downstairs for an ultra-cool evening. **CR**

◄ *The rooftop pool has an unforgettable view over
Ipanema beach and the Two Brothers mountains.*

Stay at Picinguaba Pousada

Location Near Paraty, Brazil
Website www.picinguaba.com **Price** 💲💲

"To call [Picinguaba bay] breathtakingly beautiful does not do it justice."

Hip Hotel guide

On the edge of a small fishing village in the heart of a natural park, Pousada Picinguaba is a relaxing hotel in a former colonial mansion run by an unpretentious Brazilian couple. It sits on the stunning Costa Verde (green coast), a UNESCO World Heritage Site full of spectacular landscapes.

The ten comfortable rooms are decorated with Brazilian native art. Each has a balcony with a hammock and views onto lush subtropical gardens. It is an excellent place to disconnect because there are no televisions, no Internet access, and no cell phone signal. Ceiling fans and the natural sea breeze provide all the air-conditioning needed.

Lounge by the pool on the deck by the ocean or enjoy massages carried out in a linen-draped pavilion in the gardens. Guests are encouraged to enjoy drinks and canapés together at night, although flexibility is paramount and you can eat breakfast late, or ask for dinner in a different setting. Organic food is served buffet-style using locally sourced fruit and vegetables. Fish is a specialty, from seviche to Picanha Churascos, a South American barbecue.

The adventurous can borrow the hotel's kayaks and cross the bay to Praia Fazenda, a deserted 1.8-mile (3-km) stretch of gorgeous beach ideal for walking. Guided treks, surfing classes, fishing, diving, and boat trips to deserted islands can be arranged. For a taste of town life, there are eateries, street markets, and classy boutiques a twenty-five-minute drive away in the colonial port of Paraty. Alternatively, stay in your bikini and sip the house lemonade while daydreaming. **CSJ**

🔲 *Guests can relax in the shade of the palms at the pousada, which overlooks the stunning Costa Verde.*

Unwind at Gite D'Indaiatiba

Location Paraty, Brazil
Website www.legitedindaiatiba.com.br   **Price** 💲💲

Rent Piedade Island

Location Angra dos Reis, Brazil
Website www.privateislandsonline.com   **Price** 💲💲💲💲

There is an unwritten law that the most beautiful places are awkward to get to—the farther away, the more isolated, the better. Gite D'Indaiatiba is just such a place. Situated in the rain forest between São Paulo and Rio, it is hidden in the dense vegetation at the end of a rocky, precarious dirt track 7 miles (12 km) away from the beachside town of Paraty.

The small pousada is a real gem, and definitely off the proverbial beaten track, with a main lodge and five huts dotted across the wild steep terrain of the rain forest. A tiny sauna hut overlooks the tropical paradise; the only sounds are the twitter of birds and water

---

"It was like buying an apartment in Paris. I saw about a hundred places and I knew this was it."

Proprietor, Gite D'Indaiatiba

---

cascading down to the river. There are no phones or televisions to be seen in the pink and cream bungalows; their one luxury is an open fireplace.

Activities here are few and far between: Read in the hammock on the porch, swim in the freshwater pool, or count the many different species of wild orchid. And then there is the food. The Gite's mix of Brazilian and French cuisine is so good that the helipad is used by wealthy Brazilians from São Paulo to jet across for dinner, or by their pilots flying over for takeout. Outrageous perhaps, but sitting in the dining room by candlelight sampling fish in grape sauce and the incredible tangy seviche, it is easy to see why. **RCA**

When you step ashore from your helicopter or speedboat onto Piedade Island, you are following in the footsteps of Hollywood actors, top fashion models, Formula One drivers, soccer stars, and heads of state: You are arriving at one of the world's most luxurious, exclusive escapes. This tiny island is so private that it is often rented by the South American *Caras* magazine (think *People*, *Hola*, or *Hello* magazines) for celebrity and VIP photo shoots and parties.

Piedade is halfway between São Paulo and Rio de Janeiro, in the dazzling archipelago of Angra dos Reis (King's Bay). It is just one of 365 islands in this former pirates' lair—one for each day of the year. The area is now a favorite yachting, diving, and beach destination among Brazil's richest elite, and there are 2,000 lovely, lonely beaches here, too, in case you want to get away from the "crowds" elsewhere.

The island is an all-inclusive retreat that can accommodate up to twenty-two people. If you are rich enough to rent it, you get a guesthouse with five suites, six air-conditioned bungalows (each can sleep two), and a beach house with a barbecue and gorgeous sundeck. At the top of the island is a big open-sided pavilion for entertaining, which is surrounded by a veranda where guests can lounge at their leisure and stare at the stunning view of the entire bay and its islands. Guests can travel to the different islands and beaches using Piedade's own boat, or they may prefer to use their own helicopter from the island's heliport. There are only 4 acres (1.6 ha) of lush trees and rocks on Piedade, but the facilities include four small, private beaches, a floodlit tennis court, a sauna, and even a soccer field. The full-time staff includes a gourmet chef, of course. **SH**

Visit the Harbor Town of Paraty

Location Paraty, Brazil
Website www.paraty.com.br   **Price** ◑

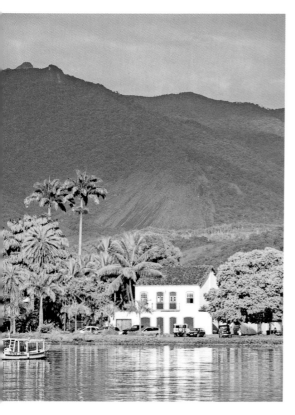

A stunning seventeenth-century colonial harbor town on Brazil's Costa Verde, Paraty is a perfectly preserved UNESCO World Heritage site. Paraty (meaning "river of fish" in the Tupi language) was founded in 1667. The town's growth was based on its location at the end of the Gold Trail (Caminho do Ouro) connecting Rio and Europe to the gold mines in Minas Gerais by the sea.

After the gold business ended, Paraty became the center of the famous Brazilian rumlike drink, *cachaça*. (The town became so synonymous with the drink that for a while the beverage was known as a Paraty.) Today it is a beautiful town surrounded by a tropical forest.

Wander the colorful, cobbled, car-free streets where horses and carts still make deliveries and take in the jaw-droppingly beautiful architecture. Churches like the Capela de Santa Rita or the Igreja Matriz da Nossa Senhora dos Remédios are immaculately preserved. Admire the pastel-painted homes adorned with mysterious masonic symbols and the riot of color that are the shop fronts flaunting bright hammocks.

Paraty is also about food, music, and, of course, *cachaça*. Try the local cuisine: fish and banana gratin or banana-and-cheese-stuffed squid in coconut milk. An acquired taste to say the least. Spend the night in any of the basic yet beautiful pousadas: simple rooms with antiques and local art on display. With no motels or fast food outlets to be seen, this is as low-key as it gets. But do not be fooled; although quiet and remote it is not undiscovered. Mick Jagger, Linda Evangelista, and Tom Cruise have all been known to visit to escape the rest of the world, and who can blame them? **RCA**

> *"Carmen Miranda sang about the man who had a Paraty instead of tea and toast."*
>
> John DeWitt, journalist

◣ *The colonial town is famed for the elegance of its architecture and the beauty of its mountains.*

Relax at Sitio do Lobo

Location Ilha Grande, Brazil
Website www.sitiodolobo.com.br   **Price** 💲💲

Lying in a hammock at Sitio do Lobo clutching a cocktail, gazing across the clear blue water to the mountains in the distance, it can feel as if you are miles away from civilization. And, in this case, you really are. The hotel is hidden among the scented tangerine trees and exotic flowers of an almost deserted island, two hours south of Rio de Janeiro.

This is definitely an escape from normal modern life. Ilha Grande is 25 miles (40 km) wide, yet has no roads. The nearest village is almost an hour away—by kayak. Sitio is a slightly ramshackle, back-to-nature sort of place, with just nine rooms blended into the jungle along the shore. It stands on the Bay of the Stars, the site of a nineteenth-century coffee plantation. Nestled among its acres of lush vegetation, the Sitio was a wealthy Brazilian family's Costa Verde retreat for twenty years. Many rich and famous friends visited, including soccer star Ronaldo and Prince Rainier of Monaco. Only recently has the luxury retreat been opened up to paying guests. And that makes for a comfortable, lived-in feeling.

This is definitely no chain hotel. Sofas are built into giant granite boulders; there are thatched massage huts and wooden verandas overlooking the sea. Bamboo furniture is embedded with tiny seashells, and exposed granite is incorporated into the walls. There are eccentric ornaments everywhere, from model boats to handmade wooden frogs. Food is simple and fresh, with plenty of seafood and local fruit. There is also a heliport, and the hotel's speedboat whisks guests around the bay. However, guests are encouraged to travel by kayak instead, to explore the surrounding national park or visit empty sandy beaches—the island has 102 of them. **SH**

Stay at Solar da Ponte

Location Tiradentes, Brazil
Website www.solardaponte.com.br   **Price** 💲💲

Standing grandly beside the beautiful main square and ancient stone bridge in one of Brazil's most historic villages, it looks like a stately official building or wonderful mansion. Yet Solar da Ponte is actually an elegant period hotel, with eighteen spacious rooms opening onto verandas, gardens, a pool, and a sauna.

The derelict building was bought by an English naturalist and his Brazilian wife in the 1970s. They have been exquisitely restoring it for thirty years, and it is now something of a monument in its own right. Solar da Ponte is regularly judged as one of the country's finest hotels. It is in the center of the colonial gold-mining town of Tiradentes, in the state of Minas Gerais.

"One of the best hotels in Brazil . . . a wonderfully civilized base for exploring."

Tatler Travel Guide

The eighteenth-century gold boom helped pay for the architecture; guests can stroll along the cobbled streets and leafy squares lined with lavish historic buildings, with the brooding São Jose mountains in the background. It is a favorite weekend retreat for wealthy families from Rio.

Inside, Solar da Ponte is comfortably full of antique furnishings, fresh flowers, and local art. There are reclaimed wooden floors, traditional wooden beds, and full-length windows that look out over the peaceful gardens, where colorful orchids bloom and exotic birds sing in the trees. Watch out for the marmoset monkeys frolicking on the lawn, too. **SH**

Enjoy Ponta dos Ganchos

Location Santa Catarina, Brazil
Website www.pontadosganchos.com.br   **Price** ⊖⊖⊖

Set amid lush tropical rain forest on a privately owned lagoon dotted with tiny islands, Ponta dos Ganchos is the ultimate paradise hideaway. The luxury resort, in the southern state of Santa Catarina on Brazil's "Emerald Coast," contains just twenty rustic-chic cabanas, some with a sauna, whirlpool tub, and infinity pool. No under-eighteens are allowed, which means that peace and quiet is a given, making the resort a hit with honeymooners and couples. With more than three staff per bungalow, the service aims to please.

There is plenty here to keep you busy. Activities range from tennis and volleyball to deep-sea fishing, canoeing, and diving. The Arvoredo Biological Marine Reserve, which has some of the best diving sites in Brazil, is less than an hour away by boat. There is also a fitness center and cinema. One of the biggest draws in the resort is the luxurious Christian Dior spa, the only one in the Americas, as well as open-air shiatsu and ayurvedic treatments. Nearby, the Island of Anhatomirim has one of the oldest forts in Brazil, and there is a pretty little fishing village just down the lane.

Menus change daily and there are no time restrictions, meaning that you can eat breakfast at midnight if you wish. For romantic dining, you can book a private gazebo on one of the islands, perhaps ordering a plateful of Santa Catarina's famous oysters and mussels, considered by many to be the best in the world. For all its opulence, much has been done to run the resort along environmentally friendly lines, with electric cars available for rent and a natural waste treatment system in the offing. **TW**

➔ *Each of the resort's bungalows has a private veranda with hammocks, sun beds, and a superb sea view.*

Discover Iguazú Falls

Location Paranà, Brazil; Misiones Province, Argentina
Website www.iguazuargentina.com **Price** 🔴

It is strange, perhaps, to think of these mighty waterfalls as an escape, unless you are planning to go over them in a canoe, in which case your mad dash might be only briefly pleasurable. But to stand at the edge of the "Garganta del Diablo" (Devil's Throat) and look down into the vast horseshoe-shaped chasm, where unimaginable quantities of water are tumbling into piling clouds of steam and great dusky swifts dart and weave through hovering rainbows, is to enter a dreamlike world of fairy-tale proportions.

The grandest falls in South America drop 242 feet (74 m) through subtropical rain forest, extending nearly 1.8 miles (3 km) in width, and encompassing 272 different waterfalls. However, size is not the issue here. The magic of Iguazú lies in being able to immerse yourself in this watery paradise, gazing at the incredible torrents from so many different angles. The Brazilian side offers a complete, far-off panorama, but for a real escape you have to enter the Argentine Iguazú National Park, take the eco-train into the forest, and prepare to explore.

The path to the Garganta del Diablo runs over the wide Iguazú River, where it flows smooth and quiet. Mounting columns of mist and a deafening roar herald the drama to come, and once you reach the falls themselves, it is impossible not to stand mesmerized by the sheer volume of cascading water. Take a boat dashing straight into the drenching spray, or hike the Macuco trail to spot abundant birdlife. Iguazú is an utterly exhilarating experience and one to which you will escape, endlessly, in your memories. **CD**

🔙 *Water cascades spectacularly down a cliff face on the Argentinian side of Iguazú Falls.*

Stay at Cabo Polonio

Location Cabo Polonio, Uruguay
Website www.discoveruruguay.com **Price** 🟢🟢

Could Cabo Polonio be the hippie ideal? Spanning miles of the rugged coastline for which Uruguay is justly renowned, this protected nature sanctuary is one of the best-kept secrets in South America: a haven for in-the-know locals looking for tranquility and unspoiled beauty amid sea lion colonies and rolling sand dunes. It is far removed from the glitz and the bustle of nearby Puntas del Este and Diablo.

With just two hotels in the vicinity (development ceased when the land was designated as protected in the mid-1900s), most visitors sleep in the rustic beach *posadas* (lodges) or rainbow-colored shacks dotting the grassy knolls behind the dunes. There are no cars

> *"Being in Cabo Polonio was like being in a galaxy far, far away."*

Kelly Westhoff, Go-Nomad.com

here (there is also no electricity for that matter), other than the odd four-by-four shepherding visitors between the dunes; at other times a neigh announces the arrival of a horse-drawn buggy into the area's epicenter, el Cabo. It is the town that time forgot, where the most notable citizens are the sea lions from the colony lying some 100 feet (30 m) into the sea, presided over by the lighthouse guarding the bay.

Gentle breezes envelop as cares are washed away with the sound of the lapping ocean; hampers are unpacked on the white sand and friendships are forged over campfires. This is the ultimate beachside idyll—protected by man and gifted by nature. **VG**

Explore the Atacama Desert

Location Atacama Desert, Chile   **Website** www.awasi.cl
Price ⊙⊙

It is hard to imagine anywhere more remote than the Atacama Desert. Stretching for nearly 1,000 miles (1,600 km) along the Chilean side of the Andes, where volcanoes are still smoking, this is the driest place on Earth. Here the skies are so clear that astronomers can see light from the earliest galaxies in the universe. Yet at its heart, there are vivid blue salt lakes where bright pink flamingos seem to hover in a perpetual haze. The silence is so profound that you can hear them sipping.

Geysers spout great columns of steam into a cobalt-blue sky, over rivers of red-hot algae. Moon Valley boasts vast dunes: the Earth twisted and eroded into such fantastic shapes it could easily pass as another planet. Particularly stunning are the sunsets over Atacama, when Licancabur volcano turns purple in the setting sun and there is a real sense of isolation. Darkness descends, the sky fills with stars—and fortunately, at this point, your dedicated guide takes you back to your sumptuous oasis, Awasi.

A world away from busy San Pedro de Atacama, Awasi is beautiful, calm, and very exclusive. A series of airy spaces, open to the sky, leads to the restaurant, offering sublime modern dishes. Traditional textiles and adobe architecture are subtly combined with contemporary furnishings, giving the local aesthetic some five-star style. The rooms are exquisite: some circular, with high thatched roofs and sunken baths. Best of all, Awasi is the only hotel in Atacama where each guest has their own dedicated guide. They find parts of the Moon Valley where no one goes, and visit the Tatio Geysers after the crowds have left. **CD**

➔ *The Atacama Desert, with its mighty volcanoes and lunar landscape, has an eerie beauty all its own.*

Stargaze at Elqui Domos

Location Paihuano, Chile
Website www.elquidomos.cl   **Price** $

In 1982 when scientists first measured Earth's magnetic field by satellite, they found our planet's center to be in central Chile's dry Elqui Valley. So it should come as no surprise that in 2005 the clear skies of this supposed magnetic epicenter were chosen to be the site for the construction of one of only seven astronomic hotels worldwide and the only lodge of its kind in the southern hemisphere.

Huddled together, the accommodation resembles some sort of futuristic, Arthur C. Clarke–style attempt at survival in a post-apocalyptic world. In reality, it represents a bold new approach to environmentally sensitive tourism. Elqui Domos is a collection of seven geodesic domes, each possessing two levels. The living area and bathroom are below, whereas the bedroom above has a removable window in the ceiling to allow unfettered observation of the night sky. A telescope is provided in each dome, just to ensure you never lose sight of the reason for coming here. Each dome has its own terrace with views of a more terrestrial nature.

Hotel staff can organize activities such as horseback riding and mountain biking, or a visit to a vineyard or the home of Nobel Prize winner Gabriela Mistral to fill up the daylight hours until the sun goes down and the exciting stuff begins. Astronomy courses and an abundance of astronomic literature are available, as are hammocks and outdoor wooden bathtubs in which to read. A number of international observatories are in the area, including the Mamalluca amateur observatory, which welcomes visitors. **BS**

◄ *Each dome at Elqui Domos comes equipped with a terrace and telescope from which to view the sky.*

Stay at Hotel el Pangal

Location Robinson Crusoe Island, Chile
Website www.enjoy-chile.org   **Price** $$

Named after the novel based on Scottish sailor Alexander Selkirk, who was marooned here between 1704 and 1709, Robinson Crusoe Island is a lonely place, ringed mostly by precipitous sea cliffs. Populated mainly by vagabonds and marooned sailors until the early nineteenth century, it is now home to the town of San Juan Bautista (population 600) and the isolated and unique Hotel el Pangal.

You can either walk to the Hotel el Pangal or arrive via an inflatable boat that will ferry you across the bay from San Juan Bautista. The hotel has a restaurant and a tea salon and is surrounded by lovely terraced gardens, but you do not come here to experience the

> *"[Robinson Crusoe Island] is the ultimate escape, an unvanquished Pacific island. . . ."*
>
> Diana Souhami, *Guardian*

hotel's fine cuisine and stunning ocean views. Robinson Crusoe Island is the Hotel el Pangal's backyard, and what a backyard it is.

Almost two-thirds of the island's vascular plants are endemic, including two species of bromeliad found nowhere else. Much of the island's original forest has been overtaken by invasive plants from South America and New Zealand, although large stands of native forest can still be found at higher altitudes. The primeval *Lactoris fernandeziana*, considered to be a living fossil, is also found nowhere else in the world, all of which helps make Hotel el Pangal much more than just a place to lay one's weary head. **BS**

Unwind at the Secret Ranchito

Location Patagonia, Chile   **Website** www.i-escape.com   **Price** ⊝⊝

The rustic delights and spectacular Andean vistas that encircle the Secret Ranchito in southern Chile will, happily, never be disturbed or eroded by the encroachment of mass tourism, its grand isolation guaranteeing to preserve it for only the most determined of souls. Getting here is an adventure in itself. An early morning flight from the Chilean capital Santiago to Puerto Montt is followed by a private charter flight to the town of Chaiten. A representative from Expediciones Chile will then take you on a four-hour shuttle into the Andes to a nondescript village called Futaleufu for the final twenty-minute walk to your accommodation. And not a moment too soon!

If you like absolute isolation totally removed from any vestiges of civilization, this is the place to come. Your luggage is brought in on top of an old ox cart, and a four-by-four vehicle is parked for your sole use fifteen minutes' walk from your lodging at the other end of a timber and rope suspension bridge strung across a small but spectacular river gorge. Fly fishing enthusiasts will delight at the abundance of brown and rainbow trout to be found in the cold, clear waters of the nearby Azul and Futaleufu rivers. Explore the river all the way to the Argentine border by kayak or by raft, or just recline on the hammock strung over the white sands of your private riverside beach.

Accommodation is a one-room timber dwelling divided into a kitchen and bedroom with wool rugs and simply furnished, with another adjacent cabin, both of which enjoy magnificent views across to the granite face of Tres Monjas. Hot showers, a telephone, radio, and CD player mean you do not have to leave all the comforts of home behind, but this is as close as you are ever likely to get to a memorably primitive sojourn surrounded by nature at its grandest. **BS**

⬆ *High up in an Andean valley, the Secret Ranchito can be reached only by foot, horse, water, or helicopter.*

Cruise the Chilean Fjords

Location Southern Chile   **Website** www.explore.co.uk; www.lata.org   **Price** 💲💲

At the southern tip of Chile, islands and icebergs feather around the tip of the mainland, and channels and straits carve routes from the Pacific to the Atlantic. Here at the ends of the earth, you will find the ultimate escape.

Along Chile's west or Pacific coast, the fjords are as deep and dramatic as their northern counterparts, but with the addition of near total isolation, ice-blue icebergs, and only a handful of native people. Cruises generally travel along the fjords from Puerto Montt, reachable by air from Santiago, to Puerto Natales, which you cannot reach by road, giving you the only access route to this part of the country. Inlets around here were navigated by Magellan in 1520 and again by Darwin in the early nineteenth century, en route to the Galapagos.

The spectacularly remote area holds beinlets, snowcapped mountains, pristine wilderness, and breaching whales, and it is not difficult to see what makes a trip here so special. In our busy world, where everything is only a click of a mouse away, just getting here is an organizational feat. The 685 miles (1,100 km) take around four days to travel at a leisurely pace, allowing you to stop and notice the smallest details, like dolphins following in the wake of the boat and seals playing along the shore, for example.

Albatross, giant petrel, and Magellan penguins are just three of the delights for bird-watchers. As the cruise ship anchors, you can take a canoe to explore the islands and inlets nearby. It is an enchanting area teeming with wildlife and very few visitors. Just a handful of fishing villages and cattle ranches stud the coastline, and penguin colonies number more than people in many areas. As night falls, the Milky Way stands out brightly in the pitch-black sky. **LD**

⤒ *A boat enters the icy waters of the Amalia Fjord in Southern Patagonia, Chile.*

Stay at Puyuhuapi Lodge

Location Chiloé Island, Chile
Website www.patagonia-connection.com **Price** 🆂🆂

It is hard to imagine a more romantic arrival. After rumbling over gravel roads between fairy-tale forests along Chile's remote but spectacular Carretera Austral, you come, at last, to a tranquil little hamlet on the edge of a fjord: Puyuhuapi. The last stretch of your journey must be done by boat, crossing the glassy waters to find a cathedral-like wooden building poised right on the water against a backdrop of virgin forest. It seems an unlikely place for a luxurious spa, and yet inside this beautiful structure there are immaculate pools, fed by three kinds of natural waters. This is Puyuhuapi's secret: There is not only clear seawater from the fjord and a spring of crystalline snowmelt, but healing, mineral-rich hot springs, too. From this rare combination, Puyuhuapi's owners have created a superb range of treatments and brought in gifted specialists to transform guests' well-being with a whole range of therapies.

Friendly, attentive staff give Puyuhuapi its warm, relaxed atmosphere. Although the accommodation is simple rather than chic, the comfortable rooms are designed with natural materials and huge windows to make the most of tranquil views onto the fjord. Fine cuisine completes the luxurious treatment, which feels particularly miraculous at this remote extreme of Patagonia. Guests can conclude their trip here with an unforgettable voyage to see the mighty glacier at Laguna San Rafael.

It is Puyuhuapi's complete contact with nature that is so special: Take a kayak out onto the water to explore, or hike to the awe-inspiring hanging glacier on the other side of the fjord. After a day of exertion, there is no better therapy than to bask in hot pools under a flawless sky and watch the heavens fill with stars. **CD**

Visit Clos Apalta Winery

Location Santa Cruz, Chile
Website www.closapalta.cl **Price** 🆂🆂

Clos Apalta is an oenophile's paradise: a tranquil retreat where visitors can live and breathe wine. Cocooned into a forested hillside of Chile's Colchagua Valley, the winery and lodge was founded by the Marnier-Lapostolle family (the producers of Grand Marnier) in 1994, but it already has the reputation of being one of the country's leading wine producers. The winery itself is beautiful; of its five storeys, three are dug into the granite hillside, providing a cool environment for the wine to age. At the heart of the building is a dramatic spiral staircase that resembles wine being poured into a glass. Visitors can watch how the wines are created as well as taste some of them.

> *"Each casita has been named for one of the primary red grape varieties planted at the vineyard."*
>
> Manos Angelakis, LuxuryWeb.com

Four luxury casitas are within staggering distance of the winery, each with its own hot tub, fireplace, king-sized bed, and terrace. These plush pads are equipped with fully stocked fridges and iPod sound systems. The food here is taken as seriously as the wine, with a local chef preparing gourmet meals, washed down with glasses of the vineyard's finest wines, plus Pisco Sours flavored with a nip of Grand Marnier. The 450-acre (182-ha) vineyard can be explored on horseback, or admired from the comfort of the infinity pool. **JK**

➡ *The striking über-modern architecture of the Clos Apalta winery stands out against the lush hillside.*

Relax at Indigo

Location Puerto Natales, Patagonia, Chile
Website www.indigopatagonia.com **Price** ⊖⊖

Arriving in Puerto Natales, with its weather-beaten tin houses and solitary air, feels a bit like winding up at the end of the world. There is good reason for this: This waterside town is just 100 miles (160 km) from the southern tip of the Americas in Patagonia—in short, the last place you would expect to find one of the country's most original design hotels.

Located on the shores of the romantically named Sound of Last Hope, Indigo works a fresh, Nordic-chic aesthetic (blond woods, whiter-than-white sheets), complementing the contemporary architecture by leading Chilean architect Sebastián Iriarrázaval. Instead of baths the rooms have rain-forest showers. There are,

---

"By far the best feature of Puerto Natales is the view from Hotel Indigo."

Christabelle Dilks, *Guardian*

---

however, three huge rooftop hot tubs, affording direct views of the indigo-colored fjord, the constantly changing hues of the vast sky, and the peaks of Torres del Paine far in the distance. Whatever the weather (most of the year quite chilly), it will not touch you in the steamy waters.

Most visitors use Puerto Natales as a base for a trip to Torres del Paine 50 miles (80 km) to the north, a national park with some of the world's most beautiful trekking circuits, taking you past glaciers, peppermint-hued lakes, and thrusting pink granite peaks. What makes Indigo stand out is its well-executed brand of laid-back luxe, ideal for post-trek pampering. **IA**

Enjoy El Manantial

Location Purmamarca, Argentina
Website www.hotelmanantial.com.ar **Price** ⊖⊖

The "wellspring of silence" is a bold claim for a hotel, and it is not made lightly here. El Manantial del Silencio is a truly peaceful retreat in the ancient village of Purmamarca, tucked away from the famous Quebrada de Humahuaca. Tourism has really boomed in this magnificent gorge of colored rock since UNESCO declared it a World Heritage site in 2002. Fortunately, most visitors charge up the center of the valley, leaving charming Purmamarca less visited. Yet here is one of Argentina's most famous views: the Cerro de Siete Colores, which boasts at least seven colors among its vivid stripes. The mountain gives a dramatic backdrop to the tiny town's popular market and traditional adobe church, which contains a series of beautiful paintings under a cactus-wood roof. Day visitors might mill around in the morning, but after noon, Purmamarca recovers its deep feeling of tranquility.

El Manantial's magic lies in its design. Inspired by early colonial architecture, its comfortable rooms echo the simple local way of life; there is an almost monastic purity to the white walls and linens and bottle-green shutters. Traditional textiles and paintings bring a welcome dash of color, but everything sits in harmony with the view of the mountain from the window. Before dining on a carpaccio of guanaco, or ravioli stuffed with handmade goat cheese made by the prizewinning chef, recline before a crackling fire with a gin and tonic. Attentive staff will arrange all your adventures in the Quebrada and beyond.

Indelibly printed on most guests' memory is the vision of the salt flats above El Manantial at sunset: A shimmering sea of white, fringed by copper-tinged clouds suspended above imposing, distant mountains, and—naturally—perfect silence. **CD**

Unwind at Estancia Colomé

Location Calchaquí Valley, Argentina
Website www.estanciacolome.com   **Price** 🜚🜚

The journey to Colomé is part of its magic. From the crumbling colonial splendor of Salta city, the road snakes up through the dramatic Cuesta del Obispo, a deep gorge cut into green velvety mountains, then streaks straight across a red plateau filled with cactus. Nothing else seems to grow here at the 26,900-foot (8,200-m) altitude. But, descend through canyons of terra-cotta rock into a remote valley of stark and spectacular beauty, and suddenly you come to a stretch of emerald green, perfectly ordered, rows of vines. Here owner Donald Hess is miraculously producing award-winning Malbecs. In the heart of the vines, surrounded by fragrant lavender, and perfectly poised for wide-open views, is another miracle: one of Argentina's most stunning hotels.

Just nine enormous, luxurious rooms, meticulously designed and decorated in deep earth tones, lead off from a central open courtyard where a Zen-like fountain murmurs. The entire estate is biodynamic, a system that sees the land and every creature on it as part of the same organism, and so owner Hess cares for the 400 Andean people living on his 96,000 acres (38,850 ha) as part of his family. Thus Colomé is utterly harmonious with its surroundings.

Whether climbing up the paths into ancient mountains, riding horses with the horse whisperer, or simply lounging around by the pool and soaking up the views, a deep sense of peace descends. As night falls, roll an inky Amalaya around your glass, sip the intense wine made from these beautiful landscapes, and blissfully unwind. **CD**

↗ *Estancia Colomé has the highest-altitude vineyards in the world, which produce award-winning wines.*

"Life is too short to look at bad art, drink bad wine, or stay in bad hotels."

Proprietor, Estancia Colomé

Explore Tierra del Fuego National Park

Location Tierra del Fuego, Argentina
Website www.parquesnacionales.gov.ar **Price** $

Close to the Chilean border, the spectacular Tierra del Fuego National Park protects 155,000 acres (63,000 ha) of the southern tip of the Andes, from north of Lake Kami to the coast of the Beagle Channel.

Miles of deserted hiking trails cross the main island of the archipelago past waterfalls, through forests, and across peat bogs to reach viewpoints looking across the panoramic scenery of rugged coastline and snowcapped mountains. On the way, it is possible to catch a glimpse of condors, albatross, cormorants, and orange-billed steamer ducks. There is color in the park throughout the year, especially from the glaciers, but autumn provides the real spectacle when the forest-clad hillsides bloom in a sea of red foliage.

Argentina's only coastal national park, Tierra del Fuego's mountains are divided by deep glacial valleys, where lakes and rivers flow. This proximity to the sea, along with dominant westerly winds, means low, moderate temperatures year-round. Even in summer, the mercury rarely goes above 50°F (10°C). These conditions mean that unique flora grows here, such as Sea Pink and Diddledee, rare lichens, and mosses.

The region's original inhabitants were the Yamana, a tribe who lived on the shores of the Beagle Channel and Lake Roca. Living off what they could harvest from the sea, they moved around in bark canoes, hunting sea lions and fishing. Ruins still remain of a settlement at Lapataia Bay. Today visitors can camp within the park to make the most of the setting, or stay at nearby Ushuaia, the southernmost city in the world. **AD**

➡ *The rugged natural beauty of Tierra del Fuego offers a fantastic landscape for hikers and eco-tourists.*

Stay at House of Jasmines

Location Salta, Argentina **Website** www.houseofjasmines.com
Price $ $

Hollywood actor Robert Duvall and his Argentinian wife, Luciana, originally bought this secluded 120-year-old colonial estate as their personal retreat. Now it has been sold to a local family who has opened it as an exclusive rustic boutique hotel. The House of Jasmines is in the northwestern Argentinian province of Salta, where the subtropical forest meets the canyons and foothills at the edge of the Andes. Guests arrive at this quiet spot down a long avenue of eucalyptus trees. At the end is the old whitewashed and jasmine-covered estate house with terra-cotta-tiled roof and verandas.

It feels intimate and personal, with just seven suites. The hotel manages to retain the feeling that this is still

> *"On foot or horseback guests are free to roam the Edenic grounds."*
>
> *Travel+Leisure* magazine

a private home. The decorative style is gently luxurious with a rustic flavor: beamed ceilings, wrought-iron chandeliers, local antique chairs and lamps, four-poster beds, and rush-matting floors. Some suites have roof terraces; all have memorable views across the garden, estate, and mountains.

The spa has masseurs, steam rooms, and saunas. There is a pool in the beautiful gardens. White wooden chairs are dotted around the lawns and under the overhanging plants for shade—perfect for relaxing with a glass of the local Torrontes wine. The hotel's land stretches along the Arenales River, and is rampant with orchids, roses, and yet more wild jasmine. **SH**

Discover Iruya Village

Location Salta, Argentina **Website** www.enjoy-argentina.org
Price $

The drive alone is unforgettable. Head north through the vast Quebrada de Humahuaca gorge, which was declared a UNESCO World Heritage site for the savage beauty of its stratified orange-ocher rock, and then strike off across wildly beautiful landscape on a rocky road that crosses several rivers before climbing to a mountain pass, the Abra del Condór, at a breathless 13,120 feet (4,000 m). From here, the track slaloms down vast slabs of mountainside. It seems incredible that anyone lives here, but finally, at the end of the road, perched on a precipitous slope above you: Iruya.

Andean village life is being changed forever by the arrival of television, modern influences, and, of course, tourism. But Iruya somehow retains its identity. With one main street giving access to provisions stores, a tiny post office, and one intermittently functioning phone center, Iruya is cut off from the world. Watch villagers driving goats into the mountains or striding out along paths threading into remote valleys, and you will want to follow. The idyllic hamlet of San Isidro is three hours' walk away. At Easter the houses are strewn with flowers, and in summer, roofs are covered with tiny peaches drying in the sun. From Iruya, there are blissful walks all around, but the real pleasure of arriving here is that you will not want to leave.

Bring a book, allow at least five days, and prepare to slow down. Stay in villagers' houses, snuggling under heavy llama blankets in winter, or in a comfortable room at Hostería Iruya. Gaze out from the terrace over the valley below; look up to a night sky filled with stars, and listen to the exquisite silence. **CD**

➡ *The mountain village of Iruya offers a rare glimpse of a vanishing way of life for Andean people.*

Ride *La Trochita* train

Location Esquel, Argentina
Website www.latrochita.org.ar **Price** ⑤

Patagonia is the definitive escape: the ultimate expanse of nothing where you can lose yourself, find yourself, or become somebody else entirely. Outlaws on the run, Butch Cassidy and the Sundance Kid, hid out here in the beautiful wilderness of Cholila. Che Guevara was filled with longing to return here "if not indefinitely, then at least for a pause while I shift from one understanding of the world to another." However, it was Paul Theroux, in his book *The Old Patagonian Express*, who gave Patagonia's narrow-gauge railway international renown.

The plan was to link the track with the national network of railways, providing vital transport to export sheepskins and livestock from remote farms. Now only 250 miles (400 km) of track remains, running through the foothills where the Andes meet the steppe, from Esquel to El Maitén, and there is no better way to see these marvelously sculpted landscapes. The original steam engine still pulls the wooden carriages, which were imported from Belgium in 1922 and are warmed in the harsh winters by quaint cast-iron stoves. As the train weaves between hills and cliffs around the 600 curves of its journey, the carriage windows frame constantly changing compositions of forested flanks, swaths of desert steppe, and rows of poplars lit golden by southern sunlight. Alight at the hamlet of Nahuel Pan and drink in the clear mountain air while local Mapuche inhabitants offer sweet fried cakes. As you peer at the perfectly polished engine, consider that *La Trochita* has far outlived the brave men who built the railway across these inhospitable lands. **CD**

⬅ *The real name of Patagonia's narrow-gauge railway is* La Trochita—*the little narrow one.*

Enjoy Posada de la Laguna

Location Los Esteros del Iberá, Argentina
Website www.posadadelalaguna.com **Price** ⑤⑤

The boat glides noiselessly across a lagoon so vast that lake merges into cloudless blue above, and you are suspended between water and sky. Then, slipping down narrow channels between floating islands, the birds appear. Jacás call from the treetops. A splash of color, and the vermilion flycatcher is spotted in a tree. Jacanas waddle on water-lily leaves, feeding noisy chicks. The Esteros del Iberá are the least visited of Argentina's many natural wonders, and yet this area of wetlands hosts more than 350 species of bird.

Posada de la Laguna is the perfect place from which to explore this magical world: the smallest hotel in a hamlet on the lagoon's edge. Owner Elsa

"[Our guests can enjoy] nightly magical boat trips down the Iberá Lagoon."

Proprietors, Posada de la Laguna

Guiraldes has created an elegant and intimate lodge, where she warmly welcomes guests as if to her own home. There are just six rooms facing the water's edge, flooded with light and designed to retain a traditional estancia feel—but with superb beds and modern bathrooms. Hammocks are slung from the veranda, and the gardens lead gently down to the water, past the swimming pool. Elsa's local guides know every single inch of the lagoon: where to see caiman, and where the birds are nesting. But the boat trips have another purpose as well: Returning at sunset, as sky and water turn deep orange, the sense of space and peace is transforming. **CD**

Explore the Ruins of The Missions

Location Misiones Province, Argentina
Website www.turismo.misiones.gov.ar   **Price** 🚻

From the early 1600s, the Jesuits built thirty missions in the area that is now northwest Argentina, Paraguay, Uruguay, and the south of Brazil. They were disciplined but harmonious sanctuaries, to which the native Guaraní flocked in their thousands to avoid the perils inflicted by Portuguese slave hunters. The priests set up *reducciones*, self-governing settlements, around the mission. The main income came from agriculture, principally the production of yerba maté, but they tended livestock, too, and these organized societies allowed some to specialize in the creation of textiles or music. "A few days ago, musicians from the nearby Yapeyú settlement performed for us . . . They sang vespers, the mass, and litanies as well as some canticles, all in such a way and with such art and grace that, if you had not seen them, you would believe that these musicians had come from India or one of the best cities in Europe," the priest Father Stroebel wrote in 1729. But in 1767, Carlos III of Spain expelled the Jesuits, and the glorious buildings were left to ruin.

The dilapidated remains still stand, however, four of them preserved as a UNESCO World Heritage site. The best on the Argentine side is San Ignacio Miní, near the town of Posadas. Visitors come to admire the ornate carving of the tumbledown walls and stroll across the flagstone terrace to rooms that once housed the library or the priests' quarters. Today the chirping of birds takes the place of Christian song, yet the spirit of the past seems somehow to pervade this place. It is as if the ghosts of the Jesuits still roam free in this haven from the chaotic world beyond its walls. **PE**

> *"Many of the inhabitants of the reducciones began to abandon them for the forests."*

Geoffrey Groesbeck, historian

⬈ *Visitors sense a profound peace amid the crumbling but imposing red sandstone walls of San Ignacio Miní.*

Visit Cavas Wine Lodge

Location Mendoza, Argentina
Website www.cavaswinelodge.com **Price** ⑤⑤

The Mendoza region produces 70 percent of all wine made in Argentina. At the Cavas Wine Lodge, a stunning property 20 miles (32 km) from the city of Mendoza in the heart of Argentina's wine country, the idea of simply drinking the wine is scorned. Instead, local *bon viveurs* believe that wine has a place not only on the dinner table, but also as part of a treatment at the in-house spa.

Cavas was the first winery in Argentina to introduce the concept of the wine bath as a spa treatment. Pioneered in 1997 in the Bordeaux wine region, it is a technique that uses the properties of wine to counter the skin-aging process. But a visit to Cavas is not just

> *"Finally there's a luxurious hotel to accommodate the wine fanatics who flock to [Mendoza]."*
>
> *Wallpaper*

about taking a dip in their trademark red, a 2005 Bonarda. Set in a 35-acre (14-ha) vineyard, the winery has apartment-style rooms tucked among the vines. They are stylishly equipped, and the roof terrace is a great place for some quality quaffing at sunset.

Back at the main house, dining is a big part of the Cavas experience, with the restaurant offering tasting dinners to choose from the 250-odd bottles in the cellars, and cooking lessons are available with prior reservation. For active visitors, the winery even invites guests at harvesttime to burn off last night's steak by working the fields. In return you can earn tokens to pay for a glass of wine with dinner that evening. **DA**

Stay at Yacutinga Lodge

Location Iguazú, Argentina
Website www.yacutinga.com **Price** ⑤⑤

Travelers to Argentina flock to the Iguazú Falls—an unbelievable quantity of water roaring over a vast, horseshoe-shaped chasm—but few explore the magnificent surrounding forest. Yet, just 60 miles (96 km) above the falls, where the Iguazú River flows wide and calm, five quaint camouflaged cabins that make up Yacutinga Lodge are hidden within pristine rain forest, thick with lianas and bromeliads.

Romantic and rustic, yet very comfortable, here guests sleep to the sounds of the forest all around them. Step out in the early morning, and the vermilion earth is strewn with confetti of fragrant blossom, as capuchin monkeys swing effortlessly from branch to branch and toucans squawk overhead. A visit here is a rare chance not only to sleep deep in the forest but also to take part in a conservation project that protects 4,000 species of plant and more than 500 species of butterfly—a private reserve in one of the world's most biodiverse areas.

The adventure begins with a gentle boat trip down the river, guided by Guaraní boatmen. Caiman alligators bask on the banks; kingfishers dart low to the water. Expert nature guides take guests deep into the forest to discover how the elements of this fragile ecosystem interrelate. You can contribute to the reforestation program by planting trees, or listen to resident biologists presenting their research. Best of all, simply wallow in the blissful pool surrounded by exotic flowers, or sit and contemplate the view from canopy-height platforms while birds and butterflies flutter all around you. As darkness descends, guests gather around the fire in the open-air bar, then set off on night walks to find the forest transformed into the habitat of a whole new set of creatures. **CD**

Relax at Estancia El Colibrí

Location Córdoba, Argentina
Website www.estanciaelcolibri.com   **Price** ⑤⑤

Blending together effortlessly the ambience and tradition of an old Argentine estancia with the style and luxury of a contemporary five-star hotel, El Colibrí is a working cattle ranch that shrugs off rustic chic for modern elegance. Set in 420 acres (170 ha) of land, it is part private garden and part national park, and the views are endless.

Its nine rooms are divided into three suites and six junior suites and deluxe rooms, all with personal details, including a roaring open fire to welcome you. Beyond the rooms, the hotel extends: The summerhouse has a relaxing bar and living room, with an Andalucian arch, tiled floors, chandeliers hanging from the high-beamed ceiling, and acid-colored, elegant furniture. No wonder *Harpers* staged a fabulous fashion shoot here; *Vogue* and *Tatler* have also tipped it as a hot retreat.

The beauty is not just skin deep: Guests say that the service and attention to detail they have experienced stay with them, whether that is wine tasting with their host in the extensive cellar, learning to play polo or dance the tango, or the superb bush barbecue out on the ranch, with grilled llama, pork ribs, and lamb.

You can look out to the Córdoba Mountains from the swimming pool, or indulge in a Finnish sauna, Turkish bath, or hot tub to soothe your aching muscles after a long jaunt on horseback, where you can learn the art of cattle rustling or sheepherding. Special indulgence is reserved for the final night, when guests are treated to a personally prepared dinner for two in the privacy of their own balcony. **LD**

← *The charming colonial-style ranch house is set in the middle of the beautiful Argentine campo.*

Ride Horses at Los Potreros

Location Córdoba, Argentina
Website www.ride-americas.com   **Price** 💲

There is something strange going on at Los Potreros, a 6,000-acre (2,428-ha) cattle ranch high in the hills of the Sierras Chicas. Everyone, from the gauchos to the kitchen girls to the guests, seems to be perpetually smiling. Maybe it is something they put in the maté.

Los Potreros has belonged to the Begg family for generations. They breed cattle, as they have for hundreds of years, but nowadays Robin and Kevin Begg run a tourist operation, too, offering luxurious horse-riding vacations. Born in Argentina but educated in the United Kingdom, Robin and Kevin appear to be quintessentially English. The farmhouse dining room blends Sheffield silverware with battered

---

"If Michelin did a Riding Tour Guide, Los Potreros would come out top."

Lord Patrick Beresford, *Ultimate Travel*

British tomes: Winston Churchill's *The Second World War,* and *Lady Chatterley's Lover.* There is homemade marmalade for breakfast. Step outside, however, and it is glorious Argentina, complete with bickering parakeets and beret-bedecked gauchos. The horses—criollos and *paso peruanos*—are well mannered and soft mouthed. Visitors can embark on multiday trail rides, play polo, or merely amble for a couple of hours in the estancia's swaying, pale-gold tussock. On your return, you will be greeted with tea, homemade cake, or perhaps even a glass of Los Potreros's own label wine to whet your appetite before dinner. Really, this is not a difficult riding vacation at all. **PE**

Stay at Alvear Palace Hotel

Location Buenos Aires, Argentina
Website www.alvearpalace.com   **Price** 💲💲

This grand old hotel, with its stately feel and chic location in the Recoleta region, is a genuine Buenos Aires institution. Indeed, this is the very place where Evita Peron—the erstwhile first lady of Argentina and a national heroine—enjoyed having afternoon tea. Today, it is still where the beautiful people hang out to enjoy the hotel's signature afternoon tea service, served in the elegant Winter Garden lounge from 4 P.M. every day. Little has changed since Eva's day, but the rhubarb pie is fresher than ever.

The hotel itself oozes with period charm: Think a decor straight from Versailles at the time of Louis XVI with historic artworks adorning the walls and Renaissance furnishings gracing the elegant suites. The in-house restaurant, L'Orangerie, also has a decidedly European feel, and the spa offers a comprehensive range of treatments. The main selling point, however, remains the hotel's Evita-rich heritage. It is just a short hop from the hotel's front door to the Recoleta Cemetery, where her body was laid to rest under cover of darkness in 1974, and a quick taxi ride across town brings you to the presidential offices of La Casa Rosada, where she delivered her most memorable and moving speeches, her fist raised and her hair scraped back in a severe bun.

Today the Alvear Palace is far more closely associated with the Hollywood A-list than with any heads of state: Actors Antonio Banderas, Catherine Deneuve, and Salma Hayek are among many of the big-name celebrities who are known to soak up the hotel's refined ambience. For Evita purists, however, the hotel will forever be her domain, and the legions of ladies of a certain age returning each afternoon to have tea are testimony to her enduring legacy. **DA**

Enjoy La Corona Sanctuary

Location Buenos Aires Province, Argentina
Website www.lacoronasanctuary.com   **Price** ⬤⬤

Just a four-hour drive southwest of Buenos Aires, among the open horizons of the pampas, La Corona Sanctuary is both a luxurious home and a working farm, owned by the same family since 1875. It also offers a complete program of yoga and holistic spa treatments, including shiatsu and Reiki healing.

La Corona's emphasis is squarely on relaxation and indulgence. There are just six rooms here: two in the pool house affording privacy away from the main residence, with French doors opening onto manicured lawns, and four rooms in the main house, including one large double room overlooking the veranda. Attentive staff are on hand to cook you breakfast,

> *"It does not take long to attune to the rhythm of this boutique resort."*

travelintelligence.com

clean your room, make you tea, and launder your clothes, leaving you free to begin your day with an hour of yoga before heading out to the bird sanctuary or taking a leisurely ride in La Corona's horse and buggy. For those after more sedentary pursuits, there are hammocks sprinkled throughout the home's lush gardens and a billiards table, and for lunch you can indulge in an *asado*, a traditional Argentine barbecue.

It is the spa that this hotel has built its reputation around. Guests are encouraged to stay a week or more so they can take advantage of the many treatments at their disposal, including asanas programs that focus on the regeneration of the whole body. **BS**

Visit Dos Talas

Location Buenos Aires Province, Argentina
Website www.dostalas.com.ar   **Price** ⬤⬤⬤⬤

Just two hours' drive from the frenzy of Buenos Aires across the flat pampas where vast fields are dotted with cattle, a long track leads between silvery elms into a plantation of soaring monkey puzzle trees and to a clearing of pristine green lawns. There sits a grand French-style chateau dating from 1893 that has sweeping staircases, balconies, and yellow awnings. Under the tall eucalyptus trees, a long table is laid for lunch and your hosts are waiting to welcome you, grilling huge, succulent home-reared steaks on a traditional Argentine *asado*. Sip a glass of Malbec, bite into a spicy empanada, and relax. You are home.

No trip to Argentina is complete without staying at an estancia, the cattle farms that made Argentina wealthy. Dos Talas is both the most romantic and the most authentic example. Here, you are a guest of the owners, descendants of the founder Pedro Luro. They will show you the park, filled with avenues of towering trees, created by Argentina's leading landscape architect, Charles Thays; they will invite you to make yourself at home in the gracious interiors, which thronged with the life of literary salons when Gatsby-style parties spilled from the high-ceilinged rooms onto the elegant terraces. The history is palpable: in the extensive library and in the evocative photographs that cover the antique tables. Guests sleep in carved mahogany beds on crisp white linen and wake to fling the French doors open onto a private balcony. Spend the morning strolling around the grounds and the afternoon sitting by the pool, gazing out over the apparently limitless plains. As the sun sinks on the curving horizon, set out with the resident gaucho to ride a horse into the sunset. Filled with peace, you will return to dine in style and sleep deeply. **CD**

Enjoy Faena Hotel

Location Buenos Aires, Argentina
Website www.faenahotelanduniverse.com   **Price** $$

Arriving at night at this decadent Buenos Aires beauty is perhaps the best way to appreciate its sumptuous decor and sophisticated brand of chic. It is certainly the best way to savor the Faena's electrifying Philippe Starck design, from the red-lit walkway into a towering, spice-scented hall, and from the wild whimsy of its Bistro restaurant to the cool splendor of one of 110 bedrooms in signature white, red, and gold.

Playing up the drama of the hotel concept at every turn, the Faena deftly marries audacious fantasy with the decadence and drama of the belle epoque. And it is appropriate, too, because the hotel is housed in what was once a grain storehouse from where Argentina's agricultural riches were exported to the world in its turn-of-the-century heyday. After a cozy aperitif to the strains of a grand piano in the rich wood and leather library, modeled on the old-fashioned luxury of a 1900s ranch, it is a deliciously shocking thrill to move on to the Bistro for dinner. There the menu treads a sure-footed line between timeless excellence and the stylishly modern. A dinner here studded with airs, foams, spherifications, and deconstructions of classic dishes is de rigueur for lovers of both fine cuisine and haute design. If you get the timing right, you can then move on into the snug cabaret theater, where one of the city's finest tango shows comes complete with an orchestra, free-flowing wine and champagne, and wonderfully saucy dancers. There, huddled at a tiny, intimate, candlelit table, the theatricality of the entire place crystallizes into a sensual, melancholy pageant of tango. **CR**

➔ *Wall-mounted unicorn heads gaze across the opulent, theatrical decor of the Bistro restaurant.*

Stay at La Pascuala

Location Tigre River Delta, Argentina
Website www.lapascuala.com   **Price** 💲💲

Just an hour from Buenos Aires, there is a wild, romantic, natural paradise only *porteños* (inhabitants of the Argentine capital) know about. Viewed from above, the Tigre River Delta is an ornate lacework of rivers strewn with hundreds of islands.

As your kayak slips away from the small town of Tigre, with its century-old rowing clubs in palatial buildings, there is a blissful sense of escaping to the jungle. The river narrows to a tunnel between tall trees and lush vegetation, with shafts of sunlight streaming through to illuminate pleasure boats cruising gently by. The banks are lined with quaint wooden houses on stilts, and families drinking maté on rickety old jetties wave as you row past. Later on, once you have crossed the Paraná River to enter the remote second section of the delta, there are few houses. The rivers are quieter here, the vegetation more wild, the domain of herons and garzas. Then, deep in the jungle, a series of tall stilts rises up from the river and, amid the trees, you glimpse the elegant buildings of La Pascuala. Concierges meet the boat and carry your bags to your room while you slip into the tub. You have arrived.

La Pascuala is a haven of good taste and luxury in the depths of beautiful wilderness. Each suite is an individual lodge on stilts, secluded by greenery, and with its own veranda where you can stretch out on loungers in perfect privacy. The bedroom is immense; the bathroom is almost equally expansive, and even the bathtub has a view. Drink gin on the terrace before slipping into the intimate dining room for a superb dinner. The service is discreet and top-notch. There is no more romantic retreat from the city. And you do not have to row: A fast motor launch whisks you here from Tigre's train station in an hour. **CD**

Enjoy Estancia Peuma Hue

Location Bariloche, Patagonia, Argentina
Website www.peuma-hue.com   **Price** 💲💲💲💲

Open the curtains and there is the lake, stretching out before you, ultramarine blue and glistening. To your side, a great wall of mountain, snowcapped and thickly forested, descends to the water. Explore trails to waterfalls through a cathedral of coihue forest—spotting the scarlet-headed Magellanic woodpecker among innumerable other birds. Take a kayak out on the water or ride with the horse whisperer to remoter lakes not reached by road: You will have it all to yourself. Argentina's Lake District is unmatched for natural adventures within a spectacular setting: dramatic mountains and lakes of all hues immersed in virgin forest. But, uniquely, Peuma Hue has its own

---

"Our first goal was to preserve Peuma Hue's pristine forests, waters, and fauna."

Proprietors, Estancia Peuma Hue

---

private stretch of lakeshore and a vast swath of mountainside, so guests can explore this natural splendor alone. No wonder that Peuma Hue means "place of dreams" in the native Mapuche language.

The estancia is the creation of owner Evelyn Hoter, whose aim is to offer complete contact with nature. She and her staff welcome guests by the fire each evening with a glass of wine before a delicious dinner, and make expert guides on hikes and adventures. Four beautiful cabins scattered in the grounds offer a spectrum from a luxurious suite with a grand bed and double whirlpool tub to the perfectly secluded mountain cabin, perfect for a romantic retreat. **CD**

Spend an Afternoon at Las Balsas

Location Villa La Angostura, Patagonia, Argentina
Website www.lasbalsas.com.ar   **Price** $

Villa La Angostura in Argentina's Patagonia is a quaint village with a friendly atmosphere. Despite being in South America, it has a slightly Swiss feel to it, which could be down to the very tempting chocolate shops on every corner, or perhaps the chalet-style homes. Set aside from the small town, Las Balsas is a hideaway in a league of its own. Hidden far down a small dirt track, within the Nahuel Huapi National Park—one of the most beautiful spots in Patagonia—this certainly is not a place you will stumble across by chance.

With just twelve rooms and three suites, it is guaranteed to be intimate. Each room has its own style, from the all dusty-pink room with its stunning views framed by the Andes to the elegant red-striped scheme. There is even a sophisticated, simple beige suite transformed with original varnished canoes cut in half and upturned in lieu of side tables. In addition to the interior and exterior pool, there is a stone spa with an incredible array of treatments: everything from a "golden face mask," with gold acting as an anti-inflammatory and antioxidant, to a full-body "chocotherapy," using chocolate as a base element.

The hotel's star attraction is definitely the restaurant and the charming wine-tasting lounge built from cypress and stone. Nibble on trout seviche, king crab with coconut milk, or venison with a blackcurrant and chocolate sauce before trying the Argentine's favorite dessert: *dulce de leche* served with red fruit sherbet and coconut cookie by chef Pablo Campoy. Las Balsas might be in the middle of nowhere, but that does not mean you have to compromise on comfort. **RCA**

↗ *The distinctive blue clapboard hotel is a luxurious paradise off the beaten track.*

"Each room or suite has its own style and a privileged view of Nahuel Huapi Lake."

Road & Travel magazine

Explore Seven Lakes Route

Location Patagonia, Argentina
Website www.patagonia-argentina.com **Price** ◑

Some say that getting to your chosen destination is as much of an adventure as the time spent there. This is certainly the case when traveling from the tiny town of San Martin de Los Andes in Patagonia to Villa La Angostura along the "Ruta de los Siete Lagos"—the Seven Lakes route.

The road, part of National Route 234, winds its way across 67 miles (107 km) of the Neuquén Province's two national parks: Nahuel Huapi and Lanin, with about 25 miles (40 km) of dirt tracks. Be warned about the lack of asphalt; the dust and gravel roads are more suitable for rally driving. The charming ski resort of San Martin is all wood and stone cabins, stores crammed with ski gear, alpaca sweaters, and scarves. Tranquil, it is the last sign of civilization until Villa La Angostura.

The scenery is so extreme that it causes visitors to catch their breath in surprise. Without veering off route, all seven lakes are visible across the flawless mountainous landscapes against the backdrop of the Andes. Machónico, Escondido, Correntoso, Espejo, Lácar, Falkner, and Villarino are each as beautiful as the last.

This is not the Patagonia of flat pampas, but rather a South American equivalent of the Alps, and magnified. You would expect bears and mountain lions to roam the hills, but instead only horses and fuzzy-headed cows wander across the road to graze where the grass is greener. Visit in the spring when melting ice and heavy waterfalls have new life sprouting vivid red and orange blooms to coat the already striking scenery. It is also the end of the ski season, which means everyone else has gone home. **RCA**

➡ *Every turn in the road uncovers a picturesque panorama of lake, mountains, and dense forest.*

Stay at Estancia Cristina

Location Patagonia, Argentina
Website www.estanciacristina.com   **Price**

As the boat leaves civilization behind and enters the more remote reaches of turquoise Lago Argentino, slipping between icebergs the size of houses, it is reasonable to wonder where you are going to end up. The three-hour journey takes visitors to the mighty Upsala glacier, past sheer walls of ice rising to a staggering 230 feet (70 m) above you, then suddenly calving off with a roar into the water beneath. As the boat approaches the end of the lake's northernmost arm, four tiny buildings can be seen, isolated on the wild shore, against a backdrop of magnificent mountains: This is Estancia Cristina.

This remote Patagonian farm, founded by a hardy English family a century ago, now welcomes visitors to stay in plush new cabins, where they can lounge by a picture window to survey the fabulous views with a fine glass of wine before dinner. Spare a thought for the original inhabitants, though, who raise sheep here through the austere winter, while you ponder whether to eat the seared salmon or the Patagonian lamb, cooked slowly over an open fire. Walking back in the chilly starlit night toward the cozy guest cabins offers just enough austerity to make you appreciate your warm room and comfortable bed.

The really unforgettable experience of Cristina, however, is to travel with your guide up to a mountain ridge where long stretches of vermilion rock, polished smooth by ancient glaciers, lead to a spectacular vista. Far below, stretching out to the distant horizon, lies Upsala glacier: silent, unfathomable, and awe-inspiring. Hike down a stunning canyon to find fossilized ammonites and mollusks, but no mark of man anywhere. Just herds of guanacos, wild horses, and rivers filled with Chinook salmon. **CD**

Relax at Design Suites

Location El Calafate, Patagonia, Argentina
Website www.designsuites.com   **Price**

Designed by world-renowned architect Carlos Ott, the five-star Design Suites hotel is a masterpiece of environmental architecture. Using only local materials, this luxury hotel encompasses an art gallery, a design shop, and a gourmet restaurant with views over Lago Argentino that defy belief. Although it is an impressive edifice, the real attraction lies in its details; a Patagonian design collective was commissioned for the furniture and interiors. Each of the sixty suites has floor-to-ceiling windows that frame a vista of the beautifully barren Patagonia, with mountainous peaks in the distance and a mirrored lake at the fore. An indoor-and-outdoor heated pool, spa, sauna, health

> *"The Design Suites cater to the design-conscious visitor. It's an impressive destination hotel."*
>
> *Wallpaper*

club, and wine bar complete a stay at what must be one of the most impressive hotels in South America. No one visits Patagonia for a hotel alone. If visitors can be dragged out of the hotel, they will walk out into El Calafate: the gateway to the famous Perito Moreno glacier. As its crumbling face crashes into the lake with clockwork regularity, visitors are all but dumbstruck at this unique sight. Beyond El Calafate are lakes and mountains perfect for skiing in winter and hiking in summer. But these are only two of a host of activities the hotel can organize. Soar over the glacier in a hot-air balloon or travel by horse up into the forests and deep into the national parks. **DN**

View the Patagonian Wilderness from Eolo

Location Near El Calafate, Patagonia, Argentina
Website www.eolo.com.ar **Price** 💲💲💲

Few places inspire a greater sense of solitude than the wild panoramas of Patagonia, near the southern tip of South America, where the treeless, uninhabitable steppes roll out interminably, and the silence is broken only by the wind. For visitors preferring white cotton and soft blankets to chilly nights under canvas, there is no finer perch from which to contemplate the Patagonian wilderness than Eolo. Its seventeen suites all have vast picture windows framing unimaginable views across the empty plains and boundless skies, punctuated only by lakes, mountains, and—on a clear day—the pointy peaks of Torres del Paine straddling the border with Chile.

This luxury lodge, on a 4,000-acre (1,618-ha) cattle ranch, sets the benchmark for indulgent Patagonian retreats. The rooms are the height of comfort (king-sized beds, fluffy towels, generously upholstered armchairs), the decor is impeccably stylish yet always discreet (rightly leaving the big statements to nature), and the helpful staff and all-inclusive rates eliminate the merest hint of hassle. Staff will even prepare you a gourmet lunch box.

Eolo redefines the vacation cliché "getting away from it all." Understandably, the owners have refrained from installing televisions in the bedrooms—the view offers something considerably more engaging. Borrow binoculars or use the huge telescope in the lounge to zoom in on the hawks, eagles, and Patagonia hares that populate the plain. Do not miss the creaking mass that is the Perito Moreno glacier, the world's largest advancing glacier, just a half-hour drive away. **IA**

↗ *The Eolo building itself sits at the top of a treeless hill, with a spectacular view of the plains below.*

"This hushed valley hideaway lies nestled in a serene landscape blanketed in tall tufts of coirón."

preferredboutique.com

See Perito Moreno Glacier

Location Santa Cruz Province, Argentina
Website www.parquesnacionales.gov.ar **Price** ●

Patagonia tempts us with its absolutes: the dry desert, the frozen seas, the dead-straight highways. But it is also a region of awesome juxtapositions. Head west across the arid steppe at the fiftieth parallel in Argentina and you arrive at the Perito Moreno glacier, cradled by ancient beech forests and framed by the jagged peaks of the Andes. The centerpiece of the stunning Parque Nacional Los Glaciares, the Moreno is surreally beautiful and beguiling. Almost discovered by FitzRoy and Darwin on their landmark voyage of 1831 to 1836, the glacier was finally sighted by its namesake, Francisco Pascasio Moreno, in 1877.

Today, visitors can choose how they want to experience this vast, creaking, ever-expanding tongue of ice. Some like to trek across the cakelike surface, others go ice climbing, or hover just below the cigar-shaped clouds in microlight aircraft. Idlers can simply take a seat and gawp from the comfort of the platform on Península Magallanes or ride in one of the numerous catamarans and cruisers that pass close to the continually collapsing—technically speaking, calving—wall. This wall reaches heights of 200 feet (60 m), whereas the glacier itself spreads over some 160 square miles (414 sq km), making it as big as the city of Buenos Aires. Impressed? Then consider that the Southern Ice Field, for which the Moreno is an outlet glacier, is the same size as Israel. The Perito Moreno ruptures every four to five years when the water flowing through the Brazo Rico undermines its east-facing central wall, causing a spectacle that brings in visitors from all over the world. **CM**

➔ *The awe-inspiring Perito Moreno is one of only three Patagonian glaciers that are not retreating.*

Cruise on MS *Fram*

Location Antarctica   **Website** www.hurtigruten.co.uk
Price 🆂🆂🆂

The most fragile environment in the world, the White Continent is overloaded with superlatives: the coldest, highest, windiest, driest, and iciest place on Earth, where you can see nature in its rawest form and wonder at its glory. Strict guidelines are set by the IAATO (International Association of Antarctica Tour Operators) to ensure the preservation of the pristine environs. The safety of passengers is also important, and Hurtigruten's highly sophisticated MS *Fram* is the most maneuverable ship sailing these waters.

The cruise passes icebergs and glaciers that look like giant white sculptures, and from the ship's lounge passengers can see spiky granite peaks, some so high

> *"We watched a wonderful golden mist, where the rays of the declining sun shone through vapor."*
>
> Ernest Shackleton, explorer

that they are shrouded in fairy-tale wisps of cloud. On deck, the silence is broken only by the occasional sound of cracking ice. Snowy mountaintops are reflected in the perfectly still water, and glacial ice tumbles down the hillside into the freezing waters, dotted with brash ice and growler icebergs the size of small houses.

At sea, albatross swoop past, looking like gray dive-bombers, gliding on the wild sea breezes. Ashore, you are able to get close to penguin colonies and see seals dozing on passing ice floes. Brash ice and smaller bergs bounce off the sides of the hull as the ship noses its way carefully through the frozen layers. In this unforgiving landscape, there is no escaping the ice. **AD**

Visit the Antarctic

Location Antarctica   **Website** www.voyagesofdiscovery.co.uk
Price 🆂🆂

The sun is shimmering on the ice-laden water, a shout goes out: "Seals on the floes to the port side." Cameras click—and this is just 7 A.M. on the first morning of an expedition cruise in Antarctica. A cruise to the White Continent has to be the ultimate escape, a chance to step ashore on a pristine land where just one hundred people are allowed at any one time, to walk through penguin colonies, get close to seals and icebergs, catch sight of feeding whales, or watch albatross floating in the slipstream behind the ship.

Big cruise lines venture to Antarctica, but they are not allowed to take people ashore. If you want to walk in the footsteps of Shackleton and set foot on the White Continent, you need to choose one of the exploration-style vessels. These are small and none too luxurious, but what you lose in style you gain in the thrill of being so far from civilization, in one of the most hostile environments in the world. So do not expect plush terminals and souvenir shops, but do pack a pair of waterproof boots, because you will go ashore on an inflatable boat, sometimes landing in water or on rocky beaches. You will also need thick, warm sweaters, gloves, and wool hats. Ships go to Antarctica during the austral summer, between November and March, when the ice is thinnest, but it is still cold.

Exploration vessels come in a variety of sizes from 100 passengers to 500. Real adventurers should choose one of the smaller ships for their voyage, but if you prefer your adventure with a modicum of comfort, Voyages of Discovery's ship *Discovery* is a perfect choice, and comes with a top team of Antarctic experts who share their expansive knowledge during lectures from the bridge. **JA**

Camp at Patriot Hills

Location Antarctica   **Website** www.adventure-network.com
Price 💲💲💲

Imagine a landscape consisting only of snow, ice, rock, and sky and where little animal or plant life can survive. This is the harsh environment of Antarctica, and Patriot Hills is the only privately owned campsite on this isolated continent, where temperatures can plummet to -129°F (-89°C) in winter. However, visitors can enjoy twenty-four-hour daylight in summer, and with endless vistas and intense solitude, Patriot Hills offers the ultimate escape by any standards.

Established in 1987, the resort at Patriot Hills is a mere 668 miles (1,075 km) from the South Pole. After an easy four-and-a-half-hour flight from the town of Punta Arenas on the southernmost tip of Chile, your plane lands on a rare, blue, ice runway in the Ellsworth Mountains, from where you have the option of either hiking the half mile to the camp or arriving more comfortably by snowmobile.

There is plenty to do when you arrive. You can take a flight over the Pole itself, or if you are feeling particularly adventurous, you can even ski there. Visit emperor penguin rookeries on the Dawson-Lambton glacier by the Weddell Sea, or just try snowshoeing and snowmobiling your way around the surrounding hills and learning about the region's unique geology in the company of experienced guides.

The dining tent is the heart of Patriot Hills—a place for guests to gather, have a warming meal, and share tales of adventure. Afterward, snuggle up in your sleeping bag and dream of following in the footsteps of explorer Roald Amundsen in December 1911, the first person to reach the South Pole. **BS**

↗ *The expedition-style tents at Patriot Hills can accommodate up to fifty people at any one time.*

"But we have been to the Pole and we shall die like gentlemen."

Robert Falcon Scott, explorer

Europe offers an enviable variety of places to stay that suit every taste and budget. Choose between a French converted windmill, a Scottish castle, a Greek island, or an Italian medieval fortress. If you want more action, try a horseback ride through the hills of southern Spain, a canal trip through Burgundy, or a train journey through Germany. The choice is yours.

← Castello Di Vicarello, Italy

EUROPE

Explore St. Helena

Location St. Helena, South Atlantic
Website www.sthelena.se   **Price** 💲💲

It is not surprising that the British chose remote St. Helena as the final place of exile for Emperor Napoleon, because this tiny speck in the South Atlantic is more than 750 miles (1,207 km) from the nearest dry land. Funding is in place for the construction of an airport that is set to commence operations in 2010, but for now the only regular scheduled way to get to the island is aboard the mail ship RMS *St. Helena*. This rugged little workhorse is the island's lifeline, bringing in some 1,500 tons of supplies and up to 170 passengers on each voyage. Visitors board in Cape Town, spend two days and nights sailing up to Namibia's wild Skeleton Coast, then head off toward the

> *"Desolate and lush by turns, it has a landscape that seems to offer the whole planet in miniature."*
>
> Jenny Diski, *Observer*

sunset into the vastness of the Atlantic Ocean for five days out at sea, to arrive in a time warp of Englishness.

A starkly barren, red volcanic rock coastline gives way to a lushly green, subtropical interior that is dizzyingly hilly. Those who have a head for heights can climb the 750 steps of the Jacob's Ladder staircase, that soars up the cliff from the friendly little capital town of Jamestown. Others might prefer to while away the afternoon watching fishermen tend their lobster pots. It is all remote but surprisingly civilized.

Returning to Europe entails another two days by sea to the even less populated Ascension Island, followed by a military flight to Brize Norton, England. **RsP**

Dogsled in Greenland

Location Kangerlussuaq, Greenland
Website www.greenland.com   **Price** 💲💲

In the snow and ice-bound wonderland that is Greenland you can witness nature at its most raw, go whale-watching, or kayak the icy waters. Most of all, though, you'll want to dogsled and, after a few days' tuition, you can even drive the dogs yourself.

Hurtling through a whiter-than-white wilderness behind a howling pack of eager husky dogs is an almost otherworldly experience. Pull on a pair of snug musk ox–fur boots and a cozy sealskin coat and liberally apply sunblock against a sun that glares fiercely from an impossibly blue sky, even with the temperature at -30°F (-34°C). Then sit yourself on a reindeer-skin-clad sled as your Inuit driver urges dogs on: Here they run side by side, six abreast, rather than in the more familiar setup of pairs in a line.

Fly into Kangerlussuaq airport, a gateway that, amazingly, cancels fewer flights because of bad weather than almost any other airport on Earth. This is the land of the midnight sun and the incredible natural light show afforded by the northern lights. The unforgiving savageness of the environment is never more than a few steps away. And, in any case, the road runs out just a few miles beyond city limits.

For 10,000 years a unique partnership between humans and their dogs has helped make this place inhabitable, and sledding with them gives a fascinating insight into this relationship. With luck you might get to have lunch in a freshly built igloo and finish your day with a glass of 30-year-old whiskey chilled by ice lumps hewn that afternoon from the 15-million-year-old polar ice cap. **RsP**

➡ *Beautiful sunsets light up the ice and cast a wonderful sheen over the frozen landcapes you sled across.*

Enjoy a Greenland Cruise

Location Greenland
Website www.hurtigruten.co.uk   **Price** 💲💲💲

Venture into the remote frozen world of the great explorers on a voyage around icy Greenland with Hurtigruten, a Norwegian-owned cruise company that is most at home in some of the world's most inhospitable places. Despite its name, Greenland, in the Arctic Circle, is a land of snow and ice—some 85 percent of the island is covered in ice, in places up to 1.8 miles (3 km) thick—huge fjords, giant icebergs, polar bears, whales, and husky dogs.

There are a few other cruise lines that offer day trips to Greenland as part of a Norwegian fjords cruise, but Hurtigruten has cut out the sailing time in getting there. Those looking for a cool cruise away from civilization can start their voyage in this land of the Inuit as soon as their flight touches down in the settlement of Kangerlussuaq, a short way from the ship's anchorage.

Fram is a modern vessel, built in 2007, but do not come expecting a luxury cruise. There are places to eat, sleep, and watch the world go by, but apart from a few lectures during the day on Greenland's history and flora and fauna, and a gym if you want to keep in shape, there is little in terms of on-board entertainment. That is fine, though, because the real spectacle is outside: polar bears (although sightings are rare), spouting whales, and icebergs the size of cathedrals.

Greenland is the world's biggest island, so *Fram* does not actually cruise all the way around. Instead there are two different itineraries that sail along the southwest coast, with stops each day so you can visit towns (getting to shore on inflatable motorboats), hike along glaciers, and even take a helicopter ride for a fabulous bird's-eye view of the fjord. **JA**

Stay at Hotel Budir

Location Snæfellness Peninsula, Iceland
Website www.budir.is   **Price** 💲💲

Just two hours' drive northwest from Reykjavik, surrounded by snowcapped mountains, extinct volcanoes, and towering waterfalls, is the Hotel Budir. It stands alone on the deserted shore of Iceland's remote Snæfellness Peninsula like a defiant custodian of civilization at the edge of the habitable world.

Inside, though, it is a haven of clean and uncluttered design. Plush red sofas stand on bare wooden floors, brick fireplaces are stacked high with logs, and dark wooden cabinets open to reveal shelves of leather-bound books. The model boats on the wall seem ridiculously playful for such an extreme environment. The candlelit restaurant is one of Iceland's finest and

> *"The ocean is turquoise, the land black, the tussocks of springy grass a pale gold."*
>
> Lucy Gillmore, *Independent*

has a long tradition of serving organic ingredients, specializing in local seafood and game. Plaice, cod, halibut, or scallops caught during the day are served at evening dinner seasoned with herbs from the lava in Budir. This desolate landscape is also home to geese, ptarmigan, guillemots, and cormorants—all of which may feature on the menu depending on the season.

The surroundings seem to inspire outdoor activities. Guests may explore the glacier by snowmobile, or take fishing or whale-watching boat trips. The sand dunes beyond the lava are a prime horseback-riding spot. You can play on the beaches or hike across dunes, lava, and rocks to distant villages and spectacular cliffs. **SH**

Unwind at Glymur

Location Hvalfjörður, Iceland
Website www.glymurresort.com **Price** 🟢🟢

Iceland's remoteness is an escape in itself, and this remote hotel offers an unusual way to experience it. Less than an hour's drive from the center of Reykjavik, Glymur is still well off the beaten track. It has views of Hvalfjörður (whale fjord) and is well situated for Iceland's wild attractions: black-sand beaches, whale-watching trips, glaciers, lava fields, and wide pastures. The views of the fjord and the mountains alone are enough to soothe you, and that is before you have taken in the best of the hotel's quirky rooms and fantastic food. Menus burst full of flavor and Icelandic specialties: cod, mountain lamb, and skyr yogurt.

As well as a twenty-two-room hotel, where all rooms are on two floors, there is a series of themed, two-person cottages. The House of Relaxation and Silence provides yoga, peace, and quiet for those in most need of a retreat and is described as "a stone to sit on while your soul catches up with you." Other cottages make use of the natural environment, like the House of Nature, which has a waterfall in its center and a cozy fireplace, and is decorated with local and natural materials. The Romantic Cottage has a large bed and a private hot tub.

The Icelandic experience is all about great nature: unpolluted skies in which to wonder at the midnight sun in summer and the northern lights in winter; sure-footed, shaggy-coated Icelandic ponies on which to explore the lava landscape; and clear mountain streams leading to gushing waterfalls in otherwise silent mountains. It is soul cleansing just to be here and experience the full force of the natural world. **LD**

↗ *There are waterfalls all around Glymur, as well as the mossy mountains and black lava rocks.*

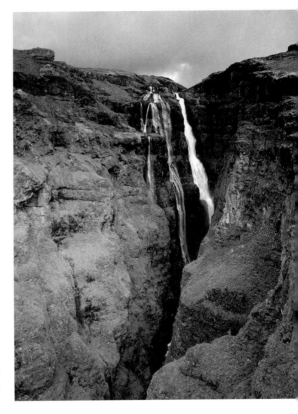

"Head [to Glymur] ... to soak in geothermal hot tubs overlooking whale-populated waters."

Sarah Barrell, *Independent*

See the Northern Lights

Location Iceland **Website** www.icelandtotal.com
Price ◑

In ancient Iceland, citizens believed that if a pregnant woman looked at the northern lights, her child would be born cross-eyed. Native Americans imagined they could conjure up ghosts and spirits if they whistled to the lights. Today astronomers' explanations are more prosaic. Through explosions and flares, the sun emits particles that travel toward Earth and penetrate its upper atmosphere at the polar regions. Molecules and atoms in Earth's atmosphere collide with the sun's particles, absorbing some of their energy. In order to return to their nonenergized state, they emit light as photons—which we see as the northern lights.

The northern lights are best seen beneath the "auroral oval," which lies around Earth's magnetic poles. Iceland sits right in the middle and, as long as the sky is clear and dark, it is one of the top places in the world to see the aurora, especially between September and March. Tour operators take guests away from the interference of the city lights, and usually provide warm shelter.

A good display can last just minutes, but is so striking that you will remember it forever. Green and red ribbons weave across black starry skies, then tumble into three-dimensional tepees before twirling heavenward like a green genie. They seem to die away, but then, just as you think the show is over, pale fingers of jade creep up from the horizon, and then grow stronger into spikes, and finally streaks that hurtle across the heavens. Now you feel that you have not only escaped the hubbub of the modern world, but reached a new universe altogether. **PE**

◄ *The northern lights dance in green ribbons and swirls across the night sky above Iceland.*

Visit Snæfellsjökull Glacier

Location Snæfellness Peninsula, Iceland
Website english.ust.is/Snaefellsjokullnationalpark   **Price** ●

There are so many stories about this area of Iceland that it is hard to know where to begin. New agers claim it as a seat of mystical energy, the country's Nobel Prize–winning author Halldór Laxness came here for inspiration, and Jules Verne chose it as the doorway to the heart of the world in *Journey to the Center of the Earth*. Mysterious lights seen here at night suggest visits by otherworldly visitors—it is nature, but not quite as you know it.

The peninsula can be seen on a clear day from Reykjavik across Faxaflói Bay, capped with the precious white peak of its cone-shaped glacier. The area around the glacier is a national park and includes winding single-track roads, cliffs full of nesting seabirds, lava-strewn pastures, and the kind of peace and quiet that you can find only up here at the end of the world.

Beaches around the peninsula show glimpses of another world; pods of orca prowl, and twisted pieces of rusty metal are all that is left of boats run ashore on the black sand in years gone by. In Djupalonssandir, great round rocks, once used by the Vikings in tests of strength, sit to the left of the path on the way to the beach. Some of Iceland's best-loved sagas took place here, and Christopher Columbus allegedly spent a winter in the region. There are not many places left in the world that can genuinely lay claim to the adjective "unspoiled," but this is one of them. Breathe in the air fresh from the glacier and feel blessed to be alive as you watch the hardy Icelandic ponies canter in deep pasture, pale manes flying out behind them. **LD**

◄ *This isolated church with its typically Icelandic red roof sits in the lap of Snæfellsjökull Glacier.*

Relax at Landmannalaugar Hot Springs

Location Near Reykjavik, Iceland
Website www.landmannalaugar.info   **Price** ●

The hot springs at Landmannalaugar have long been a popular destination for visitors seeking relief from a number of ailments. Whether you suffer from chronic arthritis, head-splitting migraines, depression, or simply stress, the hot springs are renowned for their healing and therapeutic powers.

Lying 1,970 feet (600 m) above sea level, and comprising one of the largest geothermal fields in the country, Landmannalaugar (which means "hot springs of the people" in Icelandic) is surrounded by volcanic peaks and black lava fields. This part of Iceland in the southern highlands is rich in geothermal activity—

> *"[It is] a stream that mixes with a hot spring into a shallow pool, surrounded by wildflowers."*
>
> *Observer*

numerous hot and cold springs run down from the lava field and converge in vast open-air hot baths that are popular for swimming and bathing. It is reasonably accessible in summer, although the road is a bit rough and makes for a bumpy journey.

Once you have overcome the initial heart-stopping shock of getting undressed in such a chilly climate, it is sheer bliss to plunge into the steaming hot, mineral-rich water. Aches and pains simply ebb away as the soothing heat works its magic. To make the most of the spring, ensure that you move around in order to experience the rejuvenating contrast between the hot and the icy water swirling around. **HA**

Unwind at the Blue Lagoon

Location Grindavik, Iceland   **Website** www.bluelagoon.com
Price ⊖

The Blue Lagoon may be a man-made attraction, but it seems to meld into Iceland's unearthly lunar landscape. Located about 24 miles (39 km) outside Reykjavik and about 8 miles (13 km) from Keflavik International Airport, the Blue Lagoon is (deservedly) one of the country's top attractions.

Measuring a massive 53,800 square feet (5,000 sq m), the giant outdoor geothermal baths are rich in natural mineral salts and algae, said to have a curative effect on the skin, especially for those suffering from psoriasis. Clouds of steam float above the milky blue waters, which top a toasty 104°F (40°C), making it hard to drag yourself out—especially when wearing a bikini and the air temperature is below freezing. In winter, the lagoon is often surrounded by snow, and it is then that the contrast between the icy-cold air and the cozy warmth of the water is irresistible. In fact, Icelanders believe the ideal outdoor temperature to make the most of the lagoon is a teeth-chattering 14°F (-10°C). Slather on silica mud, available in boxes around the pool, to cleanse and exfoliate, and if you get bored with bathing, head to the sauna and steam room. For a rejuvenating back massage, stand underneath the lagoon's small waterfall, which pounds away aches and pains.

The surrounding scenery is strange yet dramatic. The lagoon is nestled in among black lava rocks, there are mountains in the distance, and a power station nearby pumps the geothermally heated water from a mile belowground. Stay in until your skin is as wrinkled as a prune—it will do you the power of good. **JK**

← *Clouds of steam hang above the Blue Lagoon,
   where the waters are much warmer than the air.*

Explore the Faroe Islands

Location North Atlantic, Faroe Islands
Website www.visit-faroeislands.com **Price** $

The Faroe Islands are a daunting panorama of jagged volcanic mountains, immense sheer-sided cliffs, long dark fjords, and bleak windswept moorland. North Atlantic waves crash against black rock pillars standing alone in the sea, and basalt peaks loom through dark clouds. It looks like a scene from *The Lord of the Rings*.

The eighteen Faroe Islands are a self-governing part of Denmark, located between Scotland and Iceland. They offer one of the most authentic escapes available anywhere in Europe. Although much of the land is dramatically steep and wild, cut by deep fjords, the capital, Tórshavn, is surprisingly cosmopolitan and there are good galleries, museums, restaurants,

> *" . . . a remote land where the sheep are fearless, the birds are shrewd, and the weather is a state of mind."*
>
> Sarah Crown, *Guardian*

and bars. The hotels are products of the 1970s, with lots of mirrors and an enthusiastic use of the color orange. Stay in a bed-and-breakfast or rent a traditional wooden house with the old, dark wooden upper floor, balcony, and living grass–covered roof.

Relax and enjoy the unspoiled green countryside with stunning seascapes around every corner and the freshest air in Europe. The maritime climate means it is rarely freezing, but changeable between wet and misty, clear and sunny. Take a memorable trip by boat or subsidized inter-island helicopter to gaze at cliffs and rocks overflowing with seabirds. Whales are common offshore—and on restaurant menus. **SH**

Enjoy Storfjord Hotel

Location Sunnmøre, Norway
Website www.storfjordhotel.com **Price** $$

Small is definitely beautiful when it comes to the chic Storfjord Hotel. It is handcrafted using *lafta* (cross logging with whole timbers) and has just six rooms, exquisitely designed to ensure guests are never far from nature. Set in 6 acres (2.4 ha) of private grounds amid thousands of acres of protected forest in western Norway, the hotel lies between three mountains and a lake and overlooks the stunning Sunnmøre Alps.

A fusion of modern style and authentic tradition, each room has a luxurious bathroom and a large balcony to take in the panoramic views—some even have four-poster beds. Rooms also come equipped with a television, DVD player, and wireless broadband Internet access to keep in touch with the outside world. Spend the day kayaking in the Glomset Bay or hiking to the summit of nearby Hautua Mountain for magnificent views across the village to Storfjorden, Skodje, and the surrounding lakes and fjords. The more adventurous can take the ferry to the rugged mountains of the Sunnmøre Alps for high-altitude walking. Return to the hotel for dinner in the timbered hall in front of a roaring open fire and a nightcap on the gallery landing overlooking Glomset Bay and the snowcapped mountains in the distance.

Many guests use the hotel as a base to explore Norway's stunning west coast, with Ålesund and the islands to the west and the dramatic fjords and mountains to the east. Sitting at the gateway to the Golden Route, from here take in some of the world's most breathtaking scenery, including Geirangerfjord, a UNESCO World Heritage site. A drive through the valleys, high mountains, and deep fjords offers views of tumbling waterfalls and majestic mountains. Mother Nature has never looked so good. **AD**

Discover the Lofoten Islands

Location Lofoten Islands, Norway
Website www.lofoten.info   **Price** ◑

They look like sheer walls of mountains rising dramatically from the sea. Venture closer to the Lofoten Islands, though, and you will find sandy coves, spectacular moors, and lonesome marshes. Simple wooden buildings, often painted deep rust red, lie scattered amid the green.

The Lofoten Islands lie north of the Arctic Circle, but their climate is surprisingly mild. They have been inhabited for 6,000 years, although the fishing village of Henningsvær, the largest community in the Lofotens, has a population of only 500. It was not connected to the other islands by bridges until the early 1980s.

Alongside its fishing interests, this is an artistic community, with art displays and a glassblowing studio. Killer-whale safaris depart from here in winter—the whales follow migrating herring up the Tysfjord and Vestfjord—and there are trips to spot sea eagles in the summer months. Some of these birds have wingspans of 6.5 feet (2 m). Røst and Værøy have eider ducks, puffins, and majestic white-tailed and sea eagles. Outdoor sports enthusiasts can hike, bike, climb, and kayak in the summer months and enjoy the midnight sun. From mid-February to April, the Lofoten Islands buzz with life as fishermen from across Norway's coast stream here for the cod that swim in their millions to spawning grounds nearby.

To really experience a new way of life, try staying in a fisherman's cabin, or *rorbu*, many of which have been converted to provide accommodation ranging from rustic to luxury. Some wharf buildings, or *sjøhus*, have also been converted into guesthouses. **PE**

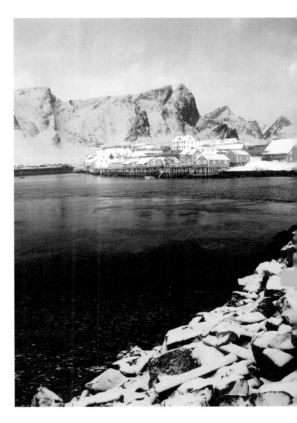

↗ *A small village on Moskenes Island—one of the Lofoten Islands—in winter.*

> "[The Lofoten Islands] have a mystical presence in the collective psyche of [the Norwegians]."
>
> *Independent*

Stay at Hotel Kakslauttanen

Location Kakslauttanen, Finland   **Website** www.kakslauttanen.fi
Price 🕦🕦

There is no experience more sublime than to be suffused by the lights of the northern lights. To do it in a glass igloo must surely be one of the more novel and cozy ways of seeing this spectacular phenomenon. The natural wonder of the northern lights is reason enough to come. At their best from August to late April, atmospheric conditions create a vast sky full of lights, from the edge of the spectrum to the full array, from a sliver to a swishing curtain of light. Seeing this is the only way to believe it.

Deep in the snowbound Saariselkä area of northern Finland, beyond the Arctic Circle, where reindeers sing to the moon and ice crystals flutter from every sentence spoken, is Kakslauttanen, an igloo and log cabin village. The cabins are built from dead standing pine and are completely self-contained lodges with kitchens and saunas. There are two kinds of igloo, constructed from ice or glass; both are surprisingly warm and utterly chic, but one is rather more private than the other.

During the day you can ski, ride on reindeer sleds, and snowshoe around the undulating and wooded countryside, then return to the hotel to feel the extremes of heat in the smoke sauna and the chill of the icy swimming pool. Dinner is then served in the largest ice restaurant, complete with an ice banqueting table, where charcoal-grilled salmon and roasted reindeer feature on the menu. Afterward, you can head off to the sparkling glass *kopa*, or Lapp tepee, which hosts cocktail parties and viewings of the northern lights until late into the night. **SM**

◀ *Kakslauttanen's glass igloos provide a novel—if not entirely private—way to see the northern lights.*

Experience a Night in the Snow Castle

Location Kemi, Finland
Website www.snowcastle.net   **Price** ⊖⊖

"The structure, the ice art, and the play of lights [are] astonishingly beautiful."

Harriet O'Brien, *Independent*

Every winter since 1996 the "world's biggest snow castle" has been built at Kemi in northern Finland—and every spring it melts away to nothing. Each year it is slightly different: Sometimes it stands 65 feet (20 m) or three stories high, or even 3,280 feet (1,000 m) long. Whatever is built, the castle attracts tens of thousands of daytime visitors. Many include it in a package of winter activities, such as a trip on an ice-breaking ship or a husky-sled safari.

Colorful lighting helps dramatize the castle's architecture and the striking carved ice sculptures dotted around the site. Among its walls, corridors, turrets, and chambers, the building always includes a chapel, a restaurant, and a hotel.

The temperature inside this huge "igloo" of snow is 23°F (-5°C), so guests must dress in serious winter clothing at all times—even in the restaurant, which has ice tables and ice seats covered with reindeer fur. Menus can include local specialties like reindeer soup, Lappish potatoes, and lingonberries. All cooked courses are served in foil to keep them warm, but cold drinks are often served in a vessel made of ice.

Some couples marry in the ecumenical chapel (complete with ice pews) and spend their first honeymoon night in a room well below freezing. Inside their windowless snow bedrooms, guests stay warm in heavy-duty insulated sleeping bags, although they are advised to wear a ski hat and socks in bed. There are toilets and a television in the lounge area (albeit on an ice table), but a shower involves a transfer bus to a more conventional local hotel. **SH**

◹ *The Snow Castle's restaurant is filled with ice sculptures and stools covered in reindeer hide.*

Cruise the Saimaa Canal

Location Southeast Finland to Northwest Russia
Website www.saimaatravel.fi **Price** 🟢🟢

As you sidle into Russia like a secret agent, the only sign that you have changed countries is a concrete post in the glassy water; it leans at such an angle that one wave might overwhelm it and erase all trace of a border crossing. Sitting on board the beautifully refurbished boat, you watch the silent and secret world of the Saimaa Canal pass by, the breathtaking countryside dotted with thick forests and open lakes through which the canal runs.

The cruise departs in the early morning from Lappeenranta, bound for the historic border post of Vyborg, just inside Russia, a town with remnants of a grand and important past, such as the castle that

> *"Saimaa is a labyrinthine watercourse . . . created by the continental ice sheet in the Ice Age."*

nationmaster.com

overlooks the entrance to the port. The total length of the canal is 28 miles (43 km). With a difference of 250 feet (76 m) in the water levels between Lake Saimaa and the Gulf of Finland (the two ends of the canal), a series of eight locks must be negotiated—an incredible feat of engineering to watch.

The leisurely journey gives passengers several hours to unwind and enjoy the scenery, and with only a handful of boats using the canal (MS *Carelia* is the only passenger boat offering cruises to Russia), those on board witness a world that would never be seen on a city visit. The boat has two restaurants and a sundeck, a great place to view the canal and locks. **CFM**

Visit Porvoo Archipelago

Location Porvoo, Finland
Website www.magnusnyholm.net **Price** 🟢🟢

With just 6.5 people per square mile (2.5 per sq km), it is not difficult to avoid the crowds in Finland. But the crystal-clear seawaters of the southern archipelago around Porvoo and Pellinki, so still that they mirror the sky's reflection, make a perfect place to escape.

Lying approximately 35 miles (56 km) from Helsinki, the archipelago takes in hundreds of small islands, with fingers of lush green land sheltered by shimmering silver birch and pine trees jutting into the Gulf of Finland. Small, brightly painted timber fishing lodges dot the landscape and make cozy places to stay, and there is barely a hotel in sight. Magnus Nyholm's beach cabin at Tirmo, surrounded by woodland, provides the perfect hideaway with fantastic views over the water. There is room for fourteen people, and visitors can use the sauna, charter a boat, or swim in the archipelago; the pure, shallow waters are perfect for swimming.

So beautiful is the area that it has provided inspiration for many writers and artists; Finland's national poet J. L. Runeberg lived in Porvoo, and Tove Jansson, creator of the Moomin characters, spent her summers on Klovharu, one of the most isolated of the archipelago's islands. The islands of the archipelago are the location for Jansson's most popular adult novel, *The Summer Book*, which describes the barren beauty superbly. Her home is open to the public for one week in July each year.

Cruises through the archipelago are available from Helsinki to historic Porvoo daily throughout the summer, but the best way to witness the sheer magic of the region is alone, finding a secret lane that runs down to the shore, or a tiny uninhabited inlet that you can call your own for a while. **CFM**

Enjoy a Snowmobile Safari

Location Luosto, Finnish Lapland
Website www.snowgames.fi   **Price** 💲💲

The northern lights, the natural phenomenon caused when electrons from outer space collide with Earth's atmosphere, light up the skies of the Arctic Circle with streaks of red, pink, and green. The native Sami people nicknamed the lights "the foxfires," believing them to be sparks brushed into the night sky by the tail of the Arctic fox. The farther north you travel, the more likely you are to see this stunning natural spectacle. It appears year-round, but is more obvious during the winter months, when the long, dark nights provide the perfect backdrop for this celestial light show.

There are many ways to enjoy the lights, from midnight snowshoe treks to husky-drawn sled rides. One of the most exhilarating options is to join a snowmobile safari. Against an inky-black night sky, the winter landscape is bathed in a soft, blue glow of reflected moonlight and the absolute silence is broken only by the nasal hum of the snowmobiles as they wind through the powdery trails. The freezing temperatures are cold enough to turn the tears on your eyelashes into icicles, but the snowmobiles' seats and handles are heated, keeping you toasty and warm inside your thick Arctic snowsuit. Cups of hot, tangy lingonberry juice help to warm you from the inside.

The sky above is painted with fiery streaks of color that dance across the heavens, shifting and shimmering like a heavenly fireworks display. The pine trees are heavy with snow, their branches buckled under the weight like bizarre sculptures. Lit up by the headlights of the snowmobiles, snow crystals make everything look like it has been dusted with glitter. **JP**

◁ *Snowmobiling across frozen Lapland is an exciting way to experience the splendor of the northern lights.*

Stay at Utter Inn

Location Lake Mälaren, Västerås, Sweden
Website www.vasterasmalarstaden.se   **Price** 💲💲

The Utter Inn (Otter Inn in English) is one of the strangest places to sleep in the world. First, you board a rubber dinghy in the port of Västerås and are taken out 0.6 miles (1 km) on Lake Mälaren. Your destination appears to be a small shed floating on a diving platform. The small red hut contains a bathroom and a hatch in the floor. Open the hatch and descend a metal ladder to find your bedroom—in a watertight chamber suspended in the water beneath the hut.

Is the Utter Inn an escape? Some find it more like solitary confinement from which they want to escape. Others enjoy the isolation, the peace, and the slight sense of danger. You are not only literally sleeping with

> *"[It] includes a sense of risk taking and adventure that tends to expand the sensory input."*
>
> unusualhotelsoftheworld.com

the fishes, but can watch them, too. Or rather, be watched by them, in a bizarre reversal of a goldfish bowl. The lake's pike and perch gather at the room's windows, peering in at their unusual visitors.

The Utter Inn is the brainchild of Mikael Genberg, a local artist. His previous work was The Woodpecker, a treehouse hotel where food was hoisted up by rope. At Utter, dinner can be delivered by boat in the evening, or else guests can paddle to shore in an inflatable canoe. A picnic breakfast is also provided. Guests can sunbathe on the floating platform and, as far as leisure facilities go, the hotel is unique in that it floats within its own swimming pool. **SH**

Relax at the Icehotel

Location Jukkasjärvi, Sweden **Website** www.icehotel.com **Price** 💲💲

> *"[T]he ice itself is completely transparent ... which makes it look otherworldly."*

Juliet Eilperin, *Washington Post*

⬆ *A woman lies on a bed covered in reindeer skins at the Icehotel in Lapland, Sweden.*

➡ *A room inside the Icehotel—the hotel changes each year as old sculptures melt and new ones are carved.*

Back in the late 1980s, a Swede named Yngve Bergqvist had a vision. In Swedish Lapland, 125 miles (200 km) north of the Arctic Circle, he would build a hotel made entirely from ice. Funding did not come easily and so the Icehotel started small. As the years passed, Bergqvist was proved right, and visitor numbers rocketed.

Now the building is an ice sculpture gallery as much as a hotel. Step through the main doors into a hallway filled with decoratively carved columns and elegant figurines of glistening beauty. Corridors to the side branch off to the ice suites, where sculptors from across the globe create their own personal visions in ice. Each winter the artworks are different: Although the hotel stores some of the larger ice blocks through the summer months, come spring the sculptures melt and slide gracefully back into the Torne River from where their material came.

Whatever the outside weather, temperatures inside the Icehotel hover around 23°F (-5°C) and guests staying the night in the cold rooms are provided with puffy purple sleeping bags, cold-weather suits, and boots. (For those a bit less bold, there are warm rooms, too, in another building.) The bed frames are made from ice, but their bases are of slatted wood, with mattresses and cozy—if slightly smelly—reindeer skins on top.

Down another passage, the ice bar serves vodka cocktails in shot glasses made from ice. The hotel uses more than half a million of these glasses each year but, on the bright side, nobody fights over who will do the dishes. Visitors must wear gloves to hold the glasses; otherwise they will slip right out of their hands. As they drink, the heat from their lips molds the cups exactly to the contours of their own mouths. **PE**

Experience the Nordic Light Hotel

Location Stockholm, Sweden **Website** www.nordiclighthotel.se
Price 🟢🟢

The Nordic Light Hotel, as the name suggests, is all about light. The responsive sound and movement systems in the lobby and multiple light settings in the rooms are intended to re-create the ever-changing patterns of the northern lights, as well as provide light therapy for the hotel guests.

The hotel has become a hip place to be, and not only for those interested in the interplay of light and color. It is the official hotel for Stockholm Design Week, alternative fashion fair +46, and Future Design Days, so Nordic Light tends to draw in a design crowd. They come to enjoy a stay in one of the 175 comfortable rooms, which offer a Scandinavian mix of minimalist white, wall projections instead of art, and light beds where guests can choose their own color, mood, and speed. Visitors can sip cocktails in the lounge (which hosts a few club nights during the week) and generally hang out and look good against some of the best designer surfaces Sweden has to offer.

You cannot get away from the light though. As well as the in-room settings, room service offers light therapy administered by professional light therapists and masseurs. This is no novelty: Not only has it been proven to help combat jet lag, but infrared light also allegedly increases blood circulation, detoxifies, and reduces swelling, as well as reducing cellulite buildup and improving the body's elimination systems. Laser acupuncture is also available, which can minimize pain and provide cures for myriad ailments—and with no side effects. If you are unsure, however, you can always book a normal massage at the same time. **PS**

> *"[T]he best thing . . . is the choice of rooms. It's like choosing clothes, [including] S, M, L, and XL."*

Jeanette Hyde, *Observer*

◥ *The lobby of Stockholm's ultra-hip Nordic Light Hotel, complete with moving light projections.*

Stay at the Grand Hotel

Location Stockholm, Sweden **Website** www.grandhotel.se
Price 💰💰💰💰

Whether it is beneath the chandeliers and painted ceilings of the opulent hall of mirrors, in the candlelit intimacy of the wood-paneled French dining room, or lounging on plush sofas between gilded pillars of the vast lobby, the Grand Hotel in Stockholm has been grand for more than 130 years. This glorious Scandinavian institution is one of the few surviving classic city hotels of Europe and is proud of its status as a Swedish national monument.

The Grand stands in the heart of Stockholm, right on the harborside opposite the Royal Palace. It is part of Swedish tradition to eat a herring smörgåsbord in the Grand's veranda restaurant overlooking the

> *"The signatures in the guest book read like an almanac of twentieth century life."*
>
> Tim Ecott, *Guardian*

paddle steamers that dock outside. Many rooms have the sense of being part of a stately home, but best of all is the four-room penthouse, which overlooks the busy waterfront. This is the Nobel Suite, where for more than a hundred years the winners of the Nobel Prize have stayed. You may even find yourself sitting in the same armchair that Albert Einstein once enjoyed.

Nobel Prize winners are just the tip of the celebrity iceberg, though. Frank Sinatra once got so drunk in the bar that a doctor had to be called, and Greta Garbo once hid in the bathrooms to avoid the staff. The Grand exudes a sense of glamour so palpable that it rubs off, making all guests feel special. **SH**

Relax at Smådalarö Gard

Location Stockholm, Sweden **Website** www.smadalarogard.se
Price 💰💰

There are few more life-affirming experiences on the planet than taking a plunge in an ice-cold pool after a wood-fired sauna, and here at Smådalarö you can set your senses to "stunned" by doing just that. With your skin dancing with pleasure at the juxtaposition of wood-smoked prickly heat and icy water, or a dip in the heated hotel pool, you will be primed and ready to enjoy a host of activities in this wonderfully calm manor house, located some forty-five minutes from Stockholm's busy city center.

Built in 1810, the fully refurbished, four-star hotel has sixty-two state-of-the-art rooms and is renowned as a top-class conference center. The open fireplaces and snug rooms add to the romantic atmosphere no matter what the Swedish weather is doing outside, with Gökboet (the Cuckoo's Nest) a favorite with honeymooners. Weather permitting, a row on the lake, a round on the nine-hole golf course, boat trips in the hotel's own yacht, rowing, fishing, walking, or a swift game of *boules* or tennis can help you meet future sauna mates; alternatively, you can stay in and relax with a game of billiards or darts, or work on your winter tan in the solarium. The Hemviken waters of this wonderful archipelago present the seasons in their myriad colors—fall has never looked as beautiful as in Scandinavia—and Dalaröhas has long been a meeting place for seafarers and trading travelers, so you are in good company historically.

The restaurant and Nämdö dining room provide haute cuisine Swedish style, with the best of the archipelago's fish and shellfish sparkling next to all kinds of local game and poultry on the menu. Plunging into Smådalarö's atmosphere is guaranteed to revitalize even the most weary of souls. **PS**

Enjoy Villa Källhagen

Location Stockholm, Sweden **Website** www.kallhagen.se
Price 🌑🌑

Villa Källhagen is a small, intimate hotel situated in Stockholm's Royal Djurgården Park—a famous part of the cityscape that has been popular with visitors for a good 200 years. As is typical in Northern European countries with long hours of daylight in the summer, Villa Källhagen's alluring architecture features a great deal of glass to enable the building—and its guests—to make the most of the light.

The twenty park-facing bedrooms have huge windows that look out onto the park and the pretty Djurgården canal, and skylights let light into the bathrooms. Rooms are spacious, a feeling enhanced by the natural light, pale woods, and pleasingly

---

"... a warm, welcoming setting in harmony with the natural surroundings of Djurgården."

countrysidehotels.se

---

colored fabrics. All rooms have balconies or terraces, too, so you can get the most of the fresh Scandinavian air. Lovers of Swedish cuisine (especially fish) will appreciate the hotel's gourmet restaurant, which specializes in traditional dishes like fried Baltic herring.

The hotel makes for a superb spring or summer escape, but the interior is remarkably cozy in winter, too, especially when the large open fire is lit, the bar is open, and the night winds howl outside. A sauna and relaxation room are also on-site, and you can rent bicycles to get out into the countryside. The villa is ten minutes from the heart of the city, making it a perfect base for those wishing to explore Stockholm. **PS**

Stay at Långholmen Hotel

Location Stockholm, Sweden **Website** www.langholmen.com
Price 🌑🌑

A book of escapes is incomplete without at least one prison: Långholmen was once Sweden's biggest jail. The grand nineteenth-century buildings on a leafy island near the city center have been converted into a hotel, with the former cells as bedrooms. The old Crown Prison was used for the capital's most notorious prisoners until 1975 and still has its original stairwell in the middle of all the old cells. It now forms an airy atrium between the bedrooms.

The cells themselves still have small windows, without the iron bars, and the old high-security doors have been retained. Inside, they each now have a shower, toilet, telephone, free wireless Internet access, radio, and cable television. Walls are decorated with newspaper clippings detailing prisoners' crimes and trials. Guests even get a copy of a former inmate's daily routine, which shows reveille at 5:45 A.M. and bedtime at 7:45 P.M., but don't worry, it is just to emphasize how things have changed.

The vast jail now has 102 bedrooms, as well as a separate youth hostel, conference center, museum, and four restaurants, including one in the basement where female prisoners were forced to spend their days at spinning wheels. Fortunately, the menus offer more than just bread and water. On top of all that, there is even a patio café where you can play *boules* in the old exercise yard.

The island itself is one of the largest among hundreds that form the Swedish capital, and its history means that it has remained an almost undeveloped piece of countryside only a fifteen-minute walk from the Royal Palace and the old city. There is even a small beach just outside the old prison walls that has become popular with summer bathers. **SH**

Recharge at Yasuragi

Location Hasseludden, Sweden **Website** www.yasuragi.se
Price $ $

Yasuragi means "inner peace and harmony," and that is what you get. A tranquil, spacious retreat twenty minutes from Stockholm, it never feels crowded, even when all 166 rooms are occupied. The Buddhist aesthetics of simple, pared-down elegance create a sense of calm, combining natural light with the soft glow of lanterns, rush matting, and untreated pale-wood walls hung with spectacular kimonos.

Once inside, a kimono, slippers, swimsuit, and towel are all you need—and they are provided. Inner peace begins with water and the indulgence of the Japanese bathing ritual. With guidance from a bath hostess, you choose a washing station in the dimly lit wet area of the beautiful washrooms and begin this slow, meditative process, alternating hot and cold water with meticulous cleansing. Afterward, time in the stone spa pool or sauna and then a few lengths of the enormous pool are the perfect precursor to a soak in the hot springs outside, surrounded by trees.

From Zen meditation classes and blissful shiatsu massage to flotation tanks and Seitai, a form of yoga, you cannot help feeling healthy—and the food helps. Breakfast takes attention to detail to new heights: eggs boiled for three, five, or ten minutes; five different types of milk; a huge variety of teas; and meat, cheese, and breads to fill you up until evening. Then, you have two restaurants to choose from. Teppanyaki has twelve grilling points, each with its own chef who explains the culinary traditions of the simple menu as they prepare and cook it over high flames—a virtuoso performance with delicious results. **OM**

> *Yasuragi's teahouse by the enormous pool is a fusion of Buddhist and Scandinavian aesthetics.*

"Simplicity has become a rare luxury, and this is what gives Yasuragi that sense of exclusivity."

Proprietors, Yasuragi

Discover Gotland

Location Gotland, Sweden   **Website** www.gotland.net
Price ❶

Holder of Sweden's sunshine record, Gotland (population 57,000) has proper seasons, but its offshore location, some 56 miles (90 km) from the mainland, means winters are mild. Ringed by silky sand beaches and stretches of pebbles dotted with limestone pillars that have been carved into strange, almost grotesque shapes by wind and rain, Gotland is a fertile, gently undulating, heavily forested island where the inhabitants even manage to produce passable wine.

With quiet roads and no challenging hills, it is perfect for exploring by bicycle or on horseback and is dotted with golf courses. Stranger sports can be witnessed at the annual Stångaspelen (The Pole Games), Gotland's very own mini-Olympics held in July. It features such challenges as tossing the caber, wrestling, and the Gotland pentathlon.

Throughout the summer months, the Roma Theatre ensemble performs Shakespeare and other classics amid the ruins of an ancient monastery, and the young at heart revel in the annual kite-flying festival that attracts addicts from across Europe.

There is a plethora of vacation cottages and condos for rent and hotels ranging from basic guesthouses to converted manor houses. Reached by air from Stockholm in just thirty-five minutes, with about twenty-five daily connections year-round, or by a leisurely car-ferry crossing, Gotland is a laid-back island where everyone enjoys the outdoor life and barbecues are an honored ritual. There are also direct flights from Germany, Norway, and Finland. **RsP**

◄ *A rock formation known as "the dog," one of many examples of limestone carved by wind and rain.*

Explore the Koster Islands

Location Koster Islands, Sweden
Website www.kosteroarna.com   **Price** 🌑

Relax at Skovshoved Hotel

Location Copenhagen, Denmark
Website www.skovshovedhotel.dk   **Price** 🌑🌑

The Koster Islands are a Scandinavian secret. Located off Sweden's Bohuslän coast, toward the border with Norway, the two islands are inhabited by just 300 people. They are a summer getaway for in-the-know Norwegian and Swedish visitors looking for an escape from twenty-first-century life. They visit for fresh air and nature in its prime, restaurants serving delicious fresh seafood, and traditional red summerhouses. As Sweden's most westerly inhabited islands, they are something of a getaway even in a country with so much space and beautiful scenery elsewhere.

Made up of two islands, North Koster and South Koster, the archipelago also has many skerries and

> *"This pair [of islands] . . . are sleepy, car-free nature reserves that visitors can tour on foot or by bike."*
>
> Siobhan Mulholland, *Independent*

rocky islets that shelter boats and colonies of seals. North Koster is the smaller of the two, and home to sixty people. It is prime walking territory, with beaches, moorland, and rocks scarred by the Ice Age, as well as a lighthouse that has been restored after falling into disuse for 110 years. South Koster is the busier island—but only in the relative sense of the word—with guesthouses, restaurants, and hotels, as well as biking trails through woodland and a half-mile-long sandy beach, Kilesand. One trail leads to the viewpoint at Valfjäll opposite a small wooden church, from which you can see the archipelago stretching out to sea. Vacationing here feels like stepping back in time. **LD**

The Skovshoved is a perfect little seaside boutique hotel that is ideal for a romantic getaway. Despite being situated only twenty minutes from central Copenhagen, you will feel a whole world away from the city in this tranquil coastal suburb.

You certainly will not be the first to realize the charms of the area, though. The Skovshoved Hotel has been around since 1660 and soon established itself as the place to be seen. Come in the summer to take advantage of the endless daylight, but even in the dead of winter, when the feeble sunlight struggles to make any impact on the gloom, it is still the most romantic place to be holed up. Cozy candlelit public areas with crackling log fires and big, squashy cream sofas are the ideal place to kick back with a glass of wine and a book.

Well situated between the two best beaches in Denmark—Charlottenlund and Bellevue—the hotel has twenty-two airy rooms, all beautifully decorated and furnished in pale Scandinavian hues of creams, blues, and grays, with stripped wooden floors and white furniture. Some rooms also have sea-facing balconies. The restaurant, which has received a Michelin recommendation, has an Italian- and French-inspired menu and has been fully booked almost every night since it opened; it manages to pull off an elegant yet casual ambience with aplomb.

If you want somewhere a bit more laid-back to enjoy a drink, there is a great little pub right next door, and a short stroll away the hotel has a private jetty from which the plucky—or foolhardy—can dive into the chilly sea for a bracing swim. The beach is a bit farther down, perfect for making the most of those endlessly long, Scandinavian summer evenings. **HA**

Explore Thy National Park

Location Thy, Denmark
Website www.visitthy.dk   **Price** 🍴

The region where the Arctic meets southern Europe is so remote that it has earned the reputation of being Denmark's last wild country. Blessed with more sunshine hours than anywhere else in the country, Thy National Park covers 61,775 acres (25,000 ha) that snake along the northwest Jutland coast and inland areas, offering epic scenery and abundant fresh air.

The park's western edge has a pristine coastline backed by a huge expanse of sand dunes and heaths ablaze with blueberries, cranberries, and orchids. The beaches are popular with windsurfers and Danish vacationers who flock there during the summer months, but they are almost desolate out of season.

> *"You can throw yourself into the sparkling waves of the North Sea or bike through dune plantations."*

Danish National Parks

Move east for rolling, fertile hills punctuated by small villages and farms with eerie wind-bent trees. Cocooned by conifer plantations, lime-rich lakes are set farther inland and are among the cleanest in Denmark, awash with aquatic plants and insect life. An abundance of carp provides a tempting reason for anglers to visit. Watch deer pass by the idyllic Nors Lake while you swim in its glassy waters.

The park's varied terrain provides great diversity for walkers, bicyclists, and horseback riders, who explore its forest and coastal trails. The paths are not well trodden, though, and it is easy to lose yourself in the scenery and wide open plains. **JK**

Stay at Steensgaard Manor

Location South Funen, Denmark
Website www.herregaardspension.dk   **Price** 💲💲

As you wander among the carved wood paneling, antique furniture, oil paintings, and suits of armor here, you will get a pretty good sense of what it is like to be a member of the nobility. Deep in the picturesque hills of south Funen, Steensgaard Manor was for many years the home of a Danish count. Now a country house hotel and restaurant, it still retains that sense of history and relaxed luxury.

The cobbled drive leads into a courtyard between the wings of the main house, which dates back to the fourteenth century. You enter the hall across a grand red and white marble-tiled floor. Walls are hung with antique weaponry and animal trophies; there is an ornate brass chandelier and imposing wooden staircase leading to a galleried landing and bedrooms. These are spacious, with great views and more antiques but no televisions or modern designer touches. Instead, it is as traditional as a royal residence, with chintz curtains, floral fabrics, and elegant dressing tables. Downstairs you may browse the leather-backed tomes in the floor-to-ceiling shelves of the library. Do not stay here too late, though—this room is said to be haunted by the ghost of a medieval owner's wife who conspired to have him murdered, and then regretted the deed for the rest of her life. The owners say that she appears at two minutes past midnight and tries to scrub her husband's blood from the floor.

Outside there is a lake surrounded by ancient trees and a Jersey cow dairy farm where the owners make their own butter and cheese, and grow herbs and vegetables for their restaurant and farm shop. Dinners at the restaurant are elaborate four-course affairs in an elegant dining room with deep red walls, creamy linen, and sparkling crystal glasses. **SH**

Stay at Sønderho Kro

Location Jutland, Denmark   **Website** www.sonderhokro.dk
Price ⓢⓢ

According to the locals on the island of Fanø, anxieties do not travel well across the water from Esbjerg on the mainland. And there seems to be some truth in the saying. Arriving in Fanø, a short ferry ride from Esbjerg, is a bit like entering another century. Most of the houses around Nordby and Sønderho date back to the seventeenth and eighteenth centuries, and any new building work must be done in the traditional style.

Sønderho Kro, on the south side of the island, has been open for business since 1722. Do not expect slick styling and neutral decor: The fourteen wooden-floored rooms, fashioned from converted fishermen's cottages, are named after prominent ships from the

---

"[T]he oldest purpose-built inn in Denmark—all wooden beams, low ceilings, and period furniture."

Paul Oswell, *Guardian*

---

island's seafaring past or names from the innkeeper's family—take your pick from the likes of Sophie, Bertha, and Olgas. For more privacy, choose to stay in the self-contained, pink painted, one-bedroom thatched cottage complete with its own garden.

The hotel serves up hearty traditional meals, not surprisingly focusing heavily on seafood. To work off the calories, bicycle around the virtually traffic-free roads, or head to the gorgeous beaches. Do not be put off by the fact that you are on an island in the middle of the chilly North Sea. You will be pleasantly surprised by how warm the water is, because it is shallow and warms up pretty quickly. **HA**

Canoe the Gudenå

Location Jutland, Denmark   **Website** www.visitdenmark.com
Price ⓢ

Get off the beaten track by exploring Denmark's lake district and paddling down the Gudenå River. Flanked on both sides by rolling green countryside, let the current push you gently downstream while you enjoy the views. Take it slow on the river's gentle waters in order to get a close look at the variety of birdlife and to keep an eye out for the perfect picnic spot.

It is possible to rent a canoe for a few hours or a few days. The Silkeborg tourist board can arrange canoe packages that are ideal for families, or you can get a boat directly from rental companies in the area. Hard-core canoeists can tackle all 100 miles (160 km) of the river in ten days, beginning at the source of the Gudenå, near Tørring in east-central Jutland, and ending up in Fladbro by Randers fjord on the east coast. The choice of accommodations on the way range from well-equipped campsites to traditional and rustic inns.

The river's banks are lined with top attractions, such as Elmuseet, a fascinating museum that specializes in anything of an electrical nature. It is well placed in the grounds of the Gudenå hydroelectric power station. At Himmelbjerget, you can leave your canoe behind to hike up a mountain. It is also worth exploring some of the passing towns, such as the scenic Silkeborg.

To escape the crowds, avoid going during the school vacations, when the river chokes with canoes. With a growing concern for the environment, this is the perfect getaway for those concerned about their carbon footprint. Days spent in a canoe and nights in a tent have a very low environmental impact indeed. **JK**

➲ *Denmark's Gudenå provides miles of canoeing for all tastes through Denmark's verdant lake district.*

Relax at Park Hotel Kenmare

Location County Kerry, Ireland   **Website** www.parkkenmare.com
Price 🌓🌓

The Park Hotel overlooks a sweep of Kenmare Bay, with grand vistas out to the Caha mountains. It is an exceptionally tranquil place to stay, yet it is just a few minutes' walk from Kenmare—an attractive town unspoiled by tourism, with an enticing set of shops, decent restaurants, and venues for Irish music. An imposing, gray-stone building surrounded by pretty gardens and lawns, the hotel has an eighteen-hole golf course on its doorstep and there are spectacular walks in the Kerry countryside a short drive away.

Unusually, its spa, SÁMAS, is open only to hotel residents, so it is an exclusive, unhurried place to escape to without the babble of day guests. There is no risk of having your stay disturbed by weddings or conferences either, because this family-owned and family-run hotel has chosen not to host them. Interiors are decked out with traditional furnishings, original oil paintings, and antique furniture, although the forty-six bedrooms also offer a flat-screen TV, DVD, CD, and MP3 player, as well as a selection of movies and music CDs. The deluxe rooms are more spacious and have sitting areas with views out to the water. The SÁMAS spa offers an indulgent set of treatments. The thermal suites share an open-air vitality pool overlooking shrubs and flowers, with the bay in the distance. If you have the energy, you can do lengths in a gleaming 82-foot (25-m) lap pool. Feast in the Park's elegant dining room, or head into town, where Mulcahy's and Packies are both chef-owned restaurants that come highly recommended. Each evening, classic films are shown in the hotel's private cinema. **CSJ**

↩ *Spa treatments at Park Hotel Kenmare finish with relaxation in a light-filled room with glorious views.*

Unwind at Temple Country Retreat and Spa

Location County Westmeath, Ireland
Website www.templespa.ie   **Price** ⑤⑤

> "A sense of calm and tranquility seemed to permeate throughout the bright, airy two-story [spa]."

Grace Heneghan, *Holistic Health*

In a 250-year-old farmhouse on the site of an ancient monastery, this adult-only destination health spa is the perfect place to escape the daily grind. Pamper your troubles away with luxury treatments in the tranquil surroundings of the rolling Westmeath countryside.

There might be an old-world charm to the location, but there is nothing dated about this contemporary spa, just ninety minutes from Dublin. An oasis of wellness, its natural light floods in to illuminate the high-ceilinged rooms that house the vitality suite, a pool with hydro-jets, the sauna, and steam room. Luxuriate in a marine body wrap, indulge in a vinotherapy facial, or unwind with a full-body massage.

The idea behind this family-run retreat is to replace what everyday life takes out of you, focusing firmly on relaxation and well-being. Choose from eighty different holistic, healing treatments in the spa, then go walking and bicycling in the 100 acres (40 ha) of parkland. Best of all, guests are actively encouraged to do absolutely nothing. It is a blissful chill-out experience that will stay with you long after you leave.

Inspired by the site's previous incarnation as a monastery, the twenty-three rooms in the cloistered spa building overlook the internal gardens. For a real treat, there are suites with whirlpool tubs and balconies. Food is healthy with an emphasis on great flavor. Only the best local ingredients make it to the table.

A cross between a bed-and-breakfast where staff offer a warm welcome and a modern spa, the Temple offers a real escape in an idyllic pastoral setting. **AD**

◸ *The Temple's twelve-seat vitality pool with therapeutic water jets is ideal for unwinding.*

Relax at Delphi Mountain

Location County Galway, Ireland
Website www.delphimountainresort.com **Price** 💲💲

A lavish hideaway on the wild, west coast of Ireland, Delphi Mountain Resort is the place to go in search of some serious pampering. Rooms look out over the mountains, and plush split-level suites have a cozy living room and mezzanine bed area.

The big draw, of course, is the spa. You can choose from massages and treatments (shiatsu, aromatherapy, Reiki), a myriad of scrubs and wraps, facials, and seaweed or detox baths. Or for something different, you can try cryotherapy: an algae wrap for the legs that is great for getting rid of puffiness. There is also a sumptuous health suite with a luxurious whirlpool tub, sauna, and dry-stone wall steam room, as well as a

> *"The thermal suite and relaxation rooms have one of the best views in Ireland."*
>
> Fionnula Quinlan, *Irish Examiner*

hydro-pool complete with star-lit canopy. The relaxed atmosphere and friendly staff make this a haven of peace and tranquility.

This is a wilderness retreat in more ways than one, though, and there is much to indulge in outdoors—from sea kayaking and bicycling to hiking. Explore sea caves, surf, and ride horses at the beach; canoe and water-ski in the nearby loch; or abseil and trek through the breathtaking countryside. The Peregrine restaurant features superb fresh local seafood, ranging from Killary mussels to scallops and sea bass; vegetables come from the resort's own organic gardens. Body and soul have never been so in tune. **AD**

Stay at Bellinter House

Location County Meath, Ireland
Website www.bellinterhouse.com **Price** 💲💲

What do you get when you take a beautiful Georgian country house set in 12 acres (5 ha) of gorgeous Irish parkland and wave a contemporary wand over it? With Bellinter House, the result is an outstanding blend of elegant stateliness and the feel of a deluxe hotel with all modern conveniences. Ireland, as the locals will tell you, is a bit like that itself, with a head set firmly on the future and a heart full of tales of wondrous myth and lush green natural beauty.

The interior of Bellinter House has been lovingly preserved, from the drawing room's plasterwork to the sash windows and floorboards. The view over the river makes the hour's drive from Dublin more than worthwhile—and that is before you take in the thirty-four rooms, individually appointed with vintage furnishings and equipped with custom-built plasma screens and an entertainment system that will keep you fully absorbed as you recline on your luxurious bed. There is also an elegant drawing room with large sash windows and wonderful views, a well-stocked library and games room, and two excellent bars. The Bellinter Bar provides a rustic warm-up for the delights of the more sophisticated basement wine bar, which hosts a superb, naturally lit restaurant (aptly named Eden) with plenty of space to enjoy the locally sourced, fresh, and imaginative menu. Try out the many fine wines or, if you prefer, pair Guinness with steak—an equally sublime combination.

Bellinter's terraces and lawns are ideal for alfresco dining, and the nearby Boyne is perfect for a spot of fishing, a relaxing way to while away the afternoon before coming home to a dip in the outdoor hot tub or perhaps another Guinness in front of a roaring open fire. Rural hospitality at its best. **PS**

Experience Ashford Castle

Location County Mayo, Ireland   **Website** www.ashford.ie
Price $ $

This is a true castle, with turrets and ramparts, armor, and oak paneling. Its first stones were laid in 1228 by the de Burgo family, and for eight centuries its inhabitants have gazed out upon the blue waters of Lough Corrib, Ireland's second-largest lake. There have been various owners, who have added a French-style chateau and, later, Victorian extensions. From the seventeenth century, the Guinness family used the castle as a hunting and fishing lodge until they sold it in 1939 and it was transformed into a hotel.

The turrets and ramparts have seen a range of high-ranking guests. The Prince of Wales, who later became King George V, visited in 1903; the billiards room was

> *"The guardian mountains which arise are as still and calm as the visions of an Icelandic god . . ."*
>
> George Moore, novelist-guest in the 1880s

built especially for his visit and the restaurant is named for him. U.S. president Ronald Reagan also stayed at Ashford; for his visit they commissioned a special bed.

Today, Ashford Castle has eighty-three bedrooms and a spa offering treatments using Ya Kon products. Outside are 350 acres (141 ha) of wooded parkland. Guests can play a round on the golf course or take a lesson in the art of falconry. There is also archery, clay-pigeon shooting, and cross-country riding. The lake is known for its stocks of wild brown trout and salmon. Alternatively, you can join the castle's resident historian for a trip to Inchagoill Island to see St. Patrick's church, built by St. Patrick in 450 C.E. **PE**

Stay at Ice House Hotel

Location County Mayo, Ireland   **Website** www.icehousehotel.ie
Price $ $

The Ice House Hotel, situated on the beautiful and tidal River Moy estuary, is a renovated ice house, dating back 150 years, where ice was stored to pack the river's famous salmon. Today, it is a great place to chill, rather than be chilled, with a luxury spa and exciting architecture that led *Condé Nast Traveler* to describe it as one of Ireland's most stylish and innovative new hotels, and a funky base from which to explore Ireland's wild, west coast.

The modern architecture is dazzling: The carefully restored white house is joined by a contemporary slate wall stylishly crisscrossed with orange lines. Inside the hotel, the thirty-two rooms and suites are divided between the iconic nineteenth-century building, complete with period furniture and sash windows, and the new wing with minimalist rooms and floor-to-ceiling windows with views of the River Moy. Bathrooms have underfloor heating, soft towels, and L'Occitane products; bedrooms are spacious with modern art on the walls and plasma televisions.

Down in the Pier restaurant, the very best local and fresh food is served up in the original vaulted ice store, with Connemara lamb, Irish beef, roast pigeon, and rabbit loin on the menu. The luxurious spa is outstanding, too, and well worth a long visit. It comprises five treatment rooms named after ships wrecked on the Moy in times gone by, plus outdoor hot tubs overlooking the river. Some of the signature spa treatments include prescription facials and body massages with warm pebbles of Inniscrone.

The hotel is also a perfect base for the west coast's many festivals, as well as hikes or salmon fishing on the Moy. It might have been cold inside once upon a time, but now this hotel exudes warmth. **LD**

Enjoy Yoga on Clare Island

Location County Mayo, Ireland   **Website** www.yogaretreats.ie
Price $

With mountain views on one side and Atlantic rollers on the other, this rural retreat is about as far away as you can get from the rest of the world. Although the dramatic landscapes are a big draw, the center offers yoga fans, from beginners to keen enthusiasts, a place to practice away from the pressures of daily life.

The traditional island cottage, which provides accommodation, has been renovated using eco-friendly materials, including solar panels and wood-burning stoves for heating. Wood, hemp, terra-cotta, and natural slate all add to the cozy feel. The new timber yoga studio has stunning views over Clew Bay and Croagh Patrick.

The center is a haven of serenity set in 240 acres (97 ha) of land grazed by sheep and horses. Organic gardens supply fruit and vegetables for the table, and there are acres of native woodland to explore after yoga classes. More than 90 percent of the fresh produce on the vegetarian menu is locally sourced, organic, or homegrown, from farmhouse cheeses and butter to freshly baked bread and homemade soy milk. Even the drinking water comes from a spring near the house.

Clare Island itself provides a unique setting for exploration and introspection—an island off an island, off an island, on the edge of Europe, this is about as remote as yoga retreats get. It is the ideal base to practice mindfulness before applying it to daily life. This is no ashram, however, and there is a relaxed and fun approach. When no courses are running, it is possible to rent out one of the houses. **AD**

↗ *Remote, peaceful, and with scenic sea views, the Clare Island retreat is the ideal place to practice yoga.*

"The dramatic scenery and invigorating sea air make a retreat on Clare Island . . . unforgettable."

i-escape.com

De-stress at Ard Nahoo

Location County Leitrim, Ireland   **Website** www.ardnahoo.com   **Price** 🌀

Ard Nahoo is a peaceful eco-retreat set along a single-track road amid the lush beauty of the North Leitrim Glens. Such a magical location as this deserves to be preserved and protected, and it is with this in mind that Ard Nahoo has been created. The three cabins that make up the charming accommodation have been built using environmentally friendly practices.

This simple health farm has built its entire ethos around the mantra of integrity. Choose from a range of holistic treatments tailored to the individual and designed to restore, rebalance, and calm the body and soul. As well as offering a variety of enticing massages and facials, there is an innovative "Detox Box," which claims to soothe muscles, clarify the skin, and burn away a fat-busting 900 to 2,400 calories a session. The Ard Nahoo yoga philosophy, with its emphasis on balance and harmony, draws on the serenity of the environment. Classes are held in the tranquil studio overlooking the grounds.

In between treatments and yoga sessions guests have plenty of time to explore the extensive grounds and the beautiful hills of Leitrim. Take part in one of the guided walks that highlight the native plants and trees, as well as explaining their connections with Irish folklore. The scenery, in the heart of Yeats country is at once uplifting and soothing. By day, there are the forty fabled greens of the Irish countryside; by night, the stars shine in the endless sky.

You could, with the simple facilities provided, cater for yourself. Much nicer, though, to order from a range of tasty vegetarian dishes prepared by local chef Maria and delivered to your cabin. Indulge yourself with delicious local food and ravishing surroundings, and let the magic of Ard Nahoo wash over you. The focus here is firmly on relaxation. **SWi**

⬆ *Ard Nahoo provides an ethical break in the middle of breathtaking natural surroundings.*

Relax at O'Fabulous

Location County Donegal, Ireland **Website** www.ofabulous.com **Price** 💲💲

Small but perfectly formed, the glamorous retreat O'Fabulous more than lives up to its name. All glittering golds and shimmering glass, this boutique hotel in the heritage coastal town of Ardara has been beautifully styled. The late nineteenth-century building has five eclectic rooms to choose from, with beautifully soft cloud beds (an ingenious design of three layers) to sink into at night. The bathrooms come equipped with roll-top baths, heavenly Jo Malone toiletries, rainfall showers, and thick, soft robes to wrap up in. The furnishings are equally opulent and luxurious, featuring billowing layers of rich velvet, Irish linen, and cool satin and silk.

If you can tear yourself away to step outside, there are glorious windswept walks with stunning mountain views from the Glengesh Pass, as well as heather-clad moors to roam. Go to Loughros Point for views out across the Atlantic, then take in lungfuls of fresh air exploring Glenveagh national park—a nature reserve with Glenveagh Castle, a Victorian folly, set amid scenic lakes and woodland. This is the perfect setting for a dramatic and romantic getaway.

In fact, it is worth staying at O'Fabulous for the Irish breakfast alone—thick slabs of homemade bread, porridge with Irish whiskey, fresh-laid eggs with succulent sausages and bacon. The passion for food carries on throughout the day, with afternoon tea served by the fire. In the evening, the menu offers Donegal crab and creamy champ (mashed potato) together with a first-class wine list. Then retire to the retro cocktail bar to kick back with a Bellini in hand.

Far away from the tourist hordes, it is everything that a boutique hotel should be. Oozing sophisticated personality and luxury, O'Fabulous always makes for an indulgent, relaxing retreat. **AD**

⬆ *O'Fabulous is a feast for the eyes—ornate mirrors, elegant wall coverings, and chandeliers.*

Explore Lusty Beg Island

Location Fermanagh Lakes, Northern Ireland
Website www.lustybegisland.com **Price** 💲💲

Derived from the Gaelic word *Lusteabeg* meaning "small and fertile," Lusty Beg Island is a tranquil Irish idyll located in the northern tip of Fermanagh's Lower Lough Erne, 22 miles (35 km) from Enniskillen.

Once a penitential retreat for monks, the 75-acre (30-ha) island changed hands between various owners through the centuries, including a Canadian aristocrat, and a captain from the British army (who built the first chalet for rent in the 1950s), before it was passed back into the hands of a local couple. The island is now a protected bird sanctuary and isolated getaway for those looking for a quiet life.

Lusty Beg is accessible only by boat or ferry, the latter of which can carry just two cars at a time and crosses the lake on an archaic rope pulley system. Once on the island, there are no roads; one nature trail circumnavigates the shore, providing countless opportunities to spot local birdlife, including a colony of breeding sandwich terns, unique to the island. Kayaks are available for those who prefer to investigate the island from the water; other facilities include a games room, tennis courts, and an indoor pool.

Accommodation is varied, with a choice of bed-and-breakfast rooms or five-star self-catering chalets with private balconies overlooking the lakes. A short stroll from the living quarters is Island Lodge, housing the one bar on the island, which regularly entertains guests with traditional Irish music, and two excellent restaurants famed for their fresh fish.

Sailors and water sports enthusiasts will love Lusty Beg and might even be seduced by the secluded setting and quiet charm of the island, a place where time seems to stand still, making it difficult to do anything but stop, relax, and enjoy. **LM**

Stay at Belle Isle Castle

Location County Fermanagh, Northern Ireland
Website www.belleislecastle.com **Price** 💲

It is easy to be king of the castle—you simply have to rent your own. This seventeenth-century castle is one of Ireland's most luxurious vacation homes. It stands on the 470-acre (190-ha) Belle Isle Estate in County Fermanagh, close to the lough water's edge amid a landscape of lakes, islands, hills, and woods.

Guests can rent cottages and apartments, but the most memorable option is to have exclusive use of a wing of the castle. The eight bedrooms are a blend of original features with antiques and modern facilities. This means beautiful old furniture, working fireplaces, and gilt-framed paintings and mirrors. Guests have use of a kitchen and seven bathrooms, too.

"Nestling close to the water's edge and set within a landscape of lakes and islands of gently rolling hills."

discovernorthernireland.com

You can opt for self-catering, bring your own chef, or take advantage of the full catering service available. With an award-winning cooking school and working farm on the estate, quality is unlikely to be an issue. Guests also have use of a banqueting room for up to thirty diners with its own minstrels' gallery. The castle also offers an all-weather tennis court, game shooting, and pike fishing. Guests have access to a wooden cruiser that can carry sixteen people around the picturesque inlets and islands of Lough Erne. **SH**

➡ *Renovated in 1993, the seventeenth-century castle has a relaxed, country-house style throughout.*

Discover Tory Island

Location Donegal, Ireland
Website www.oileanthorai.com **Price** ⬤

> "[It is] a place of bewitching beauty . . . which has also beguiled generations of artists."

Kevin Connolly, BBC journalist

It is not often that visitors are greeted personally by the king upon arrival, nor is it customary to meet him in the local pub for a drink, but this is often the case on the windswept island of Tory, 9 miles (14 km) off the coast of Donegal. Despite its relative remoteness in the harsh Atlantic Ocean, Tory has a die-hard population of fewer than 180 people, all of whom proudly speak Irish as their first language. The island's history can be traced back 4,000 years to Neolithic times and counts Colmcille, or St. Columba, as one of its more famous sons. He built a monastery here in the sixth century, which dominated island life until it was destroyed by invading English troops in 1595; now only the bell tower remains standing.

Accessing the island can sometimes be a challenge, because high winds and furious seas dictate ferry times more than the timetable, but once on the rugged rock, it is easy to feel comfortable because everyone is inviting, warm, and courteous. There are a few places to stay, including the hotel near the port and a hostel, which are by no means luxurious, but you do not visit Tory to wallow in luxury, you visit for the *craic* (good times). Listen to Patsy-Dan Rodgers, the king of Tory, a fine accordion player and artist, regale you with tales of the island in the Club Soisialta (social club); sing and dance with the locals at a ceilidh or explore the nooks and crannies of the island that hold secrets of the past.

However you choose to spend time on Tory, a visit to this weather-beaten and seemingly little island teetering on the edge of civilization is sure to be relaxing, enjoyable, and invigorating. **LM**

◤ *The jagged rocks known as Balor's Teeth are named for an evil Formorian king who lived on the island.*

Stay at Scarista House

Location Isle of Harris, Hebrides, Scotland
Website www.scaristahouse.com   **Price** ⊖⊖

Walk across the huge empty sands at Scarista Bay on the Isle of Harris in the Outer Hebrides, then look back to the shore beyond the grassy dunes where hardy sheep graze in the salty spray. Alone in the center of the bay, with heather-covered mountains rising behind, is a whitewashed Georgian manse.

This little hotel is in one of the most beautiful and remote places in the United Kingdom. Scarista House is like a cozy, miniature country-house hotel, with open fires in antique fireplaces, big, comfy sofas, and old books, antiques, and framed prints everywhere. There is even a cuddly cat called Max. Guests hardly notice the absence of television.

> *"We walked for forty minutes on the beach . . . and met precisely four people."*

Caroline Boucher, *Observer*

Instead they lounge around the house eating and drinking or take walks across the spectacular 3-mile (5-km) beach strewn with shells trying to find otter footprints. Days are filled with boat trips around Harris or as far as the deserted island of St. Kilda. Guests can visit local artists, discover the standing stones at Callanaish, or simply tour the island in their car.

Scarista is highly acclaimed for its food. Many of the staples are made in the kitchen, such as bread, yogurt, cakes, muesli, marmalade, and ice cream. There is ample use of local ingredients: Scallops and lobsters are served fresh from the bay, and the Highland lamb once roamed the surrounding hills. **SH**

Unwind at Pool House

Location Ross-shire, Scotland
Website www.poolhousehotel.com   **Price** ⊖⊖

Nestling beneath tranquil mountains at the head of scenic Loch Ewe in Wester Ross in the northwest Scottish Highlands, Pool House is a lavishly romantic hideaway that wins awards for environmental friendliness as well as luxurious pampering. This 300-year-old house was once the home of Osgood Mackenzie, founder of the famous nearby Inverewe Garden. Since acquiring the hotel in 1991, Peter and Margaret Harrison and their daughters Liz and Mhairi have transformed it into a graceful haven of elegant Victoriana, crammed with antiques, paintings, porcelain, and curiosities.

Pool House oozes country elegance. Open log fires warm the wood-paneled rooms, including an opulent library with inviting sofas—the perfect setting for a lazy afternoon tea. The cozy bar boasts a huge selection of single-malt whiskies. The suites are enormous, sumptuously furnished, and individually styled. The huge beds, some of them four-posters, and spacious Victorian bathrooms create the air of a stately home. Although most suites maintain the Victorian theme, the Nairana suite reflects the grand palaces of Rajasthan, whereas Bramble is decorated with French antiques.

Fine dining overlooking the panoramic loch, beneath a ceiling shimmering with thousands of hand-painted stars, is a memorable experience, although exquisite sunsets and occasional otter sightings can cause guests to abandon their award-winning seven courses for the photo of a lifetime. Pool House is run almost entirely by the charming owners, and without a hint of ostentation. In so many ways, Pool House comes as close as any hotel to capturing the magic of the Scottish Highlands. **ML**

Explore Uig Sands

Location Isle of Lewis, Scotland
Website www.bailenacille.com **Price** 🟢🟢

At Baile na Cille there are always more beaches than guests. The tiny hotel stands next to Uig Sands, one of Britain's most remote but beautiful bays, and there are twenty-four other beaches within walking distance. Not bad for a hotel with a maximum of sixteen guests.

This is a chance to escape to your own beach; however, rather than sunbathing and swimming in the waves, you will be walking, picnicking, spotting birds and wildflowers, fishing, photographing, exploring, and just breathing the fresh air straight off the Atlantic. When it is time to go back inside again, there is the cozy old manse waiting for you.

The house's claim to historic fame is that this was where the Lewis chessmen were first brought on their discovery in the dunes in 1831. The chessmen turned out to be early Viking examples of the game. The hotel has been created from the former big old house plus its stables and outbuildings. There are three sitting rooms: one with TV, one with a stereo, and one with billiards and foosball. If the weather is wild outside, there are board games, jigsaw puzzles, and books, but if the sun is shining, there is a garden to sit in and a croquet lawn and grass tennis court.

Meals are hearty communal gatherings with fine dishes using plenty of local produce. There are enormous Scottish breakfasts on offer, including porridge if you want. Dinner is a five-course, no-menu feast, and the bedrooms are warm, cozy, and unpretentious. At Baile na Cille a sense of remote escape pervades everything, and you will definitely not get your cell phone to work here. **SH**

➡ *The garden of the hotel overlooks the beautiful 2-mile (3.2-km) golden stretch of Uig Sands.*

Experience Rua Reidh Lighthouse

Location Gairloch, Scotland
Website www.scotland-inverness.co.uk **Price** 🄢🄢

"We had decided to take it on just from the fantastic views as we drove along the clifftop road."

Proprietors, Rua Reidh Lighthouse

Rua Reidh Lighthouse's nearest neighbor is 3 miles (4.8 km) away and it is 12 miles (20 km) to Gairloch, the nearest village. At this white-painted retreat, perched on a heather-covered peninsula in the remote northwest Highlands of Scotland, you can expect to see a greater number of dolphins than humans.

In the converted keeper's house visitors can rent by the room or take the whole place, which sleeps twenty-six. There are two comfy sitting rooms with log fires, a conservatory, a drying room for those days when the Highland weather unleashes its storms, and terrific views over to Skye and the Western Isles to be admired while sipping your evening dram of Scotch.

The big attraction of this deserted headland is its wildlife, and Rua Reidh runs nature quest weekends: Otters are regular visitors to these shores, and whales, dolphins, basking sharks, and Atlantic seals are regularly seen in the sea. The craggy cliffs around the lighthouse, meanwhile, provide nesting areas for fulmars, shags, and kittiwakes, whereas the moors inland are home to golden plover and red grouse.

The lighthouse runs guided wildlife walks and family seashore outings during which children can catch butter fish, learn the difference between a limpet and a barnacle, and delve through rock pools for red anemones and crabs. Older children learn to light a fire, cook a limpet, and identify edible seaweed. The owners also organize rock-climbing courses and can book a trek through the Torridon Mountains. The route runs for 64 miles (103 km) through dramatic peaks and broad Atlantic beaches. **PE**

◹ *Rua Reidh Lighthouse was built in 1910 by a cousin of Robert Louis Stevenson; it is now fully automated.*

Stay at Castle Stuart

Location Inverness, Scotland
Website www.castlestuart.com   **Price** 🅢🅢🅢

Over 70 years ago, the Earl of Moray wanted to prove that his home, Castle Stuart, was not haunted, so he offered a reward to anyone brave enough to sleep in it. One dark night, a Highland poacher named Big Angus retired to the three-turret, haunted bedroom at the top of the east tower. In the morning, Big Angus's body lay cold and dead in the courtyard, a look of terror etched onto his face. Now the owners of this castle-hotel ask: "Are you brave enough to stay?"

Big Angus was not the only one to suffer here. This is a building rich in bloody history. The land was given to James Stuart, half-brother of Mary, Queen of Scots, in the sixteenth century. However, he was murdered,

---

"Letting people stay in the castle means sharing the history—it's very satisfying."

Proprietors, Castle Stuart

---

as was his son, who was brutally stabbed. The castle was completed in 1625 but as soon as the last stone was laid, the MacIntosh clan took over. A few years later, the Stuart king Charles I was executed, and Castle Stuart was abandoned. It lay derelict for 300 years.

Bought in the 1980s by Charles and Elizabeth Stuart, the castle has been restored and is now run as a luxury hotel. Open fires, tartan carpets, and antique furnishings tell of the castle's colorful past. Secret stairways, hidden doorways, and priest holes abound, and there is even a camouflaged revolving door that works as a shortcut to the drawing-room bar if you do not want to walk the long way around for your whiskey. **PE**

Enjoy Auld Haa House

Location Fair Isle, Scotland
Website www.tommyart.com   **Price** 🅢

Britain's most remote inhabited island is only 3 miles long by 1 mile wide (5 km by 1.5 km). It is so small and so awkwardly positioned (alone at the top of the North Sea, midway between the Shetlands and the Orkneys) that it is often omitted from maps.

Getting to Fair Isle is awkward and expensive, too. First you have to get to the Shetland or Orkney Islands, then continue by either plane or boat, depending on the day, season, and weather. Fog and storms sometimes cut the island off altogether. Yet this rocky dot, with 70 inhabitants, 1,000 sheep, and 150,000 seabirds, has a world-famous name. The Fair Islander's traditional knitting style is more famous than the place itself. A handful of home knitters keep the brand alive, and there is a knitting museum in the old stone schoolhouse, including a photograph of a 1920s model trying to look seductive in a Fair Isle knitted hat.

Stay at the cozy Old Haa, or old hall, originally built around 1700. The house has 3-foot (1-m) thick stone walls and a stone roof that have protected it for centuries against the worst Arctic storms. It has now been converted into a bed-and-breakfast, owned by a couple of American artists who are happy to run painting weekends for creative visitors.

The island's coastline is a spectacular series of towering cliffs and swooping bays. There are two lighthouses, a quirky shop, harbors, and beaches. The island's bird observatory staff will take visitors on a cliff walk to sit among the puffin colony and be dive-bombed by territorial skuas.

As well as knitters, there are dozens of craftspeople who are only too pleased to show visitors their wares. This can mean drinking tea in their crofts and talking about the weather all afternoon. **SH**

Discover Balfour Castle

Location Orkney Islands, Scotland
Website www.balfourcastle.co.uk   **Price** 💲💲

This is the most northerly castle-hotel in the world. It was the summer home of the Balfour family from the mid-nineteenth century until 1960, when the last of its heirs died. The castle was bought by Polish cavalry officer Captain Tadeusz Zawadzki and is now run by his Scottish wife and two of her daughters.

Despite the change of hands, the castle still oozes heritage. Log fires roar amid Victorian antiques. Stags' heads adorn the walls; gas used to be pumped through their antlers to illuminate lamps upon the tips. In the library, false bookshelves give onto a secret passage through which, legend has it, the Balfour family used to scurry when unwanted guests rang at their door. The laird's bedroom features a magnificent four-poster bed into which is carved the Balfour family's coat of arms. Another of the bedrooms adjoins a turret in which a shower room is housed.

The dining room serves local meat and game, fish caught in the surrounding Atlantic and North Sea waters, and fruit and vegetables grown in the castle's own kitchen garden. Guests who wish to catch their own dinner can help the hotel staff to haul in the lobster pots. The romantically inclined can wed in the castle's tiny chapel, which holds just twenty people.

History buffs can visit the 5,500-year-old village at Skara Brae, and for bird-watchers the Orkney Islands are paradise. Puffins nest here from May to July, and visitors commonly see razorbills, guillemots, fulmars, skuas, eider ducks, and Arctic terns. For those who want to get up close to the wildlife, it is said that the local seals swim toward those who whistle. **PE**

← *You would not think that just beyond the castle walls are uninhabited islands and sea caves to be explored.*

Stay at Lighthouse Cottage

Location Orkney Islands, Scotland
Website www.orkneylighthouse.com   **Price** 💲💲💲

There cannot be many places more remote than a lighthouse keeper's cottage in Orkney, off the most northern tip of the Scottish mainland. Rugged, raw, and utterly beautiful, it is the place to see porpoises, seals, and whales, as well as an abundance of seabirds.

Choose between two cottages, both designed and built by Thomas Stevenson (father of Robert Louis) and his brother David in the 1850s. Enough original features remain to let your imagination run wild and dream of stormy days when the headland was battered by fierce winds. The cottages are private and secluded, enclosed within walled grounds, 1 mile (1.6 km) from the nearest neighbor.

> *"When the lights come out, I am proud to think they burn more brightly for the genius of my father."*
>
> Robert Louis Stevenson, Scottish novelist

The island is a place of historic interest. Delve into local archaeological finds, including the Dwarfie Stane, thought to be Britain's only example of a rock-cut chamber tomb dating from the Neolithic period or early Bronze Age. There is good sea fishing from the cliffs around the lighthouse and trout fishing at nearby Heldale Water. The most well-known landmark is the Old Man of Hoy, a sea stack of rocks rising 450 feet (137 m) out of the Atlantic, which makes a challenging climb for even the most experienced rock climbers. Visit in autumn and winter and you might be treated to the greatest light show on Earth—the aurora borealis—with a free front-row seat. **AD**

Explore Armadale Castle Gardens

Location Isle of Skye, Scotland **Website** www.clandonald.com
Price $

Find inner peace while strolling quietly through this unexpectedly tropical garden, in the midst of the rugged and green Isle of Skye. Exotic flowers and trees thrive in this 40-acre (16-ha) woodland garden thanks to the Gulf Stream that treats this part of Scotland to a warm and frost-free climate.

Surrounding the ruins of Armadale Castle, the gardens are part of a sprawling 40,000-acre (16,185-ha) highland estate that was once in the hands of Clan Donald, one of Scotland's largest clans. The Clan Donald Lands Trust took over the estate in 1971, transforming the neglected grounds into the pristine gardens seen today. Groves of 200-year-old lime trees line the castle's main driveway, as well as more recently planted thuja and monkey puzzle trees. Keen gardeners will love the attention to detail: the herbaceous borders, the ponds dotted with water plants from around the world, and the wide variety of shrubs and trees. Beneath the trees are smatterings of bluebells, orchids, and wild meadow flowers. An oasis of tranquility, this glorious location is ideal for outdoor weddings, with both religious and civil ceremonies taking place in the grounds.

Leading off the gardens are a number of nature trails that offer uninterrupted views over the lovely Sound of Sleat, the body of water that separates the Isle of Skye from the Scottish mainland. The trails provide the best vantage points to see the wealth of wildlife in the area: Keep your eyes peeled for roe deer, red deer, otters, birds, and, if you are lucky, a golden eagle. The cost of this back-to-nature experience? A small entrance fee gains you access to the castle, the gardens, a museum, and the nature trails. **JK**

Walk to the Falls of Glomach

Location Lochalsh, Scotland **Website** www.lochalsh.co.uk
Price ◑

Brave the wilds of the West Highland mountains to reach one of Britain's highest waterfalls. You will need to pull on walking boots, though, because it takes a good five to seven hours to trek the challenging yet rewarding 5 miles (8 km) to the tumultuous Falls of Glomach, accessible only on foot.

East of Duich on the Scottish mainland, the falls are most dramatic after a bout of heavy rain, although bad weather can lead to poor visibility so it is best to hire a guide to avoid getting lost. Begin the hike at the National Trust for Scotland's countryside center in the hamlet town of Morvich. While walking through the

> *"Often the mountain gives itself most completely when I have no destination."*
>
> Nan Shepherd, Scottish poet

open hill country, you may be fortunate enough to spot rarely seen majestic red deer and golden eagles. The path to the waterfall may be well trodden, but it still feels gloriously secluded. Walkers can feel the waterfall's vibrations before they see it. "Glomach" means "gloomy," and you will understand why if you visit the falls in bad weather. When the temperature drops, the falls are framed by striking ice sculptures. Although there is not as much water during the summer months, the views are unparalleled. **JK**

▣ *Set in a steep gorge, the spectacular Falls of Glomach tumble 375 feet (114 m) down into a dark abyss.*

Eat at Three Chimneys

Location Isle of Skye, Scotland
Website www.threechimneys.co.uk **Price** ⊖

It is an unlikely spot for a gourmet restaurant—tucked away in an old whitewashed crofter's house on the northern shore of a remote loch. Yet the Three Chimneys is famous as one of Scotland's finest restaurants. Owner and chef Shirley Spear is renowned for her simple presentation of the local natural larder, with ingredients like Dunvegan langoustines, Mull lamb, wild Skye game, and Hebridean oatcakes. Many local producers, growers, and fishermen deliver their supplies every day. The award-winning wine list is the result of husband Eddie's passion. Three Chimneys is an intimate place to eat, with original fireplaces, bare stone walls, candlelit rooms, and low ceiling beams.

> *"I believe that we serve the most genuinely seasonal, local fresh produce available in Scotland."*

Michael Smith, head chef

Although the crofter's cottage is more than one hundred years old, next door are six suites in a modern, five-star annex called The House Over-By. The split-level rooms have wonderful sea views and are decorated in the simple style of the old restaurant. Each room has direct access to the garden through French doors that open off the sitting area. A hillside creek babbles atmospherically through the garden from where there is a gate leading to the seashore. Breakfast is served in the morning room in The House Over-By: a light, airy room with panoramic views over the loch and west to the mountains on the islands of Harris and North Uist in the Outer Hebrides. **SH**

Stay at Isle of Eriska Hotel

Location Near Oban, Scotland
Website www.eriska-hotel.co.uk **Price** ⊖⊖⊖

The Isle of Eriska Hotel is on a private 300-acre (121-ha) island just off the west coast of Scotland. Although the location might sound intimidatingly remote, it is actually linked to the mainland by a private iron bridge and is only two hours north of Glasgow.

The main house is a grand example of the Scottish baronial style of the nineteenth century: all turrets, battlements, and bays. Today, the five-star, twenty-five-bedroom hotel has an acclaimed restaurant and spa, and is famed for its outdoor activities. Inside, Eriska is as you would imagine: a wood-paneled hall with a fire that burns every day of the year and a piano room with views of the oak trees planted in 1884, the year the house was built.

Afternoon tea is rigorously observed with a daily-changing array of pastries, cakes, scones, and pancakes. Later, have cocktails in a leather armchair in front of the fire in the library before eating in the dining room or conservatory. Menus can depend on the shellfish boats that land at the pier, but oysters, mussels, and the hotel's own home-smoked salmon are usually available, and there is always a daily roast.

Bedrooms are plush havens, with lavish canopies, cushions, armchairs, curtains, and carpets. In the garden are more modern spa suites and cottages with their own private hot tubs. The stables, beside the old formal garden, house a 55-foot (17-m) pool, sauna, steam room, treatment rooms, and gym.

Guests find there is plenty to do across the island, including a six-hole golf course and driving range, clay-pigeon shooting, fishing, tennis, croquet, mountain biking, and simply strolling around. Farther afield there are mountain walks. The hotel will even lend you a GPS unit to make sure you do not get lost. **SH**

Enjoy the Boat Shed

Location Argyll, Scotland
Website www.ardanaiseig.com   **Price** 💲💲

It is a long, winding, and ever-narrowing single-track road to Ardanaiseig Hotel, but more than worth the effort to get there. On the banks of the crystal-clear Loch Awe, the nineteenth-century baronial mansion sits glowering over the dazzling expanse of water.

Although you could opt to stay in one of the traditional rooms, decorated in sumptuous rich colors and fabrics—with not a hint of tartan to be seen—it is far cozier to hole up in the wildly romantic converted Boat Shed, only two minutes' walk from the hotel. Perched over a jetty and lapped by the waters of the loch, the Boat Shed has double-height windows and offers heartbreakingly beautiful views over the loch to

> *"The vivid purity of the air and the intense almost eerie silence … provoked sublime reveries."*
>
> Rosie Doon, nineteenth-century poet

Ben Lui. Sit on the small wooden deck, breathe in the pure, heather-scented air, and feel your worries melt away. Or for the ultimate in decadence, snuggle up in bed on the mezzanine level and enjoy the spectacular vista while cuddled up with a warming whiskey.

There are self-catering facilities in the Boat Shed, but far better to trek up to the big house and treat yourself to a delicious dinner for which Ardanaiseig's kitchen is renowned. Try the ravioli of smoked haddock followed by some divine Scotch Aberdeen Angus, although you could be forgiven for having difficulty focusing on the food because the views from the dining room are so mesmerizing. It is the lure of the loch again. **HA**

Enjoy Eilean Shona House

Location Argyll, Scotland
Website www.eileanshona.com   **Price** 💲💲

On a private island just off the west coast of Scotland, Eilean Shona House is an unassuming Victorian hotel bordered by 200 acres (80 ha) of atmospheric Scots pines, redwoods, and Loch Moidart. A lungful of the aromatic pine-laden air immediately clears away the everyday. Breathe in.

Inside the house, the contemporary artworks establish an almost bohemian impression, whereas the antiques, granite fireplaces, and the faint rattle of sash and case windows create an authenticity that "new trying to look old" can never muster. Indeed, the row of boots at the door and the old upright Steinbach make you feel as if you are attending a private party.

There are eight guest bedrooms with pleasing period features—such as windowsill seats and enamel baths with brass taps—as well as five cottages in the grounds, in one of which J. M. Barrie stayed during the 1920s when he wrote the screenplay for *Peter Pan*. The large and informal gardens that fall away to the sea are full of azaleas and rhododendrons, which provide an explosion of color in late spring.

With an ever-changing skyline, the white sands of Shoe Bay, and complete tranquility, this is the place to stay if you long for beachcombing, crabbing, investigating rock pools, or reading under a blanket on the beach. If you are lucky, you might just see a sea eagle, the scamper of a pine marten (like a weasel but cuter), or the water-slicing tail of an otter.

Every evening, dinner is served in the rather Bloomsbury-esque dining room. Oysters, langoustines, and local game abound, with everything from the bread to the ice cream made in the kitchen. As you lay your head on the pillow, you might even hear the extremely rare corncrake calling for its mate. **SM**

Relax at Holy Island Center for World Peace

Location Holy Isle, Scotland **Website** www.holyisland.org
Price 💲💲

Refrain from killing. Respect other people's property and refrain from stealing; speak the truth and do not lie; refrain from intoxicants. You would be forgiven for thinking you had stumbled across a young offenders' institution, but these are actually some of the rules of the Holy Isle Center for World Peace and Health.

Situated off the west coast of Scotland close to Arran, the Holy Isle has a long history as a sacred site, with a spring said to have healing properties and evidence of a thirteenth-century monastery on the island. The center itself is a modest environmental and spiritual sanctuary founded by Lama Yeshe Losal. Visitors are free to spend the day in any way they wish, although most courses have their own daily programs. These include everything from yoga and meditation to vegetarian cooking, Buddhism, and other courses designed to connect you with your spiritual self. Meals are at set times of the day, and there is accommodation for more than sixty people in a range of rooms.

Right from the start, the Holy Isle Project has been dependent on volunteers to do everything from tree planting to dry-stone walling, building works, gardening, organizing courses, and running the center itself. Visitors are more than welcome to get involved, although there is no pressure to do a thing; you can simply sit and absorb the peaceful vibe. If all the navel-gazing gets too much for you, take the opportunity to explore some of the beautiful surroundings, where rare plants and wildflowers flourish in the Gulf Stream climate and wild Eriskay ponies, goats, and sheep roam. The island's protected coastal waters are also spectacular, and attract several species of seal, dolphin, and even the odd basking shark. **HA**

Take a Cruise on the *Hebridean Princess*

Location Scotland **Website** www.hebridean.co.uk
Price 💲💲💲

The smallest luxury cruise ship in the world, the *Hebridean Princess* has been likened to a floating country-house hotel. Think impeccable service, fine dining, and sumptuous surroundings, the perfect way to meander around the rugged Scottish islands.

There are never more than forty-nine guests on board, soaking up the atmosphere of understated elegance while watching the countryside unfold outside. With a ratio of almost one member of staff to every passenger, personal service is second to none. Have dinner in the Columba restaurant, where chefs prepare the finest local produce. Then have a whiskey

> *"The boat's dimensions allowed us to moor in small coves surrounded by breathtaking mountain scenery."*
>
> Jennifer Wilson, *Daily Express*

by the cozy inglenook fireplace in the Tiree lounge. The top-of-the-range cabin is the Isle of Arran, with a canopied bed and Victorian-style marble bathroom.

Each morning brings a new island or strip of land to explore on privately escorted tours. Spot rare birds, whales, and seals; go walking along *machair* (coastal plains) dotted with colorful wildflowers; or venture deep into lush glens to see ancient castles and standing stones. Come back on board for a good night's sleep and sail away to the next inspiring location. **AD**

➲ *The* Hebridean Princess *is able to slip into many remote lochs for the perfect scenic escape.*

Recharge at the Witchery

Location Edinburgh, Scotland   **Website** www.thewitchery.com
Price ⑤⑤

With its lavishly indulgent, antiques-filled suites hidden within atmospheric sixteenth-century buildings at the gates of the historic castle, The Witchery offers the most romantic accommodation in Edinburgh. Centered around a merchant's house dating back to 1595, the cluster of suites is a fantasy of gothic indulgence, verging on decadence. Each suite is filled with antiques and opulent period textiles. Walls are oak paneled and hung with tapestries, mirrors, and carvings; ceilings are ornately painted and gilded.

The original Witchery suite, the Inner Sanctum, sets the standard with its antique four-poster bed, dramatic red and gold walls, separate library–sitting room, and raised breakfast area overlooking the Royal Mile. The red lacquer bathroom contains an antique roll-top bathtub big enough for two. The baroque Old Rectory suite has oak paneling and red fabric walls and a lavish bed crafted from an antique pulpit. Tall gilded bookcases flank the marble fireplace, and a separate dressing room leads to the chapel-like bathroom with a painted vaulted ceiling and mirrored and gilded walls. The bathroom of the Library suite is a book-lined hideaway reached by a secret door, and also features a bathtub big enough for two.

The downside of such a perfect lust-den is that, with just seven suites, The Witchery is often booked months in advance, often by Hollywood stars such as Jack Nicholson and Michael Douglas. If you cannot get a room, book a table in the candlelit restaurant. It serves an award-winning modern Scottish menu and boasts sensational decor and opulent upholstery. **ML**

← *The Old Rectory bathroom is romantically styled and features mirrors on every wall.*

Unwind at Fenton Tower

Location East Lothian, Scotland
Website www.fentontower.co.uk **Price** 💲💲

In 1591, James VI of Scotland, son of Mary, Queen of Scots, found himself surrounded by a rebel army in Fife. Luckily the townspeople helped him to escape, and he took a ferry over the Firth of Forth to North Berwick, where he sought refuge at Fenton Tower. If the tower is fit for a king on the run, it is surely good enough for your average twenty-first-century urbanite looking for an escape from the madding crowds.

This magnificent fortified sixteenth-century tower, which stands proud over the fertile farmland of East Lothian, offers stunning views over the Firth of Forth and is just 20 miles (32 km) east of Edinburgh. For centuries it stood in ruins after being ransacked by English invaders, but in 1998 a meticulous restoration project was undertaken, and it now provides luxury accommodation for up to twelve people, combining modern facilities with the informality of a private home. Guests can enjoy impeccable service and outstanding cuisine in a secluded environment.

The warm pink harling on the exterior matches the original and was created by combining local soil with crushed seashells. With narrow defensive windows on the ground floor, you could be forgiven for thinking that the tower would be a gloomy place inside. The unusually large windows on the upper levels flood the rooms with natural light—some have a double or triple aspect, perfect for admiring the views.

Fenton Tower is surrounded by many excellent golf courses, including the world-famous Muirfield. There is also shooting and fly fishing aplenty. If you would prefer to make the most of being the king of your own castle, the tower has 20 acres (8 ha) of private land around which you can stroll, or simply daydream by the delightful *laich* (small Scottish lake). **HA**

Discover Y Goeden Eirin

Location Near Caernarfon, Wales
Website www.ygoedeneirin.co.uk **Price** 💲💲

A weekend at this homey bed-and-breakfast in a tranquil North Wales village offers much more than just a rural escape. Named after a collection of short stories written in Welsh by the dramatist John Gwilym Jones, it is less a guesthouse and more a center of learning about Welsh culture and arts—with rooms.

The co-owners, John and Eluned Rowlands, are former academics, and the house is lined with bookcases groaning under the weight of literary tomes. Original works by Welsh artists adorn the walls, attracting a steady flow of literary societies for dinners and academics for research trips. Welsh is the first language spoken around the house, and if you are

> *"An education in Welsh culture, and a stylish spot from which to explore the country."*
>
> **Alastair Sawday, travel writer**

interested to learn more about the local culture, John leads regular study evenings. Guests can also explore the area with its walking trails and historic castles.

The guesthouse itself is cozy and relaxed with accommodation for up to six people. A home-cooked dinner, prepared on the warming stove, is served in the dining room, furnished with a traditional Welsh dresser, of course. Evenings are focused around the lounge with a carafe of sherry and a good book. Most striking of all, however, is the little boy's room, where pieces of the Berlin Wall are displayed in a glass case, and a slab of Welsh slate, engrained with political slogans, stands guard over the washbasin. **DA**

Explore the Anglesey Coast

Location Anglesey, Wales
Website www.angleseycoastalpath.co.uk   **Price** 🏷️

Anglesey, the rural island in North Wales, is a pretty sleepy place, but the inauguration of the Isle of Anglesey Coastal Path is enticing visitors to explore the superb scenery of the North Wales coastline. The 125-mile (200-km) walking path, marked with distinctive yellow signs featuring the Arctic tern, passes through twenty towns and villages, where good facilities to eat, drink, and stay overnight can all be found within easy walking distance.

The full twelve-stage trail, along terrain that is gently undulating and suitable for all abilities, passes through a picture-postcard landscape of farmland, coastal heath, salt marsh, dramatic cliffs, and pristine beaches. Equip yourself with a copy of the O. S. Explorer maps 262 (west coast) and 263 (east coast) before setting out, and allow 2 weeks to cover the whole path, walking a daily average of around 7 miles (11 km). The path has its official start and end point at St. Cybi's Church in Holyhead, but each of the twelve stages can be tackled as an individual day hike, ranging from 7 to 13 miles (11 to 21 km) per day. Some of the sections, particularly the far northern trails from Cemaes to Church Bay, make for bracing strolls against a dramatic backdrop of wild, windswept scenery.

The most popular leg starts in Beaumaris and continues via Penmon Point, with great views across to Puffin Island, toward Llanddona, a pristine beach for swimming. This 6-mile (10-km) stretch on the eastern side of the island offers a good taster for the trail. The final stretch is a tiring 2 miles (3.2 km) along the shoreline, but well worth the effort. **DA**

↗ *The lighthouse on Llanddwyn Island remains attached to the mainland on all but the highest tides.*

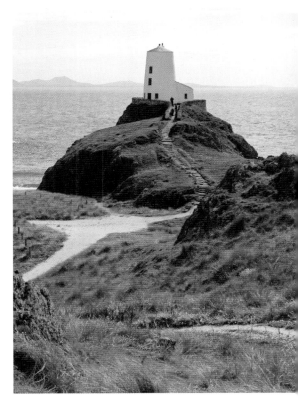

"Cemaes . . . is flanked by exceptionally attractive stretches of rugged coastline."

Isle of Anglesey County Council

Stay at St. Curig's Chapel

Location Snowdonia, Wales
Website www.stcurigschurch.com   **Price** $\ominus\ominus$

There is a wonderfully aristocratic and bohemian air to this hidden little bed-and-breakfast. The atmosphere owes something to a brazen, open-plan conversion of a nineteenth-century stone chapel and plenty to the exuberant personality of the owner.

Enjoy sumptuous distractions while you have breakfast sitting at a long wooden table, gazing out across the open space of the former apse. Around you are the chapel's original, elegant arched windows, marble pillars, stained glass, and, towering above everything, a stunning gilded mosaic domed ceiling. The dome was commissioned by William Sackville-West, a lieutenant-colonel in Her Majesty's Regiment of Grenadier Guards and local estate manager, in memory of his wife, Georgina.

St. Curig's was taken over by Lady Alice Douglas and her huge but docile dog Brecon in 1998. The renovation project was arduous, but the result is a unique and somewhat eccentric place to stay. The bedrooms are luxurious, with hand-carved four-poster beds and heated slate floors. One room still houses a stone pulpit.

There is nothing retiring about the bubbling hot tub in the corner of the former churchyard. It looks right up into the heart of the Snowdon horseshoe— the curve of peaks with Wales's highest mountain at its heart. Pen-y-Pas, the starting point of most paths up Snowdon, is a few minutes away by car. If you have just walked Snowdon, or any of the surrounding peaks, this is the perfect place to relax. Rest assured that less arduous forest paths lead right from the chapel door. Some even lead straight to a nearby pub. **SH**

➔ *St. Curig's was first opened in 1883; the B&B retains all the charm of the original chapel.*

Relax at an Eco Retreat

Location Powys, Wales
Website www.ecoretreats.co.uk **Price**

Rent Trehilyn Isaf Cottage

Location Pembrokeshire, Wales
Website www.underthethatch.co.uk **Price**

There is something stirring in the Dyfi Forest. As dawn breaks over Wales, the sun picks out an unusual array of shapes: four, 21-foot-diameter (6-m), North American Indian tepees and one 18-foot (5-m) Mongolian-style yurt in the middle of the forest. The encampment is an undeniably low-tech experience, with private compost toilets and solar showerbags to provide you with warm water, although some creature comforts can be found in the form of organic bed linen, china, and glassware.

The owners have leased the land from a local organic farm and only use fair-trade and locally-supplied goods in the welcome hampers. All the waste products go back to nourish the earth, and everything is recycled to keep the green credentials in impeccable order.

Eco Retreat is more of an experience than a mere place to stay: an escape from the trappings of modern life. There is no electricity, no running water, and, crucially, no reception for your cell phone. Cook at dusk and bed down on a plump mattress by candlelight. This is a place to let the mind wander, emerging cleaner, greener, and refreshed from the forest. Guests are invited to join a communal meditation session on their second night in camp, and a reiki/spiritual healing session is included as part of the deal. A free ticket for the nearby Center for Alternative Technology is also included. Most of all, however, this place is the ultimate chill-out zone with plenty of space, and you are guaranteed not to see a single soul from the door of your tepee as you look out over the silent forest. **DA**

⬅ *The Eco Retreat is an award-winning tourism project and offers a true get-away-from-it-all experience.*

As one of the best-preserved Pembrokeshire cottages, Trehilyn Isaf enjoys a wonderful coastal location on the Strumble Head peninsula, a landscape that is all black crags and megaliths, hills swathed in mist, and tall cliffs. If the cottage seems vaguely familiar, that might be because its restoration was filmed for the BBC television series *A Pembrokeshire Farm*. Local architectural historian Dr. Greg Stevenson advised on the program and calls the house "a complete gem."

The cottage, which is the greenest of the properties let by Welsh social enterprise company Under the Thatch, has been fully restored using authentic sustainable methods such as low-toxin paints, sheep

"The house feels alive—not in an Amityville way—and organically a part of the landscape."

Niall Griffiths, *Guardian*

wool for insulation, lime for rendering the cottage, and carbon-neutral central heating. Although the beautifully renovated old farmhouse may be environmentally friendly, this is not at the expense of modern creature comforts. Inside, the cottage is the perfect fusion of traditional features, such as a huge inglenook fireplace, and sleek minimalism. It is the kind of place you walk into and feel instantly calm.

If you can tear yourself away from your snug little sanctuary, make sure you enjoy the spectacular walk to Aber Mawr Bay, surrounded by rugged cliffs a couple of miles away, and check out the stunning views at nearby Strumble Lighthouse. **HA**

Unwind at Seaham Hall

Location County Durham, England
Website www.seaham-hall.co.uk   **Price** ⬡⬡

Seaham Hall & Serenity Spa has a great history. In the late eighteenth century, it was constructed as a vast stately home. It later became famous as the place where Lord Byron married Annabella Milbanke in 1815. Throughout World War I, the hall was used variously as a military hospital, tuberculosis sanatorium, pioneering cardiac treatment center, and nursing home until—finally—in 2002, the building was restored to its former glory and redeveloped by Tom and Jocelyn Maxfield as a world-class luxury hotel and spa.

One of the most notable things about the newly reincarnated Seaham Hall is the impressive plethora of contemporary art. Stained-glass artist Bridget Jones has created a ceiling in the lobby atrium based on Byron's poetry. The work of painters Dale Atkinson and Paul Gallagher adorns the walls, and sculptural works by Nicolaus Widerberg, Andrew Burton, and William Pye can also be found throughout the hotel. The nineteen suites are reliably modern, with "intelligent" lighting and adjustable air-conditioning. Some have two-person baths. The drawing room (where Byron married Milbanke) is still licensed for civil weddings, whereas the White Room restaurant serves up delicious, simple food at wooden tables.

Yet the hotel is only half of the story. Follow an underground tunnel to discover the Serenity Spa: Asian in design and offering more than forty-five treatments for soul, body, and mind. Amid the revitalizing scent of jasmine and the sound of flowing water, you will find a lovely 65-foot (20-m) swimming pool, black granite steam room, plunge pools, ice fountain, and traditional Turkish hammam. Not only a pretty face, Seaham Hall also delivers some quite serious inner healing, too. **PS**

Relax at Swinton Park

Location North Yorkshire, England
Website www.swintonpark.co.uk   **Price** ⬡⬡

If you like your English grandeur, then Swinton Park makes the perfect escape. This thirty-bedroom luxury castle-hotel comes complete with its own turrets, long echoing corridors, and enormous staircases leading up to what are huge, individually decorated and designed bedrooms.

Swinton Park makes an ideal retreat for anyone looking to explore the surrounding Yorkshire Dales, but with 200 acres (80 ha) of its own lakes, gardens, and parkland, there is little reason to venture farther afield. If you are feeling adventurous, you can have a go at a bit of falconry, fishing, or off-road driving. The restaurant at Swinton Park is worth a visit, too. With

> *"The view of deer, daffodils, and emerald parkland forced us into our wellies for a blustery walk."*
>
> Jill Hartley, *Guardian*

much of the produce grown in the 4-acre (1.6-ha) walled garden, the biggest of its kind in the United Kingdom, the emphasis is on delicate seasonal cuisine. The hotel is well established as a haven for culinary fans because it also has its own cooking school, run by celebrity chef Rosemary Shrager.

When you have finished your day's activities, why not retire to the games room for a frame of snooker or treat yourself to a massage in the spa and whirlpool tub? This is English country living at its finest. **RS**

➡ *Swinton Park is the kind of place where you expect to bump into Jeeves and Wooster.*

Walk the Wolds Way

Location Yorkshire, England   **Website** www.nationaltrail.co.uk
Price ◑

To the inhabitants of Yorkshire, this region is "God's own county," and it is not difficult to see why. Wild, expansive, tranquil, at times even awesome, the breathtaking scenery seems to go on forever. Hidden away in this landscape is Britain's most peaceful national trail, which was created twenty-five years ago by a group of rambling enthusiasts.

The 79-mile (127-km) Yorkshire Wolds Way remains the least visited of England's national trails. For many, that is a blessing: There is an overwhelming sense of freedom, and it is not unheard of to wander alone for days without chancing upon another soul. Walkers are more likely to catch a glimpse of some unexpected wildlife—an occasional deer grazing on a slope or a kestrel soaring high overhead.

The views are astonishing: from sweeping vistas south across the Humber to the towers of Lincoln Cathedral at the start of the walk, or north to the dramatic outcrop of Filey Brigg at its finish. You will pass by England's famous deserted medieval village at Wharram Percy, abandoned at the time of the Black Death in the fourteenth century, and the many Bronze Age burial mounds that decorate the Wold tops. The villages along the way can make visitors feel like they are stepping back in time. You do not need to arrive on horseback to call in at the Ferry Inn at Brough, although it is the place where the highwayman Dick Turpin was arrested. After a reputed 200-mile (322-km) dash from London on his trusty mare Black Bess, the long arm of the law finally caught up with Turpin in 1739, and he was hanged soon afterward at York. **SWi**

◧ *The Yorkshire Wolds Way wends through dramatic open field tops, chalk valleys, and pretty villages.*

Relax at The Samling

Location Lake District, England   **Website** www.thesamling.com
Price ◔◔

Think of The Samling as a home away from home, albeit a particularly luxurious one with beautifully rugged views of Lake Windermere, a bubbling outdoor hot tub, and a well-stocked wine cellar. From the moment they arrive, guests are made to feel that this is their domain, a place where formalities should be left at the door. It is hard not to unwind as the pretty, eighteenth-century, gabled house works its charms in minutes and cocoons you in warmth.

Clusters of colorful clematis and Virginia creeper give The Samling its lived-in appearance. There are just thirteen individual suites—many with gorgeous lake views—and each room has a unique character

> *"... nowhere in so narrow a compass with such a variety of the sublime and beautiful."*

William Wordsworth, on the Lake District

and features. For example, Methera, decorated in cool blues and greens, has a separate sitting area with fireplace and is bathed in sunlight for much of the day, whereas The Bothy is a cottage close to the main house with a Victorian bath and rain shower, and a sitting room set into a conservatory.

The decor combines traditional character with contemporary comfort, so there are lots of open fires, candles, and two-person bathtubs. The Samling is a place where visitors relish being holed up, although with 67 acres (27 ha) of land and, of course, the stunning Lake District scenery on the doorstep, there is much to experience outside, too. **LP**

Explore the Leeds and Liverpool Canal

Location Leeds to Liverpool, England
Website www.penninewaterways.co.uk/ll **Price** ⑤

There are few more relaxing ways to travel than by narrow boat. Once you have mastered the rudder system of steering—push left to go right, right to go left—off you go, at a pace slightly faster than walking.

The Leeds and Liverpool canal has 150 years of history rising up along its banks and the story of the Industrial Revolution unfolds before your eyes. Shipley, Saltaire, and Skipton may not have quite the same ring as Hamburg or Florence, but you will marvel at the grand architecture of the former millhouses and candy factories, designed and built with the care previously reserved for cathedrals. Step ashore and wander

---

> *"Vessels 60 feet long, 14 feet wide, and 3.5 feet deep can pass through its ninety-two locks."*

Leeds and Liverpool Canal Society

---

around the remarkable "model" village of Saltaire, created by the impressively named Titus Salt for his workers. The harmonious design of the houses is matched by the solid beauty of the library, gymnasium, concert hall, and factories with their majestic chimney towers, modeled on Tuscan campaniles.

Titus Salt ensured there were no pubs in Saltaire, but the Leeds and Liverpool canal has got some wonderful places to drink beer. One of the greatest pleasures during a narrow boat vacation, next to firing up the engine on a misty morning after a hearty breakfast, is mooring up at a riverside pub as the sun goes down and strolling up to the bar for a pint. **SWi**

Visit Kielder Water and Forest Park

Location Northumberland, England
Website www.visitkielder.com **Price** ❶

If it is peace and tranquility you are after, look no further than Kielder Water and Forest Park. It is famed for having the darkest night skies in England, thanks to minimal light pollution, and also happens to be situated in Northumberland, which was recently voted the most tranquil spot in the country by the Campaign to Protect Rural England.

The park is home to northern Europe's largest man-made lake and England's largest forest. With more than 232 square miles (600 sq km) to explore by bike, on horseback, or on foot, the park is so large that there is room to get away from it all and not bump into another soul for hours. For leisurely strolls or rides, there is a multitude of forest trails to choose from, including the lakeside way, which hugs the 27-mile (43-km) Kielder Water shoreline. In this haven for wildlife, expect to see deer, otters, badgers, bats, and rare species of birds. The park is also home to around 60 percent of England's native red squirrel population, the last remaining stronghold in the country.

Thanks to its inky black skies, Kielder Water and Forest Park and the Kielder Observatory are perfect for stargazing; you can learn more about astronomy in the observatory, which is open most days and occasionally in the evenings. There is also an abundance of contemporary art and architecture in this striking rural setting. With plenty of picnic spots and places to eat throughout the park, visitors are spoiled for choice when it comes to spending a day or weekend in this most peaceful area of England. **HA**

➡ *Its pure air and wilderness make Kielder Water and Forest Park stunning to walk around and explore.*

Enjoy Coombe Abbey

Location Warwickshire, England
Website www.coombeabbey.com **Price** 💲💲

Cistercian monks founded Coombe Abbey in 1150. Today, the lavish boutique hotel invites you to "come live like lordes and ladyes" at their award-winning medieval banquets. Set within 500 acres (202 ha) in the historic heartland of Warwickshire, the property has been fully restored and feels voluptuously romantic. No wonder it is so popular for weddings.

All the modern amenities are here, too, including wireless Internet access at your fingertips, satellite TV, and twenty-four-hour room service. Marvel at the historic artifacts and a plethora of special touches in every room. Modern fittings are cleverly concealed behind period details, so you may find the bathroom behind the bookcase. There are eighty-three rooms in all. Splash out with one of eight unique "grand feature" rooms such as the Chinoiserie or the Lady Craven Suite. The Chinoiserie has a lavish Asian theme with a sprawling view of the lake and formal gardens, whereas the Lady Craven Suite's centerpiece is a four-poster bed crowned with ostrich feathers.

The acclaimed medieval banquets give you the opportunity to step back to the year 1539, complete with food, music, and merriment from a bygone era. Guests are treated to entertainment by candlelight and a four-course feast of court classics, such as Baron's Broth and Royal Rib. If murder and mayhem are more your cup of tea, attend a spine-tingling murder mystery dinner set at the turn of the century. Another haunting experience awaits with "Ghostly Goings On," during which you can learn about Coombe Abbey's past before sitting down to three unforgettable courses. If those who do not learn from history are doomed to repeat it, then Coombe Abbey is the way to brush up in style. **JS**

Stay at Hambleton Hall

Location Rutland, England
Website www.hambletonhall.com **Price** 💲💲

Hambleton Hall is a former Victorian hunting lodge that was opened more than twenty years ago by banker Tim Hart. It is situated on the dreamy lakeside of Rutland Water and serves up a winning formula of fabulous food and impeccable service in divine interiors.

The seventeen bedrooms lie under the eaves and most have charmingly sloping ceilings; all but a couple overlook the lake. Beautifully decorated in a traditional yet elegant style, the rooms have big comfy beds and hunting prints on the walls. This is one hotel that has not succumbed to the trend of opening a spa. As Tim Hart says, "Why would you want to come to a place like this and spend all your time in the basement?"

"This is one of those rare hotels where guests feel not just pampered, but treasured."

Daily Mail

It would be a crime not to go out and explore the sweeping blue expanse of Rutland Water, Europe's largest man-made lake. Indeed, guests are not short of activities here, although foxhunting is no longer an option. That still leaves an array of pursuits, including walking or bicycling around the lake, bird-watching, and trout fishing. Whatever you do, be sure to build a large appetite because the food at Hambleton is stunningly good. Award-winning chef Aaron Patterson uses only the best local ingredients, and his dishes have a strong seasonal bias, which produces brilliant cooking. There may be no gimmicks or fashionable additions to this hotel, but no need. **HA**

Eat at the Olive Branch

Location Rutland, England
Website www.theolivebranchpub.com **Price** 🟢🟢

The Olive Branch must be everyone's idea of the perfect English country pub. With its thatched roof and honey-colored stone, the place is as pretty as a picture. Walk though the honeysuckle-strewn garden, push open the door, and you will find yourself in a cozy low-beamed room, complete with crackling log fire, stripped pine tables, antique chairs, and church pews laid out for lunch.

We are not talking about typical pub offerings either; the food here is simply outstanding. You do not need to take our word for it; the pub is the proud possessor of one Michelin star. With the focus firmly on seasonal and locally produced ingredients, the kitchen has the pick of trout freshly caught from nearby Rutland Water, spring lamb from award-winning butcher Nelsons, pork from the farm next door, and freshly picked berries from the hedgerows. Tuck into classic fish-and-chips with homemade tomato sauce and minted peas, or char-grilled rib eye steak with chunky fries. The wine list is impressive, too, with a fine selection of both old- and new-world wines. You may think you have died and gone to pub heaven, but it gets even better—you do not actually have to go home. Simply stagger across the road to Beech House, a charming little Georgian guesthouse under the same ownership as the Olive Branch.

The attention to detail that makes the Olive Branch such a success has been applied with equal care to Beech House. The six rooms are tastefully decorated in restful shades of green, chocolate, and lilac. Antique French beds, hand-stitched mattresses, Egyptian linen sheets, and duck-down comforters ensure a blissful night's sleep. Awake refreshed and ready to do justice to a full, tasty breakfast served back in the pub. **HA**

Relax at Cotswold House

Location Cotswolds, England
Website www.cotswoldhouse.com **Price** 🟢🟢

Situated in the center of chocolate-box-pretty Chipping Camden, in the heart of the Cotswolds hills in western-central England, the Cotswold House hotel makes the perfect retreat for a sublime weekend. It is a hotel whose owners have thought of everything to make your stay as blissful as possible. From the oversized, impossibly comfy beds and the pillow menu to ensure the perfect night's sleep, to the fabulous bathrooms with power showers and in-room TVs, Cotswold House offers every creature comfort. The bespoke minibar enables you to indulge in your favorite tipple without having to wait for room service, underfloor heating warms your toes on a chilly

> *"This luxurious 17th-century house with its elegant modish interiors offers 'à la carte' bedrooms."*
>
> Kate Simon, *Independent*

winter's morning, and free broadband connection in every room allows you to keep in touch with the office—should you absolutely have to.

The hotel is independently owned, and the service reflects a desire to ensure every guest has an unforgettable stay. Of course, the hotel is effortlessly stylish, too. The quaint and cozy cottage garden rooms come with sloping ceilings, beams, and open fires—one even has its own private garden and hot tub—whereas in Montrose House, the eight rooms have a more contemporary feel with giant stone baths and mood lighting. The wonderful Juliana's Restaurant and spa facilities make this a perfect stay. **HA**

Recharge at the Dovecote

Location Buckland, England **Website** the-dovecote.co.uk
Price ⑤⑤

Recently voted one of the most romantic hideaways in the United Kingdom, the Dovecote, situated in the grounds of Buckland Manor, near Oxford, certainly fits the bill for most lovebirds. The accommodation in this eighteenth-century dwelling is so comfortable and inviting that guests are loath to leave.

The former dovecote, which fell into disrepair in the early twentieth century, has since been restored and converted into a cozy, self-catering love nest, which can sleep up to four people. Inside the historic building, the potence remains—a technical term for the central pole and ladder—and the original 1,200

> *"Most couples spending the weekend in the . . . Dovecote don't even bother going out."*
>
> Liz Bird, *Observer*

dovecote boxes still line the walls. Dovecotes vary in size and shape, and this one is octagonal and impressively large, with exposed red brickwork. A steel spiral staircase leads up from the kitchen and dining area to a Nordic sauna and double shower. Up more stairs and you will find the bedroom, in the eaves of the building, which offers exceptional privacy.

The local pub, The Lamb, can deliver food to your door if you are feeling too lazy to cook. If you do decide to venture out, there is much to do and see in the local vicinity: Oxford is only a thirty-minute drive away, as is Sir Winston Churchill's birthplace, Blenheim Palace, with its Capability Brown landscape. **HA**

Dine at Le Manoir aux Quat' Saisons

Location Oxfordshire, England **Website** www.manoir.com
Price ⑤⑤⑤

Arriving at Raymond Blanc's Le Manoir aux Quat' Saisons, you wonder how much of an escape this can be, given that it is within roaring distance of the M40 motorway. Driving through the ornamental gateway and into the imposing front entrance, though, you are quickly transported into the world-famous chef's tranquil hideaway, nestling behind the honey-colored stone walls. This is the kind of place where the emphasis is so much on making sure you have the perfect stay that it seems your arrival has been planned in minute detail for days beforehand.

Doors are opened before you get the chance to look for a doorknob; bags are slipped out of your hand and whisked away before you wonder what to do with them. Everything is done to make you feel special, regardless of which room you are staying in. However, this is not one of those scary, pompous places where you dare not sneeze or raise your voice. Here, the overwhelming mood is relaxed and easygoing.

Great attention to detail is paid to the "food, comfort, service, and welcome" at Le Manoir, and no room is the same—perfect for repeat visits. With two Michelin stars to his name, Blanc is one of the few household-name chefs who are still very much hands-on in their own kitchen. Treat yourself to the ten-course Le Decouverte tasting menu and prepare to have your taste buds transported to foodie heaven. Make sure you also find the time to take a stroll around the hotel garden. Here grows much of the fresh produce that later will end up on your plate. **RS**

→ *Le Manoir is designed to make you feel at home from the moment you arrive in the grounds.*

Punt on the Cherwell

Location Oxford, Oxfordshire, England
Website www.cherwellboathouse.co.uk   **Price** $

When it comes to boating vessels, there can be nothing more peculiarly English than the punt, a flat-bottomed boat with a square-cut bow, designed for use on small rivers. The punter propels the boat along with a long pole by pushing it against the riverbed. Sometimes he falls in, or gets stuck in low-hanging branches, and everything goes wrong.

For those in search of a rural idyll in the heart of a bustling university town, punting in Oxford makes for a blissed-out experience. It mostly takes place on the River Cherwell, which flows through Oxford's green belt of fields and woods, before joining the Thames near bucolic Christ Church Meadow. There are various

---

"Spend the day [passing] historic Oxford colleges, botanical gardens, and tranquil English countryside."

oxfordpunting.co.uk

---

places to get on a punt, but Madgalen Bridge is too crowded and Folly Bridge is a hazard, with many long rowboats and motorized boats flying around. The pastures of Port Meadow offer good shallows for punting, but the best jumping-off point is the Cherwell Boat House. On the banks of the Cherwell, this idyllic boathouse is a restaurant, café, and punt station extraordinaire. *Brideshead Revisited* fans will be in their element, but cream flannels, Champagne, blazers, and strawberries are optional these days. **LB**

◄ *A few lazy hours on the river in a handcrafted punt is a highly civilized way to spend a summer's day.*

Experience Malmaison

Location Oxford, Oxfordshire, England
Website www.malmaison-oxford.com   **Price** $ $

On the whole you would not consider a prison to be the kind of place you might want to escape to. The former Oxford castle, which recently became the United Kingdom's first prison to be converted into a boutique hotel, offers the kind of luxurious living that former convicts could only have imagined.

Originally constructed by William the Conqueror in 1071 and later extended, the castle sits in a 5-acre (2-ha) site. On passing through a restored courtyard, visitors enter the imposing frontage of the hotel, complete with flag-adorned turrets and cruciform arrow slits. In more recent decades, the building was better known as H. M. Prison Oxford, and *The Italian Job* starring Michael Caine was filmed on location here.

Now, with ninety-four sleek and chic bedrooms, a buzzy bar, and a brasserie, Malmaison Oxford is a place where you would be more than happy to serve a lengthy sentence. On entering, the first area you encounter is the most memorable: A Wing is a vast, glass-roofed atrium with galleried landings lining the walls above. Linked by iron staircases, the whitewashed walls of these floors are studded with tiny red doors—the original cells. Three cells have been knocked together to form each guest room, and inside the arched windows remind guests they are also in a castle.

Present-day inmates are spoiled in a way that former prisoners could only dream of: extra-comfy beds, crisp white sheets, power showers, minibars, and mood lighting all conspire to make you feel utterly indulged. Little touches like the toiletries you are encouraged to take away, DVDs in every room, and a CD library all help to make Malmaison a place where you would be delighted to spend a stretch of time. **HA**

Relax at The Victoria

Location Norfolk, England   **Website** www.holkham.co.uk
Price $

Situated opposite the pine-tree-studded, sandy path that leads down to the beautiful Holkham beach, The Victoria has become the place to stay for many visitors looking to explore the north Norfolk coastline. Combining a relaxed, family atmosphere with enough edge and chic to keep the hordes of weekenders happy, The Victoria has the feel of a popular pub, mixed with the exclusiveness of a boutique hideaway.

Food at The Victoria is designed to suit the everyday palate, but the use of seasonal local produce means the menu is always changing and is full of Norfolk delights, such as crab from nearby Cromer or venison and game from the Earl of Leicester's adjoining estate. Guests quickly feel at home, be it lolling around in a compact, individually designed bedroom, or grabbing a latte in one of the quiet, cozy lounges.

The beach is the big draw here, though. It is ideal for taking long, windswept walks surrounded by blue sea and dramatic skies, or building sand castles with the kids. If Holkham looks familiar, that could be because it was immortalized in the closing scenes of the Hollywood movie *Shakespeare in Love*, when Gwyneth Paltrow got sand between her toes. After a day on the beach, head back to the hotel, where traditional English style meets the days of the Raj in the form of the claw-footed bath in your room, or the Adnams ale on tap at the bar, and the imported Rajasthani furniture and other colonial artifacts that add to the bohemian charm. If you really want to hide away, you can stay in one of the three lodges within the earl's estate that have been restored recently. **RS**

→ *Holkham Estate provides a rich and varied habitat for wildlife, including several endangered species.*

Unwind at Strattons

Location Norfolk, England
Website www.strattons-hotel.co.uk   **Price** ⊖⊖

Strattons, a beautiful redbrick Queen Anne country house in the sleepy market town of Swaffham, looks traditional enough from the exterior. However, although the service is old-fashioned—in the best possible way—there is a very modern ethos behind the running of this boutique hotel.

Owners Vanessa and Les Scott, who met at art school in the 1970s, run the hotel on environmental principles, and have a clutch of awards to show for it. They have a firm policy of sourcing organic, locally produced food whenever possible, supporting local suppliers, and recycling waste. Yet Strattons's eco-credentials do not come at the expense of comfort. Every room is individually and artistically decorated. The vibe at Strattons is decidedly eclectic. There are cowhide rugs on the wooden floors, marble busts, and sculptures artfully placed. Murals and stained glass are dotted around, and original art hangs on the walls. Each of the ten bedrooms is stunning; choose the romantic Red room, with its four-poster bed, deep-red walls, and Moroccan-styled bathroom, or the Venetian room, with its practically life-sized mural of Botticelli's *Venus* on the bathroom wall.

It is the food, though, that really impresses at Strattons. Everything on the menu, from the breakfast chocolate bread to the after-dinner chocolates and petit fours, is made on the premises. With hens scratching quietly around the lawn, it is easy to understand why the breakfast eggs taste so fresh. And feast like a king at dinner, too, when the cheese board is particularly noteworthy. Groaning under the weight of a dizzying array of Norfolk and other British cheeses, the waiter is able to discuss them all in encyclopedic detail. This is foodie heaven indeed. **HA**

Enjoy House in the Clouds

Location Suffolk, England
Website www.houseintheclouds.co.uk   **Price** ⊖⊖⊖

This strange house, seemingly 70 feet (21 m) up in the trees, is one of the United Kingdom's favorite follies, and it is now used as a vacation house with sensational views of the Suffolk coast.

Back in the 1920s, Scottish landowner and playwright Glencairn Stuart Ogilvie decided to create a vacation village at Thorpeness that fitted his visions of "life as it was when England was Merrie England." It was to be constructed around classic English pastimes, centering on healthy open-air pleasures. It sat right on the beach, with manicured lawns, pretty vacation cottages, and a man-made lake with brightly colored rowboats at its center, much as it is today.

> *"The fairies really own this house, or so the children say ... all of them moved in upon the self same day."*

Mrs. Malcolm Mason, writer, 1923

The village lacked a supply of water, so a water storage tower was built. Because its ugly exterior spoiled the skyline, Ogilvie disguised the tower as a house. From miles around, it looks like the little red house is lodged in the trees, hence its name. These days the quirky house is a retreat into childhood fantasy and a wonderful place for a family vacation. It can easily sleep twelve guests and has 1 acre (0.4 ha) of private grounds. Inside, the decor is true to 1920s English style: wood-paneled rooms, portraits on the walls, and a large oak table in the kitchen. The view from the top is the crowning glory, and small children cannot help but be fascinated by the house in general. **LD**

Stay at Tuddenham Mill

Location Suffolk, England
Website www.tuddenhammill.co.uk **Price** 🟢🟢

There has been a mill at Tuddenham for more than 1,000 years, although the present building dates back to 1775. Today, it has been brought right up to date in a renovation project that has melded the mill's original features with the best in contemporary style.

Automatic glass doors swish open to reveal a chic lobby area with flagstone floors and dark wood. A blazing fire in the corner adds a touch of warmth. The whitewashed rooms are light and airy, supported by huge exposed oak beams. The furniture is stylish, modern, and Italian, whereas the bathrooms are kitted out with Starck accessories, some with huge egg-shaped stone bathtubs big enough for two, others with state-of-the-art, walk-in showers. Oversized beds with cozy feather duvets provide the essentials for a good night's sleep, together with Jo Malone toiletries and Missoni bathrobes. Sounds come courtesy of trendy Bose hi-fi systems, and the huge flat-screen televisions are perfect for watching the extensive DVD collection. Despite these twenty-first-century luxuries, there are constant reminders of the original function of the mill; the old cast-iron water wheel has been restored and housed in a glass casing in the bar to become a magnificent architectural feature, brought to life at night by original and imaginative lighting.

Dinner is a showcase of delicious local produce served up under the stewardship of ex-Gleneagles chef Gordon McNeill. Try Cromer crab and lobster, or lamb from the neighboring Elveden Estate just 10 miles (16 kilometers) away. Afterward, take a stroll around the surrounding countryside, past the swans gliding on the millpond, and like many urbanites before you, indulge in a dream of leaving the city behind and moving to this bucolic rural idyll. **HA**

Recharge at the Elms

Location Worcestershire, England
Website www.theelmshotel.co.uk **Price** 🟢🟢

Going on vacation with children can be a contradiction in terms. The newly refurbished Elms Hotel, a fabulous Queen Anne mansion in the Worcestershire countryside, offers the perfect sanctuary for stressed-out parents. There is no need to leave the kids behind because the Elms, set in 10 acres (4 ha) of mature parkland with stunning views over the Terne Valley, is the perfect setup for families.

Leave the little ones in the day care center, or let older children entertain themselves with the air hockey machine, foosball, board games, and even an Xbox. Outside are soccer nets, croquet, a trampoline, and a fantastic adventure playground for the kids to

---

"It does make you feel as though you're staying with wealthy friends for the weekend."

Simon Hughes, *Daily Telegraph*

---

burn off some energy while you sneak off to the Aqua Sulis spa for some well-deserved pampering. Afterward, cool off in the pristine pool, which has an adults-only area so you do not have to battle with screaming kids while trying to get in a few lengths.

One of the best things about the Elms is the divine food, especially at dinnertime, when the menu really comes into its own. Get the children settled for the night, use the hotel's complimentary listening service, then settle down in one of the lounges with a large gin and tonic before succumbing to the delights of head chef Darren Bale's delicious cooking. Whoever said family vacations had to be stressful? **HA**

Relax at Hartwell House

Location Buckinghamshire, England
Website www.hartwell-house.com **Price** ⊖⊖⊖

Staying at Hartwell House, a country house of architectural interest, set in 990 acres (400 ha) of landscaped park designed by Capability Brown, is more akin to staying at a friend's home—albeit a terribly grand, well-heeled one—than a hotel. There are no bossy signs telling you what you should and should not do, and the service is discreet but impeccable.

Butlers bearing the perfect gin and tonic appear as if by magic while you snuggle up in front of a log fire. Squashy sofas and piles of magazines add to the feel that you are just hanging out with your rich friends. The rococo-style morning room with marble chimney pieces and an ornate ceiling is especially grand.

> *"[Hartwell is] a saga of historic landscape design: nearly all periods can be found."*
>
> Sir Geoffrey Jellicoe, landscape architect

Hartwell House's pedigree stretches back nearly 1,000 years; it was mentioned in the Domesday Book, and the exiled King Louis XVIII of France held court here.

The bedrooms are certainly fit for royalty; most are vast and many overlook the parkland. Hartwell does not bother with gimmicks—you will not find any huge plasma screens here. Instead the hotel focuses on what is really important. The beds are dreamily comfortable, the bathrooms are piled high with huge fluffy towels, and the water pressure is torrential.

If you are not sufficiently chilled out already, head to the spa, which offers a range of treatments to make you feel as pampered as a king—or queen. **HA**

Stay at Luton Hoo

Location Bedfordshire, England
Website www.lutonhoo.co.uk **Price** ⊖⊖

Luton Hoo in Bedfordshire is steeped in British history. The Queen and Prince Philip spent their honeymoon here, and during World War II Winston Churchill commandeered the property, the former seat of the Wernher family, as a testing ground for tanks.

Today, anyone—albeit those with sufficiently deep pockets—can stay here, because this eighteenth-century house has been turned into a luxury five-star hotel. Forget contemporary, minimalist style, however; everything here is big, bold, and on a very grand scale. Think wall-to-wall gilt, impossibly high, frescoed ceilings, dark oak paneling, swags of silk curtains, and ornate Victorian plasterwork in most of the rooms.

Luton Hoo enjoys a gorgeously rural setting but is only an hour's drive away from London, making it perfect for a weekend break from the city. There is an eighteen-hole golf course and spa, not to mention more than 1,000 acres (405 ha) of landscaped grounds designed by Capability Brown. These include two lakes and the River Lea, which wends its way through the lush parkland. What sets Luton Hoo apart from many other country-house hotels is that it does not pretend to be trendy; it simply offers good old-fashioned service in a stunningly tranquil location.

Live like latter-day aristocrats and dine in the Wernher Restaurant, one of the original state dining rooms where the decor is on such a lavish scale, with exotic marble panel work and richly colored fabrics, that it is reminiscent of the Palace of Versailles. Afterward, stroll in the terraced gardens or while away a sunny afternoon boating or fishing on the lake. **HA**

⇥ *The grand country mansion takes its name from a former occupant of the site, Lord Thomas Hoo.*

Visit Chelsea Physic Garden

Location Chelsea, London, England
Website www.chelseaphysicgarden.co.uk   **Price** $

An oasis of calm, this "secret" walled garden in the heart of London's fashionable Chelsea offers visitors a tranquil retreat from the metropolis. This lovely 4-acre (1.6-ha) garden was founded in 1673 by the Worshipful Society of Apothecaries to enable apprentices to identify different plants. Its location, on the bank of the Thames, was chosen for its proximity to the river and also because it created a warmer microclimate, allowing non-native plants, including olive and pineapple trees, the chance to survive.

Today, the garden continues to research the properties, origins, and conservation of more than 5,000 plants, and visitors are given audio guides that give an interesting commentary about the garden's history. The pharmaceutical garden offers a fascinating insight into those plants that have proven value in medicine: varieties such as Madagascan periwinkle, which is used in anticancer drugs; woolly foxglove, used to combat abnormal heart rhythms; and meadowsweet, from which aspirin was first derived. In the garden of world medicine, visitors can inspect plants used across the world, including those used by Maoris in New Zealand and Aborigines in Australia.

The perfumery and aromatics garden is a delight and contains a vast collection of scented plants and flowers, including lavender, rosemary, geraniums, and lime verbena. Along the west side of the garden is the historical walk, which shows the work of some of the characters associated with the garden's history. The café offers delicious light food, and in good weather you can sit outside and breathe in the scented air. **HA**

➔ *Steeped in botanical history, the garden is the ideal place for a pleasant stroll away from the city bustle.*

Visit Highgate Cemetery

Location Highgate, London, England
Website www.highgate-cemetery.org **Price** ⊖

"The philosophers have only interpreted the world in various ways; the point is to change it."

Karl Marx's epitaph, Highgate Cemetery

Highgate Cemetery is an unusual escape from the city humdrum. It is split into two sides: east and west. The East Cemetery is a peaceful sprawl of unassuming graves, including those of renowned novelists such as George Eliot and Douglas Adams. Most ostentatious is the surprisingly large, imposing bust that adorns the top of Karl Marx's final resting place, but the whole site is dotted with simpler areas and small, pretty, dilapidated pathways.

The West Cemetery is rather more intriguing. Although for the casual tourist access to the grounds is by group tour only, even the steps up to the first graves seem to transport you back to the Victorian era. You are surrounded by gothic architecture, grand and imposing tombs, and an enormous wealth of thick, verdant plant life, draped over and decorating the entire site. Rather than being in an active state of decay, the whole area is deliberately preserved in a permanent state of ruin.

The cemetery opened in 1839 as part of a plan to create seven new, private cemeteries around London. Appealing to Victorian society's proclivity toward grandiose funerary arrangements, many tombs were elaborately built. The impressive Egyptian Avenue captured the public's interest in the exciting Egyptian archaeological discoveries being made at the time.

It is difficult to articulate how utterly humbling, haunting, and mesmerizing a tour around the West Cemetery can be. Its stillness and atmospheric state of disrepair is like stumbling onto a film set, or into another world all together. **CW**

◹ *The tombs and statuary of the cemetery remain a tribute to the funerary obsession of the Victorian era.*

Enjoy Evensong at St. Paul's

Location St. Paul's, London, England
Website www.stpauls.co.uk **Price** ⑤

Architect Christopher Wren was commissioned to build St. Paul's cathedral after its predecessor perished in the Great Fire of London in 1666. St. Paul's was to be the new Protestant parish, a beacon of hope in a medieval city destroyed by fire. Wren wanted to make a big statement about a new-look London, and, contrary to the wishes of the Church, who wanted a spire, he topped his baroque creation with a huge dome, second in size only to St. Peter's in Rome. Particularly iconic since its survival of the Blitz, it remains the most eloquent building in the City of London and is particularly magical at night, its dome floodlit by an arc of lights.

> "Wren pursued his artistic vision: to crown the London skyline with a great domed church."

BBC History website

As the first monument to British Protestantism, St. Paul's has a different ambience from its Roman counterparts. Although there is complexity in its elaborate carvings and delicate frescoes, there is also an airiness and intelligence to the building that makes it feel modern. Unfortunately the place is rammed with tourists most of the time, making it difficult to appreciate the peace and solemnity this building is capable of generating—except at Evensong. There has been a choir of boys and gentlemen at St. Paul's Cathedral for more than nine centuries, and to hear these angelic voices is to be moved by a musical tradition that melts even the hardest heart. **LB**

Eat at Petersham Nurseries

Location Richmond, London, England
Website www.petershamnurseries.com **Price** ⑤⑤

This is no run-of-the-mill plant nursery; Petersham is utterly and magically different whatever the weather. The restaurant is a wonderful, artfully bohemian collection of shabby-chic, gently restored Victorian greenhouses furnished with an eclectic mix of mismatched, rickety, zinc and painted tables. The tables are properly and beautifully laid, surrounded by vintage mirrors, utterly covetable garden and home accoutrements, gorgeous mostly Indian artifacts, and, of course, plants spilling out of wooden crates.

It has a very special English-country walled-garden atmosphere with a great deal of space devoted to growing the most recondite vegetables, herbs, and fruit. What really elevates Petersham to a bucolic level, though, is the sensational food that veritably sings with seasonality and glows with passion. Talented chef Skye Gyngell, who originally trained with Anton Mossiman, has an innate sense of how ingredients work together to produce the most melodious flavors. While enjoying the signature rose-petal Bellini, salivate over the short, handwritten, ever-changing menu, which is only finalized midmorning, depending on what is at ripe perfection in the garden and what is available at the market.

Take the *burrata*, an extra-creamy take on mozzarella so fresh it cannot have left Italy long before, served with the most extraordinary salad. Tea-smoked wild salmon with piquant salsa verde and asparagus is a dish of pure summer, whereas a squash and tomato curry with lime delivers autumn on a plate. Desserts, especially apricot and sherry ice cream and sublime chocolate tart, are ambrosial. The whole experience is like a Fellini feast in the Garden of Eden. No wonder Mick Jagger and Madonna have eaten here. **SP**

Stroll in Richmond Park

Location Richmond, London, England
Website www.royalparks.org.uk/parks/richmond_park   **Price** ❶

Once the private playground of the British royals, Richmond Park is also open to mere commoners these days. This medieval hunting ground has changed little over the centuries and sits conveniently on London's doorstep, with a vast and varied landscape of hills, wooded glades, and grassy meadows. It is a truly urban oasis. Whether you wander over to Pen Ponds—a lake cut in two by a causeway, and a good place to see waterfowl—or to the beautifully hidden and magical Victorian woodlands over in the Isabella Plantation, you feel like you are in the wilds of nature.

The largest of London's Royal Parks, it is also renowned for its wildlife, including herds of red and fallow deer. These graceful creatures graze in clusters beneath the ancient oaks until the autumn rut, when the large males clash antlers spectacularly in an attempt to attract as many females as possible. In June you can see the fruits of their efforts as the fawns shyly peek out at you from the bracken.

Pembroke Lodge is a splendid Georgian mansion that now houses a popular restaurant. It was once the home of British prime minister Lord John Russell, and later his grandson, the philosopher Bertrand Russell.

The park has no shortage of captivating views. The most famous is from King Henry VIII's Mound, down a tree-lined "viewing corridor" that has been protected by law since 1710. It gives you a glimpse of St. Paul's Cathedral and the City of London, more than 10 miles (16 km) away. However, in 1536, it was the signaling flare from the Tower of London, telling of Anne Boleyn's execution, that Henry was looking to see. **SWi**

← *Richmond Park is the only place in London where you can mingle with around 650 free-roaming deer.*

Stay at Kemp Townhouse

Location Brighton, East Sussex, England
Website www.kemptownhouse.com   **Price** ❷❸

If you are looking for a tranquil escape from Brighton's busy hub, with its fashionable nightclubs, bars, and restaurants, then look no further than the Kemp Townhouse. Situated in the arty bohemian enclave of Kemp Town, the Regency-style townhouse is a little gem of a hotel that has been elegantly refurbished by its German owners and transformed from a run-down bed-and-breakfast into a stylish hotel. Thankfully, all the original period features have been retained.

Housed within a tall four-story Georgian house, all nine rooms have their own individual features: antique fireplaces, indulgent four-poster beds, or freestanding baths. Each room also comes with a private shower

---

"Just opened, Kemp Townhouse promises to be Brighton's chicest new hotel."

Independent

---

room, and fluffy white towels, scented candles, and exclusive toiletries complete the luxurious ambience.

The decor uses calming neutral shades of gray and mushroom to soothing effect. Soft lighting and a crackling fire greet you in the dining room, which is stuffed full of interesting objets d'art sourced all over the world. Silver pots come from Marrakech, whereas some of the paintings are family heirlooms and the twinkling chandelier was shipped over from New York.

Breakfast can be eaten in the teal-colored dining room with its sea view or in the comfort of your room. Choose from a menu including muffins, mueslis, fresh pastries, or a full English to set you up for the day. **HA**

Relax at Chewton Glen

Location Hampshire, England **Website** www.chewtonglen.com
Price $ $ $

Although the rolling lawns and ornate terraces are reminiscent of *The Great Gatsby*, it is the Maryatt family who are responsible for the country-house splendor of Chewton Glen. This is five-star luxury served up in inimitable British fashion. Muted elegance and individuality is key in each of the fifty-eight rooms: furnished with rich upholsteries and objets d'art alongside modern luxuries such as plasma screens.

The New Forest surroundings are nothing short of breathtaking. Within the grounds are a tennis court, croquet lawn, and golf course. There is even a Chewton bunny path leading to the coast via ancient woods—a smugglers' route from centuries past.

> *"A real country-house hotel with all the class, comfort, and quality you could wish for."*
>
> The Good Spa Guide

Cares are banished in the gilded serenity of the Roman-inspired spa, where a day and night sky theme permeates—from the ceiling of the stunning indoor pool to the atrium of the hydrotherapy zone. The treatment rooms are shaded brown to resemble a cocoon, and exclusive Linda Meredith facials and body care by Molton Brown are on offer.

Meals move effortlessly from the finest English fruits for breakfast to hearty fare in the award-winning restaurant by night. From the genuine yet unobtrusive warmth of the service to the flowers delivered with your coffee, the sense here is that everything has been carefully considered. Gatsby would have approved. **VG**

Stay at the Grain Store

Location Hampshire, England **Website** www.theonionstore.co.uk
Price $ $

Found by wending your way through a network of tight country lanes in deepest Hampshire, just north of the New Forest, the Grain Store is set down a garden path just beyond an unusual willow fence, and is part of a trio of lovely romantic hideaways that each appear as though in a dream.

Set in the 8-acre (3-ha) grounds of a seventeenth-century thatched house, the rustic but elegant Grain Store is evocative of chic, rural France, with huge heavy beams countered by near floor-to-ceiling windows that let the light flood in. An exotic French cast-iron bathtub complete with wood paneling graces the bedroom, whereas the bed itself is swathed in long, muslin drapes—as if it were possible to shut the world out even further. When you retire to bed, you might even discover that a rose has miraculously appeared on your pillow.

Step up to the sitting room, simply furnished with exposed wooden floorboards and dominated by a chandelier and heavy wooden table, with a door leading straight out into the wilds. Outside, the private oasis of a garden boasts a secluded black-stained sundeck enveloped by a sea of willow and other trees as far as the eye can see. It is a perfect place to have breakfast or, if the weather is unpredictable, retreat to the indoor sanctuary of the conservatory and have a coffee by the pool. The same space also offers a welcome evening retreat for solitary candlelit swims.

Refreshingly, few will find cell phone reception at the Grain Store, and there are no televisions or radios in the rooms to distract you from the delicious (if temporary) state of oblivion. The bustling and beautiful town of Lymington is only minutes away—but who wants to mix with other people? **NS**

Recharge at SenSpa

Location Brockenhurst, England　**Website** www.senspa.co.uk
Price ❸❸❸

Appearances can be very deceptive, and you have to bear this in mind when you arrive at Careys Manor Hotel, deep in the heart of the New Forest. The rather dreary property that greets you conceals an award-winning Thai spa that will literally unknot your shoulders and have you curling your toes in delight. SenSpa offers an innovative selection of East meets West treatments.

The spa's philosophy is all about inner healing and finding a balance between mind, body, and spirit. Whether you are entering the dreamy hydrotherapy pool or languishing in the superb herbal sauna, it will not be long before you start to feel any stress and tension drift away. However, you will soon be startled out of your reverie when you venture into the ice room. Here a casual tug of a cord empties a bucket of freezing cold water over you. An alternative treatment in the same room is the tropical rainstorm shower, one of several revitalizing sensory showers, which comes complete with ice-cold rain, thunder, and lightning. But some of the simplest treatments are the best. The signature Sen Fusion massage should not be missed: You will be pummeled into heavenly submission by one of the Thai-trained therapists who are expert at easing aching muscles and stiffness.

If you have any energy left, there are some beautiful trails through the New Forest—ideal for biking, walking, or horseback riding—where you can see the wild New Forest ponies. Afterward, you can feast on the delicious Thai cuisine, perfect for restoring your energy for another day of wallowing in that spa. **HA**

↗ *Even the grounds outside the therapy suites reflect the Eastern philosophy of the renowned Thai spa.*

"They have put a lot of thought into this and created an authentic Thai atmosphere."

Guardian

Unwind at Grayshott Spa

Location Surrey, England
Website www.grayshottspa.com **Price** 💲💲

Hidden away in a quiet corner of Surrey, Grayshott is the former country seat of Victorian poet Alfred Lord Tennyson. It has an air of unstuffy but polished grandeur, and an unpretentious yet sophisticated spa that combines friendliness, accessibility, and luxury in one beguiling package.

Single guests and male guests, as well as couples, are all in evidence here, and the choice of exactly how to spend your time is entirely yours. It is not unheard of to glimpse someone fast asleep by the fire in the lounge—recharging and regrouping is the name of the game—and with 47 acres (19 ha) of landscape gardens that back directly onto 700 acres (283 ha) of National Trust land, it is easy enough to sink into the quiet countryside. Spa lovers can choose treatments from cranial osteopathy to vital energy detox massage and emotional freedom techniques.

There is a real boutique feel about the stylish cream decor, expensive carpets, comfortable beds, and attention to detail, including candles flickering away on the impressive stairway. The food is memorable: The focus is squarely on healthy but delicious eating, and guests help themselves to a delectable buffet at lunchtime, laden with salad, roasted vegetables, grilled fish, and wild rice. In the evening, an à la carte menu is served in the same elegant dining room, or in the Conservatory restaurant. Evening à la carte portions are small; many guests are watching their weight. There is no compromise on taste, however.

If all that pampering becomes too much, activity seekers can take exercise, Pilates, or yoga classes, or head for the gym. A daily 8 A.M. power walk around the grounds and nearby National Trust land will sharpen your appetite for a hearty, healthy breakfast. **LC**

Enjoy Owlpen Manor

Location Gloucestershire, England
Website www.owlpen.com **Price** 💲

Owlpen, a Tudor manor house with a long history stretching back 900 years, is the ancestral seat of Lord Nicholas and Lady Mander. For more than thirty years they have been renting out a collection of buildings on their estate that have been converted into delightful period cottages offering self-catering accommodation.

They include a selection of historic buildings, and they are all unique. Sleeping between two and nine people, the cottages range from snug medieval barns such as the Tithe Barn (a romantic and secluded hideaway for two with massive oak beams full of rustic charm), to sizable farmhouses such as the Court House (a gabled banqueting house dating from 1620, which

> *"Owlpen . . . the epitome of the English village . . . evolved through centuries of rural life."*
>
> HRH the Prince of Wales

sleeps five). Grist Mill is a converted watermill built next to the delightful Ewelme brook. It dates back to 1728 and sleeps eight, whereas Marlings End is a traditional weaver's cottage with three bedrooms, stunning views, and a beautiful cottage garden.

Whichever accommodation you decide to choose, you will be absolutely entranced by the beautiful surrounding countryside. This fairy-tale hamlet is centered around the picture-perfect church and the manor house itself, nestling low in a densely wooded valley thick with copper-colored beech trees. The Mander family motto is Vive Bene (live well), and you can certainly do that at Owlpen. **HA**

Stay at Barnsley House

Location Gloucestershire, England
Website www.barnsleyhouse.com   **Price** 💲💲💲

In recent years the Cotswolds has become something of a Mecca for urban sophisticates in search of rural bliss. They flock to these parts to play lord and lady of the manor in one of the new breed of rural-glam country-house hotels. Barnsley House is one of the trailblazers of this chic country set.

This super-stylish historic manor house is set in 11 acres (4.5 ha) of gorgeous gardens designed by the former owner and legendary gardener Rosemary Verey. Visitors used to come here to admire the verdant surroundings, but nowadays that is a luxury reserved for the well-heeled hotel guests. Stroll around the sunny terraces, the ancient meadows, and the ornate formal lawns, or relax by the temple and pool garden.

The garden is not the only draw to Barnsley House. Prepare to swoon at the stunning spa; built within a sunken garden, it has floor-to-ceiling windows letting daylight flood in and a sauna, steam room, and relaxation room. Outside there is a warm hydrotherapy pool complete with back-massaging showers. Spa aficionados will be delighted with the myriad of treatments on offer.

With only nine rooms, all individually designed, Barnsley manages to retain an intimate feel, although not at the expense of comfort. Beds are huge, pillows are plump, freshly cut flowers from the garden perfume the air, and the bathrooms are decadently luxurious. Think walk-through showers, double-ended roll-top bathtubs, and funky lighting, not forgetting plasma screen televisions. Just across the road, and under the same ownership as Barnsley House, is the cozy village pub. Nip over for a drink before dinner and rub shoulders with the locals—Kate Moss and Liz Hurley are said to be regulars. **HA**

Relax at Lucknam Park

Location Wiltshire, England
Website www.lucknampark.co.uk   **Price** 💲💲💲

Turn off the leafy country road, through the old stone gate, and enter a mile-long avenue of lime and beech trees, three deep and almost 200 years old. Eventually this tunnel of trees opens out to reveal a perfect lawn in front of Lucknam, often called the quintessential English country-house hotel. In its 500 acres (200 ha) of parkland on the rolling hills outside of Bath it has a Michelin-starred restaurant, award-winning spa and indoor pool, exquisite garden dating back hundreds of years, and even an equestrian center with thirty horses, which guests may use to explore the estate.

The building dates back to a wealthy seventeenth-century merchant who earned a fortune importing

> *"Lucknam Park is the sort of hotel in which to entertain the fantasy of never having to leave."*

Kate Kellaway, *Observer*

tobacco from Virginia, then built the central part of the property. It was enlarged by successive owners and now has become a world-class hotel with an opulent traditional atmosphere.

The best bedrooms, at the front of the house, have four-poster beds, dining tables, sitting rooms, marble bathrooms, and inspiring views across the parkland. Among the antiques, ornaments, and lush fabrics, the modern touches are discreet. Downstairs, head chef Hywel Jones has been voted the best hotel chef in Britain. His menus mix traditional and modern cuisine and make ample use of the area's finest suppliers, plus Lucknam's own herb garden. **SH**

Visit Royal Crescent Hotel

Location Bath, Somerset, England
Website www.royalcrescent.co.uk   **Price** ⊝

Jane Austen fantasies come alive at this elegant hotel ideally situated in the middle of Bath's architecturally renowned Royal Crescent. The Royal Crescent Hotel occupies two historic buildings virtually unchanged since the eighteenth-century when the aristocrats of the day would visit Bath during the "season" for the water's health-giving properties.

The exterior of the hotel looks much as it did 250 years ago, while inside huge vases of scented lilies perfume the air, a fire crackles in the drawing room, and discreet staff appear as if from nowhere exactly when you need them. The bedrooms have been lovingly restored to ensure they are just as they were in the eighteenth century. Carpets, color schemes, and furniture have all been carefully chosen to ensure authenticity, but not at the expense of comfort.

For a spa, head to the Bath House, which offers a range of treatments including a warm relaxation pool where gothic windows allow natural light to flood in. After a few languorous lengths, soak in one of the toasty hot tubs before steeling yourself for an invigorating plunge in one of the icy tubs of cold water, a practice said to do wonders for the circulation.

Of course you do not need to stay for long to enjoy the best of the hotel: Do not miss out on eating at the Royal Crescent's restaurant, the Dower House, which overlooks the garden. Or on a sunny day, find yourself a seat under a flower-adorned magnolia tree in the tranquil and secluded garden, listen to the birdsong, and enjoy an indulgent afternoon tea just like those elite Georgians did back in Bath's heyday. **HA**

← *The Royal Crescent Hotel is situated in the middle of Bath's beautiful eighteenth-century Royal Crescent.*

Enjoy Thermae Bath Spa

Location Bath, Somerset, England
Website www.thermaebathspa.com   **Price** ⊝

As the sun sets across the Georgian rooftops of Bath, there is no finer place to be than wallowing in the steamy warmth of the rooftop pool at Thermae Bath Spa. It is the only spot in Britain where visitors can escape into spring water that is naturally heated. Hotel spas, even in Bath, make do with warmed tap water. Thermae uses mineral-rich spring water bubbling up from the limestone at 113°F (45°C)—just like the Romans who built the elaborate bathing complex that still stands a few hundred yards away.

There is a contemporary sense of luxury within the modern construction. More than 140 architects competed to win the contract. Nicholas Grimshaw's

> *"[The rooftop is] best enjoyed at night, when the skyline is floodlit … and the water begins to steam."*
>
> Vincent Crump, *The Times*

winning design uses traditional Bath stone, like the Georgian buildings surrounding the spa, plus giant swaths of glass and quirky round portholes.

The usual treatments are available, as well as private escapes to the restored Georgian Hot Bath and the secluded Cross Bath, a stand-alone bathhouse across the street built above the site of the original Roman cistern. At the main three-story spa, there is everything a latter-day Roman bather could want: aromatic steam saunas in circular glass pods, an indoor pool with gently flowing currents, bubbling foot baths, a huge shower big enough to soak a dozen people at once, and the highlight, a rooftop pool. **SH**

Stay at Babington House

Location Somerset, England
Website www.babingtonhouse.co.uk **Price** 💲💲

Babington House is a deliberate attempt to establish a retreat for media types and stylish urbanites looking for a country break. It is both a private members' club and a luxury hotel and restaurant, part of a small chain of boutique premises owned by British entrepreneur Nick Smith. He chose the basics well: Babington is an old, honey-colored stone mansion that dates back to 1370. Deep in rural Somerset, in England's West Country, the building stands amid 18 acres (7 ha), down a long avenue of trees.

The secret of Babington's success is the mix of classic style and contemporary cool. Everything centers on the main house, with its library, bar, and

---

" . . . material girls can check out Room Six, which Madonna loves for its bath on the balcony."

Susan D'Arcy, *The Times*

---

pool room. You eat at the informal "House Kitchen," the more secluded "Log Room," or out on the terrace if the Somerset weather allows. Across the garden the Cowshed Spa offers indoor and outdoor pools, a gym, steam room, sauna, aroma rooms, and a movie theater. In the gardens there are also grass and hard tennis courts, a cricket pitch, croquet lawn, lake (with resident swans), and a period walled garden. Bedrooms are situated either up the grand mahogany staircase in the main house or across the crunchy gravel in the converted gate lodge, coach house, and stable block. One room has a freestanding bathtub next to the bed; another has a whirlpool tub on a private terrace. **SH**

Explore Lundy Island

Location Bristol Channel, England
Website www.lundyisland.co.uk **Price** 💲

The tiny island of Lundy, 3.5 miles (5.5 km) by 0.5 miles (0.8 km), is a well-kept secret. After a two-hour ferry trip from the North Devon port of Ilfracombe, arriving on the island feels like you are stepping back in time to the 1950s. The island's craggy shoreline has been ravaged by the waves and the winds, not to mention the Vikings, pirates, and smugglers over the years, but Lundy remains blissfully untouched by the modern world. There are no cars, just a handful of people, one pub, and fields stretching to the puffin-packed cliffs full of lambs, deer, and feral goats.

Accommodation ranges from a sheltered campsite to a thirteenth-century castle, a Georgian villa, a fisherman's chalet, and a lighthouse. There are twenty-three iconic places to stay, each furnished with care and with special touches like naval charts and paintings of shipwrecks on the wall, open fires, and bookcases full of wildlife books and board games. The attention to detail makes a stay all the more special.

For such a small place, there is plenty to do. Wardens organize walks, snorkeling safaris, and boat trips around the island, during which you can hear the breeding colony of gray seals singing before you see them. Divers love the island for its pristine waters, and it is becoming one of the most lusted-after rock-climbing locations in the United Kingdom. Lundy has a timeless, wholesome feel to it, where the simple things in life take center stage, such as swimming in the sea or enjoying a pint in the Marisco Tavern. From the southern tip of the west coast of the island, there is nothing but sea between here and the United States. **LD**

➜ *The lighthouse on Lundy is one of the historic buildings preserved by the Landmark Trust.*

Relax at Gaia House

Location Devon, England **Website** www.gaiahouse.co.uk
Price §§

People come to Gaia House to escape all life's usual stresses and trappings—and a better place to unwind and de-stress is hard to imagine. Tucked away in the verdant South Devon countryside, Gaia House, the only nonaffiliated retreat center in Britain, is set in a former convent among hills and woodland. Although the retreats and courses are drawn from the wider Buddhist tradition, all are welcome, and the philosophy and atmosphere is inclusive and undogmatic.

Guests can come for either an organized or private retreat. There are many themes to choose from, including a Zen retreat, insight meditation, qigong, and yoga. The program is not for those seeking to sleep in and have time to gossip with friends: Commitment is needed, because a typical day starts at 6:00 A.M. and finishes at 9:30 P.M. Most of this time is spent in silent meditation practice, either sitting in the spacious meditation hall or walking in the grounds. The focus is on stillness, discipline, and serenity.

Retreats are held in complete silence, and there is a "no cell phone" policy, allowing guests to fully immerse themselves in the quiet. Be prepared for basic but comfortable accommodation; there are several single rooms but most are shared. There is some pitching in required, too: Guests are requested to offer an hour a day of their time toward running the house; duties include gardening, washing dishes, and cleaning. The food is no-frills but tasty and wholesome, and the vegetarian meals are eaten communally in a dining room overlooking the lawn.

Despite the busy schedule, there is time to wander the beautiful grounds and countryside surrounding Gaia House: a rare opportunity to be immersed in silence, contemplation, and nature. **LC**

Stay at Combe House

Location Devon, England **Website** www.thishotel.com
Price §§

Combe House has been dubbed one of the most romantic hotels in Britain, and it is easy to see why. Situated in bucolic Devon countryside, you approach this Elizabethan country manor via a long and winding driveway, past doe-eyed Arab mares and foals, and pheasants roaming freely around the 3,500 acres (1,415 ha) of fine country estate. Heave open the imposing oak door and you will find an opulent entrance hall, all dark paneling, snug sofas, and a log fire.

The sixteen rooms are all individually decorated. Although the rooms in the main house have a more traditional feel, the newly renovated Linen Suite is furnished in a calm, contemporary style. This one-

> *"We are fortunate to be in a stunning location with the West Country's larder on our doorstep."*
>
> **Proprietors, Combe House**

bedroom suite has a vast airy sitting room, and the spacious bathroom has, as its stunning centerpiece, a bespoke 6-foot- (1.8-m-) diameter copper bath with a powerful sunflower-head shower centered above—easily big enough for two.

For the ultimate in romantic seclusion, opt to stay in Combe's Thatched Cottage, tucked away in the woods. This cozy hideaway is a rural idyll, complete with antique pieces, a mass of freshly cut flowers, and a huge stove. The private walled garden at the back of the cottage is an absolute delight, and for special occasions, a Combe House chef can rustle up a romantic candlelit dinner for two. **HA**

Discover Polhawn Fort

Location Cornwall, England   **Website** www.polhawnfort.com
Price $

Camp at Botelet Farm

Location Cornwall, England   **Website** www.botelet.com
Price $

If you really want to escape from the world, head to Polhawn Fort. Not only does it sit at the end of Cornwall's Rame Head peninsula, but it still has a working drawbridge that could be pulled up should a severe attack of reclusiveness strike. The fort was built in the 1860s. The French navy, under Napoleon III, had just acquired the world's first steam-driven warship. In response, the British prime minister of the day, Lord Palmerston, ordered the construction of a series of "Napoleonic forts," including Polhawn. The forts never saw action and became known as Palmerston's follies.

Today, Polhawn is rather more welcoming. Step into the reception area and you will find sofas surrounding a crackling log fire. There are eight bedrooms, all facing the sea, which comfortably sleep twenty guests. The fort is often used as a wedding venue (banquets for one hundred diners take place in a vast, vaulted, brick-lined room comprising four of the original cannon casemates), but is available for vacation rental as well. There is a private beach, and guests may take a spin on Polhawn's own 50-foot (15-m) luxury yacht, the *Polhawn Whisper*. The spectacular cliffs of the Cornish coast, with their colonies of seabirds, are perfect for a bracing stroll.

One further point of interest at Polhawn is that its granite spiral staircase winds the wrong way. Staircases in historic fortifications usually wind counter-clockwise: They assume that the enemy would come from beneath and the defending soldiers, fighting from above, would benefit from having more space on the outside of the spiral because that was the side of their right, sword-bearing arm. However, Polhawn's main staircase winds clockwise because, it is thought, attack here would come from above. **PE**

Botelet Farm is a working farm that has operated as a bed-and-breakfast since the 1930s. It now also offers Mongolian yurts and two self-catering cottages to rent. The largest of these, Manor Cottage, is a seventeenth-century Cornish longhouse with flagstones, oak beams, and even a piano. There is Cornish ware in the kitchen cupboards, a blazing fire to welcome you, and bedrooms that are simply and tastefully furnished in shabby chic style with brass or wooden beds and well-faded floral fabrics. There is even an illuminated well in the kitchen that pumps delicious mineral water from deep below. Botelet is a place where guests feel at home after exploring the ancient delights of the local

---

"Down a wild-flowered drive in a hidden fold, this treasure house is a synthesis of style . . . and color."
Guardian

---

area: the stone circle at Duloe, the Neolithic fort at Bury Down, and the aged font at St. Cuby's Church.

If you prefer to get close to nature, choose to stay in one of the yurts: traditional wood-framed tents raised on posts with heavy-duty canvas on the floor and a warming wood burner. The yurts are remotely located in tranquil meadows that catch late sunsets and have prime panoramic views over farmland and out to sea. Soak up the vista while sipping a cool, freshly pressed, homegrown apple juice, or arrange for a treatment from the visiting therapist who offers massage and reflexology. Whichever of the dwellings you choose, you will be captivated by this beautiful place. **SWi**

Walk the Coastal Path from Rock to Polzeath

Location Cornwall, England
Website www.cornwall-online.co.uk   **Price** ❶❶

> *"Go . . . by the broad sands of Daymer Bay and see it's all here as [Betjeman] immortalized it."*
>
> Christopher Somerville, *Daily Telegraph*

Rock is a haven of romantic beaches, wild cliff lines, sweeping, open countryside, and fine food. However, the area gets some bad press locally, with stories of mischievous schoolboys and tiny country lanes easily blocked by overbearing vehicles. Do not let this reputation prevent you from renting a cottage in the vicinity. The wonderful Camel Valley countryside is blessed with the best Cornwall has to offer: breezy blue skies; golden sands; a rugged and romantic golf course (even if you loathe the sport, it is a wonderful place to wander); and rolling green hillsides leading down to the estuary, which has sheltered waters that are perfect for novice sailors. In summer, the golden beaches are speckled with multicolored windbreaks and kites, and are filled with the laughter of children playing in rock pools and picnicking families.

There is no surf in Rock. You can walk over the cliffs or along the beaches, through golden-hued Daymer Bay, to Polzeath, a beach cut deeply into the cliffs, where surfing and bodyboarding is the name of the game. Here the fun can be quite raucous, as novice bodyboarders shriek merrily in the surf, with their frolicking wet dogs in tow. Take a sunlit spot high on the cliffs and watch the action from a tranquil distance.

Along the way you could also visit the grave of Sir John Betjeman in Daymer Bay. He is buried in the beautiful, thirteenth-century, quaintly low-slung church St. Enodoc, hunkered down in the grass-bound dunes at the foot of Braey Hill. A couple of hundred years ago, it could be entered only through its roof, so buried was it in the sand dunes. **LB**

↖ *The coastal path sticks closely to the cliff's edge, making for some dramatic scenery on a windy day.*

Relax at Driftwood Hotel

Location Cornwall, England
Website www.driftwoodhotel.co.uk **Price** 🌀🌀

On a quiet stretch of the south Cornish coast, where the grassy cliffs roll down toward the English Channel and the Gulf Stream, there is a small private hotel. From here, take a walk for a mile or so through the protected countryside and you will reach the pretty fishing village of Portscatho. Other than this, the hotel is miles from anywhere, except the waves breaking on the shore below and the yachts turning in Gerrans Bay.

Driftwood Hotel is an informal place; some find it romantic, others escapist. Many come because of the award-winning restaurant with an unbroken sea view. Here you can eat lobster or crab caught that morning in the rocks below the hotel, and most dishes are sourced locally. On sunny days, eat out on the terrace; on warm evenings, hurricane lamps are lit in the garden. From here you will find a series of terraces leading down toward the shore and, hidden in the trees, a weather-boarded cabin overlooking the water, which provides further accommodation.

The hotel itself is tastefully fitted out with a nautical theme throughout. Relax in sitting rooms stocked with books, magazines, and board games. Each room has been simply decorated using a color scheme of seaside blue and white. The fabrics are printed with shells, and there are bits of driftwood everywhere. The wooden shutters on the windows are painted white. Bedrooms overlook the sea, of course, and ground-floor bedrooms have their own decked terrace.

Guests may take walks down a wooded path to the secluded cove or drive through high-hedged lanes to the fashionable yachting haven of St. Mawes. If you want a brief taste of the rest of the world again, from St. Mawes it is easy to take a passenger ferry across the estuary to the busy waterside town of Falmouth. **SH**

Rent Pencalenick House

Location Cornwall, England
Website www.pencalenickhouse.co.uk **Price** 🌀🌀

At the end of a winding Cornish lane, perched all alone above the still waters of Pont Pill creek, sits Pencalenick House, the luxury modernist creation of architect Seth Stein. It is truly secluded (this used to be the location of a tuberculosis isolation hospital), and with its seeded grass roof and locally sourced stone and timber construction, the house has been designed with the environment in mind.

Pencalenick is luxurious, too, though. The seven bedrooms have fittings by Philippe Starck, and each opens onto the terrace that flanks the length of the house. The open-plan living area features floor-to-ceiling windows through which pour gallons of bright

> *"Pencalenick House [is] a thrilling modernist take on the original hobbit home."*
>
> Harper's Bazaar

Cornish light. Outdoors, tables on the lawn encourage alfresco dining, and a path leads to a barbecue area in the woods. There is also a private yacht to take guests on mackerel-fishing expeditions or to explore coves. The house manager is happy to arrange canoeing trips or horse-riding forays into the surrounding countryside.

Pencalenick comes complete with a dedicated chef who plucks organic produce from the house's own garden: In keeping with Pencalenick's green tone, the kitchen favors local produce. The chef prepares whatever the guests may wish for, from seafood freshly hauled from Cornwall's crisp waters, to a casual family picnic to have on the lawn outside. **PE**

Discover the Lost Gardens of Heligan

Location Cornwall, England   **Website** www.heligan.com
Price $

There is a tragic air to this wonderfully rambling garden in the lush valleys above the fishing village of Mevagissey. It was the seat of the wealthy Tremayne family for more than 400 years. Then their enthusiastic team of gardeners went off to World War I and never returned. The extraordinary gardens were neglected, overgrown, and eventually forgotten.

Ninety years later, a team of enthusiasts stumbled on clues that there was something hidden among acres of overgrown jungle. Their romantic restoration scheme has been a triumph. More than its banks of rhododendrons (including the biggest specimen in the world), its towering tree ferns (shipped from New Zealand), and its huge *Gunnera* leaves (used as sunshades by Victorian gardeners), Heligan's main attraction is its story: how an exquisite Victorian garden was restored to its former pomp using the original gardeners' archives, tools, and methods.

The restoration has highlighted just how skillful the lost generation of gardeners were. Visitors will see the original head gardener's office—a small brick hut attached to a greenhouse. An open fire burns in the grate, shelves are packed with carefully labeled jam jars full of seeds, and an old wooden desk is stacked with planting schedules. Visitors can also see the humble apple loft where apprentice gardeners slept huddled on the bare boards, the outdoor toilet with the proud signatures of the entire Victorian gardening team on the wall, and the ingenious way the gardeners heated their greenhouses using horse manure. **SH**

→ *The Lost Gardens of Heligan in Cornwall are a magical window into the Victorian past.*

Experience Bryher Island

Location Isles of Scilly, England
Website www.tresco.co.uk/stay/hell-bay   **Price** 🅢🅢

The boat from the biggest island, St. Mary's, meanders between rocks to a stone jet on Bryher. An old four-by-four vehicle bumps along rutted tracks to the hotel. Bryher, just half a mile wide, is the smallest of the inhabited Scilly Isles. Seventy inhabitants look across to the island of Tresco, considering it rather brash because it has a concrete road. St. Mary's, at 2.5 miles (4 km) wide, with an airport, seems like downtown New York from Bryher's bracken-covered hillocks.

Bryher is also the most westward isle; its most famous landmark is its only hotel, Hell Bay. The hotel has a friendly, down-to-earth vibe: Hot flasks are offered to guests going for a walk, and after dark you

> *"Outside, there is wilderness; inside, you retreat to designer plumbing and three-course dinners."*
>
> Richard Woods, *The Times*

can borrow a flashlight. The low-rise complex of whitewashed buildings stands a few yards from a pretty sandy cove. Pray for a storm. Gales smash spray against the windows while diners feast on Bryher crab and lobster served with vegetables grown on the island.

Inside, the hotel is like a Cape Cod boathouse, with wicker chairs, wooden floors, and pastel paintwork. There is modern art everywhere, including a Barbara Hepworth, but the images commanding most attention are the views from the big picture windows. **SH**

⬅ *The coast of Bryher faces the full fury of Atlantic storms—hence the name of the hotel.*

Stay at Fort Clonque

Location Alderney, Channel Islands
Website www.landmarktrust.org.uk   **Price** 🅢🅢

Military history fans will be in their element at Fort Clonque, which was held by the Germans during their occupation of the Channel Islands in World War II. Perched perilously on an exposed rocky promontory that can be reached only by a causeway that is cut off from the mainland at high tide, latter-day guests can sleep inside this cavernous gun emplacement, which was built on the specific orders of the German High Command. Despite the 19-foot (5.8-m) thick walls, you will still be lulled to sleep by the incessant crashing of waves onto the granite rocks around you.

Fort Clonque, firmly ensconced on the steep southwest coast of the island of Alderney, at the end of a long causeway just 5 miles (8 km) from mainland France, is built into and follows the natural contours of its undulating, isolated promontory rather than being constructed on top of it all. The result is a picturesque ensemble of towers, gun emplacements, and ramparts spread over several levels.

The first defensive works here were begun in 1847, although its significance as a military outpost was not realized until the German occupation, which added many of the officer's quarters and casements still in place today. Fort Clonque offers accommodation for up to thirteen people throughout the officers' and soldiers' quarters, the gatehouse, the upper magazine, and the German bunker. There is a modern kitchen, and food and supplies can be garnered from nearby St. Anne. Care should be taken not to linger in case the tide prevents you from getting home. Alternatively, the housekeeper can do the shopping for you in advance, if you ask nicely. A log fire and upright piano help soften the harshness of the environment and create an air of romance and informality. **BS**

Discover Kinderdijk Park

Location Near Rotterdam, Holland   **Website** www.kinderdijk.com
Price 🌓

For a classic Dutch landscape that looks like an Old Master's canvas, look no further than Kinderdijk Park. Here, on the watery banks of the canal and only 10 miles (16 km) from Rotterdam, there are nineteen traditional windmills that date back to the mid-1700s. It is the largest concentration of old windmills in the Netherlands and used to perform an extremely useful function: With much of the Netherlands at or below sea level, flooding has always been a serious issue, and for more than 200 years the windmills drained the Alblasserwaard polders of excess water ensuring the surrounding land did not flood.

If you come in the second week of September, the windmills are floodlit at night, providing an unforgettable spectacle. Otherwise, come on a Saturday in either July or August when all nineteen of the mills are fully operational. Most of these beautifully preserved windmills are now occupied, although one is open to visitors. For a small entrance fee you can clamber up the steep and narrow stairs to each floor and poke around the cramped living quarters of the original miller and his family. Do not worry—even though the sails of the windmill give the distinct impression they are going to knock your head off on entering and leaving the building, their clever design means any unfortunate decapitations are avoided.

You can ride a bike along the banks of the canal, or even skate on the canal in winter if it is cold enough. If that sounds too energetic, take a boat ride along the glassy waters or simply stroll along the paths and enjoy the tranquility of this serene area. **HA**

← *The haunting beauty of the Kinderdijk windmills are a designated UNESCO World Heritage site.*

Dine at Posthoorn

Location Monnickendam, Holland
Website www.posthoorn.eu **Price** $\circleddash\circleddash$

The ornate, seventeenth-century coach house stands among humble fishing cottages in a bohemian harbor-side village just twenty minutes' drive from the center of Amsterdam. Throughout history, horse-drawn stages used to stop here, and the Posthoorn was always a well-known meeting place for dignitaries traveling along the coast road. Three years ago, the new owners restored and converted the buildings to what they call a stylish "suite hotel and restaurant." This elegant new restaurant with rooms has become a well-known meeting place for dignitaries of a different sort: contemporary Dutch TV, film, and arts celebrities.

Style and design is everything here, with dramatic antique chandeliers carefully placed together with modern, dark-wood furniture and old china vases alongside sleek, polished floors. The wood-paneled bar has an open fire and a cigar menu. There are just five luxury rooms above the gourmet dining room, and they are decorated with astonishing finesse. The bedrooms are unashamedly romantic, with candles and roses everywhere. Each suite is named and styled after a famous visitor to the Posthoorn. The Napoleon Bonaparte Suite has classic, patterned linen wallpaper and rich chocolate colors, and the Persijnen Kamer (after the Persijn family, who founded Amsterdam) is a cozy attic with exposed beams and fluffy cushions.

Downstairs, the restaurant serves modern French-Mediterranean cuisine with regional Dutch ingredients in a simple, uncluttered environment. You will sit in comfy upholstered armchairs on a polished wooden floor with modern art on the wall. There are classic, high, monumental ceilings hung with enormous modern lightbulbs. Or you can eat under the canopies of the brick-paved courtyard outside. **SH**

Stay at Hotel Julien

Location Antwerp, Belgium
Website www.hotel-julien.com **Price** $\circleddash\circleddash$

With a tram line rumbling by outside in the narrow bustling streets of the old city of Antwerp, Hotel Julien may not initially seem particularly enticing. However, on opening the huge, wooden doors of this charming pair of sixteenth-century merchants' houses joined by a tranquil courtyard, any concerns soon melt away.

Check in at a limed-oak reception desk with a glass wall that allows you to see into the light-flooded outdoor courtyard and exquisite dining room and lounge. Ornate doors and heavy paneling provide the perfect backdrop for an eclectic mix of contemporary and antique furniture. Flop down on one of the gorgeous cowhide Eames chairs close by or slip into

> *"The . . . townhouse has been spruced up . . . to create a hotel that looks like a magazine shoot."*
>
> Katie Bowman, *The Times*

the gilt-ceilinged library and enjoy, by the fire, the freshly brewed coffee and Belgian chocolates that are available around the clock, before climbing the blond-wood staircase to one of eleven stylish bedrooms.

Upstairs, the color palette is soft and neutral, with restrained shades of crisp whites, soft grays, creams, and blues. Choose a room with cathedral views and exposed timber A-frames in the attics, or a loftier-ceilinged room with a terrace and an altogether grander and more elegant feel. For breakfast, sit in the sun-dappled dining room at the communal antique Flemish table and feast on homemade breads, jam, cheese, salmon, eggs, yogurt, and fresh fruit salad. **SWi**

Unwind at Pand Hotel

Location Bruges, Belgium
Website www.pandhotel.com **Price** $\$\$$

Situated in the heart of Bruges, just a short stroll away from the canals, the enchanting Pand Hotel is run by the Vanhaecke family, who have converted this eighteenth-century house into a wonderful boutique hotel. Their quest has been aided by the convenient fact that the Vanhaeckes are also established antique dealers—so all of the wonderful pictures and furniture you see in the hotel are not only unique, but have been carefully handpicked by resident experts.

It would be easy to get the impression from this description that the Pand Hotel is somewhat old-fashioned. In truth, it blends its passion for antiques with sophisticated modern touches and even the odd funky furnishing, lending the place broader appeal. There are twenty-six bedrooms in all, which have been individually appointed. Air-conditioning and wireless Internet access are housed in refined spaces fitted with antiques and Ralph Lauren fabrics, and marble bathrooms are stocked with Annick Goutal body care products. Junior suites include a whirlpool tub and flat-screen televisions, and there are also two guesthouses—one above the canal in a sixteenth-century gabled house, the other in a manor house of the same period.

You would expect a hotel like this to have a library, and the Pand's is beautifully intimate and comes complete with an open fire, Louis Vuitton suitcases, and wooden collectibles. Equally cozy is the candlelit bar, which boasts a leather Chesterfield, mahogany furniture, and an incredibly snug ambience. A clapboard breakfast room leads onto a small courtyard, and there is even a sauna downstairs. All the services of an international deluxe hotel, in other words, with the care and intimacy of a private mansion. **PS**

Enjoy the Duke's Palace

Location Bruges, Belgium
Website www.kempinski-bruges.com **Price** $\$\$$

Amid the cobblestone alleyways and canals of the Belgian town of Bruges, the Kempinski Hotel Duke's Palace, built for Duke Philip III in 1429, has undergone an extensive restoration and is now one of the finest palace hotels in Europe.

Just a short walk from Bruges's colorful market square, it is part hotel, part art gallery. Its rooms are decorated with period ornaments and meticulously restored fifteenth-century artwork. Many historic features have been retained, including the grand ballroom and a heritage-listed chapel, with its expanses of original stained glass still intact and its walls adorned with centuries-old frescoes.

> *"[W]ith its soaring turrets and tranquil gardens, [it is] a perfect base from which to explore."*

Suzanne Cadisch, *Independent*

The hotel's gourmet restaurant serves Belgian specialties, and the bar is home to the most extensive selection of wines and beers in Bruges. Once a month, the large, landscaped garden is transformed into an outdoor exhibition area where guests may buy work from local and regional artists. Handmade chocolates are available in the lounge and are best consumed in front of the fifteenth-century fireplace and its roaring fire on a cold winter's night.

There are also three treatment rooms offering a range of massage and facial therapies, surrounded by stylishly appointed hammams and a sauna, gymnasium, and indoor swimming pool. **BS**

Visit the Royal Greenhouses in Laeken

Location Brussels, Belgium
Website www.monarchie.be/en/visit **Price** Ⓢ

Brussels's surreal side emerges in the mysterious paintings of Magritte—and in the clash of the magical and the mundane seen in the Royal Greenhouses in Laeken. Set on the edge of the city, these palatial greenhouses are where the heady scents of the colonial Congo are transported to everyday Brussels. Entranced visitors drift past orchids, azaleas, and camellias, breathing in the steamy fragrances of bitter oranges and damp ferns. The sinuous art nouveau lines reveal shifting perspectives and sudden glimpses of green canopies, cupolas, turrets, and vaulted tunnels of glass.

The city's tropical greenhouses began as a royal whim, a work of self-glorification spearheaded by King Leopold II (1835–1909). Leopold never deigned to visit the Belgian Congo, but, as a passionate plant man, he expected the Congo to be shipped to him at regular intervals. The challenge was to create "an everlasting springtime in a perfect palace of glass," teasing a tropical garden to grow in northern climes.

Leopold's architects and gardeners fulfilled his every wish, but credit must also be given to the king, whose passion for building was matched by his fascination with exotic plants and palms: from rubber plants and weeping figs to pineapples and dwarf bananas. In these winter gardens, Leopold entertained his friends, swam in his glass-canopied pool, and paraded on an African elephant. Do contact the greenhouses before you travel however, as they can only be visited in a limited summer period. **LGS**

← *This path runs through the center of Palm House in the Royal Greenhouses in Laeken in Brussels.*

Explore the Halligen Islands Archipelago

Location Schleswig-Holstein, Germany
Website www.wattenmeer-nationalpark.de/flag/engl.pdf **Price** ⬤

They are less an archipelago, more small banks of land barely rising above sea level. The Halligen Islands have always been at the mercy of the North Sea—a storm or a high tide can swamp much of the land. If both arrive together, parts of an island can be lost forever. So it is a precarious place to live—houses are built on man-made mounds of earth at least 3 feet (1 m) high to protect against flooding. Yet there is a distinctive beauty to these ten slivers of land. The skies are open and the panoramas wide. Flocks of birds wheel over thatched cottages, redbrick farmsteads, dikes, and fragile causeways. The straight lines of the horizon are

"[The] salt marshes and tidal flats of the Wattenmeer are places of constant flux."

Alan Harper, *Guardian*

punctuated only by the occasional, lone wooden windmill or sturdy stone lighthouse. It is peaceful, rural, and seems a long way from the stresses of a city.

The sea has claimed many of the Halligen over the centuries. Sometimes islands are joined to the mainland by silted causeways and then separated by tidal erosion. There is more legal protection for this watery landscape than physical protection. It is part of Wattenmeer National Park, and visitors come to take guided walks on the tidal flats and to look at migrating birds and distinctive plants. Others just enjoy the ferry trips or the ride on the distinctive narrow railways that link some islands, almost through the waves. **SH**

Visit the Island of Rügen

Location Rügen, Germany **Website** www.ruegen.de
Price ❶

Imagine a quiet island with dazzling white chalk cliffs and long sandy beaches backed by calm expanses of beech woods. Dotted among the rolling hills are pretty cottages, biking and walking trails, medieval churches, stately homes, and castles. Rügen may be Germany's largest island, but it is little known elsewhere. It lies in the Baltic Sea in the northeast of the country, yet benefits from an unusually mild climate.

The island rose to fame in Germany when it was featured in the landscapes of the nineteenth-century romantic painter Casper David Friedrich, and today it is one of the country's most popular vacation destinations. Rügen is easy to reach: A road and railway bridge connects the island with the mainland and there are many ferry connections.

The resorts on the long coastline have sandy beaches and piers, and boat trips are available to Denmark, Sweden, Poland, and neighboring German islands. Visitors simply go to the beach or explore the countryside and coastline—the island contains two national parks and a nature reserve. The spectacular wooded cliffs offer panoramic views of the Baltic Sea and Germany's coastline, and inland the landscapes range from heather-clad hills to reed beds, from woods full of wildflowers to lush, flat farmland.

Much of the architecture dates back to the spa boom of the nineteenth century, and many of the little towns and villages are linked by a historic narrow-gauge steam railway. You may not escape other tourists on Rügen, but you may feel as if you have escaped from the twenty-first century. **SH**

⇥ *The pier in the resort of Sellin on the Island of Rügen has retained its traditional architecture.*

Stay at Kempinski Grand Hotel

Location Mecklenburg-Vorpommern, Germany
Website www.kempinski-heiligendamm.com **Price** 🖲🖲

Looking like a huge, resplendent wedding cake, the Kempinski Grand Hotel Heiligendamm glitters a brilliant white in the sharp midday sun, contrasting beautifully with the azure of the sky and the pale turquoise Baltic Sea. Known as the White Town by the Sea, Heiligendamm is Germany's oldest seaside spa, a dazzling collection of six neoclassical buildings, founded in 1793 by the Grand Duke of Mecklenburg Friedrich Franz I, who came here to take in the clean salty air, lush beech forests, and tideless waters.

The building was briefly used as a sanatorium and hospital in the 1930s but, after a lavish restoration project in 2003, there is little reminder of its recent past, except perhaps for the well-heeled guests trotting to and from the super-deluxe spa in fluffy white slippers and soft, commodious dressing gowns. Tony Blair, Vladimir Putin, and Nicholas Sarkozy descended on the resort for the thirty-third G8 summit, and outside of the political arena Bono and Sir Bob Geldof, among others, have also paid visits.

Dining is taken very seriously. There is an Asian restaurant, a sushi bar, and a number of other upmarket eateries, not to mention the Friedrich Franz gourmet restaurant, one of only a handful in Germany to have a Michelin star. For the fresh-air enthusiast, many sports are available, including horseback riding and sailing. A thirty-minute bicycle ride to the pretty village of Kühlungsborn makes for an ideal day out, as does a trip on the narrow-gauge steam railway, still chugging away after more than 140 years in service. **TW**

⬅ *The Kempinski Grand Hotel Heiligendamm is right on the shore of the Baltic Sea and has lovely views.*

Escape the Crowds at Bürgerpark

Location Bremen, Germany
Website www.buergerpark.de/en **Price** 🖲

Right in the center of one of Germany's biggest cities, Bürgerpark has densely wooded surroundings that are more readily associated with rural areas than major conurbations. Unlike the gardens and parks in most cities, though, it was not devised as a playground for the ruling classes but instead developed for, and by, the Bürger—that is, the ordinary citizens.

In the 1860s, the people of Bremen formed the Committee for the Afforestation of Bürgerweide, and since then they have preserved the park through personal initiatives and donations. Apart from the forestlike terrain and the large meadows, there are also

> ## *"Bürgerpark is . . . reckoned to be one of the best landscaped parks in Germany."*
> *Independent*

landscaped park areas and an animal enclosure. One of the aims of the park is to provide a nature reserve for city dwellers—in particular children—who are unable to travel into rural areas, and the nature and adventure trail within the park provides information about plants and animals as well as their habitats.

The emphasis on furnishing a well-balanced outdoor experience is exemplified by the Finnbahn, a running track devised with a medical institution to reduce stress on the joints. In addition, several venues on the grounds stage cultural events, and the revenue from the concerts and theater performances contributes directly to the maintenance of the park. **DaH**

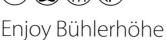

Enjoy Bühlerhöhe

Location Baden-Baden, Germany
Website www.buehlerhoehe.de   **Price** ⊖⊖⊖

Situated high up in the Black Forest and surrounded by 44 acres (18 ha) of wooded parkland, Schlosshotel Bühlerhöhe provides the ideal sanctuary from the pressures of modern life. Yet despite its seclusion, it is only 9 miles (14 km) to the elegant spa resort of Baden-Baden, the summer stomping ground of the European aristocracy in days gone by and whose old town and famous casino are still popular attractions.

The hotel's five-star attention to detail is evident in the decor, facilities, and service that maintains elements of privacy and restfulness. All seventy-seven bedrooms and thirteen suites have been lavishly redecorated and furnished with high-quality, king-size

---

"[It is] situated at one of the most breathtaking panoramic viewing points of the Black Forest."

luxurytravelmagazine.com

---

beds and luxurious mattresses. The spa and health clinic equal that of the hotel rooms for decadence, and pampering and relaxation are the order of the day. Within the wellness area of the hotel, beauty and spa treatments are offered to guests in thoughtfully decorated rooms, the subtle lighting adding to the style and ambience.

Fitness training is also available for those who desire a more active retreat, and a sumptuous swimming pool filled with the hotel's own supply of fresh springwater waits to be dived into. The surrounding woods also provide the perfect backdrop for a gentle afternoon stroll. This is luxury at its best. **TW**

Visit Planten un Blomen

Location Hamburg, Germany
Website www.plantenunblomen.hamburg.de   **Price** ❶

The German city of Hamburg is most famous for its pretty canals and waterways, its red-light district, and its vast harbor that houses some truly enormous ships. Yet it is possible to escape all the bustle in what is in fact a very green city and home to a number of parks. The most tranquil of these gardens is the Planten un Blomen (plants and flowers) park.

The public park was built on the site of the former Zoologischer Garten zoo and surrounding cemeteries in 1930 for a large flower exhibition. The expansive area remained as parkland and was redesigned in 1953, 1963, and 1973 to house various international horticultural exhibitions. The result is an oasis of green and calm in the heart of the city.

The park's extensive square of greenery reaches from the Dammtor railway station almost to the city's St. Pauli neighborhood. Visitors stroll along its pathways admiring the picturesque displays of plants and flowers or popping into various cafés for a glass of wine or a chilled beer. Tropical greenhouses packed with beautiful orchids are situated on the eastern side of the park and were once part of the Alter Botanischer Garten (Old Botanical Garden).

In the height of summer there are jazz concerts at the music pavilion, and light shows are held over the lake nightly at 9 P.M. accompanied by classical music. In winter, the park becomes home to Germany's best and biggest open-air ice-skating rink. Particularly noteworthy is the Japanischer Garten (Japanese Garden), which has a lake at its center, with an authentic Japanese teahouse on its banks. **CK**

➲ *Tulip heads in the botanical garden of Planten un Blomen park provide a diversion from the skyline.*

Cruise the Brandenburg

Location Berlin, Germany
Website www.brandenburg-tourism.com   **Price** 💲💲

With a waterway network of almost 20,000 miles (32,000 km), the area surrounding Berlin is one of the most unique ecosystems in Europe. Comprising more than 3,000 lakes and a labyrinth of scenic canals and idyllic rivers lined with castles, manor houses, timber-framed churches, colorful fields of poppies and cornflowers, and expansive gardens, it is the ideal place for a relaxing yet stimulating getaway.

Since there are no rapids, most of Brandenburg's pristine waterways are great not only for swimming, but also for sailing and canoeing, the weak currents facilitating travel in both directions. About 1,000 miles (1,600 km) of the streams are navigable by motorized

> *"The navigable waterways . . . will give anyone who loves boating a huge adrenaline rush."*
>
> germany-tourism.de

houseboats—there is no need for a special permit as long as they travel at less than 3 miles per hour (5 kph). There are moorings at every major point of interest, making it possible to visit Brandenburg's famous sights without using the area's tree-lined roads.

If it is sheer tranquility you are after, the remote river network of the Spreewald—a forest area dubbed Brandenburg's "Venice"—is a picturesque refuge southeast of Berlin, whereas those who want to be pampered should head to the Saarow Health Resort at Lake Scharmützelsee. If you are in need of urban excitement as well as relaxation, the navigable waters of Berlin present the city in a whole new light. **DaH**

Stay at Hotel Bleibtreu

Location Berlin, Germany
Website www.bleibtreu.com   **Price** 💲💲

Opened in 1995, the Bleibtreu—which translates as "remain faithful" in English—was Berlin's first design hotel. Despite a huge increase in boutique accommodation in the city, the hotel has retained its popularity and continues to appeal to a young, hip crowd. Ensconced in a renovated, nineteenth-century house in Bleibtreustrasse—one of the elegant side streets off Kurfürstendamm, Berlin's famous shopping street—Bleibtreu does not feel or look like a boutique hotel at first glance. The ground floor hosts a buzzing bar, a busy café restaurant, and a florist. Pass through the bustle, though, and a path will lead you through a glass pebble garden to the reception, slightly hidden off a tree-shaded courtyard.

Once inside the Bleibtreu, the distinctive work of designer Herbert Jacob Weinand is evident. The rooms contain individually crafted furnishings, most of them made from untreated woods (in keeping with Bleibtreu's eco-friendly policies), along with Italian mosaics and neutral color schemes. Turning his attention to the olfactory senses, Weinand has sprayed the pieces of wood in the corridors so they each have their own scent.

Taste buds are catered for, too, in Restaurant 31, where the main attraction—aside from the inventive and healthy cuisine—is a lovely, terra-cotta-tiled courtyard. Bleibtreu's basement spa is also a talking point. It is small but packs plenty in, including a steam room, reflexology, acupuncture, a personal trainer, and meditation options. Blumen 31, the hotel's florist, specializes in rare types of roses and all kinds of exotic and bizarre beauties. The hotel's location means you can easily reach all the important sights, restaurants, and cultural events in the west of Berlin. **PS**

Visit Brandenburger Hof

Location Berlin, Germany
Website www.brandenburger-hof.com   **Price** $$

You can tell you are stepping into the former grand town house of a nineteenth-century Prussian aristocrat: The imposing wooden doors open to reveal a crystal chandelier hanging from the decorative plaster ceiling between ornate white pillars and dressed stone walls. Follow the honey-colored parquet into a conservatory that opens into a courtyard of neatly clipped shrubs and stone pathways.

The Brandenburger Hof still has hints of formal Prussian style, but now that formality is diluted with the gentler decor of the Mediterranean—dark leather and shiny steel are combined with light wood and muted colors. The result is a relaxed luxury hotel with

> *"The rooms abound with splendid antiques ... [and the hotel has] a very respectable restaurant."*
>
> The Economist

a fine restaurant and spa, all tucked away on a quiet street in the former West Berlin a short walk from the boutiques of the Kurfürstendamm shopping mile.

The hotel's Die Quadriga restaurant has a Michelin star for its classic Mediterranean cuisine and an exclusive wine list of 850 German vintages. The Thaleia spa creates a feeling of exclusive pampering, serving only one guest at a time. Choose from beauty treatments and therapies like Balinese massage with aromatherapy or thalassotherapy. The suites overlook the Japanese tree garden and are decorated in a Bauhaus style under the diligent eye of owner Daniela Sauter, who manages the hotel, too. **SH**

Unwind at Hotel de Rome

Location Berlin, Germany
Website www.hotelderome.com   **Price** $$$

The former central bank of East Berlin is a grand old building dating back to 1889. It stands on Bebelplatz square, near Humboldt University and the State Opera House. In the center of the square is a memorial marking the spot where Nazis burned thousands of books one night in May 1933.

After unification, the building was a little-used conference center until international hotelier Sir Rocco Forte bought it and spent millions restoring and converting the stately building into a luxury hotel. Hotel de Rome immediately became one of the city's most prestigious hotels and a perfectly located base to explore the capital. The interior has had a modern makeover, but you can still spot clues of its past life: The bank's old underground vault is now a swimming pool and the huge cashiers' hall is a ballroom with stucco paneling, glazed roof, and mosaic floor. The best rooms have wide balconies overlooking the city, and there is an open rooftop terrace that overlooks the square below.

Hotel de Rome's grand public rooms include the Opera Court, with another original glazed ceiling, and Parioli, the acclaimed Italian restaurant, opening out onto the roof deck. The design theme is a mixture of Berlin-style glass and steel, with plenty of Germanic black, red, and gray in the palette, and some expensive and exclusive modern furniture. Suites on the first and second floors were originally the bank managers' offices and keep that dignified atmosphere, with high ceilings, wood paneling, and decorative plaster. Bathrooms boast walk-in showers, mosaic marble, and stand-alone cast-iron baths. Perhaps the best historic remnants are the World War II grenade smithereens left embedded in the wood-paneled walls. **SH**

Explore Wörlitz Park

Location Saxony, Germany
Website www.woerlitz-information.de   **Price** 🌓

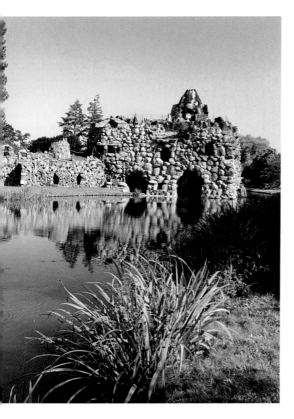

"The Garden Kingdom ... is an exceptional example of landscape design and planning."

UNESCO World Heritage Committee

In the late eighteenth century, a wealthy and well-traveled German prince employed a team of top European gardeners and civil engineers to plan and establish one of the Continent's greatest gardens. More than 200 years later, Prince Leopold's huge, English-style landscape park is still intact. Best of all, the 277 acres (92 ha) are completely free to enter and explore—just as when the gardens first opened.

The park is north of the picturesque town of Wörlitz, near a branch of the River Elbe in Saxony that supplied the water for all the features. Along with various connected smaller garden projects in the region, it has been designated a UNESCO World Heritage site, known as "The Garden Kingdom." But Wörlitz is a garden that is less about plants than design. There are indeed stately flower beds and many varieties of tree, but the park is dominated by grottoes, canals, bridges, man-made islands, temples, monuments, boats, statues, reliefs, and a huge lake. It is so big that there is one area modeled on the estate at Stourhead in England—but here it is intended just as a private garden. Another huge section of canal and islands is believed to be a version of the classical estate at Stowe, also in England.

Whether you glide around the waterways on a gondola or stroll along the pathways, the lines of sight are carefully planned. Groves of trees and sculptures were placed to draw the eye into the landscape. You may stumble upon a palm grove and mock temples, and then a pathway winding through the trees will suddenly open out into a watery panorama. **SH**

🔲 *The Stein building was constructed between 1788 and 1796 and is randomly clad with giant boulders.*

Enjoy Bülow Residenz

Location Dresden, Saxony, Germany
Website www.relaischateaux.com/bulow **Price** $\textcircled{S}$ $\textcircled{S}$

Most people are aware of the Allied bombing that ravaged the city of Dresden on Valentine's Day 1945, but the story of the city's rebirth is less well known. As one of Dresden's tourist chiefs puts it: "Dresden is the only place in the world where the number of historical monuments is growing year by year."

Some small parts of this great baroque city escaped the Allied bombardment. One or two corners of the New Town, such as the Rähnitzgasse, were preserved intact, giving an exact view of what the city was like in its heyday. This is where the Bülow Residenz is to be found—a baroque town palace dating from 1730, meticulously restored by Horst and Monika Bülow after 1989.

The hotel has twenty-five spacious rooms and five suites; on a nearby site, a new wing that will offer guests a luxurious swimming pool is being built. The public rooms are decorated with antique furniture, and there is a lively bar tucked away in the basement. Ralf Kutzner quickly ensured that the hotel's restaurant, Caroussel, gained the reputation for being the best place to eat in the city, and there is no serious challenge to that position today.

Above all, the Bülow Residenz offers the chance to see the modern miracle of Dresden. The famous skyline has been restored with the completion of the Frauenkirche in 2006. Along with the Semper Opera House, the Catholic Cathedral, the Zwinger, the "Green Vault" (containing the amazing treasures of the Saxon kings), and the Picture Gallery, Dresden remains as important as it ever was. Not to be neglected either are the unscathed villas and castles above the Elbe and the old city of Meissen with its porcelain, just a short drive along the river. **GMD**

Stay at Schloss Eckberg

Location Dresden, Saxony, Germany
Website www.schloss-eckberg.de **Price** $\textcircled{S}$ $\textcircled{S}$

Schloss Eckberg is a fairy-tale castle—complete with towers, turrets, and neo-gothic arches—perched on a hill in woodlands just outside the center of Dresden. Outside it has vineyards, herb gardens, and fuchsia rose trees sloping down to meet the river below.

This seventeen-room hotel started life in 1859 as the private residence of a local merchant and has been revamped as an exclusive hideaway that is within easy reach of the city. Each room has expensive antiques and period furniture; some have window seats that look out over immaculately pruned Italianate gardens, the curve of the River Elbe, and Dresden's old town beyond. Others, such as the

> *"Schloss's expanses of empty space . . . can be refreshing after a few days of baroque overload."*
>
> *Town & Country* magazine

honeymoon suite, are built in the towers themselves and are worthy of any princess on her wedding night.

Gastronomes will find themselves in foodie heaven. For formal dining, the walnut-paneled restaurant with its gleaming parquet floor and hand-painted gold-leaf ceiling serves up typically German dishes such as sour beef "Saxon style" and savoy cabbage and potato. To savor the wonderful view, reserve a table in the winter garden with its floor-to-ceiling gothic windows, or, if it is late in the evening, the atmospheric stone wine cellar (complete with attendant gargoyles) stocks a huge range of wines from Saxony and beyond and makes a cozy pit stop before bedtime. **TW**

Ride Brockenbahn Railway

Location Harz Mountains, Germany
Website www.harzmagic-info.co.uk/Brockenbahn.html **Price** ⊖

If you like white-knuckle train rides, you will love the Brockenbahn Railway. Chugging its way up to the summit of the Brocken, at 3,743 feet (1,141 m) the highest mountain in north Germany, this venerable old steam train twists and turns its way upward as it negotiates the steep gradients.

The Brockenbahn is one of three railways that form the Harzer Schmalspurbahnen narrow-gauge railway in the Harz Mountain region, the others being the Harzquerbahn and Selketalbahn. Most of the trains still run on steam, many using vintage 1950s locomotives. The journey takes you through the spectacularly varied scenery of Harz National Park, a place of brooding forests, soaring cliffs, and weird and wonderful rock formations. The mountains have a special place in Germanic folklore: Every April 30, known as Walpurgisnacht, Harz witches are said to join the devil at the top of the Brocken before descending with him into the underworld. The mountains were also immortalized by Wolfgang Goethe, who was so enthralled by them that he set the witches' Sabbath scene here in his famous tragedy *Faust*.

The region is dotted with picturesque medieval towns and villages, the most notable one being the hilltop town of Goslar, which has World Heritage status and has been dubbed "the Rome of the North." In winter, when the densely packed fir and beech trees are dusted with powdery snow and the rivers and streams glisten in the low winter sun, the landscape is a shimmering wonderland. In summer, you can enjoy the journey in one of the open-air carriages. **TW**

→ *A steam locomotive cuts through the frozen wonderland of snow in the Harz Mountains.*

Rejuvenate at Parkschlösschen

Location Bad Wildstein, Germany
Website www.parkschloesschen.de **Price** 🚫🚫

Parkschlösschen is not the place to rekindle a flagging love life: Guests at this charming old hotel in the rolling hills and vineyards of the Moselle Valley in western Germany are advised to remain celibate during their stay. It is not because the proprietors are particularly prudish; the sex ban is all in the name of health.

This rambling and peaceful retreat hidden among tall trees offers an escape into a world of alternative therapies and is a leading proponent of ayurveda, a 5,000-year-old Eastern healing art using detoxification, herbal preparations, nutrition, and massages. The entire 11-acre (4-ha) park and art nouveau castle are run on the ayurveda theory of "health deriving from harmony with yourself and nature." The hotel was completely renovated with natural materials like wool, wood, slate, and marble, and the water is supplied from a nearby thermal spring. All rooms have been systematically purged of the "harmful influences" of electric cables (now fitted with double insulation), and water pipes (covered with a marble shield) are decorated in gentle pastel colors.

Parkschlösschen's team of ayurveda doctors (with conventional medical backgrounds) monitor guests to ensure they get the maximum benefit from their stay. It has become a haven for stressed executives, those recuperating from illness or surgery, and health-conscious visitors. Guests swim, play tennis, or hike in the woods, and there are saunas, massages, yoga, meditation, and alternative treatments. The hotel has a no-children policy, and cell phones are actively discouraged. The gourmet meals are vegetarian and dairy-free and no alcohol, coffee, or tea is served. Instead, guests are encouraged to drink warm water. **SH**

Explore Kellerwald National Park

Location Kassel, Germany
Website www.nationalpark-kellerwald-edersee.de **Price** 🔵

What a forest! Kellerwald National Park covers the hills and valleys disappearing to the horizon, wrapping around lakes, and encasing rivers. You can walk all day and not reach the end of it. This pristine wooded wilderness is the biggest deciduous forest you will find in central Europe, flowing over hills and mountains for approximately 14,000 acres (5,665 ha). Carved by the Eder River into canyons, hills, and valleys, it makes a perfect escape from the urban world.

The sea of red beech trees here is extraordinarily old. More than a third were planted more than 120 years ago and many started growing in the

> *"The ancient trees with their countless hollows ... are already home to a number of rare species."*
>
> germany-tourism.de

seventeenth century. Kellerwald National Park is also home to rare species including the black stork, eagle owl, raven, wildcat, red kite, stag beetle, and fire salamander. You may spot a red deer, hear woodpeckers, and see bats swooping around as night falls. More than 400 springs originate in the park, uniting to form forest creeks with the highest biological water quality—perfect for brown trout.

This is such a total escape that there is not even a human safety policy in place. Old trees in danger of falling or breaking are not removed and visitors are told to proceed at their own risk, particularly after storms, and the forest is all the better for it. **SH**

Follow the German Wine Route to the Pfälzer Wald

Location Rhineland-Palatinate, Germany
Website www.germany-tourism.de   **Price** 🚻

Leaving the autobahn far behind, follow the roads through the beautiful open countryside around Kandel, Minfeld, Winden, and Bad Bergzabern and explore the quiet lanes by car, bike, or on foot. Here, orchards of apples and pumpkins provide autumn color, and small fields of corn mingle with vineyards that supply new wine sold locally from the roadside.

The *Deutsche Weinstraße* (German wine route) passes through many beautifully preserved, half-timbered villages where vines twist their way up houses and bunches of grapes hang in the sunshine; look for the signs with a wine jug indicating a place to taste the wine. The Mediterranean-like climate allows apricots, sweet chestnuts, figs, and lemons to thrive, and these too are sold in baskets at the end of driveways.

Despite the route being marked as a tourist trail, the roads are quiet in the nearby sleepy villages and not marked on the tourist maps. They become ever more remote as you climb up into Pfälzer Wald Natural Park, the woods and twisting roads hiding any habitation. The evergreen, sweet chestnut, and oak trees give way every now and again to rich glades dappled with sunshine; the river valleys of the Saarbach and Speyerbach twist below the roads in mirror image, and the hilltops provide striking views over the *wald*. Forest villages punctuate the routes, providing welcome bakeries with wafting smells of fresh-baked bread and roadside restaurants serving rustic local fare. The residents may be there, but it gets increasingly hard to spot a tourist. **CM**

↗ *These scenic autumnal vineyards line the route as you wind your way into Pfälzer Wald Natural Park.*

"Here the climate is mild, the scenery like Tuscany's, and people are warm and friendly too."

germany-tourism.de

Relax at Bareiss Hotel

Location Black Forest, Germany
Website www.bareiss.com **Price** 🔵🔵

It is well worth taking the scenic route to the Bareiss Hotel and Spa, lost in the depths of the Black Forest near Baiersbronn-Mitteltal, in southwest Germany. The winding roads snake through dark, enchanted forests, taking you deep into the Hansel and Gretel landscape.

The beauty of Bareiss is that it can be anything you want it to be: a gourmet's dream, a place of pampering, or simply somewhere to enjoy nature. With five pools, three saunas, and whirlpools, Bareiss is renowned for its state-of-the art spa. Offering everything from ayurveda to osteopathy means that whether you want to indulge in some marine-inspired Thalgo body treatments or go for an exotic Tibetan back massage,

---

"A meal at Bareiss is an assault on all the senses. Expect extraordinary, multilayered tastes."

Sue Style, *Financial Times*

---

it is all possible. Guests can also enjoy golf, fishing, or hiking, and can even take painting or cooking lessons. Among the restaurants at Bareiss is one with three Michelin stars and an 18,000-bottle wine cellar run by Claus-Peter Lumpp, who trained with Alain Ducasse. There is also a Mediterranean restaurant with light Italian meals on the menu, as well as an authentic historic Tyrolean parlor, the Dorfstuben. A rustic, wood-paneled bistro, it has an impressive collection of traditional wall-mounted clocks, and smiling waitresses in traditional garb dish up Black Forest specialties like bacon pancakes, sausage salad, and freshly smoked trout, with cool draft pilsner. **RCA**

Camp at Hopfensee

Location Bavaria, Germany
Website www.camping-hopfensee.de **Price** 🔵

A campsite unlike any other, this vast yet peaceful complex sits next to the beautiful Lake Hopfen, the verdant pastures of the King's Nook, and the Bavarian Alps juxtaposed side by side. The lake is considered one of the warmest in the Bavarian Allgäu region and is ideal for swimming, fishing, and nonmotorized water sports. The picturesque town of Füssen is 3 miles (5 km) away, and a little farther on sits one of the busiest tourist destinations in the region, King Ludwig II's fairy-tale Neuschwanstein castle. You can see the plains from the grounds of the castle, and the temptation to dodge the crowds to reach the green fields below is compelling.

In the exclusive grounds of the five-star campsite, you can escape the throng, whiling away your time in the spa—a place that "patients" visit to be "cured" of their ailments; the pure air and the relaxation alone are often enough. Based upon holistic medicine therapies developed by Kneipp, a native of the area, the registered physiotherapy practice on the campsite offers a selection of treatments for many common ailments. These must be booked in advance—up to three months for summer visits. However, for guests who simply need relaxation, the spa, situated in the center of the campsite, also offers massages, bath and beauty treatments, a sauna, and a solarium.

The campsite, with its heated indoor swimming pool, is open all year, and in winter it includes a 38-mile (61-km) cross-country skiing trail direct from the site, with skis, toboggans, and bicycles for rent. The spacious campsite spots are for trailers or motor homes (tents are not allowed—despite the name). If you do not wish to self-cater, there is an airy glass-roofed restaurant that serves superb food. **CFM**

Discover Berchtesgaden

Location Bavaria, Germany
Website www.kehlsteinhaus.de/en/index.php   **Price** $

Seventy-five miles (120 km) southeast of Munich, near the Austrian border, the breathtaking winding roads of the German Alps lead up to a mountain retreat that has been a popular vacation destination since the days when the concept of pleasure trips was still completely alien to ordinary people. Members of the Bavarian nobility first appropriated Berchtesgaden for themselves, as did the Nazis later on, before the area finally became a getaway to be enjoyed by everyone.

Within the national park itself, the snowcapped twin peaks of the Watzmann mountain loom over Berchtesgaden's picturesque church spires and the deep glacial Lake Königssee. The surrounding alpine

---

"Dramatic mountain scenery in the area offers some of the best views in the Alps."

William Cook, *Guardian*

---

meadows are populated with cattle, and ancient traditions that appear quaint to urban visitors are still upheld in Berchtesgaden. Mountain hiking and boating on Lake Königssee are among the most popular activities, with the awe-inspiring scenery inducing a sense of peace. For those who are more inclined towards physical exertion skiing is an option in winter, while the Watzmann Ostwand cliff provides a challenge for rock climbers. Meanwhile, Adolf Hitler's former residence, the Eagle's Nest, is a reminder of Berchtesgaden's links with the Nazis. Despite these links, the area's indisputable beauty and its slow pace of life make for a perfectly relaxing stay. **DaH**

Stay at Schloss Elmau

Location Bavaria, Germany
Website www.schloss-elmau.de   **Price** $$

"A place of healing for healthy people who feel burdened" was how Johannes Müller, philosopher and founder of Schloss Elmau, described the castle in 1914 when it first opened. It instantly became a magnet for artists, bohemians, and aesthetes of all kinds looking for a cultural hideaway to rejuvenate their tired minds and bodies. It is still run along the same lines, and visitors come as much for its cultural leanings (there are around one hundred events throughout the year, including a literature week, jazz festival, dance and poetry workshops, and political debates) as for the scenery and pampering.

A fire in 2005 destroyed much of the building but a complete restoration has returned it to its former glory, and more besides. Set in a valley all on its own and framed by the Wetterstein, a near-vertical rock face, the scenery is truly deserving of the much-touted epithet "breathtaking." If you have ever wondered what it must be like to find yourself in the movie *The Sound of Music*, this must surely come close: soaring mountains, wildflower-strewn hillsides, crystal-clear lakes, the tinkling of cowbells, and more than 70 miles (112 km) of hiking and mountain-bike trails to explore. The famous picture-book hunting lodge of King Ludwig II is a three-hour hike away.

Each of the elegant 140 rooms and suites in the Elmau, some with walk-in closets, comes with a Bose sound system, silk-covered walls, and gleaming floors made of polished oak or teak. There are two luxury spas, concert halls, three libraries, a bookstore, an upmarket shopping arcade, and six wonderful gourmet restaurants. Once a year, usually in November, chefs from around the world come to take part in the hotel's international gourmet festival. **TW**

Discover Ushant

Location Finistère, France   **Website** www.ouessant.fr
Price 🚻

In French the name is "Ouessant," in English "Ushant." It is a wild, rocky place 10 miles (16 km) outside of Brest and surrounded by ferocious cliffs and dangerous seas, tides, and currents. Amid the Atlantic waves, France's most westerly point seems a vulnerable little dot. It is just 4 by 2 miles (6 by 3 km) but has become world famous because of its location, its devastating winter storms, and a history of sea battles between the French and the English in times gone by. Ushant is also a regular on radio shipping forecasts, standing guard at the entrance to the busiest shipping channel in the world with its ring of lighthouses.

You arrive via a potentially choppy ferry journey from Brest or the Breton fishing village of Le Conquet. The boat docks at Stiff Bay, and it is best to travel around the island on a rental bike or minibus. To some, the treeless sheep pastures are bleak; to others the rocks, grass, and thick-walled white houses crouched against the elements are beautiful.

On the other side of the island, the one village is called Lampaul. In it you will find a couple of bars, a restaurant and bakery, two small hotels, some bed-and-breakfast accommodation, and a few *gîtes* (small vacation homes). In the summer, hydrangeas and fuchsias drape against whitewashed stone walls. In winter, you realize why windows are set 3 feet (1 m) deep into the walls for protection.

Visitors wander around breathing the bracing clean sea air deeply. You may spot seals and seabirds, or you may choose to spend your time taking photographs, painting, walking, or bicycling. **SH**

← *The Créac'h lighthouse on the island of Ushant rises high above the rocky coast that surrounds it.*

Relax on the Île de Batz

Location Finistère, France **Website** www.iledebatz.com **Price**

At just 2 miles (3.2 km) long by 1 mile (1.6 km) wide, Île de Batz is only a speck on the map just off Roscoff in northern Brittany. But it is a big step back in time to the romantic France of horse-drawn plows, old men in berets, and bicycling housewives wobbling on their way home. On the island, the sand is white, rocks are sculptures of rounded granite, and cottages shelter beneath pines and palms. The only traffic is tractors. There is not a single amusement arcade, nightclub, or noisy road in sight—just lovingly tended fields of organic vegetables, eighteen beaches, and 10 miles (16 km) of jagged coastline.

Batz is adored by Parisian high-fliers, politicians, and celebrities, who change into baggy shorts and flip-flops to taste the simple life among rugged seascapes and hedgerows teeming with fuchsias, nasturtiums, and hydrangeas. They sit at harborside cafés eating crêpes and sipping Breton cider; they stroll around the island's lighthouse, duck ponds, and overgrown forts.

The small exotic garden of tropical flowers was created by a rich Parisian in 1897 when he discovered the average temperature on the island varies by only a few degrees throughout the whole year. Frost is extremely rare thanks to the sheltered location and warm sea currents. One of the best-loved sights here is the ancient French captain who sits in the harbor every day looking out to sea cuddling his equally ancient pet tortoise.

There are two old-fashioned hotels, forty *gîtes* (small vacation homes), and a few guesthouses, but hardly any non-French speakers. Making it more difficult for outsiders is the use of the ancient Breton tongue for many signs, place and house names, and even items on restaurant menus. One of the best places to stay is a stylish bed-and-breakfast called Ti Va Zadou. **SH**

⬆ *Many small boats dot the shore of the tiny island of Batz off the coast of northern Brittany.*

Explore the Fjords of Finistère

Location Finistère, France   **Website** www.finisteretourisme.com   **Price** 🌢

The most westerly *département* in France, Finistère derives its name from the Latin for "the ends of the Earth." In the native Breton tongue, still spoken in these parts, its name *Penn ar bed* means "the beginning of the world." Whichever way you look at it, the area is renowned for its dramatic coastline and sense of isolation from the rest of the world—whether it is at the start or the end of it. Like its counterpart Land's End in England, the rough, rugged coastline is endowed with romantic tales, shipwrecks, smugglers, and myths and legends.

The wild coastline here looks out to the English Channel along the north coast of the département and is known for its *abers*, or fjords. There are three of them along the north coast: L'Aber Ildut, L'Aber Wrac'h, and L'Aber Benoît, funnel-shaped fjords that give a dramatic shape to the coast. L'Aber Ildut is the smallest and divides the Atlantic Ocean and the English Channel; L'Aber Benoît is 5 miles (8 km) long and has eight villages along it; and L'Aber Wrac'h is the most celebrated. It holds five islands within it, including Vierge Island, which has the tallest lighthouse in Europe, a popular yachting harbor, and many pretty stone villages.

Perhaps the best way to explore Finistère is by foot. It is known as the coast of legends for good reason—fairy stories abound, linking tales of King Arthur and Celtic travelers with Cornwall, and there are megaliths, Celtic sites, and holy springs to visit. You can follow *le sentier des lutins* (the pixie footpath) along the most exposed and westerly headland, La Pointe du Raz, which takes you between the moorland and the sea. The Path of Lighthouses takes you on a 62-mile (100-km) trek from Portsall to Brest, taking in 23 of Finistère's 111 lighthouses on the way. **LD**

⬆ *A wooden staircase leads down to the waters of Aber Wrac'h fjord on Finistère.*

Discover Paimpont Forest

Location Ille-et-Vilaine, France
Website www.bretagne35.com **Price** 🍷

Paimpont Forest sits in the municipality of Paimpont, a land of high moorlands, deep valleys, and dense sun-dappled woodlands. Known in mythology as Brocéliande, the brooding forest is haunted by the spirits of King Arthur and his queen Guinevere, the fabled knights of the Round Table, the wizard Merlin, and the fairies Viviane and Morgane. In fact, dozens of legends of that far-off Celtic age of courtly romance and chivalry are set in the region. Here it is easy to imagine Morgane leaning out over the Étang des Forges lake to be entranced by the Fountain of Youth or to shed a tear at Merlin's Tomb—especially if you have imbibed a little of the local cider.

> *"Whoso pulleth out this sword of this stone and anvil, is . . . king born of all England."*
>
> Thomas Malory, *Le Mort D'Arthur*

Age-old Megalithic sites pay testament to the area's rich and mysterious history, whereas the wild valleys of the Aff and Serein rivers pay testament to the power of nature. There is a wealth of marked walking, bicycling, and horseback-riding trails.

The award-winning Brocéliande Gardens at Bréal-sous-Montfort must not be missed, nor should ancient Rennes, the capital of Brittany, which today proudly flies the black-and-white Breton flag over its cobbled medieval streets. Other nearby attractions to visit include the book-lover's town of Becherel, the flour mill museum at Médréac, the park at Treffendel, and the museum at Saint Meen le Grand. **RsP**

Visit Mont St. Michel

Location Manche, France
Website www.ot-montsaintmichel.com/accueil_gb.htm **Price** 🍷

The sight of Mont St. Michel nestling in a huge bay like a medieval monastic pyramid attracts four million visitors a year. They converge on the gothic spires, tumbling gardens, and unbroken fortifications perched dramatically on an isolated mound of rock a mile offshore.

Few people know the best way to savor this amazing place, though. Simply wait until the buses and visitors leave in the late afternoon—then you have the fairy-tale island to yourself until mid-morning the next day. Better still, the cheap souvenir stalls shut as visitors leave, so the main street suddenly slips 600 years backward through time.

Stay at the fifteenth-century, half-timbered inn overhanging the ancient cobbled street leading up to the abbey. It is actually built into the island's fortifications at the back. It may be a cheap, friendly auberge, but St. Pierre's is a listed French historic monument in its own right. Inside is a creaking labyrinth of old beams, wood paneling, tapestries, leaded windows, winding staircases, ancient wooden shutters, and exposed stone walls. The restaurant is a classic Gallic affair with an open fire and red checkered tablecloths, serving dishes like shellfish from the bay and roast lamb from inland farms.

It is cozy rather than luxurious, but what five-star hotel has a door from its landing onto the ramparts of a World Heritage site? Using their hotel key, guests can pop out in the middle of the night in their pajamas to stand on the battlements and watch the tide rushing in across the vast mudflats. **SH**

➡ *The isolated, fortified island of Mont St. Michel rises high above the mudflats like a fairy-tale castle.*

Follow the Route du Cidre

Location Calvados and Orne, France
Website www.cambremer.com **Price** ⑤

As a marked tourist trail, this should be a busy place. However, the 25-mile (40-km) route, along narrow country lanes in gentle, rolling countryside, rarely sees much traffic. Explore at a leisurely pace to allow for peering over blossom-filled hedges and gazing at the views, the apple orchards, and the farms.

This circular route links a series of small Normandy villages, the traditional timber-studded houses adorned with geraniums trailing from window boxes. With small herds of cows grazing the orchards and chickens roaming the farmyards, this is a rural idyll of yesteryear. Visiting the twenty or so small-scale cider producers along the way provides perfect stop-off

> *"Its landscape of pastures and orchards . . . with half-timbered farms is . . . a perfect rural idyll."*
>
> Emily Hatchwell, *Independent*

points. You are expected (although not obliged) to taste the calvados or the local specialty, *pommeau*, and each one is different. The producers adjust the flavor according to generations of family recipes.

For drivers, tasting the refreshing *jus de pomme* is a nonalcoholic alternative, and although the route is perfect for bicyclists, remember your bike may not be capable of carrying the bounty you cannot help but acquire along the way, so bewitching is the taste. Try to make a stop in the village of Beuvron-en-Auge; it is considered to be one of the most beautiful in France, and on Sundays it fills with local families who gather in tiny *crêperies* for traditional Norman treats. **CM**

Stay at La Ferme St. Siméon

Location Calvados, France
Website www.fermesaintsimeon.fr **Price** ⑤⑤

Honfleur's loveliest hotel is not in the famous old port with its ancient houses and gray slate roofs, but on the heights above. It makes a strong claim to being the cradle of Impressionism. Painters such as Monet, Sisley, Jongkind, and Courbet were lured there by the effects of the sunlight reflected off the Seine estuary. In those days, La Ferme St. Siméon was run by La Mère Toutain, an innkeeper tolerant of painters and their eccentric habits.

The first painter to see the potential of the inn was Eugène Boudin, the son of a local fisherman, who liked to eat mackerel and drink the local cider. He introduced Monet to the hotel. When the painters could not pay, they left a painting. The Ferme was a thatched farm then, but its present appearance dates from 1888. These days it is not so much poor painters who frequent the place, but the likes of Clint Eastwood or Sophie Marceau, who avail themselves of the helipad and the plush suites. The current owners—the Boelen family—do, however, maintain the artistic tradition by inviting students from the École des Beaux-Arts in Paris to enjoy the famous light. Their bills must be paid in paintings.

Naturally the inn is now a luxury hotel with twenty-five rooms and four suites, complete with spa and indoor swimming pool and a wonderful restaurant that makes full use of the famous local ingredients: soft and cream cheeses, calvados and apples, and excellent local veal. There is a wine list to match that is worth scrutinizing—it contains some real bargains.

The Boelens also own La Chaumière (the Cottage) on the coast nearby. It has just eight rooms and less extravagant cuisine based upon local ingredients, but simple cider is still available in both. **GMD**

Taste Champagne at Reims

Location Marne, France
Website www.champagne.com/en_indx.html   **Price** 💲

Combining a bike ride with tasting champagne may sound like a recipe for disaster, but it is the ideal way to explore Reims. The pretty town is France's champagne capital, famed for being home to some of the world's best producers. Think Taittinger, Veuve Clicquot, Piper Heidsieck, Mumm, and Pommery.

The natural geology of the region lends itself perfectly to champagne production. Caves have been formed by the erosion of chalk rock, creating cellars where the wine is stored. Visitors can tour the cellars, learn about the production process, and then, of course, sample some of the good stuff. Dress warmly because the cellars are cool; the temperatures range

---

"Reims is the pretty hub of bubbly and an ideal base for a bicycling break."

Guardian

---

from 46 to 50°F (8 to 10°C). It is not always necessary to make an appointment; many of the champagne houses welcome passing visitors.

Beginning in Reims, the champagne route winds its way past perfectly preened vineyards on lush hillsides punctuated by small quaint villages. Along the way, you will pass the premises of some big names, such as Claude-Remy and Clouet-Vazard. The scenery is glorious and can be savored while bicycling leisurely between champagne houses. It is easy to rent a bike in Reims, and there are bicycle routes for all levels. Note that many of the champagne houses close in September and October, during the grape harvest. **JK**

Unwind at Les Crayères

Location Marne, France
Website www.lescrayeres.com   **Price** 💲💲

Les Crayères is a mansion that once belonged to the princes of Polignac, cousins of the Grimaldis, the rulers of Monaco. The Polignacs were also owners of Pommery champagne, and until recently the chief winemaker at Pommery was Alain de Polignac, a direct descendant of one of Champagne's most famous widows: Jeanne-Alexandrine Pommery, who ran the company with distinction after her husband's death.

Although it is on the outskirts of the art deco city of Reims, Les Crayères has the atmosphere of a country house hotel thanks to its 20-acre (8-ha) park; it also has the considerable advantage of being close to the Roman chalk quarries where the best champagne is stored. Visits to the cellars of any of the major champagne houses can be arranged through reception, but the historic link to Pommery means that if you are lucky, the staff will show you how to "saber" a bottle of champagne by running a sword along its neck and lopping off the cork. You will also have the chance to admire the chalk bas-reliefs by the artist Gustave Navlet.

The kitchens at Les Crayères achieved fame under Gérard Boyer, one of France's most distinguished three-star chefs. Boyer recently sold the mansion to Xavier Gardinier—the owner of Château Phelan Ségur in Bordeaux—and Gardinier hired the Monagasque chef Didier Elela to be the right sort of successor to Boyer. Elela was a close personal assistant to Alain Ducasse for fifteen years; when Ducasse opened in New York, it was Elela who cooked. Being in Champagne, Elela makes his dishes act as a foil to the wine. He has one menu where every dish comes with a different glass of Roederer and includes a flute of the famous Cristal with the main course. **GMD**

Enjoy Lake Gérardmer

Location Vosges, France   **Website** www.gerardmer.net
Price ❶

In the northeast of France, close to the German border and high in the Vosges Mountains, Lake Gérardmer is a haven of peace and tranquility. In the summer, the 285-acre (115-ha) lake is a playground for water sports enthusiasts—particularly windsurfers and sailors—with a backdrop of verdant mountains and pretty chalets along the shoreline. In winter, it is one of France's smaller ski resorts, far from the schnapps-swilling, après-ski crowd, where beginner and intermediate skiers can enjoy their sport in relative peace while the locals take to the 62 miles (100 km) of cross-country ski trails around the pine trees and up to breathtaking viewpoints.

Jet-set it is not, but that is the appeal. The pretty chalets and hotels surrounding the lake instead owe their attraction to the grandeur of times gone by. The Hotel Manoir du Lac, for example, was a refuge for the nineteenth-century French writer Guy de Maupassant, who had a great desire for solitude in his later years and relished the peace of the area.

These days, Lake Gérardmer is less a haunt of scholarly writers and more a natural setting for activities of every type. In early September each year, for example, the region is flooded with athletes for the Triathlon de Gérardmer, in which competitors swim the clear lake, bike in nearby mountains that have formed part of the Tour de France route, and run around the wooded hillsides. From nineteenth-century literature through to gentle ski slopes and extreme sporting competitions, Gérardmer is a true retreat for fresh-air fans of all descriptions. **LD**

➡ *Lake Gérardmer's location high in the mountains makes it an ideal escape in both summer and winter.*

Enjoy Abbaye de la Bussière

Location Côte-d'Or, France
Website www.abbaye-dela-bussiere.com **Price** 💲💲

The monks may have long since departed, but there is still an air of tranquility surrounding Abbaye de la Bussière, set deep in the heart of the Burgundy countryside. This former monastery, which dates back to the twelfth century, is situated in 15 acres (6 ha) of beautiful parkland in a lush valley between Beaune and Dijon. It is studded with fifty-one species of tree, with a small river, the Arvot, flowing through the grounds and feeding the large ornamental lake. The building has been transformed into a luxury country house hotel by English owners, the Cummings family, who are also proprietors of the renowned Amberley Castle Hotel in Sussex, England.

The grand interiors have been sympathetically refurbished and include dramatic vaulted ceilings, 20-foot (6-meter) high stained-glass windows, stone balustrades, and a romantic sweeping staircase. Although the Abbaye is unmistakably ecclesiastical in appearance, there is nothing remotely monastic about the eleven rooms: Toile de Jouy fabrics, chaise longues, and enormous beds (some four-poster) piled high with plump cushions make the rooms a far cry from their simpler origins. The bathrooms are decidedly twenty-first century, with power showers, whirlpool tubs, and Bulgari toiletries.

Although the interiors owe more than a passing nod to English country house style, the food here is undoubtedly Gallic. In a region known for its cuisine and wine, the Abbaye can hold its head high. Chef Olivier Elzer already has one Michelin star to his name, and conjures up imaginative dishes for his guests such as snails and scallops or beef and pigeon, relying heavily on local produce. Naturally, each dish is paired with fine wines from the best regional producers. **HA**

Cruise the Burgundy Canal

Location Côte-d'Or to Nièvre, France
Website www.burgundy-canal.com **Price** 💲

Cruising on the Burgundy Canal is the perfect way to discover this attractive corner of France, renowned for its wine and culture. The quiet waterway retains an old-fashioned charm with beautifully converted barges gliding past vineyards and sunflower fields, rolling farmland, and forested hills at their most glorious in autumn colors.

Itineraries vary, but a typical cruise would take a week to sail the 31 miles (50 km) from Dijon to Vandenesse, traveling by day at a leisurely pace and allowing ample time to appreciate the scenery. Pampered by captain and crew, all you have to do is relax. Deluxe barges have spacious decks with alfresco

---

"Said to be the most beautiful canal in France, it [winds] through glorious countryside."

Liz Myers, *Guardian*

---

dining and often a whirlpool tub; belowdecks, soothing decor greets guests in the lounge and dining areas, bar, library, and bright double or twin cabins.

For those who want a little more, almost anything can be arranged, from hot-air ballooning to horseback riding or golf. Passengers may hop off the boat to bike or walk along the banks and rejoin at the next lock. Predinner drinks are served on deck as the sun sets over the water and every meal is a gourmet treat, to be enjoyed with fine local wine. **SoH**

> The medieval village of Châteauneuf overlooks the Auxois plains and the Burgundy Canal.

Stay on *Bateau Simpatico*

Location Paris, France **Website** www.quai48parisvacation.com
Price 💲💲

In the world's most romantic city, what could be more romantic than staying on a boat on the River Seine, just at the foot of the Eiffel Tower? The idea is simple: *Bateau Simpatico* is a converted Dutch cargo barge moored on the Left Bank. It has been painstakingly restored and is now full of the polished brass and varnished wood that conjures up the image of classic wooden sailing ships. Now the owner rents the boat out to visitors as a floating vacation home.

You reach the *Simpatico* via a tree-lined street leading down to a cobbled riverside dock. It was once a busy working quay for the builders of the Eiffel Tower; now it is the peaceful mooring for a community of houseboats. For tourists, this is a fabulous location—within walking distance of the cafés, restaurants, shops, museums, and monuments of central Paris. Catch the waterbus nearby for trips upriver to the Louvre Museum or Notre Dame Cathedral or use the two free bicycles provided.

The old sailing barge is almost one hundred years old and surprisingly spacious. Inside there is a king-size bedroom, full-sized and well-equipped kitchen, bathroom with shower, and huge living room. The boat can sleep up to four. Amid the wood-paneled interior, you will find a leather sofa and armchairs, dining table and chairs, library of maps and books about Paris, plus assorted nautical knickknacks like an old sea chest and a pair of binoculars. The huge open deck above is a memorable spot to relax under a parasol with coffee and croissants in the morning or cocktails in the evening. **SH**

← *The* Simpatico *(center) is moored on the doorstep of the Eiffel Tower, on the banks of the River Seine.*

Explore the Marais

Location Paris, France **Website** www.parismarais.com
Price 🚶

The Marais, a neighborhood located in Paris's third and fourth arrondissements, offers ample opportunity to discover the heart of the city. Originally marshland (*marais* means "swamp"), the neighborhood was occupied by Parisian nobility in the seventeenth and eighteenth centuries and later by workers and artisans. In the early twentieth century, a thriving Jewish quarter grew up in the Marais, and it now has a large Chinese community and a vibrant gay scene.

At the heart of the Marais is the signature Paris square Place des Vosges, built by King Henry IV of France in 1605 and considered one of the most beautiful public squares in the world. Built with a small

> *"There is one thing stronger than all the armies in the world, and that is an idea whose time has come."*
>
> **Victor Hugo, French writer, lived in Place des Vosges**

public park in the center, the square is fronted on four sides by harmonious redbrick and stone facades; restaurants, galleries, and boutique stores line the arcades that run along the square. Stop for an aperitif at one of the many cafés or have an impromptu picnic in the park with a baguette, cheese, and other treats purchased from the local shops. (For a quintessential Parisian baguette, try the Levain du Marais on Rue de Turenne, one block east of Place des Vosges.)

The Marais is one of two protected areas in Paris, with strict zoning and preservation laws. Its narrow streets lined with independent cafés, stores, and galleries provide an intimate window into the past. **BS**

Discover Montmartre

Location Paris, France
Website www.parisdigest.com/promenade/montmartre   **Price** 🌓

Often regarded as the last Parisian village because of its original rural setting, the French capital's highest point is famous for its bohemian past. Named after the 425-foot (130-m) hill Montmartre, nowadays the area is a major tourist hot spot; its connection with the likes of van Gogh and Toulouse-Lautrec is thoroughly exploited on Place du Tertre, where aspiring painters sketch tourists who are willing to part with a few euros. However, once you venture beyond the various souvenir shops, the alleyways surrounding the stunning nineteenth-century Romano-Byzantine-style basilica Sacré-Coeur are a throwback to the quarter's days as a village, and offer refuge from the hustle and bustle of the metropolis below.

Another church in the area, St. Jean l'Evangéliste de Montmartre, is far less frequented by tourists yet equally intriguing. Located near Montmartre's seedy Pigalle area, the church combines Moorish influences with art nouveau to create a unique atmosphere. Not far from here, the Chapelle des Martyrs—named in honor of St. Denis, who was allegedly beheaded on the site—is another quiet spot to escape the crowds.

A short walk south, the intimate garden café at the Musée de la Vie Romantique makes for a perfect break before heading back toward Sacré-Coeur and the most surprising sight in the entire city: Les Vignes de Montmartre. The vineyard—now owned by the city of Paris—was initially created in 1930 in order to prevent investors from building new houses. These days it is the pride of the locals, and the bucolic setting makes you feel as though you are anywhere but in a city. **DaH**

> ➔ *Night or day, Montmartre bustles with activity—
> there is plenty to explore just off the beaten path.*

Visit Albert Kahn Gardens

Location Paris, France
Website www.gardenvisit.com   **Price** ◑

In the middle of Paris, there is a secret garden that even the city's taxi drivers have difficulty tracking down. The Albert Kahn Gardens and Museum in the suburbs of Boulogne-Billancourt is a hidden gem that has somehow managed to remain off the tourist radar—and is all the more lovely for it.

Albert Kahn was a French banker and millionaire philanthropist with utopian ideals who decided to use his wealth to create an "archive of the planet." His beautiful 10-acre (4-ha) gardens are a real amalgam of horticultural styles from around the world; there are Japanese, French, and English gardens, and also three

> *"On the brook below, green lily pads swayed in a chill breeze redolent of early jasmine."*
>
> Jacqueline McGrath, *New York Times*

"mini-forests" with terrain that you might find in Africa, Asia, or the United States. The gardens were a fashionable meeting place for European intelligentsia until the 1930s, when Kahn became bankrupt after the Wall Street crash and the land was turned into a public park. Today it offers a tranquil and verdant oasis from the bustle of Parisian life.

Stroll around the fragrant rose garden and admire the symmetry of the formal French garden. There is a limpid pond with water lilies and a forest of weeping birches that turn bright yellow in autumn. However, the centerpiece has to be the Japanese garden full of camellia, magnolia, and cherry trees. **HA**

Stay at Hotel Abbaye Royale de Fontevraud

Location Maine-et-Loire, France
Website www.hotelfp-fontevraud.com   **Price** ◓

Fontevraud is the final resting place of King Henry II of England, his wife, Eleanor of Aquitaine, and their son, King Richard (the Lionheart), along with other royal family members. Nine hundred years of history have passed since the royal burials, but the twelfth-century abbey, one of the largest monastic complexes in the world, remains gracefully beautiful.

Within the grounds of this magnificent complex, with its collection of cloistered buildings, courtyards, gardens, and Minster church, is St. Lazare Priory, once a place of respite for nuns, now a quiet hotel overlooking apple orchards. Set slightly away from the rest of the buildings, bordered by stone walls and symmetrical gardens, the hotel is made from the same softly colored tufa stone that is so pleasing to look at. The fifty-two bedrooms have been fully refurbished in simple but classic colors. Le Saint Lazare restaurant, within the hotel, can certainly be described as elegant, the clean lines of the cream stone and arched windows offering a relaxing backdrop to your meal, which is prepared using the local produce that the region is renowned for and, of course, is accompanied by local Loire Valley wines. A fireside salon is delightful for afternoon tea in winter, whereas the terrace offers a place for quiet reflection in the sunshine. But the hotel's greatest asset is its position within a 30-acre (12-ha) complex where respect for calm is a requisite of the stay. As a monument and resting place of royalty, the visitor's guide to the royal abbey requests, "Out of consideration for the peaceful and silent atmosphere of the site, we kindly ask you to respect the monument and its gardens, to admire them calmly, and to avoid running and shouting." **CFM**

Stay in Château Montriou

Location Loire Valley (Loiret, Loir-et-Cher, Indre-et-Loire, and Maine-et-Loire), France **Website** www.chateau-de-montriou.com **Price** ⏾

Consisting of a fifteenth-century château with a nineteenth-century neo-gothic extension surrounded by wooded parkland, the estate of Château Montriou has been in the same family for 300 years. Relaxed and unpretentious, this Loire Valley château is the family home of a French couple who invite you to stay in one of their four bedrooms or apartment, wander the extensive grounds, and eat food grown in their award-winning vegetable garden.

The owners, Nicole and Régis de Loture, offer a personal welcome to guests on arrival. Visitors are welcome to explore the grounds that include a lake,

---

"The Loire Valley is an outstanding cultural landscape of great beauty, containing historic towns."

UNESCO World Heritage Committee

---

woods, English parkland, Italian garden, orangery, private chapel of historic importance, and magnificent nineteenth-century walled vegetable garden. The garden is also renowned for its annual display of pumpkins and gourds, which hang like stalactites in the Jardin de la Princesse. Breakfast is provided in the airy and classically decorated *salle à manger*, with Le Salon Bleu (The Blue Room) and Le Salon de Chasse (The Hunting Room) managing to pull off both grand and homely at the same time.

Situated close to Angers and the beautiful River Sarthe, Château de Montriou is hidden in the most northern region of the Loire Valley. **CFM**

Explore the Loire Valley by Bicycle

Location Loire Valley (Loiret, Loir-et-Cher, Indre-et-Loire, and Maine-et-Loire), France **Website** www.discoverfrance.com **Price** ⏾

The gorgeous Loire Valley meanders across the center of France on its way to the Atlantic Coast. Also called the Garden of France, the region is best known for its dazzling architecture and fairy-tale châteaux. And with its clusters of historic villages and softly undulating terrain, it's tailor-made for bicycling.

It's difficult to imagine a nicer way to see this part of France. In the saddle of a well-oiled bicycle, free-wheeling down a quiet country lane, this is the most relaxing kind of activity vacation; fast enough to satisfy the traveler's need to see and do, but slow enough to give you time to enjoy your surroundings.

The hundreds of châteaux that pepper the low valleys of the Loire tell of centuries of wealth and renaissance building prowess. Castle after opulent castle with boxwood gardens and swan bedecked moats loom up, it seems, around every corner.

Le Château de Chambord is arguably the most impressive. With over 440 rooms and a tower for almost every day of the year, it is a magnificent monument to medieval design. From the fortress towns of Angers and Ambrois, to the indescribable beauty of the stained glass of Chartres Cathedral, there are cultural treats galore.

But this Tour de France isn't just a feast for the soul. The vineyard-laden slopes of the countryside, criss-crossed with a cat's cradle of quiet roads, will guide you to sample some of the delights on offer at the roadside hotels—an active day in the saddle more than justifies an indulgent evening at the table. Don't forget—you are in some of the best wine producing country in the world, the land of Sancerre and Pouille-fume, of Anjou and Saumur. **SWi**

Enjoy Venise Verte

Location Charente-Maritime, France
Website www.marais-poitevin-aria.com/gb/2.htm   **Price**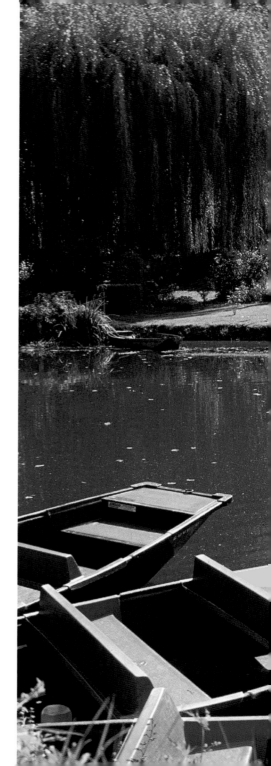

This "green" counterpart of Venice could not be further removed from the mass tourism that has engulfed the Italian city in recent decades. Located in western France, just east of La Rochelle, Venise Verte is a centuries-old canal network initially conceived to irrigate the surrounding farmland. As the waters of the ocean receded, an area of marshland (called Marais Poitevin) was created. This area became a designated nature reserve, but this status was subsequently withdrawn because of the region's agricultural importance; the beautiful, pastoral scenery still remains, however, and makes for a relaxing day out.

Situated on the River Sèvre, the village of Coulon— listed among France's most beautiful villages—is the area's hub because of its suitable location as a starting point from which to explore the marshlands. This is best done by hiring a guide with a punt so as not to get lost in the maze of canals, although maps are available for those who prefer to rent a canoe and find their way around set routes. However, it is advisable to choose the first option, because the guides also provide insights into the area's history and its significance as an ecosystem, and the small boats create an intimate atmosphere that is in harmony with the tranquil and enchanting surroundings.

The region derives its name from the duckweeds covering them, which give the canals the semblance of flat, green land. Some of the canals are barely accessible by boat, whereas others are up to 65 feet (20 m) wide, thus creating a natural habitat that is unlike any other in France. **DaH**

➔ *The canals of the Marais Poitevin provide a beautiful network to explore by canoe or punt.*

Discover Île de Ré

Location Charente-Maritime, France
Website www.hotel-de-toiras.com **Price** ❶

La Rochelle is one of the most perfectly preserved medieval port towns in France, thanks to its fastidious council, but its best-kept secret is the Île de Ré, joined to the mainland by a great curving bridge. This is a flat, narrow, and sandy isle dotted with a collection of small, exquisitely tasteful towns and villages. Every building is required to have whitewashed walls, curled orange tiles, and green-painted shutters, creating a beautiful, rustic symmetry.

This tiny Atlantic island is a place for wealthy but discreet Parisians who come here year after year. In the small, honey-colored harbor of Martin de Ré, bohemian and faintly aristocratic artists rub shoulders in charming bistros, watching the oyster trawlers come and go. To get in the thick of it, choose a spacious, opulent, ornate, French-style suite at Hotel de Toiras—perhaps the Marechal, with its splendid views of the harbor. The hotel adjoins La Table d'Olivia, a bijou restaurant. Everything in Saint Martin is about seafood, especially mussels and oysters; the northeast of the island is fringed with oyster beds.

Wandering the streets you will find local markets selling glossy fruit and vegetables, stores selling wares for the home, clothing boutiques, and plenty of well-dressed Parisians. Walk the fortifications, or rent a bicycle and head to the sandy, southern beaches. When autumn is edging in and the seasonal visitors have beaten their retreat, there is an alluring slowness to life here. The focus reverts to everything to do with oysters and mussels, and a delicious silence descends in Saint Martin's misty streets. **LB**

↩ *Building codes enforced by the local government ensure that Île de Ré remains a picturesque village.*

Stay at Le Moulin du Port

Location Charente-Maritime, France
Website www.bookcottages.com **Price** ❷❷

Nestled in the small village of Cravans, midway between Bordeaux and the coastal town of La Rochelle, the disarmingly charming and rustic nature of Le Moulin du Port is a delight. A meticulously restored old windmill converted into a contemporary bed-and-breakfast that can accommodate up to six people, it overflows with character and history, and makes an ideal escape if all you want to do is fade into anonymity and become part of the daily ebb and flow of a typical French village.

Le Moulin is set alongside an adjoining house under which flows a small, pretty stream that can be seen through specially installed glass panels in the floor.

> *"Just a short drive away are the beaches and caves of Meschers [and] the sandy beaches of Royan."*
>
> Proprietors, Le Moulin du Port

The interior of the mill is spread over two levels, ensconced within textured walls of hewn stone and exposed wooded trusses overhead. On the ground floor, the centerpiece is a magnificent grand piano set alongside an open fireplace with a steep, open-tread staircase leading up to a mezzanine level containing two small bedrooms.

The house itself has a compact and function⌐ kitchenette, a living and dining are⌐ lovingly manicured garden t⌐ through a set of double Frenc⌐ is located outdoors and the⌐ swimming pool and covered ter⌐

Relax at Château Bauduc

Location Gironde, France **Website** www.bauduc.com
Price $

Visit Les Sources de Caudalie

Location Gironde, France **Website** www.sourcesdecaudalie.com
Price $ $

If the wine from Château Bauduc is good enough for Michelin-starred chef Gordon Ramsay, then it should surely satisfy the palate of the most discerning wine drinkers. The Bordeaux Blanc is a house wine in all of Mr. Ramsay's European restaurants, and not only can you stock up on the vintage, but you can also stay in the beautiful eighteenth-century farmhouse set in the grounds of the 250-acre (101-ha) estate. A stay at La Lisière des Vignes (The Edge of the Vines), which sleeps eight people comfortably in the heart of the vineyards, is not just about relaxation—although there is plenty of opportunity for that (the owner's château is the only neighbor). It is also a chance to witness the wine-making process firsthand and to sample some of the fine vintages to boot.

The farmhouse is only 15 miles (24 km) from Bordeaux and St. Emilion, and within half an hour's drive of the international airport, not to mention the long sandy beaches of the Atlantic coast just an hour away. It is ideally situated for exploring southwest France and the châteaux of Bordeaux. That is if you can drag yourself out of the swimming pool that accompanies the farmhouse or get up from the table that sits underneath the shady vine-covered pergola in the south-facing garden.

The interior of the house is exquisitely decorated with every attention to detail considered. It has been completely renovated in recent years, using only the finest furnishings and materials. With the owner's château as the only neighbor, it is perfectly possible to feel that you have truly escaped the trappings of modern life. Rented on a weekly basis, the house sees e guests returning year after year, such is the 'ous allure of the place. **CFM**

To visit Les Sources de Caudalie is to not only treat yourself to one of Bordeaux's most luxurious spas, but also to immerse your spirit and soul in the traditions of French viticulture in a wine-growing community that can trace its beginnings to the fourteenth century.

Today the 138-acre (56-ha) vineyard of Les Sources de Caudalie includes the eighteenth-century main house Château Smith-Haut-Lafitte as well as various outbuildings reconstructed around four abandoned barns. Rooms vary in size from "comfort rooms" with king-size beds and terraces to a choice of spacious suites with terraces and fireplaces.

The hotel's heart and soul, however, is to be found in its wine. Its 15,000-bottle wine cellar, hewn out of solid rock by the hotel's owners, is the repository of generations of viticulture. Its vines have an average age of thirty years and a planting density of close to 10,000 vines per hectare. Merlots and cabernet sauvignons dominate, and the hotel also has its own on-site wine cooperative. The hotel's restaurant, La Grand Vigne, modeled after the style of eighteenth-century greenhouses, overlooks one of the property's many ponds, offering delicacies such as Arcachon Bay oysters and stuffed squid sewn with carrot.

The phrase "vinotherapie spa" was invented here after a hot spring with unusually high concentrations of minerals was found running 1,600 feet (500 m) below the château's foundations. Today various vinotherapie packages are made available: therapeutic treatments that use grape seed polyphenols to help arrest the skin's natural aging process. **BS**

➡ *You can choose to stay right by the water, in the lovely, private Île aux Oiseaux accommodation.*

Explore the Dune du Pilat

Location Gironde, France
Website www.littoral33.com/gb/dune_pilat   **Price** ◑

This mammoth sand dune is the highest of its kind in Europe, measuring a staggering 328 feet (100 m) high and 1,640 feet (500 m) wide. Snaking its way for 1.8 miles (3 km) along France's southwest coast in the Arcachon Bay area, the dune is a tremendous sight and can be found just 37 miles (60 km) outside Bordeaux. It is carved by the wind and is constantly growing and changing. With no vegetation, this desertlike landscape is magical in appearance; the constantly blowing winds create many curvy patterns and sandy ripples.

For imaginative visitors, the dune offers unparalleled adventure opportunities. Climb to the top via one of two staircases and then take an exhilaratingly sandy slide down to the sea. Fly a kite or simply take a stroll and breathe in the salty air, letting the wind whip your hair while enjoying the sweeping views of the deep-blue Atlantic on one side and the lush green of the pines on the other. Serious thrill seekers can go hang-gliding or paragliding to appreciate the sheer scale of the dune from a bird's-eye view.

At the foot of the dune is a dense forest of pine trees, beyond which lies a labyrinth of creeks and lagoons. At sunset the dune takes on an atmospheric pinkish glow, making it a popular time to visit for photographers. At this time of the day, it is also worth viewing the dune by taking a boat ride on the Bay of Biscay. When you are done with the dune, head to Arcachon for dinner. It's home to 2,500 oyster farmers, and every restaurant serves up fresh oysters with a bottle of the finest local wine. **JK**

◄ *The vast Dune du Pilat is the tallest sand dune in Europe, and is a constantly shifting desert landscape.*

Experience Camp Biche

Location Tarn-et-Garonne, France
Website www.campbiche.com   **Price** ⦵⦵⦵

High on a hill in the medieval town of Lauzerte in southern France, Camp Biche is a fitness camp with a difference. When former options trader Libby Pratt and her husband, Craig, moved here from the United States, they noticed that the French lived life a little differently. So, in 2001, Libby decided to create a luxurious hideaway where people could come to enjoy a time-tested approach to health and fitness. Camp Biche emphasizes the simpler aspects of the good life: delicious local organic food, invigorating exercise, and stunning natural surroundings. A week at the camp can undoubtedly get you in shape, but it might mark a more profound change, too.

"The traditional formula of rigorous exercise and calorie deprivation [gets] a five-star French polish."

Ian Belcher, *The Times*

The day starts at 7 A.M. with an abdominals and weights session, complete with mantras to help you feel more positive about your figure; a light breakfast follows, and then participants walk out of the door of the medieval mansion across the fields on a four or five-hour hike. Hiking is at the heart of the Camp Biche exercise program, and each walk starts with an hour of silent meditation to instill calm into your thoughts.

Lunch is back at the house, and the afternoon is filled with more glorious exercise: hatha yoga, weights, or Pilates. After a soothing hour-long massage, it is time to relax in the hot tub before a gourmet dinner with wonderful French wine. **LD**

Explore the Canal du Midi

Location Southwestern France   **Website** www.midicanal.fr
Price 💲💲

You proceed at a leisurely speed of 4 miles per hour (6.4 kph) yet life never gets boring. World War III could break out and you would not notice. Welcome to France's wonderful Canal du Midi. There is a towpath alongside the entire 150 miles (240 km) that link the Étang de Thau and the town of Sète, on the Mediterranean, with bustling Toulouse and the River Garonne (which eventually becomes the Gironde), above Bordeaux, before spilling out into the Atlantic.

Bicycle riding or rambling by the waterway is part of the fun, but the real pleasure comes when you climb aboard your rental craft. You will soon get the knack of steering the boat (available for parties of two to

> *"Light filtered through delicate foliage, at times making rainbows of color on the water."*
>
> Sarah Poyntz, *Guardian*

twelve) and negotiating the many locks—there are ninety-one in all, but you will be averaging only 10 miles (16 km) or so each day, so you are unlikely to face them all. There is usually someone there to lend a hand, and the lock-keeper will happily sell you eggs, wine, or other fresh local produce, and exchange a yarn or two. If you do not want to cook, there are plenty of enticing restaurants and cafés en route.

Try to schedule in the spectacular walled city of Carcassonne and the eight-lock staircase at Fonsérannes, on the outskirts of Béziers; another thrill is negotiating the dank and dark 570-foot (173-m) tunnel at Enserune by the beam of your navigation light. **RsP**

Go Armagnac Tasting

Location Gers, France   **Website** www.buscamaniban.com
Price 💲

Gascony, deep in rural southwest France, is renowned for its food and drink. The gently rolling landscape is dominated by hilltop castles that command stunning views over fields full of huge dazzling sunflowers. The region is also the home of foie gras, cassoulet, and most famously, Armagnac. Armagnac is the oldest brandy in France, predating cognac by a couple of centuries, and in the Middle Ages it was known for its therapeutic properties. It became very popular in the sixteenth century and went on to become a truly commercial product. Charles de Batz (better known as D'Artagnan of *The Three Musketeers*) was probably the first person to export Armagnac.

No visit to Gascony would be complete without sampling some of this local spirit, and where better to do it than straight from the producer? The biggest producer in the region is Château Laubade, but one of the most beautiful estates is that of the family-owned Château de Busca-Maniban in the Ténarèze area, where most Armagnac production is now based. Classed as an ancient monument, the château dominates 494 acres (200 ha) of vines, mainly planted in Ugni Blanc, the grape type most associated with Armagnac. This is a proper seventeenth-century château with a proper chatelaine, and, if you are in luck, Madame Flirane de Ferrone will personally show you around the salons before letting you loose on a fantastic range of traditional Armagnacs, distilled only once for an extra full body and intense golden fruit flavor. The brandies have all been aged in local oak, and the 1976 vintage is a particular treat. After a few glasses of this heady drink, it is likely you will need a lie down in order to gather your wits, so find a shady spot under a tree and snooze in the Gascon sunshine. **HA**

Walk the Pilgrim Route from France to Spain

Location From Lourdes, Hautes-Pyrénées, France to Santiago de Compostela, A Coruña, Spain   **Website** www.worldwalks.com
Price $

For more than a thousand years all roads in Northern Spain have led to Santiago de Compostela, the site of the cathedral where, according to legend, the remains of St. James the Apostle lie. It has been the site of many pilgrimages since medieval times. These days, on the walk from Lourdes to Compostela, you'll still see plenty of pilgrims, though nowadays there are fewer bare feet and many of your fellow travelers will be on bikes or in cars—but where's the satisfaction in that? Religious devotion doesn't motivate all of the thousands who converge each year on these much trammeled routes but if you are on a verified foot pilgrimage (get a Pilgrim's Passport at the start of your journey in Abbey Roncevalles) you can stay in one of the almost free roadside hostels.

Starting on the edge of the Pyrenees, the distance of the trip is 470 miles (750 km). You'll wander through spectacular mountain scenery, ancient hamlets, and wooded trails. Crumbling chapels pepper the way and you'll come across the ancient cities of Burgos and Leon too with their vast gothic Cathedrals, to give you a taste of where you're really heading.

Many aim to arrive in Santiago on July 25 for the three day festival of Sant Iago. As well as the street parties and general merry-making, the fiesta features the spectacle of the swinging of the cathedral's mighty incense holder, which traditionally carries people's prayers up to God (and was used to mask the stench of unwashed pilgrims). Whether you are spurred on by religion or emotion, there's something life-changing about a voyage as epic as this. **SWi**

↗ *The entire walk can take up to 31 days, but is easily broken into smaller sections for a more relaxing time.*

"I was suddenly transported back to the Middle Ages, when millions of pilgrims came [for] absolution."

Derek Bishton, *Daily Telegraph*

Explore Mont Perdu

Location Hautes-Pyrénées, France
Website www.worldheritagesite.org **Price** ❶

The "lost mountain" of the Pyrénées (called Monte Perdido in Spanish), Mont Perdu is the heart of the mountain chain and the dramatic natural border between France and Spain. Standing 10,997 feet (3,352 m) high, it is the Pyrénées' third-highest peak and the centerpiece of the Ordesa y Monte Perdido National Park, and is inscribed on the UNESCO World Heritage List for its classical geological landforms. What is more, it remains a European "lost world" where pastoral ways of life have been preserved.

The diversity of animal and plant life here is staggering. There are 1,500 species of flower alone, as well as mammals like the Spanish ibex, whose steady feet help it climb the precarious cliffs and crags, and wild boar, commonly hunted in the region. Eagles soar around the peaks and, if you are lucky, you might see a fabled Lammergeier, the bearded vulture native to the region, which has a wingspan of 10 feet (3 m).

Walking in the Pyrénées certainly takes your breath away—not only because of the steep climbs, but also the astounding valleys, high mountain waterfalls, and deep-blue lakes. The snow-tipped range is tackled by walkers year-round, who choose either to camp or to sleep in the small mountain huts or rustic bed-and-breakfasts along the way.

Once here, it is hard to imagine that life is going on in busy cities elsewhere. This region remains undeveloped and is home to a few scattered villages where life continues as it always has. The nature of the terrain means that things here are unlikely to change, which is reassuring to know. **LD**

◄ *The Arrazas River runs through the Tozal del Mallo Mountains in Ordesa y Monte Perdido National Park.*

Do Yoga in the Pyrénées

Location Ariège, France
Website www.yogafrance.com **Price** ❸❸

This small, elegant country château is more than 200 years old and stands in a quiet valley through the Pyrénées, among flower meadows, wooded hills, and a tree-shaded brook. In front of the house is a clear lake where the dragonflies hover and deer drink—it is also perfect for a cooling dip.

Domaine de la Grausse is a tranquil spot for a vacation, but add in the benefits of the yoga sessions here and it becomes a perfect way to escape the pressures of modern life. The special yoga breaks in this remote spot run between May and October. Guests stay in beautifully converted farm buildings on a self-catering basis. There are double and single

> *"Breathe in the pure, invigorating mountain air, a gift and joy for Pranayama yogic breathing."*
>
> **Proprietors, Domaine de la Grausse**

rooms, kitchens, and shaded dining patios. Visitors can buy fresh produce at the village market nearby or eat at the local cafés and restaurants.

The experienced resident yoga teacher, Dagmar, conducts sessions in the morning and evening. She combines the best of various schools of yoga and adapts to her pupils' needs. The sessions are suitable for all skill levels and are held either on the top floor of the château, with French windows overlooking the lake, or, on the hottest days, in a renovated stone barn built into a dramatic rock face. Guests can also unwind with guided meditation sessions and holistic therapies, including Reiki, massage, and reflexology. **SH**

Rent Moulin de Perle

Location Pyrénées-Orientales, France
Website www.pyreneesgites.com   **Price** 🅢🅢

The Moulin is an ancient water mill in a picturesque valley in the spectacular lower Fenouilledes foothills of the French Pyrénées. The owners have restored the mill and its old outbuildings to create three self-contained *gîtes* (small vacation homes), which sleep three, five, or six people. It is possible to arrange for bed-and-breakfast accommodation, and regular painting vacations are available with expert tuition. The views of vineyards, forests, rivers, and stunning gorges with historic Cathar castles perched on rocky outcrops ensure that there is plenty of inspiration for artists. Back at the gîtes themselves, visitors can expect

> *"Laze in the sun or potter around discovering the outstanding scenery and pretty villages."*

Proprietors, Moulin de Perle

exposed beams, wood-burning stoves, views of the nearby stream, charming patios, and pretty gardens. The rugged, bare stone walls, terra-cotta roofs, and sky-blue paintwork are complemented by lush, flowering creepers, potted plants, and overhanging trees. The site is surrounded by 4 acres (1.6 ha) of wild meadows where orchids flower alongside the old mill stream, which is ideal to paddle in on a hot day.

The Moulin is situated midway between two small villages, making it a very peaceful spot and a perfect base for touring the region. The local village swimming pool and tennis court are also easily accessible, only a five-minute walk away. **SH**

Explore the Black Mountains

Location Black Mountains (Tarn, Hérault, and Aude), France
Website www.blackmountainholidays.com   **Price** 🅞

The Black Mountains get their rather forbidding name from the densely forested slopes that make them seem dark from afar. Get closer, however, and you will realize why the French value this area so much. The highly protected countryside is perfect for walking, fishing, horseback riding, and exploring. It is dotted with historic castles from Cathar times, including the World Heritage site of the Citadel of Carcassonne and the stronghold of Hautpoul, Châteaux de Lastours, and Château de Saissac.

The Black Mountains form part of Languedoc National Park and join onto the southwestern end of the Massif Central in the border area of the Tarn, Hérault, and Aude *départements*. The pinnacle of the range is the Pic de Nore, a serious 4,000-foot (1,219-m) mountain that towers over Carcassonne's plain. From here the Pyrénées shimmer on the western horizon. On the hills themselves, the vegetation changes dramatically, depending on if the weather is coming from the Mediterranean or the Atlantic. In the Orb Valley, for example, you will see mimosa, olives, and cherries, but just a few miles west the prevailing winds are from the Atlantic and the fruit and flowers give way to beech trees.

The highlight of any escape here is swimming in the cool, clean mountain lakes. Several are so popular with locals they are like small seaside resorts. Lac du Pradelle and Lac du Montagne have their own lifeguards, pedal boats, tennis, mini golf, walking trails, and even a choice of restaurants. **SH**

➲ *The Rigole canal flows through the Black Mountains before feeding the Canal du Midi.*

Stay at Les Fermes de Marie

Location Haute-Savoie, France
Website www.fermesdemarie.com **Price** �$�$

Many travelers have dreamed of staying in one of those lovely old wooden farm huts you see scattered high up on Alpine slopes. French couple Jocelyne and Jean-Louis Sibuet did more than dream: They found and bought more than twenty wobbly old wooden chalets, farms, and sheds, brought them down the mountain timber by timber, and reassembled them as a sort of makeshift village on the edge of the upmarket resort of Megève.

Inside, the old rooms have been filled, not with animals and piles of hay, but with old Savoie shepherd's furniture and folk art, whereas modern features like satellite TV, sumptuous beds, and opulent marble bathrooms have been discreetly added. The extraordinary rustic feel has been retained thanks to the weathered wood everywhere and the homey details. It must have seemed risky at the time, but the plan worked incredibly well—the Sibuets have managed to create a unique luxury hotel with the feel of a group of romantic old barns in the hills.

This eccentric escape works equally well throughout the year. In winter it is a ski center with shuttle buses that whisk you to ski lifts. In summer, you can walk in the mountains, go mountain biking, play tennis, or simply relax and enjoy the hotel's facilities and Megève's shops, cafés, and bars. The hotel's well-equipped spa, gym, and pool and the renowned gourmet restaurant entice guests at any time of year. The sixteen-room spa even uses its own specially developed products created from mountain plants like horsetail and arnica. **SH**

➔ *It's almost impossible to find somewhere more quintessentially alpine than Les Fermes de Marie.*

Stay at Hotel Arbez

Location Jura, France/Vaud, Switzerland
Website www.hotelarbez.fr.st   **Price** ⊖

It is a real treat to discover a little hotel in the Alps that offers an extraordinary and memorable stay for less than the price of breakfast at some five-star escapes. Unlike many of the fabulous resorts, Hotel Arbez has a unique claim to fame: It straddles the French and Swiss border, which leads to all sorts of amusing twists. Guests can choose whether to sleep in Switzerland or France. In some rooms the border even runs through the middle of the double bed. In others, guests can sleep with their head in France and their feet in Switzerland. In one room you have to cross into France to wash your hands, and in another the toilet is over the border in Switzerland.

> *"We've made a real effort to offer specialities that reflect the cross-border character of the hotel."*

Proprietor Alexandre Peyron on the restaurant

The rooms are simple, with whitewashed walls and exposed wooden beams, with exceptional views of mountain snow in winter and flower-covered meadows in summer. It is a convenient spot for ski resorts and mountain trails in both countries.

There is also a serious side to the bizarre location. On the second floor there is a room known as "The Hideaway," dating back to the World War II resistance movement. When the Germans occupied France in 1940, the hotel became a strategic location on the border with neutral Switzerland. The owners were able to hide Allied soldiers and Jewish civilians upstairs, where German troops were not allowed to go. **SH**

Relax at La Bouitte

Location Savoie, France
Website www.la-bouitte.com   **Price** ⊖⊖

If you are the sort of person who loves to ski but cannot abide the crowds and nightlife typical of large resort-style villages, you might like to consider spending a few nights at La Bouitte, a converted eighteenth-century timber farmhouse near the hamlet of St. Marcel in a valley midway between Les Menuires and St. Martin-de-Belleville.

In 2000, the hotel's owner, René Meilleur, began to offer accommodation and, unlike many chalets and hotels in the Alps that close over the summer months, La Bouitte is open all year-round. Its five rooms are scattered around the attic in the main house and throughout its various outbuildings and are accessed via exterior wooden staircases. Ladders lead up to lofts with comfy beds draped in thick blankets; the buildings' exteriors are of the pine and stone so typical of a Savoy homestead.

René also happens to be the chef. Self-taught, he began feeding hungry skiers thirty years ago when they would turn up on his doorstep after skiing through the backcountry from Les Menuires. His simple, creative cuisine soon found its way into both the Michelin and Gault et Millau guides. René's son Maxime has since joined him in the kitchen; together they now have a second Michelin star and continue to serve fantastic regional classics. For something more sophisticated however, place a South American flower on your tongue and wash it down with essences of tomato as it slowly begins to sizzle.

Outside, watch the approaching trickle of off-piste skiers from the crowded slopes of nearby St. Martin de Belleville who may be heading your way because they once heard of an isolated farmhouse called La Bouitte that absolutely cannot be missed. **BS**

Relax at Eagle's Nest

Location Savoie, France
Website www.scottdunn.com   **Price** ⊖⊖⊖

Situated in the midst of some of Europe's best backcountry skiing runs, the Eagle's Nest is a chalet with a hedonistic fusion of contemporary design and New England warmth. It has airy open spaces, exposed timbers, and natural stone fireplaces spread across four luxuriously decorated floors and is located a mere five-minute stroll from the center of the exclusive enclave of Les Carats.

In the world of chalets, access to snow is paramount, and you can ski almost up to the front door of this chic property. It is owned and operated by British luxury tour operator Scott Dunn, whose representatives bring new meaning to the concept of customer

> *"[The chalet is] characterized by old wooden beams and natural stone fire places."*
>
> Proprietors, Eagle's Nest

service. If you are flying into Geneva, you will be met by a Scott Dunn minibus, complete with a picnic basket and champagne.

The bedrooms at Eagle's Nest, spread over its two middle levels, can sleep a maximum of twelve people and are adorned by fine examples of rough-hewn furniture. A sumptuous living room, with exaggerated exposed trusses, and separate dining room make up the upper level, with an additional mezzanine level providing an out-of-the-way satellite TV area. An indoor swimming pool, sauna, and spa combine to make up a wellness center on the ground floor, and all floors are served by an internal elevator. **BS**

Enjoy Le Saint-Joseph

Location Savoie, France
Website www.lesaintjoseph.com   **Price** ⊖⊖

Nestled high in the Savoie region of the French Alps surrounded by 375 miles (600 km) of ski trails and within easy reach of the Courchevel Valley's 200 ski lifts, the luxuriously appointed Le Saint Joseph is a boutique hotel meticulously decorated and crafted to resemble a grand country home.

Its eleven rooms and three duplex-style apartments, ideal for large groups and equipped with their own private entrances, exude a rare warmth and cosseted ambience characterized by canopied beds, thick blankets, exposed rough-hewn beams in the ceilings, and fabrics and paintings on its walls scoured from Naples, Paris, and Lyon. If money is no object, the Directoire Suite glistens in red and gold fabrics and deep sofas, and has a massive canopied bed. All bathrooms have gilt-edged mirrors and period claw-foot bathtubs. Apartments have their own changing rooms for skiwear and ski-boot warmers.

High-energy breakfasts designed to keep you powering over the slopes till dusk are a smorgasbord of freshly baked breads, fruit, and cereals. Le Saint Joseph's Italian restaurant, Le Hussard, is warmed by its monumental stone fireplace and ensconced within timber-paneled walls under a beautifully coffered ceiling, whereas the less formal Grand Café specializes in an array of authentic Thai cuisine.

The resort of Courchevel 1850 (the resort's altitude in meters) was laid out in the 1940s and was the first resort in France to be planned and constructed from the ground up, rather than around a preexisting town. It lies between the Trois Vallées ski stations, midway between Val Thorens and Méribel, and its altitude virtually guarantees exceptional skiing. Le Saint Joseph is a two-minute walk from the resort's chairlifts. **BS**

Balloon over Puy-de-Dôme

Location Puy-de-Dôme, France
Website www.france-balloons.com **Price** 💲💲

If you were to draw a picture of a volcano, it would probably look like one of these perfect lava cones. In the volcanic Auvergne region of central France, the Chaîne des Puys are one of the country's most popular attractions—more than 80 mountains lined up north to south with clear volcanic origins. Something about the way the craters rise up green from the plain makes them seem more than the result of a tectonic collision, more mythical, and certainly photogenic. And the view from above, drifting with the wind at sunrise or sunset in a hot air balloon, can't be beaten.

From this vantage point, the Chaîne des Puys betray nothing of their belligerent, violent beginnings forged over 3,000 years ago. You can see the Massif central, the Cantal mountains, and as far as Mont Blanc to the east on a good day. Puy-de-Dôme is the tallest of the 80 mountains in the chain, reaching 4,800 feet (1,463 m) high, while the smooth grassy crater of Puy de Pariou rises to 3,970 feet (1,210 m), with a walking track leading to its center.

This region brings in half a million visitors a year, many of whom walk up the Sentier des Muletiers, the old Roman way, to the top of Puy-de-Dôme and the old Roman temple to Mercury that stands there. Other temples have stood here at the top of the mountain since pre-Christian times, such is the mountain's pull. Others choose to paraglide or hang glide from the top, for different aerial views of the region. The volcanos have given their minerals to Volvic water, produced here, as well as their lava to the farmhouse roof tiles, tennis courts and roads that you'll see from above. **LD**

← *The craters of Puy-de-Dôme seem very green and soft, and show no signs of volcanic activity.*

Canoe the Ardèche

Location Ardèche, France
Website www.france-voyage.com/en **Price** 💲

The 20-mile (32-km) stretch of the Ardèche River between Vallon Pont d'Arc and Saint Martin d'Ardèche is not reserved for white-water daredevils. The only real requirement is that paddlers be over the age of seven and able to swim—there is always the risk that the stunning scenery might distract you so much that you end up taking an unintended dip.

The route runs through a chalk and limestone canyon that has been carved out through the millennia; it is the highlight of Ardèche National Park, and its starting point, the Pont d'Arc, is a natural stone bridge that soars an impressive 197 feet (60 m) above the teal-blue waters. At places, the cliffs tower an

---

"Despite terrifying names like Dente Noir (Black Teeth), the rapids are easily negotiated."

Gordon Lethbridge, *Independent*

---

incredible 1,000 feet (305 m) above you. Many companies rent out canoes and kayaks for anything from a couple of hours to two days. For the latter, there are campsites en route at Gaud and Gournier—they are equipped with showers, barbecues, and drinking water, but do need to be booked in advance.

The more adventurous might want to visit early in the season. In April and May the water is high and fast, and you can extend the trip to take in longer sections of the river. In late summer, the ride is more leisurely, with lazy sections for gentle floating mixed with faster, fun-packed rapids. And when you want a break from the water, you can stop at the beaches on the way. **PE**

Explore Tarn Gorge

Location Cévennes (Gard, Lozère, Ardèche, and Haute-Loire), France
Website www.mairie-albi.fr/eng/tourism/tarn.html **Price** ❶

If France ever had a Wild West, this must be it. In the remote Cévennes region, the shallow River Tarn carves a course through an extraordinarily deep and long limestone gorge to make one of the great natural wonders of Europe. Drivers heading down the A75 *autoroute* across the austere, lonely plateau of the Grands Causses Regional Natural Park gain a tantalizingly brief peep over it from the elegant 1,125-foot (343-m) high Millau Viaduct—a road bridge that broke world records for its height, which often stands literally above the clouds.

The gorge really deserves more than a brief peep, though. There is a magnificent walk above the point where the gorges of the Tarn and Jonte meet near Le Rozier, passing a succession of jaw-dropping viewpoints and ledges with plummeting sides that are no treat for vertigo sufferers.

You can also explore the gorge from the water, at your own pace in a two-person canoe, which you can rent at the village of La Malène. The sturdy plastic craft require no expertise whatsoever—if you have rowed a boat in the local park, you can canoe on this docile stretch of the Tarn. The amiable current takes you at sufficient speed for paddling to be reduced to occasional steering around a tree trunk or tiny rapid. Here the cliffs rise sheer and blot out half the sky beneath the aptly named heights of Point Sublime. As the tourist boats chug past self-importantly, you can feel smug at taking the ultraslow, nonmechanized option and pull up at will on the shore or on a tiny gravel islet and picnic or swim the afternoon away in this wonderfully secretive place. Farther down a flag shows you where to beach your boat, and a bus will take you back to the village where you started. **TL**

De-stress at La Chaldette

Location Aubrac (Cantal, Aveyron, and Lozère), France
Website www.lachaldette.com **Price** ❸

The healing and calming effects of the Aubrac's thermal springs have been enjoyed since the Middle Ages. Located almost 4,265 feet (1,300 m) above sea level in central southern France, La Chaldette is a state-of-the-art health resort in the tranquil village of Brion. The modernist architect Jean-Michel Wilmotte has installed stylish floor-to-ceiling windows to allow mood-enhancing sunlight inside, and a minimalist streamlined interior to clear the mind of clutter.

Stressed-out urbanites can surrender to a rainwater shower massage or a hydromassage bath with flowers and oils, then languish on an outdoor recliner, serenaded by cicadas, an occasional cow horn, and

> *"La Chaldette benefits from a healthy climate and has particularly pure air."*

Proprietors, La Chaldette

soothing springwater trickling under foot. The hotel's convivial owners have combined rustic charm with contemporary chic in their apartment-styled rooms, built around a central staircase.

The chef's *cuisine de terroir* (a modern twist on locally sourced, traditional cuisine) includes gourmet plates of duck à l'orange and crème brûlée with blueberries. Gastronomy coupled with a glass of the local Coteaux du Languedoc in the wood-fired lounge and a restful sleep swathed in crisp white cotton works wonders on the mind and body, whereas the fresh, pure air, views of unending green valleys, and cascading water restore a sense of inner peace. **SD**

Stay at Jardins Secrets

Location Gard, France
Website www.jardinssecrets.net   **Price** $ $

Arriving at Jardins Secrets, you would be forgiven for wondering whether you had come to the right address. The unprepossessing side street and nondescript door in the wall do not begin to hint at the oasis within. Walk over the threshold and you step into an enchanted garden; orange and lemon trees grow profusely, a banana plant flourishes in a corner, and bougainvillea tumbles down a wall.

Jardins Secrets, a seventeenth-century villa situated on the edge of the ancient town center of Nîmes, is more like a private house than a hotel. This impression is amplified by the lack of a reception area; on arrival visitors are ushered straight to their rooms with none of the tedious form filling that too many hotels require.

The four guest rooms are large and opulent, and stuffed full of beautiful objets d'art, paintings, thick silk curtains, and freshly cut flowers. Some rooms have four-poster beds, made up with beautiful crisp linen, and all have double doors that open directly onto the garden while green-painted shutters keep the morning light at bay. Gilt-framed mirrors and twinkling eighteenth-century chandeliers adorn the bathrooms, which are dominated by vast claw-foot bathtubs.

A baby grand piano adds a touch of class to the salon, whereas in other areas you will see piles of books and photographs, instruments, and even aviaries of tiny song birds. However, as the hotel name suggests, the garden is really the highlight, offering a wonderfully relaxing and verdant hideaway from the heat and bustle of the city. After walking around the ancient Roman remains of Nîmes, return to the Jardins Secrets for a leisurely siesta on one of the loungers in a shady spot, take a dip in the cool saltwater pool, or simply breathe in the heady perfume of the roses. **HA**

Visit Sénanque Abbey

Location Vaucluse, France
Website www.senanque.fr   **Price** $

Home to a community of Cistercian monks, the mellowed stone walls and mottled roof tiles of the twelfth-century working monastery are soothing to the eye; it is difficult not to fall in love with the architecture and the silence. Surrounded by wooded hills, guests are invited to stay for a spiritual retreat for a maximum of eight days.

Temporary residents are allowed regardless of gender or faith but are expected to partake in the life of prayer and silence; indeed silence is expected at all times, including during meals, with an exception of fifteen minutes a day. The resident monks have a structured routine beginning at 4 A.M. that includes

> *"The Sénanque abbey is one of the purest examples of early Cistercian architecture."*
>
> www.senanque.fr

five orders, such as Vespers and Mass, and those on retreat are invited to attend these services. The rest of the day is taken up with reading, meditation, and working in the gardens; the surrounding fields in summer are filled with a purple hue, the uniform lines of lavender providing an amazing display of color. The monks cultivate the lavender, as they have done for centuries, producing honey (from the abbey bees) and distilling essence.

Those staying for a retreat may leave the abbey grounds, and the terrain provides some spectacular walking territory, especially for guests who feel the need to operate their vocal cords. **CFM**

Unwind at La Mirande

Location Vaucluse, France
Website www.la-mirande.fr   **Price** ⑤⑤

In the shadows of the medieval splendor of Avignon's historic Papal Palace, the opulent La Mirande, adorned with Belgian tapestries and wallpapers printed from age-old woodcuts, is this ancient city's most desirable address and one of Europe's finest hotels.

Part of a historic complex of buildings that can trace their beginnings to the establishment of the papacy here in 1306, La Mirande first became a hotel in 1796 and for more than two centuries was known as the Hotel Pamard. Throughout its twenty guest rooms and its public spaces, attention to detail is evident, from the silk-lined curtains and antique glass windows that frame the daily life of the city to the oak parquet

> *"The culinary art of La Mirande tends to prefer the . . . harmony of unexpected combinations."*
>
> Claude Eveno, *La Mirande*

on its floors, the Carrara marble in its bathrooms, and the master paintings on its walls. Meals in La Mirande's elegant Michelin-starred restaurant are served over a floor of needlepoint carpet and beneath a magnificent renaissance double caisson ceiling, and presided over by the hotel's head chef, Julien Allano. If you would like to have dinner in a more select environment, the guest table in the hotel's nineteenth-century kitchen can be made available on Tuesdays and Wednesdays.

This is reminiscent of the great aristocratic homes of France, and it is often whispered that if the pope had been given a taste of life at La Mirande, he may not have been in such a rush to return to Rome. **BS**

See Le Grand Blanc

Location Vaucluse, France
Website www.provenceweb.fr   **Price** ❶

Lying to the east of the Provençal village of Apt, just beyond the reach of the Luberon Valley, the mountains and surrounding valleys of the Grand Luberon embody all the stereotypes of what constitutes simple, rural French living.

The 3,690-foot (1,124-m) Mourre Negre is its highest point, dwarfing the lesser summits of the nearby Petite Luberon range and towering over the flat, desolate plain of the Plateau des Claparèdes, which bursts to life in a sea of lavender fields stretching for miles all the way to the village of Bonnieux. The landscape is full of ancient hilltop villages, and everywhere you look there are reminders of a simpler time, such as the ever-present dry-stone *bories*, igloo-shaped huts of stone dating back as far as the thirteenth century and constructed for no other reason than to clear the surrounding fields of rocks to make them ready for plowing. The towering presence of Le Grand Blanc, with its vast forests of oak and cedar and limestone outcrops, is a beacon to travelers and locals alike.

A thin covering of generally poor soil is characteristic here and has prevented large-scale agriculture, allowing the many hamlets and villages of the region to maintain their traditional ways of life. Once refuges for the Waldenes religious sect in the fifteenth century, medieval towns such as Gordes and Roussillon now attract celebrities, expatriates, and sun-seeking tourists all eager to experience a region that has altered little since the creation of the Parc Regional du Luberon in 1977, which encircles the area and ensures this tiny corner of rural France will retain its charm. **BS**

➽ *Gordes is typical of the traditional medieval villages on the hillsides of the Luberon Valley.*

Visit Parc Ornithologique

Location Bouches-du-Rhône, France
Website www.beyond.fr/sites/camargue.html   **Price** ◑

The Camargue is known for its wild horses and for its greater flamingos—and it is the latter that you will see at the Parc Ornithologique du Pont de Gau. These striking pink birds with their long, gangly legs are in residence all year, but their gatherings are most spectacular during the winter months: their mating season. From December to March, as many as 20,000 flamingos gather in the Parc Ornithologique to select a mate, and each day visitors can see them dance through their synchronized courtship movements. With their graceful necks stretched taut and their beaks held high, they strut together in formation, turning their heads to the left and the right. If you are lucky, you will see them take flight together, soaring high into the sky in a great mass of pink feathers.

The park covers 150 acres (60 ha) of wetland and invites visitors to stroll around its 5 miles (8 km) of paths that weave through the marshes and lagoons where local and migrating birds—including herons, storks, egrets, teals, geese, and swans—feed. Tuck yourself into one of the specially constructed hides en route and you will be able to observe the park's feathered residents wading, fishing, and flying as if you were not there. Venture a little farther and you will find the aviaries, which house injured birds that the park staff are nursing back to health. Information boards along the pathways help visitors identify the birds and understand their habits, and guided tours offer more in-depth information. There are also eagles, hawks, harriers, buzzards, and vultures in the park, so keep one eye on the sky as you are strolling. **PE**

⤷ *Flamingos stand at sunset in the shallow water of the Parc Ornithologique in the Camargue.*

Stay at Abbaye de Sainte Croix

Location Bouches-du-Rhône, France
Website www.hotels-provence.com   **Price** ⊖⊖

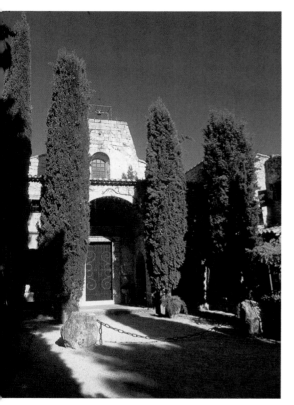

"Twenty thousand years ago, the Salounet plateau on the Abbey estate was home to the Salians."

Relais & Châteaux guide

This magnificent twelfth-century monastery, set amid perfumed gardens of lavender and rosemary, has been restored and converted into a luxury hotel. It is situated on one of the last strongholds of the Alpilles hills, and the Romanesque abbey, with arched vaulting and small windows, has been beautifully conserved.

The monks' formerly Spartan cells have been converted into twenty-one comfortable rooms and four apartments, which vary from the simple to the grand. Heavy stone walls provide respite from the blazing Provençal sun, keeping the whitewashed rooms cool in the hottest of summers—although there is also air-conditioning just in case. Vaulted ceilings, baronial fireplaces, and heavy beams all add to the rustic Provençal charm, as do the terra-cotta floor tiles scattered with handmade colorful rugs. Some rooms have views over the romantic gardens, whereas others look out over the valley. Dine on the restaurant's panoramic terrace and savor excellent local cuisine and wine while surveying the stunning landscape all around, including the nearby medieval town of Salon de Provence.

In the summer, the public sitting areas flow out onto vine-covered terraces. Rustic furnishings complement handpicked objets d'art. There is also a pool to cool down in and a tennis club next door for the energetic, but it is best just to soak up the sun with a glass of rosé in one hand and a good book in the other while reclining on the terrace listening to the chirp of the cicadas and the tolling of a distant church bell. *La vie en rose* indeed. **HA**

◤ *The Abbaye de Sainte Croix provides a luxury retreat into Provence in a setting brimming with history.*

See the Calanques

Location Bouches-du-Rhône, France
Website www.francethisway.com **Price** ◑

A few minutes' drive out of the busy town of Marseille a piece of nature survives untouched. Amid the beautiful *calanques*, pine trees, rocky cliffs, and turquoise waters, you feel as if you have stumbled upon the Caribbean. Derived from the Corsican word *calanca* meaning "inlet," the *calanques* were once ancient river mouths. They puncture the shore as far as 2.5 miles (4 kilometers) inland. These areas of outstanding natural beauty are now protected and have been left wild and unspoiled.

Some have a few small, shedlike homes dubbed *cabanons* at the edge of the water with tiny restaurants nearby. In Sormiou, Le Lunch restaurant offers plastic furniture and rather overpriced fresh fish, but it has a unique selling point: The Mediterranean gently laps at its feet while all around, the views offer only blue sea and impressive limestone cliffs. As for the others: Queyron, Podestat, En Vau, Port Pin, and Port Miou, they are all just beach, rocks, and pine forests at the edge of the translucent aquamarine water.

With access closed to traffic in the summer in order to preserve the area during the busy tourist season and prevent forest fires, getting to the beach means a long walk, sometimes up to 2 miles (3 km). Port Pin and En Vau are fantastic sights, though, well worth the hour-and-a-half trek through the Gardiole forest and down the steep hill. Although the calanques are a popular escape, thankfully, most people are put off by the robust hike.

Another option is to arrive by boat and head to the dive sites, like the grottos of "des Trémies," "des Capélans," or Castelvieil. For the lazy visitor, a drive up to the Corniche des Crêtes and Cap Canaille will give a glimpse of the paradise below. **RCA**

Enjoy Mas de la Fouque

Location Bouches-du-Rhône, France
Website www.masdelafouque.com **Price** ❸❸

Beyond the city of Arles and on the western borders of Provence—where the Rhône delta plunges into the Mediterranean—lie the wetlands of the Camargue. Glittering waters stretching as far as the eye can see and vast marshlands where wild white horses and ebony bulls still roam, there is a touch of magic in the air. With the accent on the conservation of nature and a way of life heavy with tradition, the 45,000 acres (18,000 ha) of swamps, lakes, and rice paddies are alive with folklore and legends.

Retreat to the Mas de La Fouque, a hip hideaway in the natural park overlooking the sparkling wilderness. Dreamy, chic, and full of character, it has strong

> *"All around are sea, beaches, and a wealth of wildlife (birds, flamingos, Camargue horses, wild bulls)."*
>
> Caroline Raphael, *Observer*

Moorish influences. The ultra-romantic rooms are decorated with spectacular antiques, linens, driftwood and wrought-iron four-poster beds swathed in long mosquito netting. One of the rooms is even a gypsy caravan on the edge of the lake.

Get into the spirit of things and go riding with the local cowboys through the rushes. Find out about all the Camargue's deepest secrets and see up close the glorious pink flamingos that dot the landscape, or simply while away the day by the glorious pool. The Mas has its own powerboat to cruise down the Rhône River for a private beach picnic. It brings together a relaxed vibe with rustic style naturally. **RCA**

Enjoy Le Prince Noir

Location Bouches-du-Rhône, France
Website www.leprincenoir.com **Price** ⓢⓢ

Classified as "one of the most beautiful villages in France," Les Baux de Provence cascades over 17 terraced acres (7 ha) of what was once a fortified Roman plateau. Today it is home to twenty-two historic monuments, including churches and chapels, and hewn straight out of its limestone rock face is the unique Le Prince Noir bed-and-breakfast.

Offering just three rooms, this charming, history-laden hideaway is an artist's house and the highest residence in the village. Ensconced in the center of one of the most popular tourist destinations in Provence, it makes a perfect base from which to explore the surrounding Alpilles mountains and nearby towns such as Arles and St. Rémy de Provence. The exposed rock walls of Le Prince Noir's rooms provide a natural barrier to blistering Provençal summers. There is one double bedroom, a suite with two rooms and private terrace, and an apartment with a kitchen, a master bedroom, separate living area, and two generously apportioned private terraces with panoramic views over Les Baux and the surrounding countryside and beyond to the Mediterranean. The breakfasts at Le Prince Noir are divine, but Les Baux has a small population of around 500, so you have to drive elsewhere to find one of the area's many fine restaurants for dinner.

A night at Le Prince Noir affords the opportunity to see Les Baux in much the same way as its residents do: quietly. Spend your day touring and return to Les Baux in the late afternoon when you can share this classic caricature of Provence with only the village cats. **BS**

← *The picturesque medieval village of Les Baux de Provence (population 500) at sunset.*

Eat at Baumanière

Location Bouches-du-Rhône, France
Website www.oustaudebaumaniere.com   **Price** 🌓🌓

Provence is justly famed for its exceptional cuisine, and it comes to the peak of perfection in Oustau de Baumanière. This seventeenth-century farmhouse has delighted the palates of its guests since Raymond Thullier first opened it in 1945.

Now run by his grandson, the world-class master chef Jean-André Charial, the Baumanière restaurant is the proud owner of two Michelin stars for its haute cuisine and its wonderful specialties that take Provençal cooking and contemporary techniques to a sublime standard. The signature *gigot d'agneau en croûte* (leg of lamb in pastry) alone draws gastronomes from far and wide to sample its delights.

> *"L'Oustau is a secret . . . born from the encounter between a place and a man. . . ."*
>
> Frédéric Dard, writer

Although the restaurant itself is reason enough to visit, the boutique hotel is also guaranteed to melt hearts. Comprising three vine-clad stone houses sitting astride classical gardens, Oustau de Baumanière even has a moat and drawbridge. The rooms are of the highest quality, furnished with antiques, four-poster beds, and marble baths. The sitting rooms are covered with early frescoes. Outside there is a large swimming pool and landscaped terraces that have played host to the likes of Winston Churchill, Elizabeth Taylor, and Pablo Picasso. Oustau de Baumanière also happens to be situated in Les Baux de Provence, named one of the most beautiful villages in the world. **PS**

Relax at Couleurs Jardin

Location Var, France
Website www.gigarobeach.com   **Price** 🚻

Celebrities and mere mortals have been flocking to St. Tropez since the early 1950s, but the resort became world famous thanks to Brigitte Bardot's cult film *And God Created Woman*. Today everyone from P. Diddy to Hugh Grant vacations here, and during the summer season, people-watching is a bona fide sport. Luckily it is possible to escape the ostentation just a few miles away on the other side of the peninsula in the small village of La Croix Valmer.

Unpretentious, La Croix Valmer has its own beautiful beaches and unspoiled pine forests stretching from Gigaro to the natural preserve of the Cap Lardier, covered in what locals call maquis, or low-lying, fragrant Mediterranean brush. The rough, jagged rocks contrast against the azure Mediterranean Sea along Gigaro beach. Houses are well hidden among the eucalyptus, cactus, and pine trees. The village is probably the French Riviera's best-kept secret, with just a handful of restaurants set alongside the white-sand beach, some established for more than twenty years serving yearly regulars.

The best time to visit is undoubtedly in the low season, just after Easter but before July, when the crowds arrive in the area. As the sun sets, set up camp at Couleurs Jardin, a beautifully laid-out little beach house decorated in driftwood, with the odd exotic plant, and a few splashes of bright color. The sea breeze, grayed wooden tables, frilly place mats, and candlesticks give the place a laid-back but stylish feeling. In the middle of the terrace, a pine tree grows low between the tables and the bamboo roofing. Order yourself a bottle of fresh rosé—it will come served with a smile and a clear ice bucket, a bowl of strong garlic olives, and a peerless view. **RCA**

Visit the Gardens of Rayol

Location Var, France
Website www.domainedurayol.org   **Price** 🌗

Only an hour's drive from the mayhem of St. Tropez, at the foot of the steep Maures massif, sits a tranquil house and garden overlooking the sea. The original owner of Le Rayol-Canadel-sur-Mer built a vast garden in the grounds of his domain on a wild promontory of land overlooking the Bay of Fig Trees in 1910. However, over the years, the house and garden fell into disrepair until it was acquired by the Coast Conservancy in 1989. The conservancy ensured its precious flora and fauna and unspoiled oceanfront cliffs would be preserved.

The gardens have since been transformed into a collection of gardens representing the regions of the world that enjoy a Mediterranean climate, so you can take a tour of the world's huge variety of botanical species all in one place. Wander around the Canary Islands garden, then admire the Joshua trees, cacti, and yucca from Baja, California. Pungent eucalyptus trees and cacti from Australia vie in the New Zealand garden, whereas the Mediterranean landscape is bursting with olive, pine, and palm trees. Also represented are gardens from Chile, Mexico, and South Africa. Unlike many formal gardens, the plants and trees in Domaine de Rayol are not labeled, so you will need to take a book if you want to identify them.

You cannot fail to be impressed by this beautiful garden on the headland, encircled by a verdant amphitheater of trees, and its jaw-dropping setting overlooking the Mediterranean. In the summer months, walk down the steep steps to the beach, take an invigorating dip in the clear blue water, and discover the local marine life. **HA**

↗ *The beautiful cacti on show here are from the dry, desert gardens of Baja, California.*

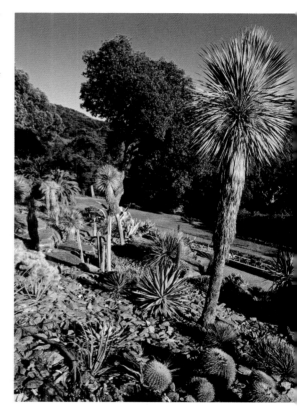

"An extraordinary garden nestles at the foot of the Maures massif at Le Rayol-Canadel-sur-Mer."

frenchgardening.com

Relax at Le Couvent des Minimes Spa

Location Alpes-de-Haute-Provence, France
Website www.couventdesminimes-hotelspa.com **Price** ⑤⑤

When Provence-based cosmetic and perfume company L'Occitane decided to open their first spa in France, they stumbled upon an ancient empty convent in the foothills of the Alps not far from their headquarters. The 300-year-old white stone walls and bell tower of Des Minimes overlook lavender fields, olive groves, and blossoming almond trees. Old wooden shutters, balustraded terraces, fountains, and terra-cotta tiles give it the perfect character for a Provençal showpiece.

After a lavish refurbishment by a specialist architect and local craftspeople, Des Minimes opened in 2008 as a small forty-six-room hotel and spa, with a fine restaurant. Any monastic hardships are certainly long gone. Rooms and suites are modern and well equipped, designed with simple pale colors and ample use of wood, stone, and fine fabrics.

Guests may lounge on private terraces admiring the views toward the mountains or cool off in the hotel's vaulted cellars tasting vintage wines. There is floodlit tennis and a heated outdoor pool, plus golf nearby. Or visitors may wander the extensive grounds discovering cloisters, the original chapel, ancient carvings, or the remains of terraced gardens that once gave the monastery a national reputation for botanical excellence. Both the restaurant and the spa use ingredients grown on-site or sourced in the immediate area: Asparagus and truffles may appear on the restaurant's menu, and local honey, lemon, olive oil, and lavender are prime ingredients in the spa. **SH**

← *L'Occitane's modernization of the 300-year-old convent preserved the building's original style.*

Explore Mercantour National Park on Horseback

Location Alpes-Maritimes, France
Website www.horseandventure.com **Price** ⊝⊝⊝⊝

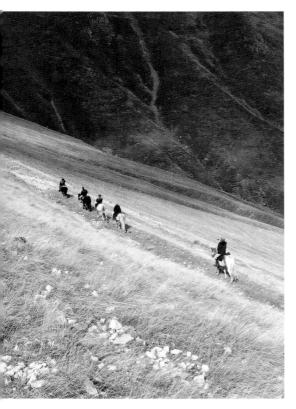

"This is the genuine ancient trail used for the transhumance of all livestock."

Horse and Venture wesbite

For centuries, shepherds and farmers have moved their livestock between their winter and summer grazing grounds in a tradition known as the transhumance. Today, native Californian Denis Longfellow, resident of rural France for thirty years, guides his troupe of Merens horses between Sainte-Agnès, just a couple of miles inland from the Mediterranean coast north of Nice, to his ranch in the mountains using the same trails that this land's inhabitants have used since ancient times. And he takes visitors along for the ride.

It is a three- to five-day journey (accommodation is in comfortable *gîtes*) down to the coast in the autumn and back up to his ranch at Le Boréon, on the edge of Mercantour National Park, in the spring. Virtually uninhabited, Mercantour National Park, known as Little Switzerland for its Alpine-style landscape, boasts 10,000-foot (3,048-m) peaks, but it also has olive groves and fields of lavender. There are some 2,000 species of plant here; many of them are rare, including edelweiss and the martagon lily, saxifrage, and gentian. The park's resident animals include several thousand chamois, marmots (visitors often hear them whistle), wild boar, and a few recently reintroduced wolves.

Visitors can ride in the park even if they do not want to embark on the transhumance because Longfellow offers half-day and day rides here in the summer and from the village on the coast in the winter. He is in Sainte-Agnès from October to mid-June, and in Le Boréon the rest of the year. The transhumance takes place at the end of September and in mid-June. **PE**

◨ *Discovering Mercantour National Park on horseback will transport you to a bygone age of cowboys.*

Stay at Orion B&B

Location Alpes-Maritimes, France
Website www.orionbb.com **Price** ⊖⊖

In the hills above Nice on the Cote d'Azur, the Orion Bed-and-Breakfast, a collection of five tree houses set in a forest of oak trees with panoramic views over the medieval, fortified hill town of Saint Paul de Vence, is helping to redefine the concept of what makes a contemporary, sophisticated getaway.

Constructed predominantly from red cedar, the tree houses are supported on stilts between the trees rather than intruding on them and are accessed via stairways and ramps, an ecologically sensitive approach to building that minimizes the impact of human intervention, leaving tiny mountain streams to run their course and the forest floor undisturbed. Be sure, however, to leave all your notions of what constitutes a rustic lifestyle at the door. Inside you will find oversized beds, massage showers, enough cushions for a slumber party, and even Internet access.

The tree houses range in size from Bagheera, which sleeps two, through to the adjoining King Louie and Mowgli dwellings, which can accommodate a family of four and overlook the pure waters of Orion's very own mountain pool. The pool is naturally filtered by a combination of gravel, carefully selected bacteria, and aquatic plants, which results in water with a level of purity that makes it good enough to drink. For those who prefer to keep their feet on solid ground, near the pool is Akela, a small, two-bedroom house with a charming kitchenette and two secluded terraces.

Orion is situated within the grounds of a 75,350-square-foot (7,000-sq-m) estate consisting of terraced spaces and tiny nooks, all set within a canopy of oak, pine, and palm trees. It provides an invitation to slow down and relax in a unique environment within easy reach of the French Riviera. **BS**

Stay at La Chèvre d'Or

Location Alpes-Maritimes, France
Website www.chevredor.com **Price** ⊖⊖

Eze is a classic village perched 1,000 feet (300 m) above the Mediterranean, a few miles to the east of Nice and close to where the Alps come down to the sea. There is no motor transportation in Eze, the streets are narrow, and the Chèvre d'Or is hidden away on one side of the village, hidden away from tourists.

The views are magnificent, and once you are out on your private terrace, you can forget the bustle outside and look down on the famously chic headland of Cap Ferrat. Some of the rooms have their own infinity pools, so you can enjoy the view from the water. There is, of course, a more sociable pool among the prickly pears where you can meet other guests.

> ## "I slept well, I laughed a lot, and I found a marvelous vigor and patience."
>
> Philosopher Friedrich Nietzsche on Eze village

The godfather to the village was the Swedish Prince William, who moved here in the 1920s after renouncing his birthright so that he could marry a woman from another social world. Eze is also famed for "Nietzsche's Walk," a grueling descent (and even more fearful climb) made by the German philosopher whose stays here inspired him to write poetry.

There is plenty to see in the village itself, not only the crafts shop, but also the church, which is a riot of Italian baroque and a reminder that Eze became French only in 1860. The hotel has three restaurants: the Michelin-starred Chèvre d'Or; Les Remparts, which is open for lunch; and Le Grill du Château. **GMD**

Enjoy Les Rosées

Location Alpes-Maritimes, France
Website www.lesrosees.com   **Price** 💲💲

Owning a vacation home on the Côte d'Azur may be an optimistic dream for most, but a visit to Les Rosées is surely the next best thing. An intimate, 400-year-old Provençal farmhouse with just four charming beamed suites, it provides a super-chic base from which to explore the village of Mougins, perched up in the hills above Cannes on the glamorous French Riviera.

The old, country-style stone buildings and wild, perfumed garden are so quintessentially Provençal you almost feel as though you could be on the set of a Hollywood movie. Elegant and unpretentious, Les Rosées—close enough to the action yet sufficiently far away to provide sanctuary from tourist groups—is the sort of place one dreams of discovering, hardly touched by time and bursting with soul.

Stay in Serguey, with its partial glass roof and wood-burning fire; dreamy Isadora, complete with an airy lounge and billowing silk curtains; St. Marguerite, boasting a private terrace overlooking the lavender-scented gardens; or St. Honorat, which has a romantic, nineteenth-century feel. All have Ralph Lauren bedding and Bose sound systems, and the attention to detail is evident throughout, with age-worn chaise longues and huge Victorian baths adding to the shabby chic feel.

For breakfast, enjoy inimitable flaky croissants each morning on a sun-soaked terrace and perhaps a dip in the pool before wandering up steep paths into the center of Mougins, a magnet for artists and poets for centuries. Above all, however, it is the level of hospitality and genuine friendliness shown by the host, Kilpérick Lhobet, his wife, Jenny, and the rest of the team that stands out and truly makes you feel at home, no matter how far away you are. **LP**

Unwind at Le Mas Candille

Location Alpes-Maritimes, France
Website www.lemascandille.com   **Price** 💲💲

Candille here refers to a line of slender cypress trees sculpted to resemble a row of Roman candles, all planted with precision and care along the shuttered facade of this delightful eighteenth-century farmhouse. More like a stately country home, Le Mas Candille is spread over 40,000 acres (16,180 ha) of terraced Provençal parkland on the northwest slopes above the village of Mougins, sequestered from prying eyes by dense canopies of pine, mature cypresses, and extensive groves of olive trees.

The hotel offers classic elegance amid the most tranquil of settings, far removed from the noise of the French Riviera, although only ten minutes by car from

---

"[The spa is] difficult to fault: you sleep like a baby and dream of the next meal."

Mel Agace, *Observer*

---

the center of Cannes. Fresh croissants and bowls of locally sourced fruit can be found throughout the day around the terraced poolside restaurant, but it is the Michelin-starred Restaurant Candille that will have you coming back again and again. Guests may savor classics like roasted wild duck and eclectic choices such as monkfish tails cooked in salt butter.

Another highlight of the Mas Candille is the Shiseido Spa, whose sole purpose is to remove accumulated stresses and strains through a combination of hot towels and shiatsu massage. The spa is surrounded by a private garden complete with whirlpool tub, relaxation center, hydrotherapy pool, and sauna. **BS**

Ride the Nice to Tende Train

Location Alpes-Maritimes, France
Website www.beyond.fr/travel/railcuneo.html   **Price** 🟢

What better way to take in some of the stunning scenery from the South of France to the Italian border than aboard a comfortable train? The *Train des Merveilles* (train of wonders) takes passengers on a two-hour journey from Nice to its destination Tende. It is run by SNCF every day in the summer and most weekends during the rest of the year.

The scenic route winds its way along the Roya Valley to cross the Alps passing under the Col de Tende tunnel into Italy. In the upper Roya Valley near Tende the train actually makes a couple of full 360-degree turns. Along the way there are many viaducts and tunnels; one of them between L'Escarene and Sospel is 3.7 miles (6 km) long. Despite the number of tunnels, the scenery is spectacular enough to make this trip a memorable one. The train travels along through wild mountains and deep gorges and valleys, and stops off at a number of lovely mountain villages along the way, such as Fontan and La Trinité, which offer great starting off places for hiking.

You can either stay aboard the air-conditioned train for the entire journey, admiring the view, or alight along the way at mountain villages to see some of the local attractions, such as the vast Mercantour National Park and the Vallée des Merveilles, famed for its mysterious prehistoric cave paintings, before catching the train back again. Alternatively you could continue your train journey over the border into historic Cuneo in Italy, which is well worth an overnight stop. However, this option requires careful planning because the services are unfortunately fairly infrequent. During the winter, the train is an excellent way of reaching the mountains to go skiing without having to navigate dangerously icy roads. **HA**

Stay at Boscolo Plaza Hotel

Location Alpes-Maritimes, France
Website www.boscolohotels.com   **Price** 🟢

Nice is one of the Côte d'Azur's most grandiose cities and the heart and soul of the French Riviera. A classic seaside town with a quaint historic center known as "the Vieux Nice," Nice has warm pebbled beaches and the famous Promenade des Anglais, which follows the Mediterranean for miles.

To take it all in without joining the crowds, head to one of the city's best-kept secrets: the rooftop bar at the Boscolo Plaza Hotel. At the very top of a meringue-style building, all white stucco, the bar and restaurant boast amazing views stretching from the city's gorgeous art-deco buildings in dusty tones of pink, ocher, and primrose to the sparkling blue sea.

"Think of class, elegance, and hospitality in a prime location in Nice."

Proprietors, Boscolo Plaza Hotel

Whether you opt for a *café crème* or a glass of chilled rosé, it is the place to catch the sunset. The atmosphere is Riviera chic: Dark wooden floors contrasting with bright white walls and low-slung daybeds create a contemporary twist. The bar itself is shaded by an intricate iron-frame latticework in belle epoque style. Staff in uniform are friendly and all smiles; pop music flows through the speakers but not too loudly.

Scan over the old narrow streets where the rooftops shield the buzzing Cours Saleya. Right below, the Jardin Albert I on Avenue des Phoceens is a green zone dotted with palm trees that turns into an improvised playground in the afternoon. **RCA**

Discover Piana

Location Corsica, France **Website** www.sipiana.com/en/index
Price ❶

Situated on the jagged west coast of Corsica, the Calanques are bizarrely shaped red rock pinnacles that provide a stunning backdrop for Piana, officially recognized as one of "the most beautiful towns in France." There is a wild savagery about the location that lends it a haunting atmosphere, which is quite appropriate: In 1489, there was a ruthless massacre by the Genoese overlords, which left just women and children alive. Blood once streamed down the narrow alleyways that today give the village much of its charm, but the mood now is of sublime tranquility.

Set on a narrow plateau some 1,437 feet (438 m) above the dazzling blue Mediterranean, Piana overlooks the Gulf of Porto and the Scandola and Senino peninsulas. Its exquisite pink-washed houses cluster around the picturesque oversize church of Sainte Marie, built with public funds between 1765 and 1795 to serve a population of only 735. From the church, a steep and narrow lane runs down precipitously to the little fishing boat haven of Ficaghjola and on through the hamlet of Vistale to the sheltered little beach at Arone, where it is safe to swim.

After witnessing a dazzling island sunset, it is hard to resist the temptation to stay, so head for the Hôtel des Roches Rouges, one of several establishments that capture Corsica's true spirit of appealingly faded-at-the-edges elegance. This one has been newly restored and now has light-filled rooms and elegant antique furnishings. Gastronomic dinner menus are dominated by the freshest of fish and seafood, caught by local fishermen and brought straight to the table. **RsP**

↩ *The pink rocks of the Calanques of Piana provide a rugged backdrop to a Mediterranean escape.*

Walk in Corsica

Location Corsica, France **Website** corsica.forhikers.com/gr20
Price ❶

The unromantically named GR20—part of the Grande Randonnée (big excursion) network in Europe and sometimes called *Fra li monti* (across the mountains)—runs diagonally from north to south across the island of Corsica. It offers visitors the chance to walk into the hills of Corsica on one of Europe's finest but most demanding trails.

This 112-mile (180-km) hike reaches heights of more than 6,561 feet (2,000 m) but you do not need to be a climber to make the journey, just confident about walking on rugged terrain. Simply follow the red and white rectangles painted on rocks and trees; it takes around fifteen days to complete. Naturally, you can

> *"Corsica [is] a sort of paradise, the kind of place we all dream of finding before everybody else."*
>
> Craig R. Whitney, *New York Times*

tackle as much or as little of the route as you like. The northern section is the most mountainous and difficult, but also the most beautiful. The northern starting point is near Calvi, and the trail ends near Porto Vecchio in the south, but there are plenty of points where you can join or leave the trail.

Between November and May, the trail is dangerous because of snow, and in the height of summer it can get too hot; June and September are therefore the best times to go. Highlights include hanging suspension bridges and climbing chains bolted into rocks at difficult spots. Along the way you will see magnificent views of nature in all her glory. **SH**

Stay at Palais Schwarzenberg

Location Vienna, Austria
Website www.palais-schwarzenberg.com   **Price** 🟢🟢

There cannot be many hotels in the world like the Palais Schwarzenberg. It sits in its own 20-acre (8-ha) park in the center of the city of Vienna, making a night here a bit like staying at Buckingham Palace in London. One notable difference, though, is that the Palais Schwarzenberg is open to all—if you have the money.

It was back in 1962 that the owners, the princes Schwarzenberg, took the unusual decision to turn a wing of their palace into a hotel. (The hotel now takes up the whole central part of the building.) The present appearance of the palace dates from 1716 when the Schwarzenbergs first acquired it and had it altered by the best architect of the time, Johann Bernhard Fischer von Erlach. The building was situated in an area of the city that was rapidly filling up with impressive noble palaces. Higher up the hill, Prince Eugene of Savoy built the Belvedere Palace, which now houses Austria's national collection of paintings.

The central dome of the Palais Schwarzenberg was destroyed by a bomb during World War II, but otherwise the building remains much as it was. There is a sumptuous marble parlor and a dining room stuffed with fine art treasures, including Rubens paintings, Meissen porcelain, and Gobelins tapestries. There are now thirty-eight traditionally furnished rooms and suites in this five-star hotel, the best of which have beautiful views looking out over the formal gardens behind. There is a lovely terrace where you can eat outside in the summer months, oblivious to the traffic on the busy Schwarzenberg Platz. The hotel has always prided itself on a French style of cooking as distinct from the more homey Viennese cuisine encountered elsewhere in the city. **GMD**

Recharge at Palais Coburg

Location Vienna, Austria
Website www.relaischateaux.com/coburg   **Price** 🟢🟢

Housed in the former town palace of the dukes of Coburg, the Biedermeyer Palais Coburg hotel opened in 2003 as Vienna's latest five-star hotel. Each of the thirty-five suites has been individually designed and the whole mass slotted into the original framework of the palace. There is even a roomy, indoor swimming pool: a rare luxury in Vienna.

Nothing of importance from the old palace appears to have been lost, and the "family parlor" is a treat. It contains portraits of all the Coburgs at the time of building and illustrates the singular success of the small dukedom that provided monarchs for half of Europe.

"Surrounded by tropical plants, the spa offers the ideal setting for relaxation . . . after tiring days."

Proprietors, Palais Coburg

With chef Christian Petz at the helm, the Palais Coburg boasts one of the finest restaurants in Vienna. It also possesses one of the very best wine cellars in the world with vintages going back to the eighteenth century, some of which may be enjoyed in the hotel's wine bar and parlors.

The Palais Coburg was built on the site of one of the bastions of the old city wall and looks out toward the famous Ring and the City Park beyond. The strong, military vaults have been exposed to make a striking lobby. The deep cellars of the bastion, where the soldiers would have slept, are still there and have been incorporated into the impressive hotel fabric. **GMD**

Relax at Hotel Schloss Fuschl

Location Salzburg, Austria
Website www.schlossfuschlresort.at   **Price** 😊😊😊

Since 1450, this fairy-tale former hunting lodge and castle has presided grandly over its tiny peninsula overlooking Austria's Lake Fuschl. A secluded, palatial world of tranquility, this classically styled hotel has been voted one of Europe's top twenty-five resorts by *Condé Nast Traveler*.

Most of the opulent rooms are within the castle proper, although six rooms in the classic Salzkammer style are available in the Jaegerhaus hunting lodge, which is set within the shadows of the castle walls. There are also six lakeside cottages that come complete with their own private terraces and replete with all the facilities one would expect of a grand hotel. More than 150 works of art, known as the Schloss Fuschl Collection of old masters, adorn the castle's extensive public spaces.

Dining at the Hotel Schloss Fuschl will be a fondly remembered highlight of any visit, with vast breakfasts served on the hotel's lakeside terrace. Lunch and dinner menus include delicacies such as smoked trout caught fresh daily from the hotel's own private fishery, complementing traditional Austrian fare in the award-winning Imperial Restaurant. Whatever else you do, be sure not to leave without having tasted the famous Schloss Fuschl tart.

If you would like to learn more of the castle's colorful history, there is an exhibition hall on-site that will take you on a journey back through the centuries. There is a library in the castle's tower, and a castle boat is available for trips across Lake Fuschl. There is also a nine-hole golf course, and the hotel's unique collection of vintage cars can be made available to guests for romantic excursions. **BS**

Visit Archbishop Dietrich Mausoleum

Location Salzburg, Austria
Website www.salzburg.info   **Price** 🚻

Located on the right bank of the River Salzach, the Linzergasse is one of Salzburg's main shopping streets and has always been an important thoroughfare in the history of the town. But sneak through the ornamental iron gates off the busy pedestrian street and you enter into the silent world that is the cemetery of St. Sebastian's Church. Occasionally the copper bells of the baroque church will break the silence, but their resonant tones tend to enhance a visit to the cemetery rather than encroach upon peaceful contemplation. Commissioned by Prince-Archbishop Wolf Dietrich in 1595, the cemetery is designed in an Italian style,

---

"Wolf Dietrich von Raitenau … brought Italian Renaissance architecture and styles to the city."

Encyclopedia Britannica

---

bordered by cloisters. In the middle stands Gabrielskapelle (St. Gabriel's Chapel). It was built from 1597 to 1603 as a mausoleum for the famous archbishop who ruled Salzburg for much of the baroque period. Inside you sit in virtual darkness, except for the light that comes in through the circular rooftop windows and plays games on the ornately colored ceramic walls. The chapel provides a welcome, cooling retreat from the heat of summer and offers brief respite when snow covers the graves. The cemetery ceased to be a burial ground in 1888, so you will not be intruding on a family's immediate grief during your period of quiet contemplation. **CFM**

Unwind at Mavida Balance Hotel and Spa

Location Near Salzburg, Austria   **Website** www.mavida.at
Price ⑨⑨

Situated overlooking the shimmering freshwater lake Zeller See and surrounded by the Austrian Alps, this ultra-modern hotel is the last word in cutting-edge chic. It is a member of the award-winning Design Hotels Group, and the interior of this smart wellness retreat is the work of the German-born designer Niki Szilagyi.

For those keen to detox, Mavida's spa offers traditional Finnish saunas, as well as unique treatments such as the Mavida Crystal Spa that uses precious stones and rare oils to help you achieve inner—and outer—tranquility. Guests who want to achieve Zen-like calm in a hurry should try the floatarium; a couple

> *"The minimalist decor confirms its status as a rival to the most sophisticated of urban retreats."*

Independent

of sessions promises to offer the same relaxing benefits as a week's vacation. Outdoor enthusiasts may take the hotel's bikes on a pleasant ten-minute ride to the southern shoreline of the Zeller See and the hotel's own private beach. The lake is surrounded by more than thirty 9,840-foot (3,000-m) peaks. The historic town of Zell am See is only a short drive away, and the hotel is adjacent to the Alpine meadows and mountain streams of the beautiful Hohe Tauern National Park. Back at the hotel, the gourmet cuisine, prepared in the exhibition kitchen, reflects traditional Austrian and Mediterranean delights and is enhanced with fresh food from the hotel garden. **BS**

Take the Cog Train to Schafbergspitze

Location Upper Austria   **Website** www.schafberg.net
Price ⑨

There are two ways to reach the Schafbergspitze Hotel, the only residence perched on the top of the highest mountain in the Salzkammergut region: walk, or take the traditional, steam, cog mountain railway. Whichever method you choose, on a clear day the journey offers stunning views. A series of seven blue glacial lakes appears far below, and snowcapped Alpine mountain ranges spread for miles across the valley. When the day-trippers depart, Schafberg Mountain is yours for the night, and you will be staying at the summit, 6,000 feet (1,780 m) above sea level.

The cog railway, the oldest in Austria, has been running from the small lakeside village of St. Wolfgang since 1893, and the journey takes about forty-five minutes, with uplifting views at every turn. The 150-year-old hotel has been run by the Pasch family since the 1960s and is open from the beginning of May to the end of October. It has twenty-five double rooms with five family rooms, all with private bathrooms, and some with south-facing balconies offering views of the Wolfgangsee (Lake Wolfgang). Simply but tastefully furnished in classic Austrian style with pine furniture, the rooms are light and airy. Wholesome and traditional Austrian food is served from the kitchen in a selection of dining rooms that includes an open summer terrace providing a birds-eye view of the region; good food is, naturally, an important aspect of the hotel given its location. Packages that include the cost of a return train fare on the cog railway are available. **CFM**

→ *The steam train chugs up slopes studded with wildflowers, traveling high up into the clouds.*

Enjoy Schloss Dürnstein

Location Lower Austria
Website www.relaischateaux.com/durnstein **Price** $ $

The baroque Schloss is the centerpiece of the quiet hamlet of Dürnstein, a picture-postcard village in the Wachau wine region which became a World Heritage site in 2000. The main street contains a number of cute cafés and bars, and the baker Schmidl, whose *Laberl*, or rolls, are famous throughout central Europe. He also makes one of the best wines in the village.

The Austrian emperor Leopold was staying in the Schloss in 1683 when he learned that the Turks had been repelled from the gates of Vienna, and the hotel is still frequented by princes and kings today. Members of the British, Japanese, and Spanish royal families have been recent guests. The building was acquired

> *"[The hotel's] decor evokes the styles of baroque, biedermeier and empire."*

Proprietors, Schloss Dürnstein

by Raimund Thiery in 1937, and his family, still the owners, have turned it into an elegant five-star hotel stuffed with fabulous antiques.

In recent years, the kitchens have improved beyond measure, and it is now a delight to eat in the main dining room, or in summer to sit on the terrace overlooking the Danube. Naturally, the collection of Wachau wines is second to none. There is a warren of gorgeous vaulted rooms on the ground floor, and many of the bedrooms contain priceless furniture. On the terrace is the lovely swimming pool. The view of the Schloss from the south side of the Danube is said to be one of the most romantic in Austria. **GMD**

Discover Mayr & Mohr Spa

Location Kärnten, Austria
Website www.mayrandmore.at **Price** $

Forget scented candles, aromatherapy oils, and frangipani blossoms: This former hospital turned Austrian health spa has a very strict results-focused approach and is not your typical indulgent spa. Think formidable matrons in crisp white uniforms, early morning starts, and a frugal diet—the staff aim to provide a life-changing experience.

The concept is based on the Mayr method, which believes that the digestive system is the key to good health. You will have a strange diet, herbal tea, medical examinations, detox massages, and urine analysis as part of your weeklong treatment. Good health is at the heart of everything—which is why there is no elevator in the hotel—and the fresh air and Alpine scenery does wonders for your well-being, too. The hotel occupies an enviable spot on the edge of Lake Worth, so you can enjoy boating on the lake, not to mention golf nearby. All the rooms in the four-star hotel have views of the gardens or the lake.

The award-winning Mayr & Mohr Health Spa might not be a chic tropical retreat or a massage heaven, but a week here can be enough to change your body and mind, providing you with something more than mere therapy. Stress therapies, burn-out solutions, and numerous other cures for hectic, unhealthy lifestyles are on offer, and because every program is tailored to suit the needs of the individual, the prescription is different every time.

Your skin will be brighter, you will sleep better, and you will be more energetic as a result of the Mayr treatments. The experience could even give you the building blocks to create a new start, leaving behind old habits and stepping forward into a new awareness and a new way of living your life. **LD**

Cross-country Ski at Ramsau

Location Tyrol, Austria
Website www.tirolarena.com **Price** 💲💲

Imagine taking giant steps and gliding with effortless ease through a snowy mountain landscape of spiky peaks and silent forests that looks like something out of C. S. Lewis's Narnia books. This is one way of envisaging cross-country skiing in the Tyrolean Alps. The rhythmic swooshing of your skis as they press down against the sparkling snow and a friendly *Grüss Gott* greeting from a passing skier make this a bewitching mode of travel.

Cross-country skiing can be as energetic or as leisurely as you like. At its extreme, it can be a complete workout for arms, legs, and just about everything else. At its most docile, it can be an amiable shuffle at walking speed from a coffee and apple strudel indulgence at one mountain café to a beer at the next watering hole.

Leutasch, not far from Innsbruck, is the king of all Austrian cross-country ski areas, with an admirable snow record and well over 125 miles (200 km) of prepared tracks beneath the pyramidal 8,730-foot (2,661-m) peak of Hohe Munde. Between the low-key villages dotted in the main valley, the track rises very, very gently, and here a procession of skiers of all ages and fitness levels makes its way along.

Farther up, the terrain becomes distinctly hillier as you head into the trees; the crowds thin out dramatically, only to reappear at the next refreshment hut. With typical Austrian precision, each route is color coded for difficulty and equipped with diagrams showing the rises, falls, and overall distance. Getting lost is never a concern. **TL**

↗ *A cross-country skier glides through a smooth patch of snow in the beautiful Tyrolean Alps.*

"How liberating to replace plastic boots with delicate skis, gliding through a silent landscape."

Stephen Venables, *Guardian*

Relax at the Posthotel

Location Tyrol, Austria   **Website** www.posthotel.at
Price ⑤⑤

At the Posthotel Achenkirch, the management and staff do not much care for the term "wellness." Recognized as having one of the leading spa and treatment centers in Austria, the Posthotel was practicing the concept of wellness to a grateful clientele twenty years before the word became commonplace in the hotel industry's lexicon.

The Posthotel's approach to the well-being of its guests now borders on the legendary, offering everything from body peels, anticellulite treatments, and oxygen therapy through to the application of various Asian disciplines such as tai chi. Anything is possible here, from a simple Shaolin massage to floating on a waterbed in a body pack while gazing through the spa's glass atrium at twinkling stars in the Tyrolean night. The Posthotel's facilities are staffed by trained therapists who continue to set the trends in holistic approaches to health and inner well-being.

The hotel's forty-three rooms are furnished in a country-house style with natural wood floors and Japanese tub-style baths filled to overflowing with scented water. Bay windows and private terraces are standard, as are the little things like complimentary fruit baskets and in-room high-speed Internet access.

The Posthotel's kitchen serves seasonal, locally sourced meals and is a regular recipient of the prestigious Gault Millau toque for fine cuisine. Tennis, squash, sailing on the beautiful Lake Achensee, or horseback riding against the backdrop of the magnificent Karwendelgebirge Mountains should leave you feeling refreshed indeed. **BS**

▣ Guests will find a five-star welcome nestled deep in
  the woodlands of the idyllic Tyrolean Achental valley.

Enjoy Liebes Rot-Flüh Hotel Spa

Location Tyrol, Austria
Website www.rotflueh.com   **Price** $ $

> "... if you keep on believing,
> the dream that you wish
> will come true."

Cinderella, 1950

This is not a hotel; it is a fairy-tale escape. "Cinderella's Castle," the spa palace, is like a theatrical stage set, with bubbling pools tucked into caves filled with stalactites, where mood and ambience have dreamlike qualities. Features include steam baths, saunas, and an ice grotto, with the attention to design second to none. More than fifty treatments are offered, too, from rose-petal baths to an invigorating massage. After your spa treatment, relax in the Mediterranean rest area filled with light and scented with fresh flowers. Or take a dip in the outdoor pool to cool down—even in winter!

All is well inside, but outside the location is phenomenal. Blanketed by winter snow or summer flowers, a backdrop of mountains, Alpine meadows and the peaceful, glacial Haldensee (Lake Halden) continues the fairy-tale setting. The location is perfect for escaping into the hills, whether walking or cross-country skiing—that is if you can tear yourself away from the open fires, lavish cuisine, and sumptuous bedrooms.

Suites are furnished in the style of Gustav Klimt, Tiffany, and country houses; no two rooms are the same, and many have their own whirlpool tubs and steam baths. Large family suites are also available, and children are well catered for with all-day supervision and entertainment programs so that you can relax in the spa knowing they are enjoying themselves, too. No wonder the hotel has won so many awards, including "best hotel in Austria" given by the *Relax Guide* and awards for the most family- and female-friendly hotel. Utter bliss and true relaxation. **CFM**

◤ *The hotel is impeccably designed, from the luxurious bedrooms to the huge, sprawling spa complex.*

Visit Lake Neusiedl

Location Austrian-Hungarian border
Website www.neusiedler-see.at   **Price** 🌐

Deep in Central Europe, straddling the border between Austria and Hungary and surrounded by screens of thick reeds, is an unlikely geographic phenomenon. The flat plains of the Hungarian Steppes drain to this spot but there is nowhere for the water to go, so a large lake has formed in a shallow basin. Lake Neusiedl is little known away from the middle of the continent, yet it covers more than 115 square miles (300 sq km). Some visitors lose themselves in more than 310 miles (500 km) of trails, walking or biking through reeds, swamps, and ponds. Others join the crowds at the lakeside water sports centers near towns such as Podersdorf and Morbisch.

"The remarkable rural architecture surrounding the lake adds to the area's considerable interest."

UNESCO World Heritage Committee

The lake is very shallow—a maximum of 6 feet (1.8 m) deep. This means Neusiedl warms very quickly in summer and creates a huge, warm, calm water playground hundreds of miles from the sea. Summer activities center around boating, swimming, fishing, and windsurfing. Activities range from kite-surfing courses to renting your own motorboat. In the winter, the shallow lake freezes easily, so ice skating and cross-country skiing are popular. The timeless, ancient villages around the lake are dotted with beautiful eighteenth- and nineteenth-century palaces. The lake has been declared a World Heritage site and is now part of a cross-border national park. **SH**

Unwind at Aquareina Spa

Location Graubünden, Switzerland
Website www.vereinahotel.ch   **Price** 💲

When it comes to old-world Alpine charm, nowhere beats the chic mountain resort of Klosters. A favorite with royalty and celebrities alike, it offers first-class backcountry skiing and more than 185 miles (300 km) of pristine white slopes.

It is not all about the white stuff. Away from the runs populated by Chanel- and Prada-clad skiers, there are luxurious hideaways such as the state-of-the-art Aquareina Spa at Hotel Vereina. Intimately decadent, it has thermal baths, Finnish and aroma saunas, and a range of treatments for some serious pampering. The vitality pool has invigorating massage jets, whereas the large indoor pool is the perfect place to practice lap swimming. The range of massages, including whole and partial body massage, foot reflex zone massage, rejuvenating massage, and maram will make you feel uplifted and refreshed. Do not leave without trying the signature treatment, the Cleopatra milk bath to revive your skin.

The sublimely luxurious chalet-style Hotel Vereina sits on the sunny side of Klosters, just a few minutes' walk from the heart of the village. Ultra-chic and elegant, it originally opened in 1890, but after a major refurbishment has made an amazing comeback in the twenty-first century.

If you can pull yourself away from its gastronomic food and piano bar, explore surrounding hiking trails and cross-country ski routes, go for a spin on the ice rink, or take the Gotschna cable car to reach the Parsenn ski routes. If you have ever dreamed of soaring over the mountains with the wind in your face, try paragliding over the Prättigau valley, taking off from Gotschnagrat. It is the closest you will get to heaven, apart from a treatment at the spa. **AD**

Stay at Chalet Eugenia

Location Graubünden, Switzerland **Website** www.descent.co.uk
Price 💲💲💲

Chalet Eugenia brings new meaning to the word "opulence." When guests take over this six-bedroom chalet, they get a team of six staff, in-house sauna and steam room, wood-paneled study, drawing room, and two beautiful dining rooms—and that is just for starters.

The style is classic and sophisticated, with each room designed to the highest specifications. Most rooms have private balconies with fabulous southerly views of the impressive Gotschna Mountain. When you feel inclined to venture farther than the front doorstep, a chauffeur is on call 24/7, naturally. Despite the extravagance of the chalet, the lure of the scenic surroundings is too much to resist. Eugenia is in a

> *"Arguably the poshest chalet in the Alps . . . The luxury of Eugenia comes as something of a shock."*
>
> Tom Robbins, *Observer*

prime position just two minutes from pretty Klosters. Lying at the foot of the Engadine, the dramatic mountain landscape is truly the stuff of dreams—it is no wonder Klosters has long been the favorite winter playground of the British royals.

It goes without saying that the skiing is great, too. There is the Madrisa region, perfect for families, and the excellent Parsenn ski area. Visitors also delight in swishing down the magical tree-lined route to Kublis and the historic journey over to Arosa. If all that sounds too much like hard work, Chalet Eugenia provides the ultimate refuge in which to hole up and watch snowflakes gently carpet the land outside. **LP**

Relax at Hotel Therme

Location Graubünden, Switzerland **Website** www.therme-vals.ch
Price 💲💲

A design aficionado's dream come true, Hotel Therme is as cutting edge as modern architecture gets. It has been said, and not too lightly, that Peter Zumthor crafted a near-religious experience out of little more than stone, water, and light at the Therme spa. It is an ultra-modernist design statement in gray Valser quartzite, and Zumthor did not stop there. He turned his attention to the faded 1960s hotel next door, and the result is the so-called Temporary rooms. Modern in style, they are all white with brightly-colored Indian rugs and chocolate leather chairs. The ambience is a million miles away from the Heidi-style chalets that characterized Switzerland for so long.

Hotel Therme was built on a hillside just below St. Peters, the natural thermal spring from which the hotel draws its water. It may offer sleek styling, but it does not come with a five-star price tag. Community-owned, like the spa, the hotel is affordable. Best of all, it offers access to the spa outside of public opening hours, and there is plenty to enjoy. The big draw is the series of vast pools: some hot, some cold, some scented with fresh flower petals. Lighting is dramatic, streaming in from blue-tinted skylights far above or lit from below. Some pools are painted bright white up to the waterline, with dark gray unfinished stone above, creating the illusion that the water is glowing. It is a thrill to immerse yourself, neck-deep in the steaming hot water and gaze at the snow-covered mountains as snowflakes gently fall on your head.

The theme is all about relaxation. Lie in the pools, sip cocktails, and worship the natural beauty of the Swiss Alps. Recordings of monastic chanting mingle with the sound of the thermal water as it bubbles into the spa. If this does not relax you, nothing will. **AD**

Discover Lake Lucerne

Location Central Switzerland (Uri, Schwyz, and Unterwalden) **Website** www.myswitzerland.com
Price 🌓

Lucerne, with its background of snowcapped mountains and its fairy-tale turrets and covered medieval wooden bridges, is one of the world's most romantic and elegant cities. Its Alpine charm hides an up-to-the-minute town crammed with attractions, from belle epoque lakeside hotels to the sleek waterside KKK (the culture and convention center) perched on the lake.

Decanted from the smooth, comfortable train ride from Zurich airport onto the lakeside quay, you come face-to-face with a truly picture-postcard Switzerland, elegant white swans dodging the paddle steamers criss-crossing Lake Lucerne, and a panorama of snowcapped mountains Rigi and Pilatus. The stunning setting makes it the perfect venue for year-round artistic events. Visit in June when the streets resound with traditional music, or in July for the Blue Balls Festival, with music from blues and soul to R&B and funk. The hills really come alive with the sound of music in August and September, when the annual festival of concerts, ballet, opera, dance, and theater attracts performers from around the world.

At any time of year, take a trip to the peak of Lucerne's snow-covered Mount Pilatus for spectacular views. Factor in lunch on the summit to get maximum enjoyment from a trip that utilizes lake steamer, cable car, gondola, and the world's steepest cogwheel railway, which climbs through meadows dotted with clumps of intense blue gentians and wooden chalets hung with geraniums. You will not hear much yodeling here, but you will find Swiss perfection. **MN**

↗ *The spectacular views over the lake from the top of Mount Rigi Kulm will leave you breathless.*

"I was literally gasping and reeling at the extraordinary beauty of the scenery."

Michael Winner, director

Recharge at Bella Tola

Location Valais, Switzerland   **Website** www.bellatola.ch   **Price** §

Dating back to 1883, it is no surprise to discover that Bella Tola is an award-winning historic hotel. It started off, all those years ago, as a typical Alpine hotel built on the foundations of a Roman villa. With additions over the years, it gradually grew to become a seriously grand hotel in this remote location.

Sitting at an altitude of 5,420 feet (1,652 m) on a terrace overlooking the mountain road on the flank of the Val d'Anniviers, Bella Tola incredibly remained in the hands of the same family for three generations before being taken over by present-day owners Anne-Françoise and Claude Buchs. Rather than modernize the grande dame of Swiss hotels, old floors and windows were carefully renovated and works of art, collectors' pieces, and antique furniture were added to set the scene for a visit to remember.

Ultimately, this is a place to rest, relax, and recharge the batteries. Opulent bedrooms are individually styled with period furniture, and some have private balconies to take in the plunging valley views. With an indoor swimming pool that features a blazing log fire beside it, a sauna, hammam, ice fountain, and massage rooms, there are plenty of treatments to ease aching muscles after a day on the slopes.

There is unspoiled skiing in the valley, or it is just a fifteen-minute drive to the cult resort of Grimentz, where you can hire a guide and enjoy fabulous backcountry skiing. Alternatively, relax in a chair on the large garden terraces and soak up the sun. The views are stunning across to the surrounding 13,120-foot (4,000-m) peaks, including the Matterhorn.

A jazz band sometimes plays in the cozy sitting room before dinner. Then wander into Tzambron, one of the hotel's restaurants, for its fondue and raclette. Perfect on a chilly winter night. **AD**

⊡ *A new wellness area offers a blissfully quiet place in which to rest and be pampered.*

Rent The Lodge

Location Valais, Switzerland   **Website** www.thelodge.virgin.com   **Price** $$$

If Verbier is the king of stylish Alpine resorts, then The Lodge is its crowning glory. Richard Branson's chic log cabin offers guests a James Bond–style, once-in-a-lifetime experience.

The ultra-modern, nine-bedroom chalet is a two-hour drive from Geneva airport. It is simply bursting with wow factors, including an indoor pool, whirlpool tub, spa, "party room," wine cellar, ice rink, and even a cinema. During your stay at the chalet, you get a personal chauffeur and ski guides on call, as well as sensational food that is tailored to suit your taste and whipped up at your convenience. No expense is spared, and a dedicated team of staff includes a beauty therapist and an activities coordinator. Even a bartender is at hand to create your favorite cocktail to sip as you admire the majestic views and warm up next to a log fire. So far, so 007. The forest setting is just as spectacular as The Lodge itself. In the winter, when the chalet operates on an exclusive-use basis only, the surrounding Swiss Alps make up a serene, glistening white wonderland, with the mountains softly carpeted in snow. In spring and summer, the landscape flourishes and comes alive with a vivid rainbow of colors. You can choose to whoosh down the trails during the winter months or swap your skis for hiking boots come summer—either way the stunning scenery will cast its spell over you.

The Lodge is conveniently located a five-minute walk from the ski lifts and stylish town of Verbier, which has a legendary après-ski scene. However, with such luxury on tap back at The Lodge, you may want to remain cocooned in your temporary abode. Yes, staying here is super expensive, but this is Branson's baby—and after a brandy or two in the hot tub, you are sure to forget all about the price tag. **LP**

⬆ *The Lodge is one of Branson's "limited edition" retreats—a rare blast of extraordinary luxury.*

Stay at Riffelalp Resort 2,222m

Location Valais, Switzerland   **Website** www.riffelalp.com
Price ⑤

Standing on your balcony, gazing out toward the majestic Matterhorn, it is impossible not to be awestruck. The Riffelalp Resort 2,222m, looming at 1,975 feet (602 m) above the hustle and bustle of Zermatt below, is blessed with stunning vistas toward the huge beast of a mountain. The view is especially enchanting in the orange glow of early morning.

In a lovely setting among Alpine forests, accessed only via hiking paths, ski trails, or the nearby Gornergrat cog railway, the large hotel provides a civilized base for a ski vacation or a summer break, when the meadows are carpeted with flowers.

Its rooms have all the contemporary touches one could wish for—whirlpool tubs, DVD players, Bose sound systems—as well as a sense of style and character that rarely comes as standard. The spacious Matterhorn and Monte Rosa suites are ideal for families and there is plenty on-site to keep visitors occupied, from a converted chapel for concerts and a home cinema, to heated indoor and outdoor swimming pools (with superb views of that famous peak), a state-of-the-art spa, and two bowling alleys.

A wine-tasting session in the cellar is a perfect way to begin an evening, followed by local specialties in one of the three restaurants—be sure to sample a cheesy raclette. Round off the evening with a digestif as the pianist tinkles away in the cozy bar. Perhaps the best feature offered by the resort however is the ski in/ski out piste access, which means that a good day's skiing starts right outside the front door. **LP**

◄ *The resort is blessed with stunning vistas toward the iconic and colossal Matterhorn.*

Camp at Whitepod

Location Berne, Switzerland
Website www.whitepod.com **Price** $

What appears at first glance to be a collection of giant white golf balls set around an Alpine chalet is actually a series of dome-shaped tents, or "pods." Perched at 5,577 feet (1,700 m) above the village of Les Cerniers, these pods make up one of the hippest eco-retreats.

The brainchild of Swiss entrepreneur Sofia de Meyer, the Whitepod experience was born from a desire to create a mini-resort that made the most of its surroundings yet did nothing to harm their beauty. Raised on wooden platforms and designed like traditional igloos, the pods are waterproof and UV resistant, flame-retardant, and insulated with fabrics that are also used by NASA. Heating comes courtesy

> *"You are gifted grand cru air quality, gob-smacking views, and a real sense of being among nature."*
>
> Simon Mills, *Guardian*

of tiny woodstoves, and each room has a comfy bed bedecked with industrial-strength comforters and pillows, organic bedding, and sheepskin. Panoramic windows offer views of Les Diablerets Massif, an Alpine chalet that dates back to 1820. It is where you will find the dining room serving up the resort's delicious cooking, all locally procured and/or organic.

Once here, guests can enjoy snowshoeing, ice climbing, backcountry skiing, horseback riding, and even dogsledding. After you have expended all your energy, you can take advantage of the camp's on-site therapists, who offer a range of treatments from hour-long massages to reflexology and osteopathy. **PS**

Stay at Beau-Rivage

Location Vaud, Switzerland
Website www.lhw.com/beaurivage **Price** $$$

Tourists have been dropping into Lausanne ever since Lord Byron arrived with the Shelleys in 1817, and Mary sat down to write *Frankenstein*. The Hôtel d'Angleterre where they stayed is still standing, and has recently been incorporated into a snazzy new extension of the venerable Beau-Rivage.

The Beau-Rivage was not around in the days of Byron and the Shelleys. It was built in 1861, marking the height of British interest in Lake Geneva. Summers in Switzerland offered the chance to enjoy the lake and the fresh air of the mountains. Every commune had its "grand hotel," but the grandest of the grand was the Beau-Rivage. Success meant that an entire new wing had to be tacked on by the turn of the century, linked to the old building by an exquisite art-nouveau ballroom.

There are glorious rooms throughout, but possibly the nicest are in the art-nouveau wing. They look out over the great expanse of the placid lake to the mountains on the French side, illuminated by the setting sun at gloaming. There is a formal garden, swimming pool, and spa. The clientele is not always the youngest; many come to service their bank accounts. Politicians are commonplace here; they are best spotted in the dreamy dining room with its encrustations of stucco and magnificent paintings. There is a choice of fine restaurants in which you may dine, but make sure you try the fish from the lake: pollen, char, and perch fillets, drunk with the marvelous limpid wines of the Vaud, from vineyards just a mile or two to the east. There is plenty to do, but a most pleasant way to relax is to take one of the turn-of-the-century paddle steamers down to the Château de Chillon, immortalized by Byron. **GMD**

Relax at La Réserve

Location Geneva, Switzerland
Website www.lareserve.ch   **Price** ⑤⑤⑤

Fresh, revitalizing mountain air, a wonderful lakeside setting, and a unique sense of style combine to make La Réserve a literal breath of fresh air. Unpretentious yet thoroughly cool, the Swiss retreat straddles the shore of Lake Geneva and sits in a landscaped park, ensuring privacy and plenty of space for relaxation. Do not get too relaxed, though, because La Réserve has a definite party edge to it: Every night cocktails flow in the bar as a DJ plays until the early hours, and the Chinese and French restaurants are buzzing with the young and beautiful people of Geneva society.

By day, hangover shaken off, the cosmopolitan city of Geneva is just a complimentary boat hop away. La Réserve's Venetian-style, elegant wooden *motoscaffo* whisks you there in minutes. Or guests can just enjoy the hotel's vibe or indulge in a range of activities, including wakeboarding on the lake.

The building may look underwhelming from the outside, but inside rooms are beautifully designed with oiled wooden floors, decadent colors, rich velvet bedspreads, and granite bathrooms. Many rooms have lake views or vistas toward the Alps, and some have generous terraces. Good looks aside, it is worth visiting La Réserve for the award-winning spa alone. In its own wing, it has seventeen treatment rooms and a varied menu of therapies, as well as indoor and outdoor pools, sauna, and hammam. Personalized programs are offered, incorporating water therapies and jasmine flower baths. But the outdoor pool is the best place to be on a sunny day, sipping a glass of crisp wine and knowing you are part of something rather special. **LP**

↗ *The sleek and, at times, daring decor is the work of hot interior designer Jacques Garcia.*

"The style is loosely inspired by African lodges, with animal-print carpets and a tented restaurant."

Condé Nast Traveler

See Piedmont by Bicycle

Location Piedmont, Italy   **Website** www.piemontefeel.org
Price 💲

The region of Piedmont is in the northwest tip of Italy, bordered by Switzerland to the north and France to the west. Renowned for its white truffles and outstanding cuisine, Piedmont is also recognized as one of Italy's greatest wine regions.

This agricultural paradise provides the perfect backdrop for a bicycle safari. Gentle slopes give way to orchards and fields of sunflowers. Winding roads unfold to reveal tiny hamlets and picturesque medieval villages. The views are never ending: from undulating vineyards to the bordering Alpine mountain ranges. On a clear summer's day, you can even see across to the majestic peak of Mont Blanc.

The capital of Piedmont, Turin, is the ideal starting point for a two-wheeled tour. There is a network of bicycle paths crisscrossing the medieval city, which allows you to view the myriad castles, cathedrals, and museums. Travel on through towns such as Bra, known as the capital of gourmet, and Alba, the home of white truffles. However, perhaps the real magic is found when bicycling between the towns, where the air is scented with wildflowers and filled with birdsong.

Quiet country roads lead you through groves of chestnut trees, alongside rushing rivers, and through lush pine forests. Recharge in the little villages along the way, stopping for lunch at one of the many gastronomical restaurants. Try to time your tour to coincide with one of the many food festivals held during the year, including those dedicated solely to truffles, snails, and cheese. After settling in each night, enjoy a glass of the region's world-famous Barolo. **JP**

➔ *Ride the gentle slopes of Piedmont to work up an appetite for the culinary delights the region offers.*

Visit a Barolo Vineyard

Location Piedmont, Italy   **Website** www.italyandwine.net/piedmont/barolo.htm
Price ⑤⑤

"The [Barolo] vineyards . . . are
the most carefully charted stands
of vines anywhere in Italy."

italyandwine.net

The road is narrow and winding as it heads through the gently rolling hills to the town of Barolo. It may be small, but Barolo is the center of a world-famous wine-making area with a big reputation. The town has given its name to a powerful and complex red wine made from Piedmont's Nebbiolo grape. This is a dark blue, highly tannic variety and means Barolo can be a hard—and therefore expensive—wine to make.

Barolo is old rural Italy at its best. Visitors can immerse themselves in a tour of the vineyards in the expert company of a local guide. You can be driven around these hills south of Alba, touring vineyards, tasting wines and visiting historic cellars.

Locals call Barolo "the wine of kings and the king of wines." Its history is closely linked to the ruling families of Piedmont. So perhaps your tour will include the Castle of Barolo, originally the home of French-born Marchesa Guilia Colbert, who first created Barolo wine. And later you may discover wineries in Barolo's eastern communes, Massolino in Serralunga and Elio Grasso or Fantino Conterno in Monforte, that are known for more structured Barolos, rich with tannins for long aging.

It's not all about sipping vintages in sun-dappled vineyards. There's plenty of eating to be done, too: Bread sticks are a local invention but Piedmont cuisine is generally elegant and hearty—truffles, mountain cheeses, veal, and hazelnuts are regional treats. You could also visit beautiful medieval castles, go shopping in historic towns like Asti and Alba, investigate the sumptuous local produce in traditional village markets, or even join a local truffle hunt. **SH**

↖ *This Barolo vineyard is planted on a suitable slope in the province of Cuneo in Piedmont.*

Enjoy La Villa

Location Piedmont, Italy **Website** www.lavillahotel.net
Price 💰💰

Perched high on a hill overlooking the vineyards of Monferrato sits La Villa, a seventeenth-century palazzo that has been converted into a sublime boutique hotel by its English owners. It offers stupendous views in every direction, framed by the Alps more than 62 miles (100 km) away. Originally a nobleman's house, La Villa has undergone extensive renovation to restore the property to its former glory. The result is a rural escape that, since opening in August 2005, has earned a reputation as the best place to stay in the region.

Every one of the fourteen rooms has been decorated in impeccable taste, combining period features with the essentials of twenty-first-century living. Locally

> "The pace [at La Villa] is relaxed, sophisticated, and comfortable all at the same time."

cellartours.com

sourced antiques and period pieces jostle alongside state-of-the-art entertainment systems. Have lunch alfresco in the shade of a large pergola, or indoors take refuge in the lounge bar, which more often than not acts as the hub of the hotel. There is also a tasting room where you can sample the superb local vintages, and with no bossy bartender to shoo you off to bed at midnight you can sit and sip a fruity Barolo or a Barbera all night if you like, courtesy of the honesty bar.

La Vie restaurant serves local produce. As the home of the slow food movement, Piedmont is renowned for the quality of its cuisine. The area is said to have the highest number of gourmet chefs in Italy. **HA**

See Pian della Mussa

Location Piedmont, Italy **Website** www.canavese-vallilanzo.it
Price 💰

At the top of the tiny Val d'Ala, a quiet Alpine valley northwest of Turin, the road gets so steep and narrow it seems as though you are approaching the very end of the mountain. Cutting past tall houses perched on the rocks where locals still live and farm, winding around impossibly tight corners, there is a moment of genuine awe and pleasure when the track levels out and broadens into an extensive, impressive plateau. Arriving at Pian della Mussa is like entering a lost world.

Mischievous old women will tell you Pian della Mussa is filled with fairy folk, and it is easy to see why such tales abound. Its sheer sides are dotted with a plethora of mineral-white waterfalls that throw light mists and spray around the plain, and a large population of chittering marmots and rambunctious mountain goats perches on the unlikeliest of outcrops, surveying the grazing ground below. The mountains themselves, straddling the Italian–French border, are served by trails that are peppered with stone refuges dating back to the 1880s, each with their own unhappy history of bloodshed and battle, particularly of resistance fighters in World War II.

There is no better place to ponder Pian della Mussa's historic and natural wonder than the thick wooden bench of a rustic, family-run café in the center of it all. The very friendly, generations-old "Cristina" has a commanding view of the entire plain and mountain range, and serves heartwarming zabaglione, a mixture of egg yolk, sugar, and strong sweet wine that has been enjoyed by Alpine hikers for hundreds of years. It is the perfect place to sit and meditate, or for the more adventurous to begin their hikes up to the various lovely isolated lakes in the area, providing the very best in simple, alpine pleasures. **CW**

Stay at the Petit Palais

Location Lombardy, Italy
Website www.petitpalais.it   **Price** 💲💲

Milan is the kind of city that appeals to those with expensive tastes and a feel for culture and fashion. A semicontained universe of chic boutiques, haute cuisine, and centuries of fascinating history, Milan lures travelers from far and wide. Some of the most discerning visitors end up staying at Petit Palais, an elegant seventeenth-century mansion recently converted into a charming, intimate apartment hotel.

This is the type of hotel where quality is paramount: The chandeliers are Murano, the rugs are hand-woven, and the glassware is crystal. The eighteen suites and junior suites are each individually and tastefully decorated, featuring refined drapes, period furnishings, and original stucco work, as well as unobtrusive modern conveniences. The bathrooms are made from the best Italian marble and offer whirlpool tubs and enormous showers. Some of the suites boast private terraces or access to the delightful patio, and the three royal suites have their own fireplaces, too. Afternoon tea or an aperitif can be enjoyed in the lounge, whereas breakfast is served in the wonderful vaulted cellar room (or you can of course request it in your suite).

Despite the peaceful atmosphere at the hotel, Petit Palais is, remarkably, only a ten-minute walk from Milan's countless shops, boutiques, restaurants, and bars, as well as some of the city's most famous cultural landmarks: Piazza Duomo, La Scala Opera House, and the Santa Maria delle Grazie are all mere minutes from the door. Matching comfort and tranquility to upmarket chic on the inside, and boasting a host of pleasure-seeking on the doorstep, the Petit Palais is one of those wonderful all-around escapes that will leave you both stimulated and soothed. **PS**

Discover Lake Maggiore

Location Lombardy/Piedmont, Italy
Website www.illagomaggiore.com   **Price** 💲

There are thirteen lakes strung along the north of the Lombardy region like jewels on a glittering necklace. Seasoned visitors will tell you that each lake has its charms, but it is Maggiore, the "big" lake, that surpasses the others. Famed for the belle epoque resorts of Stresa and Baveno and its beautiful trio of Borromea Islands, Maggiore has it all.

At 33 miles (54 km) it is too wide to swim, although the crystal waters are clean and clear enough for a refreshing dip. The islands in the middle of the lake are owned by the Borromeo family. Isolas Bella and Madre are grand and majestic; they consist entirely of gardens embellished with the rococo Borromeo family palaces.

> *"One can't describe the beauty of the Italian lakes, nor would one try if one could."*
>
> Henry James, author

Isola Superiore is the island of fishermen. Covered with a tumble of rustic houses, it has a shoreline studded with *pescatori* mending their nets beside their boats.

Lake Maggiore ought to be seen in different seasons and under a variety of skies, although the famous microclimate sometimes makes this possible in a single day. Morning can reveal a vast gossamer cloud that is slowly punctured by pinpricks of sun. When the haze lifts, and the slick of water basks in the light, the sparkle is simply dazzling. **SWi**

▣ *Whether enjoyed from the water or from the stability of the shoreline, Lake Maggiore is spectacular.*

Experience L'Albereta

Location Lombardy, Italy
Website www.relaischateaux.com/albereta **Price** 😊😊😊

Set in the hills of Franciacorta, L'Albereta offers a perfect getaway for foodies and sybarites. It has been stylishly turned into a chic country house hotel, which is home to a world-class, two-Michelin-starred restaurant, presided over by Italy's most feted chef Gualtiero Marchesi, and an equally impressive spa.

Marchesi trained with the Troisgros brothers in Roanne and was the first Italian to gain three Michelin rosettes. In recent years he has been designated a national treasure and has his own "national" cooking school. At L'Albereta he interprets Italy's grandest traditions in a French way: Risotto is made with the finest chicken stock, saffron, and a little cheese, with a

---

"Marchesi's cooking is influenced by his love of art, most obviously in dishes inspired by paintings."

theworlds50best.com

---

perfect square of gold leaf in the middle. Another item on the menu to try is his version of the classic "tournedos Rossini." Marchesi uses veal rather than beef fillet, rendering the meat all the more succulent.

The hotel boasts every comfort, including elegant drawing rooms, an indoor swimming pool, and a helipad. One room even has a retractable glass roof. L'Albereta's location is perfect for excursions to this little-known corner of Lombardy. A must-see is the city of Bergamo, for its churches and art collections. **GMD**

← *The rambling nineteenth-century villa seems to rise organically from the surrounding vineyards.*

Ride Through the Tyrol

Location South Tyrol, Italy **Website** www.theridingcompany.com
Price 😊😊

You may wake up and wonder where you are: Although South Tyrol is in Italy, the majority of its inhabitants speak German as their mother tongue. Nestled right on the Austrian border, it is a land of chocolate-box mountains and verdant valleys, of orderly apple orchards and sweetly clanging cowbells. It is also home to the Haflinger horse—a small, chestnut-colored breed with a striking white mane and rhythmic gait that was first developed in this part of the Dolomites in the late 1800s.

Head to the riding stables at Tolderhof and you will be able to saddle up a Haflinger and take half-day or full-day rides into the surrounding Alpine scenery. There is also an indoor riding school where dressage and jumping are taught, and anyone wishing to build up their confidence before braving the outdoors can do so. Riding is certainly not an indoor occupation, nor is it just a summer occupation here: In winter, you can canter through the white, virgin snow. You can even try your hand at ski jeering, in which a skier is harnessed to a horse and travels behind it like a water-skier on snow. You will need to be able ski, but previous riding experience will not be necessary.

Accommodation is available in the four-star Hotel Post, which comes complete with a spa offering massages and aromatherapy soaks for those with sore muscles. The hotel also features a gourmet restaurant that serves up five-course dinners—plenty of food to keep you going on your rides. Alternatively you can stay in an apartment next door to the riding stables, where you will still have access to the hotel's facilities. There is also an art-nouveau villa, Villa Prugger, which can accommodate up to thirteen people and has its own large garden. **PE**

Enjoy Vigilius

Location South Tyrol, Italy   **Website** www.vigilius.it
Price 💲💲

Accessible only by cable car, the remarkable Vigilius Mountain Resort sits 4,920 feet (1,500 m) above everyday life and has jaw-dropping views of the dramatic Dolomites. Come here to escape the pollution and stress of the city—larch wood scents the pure, clean air, and the resort is shrouded in serenity.

This modern lodge is a bold departure from traditional Tyrolean chalets. The ultimate in eco-chic, star architect Matteo Thun has used glass and local wood to skillfully integrate the low-lying building into its natural setting. His inspiration was a wind-fallen tree, and guests will find the reception in the upturned root and bedrooms in the trunk. The grass-covered roof helps energy conservation, whereas inside, open-plan rooms are styled with minimalist furniture and are cleverly divided with internally heated clay walls. Furnished in the main with exposed timber, all rooms have balconies or terraces to take in the views.

The sophisticated spa has a range of treatments and massages, along with a steam room, sauna, and yoga classes. Try the signature hay bath for a circulation-boosting treat. Hearty Tyrolean cooking, from stews to strudels, features on the menu at the Parlour Ida restaurant, whereas the vegetarian 1500 serves Mediterranean-inspired dishes. End the night with a drink by the log fire in the lounge or step outside to the terrace to enjoy the celestial views. In winter, when the mountain is blanketed in snow, go tobogganing, skiing, and snowshoeing. Alternatively, in summer, walk some of the 31 miles (50 km) of hiking trails, or try Nordic walking, paragliding, and archery. **AD**

→ *Go for a dip in the infinity pool for the sensation of swimming into the mountains.*

Experience the Dolomites

Location South Tyrol, Italy
Website www.valgardena.it/en   **Price** ❿

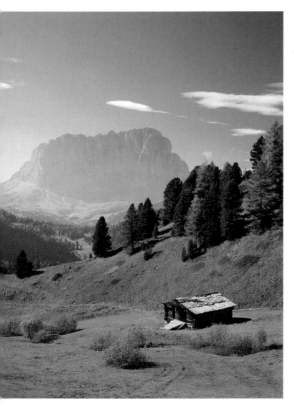

" ... wooded valleys and savage, almost lunar landscapes towering like melted tombstones."

Nick Redman, *Observer*

There may be taller peaks in the Alps, but the Dolomites are perhaps the most startling in shape and sheer drama. The mountains appear improbably jagged and fantastic, and the landscape is almost made for exploring on foot. Although the high summits are climbers-only terrain for the most part, there is plenty of scope for easier walks, with chairlifts and cable cars getting you up from the valleys.

Go in early summer, before the meadows are cut, and you are greeted by the sight of spectacular wildflowers. The best place is the Alpe di Siusi, a high, grassy plateau above the Italian town of Ortisei, also known by its Austrian name of St. Ulrich, in an area where German, Italian, and the local Ladin dialect are all spoken. Miniature rhododendrons and brilliant blue gentians speckle the landscape, along with hundreds of other species. The walking here is almost effortless, along gentle tracks, with the soaring form of Sassolungo looming over everything.

The Sassolungo hut is one of the most enchanting and old-fashioned haunts of climbers and walkers. By staying overnight high up in this or one of the many other mountain huts, you have the glorious reward of stepping out into a mountain wonderland the next morning and having it all pretty much to yourself. You might even spot edelweiss as you find the path threading from the top of the Seceda lift over the rocky landscape around the Alpe del Puez. After a long, steep haul to the Pisciadu hut, a path crosses the Sella (a snowfield even in summer), making this one of the most exhilarating hikes imaginable. **TL**

⬈ *Stay overnight in a small wooden hut high up in the Val Gardena for a quintessential Dolomites experience.*

See Dobbiaco/Toblach

Location South Tyrol, Italy
Website www.dobbiaco.info   **Price** ❶

With the rocky outcrops of the Dolomite Mountains on one side, the Alps on the other, and the bubbling Rienza mountain river refreshing the Alta Pusteria and Landro valleys, the beautiful village of Dobbiaco/Toblach enjoys, without doubt, a spectacular position. Situated in the South Tyrol region of Italy, close to the Austrian border, both Italian and German are spoken; hence the two names of the village.

The compact village has only 3,200 residents, and its green and white, onion-domed tower of the Parish Church of St. John the Baptist is a local landmark. In winter, Dobbiaco is a paradise for skiers, but throughout spring and summer the Alpine pastures remain alluring, and the crowds disappear. With its high altitude, the fresh smell of the larch forests that climb the lower slopes spreads through the clean mountain air every now and then, the surrounding countryside oozing tranquility. The quietness of the area is appealing, but it is not completely isolated because a handful of old farmhouses, mountain huts, and chapels are dotted about, and the scenery is so magnificent that you want to feel a part of it. Hiking trails abound through the forests and the Sesto Dolomite Nature Park, within which the village sits. Scenic trails can be followed around the crystal-clear waters of Lago di Dobbiaco, and the famous Tre Cime (Three Peaks) mountain range offers further walking possibilities, if only to gaze upward and admire.

Pick any hotel you like in the village; they all offer superb spa facilities and take advantage of their rejuvenating natural landscape. The Bohemian composer Gustav Mahler was a famous summer guest, composing his 9th and unfinished 10th symphonies between 1908 and 1910 in the village. **CFM**

Explore Prosecco

Location Veneto/Friuli-Venezia Giulia, Italy
Website www.prosecco.it   **Price** ❺

The Veneto region is Italy as you always imagine it: beautiful landscapes, elegant architecture, and delicious food and wine. It is in this sublime region, tucked beneath Venice and the foothills of the Alps, that prosecco is made and where, in 1966, the first Italian wine route was inaugurated.

Stretching for 29 miles (47 km), the Strada del Vino Prosecco meanders all the way between Conegliano and Valdobbiadene, the acknowledged joint capitals of this wine region. The route begins in the imposing Conegliano castle, then sets off along the ridges of the hills to San Pietro di Feletto. In a scenic position on the plains, encircled by mountains, you will find Molinetto

> *"... recognizable by its pale straw-yellow color, its moderate body, and its exclusively fruity aroma."*

Prosecco DOC of Conegliano-Valdobbiadene

della Croda, a sixteenth-century water mill planted in the rocks next to a large waterfall and described as "a pearl set in stone." It has, over the centuries, been fêted and painted by many a prosecco-fueled artist and poet.

The next stop is the Santa Maria Abbey of Follina. The industrious monks founded a wool-processing business here long before the bubbles of prosecco had started to fizz. The wine route continues through a landscape that features patrician villas, chestnut woods, and ridges of terraced grapevines. The main road looks out over the open vineyards below, before reaching its final destination, nestling in a valley at the foot of the Alps in Valdobbiadene. **SWi**

Stay at Bauer Palladio

Location Venice, Veneto, Italy **Website** www.bauerhotels.com
Price ⑤⑤

Arriving in Venice feels much like walking onto a movie set, so incredible are the vistas. While you are visiting the city, you might as well go the whole way and stay at the exclusive Bauer Palladio Hotel on the secluded island of Giudecca. This landmark of Venetian history is situated just yards from the world-famous Hotel Cipriani and is a must for those who like to brush shoulders with celebrities yet keep one foot firmly in the past. The hotel is just the other side of the Grand Canal but feels like a million miles away from the hordes of tourists at St. Mark's Square.

The building is a converted convent, originally designed in renaissance style by Andrea Palladio, and combines an imposing exterior with a somewhat austere interior. However, its cavernous sitting and dining rooms are beautifully decorated to give a surprising sense of intimacy. At the hotel, the thirty-seven rooms and thirteen suites are subtly designed with antiques, tapestries, and handcrafted touches, with either a garden or lagoon view. Great pains have been taken to keep many of the Renaissance features.

The hotel's spa offers postcardlike views of the Venice lagoon, and there you can enjoy a range of treatments. However, the highlight of any stay here has to be the private solar-powered shuttle that ferries guests from the hotel across to Bauer's sister hotel, Il Palazzo, just yards from all the Venice landmarks. Hot and tired from a day of shopping and exploring, simply walk down to the jetty, skip onto your private boat, and be whisked over the glittering lagoon to the tranquility of your hotel just five minutes away. **RS**

◄ *The elegant hotel has been carefully restored and is located on the waterfront, providing wonderful views.*

Visit Cinque Terre

Location Liguria, Italy
Website www.lecinqueterre.org/eng **Price** 🌓

"Each town is a unique destination carved rather amazingly into the steep terraced-vineyard coastline."

Ariel Foxman, *New York Times*

Cinque Terre (five lands) is a UNESCO World Heritage site made up of five small villages, linked by a picturesque walking trail. Each village can be reached by train or boat, but the only way to explore the rugged coastline is by foot.

The southernmost village, Riomaggiore, was established many centuries ago as the perfect location to plant olive trees and grapevines. The pretty stone houses are built vertically, like multilevel towers, to accommodate the steep terrain. Vertiginous staircases allow access between the homes and buildings. Here you will find the start of the famous Via dell'Amore, or Lover's Walk. This 0.6-mile (1-km) paved pathway links Riomaggiore with its closest neighbor, Manarola. Cut into the rock face, it takes just twenty minutes to walk and allows visitors spectacular views back over the village and out across the Mediterranean.

The route from Manarola to Corniglia takes around an hour. The middle of the five villages is surrounded on three sides by ancient stone terraces and lush green grapevines. Vernazza is a traditional fishing town with a natural harbor. It is accessible only by foot because the locals decided long ago not to build road access, in order to retain the character and quiet pace of life. The final leg of the Cinque Terre walk stretches to Monterosso and takes around ninety minutes. This is the steepest and most demanding part of the walk, but also one of the most beautiful. The hike will lead you through winding olive orchards and verdant vineyards, and will reward you with dramatic ocean views you will not want to leave. **JP**

◥ *The small town of Manarola is the second-smallest of the Cinque Terre, perched on rocks above the sea.*

Discover Emilia-Romagna

Location Emilia-Romagna, Italy
Website www.emiliaromagnaturismo.it **Price** $

Stay at Casa Argento

Location Tuscany, Italy
Website www.invitationtotuscany.com **Price** $$

From the spectacular scenery to the frantic bustle of the cities, there is no doubt that driving through Emilia-Romagna is an experience in itself. The Italians drive like they live: with passion and excitement. You either keep up—or get left behind.

Emilia-Romagna is renowned for its beautiful landscapes and outstanding food. It is the perfect location for a driving tour that takes in all the wonderful scenery and all the culinary delights. Fly in to Parma, nestled in the lush valley of the Po River. The city is famous for its cured ham, prosciutto di Parma. From there it is a laid-back drive to Reggio-Emilia, where you may sample another local gastronomic favorite: Parmigiano-Reggiano cheese. Drive east and you will hit Modena, the home of the eponymous balsamic vinegar. Production of this sweet-and-sour ingredient can be traced as far back as the eleventh century. While in Modena, there is no more fitting stop than Maranello—also known as the city of the Ferrari. The town has been home to the famous sports car since the early 1940s. Creator Enzo Ferrari moved to Maranello after bombs destroyed his original factory in Modena during World War II.

After admiring the finest in Italian automotive engineering, continue the drive through green countryside, along the foothills of the Apennine mountains to the capital of Bologna, known with good reason as the gastronomic capital of Italy. Sample the famous meat-based pasta sauce that the locals refer to as *ragù* but the rest of the world knows as Bolognese. The hills behind Bologna are dotted with rustic Italian villages and towns to explore. From here it is an easy journey to Ravenna, where you can marvel at the ornate Byzantine architecture. **JP**

The views from this stylish mountain retreat are so spectacular that you can see all the way to Corsica. Perched high in the Apuan Alps, above Camaiore and Pietrasanta, this is the place to come if you want to leave the stress of city life far behind.

The restored house was once part of the nearby medieval silver mines. Guests may rent the whole house, sleeping up to six, or just the upper section, for three people. Either way, absolute privacy is promised because no one else shares the property with you.

Head for the hills and spend your days following paths snaking around the mountains and surrounding valleys. Then come back to cool off with an outdoor

"If Tuscany had only Florence it would still be a region to love. But it lays claim to several more gems."

Sir Arnold Wesker, British playwright

shower in a cave carved out of the rock and soak in the open-air whirlpool tub. Placed on the terrace looking out across the Mediterranean, it is the perfect spot to unwind with a glass of wine in hand.

There is much to do in the surrounding area. In summer, spend the day at the beach, just twenty-five minutes away, or take a drive to find cozy restaurants with traditional menus in local villages. Combine a visit to the quarries, where the white marble came from for Michelangelo's *David,* with a trip to nearby Pietrasanta, a center for local sculptors who exhibit their work there throughout the year. There is also sightseeing aplenty in the cities of Lucca and Pisa. **AD**

Relax at Grotta Giusti

Location Tuscany, Italy
Website www.grottagiustispa.com   **Price** ⑤⑤

Grotta Giusti Spa's claim to fame is its natural grotto turned sauna. The amusingly named Hell, Purgatory, and Paradise "rooms" have 100 percent humidity and increases in temperature. However, the resort is not all about the bat cave. The nineteenth-century edifice is a graceful villa full of antiques and paintings with classic old-world charm. Plush velvets, grand lounges, but, most of all, marble features add an air of grandeur.

The real attraction is the natural thermal water, rich in bicarbonate, sulfate, chloride, magnesium, and calcium. It was discovered in 1849 and has had crowds flocking to it ever since. At an admirable 93°F (34°C), it is recommended for everything from muscular to

> *"Verdi called the Grotta the 'eighth wonder of the world' . . . That said, it's not for claustrophobics."*
>
> *The Times*

cardiovascular problems. What is more, the waters even gush out of the taps in the marble bathrooms. In the modern well-being center there is an Asian area, a gym, an open-air thermal pool with a waterfall and underwater hydro-massage, and even a medical aesthetic center offering both ancient and cutting-edge techniques. The treatment menu includes mud therapy, Swedish massage, and Namikoshi shiatsu massage, for example, and the aromas of dog rose, liquorice, sea tangle, and olives hang in the air. Grotta Giusti is a lot more than a thermal spa; it is now a fully fledged resort with pools, tennis courts, and a gourmet restaurant. Nothing like purgatory. **RCA**

Explore Boboli Gardens

Location Florence, Tuscany, Italy
Website www.firenzemusei.it   **Price** ⑤

Florence's—indeed Italy's—most famous garden may be listed in every guidebook, but climb the calf-crushing steps to leave the Pitti Palace behind and you can soon find yourself "lost" in areas of garden that barely see visitors. As a whole, the garden's 111 acres (45 ha) are a great place to escape the rigors of sightseeing in Florence; however, some areas are less frequented than others, so if you crave total peace (and respite from the Tuscan sun), avoid the amphitheater directly behind the Pitti Palace leading up toward Neptune's Fountain. Here the garden consists of symmetrical lines and patterns made from neatly clipped box hedges around formal pools with gruesome stone statues.

Elsewhere, particularly to the west of the palace (with the palace behind you and turning right), the secret, winding paths are your solace, and the hazel bushes, tall pines, and cypress trees your cover, protecting you from the heat of summer days—and the visitors thin out. The hedge-lined, soft-grass plots, small groves, and meadows are perfect for afternoon siestas and for wearing out young children safely, away from the busy city streets. There are good views of Florence from the eastern side of the garden, where a small café also serves refreshments.

Most visitors enter the gardens via the Pitti Palace at the Piazza dei Pitti, but there is a much quieter entrance/exit through the Forte di Belvedere that leads out onto a quiet, suburban street with open fields. Be warned however that the gardens are closed on the first and last Monday of each month. **CFM**

➔ *There are some quiet, shady spots in addition to the manicured gardens and formal pools by the palace.*

See Castello Vicchiomaggio

Location Tuscany, Italy
Website www.vicchiomaggio.it **Price** $ $

Leonardo da Vinci is said to have stayed here while painting the *Mona Lisa* and it is easy to see how the stunning setting of this *castello* would provide artistic inspiration. Overlooking regimental rows of cypress trees, olive groves, and fields of corn, the fifteenth-century Castello Vicchiomaggio, with its crenellated tower, stands guard over a Tuscan hillside. Its warm stone walls harbor small, sun-drenched courtyards, with giant terra-cotta pots adorning each corner. A private swimming pool is surrounded by gardens against the magnificent backdrop of the Tuscan hills.

The 286-acre (130-ha) estate, which produces both wine and olive oil, sits partway between Florence and Siena in the heart of Chianti country and within a five-minute drive of Greve in Chianti, a quintessential Tuscan town with small food stores from which to buy local produce to prepare back at the castle. Spacious suites and apartments accommodate guests with elegant and tasteful furnishings in rich reds and natural colors that highlight the beauty of the architectural features. All the rooms have magnificent views over either the vineyards or the surrounding countryside. In addition to modern bathrooms, apartments include small kitchens for self-catering, although the restaurant prepares delicious food gathered from the estate.

Sampling a bottle from the estate's vineyard is a must, too. The castle has made a name producing award-winning Chianti, and the owner, John Matta, has been awarded the title of "Italian Wine Maker of the Year" over three separate years. Guests receive a complimentary tour of the vineyard and cellar. Whether using it as a sightseeing base or remaining on-site, guests will find their stay utterly sublime. **CFM**

Stay at Villa San Michele

Location Tuscany, Italy
Website www.villasanmichele.com **Price** $ $

With a facade said to be designed by Michelangelo and interiors like precious works of art, Villa San Michele is a stunning base from which to explore the classical treasures of Florence. The former fifteenth-century Franciscan monastery is nestled in the woodlands of the Fiesole Hills, outside the traffic and noise of Florence, yet only a few minutes from the historic center of the city.

Apparently named after the church of St. Michael the Archangel, the villa's facade and imposing loggia date from 1600 when the building was enlarged and completely renovated by Giovanni di Bartolommeo Davanzati. It has been expertly refurbished in recent

---

"There is no nicer place on Earth to lounge with a book than the hotel's wisteria-shaded lemon grove."

Condé Nast Traveler

---

years into a luxurious villa set amid beautiful gardens. The rooms have spectacular views of the glorious sweeping vista spreading right across Florence and into the Chianti countryside. The chapel, a small seventeenth-century *cappellina* that was used by the monks for prayer and meditation, is now a lavish honeymoon suite.

A complimentary shuttle service takes guests into the city center where they can visit the Uffizi, Duomo, Ponte Vecchio, and other famous Florentine sites. Then it is back to Villa San Michele for rest and relaxation. Sleep comes easily in these hallowed walls; this once was a monastery, after all. **AD**

Experience Montelucci

Location Tuscany, Italy
Website www.montelucci.it **Price** $

In the heart of Tuscany, far from the madding crowds, a rustic yet chic farming estate has turned into one of agritourism's best success stories. With farmhouses offering a taste of rural life, literally, it is a chance to sample the local fare direct from the source. Rest assured, though, this is nothing like an industrial farm.

Montelucci chose to aim for a luxurious yet simple approach, focusing on all things homemade, homegrown, and organic in comfort. Its raison d'être is to give visitors an insight into local activities and produce, from fruit and vegetables to the naturally raised livestock. Its pride and joy are the Chianina cows with their white coats and long horns. One of the oldest breeds of cattle in existence, they are renowned for their excellent meat.

Fruity and fresh olive oil is made on-site from a blend of four types of olives, whereas the Chianti wine comes from the vineyard's Sangiovese grapes. In addition to sampling the food, there is horseback riding, walking, hunting, mountain biking, and cooking classes. It is also a great base from which to explore Tuscan towns like Florence and even spend a little time at The Mall, the Italian designer outlet for Prada, Gucci, and Armani.

Surrounded by nature, Montelucci exudes effortless charm with its inviting pool and views over the rolling hills of the Valdarno. Whether it is in the organic restaurant or in the simple yet stylish bedrooms, the decor is unique and traditional, but surprisingly elegant. Neutral color schemes, wrought-iron beds, and wide-striped chocolate sofas blend well with potted cacti and the stylish, modern bathrooms. Staying at Montelucci is like savoring a delectable slice of Tuscany with the rarest ingredients. **RCA**

Enjoy The Hill That Breathes

Location Tuscany, Italy
Website www.thehillthatbreathes.com **Price** $$

Set up by Englishman John Parkin, author of the irreverent and witty guide to spirituality, *Fuck It*, The Hill That Breathes runs personal development courses with a down-to-earth approach that will not scare you off if you have never been personally developed before. It is set on a horseshoe-shaped hill, surrounded by mature woods with running water on three sides.

Although the summer months are hot and dry, there is a near-constant breeze around the hill, so that The Hill That Breathes really does appear to breathe. Courses include various styles of yoga, qigong, and shamanism, as well as the popular "Fuck It" weeks that inspired John's book. Do not be put off by the name—

> *"John's approach to tai chi was identical to his approach to yoga . . . it was free yoga."*
>
> Emily Hynes, *Yoga Magazine*

the "Fuck It" philosophy is about fun and friendship, not nihilism and delinquency, and includes trips to the nearby hilltop town of Urbino and plenty of cake as well as deep soul searching.

You will sleep in a tastefully renovated, traditional Italian farmhouse made of local sandstone, usually in shared rooms. Classes take place in a huge tepee on top of the hill and on a wooden platform jutting out over the valley—during the day you will be serenaded by the whir of cicadas. There is a saltwater pool and 100 acres (40 ha) of fragrant pinewoods to lose yourself in—massages and other treatments are carried out in smaller tepees hidden in the woods. **CSJ**

Stay at Castello di Magona

Location Tuscany, Italy
Website www.castellodimagona.it   **Price** 💲💲

There are few better ways to enjoy the considerable pleasures of Livorno than in your own sixteenth-century castle. Looking out over the Maremma coastline, just opposite the island of Elba, stands the Castello di Magona, an enormous mansion within landscaped gardens. It has been the former home of many grand Tuscan dukes, but it was Leopold II who really stamped his noble credentials on the place.

Within this beautifully restored Renaissance residence, you can breathe in 500 years of history while reveling in the lap of luxury. Inside are vaulted dining rooms with terra-cotta floors topped by beautiful, intricate Asian rugs. There are ornately

> *"[Leopold II was] one of the most advanced advocates of material progress, liberty, and toleration."*
>
> **Obituary of Grand Duke Leopold II, *New York Times***

carved, wooden-ceilinged galleries full of enveloping sofas, bursting bookshelves, and the occasional display of ancient broadswords. Bedrooms are painted in delicate colors and have views over the cypress and olive trees that dot the Tuscan hills. The furniture is more than a match for the rooms: huge wooden wardrobes, specially made canopied beds, and vast gilt-framed paintings of armor-clad ancestors.

Your surroundings will transport you to the indulgent world of sixteenth-century nobility, so much so that you will half expect to round a corner and find Duke Leopold himself lounging on a sofa with his bustling staff in rapt attendance. **SWi**

Discover Elba

Location Tuscany, Italy
Website www.elbatuttanatura.com   **Price** ❶

According to ancient mythology, the goddess Venus emerged from the waters of the Tyrrhenian Sea and, as she did so, her necklace snapped, scattering seven pearls that reemerged as the seven islands of the Tuscan Archipelago. Thus, Elba, the largest of these, was born, and the island retains some of this mythical appeal to this day.

Elba is known for its sparkling waters—some of the clearest in Europe—and the beaches of fine, white sand bordered by pine and ilex woods. Its ancient, chestnut-scented woodlands hold an enduring allure to travelers. The fact that this special island is part of Europe's largest marine park is an added attraction. Red coral provides a visual underwater feast for adventurous divers, whereas wild orchids, cornflowers, and violets reward walkers as they ascend Monte Capanne, the highest peak on the island.

Elegant buildings in shades of ocher line the streets of the old harbor in Portoferraio, the island's capital. Leave the bustling ports behind and head inland to explore ancient villages, follow age-old shepherds' paths as they meander over scented hillsides and shady forests, or find serenity in a quiet cove.

Fetovaia, in the southwest, is particularly appealing with its alabaster sand and granite rocks. Climb the steep passageways between the narrow streets of ancient Marciana and immerse yourself in the sense of history that abounds here. Napoleon, exiled to Elba in 1814, must surely have savored the beauty of his gilded prison and watched the crimson sunsets over Corsica, island of his birth. **KF**

➡ *The town of Poggio on Elba is surrounded by rich forests and its streets are typically paved with granite.*

Stay at Castello di Vicarello

Location Tuscany, Italy   **Website** www.vicarello.it
Price ⓢⓢ

A secluded estate in the Grosseto area surrounded by the rolling Tuscan greenery of olive groves and vineyards, Castello di Vicarello sits perched on top of a hill like a fairy-tale castle. The exquisite eleventh-century *castello* blends historic atmosphere with modern luxury to create an intimate rustic hideaway. There are four suites and one villa to choose from, filled with antiques and elegant furniture in a seamless blend of Italian and Asian styles.

Two infinity pools set among olive trees, a cobbled courtyard, and lush grounds with plenty of shady corners in which to curl up with a book or eat an intimate lunch tick all the boxes when it comes to romantic surroundings. There are terraces to relax on, honey-colored gravel paths to wander, and comfortable rattan chairs to ease into and enjoy a drink in as the sun goes down. A small spa offers soothing treatments and yoga sessions. Suites looking out over the panoramic views have low-beamed ceilings, large windows, and thick stone walls.

Traditional Tuscan and Mediterranean cuisine, using homegrown ingredients, is the highlight of the kitchen. Think pan-fried pigeon with bacon, sage, and white grapes, washed down with a glass of Castello di Vicarello, a blend of cabernet sauvignon and cabernet franc from the estate's own vineyard.

It takes no time at all to adapt to the deliciously slow rhythm of life and be seduced by the evocative scenery. Take a walk around the gardens, among roses, trailing jasmine, lavender, and mulberry trees. On clear days, the fresh salty sea breeze blows inland and the shimmering water can be seen in the distance. Siena is an hour's drive away, or you can explore Uccellina National Park and the springs at Saturnia. **AD**

Unwind at L'Andana Hotel

Location Tuscany, Italy   **Website** www.andana.it
Price ⓢⓢ

L'Andana was once the hunting lodge of the Grand Duke of Tuscany, Leopold II. It is situated in a secluded spot, nestled amid centuries-old olive groves and vineyards in the Maremma, with nothing to disturb the tranquility except the background hum of cicadas and the cooing of doves.

The property has since been converted into a luxury hotel by world-famous restaurateur Alain Ducasse in partnership with spa innovators Espa to cook up L'Andana, a thirty-three-room gastronomic retreat and spa. The rooms are elegant and stylish, with beautiful silk curtains, Italian fabrics, Tuscan antiques, and sumptuous, richly colored bedspreads. However, it is

> *"L'Andana is a reflection of the Maremma . . . unique, authentic, generous."*
>
> **Alain Ducasse, cofounder**

the bathrooms that really impress; they are wall-to-wall marble, some with vast bathtubs that are big enough for an entire football team.

For the ultimate in pampering, be sure to try the deeply relaxing holistic back, face, and scalp massage with hot stones. Surrender to the skilled ministrations of the therapist and drift off into a heavenly half slumber. Afterward, take a dip in the vitality pool, or be tempted by a range of mouthwatering snacks from the gourmet spa menu. To work off all that overindulgence, take a stroll around the lovely gardens. There is also a three-hole golf course and a tennis court if you are feeling energetic. **HA**

Experience Ripa d'Orcia

Location Tuscany, Italy   **Website** www.castelloripadorcia.com
Price ⑤

The walls, battlements, and towers of Ripa d'Orcia Castle still stand on an isolated hilltop in Tuscany, as they have done for centuries. You reach the castle by traveling along a gravel track winding up through the woods along the Orcia Valley. At the hilltop, enter the fortifications through a gatehouse. There is no drawbridge these days, but you still feel like you are intruding into the medieval world. Inside is a hamlet and church, plus a maze of stone stairways, paths, gardens, outbuildings, and turrets. It feels like a museum village—still with its bakery, carpentry workshop, blacksmith's forge, olive mill, and granaries.

The castle has long been the home of an aristocratic Sienese family who painstakingly maintain it. They still live in the main castle but have opened hotel rooms and vacation apartments in many of the other houses inside the ramparts. Inside, you will find nothing has been spoiled. Rooms are simple and rustic, with wooden Tuscan furniture, exposed beams, terra-cotta tiled floors, and heavy window shutters. Some have open fireplaces and private terraces, and all offer terrific views. Rooms have no televisions or telephones but there are modern bathrooms. The only concession to modernity is that on a terrace with panoramic views they have built a fabulous open-air swimming pool.

The communal dining room serves hearty dishes using fresh produce from the castle gardens, and guests can use a reading room in an old converted granary that has a big open fireplace. The castle still has an 800-acre (324-ha) estate and makes olive oil and vinegar as well as red, white, and sweet wine. The ancient wine cellar has been converted into a beautiful tasting room for the estate's wines and extra-virgin olive oil that can be bought on-site. **SH**

Relax at Terme di Saturnia

Location Tuscany, Italy   **Website** www.termedisaturnia.it
Price ⑤

Natural springwaters have been flowing into a volcanic crater in front of what is now the Terme di Saturnia Spa and Golf Resort for more than 3,000 years. The chic, minimalist hotel set at the foot of the ancient village of Saturnia in the Maremma region has one of the most famous spas in the world, renowned for its medical care as much as for its conventional beauty treatments, which take place in any one of fifty treatment rooms.

The water follows a subterranean route that filters slowly through micro-fissures in the rock, absorbing salts and minerals on a journey that takes more than forty years to reach the hotel's thermal pool, which

> *"The pool is a crater of an extinct volcano filled with rainwater filtered through the ground."*
>
> Denis Campbell, *Observer*

bubbles night and day. There are 140 rooms, one indoor and six outdoor pools, two restaurants, a fitness center, tennis courts, and a replica of a traditional Roman bathhouse, as well as a championship eighteen-hole golf course.

The Tuscan landscape, with its ocher-brown hills and lush vineyards, hilltop villages, and medieval castles, has been seducing visitors for centuries; in the Maremma, cowboys still ranch cattle the old-fashioned way and Etruscan ruins dot the landscape. The nearby medieval town of Montemerano and the magical town of Pitigliano are well worth dragging yourself away from the hotel for a day. **TW**

Stay at Borgo Santo Pietro

Location Tuscany, Italy
Website www.borgosantopietro.com **Price** 💲

Around 700 years ago, Borgo Santo Pietro was a resting place for pilgrims from all over Europe on their way to Rome. The tiny settlement dates back to the thirteenth century and stands on a rise among cherry orchards and ornamental gardens. The pretty village of Palazzetto is a five-minute stroll down the old Pilgrim's Way. Siena and the Tuscan coast are both half an hour away.

The old villa and its outbuildings have only recently been lavishly converted into a boutique hideaway. The Borgo has become all you would expect from a luxury Italian escape, with state-of-the-art spa treatments in the old bakery, fresh-off-the-vine food from the

---

> *"Cortona was the first town we ever stayed in and we always came back to it."*

Frances Mayes, *Under the Tuscan Sun*

---

organic garden, and a chemical-free, freshwater infinity pool surrounded by immaculate flower gardens. Yet it is intimate, too, with only eight bedrooms. They are packed with period style; you will find details like ornate plasterwork, gilt-framed mirrors, tapestries, beamed ceilings, freestanding bathtubs, and open fires. The enormous beds have special handmade mattresses from Denmark.

Guests can eat in the villa's ornate candlelit dining room, outside by the colonnaded terrace, or in the garden beside the pool. Expect menus of the finest Italian dishes, using produce from the hotel's garden or local farms wherever possible. **SH**

Explore Monte Amiata

Location Tuscany, Italy
Website www.sienaonline.com **Price** 💲

In the distance the peak rises majestically, dominating the Tuscan skyline. Monte Amiata is the second-highest volcano in Italy, after Mount Etna. Reaching 5,680 feet (1,731 m) high, it is the northernmost peak of the Tuscan anti-Apennines, a string of volcanoes dotted along southern Tuscany.

Although it last erupted 180,000 years ago, the superheated core still fuels the hot-water springs found at its base. For centuries, Italians and other visitors have flocked to these hot-water springs. The mineral-rich waters are considered to have relaxing, healing properties. There are many health centers in the vicinity, most offering year-round bathing in the heated waters. Some have built spa complexes around the springs; others are untouched pools, carved by nature into the surrounding landscape.

However, soaking in the geothermal hot springs is just one of the many ways to enjoy Monte Amiata. Marked walking paths crisscross the dormant volcano, making it a popular destination for hikers. The upper slopes are covered with thick forests of beech, fir, and chestnut trees, whereas lower down you will find olive trees and strangely shaped volcanic boulders. From December to March these trails are blanketed with fresh snow. Skiers can opt to go cross-country through the forests or to visit one of the mountain's ski fields.

There are hundreds of different walks that take in the fascinating and diverse sights of the mountain, from freshwater springs to the tiny villages and towns that coexist on the slopes of the volcano. One of the most famous is the town of Abbadia San Salvatore. Built around one of Tuscany's oldest Benedictine monasteries, the town is a perfectly preserved example of eleventh-century architecture. **JP**

Discover the Maremma

Location Tuscany/Lazio, Italy
Website www.lamaremmafabene.it **Price** ◑

If you think Tuscany has become too tame and touristy, think again. The Maremma, a spectacular area of coast, forest, and mountain that straddles southwest Tuscany and northern Lazio, still clings to its wild side. It is famous, in particular, for its 100 miles (160 km) of rocky coastline scattered with fishing villages and pretty bays that are perfect for swimming.

Those who like their wilderness amply peppered with eateries should head to the Gulf of Follonica, whose beaches at Cala Martina, Cala Violina, and Castiglione della Pescaia always provide plenty of opportunities for feasting between sunbathing stints. Try the local pecorino cheese, washed down with a glass or two of Morellino di Scansano. Alternatively, the islands of Giglio and Giannutri feature cliffs that plummet into the jade Mediterranean Sea, or visit the promontory of Monte Argentario, which is known for its scuba diving.

The pine forests that border the beaches are spotted with lagoons teeming with waterfowl and other birdlife; this whole area was marshland until Mussolini had it drained. Bird-watchers should head to L'Oasi della Laguna, a bird sanctuary open to visitors from September to April, or to Lago di Burano, which is the most important birding site in Italy: More than half the species that live or migrate in the country can be seen here.

If you visit during one of the festivals, keep your eyes peeled for the *butteri*, or cowboys, who saddle up for special events and ensure that, still today, the Maremma delights in its wild side. **PE**

↗ *Its marshes drained less than a century ago, the Maremma remains relatively undiscovered.*

"Landscapes are the equal of anything in Tuscany, especially the Argentario."

Tim Jepson, *Daily Telegraph*

Explore Perugia

Location Umbria, Italy   **Website** www.comune.perugia.it; http://tourism.comune.perugia.it   **Price** ❶

Perugia is a fascinating fortress town of massive stone walls and red-tiled roofs, ancient gates and archways, sun-drenched, classical frescoes, and panoramic views. It is the quintessential Italy portrayed in early renaissance art. If you look out from the Duomo at the city's highest point, you'll see the endless lines of hills, with their willowy cypresses and steep terraces of olives and vine, stretch away into the distance. But with so much of interest within the ancient ramparts, it's the perfect place to engage in that most Italian of pastimes—the *passeggiata*, or "stroll"—and take in all the cultural delights while you're at it.

The many styles of Perugia's architecture offer a portal into its remarkable past. The massive Etruscan city walls and Arch d'Agusto were built in the 4th century B.C.E. (a reminder of the existing civilizations that the Roman bully-boys hijacked) while the more recently built medieval Priors' Palace, with its delicate patterning of white and pink stone, houses the National Gallery of Umbria. Next to it, in the Cathedral square, extraordinary 13th century sculptures decorate the Fontana Maggiore, and the sound of modern life chimes in with the tolls of the bells in the background.

To get a taste of Perugia's more bloody past go down into the bowels of time. An escalator will take you to the Rocca Paolina—once the headquarters of the Baglioni family. This bloodthirsty clan once dominated the city until the equally unpleasant Pope Paul III murdered the lot and buried their remains under the rock of their fortress—along with their palaces, seven churches, and 138 houses. **SWi**

➔ *The medieval Fontana Maggiore, sculpted by Nicola and Giovanni Pisano, was designed by Fra Bevignate.*

Relax at Todi Castle

Location Umbria, Italy   **Website** www.todicastle.com
Price 💲💲💲

This imposing family-owned medieval fortress stands amid the rolling green hills of Umbria in central Italy and offers you the chance to escape to your own Italian castle. Although Todi Castle may be a perfect mix of relaxed self-catering and luxury service now, this was once the real thing: a fortified stronghold with a long history of conflict. In the Middle Ages, vats of boiling oil were thrown from the battlements, and the remains of many dead soldiers have been found around the site. The high stone walls, tower, arrow slits, and secret underground escape passages remain, as does a sense of history in everything you touch.

Your rental includes having breakfast prepared, rooms cleaned, and quality linen and towels provided. After that, the castle owners provide as little or as much service as you want—you can use the well-equipped kitchen yourself, or have lunches and dinners prepared for you.

There are four bedrooms in the main castle, plus a separate wing that sleeps three more, and three other villas on the estate that are available to rent. Outside is a garden with a swimming pool, terraces with panoramic views, and sloping green lawns leading to olive groves, vineyards, and a fenced deer park, all bordered by rows of cypresses. Apart from that, there is plenty to do in this remote spot. The owners provide private tours, mountain bikes, treks, visiting massage, personal trainers, food tasting, and cooking demonstrations—including a course in making your own pasta. They will even take you on a tour of the local wine cellars, farms, and olive oil mills. **SH**

⬅ *The west view of Todi Castle in Umbria, with its sloping green lawns and orchards.*

Visit Italy's "Other" Lakes

Location Lazio, Italy   **Website** www.lagodibolsena.org/en
Price 💲

Forget Garda, Como, Lugano, and Maggiore and try this trio of volcanic lakes in Lazio, north of Rome. Lake Bracciano might be better known for its lakeside castle, the setting for Tom Cruise and Katie Holmes's wedding in 2006, than for its lake, but that is definitely a good thing. Undiscovered by mass tourism, the lake provides respite from Rome's hot summers, with plenty of water sports, including sailing and waterskiing, all surrounded by forests, olive groves, and gardens. The castle itself can be visited, and you can discover the legends of loves lost, death, secret passageways, and medieval mischief, as well as walk around its candlelit ramparts.

"There is no heavy industry in this area, which means the waters are mercifully clear of pollution."

Stephen Pritchard, *Observer*

Lake Bolsena is the largest volcanic lake in Italy, a circular 71-mile (115-km) lake with two small islands in the center. Surrounded by low, vine-covered hills, it has some great swimming beaches and is one of Europe's cleanest lakes. On the uninhabited side of the lake, there are small secluded beaches, and the lake is popular with sailors and snorkelers, too.

Lake Vico is the smallest lake, still stretching to over 7 miles (11 sq km), and is a volcanic crater surrounded by nature reserves and overlooked by Mount Venere; according to legend, it owes its origins to Hercules. He defied local orders to pick up his club and, when he did so, a river appeared and created the lake. **LD**

Stay at Sunflower Retreats

Location Lazio, Italy
Website www.sunflowerretreats.com   **Price** 💲💲

When Rome fell, Casperia was born—a fortified hilltop haven that protected the natives from any invading barbarians. Just forty-five minutes from Rome, the sun-baked medieval village now provides an atmospheric setting for Sunflower Retreats yoga vacations. From the mysterious Forani Palace within the village itself to the nearby caves where St. Francis of Assisi lived and taught, there is a spiritual dimension that lends itself perfectly to the more contemporary pursuit of well-being.

Yoga is central to the Sunflower Retreats experience. In a converted barn there is a studio with a freshwater spring bubbling away beneath the floor. Daily classes

> *"Enjoy an authentic Italian village lifestyle and benefit from a truly holistic and spiritual experience."*
>
> The Italian Magazine

as well as massage, Reiki, and beauty treatments help to banish any work-related weariness. You can also while away the hours with a little wine tasting or Italian cooking classes. The inviting lounge café is shared by guests and locals and has organic breakfast buffets, snacks, drinks, and evening entertainment.

With olive groves, shady woodland, and mountains to explore, as well as neighboring villages, this is a place to be active, even if the pace stays slow. Sunflower Retreats creates a companionable group vacation for single travelers, but it works just as well for friends and couples with a fondness for yoga and passing time in the idyllic countryside. **OM**

Enjoy La Posta Vecchia

Location Rome, Lazio, Italy
Website www.relaischateaux.com/posta   **Price** 💲💲💲

It is a setting reminiscent of a painting by the French seventeenth-century master Claude Lorraine. La Posta Vecchia sits next to a gothic castle, the foundations of which appear to go down into the water itself. Despite the feeling of being transported back in time, it is only a short taxi journey from the center of Rome, and at night you can see the twinkling lights of the Lido di Faro, close to the city's main airport.

La Posta Vecchia was originally a guesthouse for Prince Odescalchi, who owned the castle next door; then it was a posthouse (hence the name) before being left derelict for a century. The American millionaire John Paul Getty bought it in 1965 and called in archaeologists who discovered the house was built on the site of a Roman villa. The finds they made are housed in the basement of the hotel.

The place is still filled with some of Getty's collection of antiques: A magnificent tripod table and Marie de Medici's dowry chest are just two such objects. Some of the treasures are in the bedrooms, including a seventeenth-century bed that formerly belonged to the Prince Colonna in one of the suites.

La Posta Vecchia opened as a hotel in the early 1990s, and a dining room and a swimming pool now fill the previously open arcades at either end of the building. Most of the wine is of the standard luxury Brunello and Barolo types, but there are local wines, including some top Frascatis that make you want to revise your opinion of this oft-derided grape. In the summer, you dine on the terrace, just above the lapping waves of the Mediterranean. **GMD**

↪ *The front of luxury retreat La Posta Vecchia, formerly the guesthouse of Prince Odescalchi.*

Visit the Sabine Hills

Location Lazio, Italy **Website** www.sabina.it/index-i.html
Price ◑

Less than an hour from Rome, the Sabina landscape is a mass of rolling hills dotted with medieval villages draped on their peaks. One such tiny village is Roccantica, with its maze of cobbled streets overlooked by a medieval fortress. Every August, Roccantica hosts a four-day festival that includes falconry displays, flamethrowers, and banquets of wild boar, culminating in a colorful medieval pageant for the Procession of the Assunta. If ambling around this charming village is not energetic enough, take a full-day trek to Monte Pizzuto, which at nearly 4,265 feet (1,300 m) is the region's highest peak. Its summit rewards you with spectacular views of Monte Terminillo covered in winter snow, the Tiber River cutting through the valleys below, and—on a clear day—the Tyrrhenian Sea beyond Rome.

However, you do not need to go this high for magical views and peaceful, unspoiled hikes. Casperia, another hilltop village of honey-colored stone, towers, and turrets, is the starting point for several more gentle walks along old mule tracks and wooded trails, through forests of green oak alongside silvery olive groves and vineyards. If you prefer ambling around ancient historic buildings, be sure to stop at the abbey in Farfa or the Church of Santa Maria in Vescovio, a former cathedral whose beauty lies in its simplicity, much like Sabina itself.

Finally, before heading back to the city, treat yourself to a glass of wine in the piazzas of Poggio Mirteto or Casperia and sample the delicious local extra-virgin olive oil, another of Sabina's great secrets. **SWa**

➡ *The village of Toffia (population 850) rests on top of the Sabine hills to the north of Rome.*

Enjoy Villa Dragonetti

Location Abruzzo, Italy **Website** www.villadragonetti.it
Price 😊😊

The Hotel Villa Dragonetti is a masterpiece of Italian art. Originally built as a summer residence for the Dragonetti de Torres family, this sixteenth-century property has been carefully restored to its glorious former status. Hidden away in the small, largely undeveloped village of Paganica at the foot of Abruzzo's soaring Gran Sasso mountain range, the villa is immediately striking from the outside, with its spacious, verdant grounds, garden maze, and pool.

The architecture of the villa dates back to the sixteenth century, but the interior was redecorated in the eighteenth century by specially commissioned French artists; their dramatic frescoes of flora and fauna cover the interior of Villa Dragonetti from top to bottom, lending the place an ornate and sophisticated time-warp feel. There are just four double rooms and three junior suites available. The limited occupancy creates an authentically intimate atmosphere. Rooms are reasonably spacious, decorated with frescoes or wall paintings, and also come furnished with authentic period antiques like big dressing tables, armoires, and heavy curtains. The bathrooms are equally flamboyant and distinctive, and there are three more rooms in the guesthouse in addition to a small patio.

Villa Dragonetti's restaurant is very well known in the local area, chiefly for the regional dishes that are its specialty, although guests will also appreciate the delicious homemade breakfasts that greet them every morning. The gardens are lush enough to be used for weddings, and there is an outdoor swimming pool where guests can enjoy an aperitif before their evening meal or a dip before lunch. Dragonetti makes a beautifully refined base for skiers, hikers, or just admirers of cultured accommodation. **PS**

Stay at Sextantio

Location Abruzzo, Italy **Website** www.sextantio.it
Price 😊😊

Sextantio Albergo Diffuso, set in a timeless medieval Italian town known as Santo Stefano Di Sessanio, is not so much a hotel as an ambitious cultural project. Just a few years ago, this tiny hamlet was all but a ghost town. Daniele Kihlgren, a Milanese entrepreneur, fell in love with the place while passing by on his motorcycle and decided to launch a rejuvenation project. His aim was to boost tourism in the area while preserving the centuries-old culture and folklore.

Kihlgren and a carefully selected team of specialist archaeologists and researchers have crafted a hotel that is as close to the Middle Ages as possible. This means the rooms, hewed naturally from rock and

---

> *"With its architectural beauty and hilltop setting, Santo Stefano gives a real sense of going back in time."*
>
> Marc Zakian, *Town & Country* magazine

---

stone, are cavelike and come with immense, wooden doors (with long iron keys) and natural fireplaces. The bed linens are woven by hand in a local workshop, and food is cultivated locally, too. Touches like designer bathrooms, heated floors, and remote-controlled lighting have also been added to ensure comfort.

The hotel has functioning medieval-style workshops, a Middle Ages–style restaurant, and exhibition spaces. Outside the Sextantio complex, life goes on in the village much as it has done for all those centuries. **PS**

🔁 *Sextantio has been sensitively restored to resemble how it would have looked not 50, but 500 years ago.*

Walk in Majella National Park

Location Abruzzo, Italy
Website www.parcomajella.it/LgENG/home.asp; www.uplandescapes.com   **Price** ◑

Deep in the heart of Abruzzo, far from the crowded coast, sprawls the Majella, Italy's little known haven of mountains, meadows and medieval hermitages.

The National Park encircles the massif of Monte Amaro, the second highest peak in the entire Appenine range. The sheer height of the Majella's own mountain offers a huge variety of terrains to walk in. The lower landscapes of alpine meadows and forests gradually give way to the higher reaches of desert-like landscape and pockets of year-round snow.

Decontra is the ideal village base. At 2,650 feet (810 m), this little mountain hamlet has stunning south-facing views over the gorge's wild upland pastures. Many routes set out from here and you can choose whether to embark on a challenging full day summit bid or stay among the wildflowers.

You could spend half a day trekking to San Bartolomeo. Following a broad gravel track past meadows and cultivated fields you'll cross the plateau of the Valle Giumentina to this medieval sanctuary. Gravel tracks wind past grazing sheep and grassy paths pass curious conical stone dwellings no longer inhabited by the shepherds that built them. It's said that years ago, whenever a lost Christian missionary happened to get in the mountains, they would hide themselves in a cave and form a new faction.

You'll find more of these ancient rock hermitages if you delve into the deep magical world of the Orfento Gorge. Along the gorge bottom snakes the Orfento River with shady banks of lush greenery and secluded footpaths skirting the crystal waters. **SWi**

> *"It was clear and cold and dry and the snow was dry and powdery and hare-tracks in the snow."*

Ernest Hemingway, American writer, on Abruzzo

◰ *Even when viewed from ground level, the mountains of the Majella retain a sense of romance and mystery.*

Enjoy Santo Spirito

Location Abruzzo, Italy
Website www.monasterosantospirito.it   **Price** ⓢ

Monastero Santo Spirito, built in 1222, was one of the first Cistercian settlements in Abruzzo—a tranquil, historic region of southern Italy primarily made up of wonderful landscapes, medieval villages, and national parks. Several years ago it was transformed into a highly atmospheric guesthouse whose distinctive rectangular shape, characterized by high stone walls and a tall bell tower, rises majestically from the undulating landscape.

As soon as you pass through the old iron gates, stillness descends and you automatically find your voice dropping to a whisper. The monastery has been impeccably restored—so much so that it succeeds in

> *"Hidden by tangled and untamed woodlands, wolves, deer, and martens move stealthily around."*
>
> Monastero Santo Spirito website

retaining the mood and essence for which it was originally conceived. Once inside you will find a large, square courtyard—originally a cloister—around which are arranged a church that boasts frescoes dating back to 1280, a refectory, a dormitory, and twelve unadorned guest rooms. The rooms, formerly monks' quarters, are simply furnished but far from monastic. All have views onto the central courtyard and modern wooden furnishings.

The monastery even squeezes in a small gym and sauna, a reading room, and a lovely patio where you can gaze out at the timeless countryside. This is a place to relax and meditate, reflect and philosophize. **PS**

Unwind at La Reserve

Location Abruzzo, Italy
Website www.lareserve.it   **Price** ⓢ

La Reserve is a dedicated luxury spa that offers accommodation, not a hotel with a spa added on as an afterthought. Having said that, it is still a lovely place to stay. The striking modernist concrete-and-glass block rises out from the evergreen wooded hillside like a friendly fortress. There are great views of the surrounding Majella National Park from all sides.

Inside this imposing modern hotel architecture, there is a quiet atmosphere of well-being that cannot help but rub off on guests. This calming influence starts in the lobby where white walls, designer seating, and polished wood floors create an easy ambience. Floor-to-ceiling black-and-white photographs and contemporary sculptures are dotted around the spa, and a giant round skylight floods the building with natural sunlight. Bedrooms are bright and airy with whitewashed walls and simple color schemes.

The spa was built here because of the springs of warm sulfurous water in the surrounding Apennines, and it is this water that is at the heart of the spa. Perhaps the highlight is the large outside thermal water swimming pool that glows blue at night when illuminated and is surrounded by sunny terraces with engaging panoramas by day. The oval indoor spa pool is a stunning environment, too, surrounded by wood decking and pillars.

There is a vast choice of treatments and a team of professional therapists on-site. Water treatments are the specialty, and guests are even encouraged to drink the water for its detoxifying properties. Guests can also sample cutting-edge treatments like breathing regenerations, massages, thermal cures, and dietetics. There is even the chance to be covered with a thick layer of the local therapeutic thermal mud. **SH**

Relax at Regina Isabella

Location Campania, Italy   **Website** www.reginaisabella.it
Price ⑤⑤

Regina Isabella, on the island of Ischia in the Bay of Naples, is right on the water's edge, framed by rocky outcrops and tumbling greenery. A stone breakwater keeps the sea tranquil and provides extra sunbathing space; to the side is a secluded private sandy beach with the pretty village and mountain beyond. Behind the hotel is a little square with a church, museum, and antiques market.

It is easy to see why a wealthy Italian film producer established the hotel on this spot back in the 1950s—and why Regina Isabella soon became a retreat for the international jet set. Inside you can still imagine old regulars like Richard Burton or Charlie Chaplin pacing the beautiful tiled floors and lounging in specially made Neapolitan furniture. The walls are decorated with tapestries, mosaics, and modern art—and you catch spectacular glimpses of the sea through every window.

Bedrooms exhibit traditional Italian design flair, and suites have private terraces and pools. You can recline on period wicker furniture on the veranda or dine in one of the restaurants, where fresh seafood is the specialty and stunning views are the distraction.

The hotel was built above mineral-rich thermal springs that have attracted bathers since classical times. Today there is a luxurious two-story spa that offers therapeutic treatments using local volcanic healing mud. One of the hardest decisions will be which pool to use: There are four. Perhaps the best is full of purified seawater and overhangs the sea at the front of the hotel with a spectacular view. **SH**

➔ *This is one of Regina Isabella's four swimming pools, which overlooks the Bay of Naples.*

Unwind at Micalò

Location Naples, Campania, Italy **Website** www.micalo.it
Price ⊖⊖⊖⊖

So blessed with natural wonders is the Bay of Naples that the crazy and fascinating baroque city itself is often overlooked by visitors. Micalò is an inspiring and relaxing haven in the city's upmarket Chiaia district. Outside on the Riviera di Chiaia, where Spanish viceroys and local aristocrats built handsome residences, the street life is colorful and noisy.

It may be a crumbling seventeenth-century palazzo on the outside, but once enclosed within Micalò's dreamy interiors a wonderful atmosphere is just the tonic after a Neapolitan adventure. Curvy white walls blend with creamy marble floors, giving the place an ethereal quality. Alluring artworks by emerging

---

"The high-ceilinged rooms are minimal, crisply designed, richly furnished, fully connected."

Sunday Herald newspaper

Neapolitan artists add splashes of color, whereas dwarf plants and beautifully sculptural volcanic rocks sprout here and there. Many of the nine guest rooms are cavernous, with tall walls punctuated with art and Zen-inspired mezzanine bathrooms that tower over enormous beds.

From the stylish Art Bar hewn from Italian marble—where a fine breakfast, refreshments, and Neapolitan food are served—there are glimpses of the Villa Comunale gardens and the sea. Chiaia has lots of chic shops, galleries, and fabulous restaurants, and the Mergellina jetty is the best place to hop on a hydrofoil for the bay's islands and coastline resorts. **NB**

Stay at La Minervetta

Location Campania, Italy **Website** www.laminervetta.com
Price ⊖⊖

A designer dream come true, this 1950s restaurant turned exclusive hotel sits perched on Sorrento's cliffside. More like a contemporary Mediterranean loft apartment than a typical hotel, it would not look out of place on the pages of a trendy interiors magazine. Warm Neapolitan sunshine floods in through floor-to-ceiling windows, illuminating sleek furniture with a retro twist. The colors contrast perfectly with showpiece works of art and ceramic collections displayed in alcoves and shelves.

There is a warm, welcoming feel to this stylish establishment, yet it never looks overstyled. From the old ships' maps on the walls to the carefully positioned bowls of fresh lemons on the coffee tables, there is a real homey touch. There are twelve captivating rooms, some with wraparound glass walls for 180-degree views of the azure water below. Sleep with the blinds rolled up to wake when the sun appears over these wonderful surroundings. Listen for the sound of church bells ringing in the village below, then wander down to the kitchen for breakfast, where pastries, cereal, fresh fruit, and foaming cappuccinos are served at the huge table. Spend the day on the hotel's stretch of private beach, where you can take the hydrofoil to Capri, Ischia, Naples, and Positano. Or take the 300 steps down to the traditional fishing harbor of Marina Grande to soak up the atmosphere and join the evening *passeggiata*.

Terraces have sofas, daybeds, and chaise longues to sink into and soak up the panoramic views. Sip a cocktail and watch the sun go down, or have a soak in the whirlpool tub, looking across to Mount Vesuvius and the shimmering Bay of Naples. Meanwhile, the pool appears to lean across the cliff edge. **AD**

Relax at Le Sirenuse

Location Campania, Italy **Website** www.sirenuse.it
Price 🄢🄢

For 250 years, this was the summerhouse of the noble Neapolitan family Marchesi Sersale. Today it still feels like a grand home, maybe because it is still run by the family. The undisputed prima donna of Positano hotels, it has attracted legendary writers and Hollywood stars since the 1950s. Rising above the sun-drenched seaside town, the distinguished Le Sirenuse is covered with climbing grape trellises and feels a million miles away from the streets below.

Take the elevator to the sun terrace, where you will find a pool and pristine white deck chairs as well as a glassed and vaulted dining area. Best of all, come here for the view, past Santa Maria's majolica dome, which

> *"The Pompeian red building of Le Sirenuse is an icon of Italian hospitality."*
>
> *Condé Nast Traveler*

looks close enough to touch, to the sinuous profile of the Islands of the Sirens, from which the hotel takes its name. The heated lap pool looks down over the pastel-painted town of Positano, whereas the spa has a Turkish bath and bio-sauna to take you to another world of relaxation.

If it gets too hot, retire to one of the elegant drawing rooms or find a shaded corner on a flower-filled terrace. You are welcome to make use of the hotel's boat for cooling dips, then return to Positano's sandy beach, just a five-minute walk away. Splash out and book a room with a balcony and a bathtub that faces out to sea—you will never get tired of the view. **AD**

Enjoy Casa Angelina

Location Campania, Italy **Website** www.casaangelina.com
Price 🄢🄢🄢

Sitting on a cliff top overlooking the fabulous Amalfi Coast, it can prove tricky to pull yourself away from the modern, minimalist chic of Hotel Casa Angelina to explore this fascinating stretch of coastline. The hotel is in the small town of Praiano, sandwiched between Amalfi and Positano. Take the private panoramic elevator down to the beach to relax under an umbrella with a cocktail or go for a swim in the pool, looking out across the coastline. Inside, a heated hydrotherapy pool bubbles away under a constellation of fiber optics on the ceiling.

Beach chic does not come more stylish than this, with elegantly furnished simple white rooms. Some have wide terraces, complete with sun beds and chairs for a sunset drink. Sit back and smell the roses from a series of tiered gardens at one end of the hotel. The flowers release their scent at dusk for a heavenly experience, which wafts across the balconies in the evening. For complete privacy, book into Eaudesea, the four apartment suites by the sea. The fishermen's houses are perfect for couples on romantic breaks.

Restaurant Un Piano nel Cielo offers traditional Mediterranean cuisine with the aromas and flavors from the Amalfi Coast. The food is complemented by their excellent wine—get a table on the edge of the terrace for dramatic views. After dinner, take a stroll to the cocktail bar, stopping to admire the pieces of contemporary art in the hotel, including beautiful Murano glass, stunning paintings, and bronze sculptures. Connoisseurs can stop in the Cigar Room for a glass of grappa and soak up the views outside.

The towns of Amalfi, Positano, and Ravello are all within easy driving distance—if you manage to pull yourself away from Casa Angelina, of course. **AD**

Enjoy Villa Rufolo Gardens

Location Campania, Italy **Website** www.villarufolo.it
Price $

Nestling in the greenery, a square tower marks the entrance to the grounds on Piazza Vescovado. Beyond the archway, lime and cypress trees lead to the villa built in the thirteenth century by the wealthy Rufolo family, patron of the arts. Though altered by successive owners, Villa Rufolo retains many original features.

This is a place to relax among atmospheric remains, amid scattered sculptures, old archways, Moorish courtyards, and cloisters with exquisite colonnades and loggias. Myriad writers and artists have found inspiration on this site, most of all in the luxuriant nineteenth-century gardens, laid out by Neville Reid in true romantic fashion. Clinging to the hillside 1,150 feet (350 m) above the Mediterranean, the upper and lower terraces reveal a fabulous panorama of the Amalfi Coast and Capo d'Orso framed by precipitous cliffs and hills draped in vineyards and lemon groves.

Fragrant and bursting with color, the gardens are delightful whatever the season, but the highlight comes in the summer, between April and November, when a world-famous music festival is staged in their superb setting. The festival was first held in honor of Richard Wagner, who immortalized the site as "the enchanted garden of Klingsor," in his last opera, *Parsifal*. Today the emphasis is on diversity: Chamber music, orchestra, ballet, and musical promenades are performed in a number of venues in Ravello, but none more stunning than the Villa Rufolo gardens. As the moon rises and the audience sits spellbound among the flower beds, the stage built out over the edge seems to float between sky and sea. **SoH**

→ *The gardens of Villa Rufolo rise high above the Amalfi Coast, providing stunning views of the bay.*

Unwind at La Masseria San Domenico

Location Puglia, Italy **Website** www.masseriasandomenico.com
Price $ $

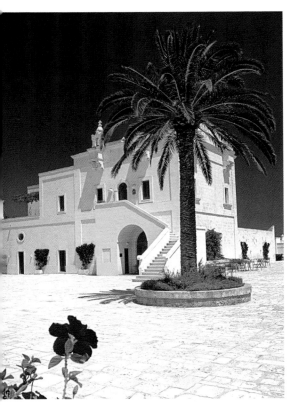

Indulge in luxurious seclusion at this lavishly styled five-star resort on the Puglian coast, deep in Italy's heel. The dazzling white, fifteenth-century *masseria* is a restored farmhouse with an ancient watchtower where the Knights of Malta once defended themselves against Ottoman attack.

There is a magical Moorish feel to it all. The thirty-two rooms and sixteen suites have wrought-iron beds and luxurious soft furnishings. French doors open straight onto the olive groves, and mesmerizing views look out across the lush estate to the dazzling Adriatic. In the center of the manicured grounds, surrounded by olive trees, sits a magnificent free-form saltwater swimming pool fringed with rocks. Fifteen minutes away is a stretch of private beach with chic cabanas—just a short hop on the free golf cart shuttle.

The spa offers thalassotherapy to detoxify and cleanse the body and soul, using seawater and mineral-packed seaweed from the Adriatic. There are tennis courts, a water gym, and an eighteen-hole golf course as well as windsurfing and diving. Meanwhile, around Puglia there are caves, stalactites, and rock formations at Castellana Grotte, near Bari, to explore. The baroque town of Lecce is the nearest big city and has plenty of buzz, whereas the nearby hilltop towns of Ostuni and Martina Franca offer a wealth of historic churches, cafés, and art galleries.

Dress up for dinner at the San Domenico restaurant, with its dramatic columns and arched stone ceiling. Once used as an olive press, the dining room now serves ingredients straight from the resort's farm. **AD**

> *"You're slathered in mud and placed in a plastic pod. Warm jets of water help detoxify your skin."*

Tatler

◪ *The gleaming white stone of the restored farmhouse keeps the* masseria *cool even in the hot summers.*

Discover Puglia by Car

Location Puglia, Italy **Website** www.viaggiareinpuglia.it/hp/en
Price $

Puglia is Italy's heel. Surrounded by ocean—this is where the Adriatic and Ionian Seas meet—it is a land of whitewashed houses perched on spectacular cliffs, of olive groves and vineyards, of monumental cathedrals, and quaint, cobbled lanes. Mass tourism has never made it here (do not forget your phrasebook) and, with its panoramic views and regular points of interest—from historic shipyards to white-sand beaches and family-owned eateries serving handmade pasta—this is the perfect place for a road trip away from the crowds.

There are many routes to choose between, but those with a penchant for sea views may like to take a coastal drive starting in Margherita di Savoia, known for its salt mines and salt mine museum. Admire views over the Strait of Otranto as you continue to Trani, a historic fishing port: Visit the dramatic cathedral before heading to the harbor for some freshly caught fish. Next stop is Molfetta where the lively beaches attract the surfers. Monopoli is another attractive old town a little farther southwest.

Make time to stroll around Brindisi, which bristles with ancient brickwork, before admiring the prehistoric cave paintings near Otranto, Italy's most easterly town. (Gothic novel enthusiasts should pack Horace Walpole's *The Castle of Otranto* as their vacation reading.) Around the cusp of Italy's heel you reach Gallipoli—not to be confused with the World War I battleground. This Gallipoli sits on a breathtaking stretch of beach, and its old quarter perches on a limestone island linked to the mainland by a sixteenth-century bridge. Finally, drive up the Ionian coast, whose beaches have crystal-clear water. The villages around Ginosa are particularly picturesque. **PE**

Stay at Parco del Vaglio

Location Puglia, Italy **Website** www.cvtravel.co.uk
Price $ $ $

Puglia's landscape is distinctively hot and arid, with plains covered with lines of olive groves. Its distinctive architectural feature is the "trulli" house. These dwellings are mysterious, whitewashed, circular stone buildings with conical black slate roofs, like windmills without sails. Most date from the fifteenth century, and they are believed to have been a popular way of avoiding taxes. Trulli houses were constructed without concrete and could be dismantled to evade housing tax inspectors, then rebuilt when the coast was clear.

Despite these humble origins, thousands of the hobbitlike dwellings have survived. The best collection of trulli can be found in the World Heritage–listed

> *"[Alberobello] is of outstanding universal value . . . an exceptional example of a form of building."*
>
> **UNESCO World Heritage Committee**

town of Alberobello, where there are more than 1,500 examples, many still inhabited. Tourists flock there making it very busy, especially in summer; a trullo in the countryside provides a more authentic escape.

Parco del Vaglio is one of the very best—a gorgeous group of carefully restored trulli that have been combined to form one big self-catering vacation house that sleeps up to eight. Or it can be partitioned to form smaller units. Within the traditional thick stone walls, the single-story house stays cool in summer without air-conditioning. There are original stone floors and high vaulted ceilings, too, plus modern luxuries and en suite showers. **SH**

Relax at La Sommità

Location Puglia, Italy   **Website** www.lasommita.it
Price ⑤⑤

Hidden away in a maze of tiny alleyways at the top of whitewashed Ostuni is the luxe design den La Sommità. The historic palazzo looks out across olive groves and down to the glittering blue Adriatic Sea. It might be the ultimate in Italian chic, but it has still held on to sixteenth-century features such as cool vaults, twisting staircases, stone walls, and sculpted columns.

Guests are cocooned in rooms with cream-colored walls and fabulous furniture—the minimalist interiors are from Milanese boutique Culti, which has a stake in the hotel. If you like what you see, you can buy it and have it shipped home. Bag a room with a terrace and views out to sea for a private breakfast or evening

> *"Ostuni is a circular town built around a hill and La Sommità is right at the top."*
>
> *Condé Nast Traveler*

aperitif. There is a winter sunroom to relax in when the temperature is not soaring outside and a subterranean spa in the old wine cellars, which offers bespoke treatments to ease away the aches and pains of traveling. Best of all is the dining room serving authentic Puglian cuisine. The locally caught fish is cooked to perfection, and wines and pastas are second to none. Grab a table outside in the Spanish garden, among orange blossom and olive trees.

La Sommità does not have a pool, but guests instead have access to a private strip of beach. Horseback riding and biking are available, and Italian cooking classes can also be arranged. **AD**

Stay at Torre Camigliati

Location Calabria, Italy   **Website** www.torrecamigliati.it
Price ⑤

Although many of Calabria's old baronial buildings now lie in ruins, Torre Camigliati, an eighteenth-century hunting lodge set in the heart of the Sila Grande region, has been lovingly restored to its former splendor. Part hotel, part cultural center, and part literary park, the lodge principally celebrates the life and work of British author Norman Douglas, who wrote the nineteenth-century Grand Tour travelogue *Old Calabria*. Surrounded by a 200-acre (80-ha) private estate, there is a fantastic sense of intimacy and tranquility about the place.

On the first floor are several reception rooms resplendent with nineteenth-century furniture. Twelve guest rooms have been similarly refurbished in period style, with iron beds, antique wardrobes, and views onto the park outside conjuring up a timeless ambience. More modern are the six mini-apartments nearby, which have been converted from workers' cottages and offer self-contained accommodation for couples and families. The public areas continue the lodge's grand theme, with large living rooms and fireplaces, an attractive breakfast room, and a spacious hall that is occasionally used for concerts and exhibitions. On the ground floor lies the visitor center: a vast selection of books on the Grand Tour, exhibitions by photographers such as Mimmo Jodice, and a shop selling Calabrian crafts.

The immediate surroundings are perfect for contemplative hikes and quiet strolls; press a little farther and you will discover a network of medieval villages, Byzantine churches, seductive countryside, ancient Albanian communities, and even evidence of Grecian settlements. Guided walks and excursions to nearby places of interest are happily arranged. **PS**

Explore the Aeolian Islands

Location Sicily, Italy **Website** www.italiantourism.com/island6a.html
Price 🌓

Smoldering volcanoes, bubbling mud baths, and steaming fumaroles—this has always been a volatile part of the world. These islands are seven volcanic sisters—Lipari, Vulcano, Salina, Panarea, Stromboli, Filicudi, and Alicudi—that lie off the coast of Sicily, and they are hot in the literal sense of the word.

Stromboli and Vulcano are active volcanoes, and volcanic activity is everywhere on this archipelago, but each island has its own character. On some, volcanoes with smoldering craters are staggered by canyons. Some have black-sand beaches, whereas others are sugar-white; some are barren, others verdant. There are splintered coasts that fall sheer to the sea with rocks that nature has modeled into strange shapes next to the deep, impossibly blue sea.

In addition to varying terrain, each island has a different vibe. The jet set favors glamorous Panarea, rammed with super-yachts in summer, whereas Alicudi is a rustic island of donkeys, where the eighty or so permanent residents are said to detest the sight of one another. Salina is the most verdant, and stunning Stromboli has little coves of black sand tucked into lava crags. Unpretentious Lipari, a place of rustic restaurants and flower-strung gullies, has a year-round population and a sizable town. There, you can eat dishes with delicious local ingredients such as wild fennel, cherry tomatoes, and endless varieties of local fish in its cobbled streets. If you can stand the sulfuric stench in Vulcano, you must wallow with all the visiting Italians in the baths said to cure joint diseases and neuralgia and do wonders for the skin. **LB**

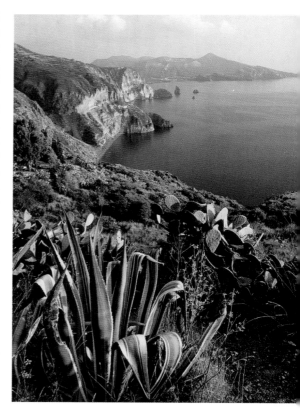

🗗 The island of Lipari, the largest of the Aeolian Islands, located off the coast of Sicily.

"They are a mixed bag of rough and sparkling jewels that attract an equally mixed crowd."

Condé Nast Traveler

Discover Mondello

Location Sicily, Italy   **Website** www.palermotourism.com
Price

Think Palermo and you probably imagine crowded city streets rather than golden beaches. But just twenty minutes' drive from the bustle of the inner city is the seaside town of Mondello. Once a thriving fishing village, the locals historically made their living catching tuna off the west coast of Sicily. When the industry dried up, locals quickly recognized the potential of the wide, picturesque bay. With its fine, golden sand and clear turquoise waters, Mondello became a popular destination for wealthy Sicilians.

Today, rows of pastel-colored beach huts snake across the sand. Mahogany-hued Sicilians laze on sun beds while enterprising locals trawl the hot sands selling ice-cold drinks. Farther out to sea, windsurfers and sailboats dot the horizon.

Follow the palm tree–lined streets to the tiny town center, and you will see that Mondello still trades heavily on its fishing heritage. The marina is full of pleasure crafts and fishing boats. A clutch of waterside cafés and restaurants serve calamari, sea urchins, and shrimps, literally plucked from the ocean and served onto your plate.

From here you have a clear view across the bay to the imposing rock slopes of Monte Pellegrino, where the bones of Santa Rosalia, the patron saint of Palermo, were discovered in a cave in 1624. Santa Rosalia is believed to have saved the city from the Black Plague, and every year, on July 14, locals celebrate with a festival and a procession through Palermo. From the summit of Monte Pellegrino, you can enjoy sweeping panoramic views across the Mediterranean. **JP**

← *These boats are more than merely picturesque and are used for fishing in the Gulf of Mondello.*

Stay at Villa Ducale

Location Sicily, Italy   **Website** www.villaducale.com
Price 🟢🟢

Imagine a romantic evening spent sipping a glass of prosecco on your own private terrace overlooking the blue Ionian sea at the Villa Ducale, or gazing up at snowcapped Mount Etna, whose wispy puffs of smoke and occasional fiery lava flows add a frisson of excitement to the otherwise tranquil scene. A stay in this former aristocratic Sicilian country house, now a small, elegant hotel run by Andrea and Rosaria Quartucci, is to truly experience Sicily—and Taormina.

The Mediterranean garden, with its small spa and a terrace where breakfast is served, never fails to win plaudits; the use of terra-cotta, painted ceramics, and wrought iron in the public rooms and the lovely

---

"The owners have recreated the atmosphere of a private villa . . . [the] staff are genuinely warm."

Mary-Clare Jerram, *Daily Telegraph*

---

local products and furnishings in the bedrooms all complement each other in a way that manages to be sophisticated without being too formal.

Tearing yourself away from Villa Ducale can be difficult, but the historic center of Taormina is only ten minutes away on foot. The town's dramatic hilltop setting, its picturesque ruins, and its elegant shops and restaurants have attracted writers, royalty, and Hollywood stars for decades. They come for its spectacular Greek amphitheater, for the views of Mount Etna, and for Castelmola, an ancient medieval village not far from the hotel. They come also for the sinfully rich, delicious Sicilian food. **MN**

Visit Cala Brandinchi

Location Sardinia, Italy   **Website** www.sardegnaturismo.it
Price 🟠

Soft white sand forms a neat half-moon around the shallow turquoise waters of the Mediterranean Sea. Such exotic views have earned Cala Brandichi, on the northeast coast of Sardinia, the nickname "Tahiti." Situated near the popular resort town of San Teodoro, Cala Brandinchi is slightly farther up the coast than its famous rival, La Cinta. Both feature the powdery white sand, crystal-clear waters, and sandy sea beds that visitors expect from this glamorous island off the western coast of Italy.

The waters around Sardinia are some of the cleanest in the Mediterranean, and the tourist beaches are swept and cleaned daily. There are eighteen beaches dotted along the coast of San Teodoro, but Cala Brandinchi easily stands out, with its wide, sweeping sands and quirky views. Soft beach gives way to gently rolling dunes, blanketed with juniper bushes, which back onto thick pine forest. In summer, the scorching temperatures are mitigated by a cooling sea breeze, and even in winter the weather is pleasantly mild.

From the beach you can gaze out to the island of Tavolara. Once a tiny kingdom, the island is home to just a handful of families. Only 3 miles (5 km) long, its highest peak, Monte Cannone, rises 1,854 feet (565 m) above sea level. Tavolara has been a protected marine reserve since 1997, and the clear, warm waters that surround the island are a popular spot for scuba divers. Wildlife is abundant around this unspoiled stretch of coastline, and you might see cormorants, seagulls, ducks, herons, and maybe even flamingos.

When you have finished relaxing on the wonderfully soft sands, you can make the short trip back to San Teodoro for a drink and a bite to eat: without a doubt it's the perfect end to an idyllic Sardinian day. **JP**

Kayak the Sardinian Coast

Location Sardinia, Italy **Website** www.locationsardinia.com
Price $

With almost 1,250 miles (2,000 km) of coastline surrounded by the warm, clear, calm Mediterranean Sea, Sardinia promises plenty for kayakers. The crenulated coast along the north and east coasts of the island is punctuated by hidden coves and secret beaches, inaccessible from the shore, with seabirds nesting along the cliffs.

Start your kayak adventure with a visit to the closest offshore islands, many of which are uninhabited and are just a few miles away. The white-sand beaches offer a comfortable camping area once you have soaked up the rays and exhausted your arms. There is plenty to look at as you paddle across the famously

> "A fantastic archipelago of sea-weathered granite sculptures and islands dominates the northeast."

Jim Krawiecki, *Guardian*

clear sea: Several of Italy's millionaires have villas on the coast, and from your kayak you will have a great view of their excesses, not to mention the windblown rock formations and the island's Bronze Age remains.

If you want to spend more than an afternoon on the water, there are plenty more ambitious kayak trips to be had. Around 7 miles (12 km) away, the Bonifacio Strait separates Sardinia from Corsica and are a reasonable challenge. You will have to paddle against the famous wind that blows through the strait, with views of great white cliffs. There are also several uninhabited islands to visit en route: Spargi, Santa Maria, Razzoli, and Budelli are all good choices. **LD**

Visit Xara Palace

Location Mdina, Malta **Website** www.xarapalace.com.mt
Price $ $

The taxi starts winding through dusty lanes toward a rocky ridge in the center of the island. Eventually, the imposing turrets and towers of the medieval walled town of Mdina appear on the crest of the hill. Because the taxi carries a guest of Xara Palace, the car sweeps past "no traffic" signs, across a narrow bridge over the moat, through an ancient gatehouse, and pulls up on the worn stone slabs of a grand Norman courtyard in front of an ancient mansion. It is an approach befitting the historic pedigree of Malta's finest hotel. Xara Palace was built right into Mdina's ramparts by Sicilian grandees back when the Crusader Knights of St. John ruled the island.

A decade ago, a local family bought the derelict building and spent years renovating and decorating it with Maltese antiques and paintings. They did a fantastic job, from planting gnarled olive trees in the atrium to putting an authentic wind-up gramophone on the landing. The contemporary restaurant on the roof has panoramic views to the coast that attract diners from all over the island, and the intact history of Mdina is perfect for after-dinner strolls. Mdina is known locally as "The Silent City" because traffic is normally banned from its maze of narrow alleyways between towering palaces, convents, and churches. Little wonder that Xara has become a celebrity retreat, regularly welcoming high-profile guests such as Brad Pitt, Sir Roger Moore, and Bruce Willis.

The best of the seventeen rooms is the romantic suite hidden up a twisting stone staircase and complete with a huge illuminated outdoor hot tub on a private section of the town's battlements. It is particularly inviting at night with a cocktail in hand and the lights of Valetta twinkling in the distance. **SH**

Explore Las Islas Cíes

Location Galicia, Spain   **Website** www.turgalicia.es
Price $

The wild and stunning Atlantic coastline of Spain surely has to be the ultimate place to go for dramatic stretches of unspoiled beaches. Just north of Portugal, the Galicia region is where you will find Las Islas Cíes. An archipelago off the northwest coast by the city of Vigo, it was once a pirate haunt and nowadays is an uninhabited and pristine national park area that is open to the public only in the summer months.

Take the ferry from Baiona to spend some long, lazy summer days on the Praia das Rodas, a perfect crescent of soft, pale sand backed by small dunes sheltering a calm lagoon of crystal-clear sea. It is the closest you will find to a Caribbean idyll this side of the Atlantic, with turquoise water, white sand, and shady pine trees lining the shore. A campsite has views out to sea, but it is not all Robinson Crusoe fare. There is a good restaurant with fantastic seafood in this tranquil setting, although you will have to carry your bags and camping gear more than half a mile (1 km) from the ferry to the campsite.

On the western side, towering granite cliffs take the full force of the pounding Atlantic, surrounded by numerous caves. Three main islands—with two linked by a sandbar—are fringed by smaller islets and rocky outcrops. Although a big draw here is the quiet beach, the wildlife also attracts a fair share of visitors. Inland, the islands are covered with pine and eucalyptus trees, dotted with purple foxgloves and white asphodels.

Spend the day wandering marked trails and looking for wildlife, then laze on the beach. There is even a designated nudist beach for those so inclined. **AD**

← *Las Islas Cíes archipelago forms part of a protected nature reserve that is home to colonies of seabirds.*

Stay at Hostal dos Reis Católicos

Location Galicia, Spain
Website www.parador.es/en **Price** 💲💲

The Hostal dos Reis Católicos is the king of all Spain's paradors. These eighty-five state-funded hotels and hostels are housed in some of the country's most important historic buildings. The Católicos sits on the Plazo do Obradoiro, flanked by the equally spectacular Romanesque cathedral and military college.

Said to be the oldest hotel in the world, it began life in 1499 as a hospital for the thousands of pilgrims who converged on the holy city of Santiago de Compostela (now a UNESCO World Heritage site). In keeping with 1,000 years of tradition, modern pilgrims are still given free food and lodging if they complete the Way of

> *"Even if I were not able to find my sword, the pilgrimage ... was going to help me to find myself."*
>
> Paulo Coelho, *The Pilgrimage*

St. James (whose remains are said to lie beneath the cathedral). Today, apart from modern bathrooms and some luxuries, the building looks much as it must have done originally. Delicious food is served in the atmospheric restaurant that was once a stable. Looking at its cloisters, manicured herb gardens, and four-poster beds, you could be forgiven for thinking you had stepped back 500 years. If further evidence were needed of the hotel's grand status, kings, queens, and presidents have all graced its hallowed halls. **TW**

⬅ *The 500-year-old courtyard of the Hostal dos Reis Católicos in Santiago de Compostela.*

Relax at Hotel Posada del Valle

Location Asturias, Spain
Website www.posadadelvalle.com **Price** 💲💲

Luxury and pampering are resolutely not the name of the game at this characterful farmhouse nestling at the foot of the Picos Mountains in northern Spain. But if stunning countryside, strong environmental values, extensive walking, and homegrown food are high on your list, Hotel Posada del Valle will fit the bill.

Owners Nigel and Joann Burch converted this stone-and-wood farmhouse to a traditional twelve-bedroom hotel in the mid-1990s. He is a renowned horticulturist and she a chef—a winning combination for a hotel operation dedicated to serving fine, locally grown food. The house sits in its own EEC-registered, 18-acre (7-ha) organic farm, complete with goats, a breed of rare Xaldas sheep, free-running chickens, and two Asturian ponies. The farm also has traditional hay and wildflower meadows, and produces cider.

Early in 2008, the business won the Spanish Organic Food and Biodiversity award for its restaurant, which serves delicious meals sourced, where possible, from ingredients grown on the farm. Guests are treated to fresh apple juice and homemade bread at breakfast time. The hotel is tucked away in rolling, dazzlingly green countryside and the nearest town with restaurants is a forty-five-minute hike, but guests are well catered for by the imaginative evening menu.

It is entirely possible to enjoy a wonderfully peaceful vacation here without a car—Nigel and Joann have compiled at least a week's worth of walks starting from the hotel, and taxis are available for those wanting to stray farther afield. Within a twenty-minute drive, the magnificent, unsung beaches of northern Asturias are there for the taking, and the lovely city of Oviedo is ninety minutes away by FEVE train. **LC**

Stay at Marqués de Riscal

Location Basque Country, Spain
Website www.starwoodhotels.com   **Price** ⬡⬡

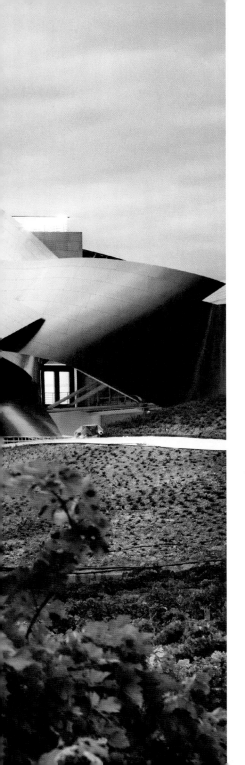

Love it or hate it, Frank Ghery's makeover of the Spanish Marqués de Riscal winery has dragged the tiny village of Elciego into the future. There is a feeling of exclusivity as you walk the hotel's red carpet toward the sleek rooms, where pale maple wood, leather touches, and dark marble bathrooms ooze luxury. The bedrooms are definitely twenty-first century, complete with sleek Bang and Olufsen flat-screen televisions. Ghery's personal touch is everywhere. He handpicked the interiors: everything from the Alvar Aalto inspired furniture and the bright red Ligne Roset "pop" chairs.

Take a tour of the ancient winery, dating back to 1858, and do not miss the extraordinary "cathedral of wine." Slightly spooky, the "crypt" contains around 16,000 bottles from every single year since its first vintage. Bottles lie covered in dust, like forgotten treasures. To sample the wine while taking in the view, head to the hotel's fabulous rooftop lounge. Overlooking Elciego's medieval cathedral, it is the perfect spot to try one of the 1,000 bottles from the Vinoteca bar, a gigantic library of Riojas, Rosados, and white Ruedas. For dinner, try the impeccable gourmet restaurant. Simple, yet sophisticated, it has won several awards for its croquettes, and the meatballs with truffle are a must.

After that you can relax at the Caudalie Vinotherapy spa, with its beautiful pool and serene lounge. Soak in a giant barrel-shaped whirlpool tub filled with a potent mix of crushed grape seed while sipping a restorative grape infusion, of course. Who knew that there were so many ways one could enjoy vino? **RCA**

⬅ *Slightly surreal, Ghery's distinctive titanium wave-roof stands out proudly amid the Riojan vineyards.*

Unwind at Mas de Torrent Hotel and Spa

Location Catalonia, Spain   **Website** www.mastorrent.com   **Price** ⑤⑤

This former *masia* or farmhouse is the kind of place where you can hide away for days. Sitting deep in the Catalonian countryside between Barcelona and Girona, the hotel has managed to retain enough of its original characteristics to enable you to imagine the sprawling eighteenth-century rural home it must have been. An olive press still stands in what is now the games room, whereas each of the ten self-contained bungalows has antique furnishings that add to the charm.

The hotel spills out into the expansive grounds, where orange trees line paths leading to each of the bungalows. They have everything you need to feel perfectly at home, including two bathrooms, an enormous bedroom, and a separate living room. Seven of these bungalows, the luxury suites, also have a private pool. The hotel even provides a thoughtful selection of books for guests to dip into while they lounge in the sunshine, and the array of toiletries in the bathrooms are ideal for pampering. If your tension is more deeply rooted, visit the Mas Spa or arrange for a masseuse to come to your room and treat you to a thorough full-body massage.

So much relaxation can build up an appetite, so order room service or venture over to the gastronomic restaurant, where you can indulge in the extraordinary "tasting" menu, sampling an aperitif, four starters, a fish dish, meat dish, predessert, and dessert, all created using the wealth of fresh seasonal produce available in the region. The hotel also has its own herb and vegetable gardens.

After so much feasting, you may feel that some exercise is in order the next day, so head to the hotel's vast outdoor pool for a few lengths, play tennis, or borrow a bike from the hotel and head out to explore the surrounding countryside. **JED**

⬆ *The yellow-stone hotel maintains the look and feel of the eighteenth-century farmhouse it once was.*

Stay at Hostal Sa Rascassa

Location Catalonia, Spain   **Website** www.hostalsarascassa.com   **Price** ⊖⊖

Hostal Sa Rascassa counters all the preconceptions that great escapes should be expensive and luxurious. A wonderful getaway, Sa Rascassa has only five simple rooms, and none of them have telephones. Spread out under a canopy of pines, the hotel was built in 1916, but has the feel of an ancient landmark. It's just 130 feet (40 m) from the seashore at Cala d'Aiguafreda, and guests come here to soak up the stunning scenery, from the Pyrénées all the way down to the empty beaches. There are no bars or discos for miles around; this is blissful seclusion at its very best.

Decorated in Mediterranean colors with traditional oak furniture, rooms are cozy and have heating for cooler autumn months. The restaurant offers a fine selection of Spanish cuisine with distinctly local touches, from Iberian pork and grilled cockles to freshly caught sardines, sea bass, and monkfish. Eat inside or take a table out in the courtyard, sitting under twinkling lights strung between the pine trees.

Find a quiet corner looking out across the cove and take in the views with a glass of Rioja and a bowl of olives. It is a tranquil delight.

At the end of a narrow road in an idyllic bay, just a few miles from Begur, Hostal Sa Rascassa is the perfect base from which to explore the coastline. Follow walking trails around the rocks, go swimming in the sea in warmer summer months, and explore the local region. This is the real Spain, a million miles away from packed beaches and rowdy bars. It is actually where Barcelonans come for weekends. Visitors can wander the cobbled streets of Begur shopping for antiques or browse the work of local artists at the weekly craft market. Drive on to find the charming medieval towns of Pals and Peratallada and Salvador Dalí's museum at Figueres. It is like taking a step back in time. **AD**

⬆ *The hostal's restaurant opens onto a charming courtyard that is illuminated with lanterns.*

Visit Montserrat Monastery

Location Catalonia, Spain   **Website** www.abadiamontserrat.net
Price ❶

In the year 880, a group of shepherd children saw a light descend from the heavens in the mountains of Montserrat—angels sang and the children's hearts were filled with joy. For a month the visitations continued and were traced to a mountain cave. When local priests explored the spot, they found an image of the Virgin Mary. Later, in the eleventh century, Abbot Oliba founded a small monastery on the site, and today eighty Benedictine monks still welcome pilgrims to their rocky mountain home.

A pilgrim is any person who knocks on the door with the intention of spiritual quest, and the Montserrat monks share their prayers and meals with guests. Visitors can tour the museum; its building was designed by Josep Puig i Cadafalch, who created many of Barcelona's landmark buildings (including La Casa Martí, also known as the restaurant Els Quatre Gats). The museum houses more than 1,300 pieces, from an Egyptian sarcophagus to a twenty-first-century sculpture. There is also a boys' choir at Montserrat (there has been a music school here at least as far back as the fourteenth century) that enjoys international prestige.

The massif at Montserrat is protected as a nature reserve and features walks, including the hike to the peak of Mount Sant Jeroni, which offers spectacular views over the rugged landscape (Montserrat means "serrated mountain" in Catalan). Many people come to Montserrat on day trips from Barcelona, but those who wish to stay longer can book into the Hotel Abat Cisneros or the Abat Marcet Apartments nearby. **PE**

← *The monastery sits in the shadow of Mount Monserrat, a unique and memorable location.*

Relax at Six Senses Spa

Location Barcelona, Catalonia, Spain
Website www.sixsenses.com   **Price**

The Six Senses Spa sits on the forty-second and forty-third floors of the Hotel Arts, Barcelona, with views stretching over the Mediterranean Sea. It is a unique location. Hotel Arts overlooks the Port Olímpic and, of all its rooms and facilities, the Six Senses Spa takes the very highest panorama. In the saunas, the sleek Scandinavian lines of the pale-wood benches complement the geometric frames of full-length window walls, yet invite in the brash blue of the sea and bright Catalan sunshine. There are also two outdoor terraces that gaze out over the city.

Treatments include the exclusive Art of Stone therapy, a massage that combines the natural healing properties found in the Earth with a human touch to restore balance and vitality. The signature Six Senses Sensory Journey lasts for nearly three hours, but passes quickly. Color therapy, or chromotherapy, is also used: all of the treatment and steam rooms are decorated with six individual colors to enhance the well-being of body and mind.

If the city smog has clogged your pores, try a natural Thai facial, which cleanses and exfoliates your skin using honey, yogurt, sesame, and jojoba oil; or try a luxury hot and cold stone facial, an essential-oil massage employing warm and cold stones to massage face, neck, and shoulders. The more adventurous might like Hopi ear candling, an ancient therapy used by the indigenous peoples of North and South America. Specially designed candles are lit and held inside the ear to promote a healthy atmosphere in the ears, sinuses, and throat. If that sounds like too much healing, you could just go for a workout. The Six Senses Spa also features a state-of-the-art fitness center with yoga, tai chi, and pilates classes. **PE**

See Montjuïc Garden

Location Barcelona, Catalonia, Spain
Website www.barcelonaturisme.com   **Price** ❶

The Jardins de Mossen Costa i Llobera are both perfectly in keeping with the crazy, cool vibe of Barcelona and at once a complete breath of fresh air for visitors exhausted by Gaudí's flights of fancy. Leaving the city behind, by foot, funicular, or cable car, visitors can climb Montjuïc and find the cactus gardens, clinging to the side of the hill looking out over Barcelona's port, at the top entrance at Miramar.

The gardens were created by the architect Joaquim Casamajor i d'Espona. They were planted by Josep Panello and are dedicated to the Majorcan poet Miquel Costa i Llobera. There is a monument in the gardens dedicated to the Pine Tree of Formentor, the

> *"Montjuïc is, together with Tibidabo, one of the two mountains that give our city character."*
>
> **Barcelona City Council**

inspiration for Catalan poet Costa i Llobera's most famous poem. More than 200 species of cactus and succulent thrive in the gardens, from countries as diverse as Kenya, Ethiopia, and Mexico, and some of them stand more than 20 feet (6 m) tall. There are also more than twelve species of pine tree here, providing welcome shade for visitors.

The oldest cactus that can be found in the park, *Oreocereus neocelsianus*, also known as the "Old Man of the Andes," was imported to the gardens from Italy and is more than 200 years old. In the heat of the Spanish sun, the Montjuïc cacti throw amazing shadows and appear otherworldly. **EP**

Unwind at Hotel Omm

Location Barcelona, Catalonia, Spain
Website www.hotelomm.es **Price** 🟢🟢

Barcelona is not exactly lacking in design hotels, but Hotel Omm is one of its most unique. Located in the city's fashionable Passeig de Gràcia district (which is great for shopping), Omm is the joint creation of architect Juli Capella and interior designers Sandra Tarruella and Isabel López. The futuristic design and low lighting immediately make you feel like you have stepped into a surrealist, funky mothership. The reigning style is very much postmodern minimalism, but Omm's designer luxury is balanced with a sense of new age tranquility implicit in its name.

Consider the open-plan lobby, which has a floating fireplace; or the decked roof terrace, which offers not only fabulous views of Gaudí's La Pedrera and La Sagrada Família, but also a sexy plunge pool. The rooms are light and bright, with lasciviously curved walls and a host of high-tech gadgets. Front-facing rooms have balconies, whereas those at the back have terraces and upper rooms that overlook Gaudí's Casa Milá.

The restaurant—Moo—is equally well conceived and is entered via a glass-fronted courtyard garden that features giant bamboos and stainless steel sculptures. The kitchen serves exquisite, modern Catalan cuisine courtesy of the Michelin-starred Roca brothers (Joan, Josep, and Jordi). Postprandial entertainment is provided in two bar lounges where cocktails are served while DJs and live music play through much of the week and on weekends. It might all sound a little overstimulated for an escape destination, but it is not: Omm ensures that every facet of your experience is unrushed, sophisticated, and relaxing. In any case, you can always head down to the in-house spa and indulge in any one of a range of therapies, including underwater massage. **PS**

See Muntanyes de Prades

Location Catalonia, Spain
Website www.ctv.es/USERS/albertb/english.htm **Price** 🔴

The Muntanyes de Prades lie 37 miles (60 km) north of Tarragona in Catalonia—a green but rocky landscape dotted with remote villages and snowy peaks. Most people will only ever see these sights in the pages of *National Geographic* because the best of the mountains is only accessible on foot.

Below soaring snowcapped peaks, through seemingly endless forests of pine, or looking down upon quaint stone villages, walking in the Prades Mountains offers plenty to see. However, it is the contrasts of the Prades that are especially intriguing. From the bracing experience of looking out across the canyon of the Barranco de Garx to sitting in a café

"Its many rivers, streams, and springs allow magnificent oak and pine groves to flourish."

World Travel Market website

---

filled with shepherds singing folk songs in one of the mountain villages, there are countless wonderful experiences to enjoy. These peaks are as much loved by locals as they are by visitors, and a trek past some of the imposing limestone palisades here will show you the cliffs and gorges that inspired a young Picasso.

The area is populated by unusual creatures such as the wildcat and Eurasian badger and is replete with beautiful maples, hazels, and oaks. Granted state protection, its unspoiled beauty is timeless. Nobody will reach you on your cell phone here, and you will finally remember what silence sounds like. And it's all right there on Barcelona's doorstep. **SWi**

Visit the Natural Reserve Sierra Y Cañones de Guar

Location Aragon, Spain   **Website** www.guara.org/ingles
Price 🌓

This protected reserve in northeast Spain is most famous for its canyons. Four rivers—the Guatizalema, the Alcanadre, the Mascun, and the Vero—traverse its karst landscape and, together with the wind and rain, they have carved it into striking caves and canyons.

There are around 90 canyoning routes in the reserve. One of the most popular is the River Vero canyon. Here you need to be able to walk and swim, but there's no rappeling, so it's a good choice for beginners. Those who like a view from up high might like to try the River Formiga canyon, with the option to rappel down; its highlight is a beautiful waterfall with

> *"There are caves, potholes and canyons . . . in short, a landscape of unusual beauty. "*

Aragon Tourism website

a cave behind its curtain of gushing water. Or there's the Lower Peonera canyon, known for its otherworldly caves and clear rock pools. The reserve also has excellent hiking and mountain biking trails for those who want to keep their feet (or wheels) on the ground.

But there's more to this natural wonderland than its adventurous side. Bird species include the Griffon vulture, the bearded vulture, and the golden eagle. There's prehistoric art, too: More than 60 caves and rock shelters feature paintings dating back to the Upper Palaeolithic period. And if all that works up an appetite, a number of scenic hilltop villages in and around the reserve serve up hearty local dishes. **PE**

Walk in the Picos de Europa

Location Picos de Europa, Spain   **Website** www.spain.info
Price 🌓

The Picos de Europa (the peaks of Europe) are one of Europe's last mountain wilderness escapes. These limestone ridges run for 25 miles (40 km) between Asturias and Cantabria near the north coast of Spain, and their jagged peaks reach to nearly 8,700 feet (2,648 m). The region has been a protected National Park for almost 100 years, so it is now an area of dazzling wildlife and plants. You may even see brown bears, wolves, lynxes, vultures, and wild boar in the more remote spots.

The distinctive features of the Picos are the deep gorges carved out by north-flowing rivers over thousands of years. They help walkers discover views of sparkling mountain streams, peaceful lakes, snowy peaks, and green valleys, with ancient beech and oak woods and lush pastureland. Serious mountaineers tackle the high peaks where there is a network of mountain refuges. Cavers explore an underground world that includes some of Spain's deepest caves.

Walking through steep mountain gorges you may have only donkeys and goats for company. Then wandering down through sleepy stone-built villages, with traditional farms that have remained unchanged for centuries, you could see cherry trees laden with fruit, bright clouds of butterflies, and wildflower meadows buzzing with insects.

Many visitors base themselves in the busy little town of Potes at the center of three big valleys. From here you can drive to Fuente Dé and give yourself an easy start by taking a cable car partway up. **SH**

➡ *The Picos de Europa would have offered sailors their first sight of Europe when returning from America.*

Walk in Primo Rivera Park

Location Aragon, Spain
Website aragonguide.com   **Price ◐**

The elegant inhabitants of Zaragoza say the Parque Primo de Rivera—which they usually call the Parque Grande or Great Park—is the lungs of their hometown. Inaugurated in 1929 by Miguel Primo de Rivera, the dictator who ruled Spain for seven years during the 1920s, it provides residents with 100 acres (40 ha) of green, recreational space.

It is a very Spanish affair, of course. Although in New York's Central Park people jog, and in London's Hyde Park they lounge about on striped deckchairs, Spain's park goers are dedicated predominantly to the paseo—the art of strolling. They dress up, meet, greet, and are seen. The Parque Grande's setting is certainly stylish enough for this and worthy of the fourteen years that were needed for its design and construction. Its main entrance opens onto the imposing Avenida de San Sebastián, which is filled with fountains and flanked by gardens inspired by Versailles. Meanwhile, on Buenavista Hill, the Carrara-marble statue of King Alfonso I of Aragon stands 20 feet (6 m) tall—he conquered Moorish Zaragoza in 1118, reclaiming the city for the Christians.

There are botanical gardens, too, where the more horticulturally minded can commune with local Aragonese flora, as well as a Winter Garden, a large wild area planted with pine trees, and a garden dedicated to Símon Bolívar. If these are not entertainment enough, there is also a tourist train and an amusement park, and bicycles and tandems are available to rent. All in all, it is the perfect place to escape the noise of the city traffic beyond. **PE**

← *The monument to King Alfonso I El Batallador (the Battler) stands tall in Primo de Rivera Park, Zaragoza.*

Stay at A.C. Santo Mauro

Location Madrid, Spain
Website www.ac-hotels.com   **Price ◐◐**

Madrid is a warren of undiscovered and often opulent gems, so it is little surprise when the A.C. Santo Mauro looms into view in the leafy streets of the wealthy Chamberi district. Built by architect Louis Legrand under the instruction of the duke of Santo Mauro, this neoclassical mansion has, since the last stone was laid in 1894, existed through various incarnations. Once the residence of the marquis of Santo Mauro, the building eventually opened as a hotel in 1991.

The exterior of the building is immediately striking, but the interior is even more magnificent. Subtle blacks, whites, and grays complement the grandiose architecture, and the recent renovations lend the hotel

> *"When you get to know it, [Madrid] is the most Spanish of all cities, the best to live in, the finest people."*
>
> Ernest Hemingway, *Death in the Afternoon*

a contemporary ambience. The fifty-one spacious rooms include studio apartments and duplex suites, some of which are housed in the former stables of the mansion. Expect antique furnishings, silk curtains, Persian carpets, and the kind of luxurious details that would make a marquis blush.

The old and the new work together perfectly here. The restaurant, for example, is situated in the former library. The bookshelves have been kept intact, and the glass-encased books give the dining experience extra cultural elegance. The conference room is in what used to be the ballroom, and there is an Arabian swimming pool and a very well-appointed gym. **PS**

Unwind at Hotel Urban

Location Madrid, Spain
Website www.derbyhotels.com   **Price** ⊖⊖

Since opening in late 2004, the six-story glass glimmer of Hotel Urban has added a dash of the ultrachic to Madrid. Situated equidistant from the Thyssen-Bornemisza and Prado museums, Puerta del Sol, and the titillating tapas paradise of Santa Ana, there is already plenty to recommend a stay here without mentioning the wonderful art collection.

Owner Jordi Clos is a renowned collector and head of an archaeological society. The hotel displays the society's superlative collection and also boasts distinctive artistic touches, such as white marble from Thasos, Papua New Guinean figurines, 300-year-old Chinese portraits, and a superb set of nineteenth-century Hindu figures. The lobby showcases the prestigious collection with a dedicated Egyptian art museum notable for its sculptures of pharaohs and their retinue; pieces date from as far back as 300 B.C.E.

The artistic sensibility of the Urban extends beyond objets d'art, however—the lighting and interior design of the public spaces is exquisitely delivered. The lobby's reception desk mirrors the glowing column of alabaster that soars in the middle of the atrium; fluorescent tubes adorn the walls, and glowing globes additionally convey messages of modernism's focus on razor-sharp minimalism and white heat. The ninety-six contemporary bedrooms are decorated with an additional piece of art (complete with notes).

The Mediterranean/new-Spanish fusion fare here is noted for its excellence, and Urban's Glass Bar is, as the name suggests, a glass-covered area where guests can sit and join the movers and shakers sipping cool cocktails and shucking fresh oysters. Urban living really does not get any better than this. **PS**

Stay at the Parador de Chinchón

Location Chinchón, Madrid, Spain
Website www.paradores.es   **Price** ⊖⊖

Just 31 miles (50 km) from the sleepless city of Madrid, the Parador de Chinchón is an oasis of calm. It used to be an Augustinian monastery, founded by the lords of Chinchón in the seventeenth century. They brought the first monks here to live beneath the protection of the neighboring castle. Still, the monks did not have an easy time. Over the centuries, they were banned and reinstated, and then had their property confiscated. Finally, the building was destroyed by fire in 1929.

Restored by architect Juan Palazuelo, today the parador retains its original baroque appearance and renaissance features. Adornments include impressive

---

"The picture-perfect town of 4,400 souls has retained its stage-set 16th-century plaza mayor."

New York Times

---

floor-to-ceiling tapestries, ornate murals of religious figures, and ceilings fabulously painted in tones of ocher. In the bar, the walls are tiled in traditional blue and white, and the worn leather-backed chairs could surely tell stories if only they could talk.

Cypress trees, roses, and wild privets grow in the garden, and fountains enhance the sense of peace. The bedrooms are simply furnished, but do not lack comfort. One has a private terrace with views over the castle. In the past this room has been booked by bullfighters when performing in Chinchón's bullring. Maybe, after the *corrida*, they enjoyed soothing their battered limbs in the hydromassage bath. **PE**

Discover Parador de Guadalupe

Location Extremadura, Spain
Website www.paradores.es   **Price** 💲💲

Cáceres, in the autonomous region of Extremadura in the west of Spain, is too rarely on the tourist agenda. A pretty town of stone and cobbles, Cáceres and its surrounding area played a vital role in the exploration of South America. Many of the conquistadors were from here, including Francisco Pizarro. Guadalupe, for whom the parador is named, is local, too. The small black statue of Our Lady of Guadalupe was found nearby in the fourteenth century. A monastery was built, and her name traveled all over the New World.

The Torreorgaz Palace, in which the parador is housed, dates from the same era. Originally gothic, it has been revamped with, for example, an eighteenth-century facade, and its stonework is adorned with the coats of arms of different noble owners. The oldest structure of the hotel is its brick and granite tower.

Inside, the building is delightfully labyrinthine. An interior courtyard features walls that are painted deep terra-cotta, a tall, arched gallery, and windows with wrought-iron grilles. These colors are echoed in the rich reds and ochers of the lounge's decor, contrasting with the parador's plain exterior. The largest of the bedrooms is the Comendador de Alcuéscar, which has an en suite living room and whirlpool tub, with views over the sanctuary of Nuestra Señora de la Montaña (Cáceres's patron saint) and the garden.

Beyond the hotel walls, points of interest include the cave paintings at Maltravieso and the Roman theater, amphitheaters, and museum at Mérida. The area surrounding Cáceres was once a vital foothold of the Roman Empire, and the artifacts are of outstanding quality—yet few visitors turn off the tourist trail to reach this undiscovered gem of Spain. **PE**

Explore Parque Nacional de Monfragüe

Location Extremadura, Spain
Website www.spanish-fiestas.com/extremadura   **Price** 💲

Within Extremadura, the least inhabited region of Spain, lies the Parque Nacional de Monfragüe. A Natural Park since 1979, it was designated as such in 2007 with the added protection of a UNESCO Biosphere Reserve.

The vast emptiness of the area makes it ideal for wildlife. You are more likely to have the company of soaring eagles than people, so it is worth carrying a pair of binoculars at all times. The empty road from Plasencia to Trujillo takes you through the heart of the park, the countryside offering up wild and stunted olives, cork, and holm oaks laid out among the sun-baked grassy scrub. This is one of only three roads

> *"Thousands of visitors come every year . . . to 'preserve and rediscover' nature."*
>
> **UNESCO's Man and the Biosphere program**

within the park, all of them in the most northern stretch, allowing the remainder to be explored on foot. Rocky outcrops appear occasionally, which can be the best places to spot birdlife, such as peregrine falcons, eagles, and the world's largest colony of black vultures. Two sparkling, wide rivers cross the park, the Río Tajo and Río Tiétar, adding even greater beauty to the sparse landscape. Deer, wild boar, otters, and the rare Iberian wolf and lynx are known to inhabit the area.

Villarreal de San Carlos is the only habitation within the park and has a population of just thirty. There is a water protection center, nature center, and visitor center if you wish to learn more about the park. **CFM**

Relax at Parador de Almagro

Location Castilla-La Mancha, Spain
Website www.paradores.es **Price** ⊖⊖

Fourteen inner courtyards grace the Parador de Almagro in Spain's La Mancha. The building used to be a convent consecrated to San Francisco; it was built by the Davila de la Cueva family in 1596. Monks would file from their cells to the chapel at midnight, then kneel and pray for three hours. They would then return to their beds, only to rise again at dawn for more prayer.

Today visitors sleep in the former monks' cells, which have, presumably, improved in comfort. Now the rooms have canopied beds and elegant antique furnishings. This air of historic sophistication follows through into the public areas: The lounge and dining room feature

---

"Every wall, gallery, and courtyard oozed with the tranquility of its former occupants."

Tom Reynolds, *The Sunday Times*

---

polished tile floors, beamed ceilings, and sweeping arches. It is the outside area, though, that really inspires serenity. The many courtyards of the Parador de Almagro are filled with fountains and greenery. There is also an outdoor swimming pool flanked by terraces.

Outside the convent walls, guests can visit Almagro's famous open-air theater, which dates back to the seventeenth century. The nearby Tablas de Daimiel nature reserve attracts bird-watchers from across the globe, as well as migrating birds such as herons, egrets, bitterns, and pochards. This is also Don Quixote country, so there are plenty of cheeses and wines to enjoy, not to mention a few windmills. **PE**

Stay at Palacio Condestable Davalos

Location Andalucía, Spain
Website www.paradores.es **Price** ⊖⊖

Condestable Davalos was a soldier who fought for the Christians during the reconquest of Spain. He was captured and imprisoned by the Moors. Upon his release, King Juan II bestowed on him the title of "condestable," or high constable. Now Davalos's portrait hangs in the hotel restaurant—but in fact the man never lived here. Instead, the retreat was once the palace of Dom Fernando Ortego Salido, the dean of Malaga.

Built in the sixteenth century but reconstructed in the seventeenth, this is a parador of grand proportions. From the outside, the honey-colored stones present a flat facade. It almost looks austere, but step within and you will find yourself in the inner courtyard, which features a double gallery of elegant stone arches—the upper section is glazed, and full-length white linen curtains hang at its windows. The patio creates an intimate oasis with its potted trees, stone fountain, and wrought-iron tables and chairs. From here, a wide stone staircase leads to the upper level, adorned with an ornate fireplace, wrought-iron lamp fittings, and suits of body armor that hark back to the days of the reconquest. The bedrooms feature floors tiled in terra-cotta, and antique desks and chests alongside comfortable sofas and armchairs. In the restaurant, the chef serves up local specialties such as stewed kid.

The parador forms one side of Úbeda's Plaza de Vasquez. Neighboring buildings are some of the most esteemed in the city: the Church of El Salvador, the Church of Santa Maria, the Palacio Vazquez de Molina, and the Palacio de El Marques. **PE**

→ *The sixteenth-century renaissance palace is also known simply as Parador de Úbeda, after its location.*

Enjoy Parador Castillo de Santa Catalina

Location Andalucía, Spain
Website www.paradores.es   **Price** 💲💲

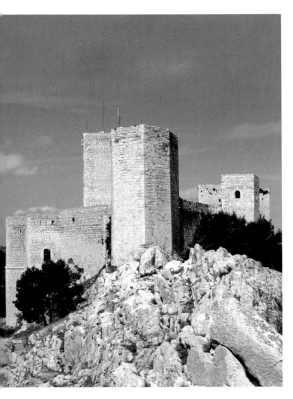

"You half expect Charlton Heston as El Cid to come riding out of legend for a beer at the pool bar."

David Clement-Davies, *Guardian*

Overlooking the Andalucían city of Jaen, this parador is a hotel with atmosphere. Its public rooms have vaulted ceilings and arches that stretch to more than 65 feet (20 m) high. Many of its forty-five bedrooms harbor four-poster canopied beds, are hung with tapestries, and feature balconies with extraordinary views out across the olive groves and rocky mountains of the Sierra Morena and Sierra Nevada. The dimly lit dining room keeps the Arabic architectural theme, and serves up local specialties such as *ajo blanco* (cold garlic soup); *ensalada de perdiz* (partridge salad); *pipirrana* (mixed salad); and *morcilla en caldera* (stewed black pudding). If you need a little exercise to work all that off, there is also an outdoor swimming pool.

The hotel is not as old as it seems. Although it butts up against the ancient *castillo*, the hostelry dates back only to the 1960s. The castle was built during Moorish rule, but fell into Christian hands when Ferdinand III's troops stormed it in 1246. For the next two centuries, the Moors continued to attack, but the Christians held firm, building their own fortress and chapel on the site. The Christian monarchs, Ferdinand and Isabel, finally threw the Moors out of Spain in 1492, but this did not mean that peace would reign over Jaen. Napoleon invaded in 1810, and threats during the Carlist wars of the late nineteenth century inspired more fortifications.

It is all quiet now, though. Indeed, the buildings and their lush surrounding gardens exude an ambience of such peace and serenity that General de Gaulle chose this escape in which to write his memoirs. **PE**

🔲 *The parador is on the site of a thirteenth-century Arabic fortress, high on Santa Catalina hill.*

Stay at Hospes Palacio del Bailio Spa

Location Córdoba, Andalucía, Spain
Website www.hospes.es **Price** 💲💲

Understated luxury is the order of the day at Hospes Palacio del Bailio. Hidden among the narrow backstreets of the ancient city of Córdoba, this beautiful hotel is housed in a sixteenth-century mansion that, by turns, has also served as a military headquarters and a stables.

Like many Andalucían buildings, it is set around a central courtyard in the Moorish style, this one filled with the tangy scent of citrus from the immaculately pruned orange and lemon trees and the soothing trickle of an eighteenth-century stone fountain. As well as being stunning, the hotel conceals a rare treasure: the remains of a Roman house, discovered by

> "This hotel is … 'the evolutionary surprise that allows you to express your inner self.'"
>
> *Condé Nast Traveler*

chance by a previous owner. Today the remains lie underneath the five-star restaurant's glass floor and are lit up to spectacular effect at night.

A dip in the infinity pool is the perfect antidote to the effects of the hot southern European sun. The Bodyna spa is a major feature of the hotel, part of it situated in a courtyard flanked by stone columns, with a further three spas on the lower ground floor built around original Roman thermal baths. Just a fifteen-minute walk away you will find the wondrous Córdoba *mezquita*, the most magnificent mosque built by the Moors and rightly deserving of its designation as a UNESCO World Heritage site. **TW**

Visit Coto Doñana

Location Andalucía, Spain
Website spainforvisitors.com/sections/donana.htm **Price** 💲

Wildlife-watching can be frustrating at times. No matter how meticulous your preparations, you can never guarantee that the animals are going to put in an appearance. What makes a trip to the Parque Nacional del Coto Doñana such a rewarding and ultimately stress-free experience is that the sheer abundance of wildlife here means the odds of spotting something of interest are very much in your favor. With the park home to more than 300,000 birds, you would be unlucky not to see anything noteworthy.

The park's name derives from the famously antisocial Duchess Doña Ana de Silva y Mendoza, who built a residence for herself here, as far from civilization as possible. Doñana encompasses more than 500 square miles (1,300 sq km) of coastal territory, made up mostly of sand dunes, marshland, and lakes that provide perfect living and breeding conditions for around 125 bird species—among them some of the few surviving pairs of the rare Iberian eagle. Another 125 species, including red kites, bee eaters, hoopoes, and golden orioles, are migratory visitors, not to mention tasty treats for one of the park's other celebrated residents, the pardel lynx, for whom Doñana is one of its last remaining refuges.

You can tour parts of the park on foot, along trails that link the main visitor centers—where there are exhibitions on the local wildlife—and take you past marshes and lakes where hides have been set up for observing the wildlife. For an in-depth exploration of the park, however, your best bet is to prebook a four-wheel-drive tour with a guide, who will be able to take you into some of the park's more inaccessible areas to the very best wildlife-watching vantage points. **JF**

Explore Zuheros

Location Andalucía, Spain **Website** www.zuheros.com.es
Price ❶❶

It is a vision of Spain that you will remember for years to come: one of Andalucía's most celebrated *pueblos blancos* (white villages) nestled in the rocky mountains, with blue sky above and olive groves leading to it. Zuheros, in the center of the Cordoba/Malaga/Granada triangle, is one of the best examples of the country's Moorish villages, with narrow streets and a history dating back to pre-Roman smugglers.

The town has fewer than 1,000 residents and only a handful of inns and hotels, but that has not stopped it from attracting tourists of all stripes. Little local restaurant Los Palancos, Llana 43, serves hearty, rustic dishes—including young goat, rabbit, and suckling pig—and attracts those looking for tranquility and a hideaway in the Andalucían mountains. Hard to believe, really, that it is only an hour and a half from the fleshpots of Malaga and Marbella.

Zuheros is on the fringes of the Sierra Subbetica natural park, which has great walking potential, and the old railroad running through the village has been transformed into a walking and bicycling route. Just 2.5 miles (4 km) uphill from the village, the big must-see is Las Cuevas de las Murcielagos (cave of bats), which is full of stalactites and stalagmites as well as its famous mammals. There is plenty of evidence of Neolithic life in the caves of the region, too, including cave paintings. Las Balanchares goat cheese factory in the center of the village is internationally known, and the cheese is very popular grilled as a tapa dish in the area and beyond. Bring some home, with a bottle of local olive oil, to prolong that vacation feeling. **LD**

→ *The village of Zuheros in the mountains of Andalucía is one of the best examples of a pueblo blanco.*

Stay at Hacienda de San Rafael

Location Seville, Andalucía, Spain
Website www.haciendadesanrafael.com   **Price** ⑤⑤

The Hacienda de San Rafael is the kind of place in which those looking for complete seclusion stay when they want to leave the world behind. Set deep in the Andalucían countryside down a long sweeping driveway fringed with olive trees, it looks exactly how a Spanish hacienda should: whiter than white whitewash, gardens full of sweet-smelling herbs, and sunflower fields stretching as far as the eye can see.

The property dates from the seventeenth century and has been in the same family for the past 150 years. After starting life as an olive estate, it now operates as a luxury boutique hotel and has been meticulously

---

"This small boutique hotel feels more like staying in your own big villa. The interiors are exquisite."

Independent

---

refurbished by its Anglo-Spanish owners, brothers Anthony and Patrick Reid, who are also the brains behind the award-winning Corral del Rey in Seville.

Each of the eleven deluxe rooms is set around a bougainvillea-strewn courtyard, where migrating swallows come every year to nest, dip, and dive as you sip your sangria or dine by candlelight on beautifully prepared Mediterranean food. For total privacy, you can stay in one of three *casitas* (cottages), each with its own garden and a shared infinity pool that is out of bounds to the other guests staying in the main house. You can even order breakfast to be eaten alfresco from the comfort of your own gazebo. **TW**

See the Jardines de las Reales Alcazares

Location Seville, Andalucía, Spain
Website www.gardenvisit.com   **Price** ⑤

The setting is more Morocco than Europe—the garden of this stunning *alcazar* (fortress) was built on Moorish ruins and is bursting with palm, cypress, orange, myrtle, and lemon trees that shelter visitors from the scorching Andalucían sun. With its whitewashed buildings, cobbled streets, and tall palms, Seville is one of Europe's most evocative cities, and the Reales Alcazares and its gardens attract numerous visitors.

This impressive monument is Seville's royal palace. Originally a Moorish fort, the palace and its mosaic-covered rooms have been expanded on several occasions, and most of the modern buildings were built over Moorish ruins for King Pedro of Castile, who ruled from 1350 to 1369. The city's palace was built to be one of the greatest examples of mudejar architecture—a style prominent under Christian rule in Spain but heavily influenced by Islamic architecture. The later addition of gothic elements contrasts with the dominant Islamic style.

The Alcazar's extensive gardens, or *jardines*, are a perfect location for relaxing under shady palms: Small, Arabic courtyards are set between sparkling pools, fountains, and seats tailor-made for some Eastern-style peaceful contemplation. In spring—perhaps the best time to visit Andalucía—orange trees drop their fruit and scatter their world-renowned marmalade scent. Despite the popularity of this city-center oasis, there are plenty of quiet corners where visitors can rest, daydream, or take in the atmosphere. The gardens are open all year-round but are closed on Saturday and Sunday afternoons. Finding a more restful urban hideaway is difficult to imagine. **LC**

Visit Parque María Luisa

Location Seville, Andalucía, Spain
Website www.spain.info **Price** 🌓

Sitting under orange trees that provide respite from the sun and listening to the trickling of the fountains, it is quite easy to close your eyes, relax, and drift away. The Parque María Luisa is Seville's main urban park, and its extensive grounds, with clusters of mature trees, are exactly what is needed to escape from the heat and dust of the city streets.

Just south of the city center, the park was designed by the French landscape gardener Jean-Claude Forestier (who also worked on the Bois de Boulogne, the main park in Paris) to provide a setting for the pastiche buildings that were constructed for the Ibero-American Exhibition in 1929. The legacy is astounding. People gather around landmarks like the Plaza de España, a few steps away from the leafiest sections of the park, but the area is sufficiently large that there is no problem finding a quiet, private place to cool down and recharge—and it is the heat from which visitors mostly want to escape.

The extensive grounds, given to the city by Princess María Luisa d'Orleans in 1893, are filled with tree-lined avenues and paths, colorful flower beds and gardens, ponds, pools and cascading waterfalls, statues, water fountains, and monuments dedicated to national literary figures like Cervantes. In the center of the park is a larger lake, complete with an island upon which stands a gazebo, where you can sit quietly to watch the waterbirds that swim around the lake. Parque María Luisa has often been described as one of the most beautiful urban parks in Europe. **CFM**

🡕 *Moorish design elements are introduced by ceramic tilework throughout the park.*

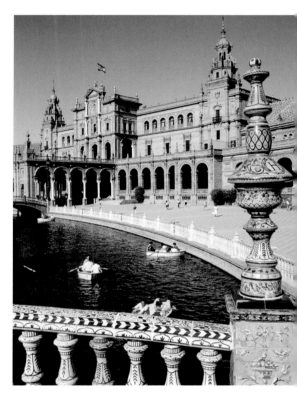

"[Forestier's achievement] is an enduring testimony to creative interpretation in landscape design."

Alan Tate, *Great City Parks*

Explore Andalucía by Horseback

Location Andalucía, Spain   **Website** www.ridingandalucia.com; www.spain-horse-riding.com   **Price** 💰💰

What better vantage point is there to admire the stunning Andalucían scenery than from the back of a horse? Not only do you get a finer view than on foot, you are also able to cover far more ground.

There are scores of companies offering riding vacations in this beautiful part of Spain, from complete beginners to those who were born in the saddle. Whatever your ability or the company you choose to go with, this is a great way to feel at one with nature.

In the heat of the summer, days start early, before the sun has risen and the high temperatures render even the mildest of exertions too much effort. You'll saddle up your Andalucían steed and head off into the mountains of the Sierra Nevada. Follow ancient bridle paths and drovers' routes that date back to the Moorish occupation and beyond. As you climb into the pine-scented hills, breathe in the fragrant perfume of rosemary and thyme as they are crushed under your mount's hooves.

You'll find yourself riding though eucalyptus-lined rivers, passing by orange, lemon, and almond groves. From time to time you'll stop to give both horse and rider a much needed break and some refreshments. With no fences or tarmac roads, there is a wonderful sense of freedom and space.

When the pace picks up you'll find yourself flying over the ground, with hooves thundering. When you stop, a delicious picnic lunch will be provided, usually consisting of locally baked bread, cheese, and chorizo washed down with local wine and beer. **HA**

→ *Andalucía is very diverse: You can explore volcanic landscapes, mountains, green hills, and beaches.*

Unwind at Trasierra

Location Seville, Andalucía, Spain
Website www.trasierra.co.uk **Price** ⊖⊖⊖

If the prospect of your average health retreat conjures up images of sadistic boot camps and cold showers, then think again. Trasierra is a sixteenth-century, family-run hotel that has been designed for people who appreciate beauty, comfort, good food, and peace. You can also come here to kick start a new healthy lifestyle, as twice a year Trasierra is taken over by In:Spa, experts in residential health retreats

The sun-scorched Sierra Morena mountains form a wild, romantic landscape of olive and chestnut trees where wild boar roam and bulls shade themselves beneath branches. In a remote valley lies Trasierra, amid 3,000 acres (1,210 ha) of olive and orange groves

> *"There is nothing ordinary to be found at Trasierra; this is a place that nurtures dreams."*
>
> *Independent*

and consisting of a collection of whitewashed buildings linked by terra-cotta walkways. Archways lead to carefully tended aromatic gardens, and inky water shimmers in a deep pool with red-earth vistas beyond. Inside, the rooms are decorated in a blend of English country house and traditional Spanish style.

The day starts early with a poolside yoga class as the sun rises behind the mountains. At breakfast time, feast on delicious fruit salad, porridge, thick smoothies, and freshly squeezed juices. Then a morning of hiking in the wild mountains will set you up just in time for a light, detoxifying lunch. Afternoons are spent having massages, reflexology, or simply lazing by the pool. **HA**

Stay at Hotel Cortijo Fain

Location Andalucía, Spain
Website www.arcosgardens.com **Price** ⊖⊖

This boutique hotel may be compact, but the bedrooms themselves are as spacious as some city-center apartments. Even the smallest rooms have sitting areas that open onto immense bathrooms with deep bath and separate wet rooms. Shutters mean you can leave the windows open all night and enjoy the scent of air softly scented by eucalyptus trees. However, this will mean you are likely to be woken by birdsong, before rolling over and giving in to a few more hours' sleep in the extremely comfortable beds.

The setting exudes romance, with each room in the *cortijo* (farmhouse) named after one of the many poets inspired by nearby Arcos de la Frontera, the prettiest of Andalucía's *pueblos blancos* (white villages). The hotel is based around a 300-year-old central courtyard, complete with a fountain and bright bougainvillea. Many of the hotel rooms have windows on two sides, enhancing their natural lightness and allowing guests to take in views of the courtyard as well as gardens planted with hundreds of ancient olive trees. These trees shade the pool so that while you swim you may hear the occasional plink of an olive dropping onto the surrounding flagstones.

The design is quintessentially Andalucían, with the *cortijo*'s original architecture preserved as much as possible, and the original stables converted to a charming tapas bar. Further accommodation is available in the town-house hotel suites, which can be found between the first and ninth holes of the eighteen-hole golf course. The course itself offers outstanding views of Arcos de la Frontera. Prime time for this is in the late evening, when you can borrow a golf cart and drive out as the sun sets, watching rabbits and grouse scattering across the greens. **JED**

Relax at Escondrijo

Location Andalucía, Spain
Website www.escondrijo.com **Price** 🚫🚫

Vejer de la Frontera is a whitewashed Spanish *pueblo* (house) that seems to have stood still in time. Tucked into the village's maze of cobbled lanes sits Escondrijo, a boutique hotel with just five elegantly appointed suites. The house has been built from the remains of the ruined Vera Cruz Chapel, and some parts of the house date back to Moorish days, as can be seen from the galleried interior courtyard and twelfth-century well.

The rooms are both comfortable and contemporary, and each one is decorated with its own particular style. The high ceiling creates a sensation of great space in one open-plan room; another room has a more sultry feel with shuttered windows and walls

---

"[Escondrijo] is not just some self-catering duplex . . . it is a dream of the Spanish Golden Age."

Juliet Kinsman, *Observer*

---

and drapes in gloriously wanton red. The upper-floors have private terraces with spectacular mile-long views.

Away from the house, guests can drive to the dune-backed beaches of the Costa de la Luz in minutes. Activities include windsurfing and kite surfing, scuba diving, and whale- and dolphin-watching. You can walk through the pine trees that perch on the cliffs above the crashing waves, or ride horses through the surf. You can also hire mountain bikes, play a round of golf, or indulge in a spot of bird-watching. For the best of Spanish culture, Cadiz, Jerez, and Seville are all just a day trip away, so guests can tour the sights and still be safely back on the Escondrijo terrace for sundown. **PE**

Enjoy Casita La Laguna

Location Andalucía, Spain
Website www.vivatarifa.com/laguna **Price** 🚫🚫

This secret hideaway for two is in a truly beautiful location. Looking out across the straits to Morocco, there is just your loved one and the sea for company. The tiny *casita*, south of Tarifa, is hidden among the sand dunes and pine trees at the end of a narrow track, and romantic seclusion is what it is all about. Cuddle up and enjoy the views across to North Africa and the lights of Tangiers glittering in the distance.

Inside, the interior is cool and uncluttered, decorated with Moroccan-style lanterns and ceramics. High windows let light flood in, and a wood-burning stove offers heat on cooler nights. The *casita* is also eco-friendly, with electricity from wind and solar energy and water from the nearby spring. Outside there is a wonderful terrace where you can sit to watch the blistering sunset, and the sheltered garden leads to the deserted beach for sunbathing and feasting on picnic lunches far away from the crowds. If you hanker to do more, the *casita* is attached to a farm, where you can hire horses and ride through the pine forest and along the beach to the fishing village of Bolonia.

From the *casita* it is a fifteen-minute drive to Tarifa, where it is easy to spend a pleasant day wandering the winding streets, stopping to sample traditional tapas, before exploring the castle and harbor. Alternatively, take a day trip across the water to Morocco, only forty-five minutes by hydrofoil. At night, wander down the road to the local fish restaurant or cook dinner for two and eat outside on the terrace under a star-studded sky. The local market in Tarifa is a great place to stock up on supplies, from freshly caught fish to locally grown herbs and vegetables. Then fall asleep to the sound of Atlantic rollers pounding on the beach. This *casita* has to be the very definition of tranquility. **AD**

Stay at Hoopoe Yurt Hotel

Location Andalucía, Spain **Website** www.yurthotel.com/about.html
Price 💲💲

> *"Life in a yurt is as romantic as you imagine it to be, but that doesn't make it easy."*

Tiffanie Darke, *The Sunday Times*

"Getting back to nature couldn't be easier at this solar-powered retreat," enthused a journalist for the United Kingdom's *Independent* newspaper. Tucked away in a spectacular corner of Andalucía, the yurts bask in 7 acres (3 ha) of olive groves and cork oak trees, nestled twenty minutes' walk away from the picturesque village of Cortes de la Frontera.

Private views of the mountains are part of the deal for guests staying here. Each yurt—and there are now five—boasts spectacular views of the blue-hazed Grazalema Mountains, plus its own private meadow, equipped with hammock, outdoor furniture, and private bathroom. Anyone deterred by the thought of alfresco showering and trips to the outside compost toilet could do well to suspend judgment. Your flower-strewn meadow really is private.

The Hoopoe Yurt Hotel is for anyone who relishes spending time outside, far away from modern trappings yet within walking distance of bars and shops. It is difficult to imagine a more restorative sanctuary. You will wake to the sounds of goat bells plus an army of resident birds: sparrow hawks, turtle doves, and honey buzzards. It may all be wonderfully "back to nature," and impressively environmentally friendly, but the yurts are large and comfortable, with indoor furniture in case the weather falters.

Foodies will rejoice. Young British owners Ed and Henrietta organize a three-course, locally sourced, mostly organic meal with wine four days a week. Dinner is enjoyed under a pergola, lit by Chinese lanterns, perched by the swimming pool. **LC**

↖ *Comfort is a big part of any stay here. The yurts all have double beds and private bathrooms.*

Experience Los Castaños

Location Andalucía, Spain   **Website** www.loscastanos.com
Price 💲💲

Los Castaños is a five-bedroom hotel in Cartajima, one of the *pueblos blancos* (white villages) behind Marbella and Ronda. Here the hills wind steep and scenic. Vertiginous gorges and stomach-lurching switchbacks vie for your attention with mind-boggling views. The mountain roads here were once famous for their bandits.

Survive the road and it is relaxation all the way. The mother and daughter owners aimed to create a laid-back, rural idyll, and they have succeeded. The rooftop terrace with its plunge pool, the plush sofas and open fire, and the massage room all ensure that your stress levels plummet. Should guests insist that they achieve something during their sojourn here, there are sketch

---

"... you begin to appreciate the harmony of an older, slower, and more peaceful way of life."

Scotsman

---

pads in each room. If the environs inspire you, Los Castaños hosts painting vacations, with tuition from a local artist. There are writing courses, too. Alternatively, a local ornithologist will take you on a bird-watching walk—four species of eagle inhabit this area. Energetic guests can hike the walking paths that link the seven villages of the Alto Genal; trails run through chestnut groves and over limestone crags. Or why not swim in the river, or ride horses in Ronda? The brave can try out caving or rock-climbing in the Los Riscos. At the end of the day, guests return to the hotel to eat a candlelit dinner and compare stories as they dig into Andalucían and African flavors. **PE**

Relax at La Cazalla

Location Andalucía, Spain   **Website** www.lacazalladeronda.com
Price 💲💲

Ronda is a much-visited beautiful town in Spain's Andalucía region. Its whitewashed old quarter stands along the precipice of a dramatically deep gorge crossed by an eighteenth-century stone bridge. Just ten minutes from the bridge, down a rough track, you will find the most secluded place to stay—a tiny and romantic six-room hotel in an undisturbed valley surrounded by mountains and oak forests.

Owner Maria Ruiz looked long and hard for a site to build her hotel, and she has used the secret spot to create a charming rustic hideaway that feels more like a wonderful private house than a hotel. It is certainly a total escape. You can either relax, slumped among the cushions, drapes, Moorish tiles, and antiques, or wander the hills all around. Some guests play boules in the garden; others simply sit in the quiet and read.

The hotel is quirkily luxurious, with arabesque arches, whitewashed walls, old paintings and books, fans, and mosquito nets. There is a hidden outdoor swimming pool but no televisions, cell phone reception, or air-conditioning. It is like staying with a lovely old aunt. You will find a bowl of walnuts by the fireplace, a sprig of scented rosemary on your pillow. A well-stocked fridge in your room includes cold meat, cheese, wine, and beer. Whichever way you look, there are great rural vistas, and there are also binoculars in each room, for gazing at the view and spotting the beautiful local birdlife.

La Cazalla has no menus, but the fine dinners are cooked with the very best ingredients that the kitchen staff can find in the local markets, plus their own award-winning homegrown herbs, vegetables, and fruit. It is most enjoyable to eat outside savoring the silence by flickering candlelight. **SH**

Visit the Generalife Gardens of Alhambra

Location Granada, Andalucía, Spain **Website** www.alhambra.org
Price $

"A pearl set in emeralds" is how one Moorish poet described the ancient Alhambra complex in Granada, Spain. Once the lavish home of the Nasrid sultans in the thirteenth century, this walled complex includes a stunning former palace and the Alcazaba Fortress. Surrounding it are some of the world's most beautiful, traditional Islamic gardens.

Gardens are considered a vital element to the Islamic way of life. They are seen as an escape from the baking heat of the desert, and water plays a vital part in their design. Flowing water not only soothes the soul, but also cools the stone buildings. The gardens of Alhambra are known as *Generalife*, which translates to "garden of paradise," "orchard," or "garden of feasts."

Built in the fourteenth century, the Patio de la Acequia lies at the heart of the gardens, a long, thin irrigation trough decorated along one side with more than a dozen fountains, each sending a thin stream of water arcing through the air. Continue through the northern portico to the Patio de los Cipreses. Here you will find a rectangular pool framed by a low, neatly manicured hedge. In the center sits a second, smaller pond, with a stone fountain trickling in the middle. The design is unexpected and perfectly symmetrical.

Most of the gardens follow this same ordered, geometric feel. You will find box hedges sculpted into exotic shapes, from turrets to triangles to perfectly formed stars. Every corner reveals another beautiful view; every courtyard holds another stunning example of Arabic art and architecture. **JP**

← *These fountains line the beautiful Moorish Patio de la Acequia in the gardens of Alhambra.*

Stay at the Parador de Granada

Location Granada, Andalucía, Spain
Website www.parador.es   **Price** $ $

Few hotels in the world can rival the magnificent surroundings of the Parador de Granada. This popular, state-run hotel chain has successfully converted close to one hundred historic buildings into grandiose places to stay for tourists, yet all are surpassed by the beauty and wealth of history that exists at Granada.

The building resides in the heart of the majestic Alhambra, the vast fortress complex that stands imperiously against the backdrop of the Sierra Nevada. Built in the fourteenth century, it formed part of a palace and mosque at a time when Granada was one of the most flourishing and envied cities in the Islamic

---

"It fulfils one of the romantic traveler's greatest dreams: to sleep inside the walls of the Alhambra."

Condé Nast Traveler

---

world. With the Christian reconquest of the city in 1492, the building was converted into a Franciscan monastery and chapel. Subsequent years saw the building slide into dilapidation, leaving scant trace of the original features, yet the appearance today is one of Moorish-inspired architectural touches, soothing fountains, and gardens flourishing with wisteria. Numerous works of art and classical furniture line the cloister and interior rooms, from which all windows offer breathtaking views, especially those above the Albaicin. **SG**

◄ *The monastery was the first holy place built in Granada on the orders of the Catholic monarchy.*

Discover the Cuevas Pedro Antonio de Alarcón

Location Andalucía, Spain
Website www.andalucia.com/cavehotel   **Price** $

You do not need to be a caveman to live in a cave, the residents of Guadix, near Granada, are keen to point out. More than half the population of this town is troglodyte (this is the largest concentration of inhabited caves in Europe), and their dwellings boast all modern conveniences—Internet, electricity, running water, and the rest. In the Cuevas Pedro Antonio de Alarcón, the "cave hotel" that lies a little way out of town, there is even one suite with a whirlpool tub.

People in this part of the world have been living in caves since the eighth century. Some stories relate that the caves became better developed when the Moors, escaping the Christian reconquest, fled to the hills and burrowed beneath the ground. Whatever the reason for their existence, caves have their advantages. Their temperature is constant year-round, with the mercury hovering at about 66°F (19°C). Log fires warm the caves when necessary, with smoke puffing up through whitewashed chimneys that poke skyward from the rich, brown soil of the hills. Some people report improved sleeping patterns—something to do with a connection to the earth, apparently—whereas others cite the individuality of their dwellings as the main attraction. After all, no two caves are alike.

The Cuevas Pedro Antonio de Alarcón complex has twenty-three apartments, each with views over Guadix and the Sierra Nevada. There is central heating, hot water, TV, telephone, bathroom, kitchen, and a private barbecue for each. There is also a restaurant and swimming pool. Nearby attractions include horseback riding and climbing in the surrounding hills, and the Roman thermal baths in Guadix. Wearing skins and clubbing down your dinner are not encouraged. **PE**

Enjoy Los Jardines de Palerm

Location Ibiza, Spain
Website www.jardinsdepalerm.com **Price** 🖲🖲

Ibiza may be known for its clubbing scene, but there is one tiny corner where visitors can reach absolute relaxation. Los Jardines de Palerm is a bijou hotel (there are only nine rooms) created from a converted seventeenth-century finca. Overlooking the bay of San Antonio, it is a haven of peace and quiet, yet near to the beaches and the nightlife if you want them.

Most guests remark on the tranquility of the exotic water gardens and infinity pools. Terraces with loungers are scattered through the landscaped grounds, so guests have no trouble finding a peaceful corner to call their own. Minimalist, white rooms decorated with pretty Chinese ceramics and antique

> *"[It] allows total privacy in grounds punctuated with water gardens and two stylish infinity pools."*
>
> *Harpers Bazaar*

manuscripts inspire further serenity. There is no restaurant, but breakfast is served, and kindly staff even rustle up food for those who partied into the small hours and missed the official meal. The chef will also conjure up a sandwich or salad for those who cannot tear themselves away from their lounger at lunchtime, and there is an honesty bar so people can help themselves to drinks.

The atmospheric town of San José is just minutes away by foot, with its whitewashed buildings, palm trees, and pottery shops. Sit quietly and enjoy the view from a tiled bench in the main square but not for too long; Los Jardines de Palerm is calling. **PE**

Explore Formentera

Location Formentera, Spain
Website www.turismoformentera.com **Price** 🖲🖲

Although Formentera lies just a few miles to the south of Ibiza, it seems a world away from its nearest neighbor. If Ibiza is Spain's party island—filled with pumping nightclubs, heaving bars, and hordes of sweaty revelers—then Formentera is very much the chill-out alternative. Situated off the east coast of Spain, and accessible only via ferry (one hour) or hydrofoil (twenty-five minutes) from Ibiza, the island has yet to succumb to the ravages of mass tourism.

Those few tourists who do make it here, most of whom are day-trippers, will find a tiny place—its 32 square miles (83 sq km) make it the smallest of the inhabited Balearics—of great bucolic charm. Rolling hillsides blanketed in olive trees and dotted with small stone villages lead down to beaches that are among the most pristine to be found anywhere in Spain. The clean white sand and clear blue waters give the coast an almost Caribbean appearance.

Windsurfing is popular, and snorkeling and diving equipment can be rented by those who want to get in among the colorful fish that inhabit the coastal waters. A network of bicycle tracks allows for easy, relaxed exploration of the island, taking you past the beaches and up into the wild, windswept countryside at the center of Formentera.

The nightlife is as relaxed as the gentle lapping waters of the Mediterranean, with the island home to a fine collection of small, cozy restaurants, many boasting idyllic beachfront locations. Those on the northern shore, facing Ibiza, provide picture-perfect sunset-watching opportunities. **JF**

→ *The sunsets are spectacular from any angle as the color of the rocks is gently transformed before you.*

Relax at Finca Son Palou

Location Mallorca, Spain
Website www.sonpalou.com **Price** ⊖⊖

Just 25 miles (40 km) from Palma is the tiny hamlet of Orient. With only a handful of honey-colored stone houses scattered along the cobbled streets, nothing much has changed over the years. The bell still tolls at the tiny church of Saint Jordi, and now and again a wedding takes place and everyone turns out to watch.

Orient lies in a fertile valley surrounded by the majestic Tramantuna Mountains, and the Finca Son Palou is perfectly placed for visitors to take in the incredible scenery and immerse themselves in the peace and tranquility of the area. Originally a fourteenth-century manor house, this family-run finca has been renovated to high standards yet keeps a rustic feel. Set in a private estate that provides the hotel with organically grown produce, there are miles of footpaths and bike trails to explore and an infinity swimming pool with views along the valley. The spacious guest rooms are all individually designed and create a cool and relaxing haven on a hot day and, with central heating, are cozy and welcoming during the winter months. Stone floors, whitewashed walls, and exposed beams combine with tasteful furnishings to give a sophisticated simplicity.

Breakfast is a leisurely affair and, during the summer months, is served on the terrace. Sip freshly squeezed orange juice from locally grown fruit, bite into a freshly baked flaky croissant, and relish the strong coffee with just birdsong and the occasional sheep bell as accompaniment. For lunch and dinner, the finca prides itself on providing modern Mediterranean cuisine using the best locally grown ingredients; on a balmy summer evening, dinner can be enjoyed outdoors against a backdrop of mountains that dramatically change color as the sun goes down. **SD**

Unwind at La Serranía

Location Mallorca, Spain
Website www.laserrania.com **Price** ⊖⊖

During the spring and autumn, artists, writers, and yogis alike find life-altering inspiration at this tranquil retreat in the foothills of the Tramuntana Mountains, 6 miles (10 km) from the historic town of Pollensa. Nestled in 10 acres (4 ha) of private grounds, La Serranía both respects and draws on its surroundings.

The lofty ceilings and expansive windows create a bright, open space, highlighting the exquisite marble and oak floors, limestone walls, and cedar woodwork. It is no wonder this breathtaking property is also a popular location for film and photo shoots as well as a favorite for corporate retreats and group vacations. Yet you will find plenty of privacy here.

"Would suit anyone in search of inspiration, insight, or an escape from everyday life."

Harpers & Queen

This is minimalist yet stylish luxury, with sleek marble private bathrooms, maid service, and private terraces. There is a meditation room for those seeking even more tranquility, or let yourself go at the hands of an expert masseuse. Take time to reflect in La Serranía's large pool, but keep your head above water to catch the incredible views of the valley dotted with almond, olive, and oak trees. During the summer, you will get ample water time and an optional daily yoga class as well as full brunches and dinners you would not dream of skipping. Plenty of free time means you will also have the chance to sample some of the vibrant local cuisine. Soul soothing? *Sí, señor.* **JS**

Stay at Son Gener

Location Mallorca, Spain
Website www.songener.com   **Price** 💲💲

Stay at La Residencia

Location Mallorca, Spain
Website www.hotellaresidencia.com   **Price** 💲💲💲💲

The eighteenth-century stone farmhouse was lying derelict on a hilltop among the farmers' fields of northeast Mallorca. Local architect and designer Toni Esteva spotted it and invested many years converting it into one of the island's most alluring small hotels. Son Gener is now a chic ten-room finca, surrounded by rolling hills of olive groves and orchards. It has its own organic fruit and vegetable gardens, and there are views of the Mediterranean sparkling in the distance. The nearest day trip is to the historic little town of Arta, where you can wander along stone alleyways to a hilltop chapel. Son Gener is also close to some of the island's least spoiled beaches.

Inside the hotel, Toni has created a showcase of uncluttered design. Explore the maze of exposed stone walls and old wooden beams, amid plenty of whitewash, limestone floors, and antiques. It is neither fussy nor opulent, just quietly understated with large rooms decorated in pale neutral colors, stone stairways, and the occasional bouquet of fresh flowers to lighten the mood. There are open fires in cool weather, and double doors open out onto the extensive gardens.

Big bedrooms come with private terraces, four-poster beds, high wooden ceilings, and creamy linen-covered armchairs. Bathrooms are swathed in limestone. Some rooms offer roof decks with sea views. The small spa furnished in stone, glass, and dark wood has indoor and outdoor pools, a sauna, steam room, whirpool tub, and massage room. There is no fine cuisine here, though: The food is tasty, fresh, and rural, and you can eat outside among the bougainvillea.

It is very quiet here, sometimes silent. As you lie, totally relaxed on your terrace, occasionally you will hear a goat's bell jingling in the fields. **SH**

Overlooking the mountain village of Deiá, this splendid hotel has spectacular views of the Tramuntana Mountains and the sparkling Mediterranean Sea. It is set in 30 acres (12 ha) of grounds, which feature landscaped lawns and flower gardens, fragrant citrus groves, and working farmland. Originally three manor houses, La Residencia is furnished with a mixture of Mallorcan antiques, simple rustic fabrics, and a wealth of local art. The hotel manages to combine a feeling of absolute luxury with the rusticity of a hacienda.

La Residencia rambles and sprawls over soft ocher-colored steps and through a labyrinth of beautiful rooms and gardens. Whether you are enjoying the

---

"The rooms are decorated in traditional Mallorcan style (plus a dollop of posh hotel style)."

The Sunday Times

---

quaint, creaking charms of the rooms in the old house or the less restrained opulence of the luxury suites, you will experience a splash of Iberian glamor. It is lovely to dress up for dinner at the El Olivo restaurant—set in the sixteenth-century olive press, you will choose from a gourmet menu of tantalizing locally inspired dishes—or at the Son Fony, a restaurant with a more casual atmosphere but no less delicious cuisine.

The easygoing ambience of Deiá, a charming village that has been a popular haunt for artists, writers, and poets over the decades, infuses this memorable hotel. The atmosphere is unhurried and tranquil, but the village oozes with character, like the hotel itself. **SWi**

Stay at Abama

Location Tenerife, Canary Islands
Website www.abamahotelresort.com **Price** ⓈⓈⓈ

This deluxe resort on Tenerife's west coast sits on white sands nestled by palm trees beneath the foothills of Mount Teide. Abama is ideal for those whose idea of escape is to be active. Large and packed with facilities, it has eight swimming pools, a private beach, and a dedicated eighteen-hole golf course. There are ten restaurants with cuisine ranging from sushi to Argentine *parrilla* (grill), and from seafood to Italian classics. There is a choice of accommodation, too. You can either stay in the Citadel, which is in the center of the resort and has views over the golf course and gardens, or in the Villas, located in a quieter spot. Each spacious villa has a private balcony and the decor looks back to Moorish days—sultry terra-cotta, dark wood, and plush rugs.

At the beach club, guests can choose between sailing, scuba diving, or deep-sea fishing. Or you can just lie back and enjoy a massage in the sun. There is a tennis academy offering courts, equipment rental, and lessons. There is also a gym, where classes include yoga, Pilates, aerobics, and tai chi. And at the Wellness Club, the options for relaxation are enough to have guests reaching for their dictionaries. There is a tepidarium, a hammam, an African sauna, an herbal steam bath, a Kneipp trail, a hydrotherapy pool, a snow cabin, and a spa garden.

Activities include reading clubs, salsa classes, belly-dancing workshops, and bridge and billiards competitions. And to keep the children happy, there are kids' clubs with activities including cake baking, necklace making, discos, and outdoor games. **PE**

← *There are plenty of spectacular views to be had from Abama, on a variety of spacious terraces.*

Relax at Hotel San Roque

Location Tenerife, Canary Islands
Website www.hotelsanroque.com **Price** ⓈⓈ

On the far side of Tenerife, away from the crowded beaches of the south coast, amid the more lush and tropical northwest coast, lies the little fishing village of Garachico—a small huddle of whitewashed houses. Not much of Garachico survived an eruption 300 years ago, and you can still see the deadly trail of the lava. There are a few cafés, a church, and a shop. Just off the tree-lined main square you will find an eighteenth-century mansion that has been converted into a world-class boutique hotel.

The bold terra-cotta-washed outer walls hint at the style and atmosphere within. Guests enter through the cloisters and arched stone doorways into dark,

> *"Friendly San Roque provides a subtle mix of Havana-style charm with cutting-edge mod-cons."*
>
> Louise Roddon, *Daily Telegraph*

cool rooms with heavy beamed ceilings, big wicker sofas, and striking Spanish art. Cream drapes sway in the breeze from open windows and doors. Up a spiral staircase, the three-floor Tower Suite has a private roof terrace with views of the mountains and sea. A small round window above the bed offers a view across the rooftops of Garachico.

The simple pool fills one courtyard and is floodlit at night. The sea is only a minute's walk away, and, although there is no beach, swimmers can use pools in the lava shoreline. Fishing rods are available to borrow at reception, and if you catch something, the chef will cook it for your dinner. **SH**

Walk in the Highlands of Gran Canaria

Location Gran Canaria, Canary Islands
Website www.uplandescapes.com **Price** 🌗

While most of the island's visitors head south to the sandy beaches and picturesque fishing harbors, Gran Canaria's highlands provide a refuge for those who are in search of solitude amidst spectacular scenery: volcanic mountains connected by palm- and flower-filled valleys and lush meadows. Rising up to 6,230 feet (1900 m) above sea level, the mountains are all interspersed with quaint and isolated villages that are linked by ancient royal pathways (Caminos Reales). Even high up in the peaks the temperatures average 60°F (15°C) or more during the cooler season, making for agreeable walking conditions in the months from October to April.

Accommodation on these walking vacations in Gran Canaria's highlands is provided in stylish cave houses that are rented out to individuals or groups of up to five people. Alternatively, you can stay at the hotel Fonda de la Tea in the sleepy mountain village of Tejeda, where a few shops and restaurants, and even a museum, provide a charming counterpoint to the peace and quiet in the surrounding mountains. A rental car is included in the price, although visitors can opt for eco-friendlier group airport transfers and arrange other transportation according to their needs.

But above all, the walking vacations in Gran Canaria's highlands are about the walks, which visitors can embark on independently of organized groups if so desired. And walking down a pilgrim's path, the smell of pine trees in the air will surely make you forget about your life back home. **DaH**

➡ *The stunning volcanic scenery will provide an unforgettable walking vacation.*

Enjoy Finca Las Longueras

Location Gran Canaria, Canary Islands
Website www.laslongueras.com **Price** 💲💲

Built in 1895, this large rural mansion on the island of Gran Canaria is situated in the middle of an agriculture plantation growing bananas, oranges, avocados, and papayas, intoxicating the visitors who stumble across it with its heady, tropical perfume. Even those who discover this place of wonder—situated at the end of a winding gravel road high up in the hills—can easily find themselves lost again, adrift in the maze of paths meandering through the plantation.

This luxury rural hotel, also known as the Red House (La Casa Roja), is inspired by colonial style with its white, decorative arched porch and high ceilings, and was formerly home to an aristocratic local family.

"Contemplate romantic sunsets amid tropical surroundings, perfumed by orange blossom."

Proprietors, Finca Las Longueras

The sense of grandeur lives on, from its ornate brass bedsteads and long corridors to its huge arched windows and vast antiques collection.

Finca Las Longueras has nine double bedrooms, but you need never see another soul in these sprawling 427 acres (173 ha) perched on the edge of the Atlantic Ocean. Sit amid the orchards with a glass of wine and watch the fireball of a sun sink behind the mountains, or start the day with an orgy of fruit, fresh from the trees that surround you. If the scent of orange blossom becomes too overwhelming or the sense of pure isolation becomes too much, this gem is just 20 miles (32 km) from the hubbub of Las Palmas. **NS**

Stay at Finca Malvasia

Location Lanzarote, Canary Islands
Website www.fincamalvasia.com **Price** 💲

In the 1700s, looming volcanic cones sprayed Lanzarote with molten lava, redefining the vista into a surreal, jagged environment. To some, bedding down in a valley between two volcanic cones may not sound like a sleep-inducing experience, but British owners Tarnya and Richard Norse-Evans have created a tranquil hideaway here on the island.

Four retro-rustic cottages form an L-shape around a carved swimming pool, an oasis of gleaming white and tropical flora amid a landscape of ash-black lava. Bougainvillea clambers over the ocher rooftops, and palm trees shade the private gardens. The cottage interiors pair old with new: high-tech entertainment systems housed on bare stone shelves; terra-cotta floor tiles splashed with bright rugs; and stylish bathrooms dominated by indoor foliage. At night, the silence is overwhelming. With near-zero light pollution, the razor-sharp sky feels only a stretch away.

The hotel's relative isolation certainly does not mean there is nothing to do. Spa treatments and massages are on offer in a stone yoga yurt, sandy beaches are less than 6 miles (10 km) away, and a network of trekking trails for the more adventurous crisscrosses the region. Creative writing, cooking, and painting classes are also arranged on request. Although self-catering, organic breakfasts featuring homegrown fruits are delivered to the secluded terraces. For stocking up the fridge, a local farmers' market sells cheese, fruit, vegetables, and fresh bread every weekend. For stressed-out suits in need of some "away-from-it-all" time, couples seeking the perfect anti-resort, or artists searching for an inspirational retreat, the volcanic cones of Lanzarote's interior are the ideal subtropical escape. **JC**

Unwind at Aquapura

Location Douro Valley, Bragança to Oporto, Portugal
Website www.aquapurahotels.com **Price** ❸❸❸

The Douro River winds between the green hills of northeast Portugal. The slopes above the river are still covered with terraced vineyards as they have been for hundreds of years. This unspoiled historic valley is a World Heritage site and is famous for its port wine.

Aquapura is a luxury hotel and spa, based around a striking terra-cotta-colored mansion on the south bank of the river, facing the historic town of Peso da Régua. A chic modern glass extension holds a huge spa center. Its Asian-themed interior mixes flickering candles with dark-wood surfaces. The treatment rooms use local natural products and have huge picture windows overlooking the Douro Valley.

> *"[A] long tradition of viticulture has produced a cultural landscape of outstanding beauty."*

UNESCO World Heritage Site Committee

In the hotel restaurant, expect to find Portuguese regional specialties reinvented by a French chef. He uses local olive oils and ports for many of the sauces. Eat outside under wicker umbrellas on the patio or inside in the modern formal restaurant.

The Aquapura holds nothing back in the quest for luxury and style. The elegant and spacious bedrooms have a relaxed minimalist theme and offer twenty-four-hour, decadent in-room dining, luxurious double bathrooms, four-poster king-size beds with crisp cotton linen, and in-room spa treatments. Some have balconies overlooking the historic cloisters and, of course, the River Douro below. **SH**

Relax at Flor Da Rosa

Location Portalegre, Portugal
Website www.pousadasofportugal.com **Price** ❸❸

If you want turrets, then look no further. Although it began life as a monastery, this building seems more like a castle than a religious establishment. It was built in 1356 for the knights of the Order of Malta and was audaciously—and highly successfully—renovated by Portuguese architect Carrilho da Graca. The building is steeped in history and has magnificent vaulted ceilings and medieval cloisters.

One of the most dramatic rooms is the bar. Once the monastery's refectory, it keeps its vaulted ceilings, arched windows, and stone pillars and blends these with sleek, geometric sofas in brown leather and lime-green linen. In the bedrooms, crisp white linen-covered armchairs sit before eons-old stone walls. There are just twenty-four rooms—and most guests concur that the three in the tower are the best.

The pousada sits in a sleepy little Alentejo village, not far from Crato, which is famous for its pottery, still made in the traditional way. Also nearby is the picturesque walled town of Portalegre.

Flor Da Rosa also has a pool, on whose blue waters the imposing turrets reflect strikingly. For those who want peace and quiet, this is the perfect spot to stay and be still, to lounge by the pool in the daytime, eat in the pousada's restaurant—which serves up excellent local fare and offers wonderful views from stunningly modern panorama windows—and perhaps sip a little *vinho do porto* on a super-chic sofa before sinking into bed. For those wanting a bit more action, there is a golf course, tennis court, horseback riding, fishing, shooting, and bird watching nearby. Oh yes, and there is cable TV, wireless Internet, air-conditioning, and the rest—but then, what else would you expect from a fourteenth-century monastery? **PE**

Explore the Serra de Estrela

Location Serra de Estrela, Portugal
Website www.quintadoriodao.com/eng/out/estrela.html **Price** ◑

Soaring to a lofty 6,541 feet (1,993 m), the appropriately titled Mountains of the Stars—the tallest peaks in mainland Portugal—really do reach for the heavens. Unusually, you can get to the top quite easily because there is a paved road up to the summit plateau and the point known as the Torre (tower). Views look out as far as the sea, about 100 miles (160 km) away.

A massive granite ridge stretching for more than 60 miles (100 km) and with more than half its area set at over 2,300 feet (700 m), this is a truly awesome showcase of what nature can accomplish. Strangely shaped crags, deep gorges, rushing mountain streams, and placid lakes pepper the unique landscape.

> *"Near [its] top there was said to be a lake in which the wrecks of ships floated up to the surface."*
>
> Herman Melville, *Moby Dick*

The Mondego—the longest river flowing entirely within Portuguese territory—has its headwaters here, as do the Alva and the Zêzere. A protected nature park, the range has a thriving ski resort at Loriga and gives its name to a hardy breed of dog, a type of smoked sausage, and a tasty hard cheese.

There is abundant wildlife and a wonderland of waterfalls, woods, and mysterious caves. The bears are gone, and wolves are now extremely rare, but you will likely meet otters, water voles, and many rare birds. **RsP**

⮕ *The small and picturesque village of Belver sits on the Tagus river in the Serra de Estrela.*

Unwind at Penha Longa

Location Near Lisbon, Portugal
Website www.penhalonga.com   **Price** ⑤⑤

"The building is a graceful palazzo-style structure set among rolling hills, clear lakes, and lush gardens."

New York Times

Only a short drive from Lisbon, this hotel feels like it is in a different world. Your first glimpse is likely to be the Penha Longa itself, the long rock that inspired monks to build a monastery here in the belief it was a holy site. Today the place still exudes much of the peace from its secular days, and the fourteenth-century monastery still stands—you can even arrange to get married in the small chapel there.

Close to this ancient building, and before the modern hotel, you will find the Asian-inspired spa where guests are served fruit teas and may lounge beside water features inside or out while waiting for or recovering from a treatment such as the seaweed wrap. If you can tear yourself away from here, there is a fabulous pool to wallow in, overlooking the expansive greenery of the Atlantic golf course. Then there is the elegant 194-room hotel. It currently has four different restaurants, including Serra, by the pool, and Midori, offering Japanese cuisine. The newest addition is Arola, where chef Julio Pereira creates Portuguese cuisine with a contemporary twist. Breakfast is served in Assa Massa or the club lounge, with an array of fresh fruit, muesli, breads, and a fantastic selection of homemade preserves to choose from, reminiscent of the best kind of delicatessen.

The broad balcony of the club lounge is situated in the perfect spot to offer the best view of the sun rising over the surrounding hills, so sit back, dig in, and watch the holy Penha Longa rock slowly illuminate with the early rays of the sun. **JED**

↖ *The blue agapanthus, or Lily of the Nile, planted in front of Penha Longa give off a wonderful scent.*

Experience
Lapa Palace

Location Lisbon, Portugal
Website www.lapapalace.com **Price** 💲💲💲

Lapa Palace was originally built in 1870 for the Count of Valenças. Its elegant pink facade and inner combinations of marble stucco, carved wood, and beautiful azulejos tiles have been lovingly cared for over its years of private ownership. Since opening as a hotel in 1992, Lapa Palace has won accolades galore, and it is not difficult to see why.

The hotel's central Lisbon location amid beatific gardens, streams, and ornamental fountains is on a hill that allows both easy access to the city center and exceptional views of the Tagus river. Some 109 rooms are available, with even the most standard enjoying terraces or balconies, reproductions of French and English furniture, marble bathrooms (some with bas-relief and whirlpool tub), and classic eighteenth-century design. Twenty-two individually decorated palace rooms and suites feature restored antiques from the original palace, and the fourteen Italianate villa rooms situated in the former stables have their own private gardens—perfect for whiling away the southern European warm evening sunshine.

The hotel has attracted its fair share of high-profile guests, most of whom are drawn to the Royal Suite, with its pastel rococo styling, or the honeymooners' favorite, the Tower Room, which has an Elvis-style pop-up TV at the end of the bed, a two-person whirlpool tub, and a private turret to dine in. After a workout in the wellness center or the heated pool, have one of the fifty varieties of tea in the Rio Tejo bar. The in-house restaurant Cipriani is regarded as one of the best restaurants in Lisbon and has an excellent reputation for its contemporary cuisine. All in all, it is aristocratic quality you can count on. **PS**

Recharge at
Palácio Belmonte

Location Lisbon, Portugal
Website www.palaciobelmonte.com **Price** 💲💲

When Maria and Frédéric Coustols bought Palácio Belmonte, it was a crumbling building in need of restoration. Several years and millions of euros later, it is now a ten-suite hotel and a classified National Monument, mere cobblestones away from São Jorge Castle in the old Jewish medieval quarter of Alfama.

Although the owners have introduced some modern touches, perfectly preserved nineteenth-century bathtubs and original blue and white tiles are just some of the older features. The suites, all named after prominent Portuguese individuals (ecologists, writers, inventors, and so on) are appointed with genuine

> *"Made from the shell of a former count's palácio, the Belmonte is still fit for nobility."*
>
> *Condé Nast Traveler*

eighteenth-century furnishings: mirrors, armoires, canvases, and drawings. Romantics may want to request the Bartolomeu de Gusmão Suite, on top of one of the Moorish towers with its own terrace overlooking Alfama and the Tagus river.

The garden completes the hotel's charm—an Eden of whitewashed walls, fruit trees, and bougainvillea. The black marble swimming pool is another talking point, as is the library, which holds more than 4,000 books and publications in a variety of languages. The Belmonte even has its own chapel. An all-around cultural experience as well as a chic luxury destination, Palácio Belmonte is a once in a lifetime indulgence. **PS**

Stay at the Ritz

Location Lisbon, Portugal
Website www.fourseasons.com/lisbon **Price** 💲💲

If it is luxury with a capital "L" you are after, it does not get much better than Lisbon's Ritz. At first glance the hotel may seem like one of Lisbon's many period buildings, but it is its interior details that stand out.

The hotel is built on one of Lisbon's seven hills, and the views across many of the city's well-known landmarks (including Edward VII Park, St. George's Castle, and the Tagus river) are immensely impressive. Once inside, the public areas do not fail to seduce: a riot of tapestries, paintings, and antique reproductions, including pieces commissioned by Portuguese artists of the period. The accommodation features suites that are enormous and beautifully furnished with marble

> ## "[The] suites boast the finest decoration you'll see in any major Portuguese hotel."
>
> *New York Times*

bathrooms, large mahogany canopied beds, antique satinwood dressing tables, and very plush carpeting.

The hotel restaurant, Varanda, is one of Lisbon's top dining spots and consequently manages to attract the city's glitterati. The lounge bar has a great terrace that overlooks the park. On the subject of fantastic views, even ardent relaxation aficionados might want to take a peek at the rooftop gym, which boasts a running track with wonderful 360-degree views of the city, before popping back down to the in-house spa, a Zen-inspired creation with great steam baths, foot massages, blissful treatments, and changing rooms with heated limestone floors. **PS**

See Jerónimos Monastery

Location Lisbon, Portugal
Website www.mosteirojeronimos.pt **Price** 💲

For a sense of peace close to some of Lisbon's most popular tourist attractions, the sixteenth-century Jerónimos Monastery in the Belém quarter is unbeatable. Although most tourists flock to the nearby Antiga Confeitaria de Belém to feast on pastries, or head to the riverside to explore dramatic edifices such as the Monument of the Discoveries, the monastery is large enough to swallow up crowds of curious tourists without losing any of its overwhelming serenity.

Corridors spiral around each other, unfolding into rooms where you will find the tombs of poet Fernando Pessoa and historian Alexandre Herculano, along with those of hundreds of Jerome monks. Other paths lead into the central apex where the only roof is the sky, seemingly held up by pinnacled towers. Every surface is pure white stone embellished by the imaginations of sailors who paused here to pray before setting out on endless voyages. Those who returned gave thanks in the form of fantastical depictions of their travels: the things they saw or dreamed up while overseas.

The monastery captures the state of mind of these brave adventurers, and among their fairy tales you will find scenes from the Bible. Noah's ark is a particularly fine example, with hordes of animals spilling over the bows of an archaic ship, not unlike the flimsy vessels in which the sailors searched for new worlds.

The church here still hosts Mass, and sitting in the rear of the church listening to the murmuring Portuguese is sure to lull you. Just be careful not to fall asleep. Who knows what kind of dreams you might have in this magical place? **JED**

⮕ *The structure seems strangely organic, as though the place has grown from the earth rather than been built.*

Visit Nossa Senhora Do Monte

Location Lisbon, Portugal   **Website** www.golisbon.com
Price ◐

Lisbon is built on seven hills. On the brow of the highest stands Nossa Senhora do Monte, Our Lady of the Hill. Dressed in white, with one hand slightly raised in benediction, she gazes upon the red rooftops of the city and the waters of the Tagus river beyond. Behind her stands her chapel, which was originally built in 1243. It is on the site where the first bishop of Lisbon, São Gens, was martyred in the fourth century C.E.

Around the chapel, a viewpoint (Miradouro) has been thoughtfully landscaped. There are pretty, tiled, terraced areas and benches beneath the trees. Shift your gaze to the left and you will see the fabulous crenellations of the Castelo de São Jorge. The castle is just a short walk from the Miradouro and well worth a visit, too. Here you can climb the towers and walk along the ramparts. Grab a coffee and sit at one of the restaurant's outside tables and you will be rewarded with yet more incredible views across the city.

If you cannot bear to climb up here (it is about a thirty-minute hike from the city center), take the number 28 tram. Lisbon's trams are famous for their retro design, and the number 28 route, which tours the city's hills, is one of the highlights of any trip.

Locals say that the best time of day to come up to the Miradouro is at sunset. In good weather, the sky turns deep blue, then melds into a dusky pink where it meets the dark, inky waters of the Tagus. Our Lady of the Hill shines brightly, illuminated in her own glass sanctuary, while far below the lights of the city twinkle yellow and orange in the warm Lisbon twilight. **PE**

→ *Nossa Senhora do Monte sits atop Portugal's highest hill—it's a steep walk to get there, but well worth it.*

Stay at Pousada de Estremoz

Location Évora, Portugal
Website www.pousadas.pt **Price** $

Estremoz is a former garrison town on the Spanish–Portuguese border, whose raison d'être was to prevent incursions by the detested Spanish. There are still plenty of soldiers around, billeted in the many old convents built in white marble extracted from local quarries. The pousada Rainha Santa Isabel in Estremoz is lodged in a royal palace next to an impressive fourteenth-century keep in the upper town, with its star-shaped ramparts inspired by the French military engineer Vauban. At 1,300 feet (395 m) above sea level, there are magnificent views toward Elvas, Évora, and Badajoz, across the border, which can be enjoyed in full from the private palace gardens.

The palace was built for the wife of King D. Diniz, and the saintly Queen Isabel died here in 1336. It was first opened as a hotel in the 1960s. On the first floor of the keep there is a vaulted octagonal room. There are period features and fabulous antiques everywhere, including ancient four-poster beds, as well as an array of armor and ancient weapons in the plush bar. The food is simple Alentejano fare: bread soups called *migas*, the Portuguese *arroz* (a sort of paella with shellfish), and sun-dried Elvas plums.

In Estremoz, there is a huge central *praça* where lively markets are held on Saturdays. Look out in particular for the rough sheepskin waistcoats and traditional slippers worn by shepherds, characteristic terra-cotta pottery, and ewes' milk cheeses. The local antiques shops have been known to stock rare gems, such as eighteenth-century English pewter. It is also worth visiting the museum of Alentejo, the church of the Convent of São Francisco, and the other buildings of the royal castle complex. **GMD**

Unwind at Monte do Chora Cascas

Location Évora, Portugal
Website www.wonderfulland.com **Price** $ $

Blissful isolation can be found at the end of a long road winding through the Portuguese countryside where a traditional farmhouse has been restored by owner and architect Sónia Estima Marques and transformed into an intimate country hotel.

With only seven rooms, identified by color rather than number, there is not a chance of feeling swamped in the way you might in a huge hotel. Furnished with cast-iron beds, bright walls, and crisp white linen, Monte do Chora Cascas oozes understated style. The wooden ceilings are a reminder of its origins, with lavish bathrooms bringing it bang up to date.

> *"It is currently the reflection of enormous dedication and strong emotional investment."*

Proprietors, Monte do Chora Cascas

The large public living room has plump sofas to sink into, a baby grand piano in the corner, Chinese woodcarvings, and delicate glass vases overflowing with fresh flowers. Wander outside to find a pretty courtyard, lush gardens to explore, and wonderful views across the valley to the town of Montemor, sitting on the side of a hill. Lie back on a lounger by the pool with a glass of *vinho verde* in hand and soak it all up. If you crave something a little more strenuous, head to the tennis court. There are also bicycles to take out, and there's even a tree house for children. For a memorable day trip, take a stroll around Montemor, with its eighteenth-century manor houses. **AD**

Stay at Pousada Vila Viçosa

Location Évora, Portugal
Website www.pousadasofportugal.com **Price** 💲💲

Portuguese pousadas are a network of state-owned hotels occupying historic buildings, decorated to reflect the culture and heritage of their region. The Pousada Vila Viçosa (also called Hotel Dom João IV) is one of the finest—set in the sixteenth-century Convento das Chagas de Cristo in the charming old town of Vila Viçosa. The town was once the royal seat of the kings of Portugal. The convent stands on the grand main square, next to the former royal residence: the Paço Ducal. In the center of the marble square is a huge statue of Dom João IV on horseback, the first king of the House of Braganza.

Vila Viçosa is famous for its marble quarries, so it is no surprise to find the pousada's reception area dominated by cool white marble—although the preserved nuns' latrines alongside diminish the sense of grandeur somewhat. Wander through the ancient corridors and you will find that the floors become stone, and then wooden in the bedrooms. Marble is reserved for staircases and bathrooms.

It is not only the history of the hotel that attracts its guests—you will find a small gym up a narrow stone spiral staircase and a large outdoor pool. There is also a courtyard where guests eat in the summer and cloisters to sit in the shade. The peaceful garden has orange trees, vines, and lavender bushes.

Guests may relax on velvet sofas by the open fireplace in the grand sitting room under a domed ceiling, or chat in the bar, with leather-topped tables and framed equestrian prints. The pousada itself may not be a museum, but next door you can browse a fine collection of porcelain, tiles, and tapestries in the impressive Paço Ducal. **SH**

Unwind at Pousada Dos Loios

Location Évora, Portugal
Website www.pousadas.pt **Price** 💲💲

One of Portugal's most beautiful hotels is the former monastery of St. John the Baptist founded in 1485. The magnificence of the manueline, gothic building is revealed only once you pass through the relatively simple baroque facade. The monastery was disbanded in 1834 and the building put to various uses, including housing conscripts, but in 1965 it became one of Portugal's historic state inns, or *pousadas*.

The guests sleep in thirty-one well-appointed monks' cells. There is no longer communal washing in the lavatorium, however—every third cell has been divided in two to make bathrooms for the rooms on

> *"Loios is reliving history itself in each stone, each glance, and each object."*

distinctiveportugal.com

either side. The dining room is on the lower level of the two-story former cloister, next to the sacristy, with its stunning, double-horseshoe manueline door. The restaurant offers Alentajano specialties, such as *Porco preto* (Iberico) ham, and typical desserts (*morgado*) include *pao de rala* (grated bread with big chunks of sweetened pumpkin). Naturally the emphasis is on the red and white wines of the Alentejo region. Splash out and try Pera Manca, Évora's most prestigious wine.

Staying at Dos Loios gives visitors a chance to explore the World Heritage site of Évora. Its whitewashed buildings covered in blue tiles suggest very little has changed here since the eighteenth century. **GMD**

Explore the Tagus Valley

Location Castelo Branco to Lisbon, Portugal
Website www.portugal.org/tourism/regions3.shtml **Price** ●●

The Tagus is a river. Not just any river though; many would say it is probably one of the most important rivers in the whole Iberian region. It begins in Spain and ends in Portugal, where it becomes the Tejo, but that is just the start of the story. It forms the natural border between the two countries for more than 29 miles (47 km); it is the heart and soul of Lisbon, one of the most beautiful cities in the world; it provides both countries with drinking water; and its wetlands, in the eastern side of central Portugal in the Reserva Natural do Estuario do Tejo, are home to more than 40,000 birds encompassing some 154 different species.

The park is an area of outstanding beauty and has been the must-see destination for bird-watchers for centuries. Imagine sitting under a shady tree looking down onto the Tagus glistening in the valley below and watching majestic eagles gliding around above, or spotting colonies of the distinctive Black Stork, the park's symbol, wading in the lush marshes.

There are more than 100 square miles (259 sq km) of park to explore, and whether you are walking, bicycling, or simply taking a leisurely drive, you will absorb the visual feast and commit it to memory. In addition, following the route of the Tagus are some of the most picturesque towns and villages in Portugal, and two of the best are the medieval walled town of Obidos and the UNESCO World Heritage site that is Sintra. Strolling around the ramparts in Obidos, you will take in the terra-cotta roofs over little whitewashed houses lining narrow cobblestone streets. Sintra is a fairy-tale mix of palaces, gorges, and woodland. **AM**

→ *The Monastery of San Juan de los Reyes sits next to the San Martin Bridge that crosses the Tagus river.*

Explore Alcácer do Sal

Location Setúbal, Portugal
Website www.pousadasofportugal.com **Price** 🎟️🎟️

There are pousadas in unique settings all over Portugal. They normally offer a chance to learn about the country from owners who are friendly, interesting, and full of local stories. Some pousadas are in old historic monuments; others are totally modern. Pousada Dom Alfonso II, in Alácer do Sal, is a bit of both.

The hotel stands within the imposing stone walls of a castle with a history dating back 5,000 years. The castle is high on an escarpment overlooking an ancient village and beautiful river valley. A leading Portuguese architect was employed to convert the old turreted castle into a hotel with modern facilities. The knights of yesteryear would not recognize their stronghold now—there is a pool with underwater lighting for evening swims and a spectacular illuminated glass cube in the center of the colonnaded courtyard. It is that mix of old and new that makes this *pousada* so interesting: the chic parasols and sun loungers next to the old bare stone ramparts; old wooden window shutters against the clean lines of modern furniture and polished wood floors; and, amid bright white pillars, a fine high-ceilinged restaurant featuring traditional regional specialties such as Sado fish soup, tomato rice with fried eel, lamb stew with cream, and local egg pudding.

Guests spend their days here enjoying a range of activities, including canoeing on the river below the castle, strolling along the paths of the Sado estuary, venturing up in a hot-air balloon, or enjoying the sandy beaches of the Troia peninsula. Alcácer do Sal itself is a pretty village with plenty of cafés and craft shops among the ancient streets, medieval houses, and old churches of Muslim origin. It is a perfect place for a day's exploring. **SH**

Discover Monchique

Location Faro, Portugal
Website www.monchiquetermas.com **Price** 🎟️🎟️

People have been visiting the small mountain town of Monchique, set cozily in the saddle between the Picota and Foia peaks, since Roman times. They come to "take the waters" that emerge from natural springs at a constant temperature of 89.6°F (32°C), and with a pungent aroma of sulfur.

Kings of Portugal and Italy, and a host of celebrities, have made the health-seeking pilgrimage, and commercially marketed bottles of Monchique water grace respectable dining tables far from the source. However, this town of 10,000 people has somehow managed to stay virtually untouched by the waves of mass tourism that have beset the nearby coast.

> *"Monchique has been a spa at least since Roman times . . . its tasty water is the best in the Algarve."*

Paul Lewis, *New York Times*

Picturesque, steep, cobbled streets; mysteriously shaded doorways; and the tucked-away workshops and studios of artists and craftspeople create a truly spellbinding ambience. The far-reaching panoramic views from the dilapidated seventeenth-century Franciscan monastery encapsulate and evoke the true spirit of rural Portugal.

Among the colorful gardens and verdant woods, seek out the sophisticated retreat of the Hotel Villa Termal das Termas de Monchique. It has been lavishly refurbished and now boasts all modern amenities yet is time-warped in a more leisurely age. The nearest beach is only 11 miles (18 km) away. **RsP**

Taste Madeira at Blandy's

Location Madeira, Portugal
Website www.symingtonfamilyestates.com/winelodge   **Price** $

Honey and raisin, caramel and vanilla, toffee, lemon, and lime. With a list of flavors such as these, you would be forgiven for thinking that you were about to choose a dessert rather than browse the tasting notes in an atmospheric wine cellar.

The centuries-old Blandy's winery is tucked behind the promenade of the Madeiran capital, Funchal. This former Franciscan monastery is suffused with a liquor-laden haze, and the much-trampled stones of the atmospheric courtyards and cellars lead you first through a museum history of the island's tipple and then sit you down to savor a drop yourself.

Legend has it that this fortified wine was developed entirely by accident, when a forgotten case baked inside a ship during a long sea journey to the Americas. On its return, the liquor was found to have "burned" to a mellow deliciousness that sent the vintners scurrying off to roll all their barrels into the Madeiran warmth. Today, the wines are more simply heated to high temperatures in a process known as *estufagem*.

Bottles and barrels line the cobweb-strewn walls, and much is made of the fact that although the grapes are grown and pressed out on the volcanic slopes of this beautiful Atlantic island, it is the time spent in wooden casks in the wineries of Funchal that allows the nuances of age and oak to develop.

Pull up a stool at the bar in the main tasting cellar where a selection of young Madeiras will be poured out for you to try. From Sercial, the driest and the lightest of the wines, to the rich and sweet Malmsey, there is a Madeira for everyone. **SWi**

↗ *Depending on how far your wallet stretches, you can taste Madeiras going back several decades—or more.*

"The vintage was 1803 . . . and it was still fresh and vibrant . . . a window into another time."

Junior Vianna, Master of Wine

Stay at Reid's Palace

Location Madeira, Portugal
Website www.reidspalace.com **Price** $ $

"Winston Churchill retreated to the hotel to lick his wounds after losing office."

Adrian Mourby, *Independent*

Reid's Palace is a piece of living history. It was here, in the mimosa-scented air, that Winston Churchill painted and wrote his war memoirs and playwright George Bernard Shaw learned the tango. Both renowned men loved the often overlooked island of Madeira, a sparkling gem in the Atlantic Ocean.

As its name suggests, Reid's Palace is a royal destination. The atmosphere is glamorous and the clifftop setting gives a privileged view over the Bay of Funchal. It is hardly surprising that the caliber of guests since the hotel opened in 1891 more than matches the mood. Captain Scott called in 1901, en route to the Antarctic; newlyweds Rita Hayworth and Prince Aly Khan sought privacy beyond its walls in 1949; and Cuban dictator General Fulgencio Batista and his entourage took up residence after his defeat by Fidel Castro in 1959. But whether royalty or regular folk, each guest is treated with uncommon courtesy.

The elegant hotel is set among 10 acres (4 ha) of dense, beautiful, subtropical gardens and, although only a leisurely walk away from Funchal's shops and restaurants, a sense of complete peace pervades. Restful days are spent sitting by one of the three pools, unwinding at the ocean-view spa, and dining at the excellent restaurants, not forgetting to enjoy a dignified afternoon tea with all the trimmings—a signature Reid's Palace tradition. The tranquil setting and views conspire to make visitors reluctant to leave the palace's grounds, and if you use your imagination you can almost picture Winston Churchill having tea on the terrace in the afternoon light. **LP**

⬉ *Reid's Palace has spectacular views over the Bay of Funchal and its dramatic cliffs.*

Relax at Choupana Hills

Location Madeira, Portugal
Website www.choupanahills.com **Price** 💲💲

Some hotels are all about the gastronomy or the spa. Although both of these are outstanding at Choupana Hills Resort and Spa, the emphasis here is firmly on the views. The drive to Choupana Hills from Funchal leads past orange groves with trees leaning at astonishingly crooked angles because of the steepness of the road. Do not be surprised if your ears pop, or if you pass one of the hardy locals hiking up the hill without so much as pausing to catch their breath.

At the hotel's reception, dark gleaming wood and discreet Tibetan artwork lead the eye to an immense window, running from the floor to the peaked ceiling, revealing a sweeping view of the hillside dotted with

---

"Guests breathe in eucalyptus-scented breezes while admiring the view of the ocean."

Town and Country Travel magazine

---

eucalyptus trees and, far below, the picturesque curve of Funchal Harbor. This is nothing compared to the views from the rooms, however.

Each bungalow is designed to make the most of its individual vista, so you can lounge on your private balcony and drink it in, or gaze through the immense glass patio doors from your bed. Even the shower's frosted glass ends at the perfect height to allow you to admire the view. The only time you will see another soul is if you visit the Xôpana restaurant, venture to the indoor or outdoor pool, or take advantage of the turndown service. Otherwise, you can hide away and revel in the feeling of absolute seclusion. **JED**

Enjoy Quintinha de São João

Location Madeira, Portugal
Website www.quintinhasaojoao.com **Price** 💲💲

Arriving at Estalagem Quintinha de São João feels more like coming home than checking into a hotel. Located on a discreet side street close to the center of Madeira's capital city, Funchal, the hotel has the air of the home of friends with impeccable taste, enhanced by the warm welcome from reception staff. That there are only forty-three rooms adds to this, so by the time you walk into your room, you feel like one of the family.

This is the perfect place to relax between bouts of sightseeing, with spacious balconies overlooking the rooftop pool, gardens, and surrounding hillsides. The pool opens early, so a swim is a great way to wake up, followed by sumptuous breakfast served in the A Morgadinha restaurant. If you prefer more privacy, arrange to have croissants, cereal, fruit, and coffee brought to your room and wait for the caffeine to kick in. Each room has a spacious living area; suites have separate living space and bedrooms with a balcony opening out from each so you can choose where to relax. You can have a masseuse come to your room, or visit the hotel's spa with three treatment rooms plus whirlpool tub, a sauna, and hammam steam bath.

If you do not feel like leaving the hotel, there are plenty of comfortable, shady corners in the garden, as well as comfortable nooks with fat armchairs, tables, and sofas where you can read quietly, plug in your laptop to catch up on your e-mail, or else write those long overdue postcards.

In the evening, sample some cocktails in the Vasco da Gama bar or ask general manager André Barreto to have a romantic meal served to you in the gardens, beneath an arbor of sweetly scented jasmine blooms. By the time the stars come out, you may well decide that you never want to leave. **JED**

Swim with Dolphins

Location Pico, Azores
Website www.dolphinconnectionexperience.com **Price** $

On the volcanic island of Pico in the Portuguese Azores, you can be inches away from dolphins and whales feeding in the warm and unpolluted currents of the Gulf Stream each summer. Pico is one of the most naturally beautiful places on the planet, attracting scientists, divers, and photographers to marvel at the resplendent green landscape, clear blue sulfur volcanic rock, and fascinating marine life.

A former world-famous whale-hunting location, the tranquil fishing village of Lajes do Pico is now a dolphin and whale hot spot. When whale hunting was banned in the 1980s, islanders began taking tourists out on boats from the Espaço Talassa (whale-watching center). By adopting the honed skill of the "Vigia" (the original whale hunters), along with modern sonar, the guides can track down schools of up to 200 dolphins.

The Dolphin Connection is an environmentally conscious company offering swimming-with-dolphin vacations to rebalance, rejuvenate, and change your life forever. Don your wetsuit and speed out to sea on a hard-hulled boat to spot calm, peaceful Rissos and Sperm Whales. Slip into crystal clear water to lie on the surface while Bottlenose dolphins dance beneath you, or splash about with Spotted dolphins as they cut through waves at extraordinary speed, and get high on hormones released by the brain after the exciting dolphin encounter. When you are not in the water cavorting with cetaceans, wander around Pico, where baroque churches, tiny squares, cobbled streets, and quaint buildings reveal a land and lifestyle that is untouched, unhurried, and calm. **SD**

← *Encountering a school of dolphins in the wild is one of the highlights of a trip to Pico.*

Discover Casa Dos Barcos

Location San Miguel, Azores
Website www.casadosbarcos.com **Price** $ $

Fly to the middle of the Atlantic, land on a small volcanic island, and head into the forested hills. On the lush southern shores of a lake, formed by the crater of an extinct volcano, stands an elegant historic boathouse, available to rent by the night.

Casa dos Barcos stands beside Lagoa das Furnas, the most beautiful natural sight on San Miguel island. It is about an hour's drive from Ponta Delgada, the island's main town, and 3 miles (5 km) from the village of Furnas, famed for its hot springs, "caldeiras" (geysers), thermal baths, natural warm-water swimming pool, and stately parks and gardens. The Casa is part of a nineteenth-century estate created by

"Furnas is a picturesque village inside a huge crater ... [with] lush vegetation and thermal springs."

Cathy Packe, *Independent*

José do Canto, a local aristocrat, who employed leading botanical, landscape, and architectural firms from London and Paris. Behind the Flemish-style boathouse are landscaped gardens with paths, streams, and exotic plants. It has become famed for the walks through old camellia trees that flower spectacularly between December and March. Just along the sandy shoreline is the estate's gothic chapel.

Guests at the Casa can use free canoes and bicycles, and there are stables close by. Other highlights include the man-made, hot-water swimming pool in the Parque Terra Nostra in Furnas and the steaming caldeiras on the opposite shore of the lake. **SH**

Hike Through Vikos Gorge

Location Vikos-Aoos National Park, Greece
Website www.meteo.noa.gr/Primavera/index.htm **Price** ❶

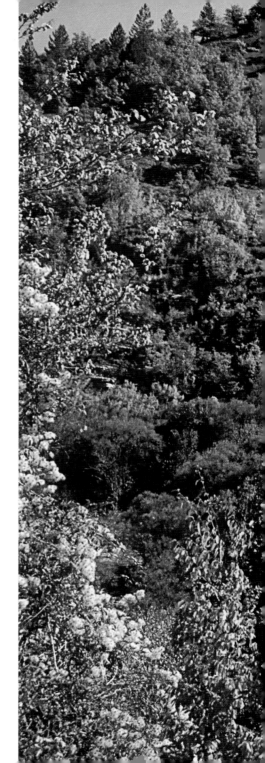

There is a lot more to Greece than sun-drenched islands and ancient ruins. The Vikos-Aoos National Park in northern Greece includes the extraordinary Vikos Gorge: one of the natural wonders of the world. It is 7 miles (12 km) long and is officially categorized as the deepest gorge in the world, with limestone walls more than a mile high. It runs along the Voidomatis River and you can hike right through it.

The ancient trails of mule caravans and nomadic shepherds will take you along the gorge, climbing steep paths to villages and chapels along the way. Sometimes the path follows a ledge winding up through broad-leaved forests; other times a cobbled trail will cling to the banks of the river. The park is an unspoiled 49 square miles (126 sq km) of forests, mountains, and remote villages. Hikers will discover springs, gorges, pine forests, rocky pinnacles, river pools, wildflowers, lakes, and ancient stone bridges. If you are lucky, you may spot bears, boars, foxes, trout, and deer. In spring, you may find yourself tramping through huge swaths of wild-growing crocuses.

There are serious peaks in the park, such as Gamila at 8,192 feet (2,497 m). Trek up here to find Drakolimni —the Dragon Lake—and breathtaking views. Farther into the Pindos Mountains are monasteries perched on impossibly steep pinnacles. Despite the old stone paths, hiking is challenging and strenuous. Respite is provided by gentle Alpine-style pastures and tiny traditional villages of slate houses and farms. Visitors can stay in small family hotels or village pensions. Rooms are clean, comfortable, and very cheap. **SH**

→ *The Vikos-Aoos National Park offers some of the most dramatic and rewarding hiking in Europe.*

Discover Meteora

Location Thessaly, Greece   **Website** http://odysseus.culture.gr
Price ◐

As you pass the village of Kalambaka, prepare for an unexpected sight. Rising out of the ground like a series of giant stalagmites are towering rock formations, framing the horizon with their unearthly presence.

As if this natural wonder were not enough, you soon discover that their peaks house a cluster of settlements, an architectural miracle in itself. Their history dates back to ascetics of the eleventh century who first dwelled in caves and huts. Yet food, supplies, and even people were eventually ferried up there using a system of ropes, ladders, and pulleys.

Scientists believe that the rock towers were once part of a vast inland sea, later shaped and formed by earthquakes and the elements. Poets, thinkers, and travelers have all come here to reflect both on the spirituality of this area and the sanctity of the monasteries. Today, the six buildings that are still functioning contain beautiful religious art, frescoes, mosaics, and paintings, which show the dedication of the monks and nuns to their way of life. Although access to some places, like the Great Meteoron and Agia Triada, requires myriad steep steps, others like Varlaam and Roussanou can be accessed by bridge. This has prompted plenty of tour buses and souvenir stalls, but most monks are happy to have a chat with visitors, and the nuns sometimes offer sweets as you relax in the shady courtyard. When you have visited the museums inside, outside the views of the green hillsides and snowcapped mountains in the distance make this a place in which to reflect on the ways of the modern world—and take a glimpse into the past. **JW**

◁ *It remains a mystery how the Byzantine monks built the monasteries in this seemingly inaccessible spot.*

Discover Argentikon

Location Chios, Greece   **Website** www.argentikon.gr
Price ◐◐◐

This site has been dedicated to luxury for hundreds of years. Behind its high stone walls and heavy bronze-studded gates, Argentikon was the summer residence of the Argenti, a wealthy Genoese family who came to administer this distant Mediterranean island colony in the Middle Ages. The green valley of Kambos was the prettiest, most sheltered part of the island—now known for its walled orchards—and the Genoese aristocrats built their villas there. Chios has long since returned to the ownership of Greece, but Argentikon still stands as a monument to a wealthy colonial past.

Among the period buildings, there are now just eight suites. Guests will find exposed beams, frescoed

> *"Chios is so unique, so genuinely odd, that at times you don't feel like you are in Greece at all."*
>
> Jonathan Futrell, *Guardian*

ceilings, and Venetian furnishings inside. The rooms are more like museums than hotel accommodation. The bedrooms have fireplaces, marble bathrooms, and balconies. There is a spa, sauna, massage room (in the old chicken house), outdoor swimming pool, and gardens lush with palm trees, roses, and citrus groves and dotted with carved marble. The fertile estate is useful in other ways, too. The kitchen uses plenty of the fresh vegetables and fruit for its menus, complementing the fish bought straight from the quaysides of Chios. You can also drink wine that has come from the estate's own vineyards, and even eat marmalade made from its own orange groves. **SH**

Explore Hydra

Location Hydra, Greece **Website** www.hydra.com.gr
Price ❶

Only 38 miles (70 km) from the busy port of Piraeus, this gorgeous island has a pretty port town crammed with donkeys and cafés. It has always been a place of maritime success. At its zenith, during the eighteenth and nineteenth centuries, Hydra had the most successful commercial fleet in Greece; it even ran the blockade during the Napoleonic Wars. When Greece rose up against the Turks in 1821, the wealthy maritime merchants—responsible for building all the wonderful mansions, or *arondika*, of Hydra town—rose up, too, converting their merchant ships into battleships.

Later, in the 1950s, the writers and artists started coming—and have never stopped. Many, such as Leonard Cohen, have become semipermanent fixtures, lavishing money and loving care in the restoration of the old sea merchants' homes, or in the creation of galleries, museums, and shops.

One of the many simple joys of Hydra is the fact that all motorized vehicles are banned. Water taxis are available to whisk you off to various beaches and tavernas dotted around the coast, or you can simply use your legs or rent a bike.

Hydra is wonderful for walking. Start with a climb up to the Mansion of Lazaros Koundouriotis, once the home of a wealthy merchant, now the home of the Historical and Folk Museum and the public art gallery. A strenuous walk to the Profitis Ilias monastery and Agias Evpraxias nunnery will reward you with views of the Peloponnesus. Boundouri is a path that leaves the port toward the fishing village of Kamini; it is magical at night, with its own small, delightful harbor. **LB**

→ *Hydra rises amphitheatrically above its harbor like a romantic whitewashed stage set.*

Explore Lycabettus Hill

Location Athens, Greece **Website** www.tourtripgreece.gr
Price 🔴

Athens is the ultimate city of contrasts in its relentless concrete sprawl, traffic chaos, ancient monuments of soaring beauty, and wonderfully atmospheric streets. Every day, hordes of tourists make the trek up Acropolis Hill, as much to look out over the metropolis as to enjoy the Parthenon. If you can linger a little longer, consider Lycabettus Hill, a patch of pine-studded wilderness in the dusty city which, at 909 feet (277 m), offers a wonderful panorama of the Acropolis, most of Athens, and across to Piraeus and the Saronic Gulf.

Ancient mythology says that Athena created Lycabettus when she hurled a missile at the daughters of King Cecrops in a fit of pique, but missed, and created the hill instead. Although most tourists access Acropolis Hill from the chaotic streets of Monastiraki or Plaka, Lycabettus is in the middle of Kolonaki, whose broader and wealthier streets offer a calmer vibe. It is possible to drive to the summit, but better to take the funicular railway, which departs every half an hour from the corner of Aristippou and Ploutarchou Streets in Kolonaki. Alternatively, there are three options for actually walking up the hill: the gentle circular route (Sarantapichou), the steep Ploutarchou, or the even steeper woodland paths that snake to the top.

At the top, you will find the eighteenth-century Agios Georgios, a modest church. At midnight on Good Friday, Athenians appear in large numbers to watch the procession of the Easter flame from here. On the way, you will also see a beautiful open-air amphitheater that overlooks the city. After a sunset drink at Orizondes, the restaurant at the peak, or Prasini Tenta, the informal café halfway down, make your descent through the shade of the pines, back into a land of sirens, horns, and frenetic activity. **LB**

Stay at Porto Zante

Location Zakynthos, Greece **Website** www.portozante.com
Price 🟢🟢

A hidden treasure lies on the unspoiled island of Zakynthos, just west of Greece's mainland. Tucked away in a secluded bay, Porto Zante De Luxe Villas occupy a sandy slice of private beach in the area of Tragaki, on the island nicknamed Flower of the East by the Venetians who ruled it during the Middle Ages.

The boutique-style, all-villa hotel makes the most of the natural beauty of its surroundings, decorated thoughtfully with luxurious furnishings and paintings by prominent Greek artists. There are several types of villa, the most indulgent being the four-bedroom Imperial Spa Villa with a heated pool and in-room spa. Many of the villas have private pools and gardens and

---

"Even just arriving here is luxurious, with limousine transfer included to and from the airport."

Condé Nast Traveler

---

occupy heavenly spots on the seafront; each is finished with luxurious touches such as sumptuous bedding, Bulgari toiletries, and Valentino bathrobes.

There is just enough here to keep guests quietly occupied: The Club House restaurant whips up tasty Greek specialties with a modern slant, there are thalasso therapy treatments in the spa fit for island beauties, or you can devour a book while swaying peacefully in your poolside hammock. The more adventurous visitors can also charter a yacht. **LP**

➡ *With a view like this to sit at all day long at Smugglers' Cove by Porto Zante Villas, why go anywhere else?*

Experience Pelion

Location Pelion, Greece   **Website** www.pelion.gr   **Price** 🌓

Some call the Pelion region of Greece "The Mountain of Four Seasons," and it is not hard to see why. Situated west of Skiathos, Pelion is a mountainous peninsula flanked by the Pagasetic Gulf to the east and the warm waters of the Aegean Sea to the west. In an area of just 78 acres (31 ha), the landscape switches from coastal villages to dense forest, to a peak of 5,000 feet (1,500 m). In summer, there are myriad trails and nature walks through thick glades of beech, oak, maple, and chestnut trees. In winter, you can ski while looking out over the spectacular sea views.

Traditional Pelion architecture is unique and striking. Stone is used for the ground and middle floors, whereas the upper levels are constructed from a mix of stone and timber. You will not find this style anywhere else in Greece. The villages that line the west coast are undeniably Greek, with gently sloping hills blanketed in olive groves and eucalyptus trees. On the southern tip, and stretching around to the eastern coast, the scenery seems to take on a more Tuscan look, with snaking lines of Mediterranean cypress and poplar trees. The northeastern corner is arguably the jewel in the crown of this lovely landscape.

Four hours' drive from Thessaloniki, you will find the charming seaside village of Damouhari. This close-knit Greek village, situated on the mainland in the Pelion peninsula, has a beautiful backdrop of olive groves and a tiny pebble-beach harbor overlooking the blue-green Aegean Sea. It provided the beautiful backdrop for several key scenes from the smash-hit musical-turned-movie *Mamma Mia*. This unspoiled chunk of Pelion has long been a favorite hideaway for Greek vacationers, but is for the moment still largely unknown to foreigners. We hope the success of the *Mamma Mia* movie does little to change that. **JP**

⬆ *There are many hidden bays such as this in Pelion, with lush vegetation and pebble beaches.*

Relax at Elixir Spa

Location Attica, Greece **Website** www.grecotel.com **Price** ❺❺❺

Wallowing between mock-classical pillars in the bubbling spa pool, you can gaze through a glass wall to the Temple of Poseidon on the southernmost point of the European mainland. Surely, this fabulous octagonal spa was inspired by the Greek gods? Well, no, actually, say the owners, it was inspired by the James Bond film *Dr. No*. You can easily see the 007 influences: It is part of a money-is-no-object lavish modern resort in a fantastic Mediterranean landscape, but there is no evil genius at work here. In fact, it is a luxurious paradise that even the heroes of Greek mythology would have enjoyed.

You enter the spa through a huge round bronze door, a bit like stepping through a porthole. Private treatment rooms have an intimate atmosphere with scented candles and soothing music. Therapies include shiatsu, aromatherapy, reflexology, and hot stone therapy. The local specialty pays proper homage to the sea god—the "Poseidon Elixir" is inspired by grooming rituals of the classical era. Finely ground olive seeds, natural sea salt, and rich clay are applied in successive scrubs and rubs, combined with sessions in the sauna, to remove toxins. The sequence culminates in a theraputic, forty-five-minute, four-hand massage with a natural deep-penetrating cream of dandelion and pear extracts that is guaranteed to leave the skin silky smooth and glowing.

The spa is part of the Grecotel Cape Sounio resort: a five-star collection of 124 luxury bungalows covering 75 acres (30 ha) in an amphitheater landscape facing the brilliant blue sea. Many of the fabulous terra-cotta bungalows have their own private pools and gardens, balconies, and amazing views. The resort boasts five restaurants, three pools, a private beach, and its own yacht. Dr. No would have been impressed. **SH**

⬆ *The spa rooms are eight-sided, and glass exterior walls showcase memorable sea views.*

Relax at Grand Resort

Location Attica, Greece **Website** www.grandresort.gr
Price 🟢🟢

Here is the ultimate in sun and sea hotels. The Grand Resort occupies a peninsular 22 miles (35 km) south of the Greek capital, Athens, and is one of the most luxurious hotels you can find, not just on the Athenian Riviera, but anywhere on the Mediterranean.

The Grand Resort lives up to its name: It offers every conceivable extra from personal trainers to electric shuttles that trundle around the 72-acre (29-ha) site. If your idea of luxury means not moving from your room at all, you will appreciate the in-room dining (with a personal chef), in-room tailors, pianists, hairdressers, and spa therapies. Facilities that other hotels would boast about, such as the beachside spa, gym, and

---

"The resort is stunning architecturally, quietly joyous in a pre-Zorba the Greek way."

Helena Smith, *Guardian*

---

waterfront ballroom, are hardly worth mentioning among jet-set glamor like this. The quality of the resort's helicopter services, yacht rental, and private chauffeurs are more important to guests.

As for the rooms and villas, rest assured there is a comprehensive range, starting from palatial and reaching right up to extraordinary. Many of the villas are on the water's edge, and have private infinity pools, marble bathrooms, heated floors, and a choice of pillows. More highlights of the resort include sixteen private sandy beaches, ten restaurants, an Olympic-sized seawater pool, and facilities for just about any sport you could wish to try on vacation. **SH**

Visit Amorgos Island

Location Amorgos, Greece **Website** www.amorgos.net
Price 🔴

Glistening in the sunlight, the whitewashed facade of the Byzantine monastery of Panagia Hozoviotissa juts out of the cliffs toward the Aegean Sea, affording an azure vista far out into the horizon. It was this mixture of drama and solitude that drew French director Luc Besson to Amorgos to film his 1988 classic *The Big Blue*. Today, the island continues to beckon the faithful back every year, to revel in its rugged natural beauty.

The north-to-south coastal road winds its way through the mountains, with a sheer drop giving way to deep, crystal-clear waters and hidden coves. It is a long, lonely drive, except for a few stray goats, and the undulating road gives the feeling of flying as it takes you between the island's three towns. Even in the main "resort" of Aegali, the pace is always slow. Priests play backgammon in the tavernas, shading themselves from the afternoon sun. If the slightly larger crowd in mid-August is too much for you, take a small boat from the harbor to your own secluded (possibly nudist) stretch of beach, or out to one of the mysterious, uninhabited islands. Alternatively, arm yourself with a map and clamber over the scrub and barren paths to your own spot beyond the bay—be it shallow and sandy, or just rocky with a leap into the big blue itself.

Many of the island's 1,900-strong population reside in the capital, Chora, one of the best-preserved towns in the Cyclades. Pause for a while among the houses of blue and white, and look up toward the Venetian castle on the hill. Pirates, Roman exiles, and Minoans have all walked here, and the island's history dates back to 4,000 B.C.E.—at times lawless, always atmospheric. **JW**

➡ *As you climb the myriad dusty steps leading to Panagia Hozoviotissa, time appears to stand still.*

Experience Skyros Island

Location Skyros, Greece **Website** www.skyros.co.uk
Price ⑤

Visitors are encouraged to come to Skyros island with an open mind. Stay here to chill out, be creative, learn a new skill, or socialize, and, if you need to, find the inspiration to change your life.

Courses led by experts cover everything from qigong, yoga, and massage to filmmaking, art, and singing. Workshops take place at the Skyros Center, tucked away in the cobblestone town, where you can stay in one of the modern rooms with private bathrooms. For a more authentic slice of Greek island life, you can book into a traditional house run by a local landlord. Atsitsa is a more basic, bohemian course center, set by the sea and surrounded by pine forests. Here there is a greater emphasis on physical activities such as sailing and windsurfing. Up to ninety people can be accommodated in this spacious stone villa, sleeping five to a room, or in very rustic, two-person bamboo cabins under the trees. This is the place to get back to nature, with open-air showers and meals eaten outside, but if you want a tad more luxury, upgrade to the nearby Atsitsa Taverna.

Each day after breakfast, there is an hour for the communal *Demos*, or people's assembly, when facilitators outline the day's schedule and guests offer feedback. Most guests are in their mid-thirties and upward, but age becomes rather irrelevant. Whoever you meet and whichever course you choose, you will have plenty of free time for the beach, massages, suppers out, moonlit walks, midnight skinny-dipping, cheesy disco dancing, philosophical debate, group hugs—whatever floats your boat. **CSJ**

← *The island is dedicated to holistic well-being and is home to a magical community.*

Stay at Nafplia Palace

Location Nafplion, Greece **Website** www.nafpliapalace.gr
Price ⑤⑤

Sometimes all you need is a drink, somewhere to sit, and a great view. The Nafplia Palace was built on that simple principle. The architects sited it within the Bronze Age fortress of Akronafplia, on the rocks above the old town of Nafplion, the first capital city of Greece.

The views from here are stupendous: right across the tiled rooftops of the city, along the coast past sandy beaches and plunging cliffs, across the crescent of the Bay of Argolis to the misty mountain peaks in the distance. By day you can admire the bougainvillea trailing across the walls of the town below; by night guests can sit and watch the lights twinkling right around the bay, looking up to the stars if they wish.

"[Greece's] only hotel in a historic monument. . . . There are grandiose sea views from the elegant rooms."

Dana Facaros, *The Sunday Times*

A view this good influences the whole hotel experience. All the newly renovated modern rooms and villas face out across the bay, whereas the two bars and three restaurants are perched on the cliff to take advantage of a panorama that can distract even the hungriest diner. Many of the villas have private infinity pools and outdoor whirlpool tubs facing the sea. Others boast exclusive terraces—for soaking up that memorable vista. There is a deliberate attempt to create a luxurious atmosphere. The view is so important that the best rooms offer guests remote control mattresses so they can prop themselves up and simply stare at the vision out of the window. **SH**

Explore Kastellorizo Island

Location Kastellorizo, Greece   **Website** www.kastellorizo.de
Price ◑

"The famous aqua-colored cave of Kastellorizo is one of the rarest geological phenomena."

Kastellorizo municipality website

Greece's remotest island is a hidden gem. It is only a stone's throw from the Turkish coast, but visitors normally reach the island by taking a flight, ferry, or catamaran from Rhodes, 60 miles (96 km) away.

Kastellorizo has retained its underground status by staying out of the travel brochures and off the tourist trail. With a surface area of only 3.5 square miles (9 sq km), it is virtually impossible to get lost on this tiny island, which has just 250 inhabitants, most of whom are fishermen. At the beginning of the last century, the island had 15,000 inhabitants, but the majority of them emigrated to Australia when Greece was bombed during World War II, and the population has remained small ever since, lending the island an air of tranquility.

Kastellorizo's attractive horseshoe-shaped port is dotted with vibrantly colored, neoclassical houses that date back to the Byzantine period when the color of the homes reflected the social status of the residents. Behind the port are crumbling and abandoned homes that line the backstreets like an atmospheric ghost town, with history oozing from every brick. Beyond the island's only settlement are rocky cliffs, and at their peak are the ruins of a fourteenth-century castle, Castello Rosso, after which the island is named. There are no roads and few guesthouses, but a raft of charming portside tavernas and top-notch restaurants, serving up grilled fish and home-cooked Greek fare, provide a place for visitors to while away the evenings. The island is traffic-free, but it is easy to get around on foot—there is no need to rush, because there is a real feeling that time has long forgotten this spot. **JK**

◸ *Kastellorizo may not have any beaches, but its clear waters are awash with dolphins, turtles, and seals.*

Unwind at Perivolas

Location Santorini, Greece **Website** www.perivolas.gr
Price 💲💲

Stay at Santorini Grace

Location Santorini, Greece **Website** http://santorinigrace.com
Price 💲💲

If the Perivolas infinity pool looks familiar, you have almost certainly seen it before, gracing the front cover of every quality travel magazine worth its high-gloss pages. After seeing it, it will be no surprise that this stunning hotel is consistently voted among the best in the world because romantic hideaways do not come much better than this.

Just a short walk away, the town of Oia pulses with the constant flow of tourists flocking to see the awe-inspiring volcanic geology of the Santorini caldera, but at tranquil Perivolas a peaceful atmosphere prevails. Faithful to Santorini's unique traditional architecture, Perivolas is fashioned from a series of 300-year-old

"The stunning infinity pool overlooks Santorini's famous flooded volcano."

Condé Nast Traveler

caves, previously the homes of local fishermen and farmers. The original shape of the caves has been preserved in each of the seventeen private houses' uniquely structured, sloping whitewashed walls, but the cave comparisons end there. Each house is kitted out in modern, understated style and comes complete with a private stone terrace with stunning views.

For something special, check in to the Perivolas suite. A central sitting area leads onto the bedroom, a spa facility with steam bath and massage pool, and a private pool with views of the Aegean. As the sun sets over the caldera, guests can finish the day in the candlelit bar, which opens onto the pool terrace. **HO**

Location, location, location is what makes Santorini Grace such a winner. Situated in the beautiful village of Imerovigli on the northwest of the volcanic island of Santorini, and high above the caldera—a deep basin formed by the volcano sinking into the sea—the newest hotel from the award-winning Grace Hotels stable offers the perfect vantage point from which to admire the famous Santorini sunsets over the Aegean.

You realize you are somewhere special as soon as you arrive. A welcoming glass of champagne is proffered, as well as an iced towel to cool you down. This stylish, chic property comes with nine individually styled rooms decorated in pale calming shades, and will appeal to those seeking a relaxing and romantic escape. It combines first-class service and the finest food and drink with a real sense of privacy and serenity. From deluxe rooms with plunge pools, to superior suites facing the sea, junior suites with jaw-dropping views, and the ultimate in exclusive accommodation (the honeymoon suite and the Grace suite), whichever room you find yourself in, king-size beds, luxurious bed linen, and a pillow menu all guarantee a good night's sleep. There are Korres toiletries with which to pamper yourself and satellite TV, DVDs, wireless Internet, and iPod speakers for your entertainment.

The hotel also has an intimate restaurant serving up Mediterranean fusion cuisine. It has a beautiful domed ceiling, but best to dine alfresco under the starlit sky to make the most of the stunning panoramas. If you get carried away by the sheer romance of the Grace, then you can tie the knot in the tiny church of Agios Ioannis Katifois nearby, which dates back to the fifteenth century. A more idyllic setting for a wedding would be difficult to imagine. **HA**

Stay at
Elounda Peninsula

Location Crete, Greece   **Website** www.eloundapeninsula.com
Price $$$

"It enjoys unparalleled views and a tranquil setting. . . . The view is blue as far as the eye can see."

greekhoneymoon.com

If only life were always like this: straightforward, with no decisions to make except which treatment to have in the spa, whether to play golf or take out a yacht for the day, or where to enjoy a predinner cocktail. Fortunately, life can be like this some of the time; at least it can at Elounda Peninsula in Crete. While hordes of tourists noisily congregate around busy corners of the island in their organized groups, the prevailing ambience here is one of tranquility.

Stretched out on a peninsula overlooking the Bay of Elounda, Mirabello Bay, and the glittering Aegean Sea, the hip hotel, which has no guest rooms, only suites, is permanently bathed in a swath of blue. Luxurious marble bathrooms offer spectacular vistas toward mountains and the ocean, so that you can even admire the view while you are splashing about in the bathtub. For those with serious cash to flash, there is the once-in-a-lifetime experience of staying in the Peninsula Palace. Located directly on the water's edge, it is exquisitely furnished and comes with immaculately manicured gardens and staff quarters, as well as a stylish private sailing boat.

To top it all, the hotel complex has a first-class Six Senses Spa offering a full range of holistic treatments and an authentic Turkish hammam. Have your body and feet polished with Cretan olive stones after a day spent exploring the island—if you can drag yourself away from the beach, that is. It promises to appeal to the five senses and awaken the sixth. An escape truly fit for Greek gods and goddesses. **LP**

↖ *The jetty bar offers a wonderful setting to enjoy drinks, with views through the floor to the sea below.*

Unwind at Blue Palace Resort

Location Crete, Greece **Website** www.bluepalace.gr
Price ⦵⦵

The Blue Palace Resort and Spa is made for romance. Highly popular for weddings and honeymoons, it even has its own romance department. The dedicated staff are highly attentive, and the Greek tradition of *philoxenia*—love of the stranger—is here in full swing.

The resort lies just outside the village of Elounda and close to the fishing village of Plaka, hugging a steep hill on Crete's northern coast. Facing the picturesque isle of Spinalonga, a former leper colony, the hotel is blessed with natural beauty but has also been cleverly designed to reflect its heritage. Upon entering the barrel-vaulted lobby, one is immediately

---

"This peaceful resort is set on a beautiful and otherwise undeveloped stretch of coast."

Lynne Truss, *The Times*

---

transported to a bygone era, because the building has been carefully modeled on the sixteenth-century Venetian arsenals of Heraklion, Crete's capital. The original design of the 36-foot (11-m) high columns has been imitated, and they are spectacularly lit up at night. Five tempting restaurants, where dishes are concocted from the very best local produce, mean that there is never a lack of choice when it comes to dining, but it is the hotel's hedonistic spa that particularly stands out. Thalasso treatment pools are filled daily with fresh, heated seawater drawn from the Cretan Pelagos, and Cretan herbs are used in the hydromassage bath for the ultimate in relaxation. **LP**

Visit the Restored Settlement of Milia

Location Crete, Greece **Website** www.milia.gr
Price ⦵⦵

"Don't imagine we're some group of extremists living off spring onions and wearing potato sacks," say the owners of Milia village. In fact they simply own houses and land in the same area and are united by a passion for all things natural and traditional. Their little Cretan mountain village has become a world-renowned haven of tranquility, recycling, and sustainability.

The stone houses have been immaculately restored and stand on fertile slopes above a stream, amid olives, pears, herbs, and flowering shrubs. Visitors stay in one of thirteen rooms in the old village houses. Do not expect the Ritz Carlton; they are simple homes, but prettily furnished with reclaimed furniture and colorful textiles. Some houses are built right into the rocky slopes, so huge boulders appear along the side of rooms. Solar energy provides electric power, although guests are encouraged to use candles. Comforts are basic, but rooms have private bathrooms and fireplaces for heat during the winter. They all have a balcony, small terrace, or garden where guests linger to admire the views across the valley.

The atmosphere is friendly and relaxed. You will sit at chunky monastic tables in the communal dining room to sample delicacies made from produce cultivated organically on the village farm. Meals include rabbit with mizithra goat cheese; potato, chestnut, and onion stew; pork with orange cooked in the woodstove; and *kalitsounia* (small cheese pies). Days are spent exploring footpaths into the hills or using the village's mountain bikes. There are lessons in traditional Cretan cooking and wine tasting, and some guests enter into the spirit of Milia so enthusiastically that they spend their vacations helping with jobs around the village. **SH**

See Valley of the Butterflies

Location Rhodes, Greece
Website www.rodosisland.gr   **Price** ❶

Every year, a gorge in Rhodes becomes a temporary home to millions of delicate Jersey tiger moths. Despite this misnomer, Valley of the Butterflies attracts half a million tourists annually. You can get here by catching a bus from Rhodes town or you can drive, but if you are staying in one of the resorts on the north coast, such as Tholos, you might like to try the hour-long walk to reach the natural park. Your efforts will make the lush greenery of the Petaloudes Valley all the more refreshing. Waterfalls gush and leafy trees cast deep pools of shade where log bridges stretch over the River Pelekanos.

At the beginning of June, the first few moths flutter into the valley, and the best time to soak up the true tranquility of this place is with these early arrivals. Although the highest numbers of moths are here in July and August, this period is also when most tourists visit, transforming the valley paths into thoroughfares. However, in June, you may have the valley to yourself, apart from the occasional moth wafting by, to feed on the pine resin that fills the valley with its heady scent, and giving you the chance to admire its flashing red, black, and brown wings. After a couple of months of replenishing their strength, the moths go into a gentle frenzy of reproduction in August, before drifting away from the valley in September.

There is also a museum here with displays on the valley's plants and animals. Even when the moths are not here, this is a wonderful place to meander in the dappled sunlight and enjoy the cool air, dampened by spray from the waterfalls. **JED**

⬅ *Arriving at the Petaloudes Valley is like coming across an oasis in a desert, quite unlike the Rhodes terrain.*

Stay at the Anassa

Location Latchi, Cyprus
Website www.anassa.com.cy   **Price** ❺❺

Sleep with the balcony doors open and wake to cream drapes swaying in a warm Aegean breeze. Walk outside and gaze at the long, long beach, hazily disappearing toward the hills of the Akamas National Park and the Baths of Aphrodite in the distance. The Anassa's dreamy atmosphere is helped by its peaceful location, alone on one of Cyprus's best beaches and backed by pine-forested mountains. Guests stay in a cluster of whitewashed villas under terra-cotta roofs surrounding the grand neoclassical palazzo of spas, restaurants, and cool, airy public rooms. Tall windows and balconies overlook paths winding through landscaped gardens to a quiet seashore.

"The 'It Girl' of the Mediterranean hotel scene; glamorous, fashionable and dripping in style."

Food and Travel magazine

The Anassa may feel like a five-star ancient monastery but is really a late-twentieth-century construction. Everything you touch is either marble, polished wood, fine linen, wrought iron, clean stone, or lush cream fabric. The hushed indulgence reaches its epiphany at the Romanesque spa and in the arched stone cellar where the finest of the four restaurants is housed. It serves a nine-course gourmet menu. But reverential tranquility is not compulsory—you can eat barbecued fish on the beach serenaded by bouzouki players. There are water sports, diving, and tennis on tap, and the best view of the rugged Akamas peninsula comes from the deck of the Anassa's private yacht. **SH**

Stay at Hotel Vila Bled

Location Upper Carniola, Slovenia
Website www.relaischateaux.com **Price** 💲💲

Taking in the glorious view across sparkling Lake Bled to the soaring peaks of the Julian Alps, you would be forgiven for thinking you had landed in an alpine paradise. St. Mary's Church sits atop a huge rock on a tiny island before you, and all is still, except perhaps for a few people canoeing or jogging around the lake.

The snapshot is from Vila Bled, once the private residence of the leader of the former Yugoslavia, Marshal Tito. It is clear to see why it was here that Tito set up home, as did princes from imperial Austria and Yugoslav royals before him. There are rowboats, tennis courts, and swimming from a private lido, perfect for entertaining visiting statesmen and -women, and

> *"[It has] breathtaking views of the lake . . . and many of its original fifties socialist-chic furnishings."*
>
> Robert Boynton, *Travel+Leisure* magazine

ample opportunities for horseback riding, fishing, and hunting. The estate, set among 12 acres (5 ha) of colorful flowers and greenery, also offers a spa, sauna, and hammam, but it is the picturesque lakeside setting that makes it extra special.

Inside, there are austere marble staircases and wooden floors, an atmospheric piano bar, and some enormous suites. There are also features reminiscent of its fascinating communist past, such as the ballroom covered in Tito's prized murals depicting the victories of the People's Red Army. Beyond the estate are dense wild forests, and Slovenia's capital, Ljubljana, is 31 miles (50 km) south. **LP**

Relax at Kendov Dvorec

Location Goriška, Slovenia
Website www.kendov-dvorec.com **Price** 💲💲

Escape the hustle and bustle of city life by going back in time to an era when life moved at a far slower pace. Nestled in among the Slovenian mountains an hour's drive from the lively capital, Ljubljana, Kendov Dvorec (meaning "Kenda Manor") dates back to 1377, a time when Kenda landowners farmed the Idrija Valley. The area is still as richly green and full of fresh air as it was all those years ago.

Now a calm retreat that oozes class, Kendov Dvorec's eleven plush guest rooms are all named after former members of the Kenda family and are individually decorated, decked out with nineteenth-century antique furniture. Think hand-carved beds and oversized wardrobes. Pretend you are the lord of the manor by staying in his former room, a spacious affair beautifully decorated in a baroque style and enjoying stunning panoramic views over the old city center and church, backed by wooded peaks. It might have once been home to the region's most powerful men and women, but this five-star bed-and-breakfast has a very homey feel, with local handmade lace decorating the tablecloths, curtains, and bedcovers, plus a fabulous garden cloaked with flowers and hundred-year-old apple trees.

The house restaurant serves up Slovene cuisine with a modern twist, using only the best ingredients. There is no menu, so the chef will explain the dishes on offer, normally local specialties washed down with wine from nearby vineyards. Do like the locals and swim or fish for marble trout in the Idrijca River; bike or hike to alpine lakes and waterfalls, or go rafting or kayaking. Most important, take every opportunity you can to inhale deeply, filling your lungs with the crisp, pure alpine air. **JK**

Enjoy Nebesa

Location Goriška, Slovenia
Website www.nebesa.si/ang/nebesa.html **Price** 💲💲

These four Alpine cottages for two sit 2,950 feet (900 m) up the slopes of Mount Kuk. Perched so high that you are even above the cloud level, there are staggering views across snowcapped mountains and green valleys. The wooden and stone chalets are simple but stylish, with a full glass wall looking out to the meadows and woodland rolling down the steep hillside, dotted with roaming wild deer.

A large sitting room downstairs leads to a kitchen and bathroom. Upstairs, the attic bedroom has low eaved ceilings and a comfy double bed. It is minimalist without being too fashionable, with contemporary chrome lights and coffee-colored wool sofas to add

---

"Glass-walled fronts mean views are ever present and wild red deer wander through the meadows."

i-escape.com

---

warmth. Nebesa offers guests only bed-and-breakfast, though there is a kitchen. Help yourself during the day to drinks and snacks, from local wine to cheese and cold meats, all of which are included in the price. Breakfast is put in your fridge to eat at your leisure.

The nearest town is a fifteen-minute drive away, so you will need a car to get around. That just adds to the magical sense of isolation. If you can pull yourself away from the views and the fantastic wellness center—complete with sauna, whirlpool tub, and heated pool—go hiking for panoramic views from Slovenia all the way to Italy. Alternatively, drive to Kobarid for walks around the Soča River. In winter there is great skiing. **AD**

Dine at Hiša Franko

Location Goriška, Slovenia
Website www.hisafranko.com **Price** 💲💲

Located in the Soča Valley in the far west of Slovenia, near the border with Italy, Hiša Franko is a small boutique hotel that has been making waves far and wide. Deep in the least developed region of Slovenia, the restaurant alone is worth the trip.

Run by husband and wife team Valter and Ana, the menu is eclectic—expect nettle risotto alongside scallops, bitter cacao noodles, mountain lamb, rabbit, and Mediterranean tuna. Desserts like fruit sorbet and Cuban chocolate soufflé finish the meal with a flourish. All the food is organic and local. It is served in a relaxing red room with starched white tablecloths and dark-wood furniture and matched with Italian or Slovenian wine: Valter is an expert sommelier and is happy to lend his expertise to interested parties. Five and eight-course tasting menus are also roundly celebrated for their inventiveness and exquisite presentation. Although there is accommodation at Hiša Franco, guests visit for the food experience: It is an inspiring place for those who know their cuisine. In the summer, dining takes place in a glass-walled room, and there is also a private dining room for special occasions. Such is Valter's enthusiasm for Slovenian wine that you will inevitably join him in the cellar for a tasting session and take home a few bottles of your favorite wine at cost price.

Rooms at the restaurant exhibit a similar attention to detail, with plenty of creative touches. Rooms 9 and 10 both have a separate enclosed terrace, and all are individually decorated in a modern, sleek style. The surrounding countryside is fantastic to explore, either by foot, bike, or by heading down one of the rivers on a kayak or white-water raft, and Ana can provide luxury packed lunches for all excursions. **LD**

Explore Slovenia by Bicycle

Location Slovenia **Website** www.slovenia.info
Price ⊖⊖

Its glorious countryside crisscrossed by an extensive network of bicycle paths, Slovenia has in recent years become one of Europe's best destinations for biking vacations. It may be small, but Slovenia manages to pack meandering rivers, snowcapped mountains, craggy caves, ancient villages, primeval forest, and rolling farmland into its compact dimensions.

There are several options for those who like their biking to be freewheeling and easy. The region to the southwest of the capital, Ljubljana, which heads down toward the Italian border and Adriatic coast, is filled with quiet, idyllic country lanes. For a bit of pampering, visitors could try the northwest, around Maribor, a wine-growing region famous for its spa towns and vineyards. After a hard day in the saddle, riders can fortify themselves with a dip in the healing, thermal waters of the local hotels and a glass of regional wine.

To appreciate the best views the country has to offer will require a little more exertion. Narrow paths lead up into the Slovenian Alps, winding past verdant peaks, pine-clad slopes, and crystal-clear glacial lakes. One of the most popular rides is to Lake Bled, whose tranquil waters have been guarded by the famous Castle Bled, which has perched upon a 425-foot (130-m) cliff for more than a thousand years.

If you do not feel up to mountain riding, you could always head in the opposite direction. Peca Mountain offers a very unusual bicycling experience. Instead of making a lung-bursting trip to the top, cyclists put on headlamps to guide themselves along a 3-mile (5-km) subterranean path through a disused mine. **JF**

→ *A cyclist rides through the valley of Voje above Bohinj in the Julian Alps, Slovenia.*

Discover Pristava Lepena

Location Goriška, Slovenia   **Website** www.pristava-lepena.com   **Price** $

Gazing across the churning jade waters of the Soča River, it is easy to see why this magical corner of Slovenia was chosen as the background for the Chronicles of Narnia film *Prince Caspian*. Luckily you do not have to travel to another world to enjoy this unspoiled alpine wilderness.

The Soča River flows through the Triglav National Park, where the fresh Alpine air collides with the balmy Adriatic breezes from neighboring Italy. Over thousands of years, the icy, clear waters of the river carved out the Trenta Valley. Today it is lush with green meadows and brightly colored wildflowers. Tucked in the fertile valley, overlooked by the majestic limestone peaks of the Julian Alps, is Pristava Lepena.

Owners Milan and Silvia Dolenc have created the perfect getaway for outdoor enthusiasts. A cluster of eight traditional wooden and stone chalets, Pristava Lepena both blends in with and takes full advantage of its magnificent natural surroundings. Guests can choose from a myriad of activities. Horse lovers relish the opportunity to trek through forests and mountain ridges on one of the village's purebred Lipizzaner horses. Alternatively there are walking or mountain biking trails, tennis courts, and a swimming pool. The river hosts a range of water sports, including rafting, kayaking, and canyoneering. But it is the top-notch fly-fishing that attracts keen anglers from all over the world. Marble, rainbow, and brown trout can all be caught in the cool, clear waters.

The restaurant offers locally sourced, traditional cuisine, such as fresh lamb on a spit and grilled trout. Braver souls might even attempt the homemade spirits. Afterward, you can warm yourself by the open fire or sit out on your private terrace and soak in the surrounding Alps. It is a truly unforgettable view. **JP**

⬆ *Pristava Lepena's location in a secluded valley high in the Julian Alps is perfect for enjoying the mountains.*

Stay at the Pucić Palace

Location Dubrovnik, Croatia   **Website** www.thepucicpalace.com   **Price** 💲💲

Amid all the hustle and bustle that is Dubrovnik on a typical summer day, the five-star Pucić Palace Hotel is a romantic haven. Though right in the center of the Old Town, it is a million miles from the camera-toting tourists who pack the city's narrow streets.

Across from the Gundulić Square, named after a seventeenth-century Dubrovnik-born dramatist and poet, the Pucić Palace was once one of the finest noble homes of its time. It was converted into a hotel at the end of the nineteenth century. Originally a three-star hotel, it was renovated and reopened in 2002 with just nineteen rooms, each named after a writer or artist from the city's past.

There are two suites and one single room, but mainly deluxe and executive rooms—the latter with better views than the deluxe rooms—all exquisitely finished with high-beamed ceilings and dark-oak floors. They are furnished with antiques but feature every modern convenience a twenty-first-century traveler could possibly want. A notebook, printer, scanner, and fax can even be provided on request. Bathrooms are equally luxurious, with freestanding tubs, soft cotton bathrobes, and Bulgari products.

The rooms are superb, but the pièce de résistance has to be Defne, the rooftop restaurant, where you can feast on Eastern Mediterranean cuisine to the gentle sounds floating up from the street below. The Café Royal brasserie on the ground floor has seating inside and out, in Gundulić Square, during the summer. Do not miss the stone soup, literally flavored with minerals from pebbles taken from the Adriatic Sea. Razonoda wine bar is a great place to hang out in the early evening with a glass of your favorite tipple, served with traditional, local nibbles such as Dalmatian smoked ham and homemade cheese. **JA**

⬆ *The Pucić Palace offers an intimate luxury experience in the heart of Dubrovnik's Old Town.*

Unwind at Villa Dubrovnik

Location Dubrovnik, Croatia   **Website** www.villa-dubrovnik.hr
Price ❸❸❸

"Watch the sun go down over the Adriatic from one of three vine and flower-covered terraces."

Liz Bird, *Guardian*

Built as a resting place for Tito's officials in the 1950s, this intimate and upmarket pad has a colorful past. Communism may be long gone—along with the officials—but Villa Dubrovnik remains a relaxing haven for those in need of indulgence.

Clinging onto a cliff's edge, its low-rise terraces spectacularly draped over the Adriatic Sea, this charming hotel affords fantastic views of ultra-chic Dubrovnik. More than sixty steep, cypress tree–lined steps lead down from the road to the creamy-colored villa's main entrance. Once inside, the style is completely minimalist, with sleek white walls and simple furnishings lending the place a light, airy feel.

Rooms are also simple but clean, all with French doors opening out onto balconies offering stunning panoramic views of the sea, the island of Lokrum, and the ancient city walls in the near distance. All communal areas have generously sized terraces with plenty of loungers, shaded by vines and umbrellas, and every meal is served up on a different level. An à la carte restaurant cooks up divine food, and a bistro offers snacks. There is also a well-equipped fitness studio for those who fear overindulging.

Wander down to the water's edge via the hotel's verdant gardens (or by taking the elevator), where there is a small and secluded private pebble beach for sun worshippers and swimmers. You can reach the shops, bars, and restaurants of Dubrovnik's Old Town by taking a leisurely twenty-minute stroll or, better still, by using the hotel's private boat service. **JK**

🔼 *All rooms in the glamorous Villa Dubrovnik have terraces with views of the sea and the Old Town.*

Visit Mljet and St. Mary's Church and Monastery

Location Mljet, Croatia   **Website** www.visitcroatia.com
Price 💲

With an almost otherworldly beauty permeating Mljet, it is no wonder that the tiny island is a treasured national park. It is liberally sprinkled with hallmarks of the Croatian countryside—emerald green valleys, bristling conifers, and fascinating stone architecture—from the man-made gothic turrets of the villages to the natural wonders of its karst cliffs.

With salt lakes, pine forests, sleepy villages, and a unique ecosystem, Mljet is an island whose lore precedes it. Its roots stem from the Illyrians; its history, like its country's, is peppered with occupations, settlers, invaders, reclamation, and myth. Such is its legacy that this little island, seemingly lost in the sea, is even said to be the place where Calypso ensnared Odysseus, keeping the mighty warrior captive in a cave for seven years.

Then there are the sunken lakes that, like the snakes eaten up by the illustrious mongeese still flocking over the island, the elusive seals, and the bura winds that clip the island's hinterland and shores, appear and vanish like its legends. These lakes, great and small, have been providing an attraction to visitors from nearby Dubrovnik and beyond for eons.

A boat carries visitors from the shore to the tiny islet in the center of the Great Lake. Stretched across its curious surface are the Benedictine Monastery and enchanting Church of St. Mary, remnants from the years when Mljet was under the jurisdiction of Benedictine Monks. The charming stone monastery has been an epicenter of culture and spirituality throughout the ages, hosting famous poets as its abbots, such as Ignjat Đurđević, and drawing Benedictines from across the neighboring lands. **VG**

Recharge on Palmižana Island

Location Near Hvar, Croatia   **Website** www.palmizana.hr
Price 💲

Set in 740 acres (300 ha) of unspoiled and uninhabited wilderness on a tiny island in the Adriatic, Palmižana resort is a ten-minute boat ride from Hvar. The air is rich with the scent of exotic flowers, pines, and wild herbs, and tropical vegetation, such as cacti and eucalyptus, flourishes.

Under the shade of the century-old pine forest are stone bungalows that can accommodate sixty guests; all are individually decorated and brightly colored with highly patterned bedspreads and modern Croatian artwork. Run by members of the Meneghello family, who have managed the estate for over a hundred

> *"My kids were wild about the Palmižana beach, which is sandy and shallow and lined with caves."*
>
> Josip Novakovich, *New York Times*

years, the two restaurants, Toto's and Palmižana Meneghello, are renowned for their fish dishes. Guests may even accompany the chef on his purchasing trips to vineyards and the fish market.

A short walk across the pine forest leads to the beach, studded with secluded coves and hidden bays where you can strip off and bare all if you feel like it: Palmižana has a long tradition of nudity, and skinny-dipping is commonplace. Warm temperatures last from April to November, and the island is famed for its high number of sunshine hours. The waters surrounding the island are a haven for divers, awash with shipwrecks and tropical fish. **JK**

Visit the Kornati Islands

Location Kornati, Croatia **Website** www.kornati.hr
Price $

When George Bernard Shaw traveled around the Adriatic, he stopped on the coast of what is now Croatia and fell in love with the archipelago of the Kornati Islands. They are still as beautiful today as they were all those years ago.

The 140 islands cover an area of 124 square miles (320 sq km), much of it protected by a national park. Within it are crystal-clear waters, hidden coves, underwater reefs, ancient archaeological remains, and the famous crowns (sheer rocks soaring out of the sea). These fascinating steep cliffs are the sides of a large tectonic rift that stretches from Istria and ends in Middle Dalmatia, caused by the northern motion of Africa and its collision with Europe.

There are no permanent residents on the islands, and most of the region belongs to the people of Murter Island, who come to tend the olive groves, the vineyards, and orchards. They stay in cottages when there is work to be done, and rent the accommodation out to vacationers when the farming is finished. With no electricity or running water, these traditional retreats are as far removed from the outside world as you can get. Alternatively, you can take a day trip from Zadar, Sibenik, or Split.

Some of the most beautiful islets to explore by boat are Koromacna, Opat, Stiniva, Striznja, Sipnata, and Lopatica. You can stop at one of the many piers dotted around the islands for a delicious lunch at a seafood taverna. There is good diving and snorkeling in the surrounding waters, or you can hike across the desertlike landscape for panoramic views. **AD**

← *The islands of the Kornati archipelago provide an echo of the untouched, rugged Mediterranean.*

Sail Croatia's Coast

Location Croatia   **Website** www.dalmatiancoast.com
Price 💲💲

There are more than a thousand islands scattered off Croatia's Adriatic coast, creating between them a coastline that stretches to 3,600 miles (5,794 km) in length. For nautical enthusiasts, this archipelago is heaven-sent. There are numerous yacht-charter companies along the coast that rent out vessels, whether you are after a bareboat charter or a luxury yacht with skipper and crew. The waters are blue, the weather is gentle, and the islands, of which about fifty are inhabited, are close enough to reach with the tiniest of hops.

Above all, though, it is the diversity that keeps the sailors happy. Some islands are long established on the tourist trail. Take Rab, for example, which was declared a health resort by the local council as far back as 1889. More than half a century later, Britain's Duke of Windsor (formerly King Edward VIII) came to the island with his wife (Wallis Simpson); it is said that he was the first to swim here without clothes and thus started the island's tradition of nudism. You might stop in Silba, which has restaurants and stores but no roads, ensuring back-to-nature tranquility, or Pasman, whose many white-sand coves attract those in need of a rest.

Many like to visit the Kornati Islands, an archipelago of 147 different islands, islets, and reefs that together make up a national park. Here you will find traditional fishing villages and quiet bays. Between the islands winds a labyrinth of marine passages: Local legend has it that the islands were created when God had finished making the world and, finding he had some materials left over, simply threw them into the sea. **PE**

← *The warm, limpid waters off of Croatia's coast are perfect for exploring by boat.*

Stay at Zabola

Location Transylvania, Romania   **Website** www.zabola.com
Price 💲💲

Zabola, the estate of the Count Mikes family, dates back to around 1400 and was at one time a fortified building with a tower and ceilings intricately painted with frescoes. The grand house sits at the end of a tree-lined estate with a stunning lake in 84 acres (34 ha) of parkland at the foot of the Carpathian Mountains. Six airy guest rooms are housed within the Machine House, which once held generators for the hospital set up here under communist rule.

Today, open fires roar a warm welcome and the red room, with blood-red walls, is the closest thing you will find to a spooky Dracula encounter. Soak in the freestanding bathtub surrounded by antler-clad walls

> *"[U]pmarket accommodation that conveys both colonial-era India and old school Transylvania."*

Andrew Eames, *CNN Traveler* **magazine**

for a real-life gothic experience. Then enjoy the fruits of the chef's labors in the kitchen, from venison and beautifully cooked wild mushrooms to homemade dips and jams, all made using local produce.

There is much to explore in the surrounding area, although hunting has now been replaced with more nature-friendly bear-watching trips. Take a guided trek through fairy-tale woodlands, or take the estate's horse and trap on a tour of carefully preserved local villages. Farther afield is the medieval settlement of Sighisoara, the birthplace of the infamous Vlad the Impaler, who skewered his enemies on wooden poles and inspired Bram Stoker's Count Dracula. **AD**

Explore the Danube Delta by Boat

Location Danube Delta, Romania
Website www.deltadunarii.ro/?lg=en   **Price** 💲

Dubbed Europe's avian Serengeti due to the 300 species of bird that live here, the Danube Delta is one of the last surviving great wildernesses on the continent. After a 1,700 mile (2,735 km) journey winding across Europe, the Danube finally reaches the Black Sea, where it splits into many channels. Vast expanses of swamps, forests, and lakes, surrounded by thick reed beds, provide a sanctuary for the vast diversity of wildlife, plants, and trees. Herons, pelicans, red breasted geese, pygmy cormorants, and a fantastic collection of mammals including otters, mink, muskrat, and wild boar reside here. It was named Landscape of the Year 2007-2009, and UNESCO has given the status of Biosphere Reserve to large swathes of it.

One of the best ways to explore this watery wilderness is to take a boat trip deep inside the delta for bird-watching and fishing, or simply relaxing. To really immerse yourself in the Delta, however, spend a few days on a houseboat, or floating hotel as they are known locally. Explore wooded islets, marshes, sand dunes, and villages before mooring in a convenient spot. Smaller boats enable you to navigate some of the narrower channels and backwaters.

But if you'd rather keep your feet on dry land, the luxurious Delta Nature Resort is the place to stay. It offers comfortable villas with large terraces that provide sweeping vistas over the Delta. Facilities include a gloriously well-positioned pool, and an observation tower to give you a bird's-eye view of the wonderful natural spectacle. **HA**

⮕ *The scenic Danube is home to 160 varieties of fish, and 1,200 species of plant.*

Enjoy Aquacity

Location Poprad, Slovakia   **Website** www.aquacity.sk
Price ⊙

Chill down to minus 186°F (-121°C) in the world's coldest place, all in the name of a health kick. It might sound like the stuff of science fiction, but it is considered a wonder treatment for top athletes and is available for everyone at Aquacity, a water park and spa center in Slovakia, situated at the foot of the snow-peaked High Tatras Mountains. Exposing bodies to temperatures this low is part of a process known as cryotherapy.

The treatment is carried out under strict medical supervision, and patrons wear insulated shoes, socks, ear protectors, gloves, and a paper mask to cover the nose and mouth, plus shorts and a T-shirt. The experience begins in the antechamber, chilled to a mere minus 76°F (-60°C), where people undergoing the treatment stamp their feet and huddle together for up to a minute to eliminate moisture from the surface of the body.

Next up is the mother of all freezers, the cryo-chamber itself, chilled to an inconceivable minus 186°F (-121°C)—that is colder than the Antarctic, where the coldest temperature ever recorded was only minus 128°F (-89°C). The temperature is so extreme that people feel nothing but a tingling sensation, but you can leave the chamber at any time if the cold becomes unbearable.

After treatment, users undertake a supervised low-impact gym workout to get the blood flowing to the muscles and joints. Patients report a reduction in pain thanks to an increase in blood flow. It is also said to help conditions such as arthritis, lower-back disorders, and osteoporosis. The release of endorphins during the treatment is also considred to be helpful for people suffering from depression. **JK**

Discover Spiš on Foot

Location Spiš, Slovakia   **Website** www.slovakia.travel
Price ⊙

In a country blessed with a multitude of beautiful landscapes, Spiš is considered a little bit special, even by the Slovaks. Interestingly, the region has no official status within Slovakia. It is not an administrative area, but rather a place defined by its shared culture, dialect, and dress. For the Slovakians its influence is profound—everyone can tell you how to get there—yet its name appears on no maps.

Its borders are generally defined as being the Tatras Mountains to the north (known as the "miniature Alps"), the Lovoca Mountains to the east, and the Slovenské Rudohorie Mountains to the south. It is a rolling, hilly place filled with beautiful walking routes

> *"Summers in mountainous Spiš are lazy and relaxed, and the fields and forests fill with hikers."*
>
> Jaime Gill, *Guardian*

that take you along steep, forest-clad canyons, dotted with waterfalls and fast-flowing streams, and past great, snowcapped peaks. In the summer people come to hike the trails and soak in thermal spas, and in winter they come to ski.

Spiš's attractions are historic as well as natural. Its major landmark is the majestic Spiš Castle—one of Europe's largest fortresses—which looms on perilous cliffs 2,080 feet (634 m) above sea level and provides towering views of the surrounding landscape. **JF**

➩ *The World Heritage site of Spiš Castle, the largest ruined castle in the country.*

Unwind at Hotel Josef

Location Prague, Bohemia, Czech Republic
Website www.hoteljosef.com   **Price** 🟢🟢

You cannot fail to miss the pink and orange facade of one of the only boutique hotels in Prague. One peek inside Hotel Josef's eye-catching, glass-fronted reception is enough to tell you that this is a special place. Designed by Czech architect Eva Jiricná, her minimalist chic is evident pretty much everywhere, extending from the lobby—which boasts floor-to-ceiling windows and a magnificent glass and steel spiral staircase—to the ultra-modern rooms and the beautifully beige-colored corridors.

There are 109 rooms, all of which are soundproof and continue Jiricná's meditation on light and space. In them, a provocative mix of natural light and glass

---

"There are so many impressions in Prague. . . . Your eyes need a rest. The hotel cleans your mind."

Proprietors, Hotel Josef

---

compensates for an absence of wall art and helps make these spaces unique. The color schemes are pleasingly natural; thirty-five of the rooms have glass bathrooms, and rooms on the seventh and eighth floors have balconies—some of them have views of the towers of Prague, including the castle, whereas others face the courtyard.

Back downstairs, the Josef's atmospheric all-glass bar is a designer masterpiece; pull up one of the pristine white stools, order a superlative martini, and feel like James Bond. There is also a rooftop gym (with a sauna and massage room) and a pleasant grassy courtyard with patio seating for the summer. **PS**

Relax at Mandarin Oriental

Location Prague, Bohemia, Czech Republic
Website www.mandarinoriental.com/prague   **Price** 🟢🟢

The Mandarin Oriental Hotel is a new, tranquil, and luxurious retreat just a couple of minutes away from the bustling gothic grandeur of Charles Bridge and Prague Castle. This exquisitely converted fourteenth-century monastery sits amid picturesque historic houses, red-tiled rooftops, and ancient spires of the peaceful Mala Strana quarter in the heart of the old cobbled streets of Prague's Left Bank. Many highlights are within strolling distance and most rooms overlook the medieval palaces, churches, and gardens of Mala Strana, which is like an open-air museum of every architectural style from gothic to renaissance.

Contemporary straight lines have been blended with the beautifully preserved period architecture to create the new hotel. Its modern, world-class spa, for example, now sits within a renaissance chapel that was part of the old monastery. The monastic cloisters are now a lounge where guests drink tea or read newspapers among baroque colonnades, and the lobby is the former nave of the chapel.

The spa has been voted the best in the country, and for complete privacy, guests enter in their robes through an underground passageway linked directly to their rooms. The two-floor center includes seven private treatment rooms, a hydrotherapy pool, steam showers, and water massage area. A trademark ritual involves a fragrant and relaxing linden-blossom body scrub, inspired by the therapeutic properties of the Czech Republic's national tree.

Similarly, the hotel's Essensia restaurant is one of the city's finest. Under the vaulted renaissance ceilings, enjoy a mix of authentic Asian and modern European cuisine that could see coconut prawns with chili salsa sharing a menu with foie gras ice cream. **SH**

Enjoy Château Mcely

Location Bohemia, Czech Republic
Website www.chateaumcely.com **Price** 🅢

This seventeenth-century restored château oozes neoclassical romance and boasts exquisite interiors—glittering chandeliers, sumptuous fabrics, and a long, sweeping staircase—behind its imposing white facade. But although it undoubtedly provides an escape far from the madding crowds, the lively hub of Prague is just 34 miles (55 km) away.

The château is devoted to pampering guests, from luxuriant massages in the spa to afternoon tea with a harpist strumming in the background. Dinner is a gourmet affair and incorporates many excellent local ingredients, whereas the aptly named Alchymist Club in the cellar bar mixes up enchanting elixirs to promote

> *"[At Mcely] the ritual of high tea is honored again . . . so many appetites to be satisfied at once."*
>
> Ed Gutierrez, *Lifestyles Magazine*

health and love. Any pangs of guilt triggered by such indulgence may be tempered by the strength of Château Mcely's green credentials: It is proud to be the Czech Republic's first eco-chic five-star hotel.

There is much to do beyond the castle walls, too. Set off on a walking trail through the Jabkenice Game Park and spot wild deer, or try a sulfur-rich mud treatment at the local Toušeň Mud Baths. A romantic horse-drawn carriage ride through the forest should also not be missed. However you spend your time, do not rush to bed at the end of a blissful day. Take a moment first to gaze up at the night sky from the château's rooftop observatory. Pure magic. **LP**

Stay at Bursztynowy Palace

Location Middle Pomerania, Poland
Website www.hotel-bursztynowy-palac.pl **Price** 🅢🅢

Just minutes away from the Baltic Sea coast, 6 miles (10 km) south of the town of Koszalin, the Bursztynowy Palace Hotel is a collection of three historic buildings built in the eighteenth century for the aristocratic von Kamecke family. They include the Bursztynowy (Amber) Palace, the White Palace, and the Hunter's Cottage, and all are set in the midst of an immaculately landscaped park that reflects the principles and charm of a traditional French garden.

In a setting straight from the pages of a Hans Christian Andersen tale, the hotel's sixty-seven rooms include forty-nine standard rooms and four suites in the Amber Palace, six rooms in the White Palace, and twelve rooms in the Hunter's Cottage. A wellness spa includes a whirlpool tub and Finnish-style sauna, and trained physical therapists can offer traditional pursuits such as aerobics and yoga. For the more adventurous, there is a course of muscle electro-stimulation and sophisticated inhalation techniques.

Centuries-old local recipes are constantly on the dinner menu and are served with pride by a dedicated team of chefs in the hotel's gilded, sumptuous Mirror Chamber and Ball Room. The chefs delight in specializing in traditional Polish feasts such as wild game or roast lamb, and waiters are dressed in traditional Polish outfits. Meals are often accompanied by live classical music. The ambience of the fireplace room is the perfect venue to relax at the end of the day with a folk concert featuring the music of the local Jamno and Kaszuby regions or a classical concert with musical themes from baroque to contemporary. History buffs may enjoy a course in crossbow shooting. Whatever your tastes, the Bursztynowy Palace Hotel has, in all likelihood, already anticipated them. **BS**

See Slowinski National Park

Location Middle Pomerania, Poland
Website www.mos.gov.pl **Price** 🌓

Hauntingly beautiful sand dunes are a unique feature of Poland's coastline. Set in Slowinski National Park between the pretty towns of Rowy and Leba, these giant, desertlike dunes can rise up to a colossal 138 feet (42 m) above sea level. Shifting up to 32 feet (10 m) per year, the dunes leave behind dead tree stumps, evidence of a deeply buried ancient forest. This stark sight adds to the mysterious and desolate beauty of this vast open space that stretches for miles.

Perfect for those people who like to explore and really get back to nature, the dunes are rich in flora and fauna. Heathers, crowberrys, orchids, and pines dot the otherwise barren landscape. A designated UNESCO Biosphere Reserve, the rolling dunes are home to 250 species of resting and migratory birds, including rarely spotted varieties such as the white-tailed eagle and the black stork.

Cars and buses are banned from the pristine white sands, helping to maintain its peaceful charm. Walk through the park to reach the dunes and make the return trip to Leba by walking 5 miles (8 km) along the beach, or even by swimming back.

During the balmy summer months, the sun beats down on the dunes, but the relentless sea breezes that whip up the sand and keep it on the move ensure the temperature remains pleasant. Alongside the dunes are several clear lagoons, where deer and boar often gather on the shores. Beyond this is a dense pine forest where elk, raccoons, and badgers roam. Spend the night in the nearby tranquil town of Leba, surrounded by pine forest, and enjoy the wildlife. **JK**

◄ *Huge sand dunes stretch to the horizon in Poland's Slowinski National Park.*

Explore Białowieża Forest

Location Podlaskie Voivodeship, Poland
Website www.whc.unesco.org **Price** 🌓

Białowieża Forest is as wild and magical today as it was 500 years ago when the Polish royal family banned logging and settling to safeguard it as a hunting ground. A model of tranquility and nature, it remains unspoiled and undeveloped by man. Sprawling across Poland's border with Belarus, this peaceful region clings to the past, with farmers still tending to their land with horse-drawn plows.

One of Europe's last remaining primeval forests, which once spanned the entire continent's lowlands thousands of years ago, this is the landscape of fairy tales. A dense and beautiful network of oak, spruce, and hornbeam trees is mixed together with marshes,

> *"[T]his immense forest range . . . is home to some remarkable animal life."*

UNESCO World Heritage Committee

peat bogs, and streams. The numerous decaying trees add to the serene yet eerie atmosphere. Rich in wildlife, Białowieża throbs quietly to the sound of woodpeckers and the song of the 228 bird species that make the forest their home. The world's last remaining herds of bison, the largest land mammal in Europe, are kept in a reserve here. Watching these huge, slow-moving animals trudging through the snow in winter is a moving experience.

Trails for walkers, bikers, and horse riders mean it is possible to visit the forest without a guide, giving visitors the chance to soak up the fresh pine-scented air and enjoy the beauty of the area at a relaxed pace. **JK**

Visit Kazimierz Dolny

Location Lublin Voivodeship, Poland
Website www.kazimierz-news.com.pl **Price** ❶

Landscape artists flock to Kazimierz Dolny because it is thought to be blessed with an effervescent light. The appeal of the tiny, sleepy town has not been lost on film directors, either, who have often used its atmospheric streets as a setting for romances and historical thrillers. Sitting proudly on the banks of the Vistula River, Kazimierz Dolny in eastern Poland is flush with peaceful cobbled streets lined with historical buildings. A laid-back retreat for stressed-out city dwellers who swarm here during the summer months from the nearby cities of Warsaw and Lublin, Kazimierz Dolny's large population of artists and writers helps maintain its bohemian ambience.

The town was founded in the fourteenth century by the much-loved King Kazimierz the Great as a community for the Jewish population, and he built a castle here as his summer residence. The gothic castle was destroyed by the Swedes in the 1650s, but its ruins are still open to the public today and offer sweeping views of the city and the River Vistula from its hilltop vantage point. Both World Wars shattered much of the town, with the second wiping out almost its entire Jewish population, but authorities worked wonders to restore the medieval houses to their former splendor, and every corner of the town tells a historic tale.

Rynek, the market square, is the prettiest part of town, with a well marking its center. It is here you will find several opulent houses, dating back to 1615. All town houses have roofs covered with wooden tiles, and in the balmy summer heat there is a faint yet pleasant smell of pine in the air. **JK**

➡ *A view of the traditional town center of Kazimierz Dolny from the "Hill of the Three Crosses."*

Enjoy Schlössle Hotel

Location Tallinn, Estonia   **Website** www.schlossle-hotels.com
Price 💲💲

Stumbling across the Schlössle Hotel, tucked away in one of Tallinn's intricately winding narrow cobbled streets, is like finding yourself suddenly on the set of an elaborate costume drama. A fifteenth-century merchant's house overflowing with old-world charm, it has giant wooden beams, antique furnishings, and vaulted ceilings that create a baronial feel right in the heart of Estonia's capital city.

There is a cozy fireplace in the Great Hall, and there are tapestries hanging on the ancient stone walls, a pleasant courtyard garden, and medieval portraits dotted around, plus elegant rooms and suites with all the creature comforts contemporary travelers

---

> *"The seasons up here . . . are indeed a source of inspiration. The autumn is especially exciting."*

Tōnis Siigur, head chef of Stenhus

---

demand. The jewel in the small boutique hotel's crown, however, is its atmospheric Stenhus restaurant in the vaulted cellar. Eating gourmet Baltic dishes—perhaps grilled Estonian elk or baked langoustine—by candlelight, a huge log fire crackling comfortingly on a cold winter's night, you can imagine groups of nobles doing the exact same thing centuries ago in this extraordinarily intimate setting.

For an unforgettable stay, visit between December and early January, when the city, in the northeast corner of the Baltic Sea region, is blanketed in romantic snow and the bustling Christmas markets make for a wonderful treasure trove of delights. **LP**

Stay at Three Sisters Hotel

Location Tallinn, Estonia   **Website** www.threesistershotel.com
Price 💲💲

How times have changed in Tallinn. Having almost completely shaken off the remnants of its Soviet past, this medieval city has become a hip and exciting destination for culture lovers and fun seekers alike. Its labyrinth of cobbled streets and needling spires jostles with the buzz and bustle from the bars, ultra-cool cafés, and nightclubs that have flourished since the iron grip of communism was relaxed.

Renovated in 2003, the Three Sisters Hotel has embraced this new-meets-old mentality with stylish aplomb. From its high ceilings, chalky walls, and crimson color washes to its restored frescoes, old wooden staircase, and dark, centuries-old beams, everything about the hotel oozes eclectic flair. Three fourteenth-century merchant houses (the "sisters") have been joined to create one hotel, and each of the three buildings has its own character. The third sister's rooms are spacious and private, whereas the middle sister's rooms are more flamboyant, using richer colors and muslin-draped four-poster beds. The hospitality is left to the big sister, who dishes it out effortlessly. The enormous arch of the hotel doorway beckons you into a haven of restrained luxury. In the lobby, low lighting bounces off softly colored walls to cozy effect, whereas the cavelike bar attracts a trendy, cocktail-sipping crowd. If you want to, you can join the chef in the kitchen and watch him whip up a six-course meal for you. The cobbled courtyard is a lovely place to eat, too, during the long, light summer evenings.

Tallinn's old town area is compact enough to explore on foot in a couple of days and is bursting with cultural treats and historic attractions, such as the Town Hall Square, and the green parks around the ancient ramparts are perfect for a quiet stroll. **SWi**

Unwind at Pädaste Manor

Location Muhu Island, Estonia **Website** www.padaste.ee
Price ⊖⊖

Guests may not expect to find a luxury country house hotel on a small island off the coast of Estonia. Certainly Pädaste Manor is a unique escape: a fabulous conversion of a historic estate in a stunning location.

For 700 years, Pädaste was the country estate of the Von Buxhoeveden family. The crescent of grand buildings facing the sea dates from the nineteenth century, to when the wealthy Baron Axel von Buxhoeveden was imperial hunting master at the court of Czar Nicholas II. This was his family's summer home, but Von Buxhoeveden was assassinated by revolutionaries as he left the manor one day in 1919.

In the Soviet era, the manor became a fish distribution center and home for the elderly and was completely abandoned twenty years ago. It still stands in a landscaped park surrounded by meadows and forests looking out across Pädaste Bay and is now an opulent country house hotel, with all the crackling log fires, squashy sofas, and wood paneling that implies.

The fourteen rooms have lavish fabrics, simple wooden floors, and thick rugs. Guests are treated to unobtrusive technology, and spa treatments are available in traditional period rooms. The balconies and terraces all have wonderful views across the island shores and softly breaking waves.

True romantics should choose Room 15, which has its very own poetry loft. You will climb a farmer's ladder to the tiny mezzanine, which is crammed with a fine collection of poetry. A small window opens up to the sky, and you may lean back in your chair and escape into the world of verse. **SH**

⊿ The main building of the luxury estate of Pädaste Manor dates back several centuries.

"We don't want a wow factor. Pädaste is about remoteness and nature."

Proprietors, Pädaste Manor

Visit Kizhi Island

Location Karelia, Russia
Website www.kizhi.karelia.ru   **Price** ❶

The Karelian Republic, a fairy-tale land of pine and birch forest, marshes, and lakes in their tens of thousands, is a boundless wilderness. The area around the city of Petrozavodsk, in Karelia, is one of the most beautiful regions in the whole of Russia for hunting, fishing, hiking, and camping.

The most beautiful attraction in the region is the exquisite island of Kizhi on Lake Onega, an old pagan ritual site where twelfth-century Russian colonists settled, creating a parish of extraordinary wooden buildings that remain today. The Cathedral of the Transfiguration has twenty-two picturesque onion domes, and the building has wonderful decorations and gables to keep the rain from getting in. Also on the island is the nine-domed Church of the Intercession, full of icons; the fourteenth-century Church of the Resurrection of Lazarus, the oldest in Russia; and the Chapel of the Archangel Michael. Not a single nail or piece of metal was used in the construction of these buildings; instead, scribe-fitted horizontal logs and interlocking joinery keep the structures aloft.

In summer, students from nearby Petrozavodsk play the bells here, and young pale-skinned waifs dressed in traditional costume sing mournful folk songs about the sad forests. The island is a glorious idyll of long grasses, wildflowers, country lanes, and silence. If you can, stay at Sennaya Guba, where vacationing Russians flock. You will be taken care of, with a boat to take you to Kizhi, a wooden jetty to loll on, and very likely a wooden *banya* (sauna) on-site. **LB**

← *The domes of the Cathedral of the Transfiguration on Kizhi Island shimmer in the sun.*

Stay at Kempinski Moika 22

Location St. Petersburg, Russia
Website www.kempinski-st-petersburg.com   **Price** ❸❸

The one-time capital of Russia, founded in 1703 by Peter the Great, is like a living museum where white is a recurring theme. To live out those Dr. Zhivago fantasies, visit in winter when a dusting of snow covers the city's golden cupolas, whereas in summer, the sun shines all night during the "White Nights." Magical, full of history and charm, the Venice of the North's highlights include the Winter Palace, home to the Hermitage Museum's amazing three million pieces of art. Spoil yourself and book into the Kempinski Moika 22 overlooking the Hermitage. Located in a traditional St. Petersburg mansion, it dates back to 1853, during the reign of Czar Nicholas I.

> *"At the Winter Palace, the former royal rooms . . . are as captivating as the art."*
>
> Clifford J. Levy, *New York Times*

Although the building's facade is unchanged, the interior has been updated and modernized. Cozy duplex rooms with a nautical theme are plush and romantic, especially thanks to the daily delivery of fresh roses: a nice touch on the windowsill against a backdrop of snowflakes. Another bonus is the daily English high tea, especially when it is well below freezing outside. The dedicated Tea Room blends England and Russia's finest traditions: The national ritual loved by the likes of Pushkin and Chekhov has been adapted with pastries and cakes, but also very English cucumber sandwiches, alongside the antique samovar bubbling away brewing zavarka tea. **RCA**

Take the Grand Express Train to St. Petersburg

Location Moscow–St. Petersburg, Russia
Website www.grandexpress.ru/en   **Price** 💲💲

It might not be the same as a two-week Trans-Siberian extravaganza, but the Moscow to St. Petersburg overnight Grand Express offers the best of old and new Russia on wheels. The departure platform in the Russian capital is unchanged; from its name "Leningradskaya" to the austere atmosphere complete with James Bond–movie steam and attendants in sharp red uniforms and matching pillbox hats.

Stepping onboard Russia's first privately owned and operated luxury passenger train is a throwback to the time when travel was glamorous. The fourteen-car train is entirely decorated in red, with a very strong

---

"The journey on the Grand Express is nothing short of fantastic and ideal for a romantic evening."

James Logan, *Passport Magazine*

---

art-deco influence, from the deluxe cabins with their freshly laundered crisp sheets on the twin berths to the beautiful wood-paneled bar.

You are greeted with a hot cup of tea in a traditional tea glass with an intricately designed silver holder. Join other diners in the restaurant, reminiscent of a golden era movie theater, to nibble on tiger shrimp, assorted cold cuts, or caviar sandwiches. The train moves slowly throughout the night, and with the gently rocking steady motion, sleep comes easily. However, you would be forgiven for staying awake to take in the scenery. For miles, watch the countryside blanketed in snow, dark forests, and towns bathed in light. **RCA**

Visit the Cathedrals of the Kremlin

Location Moscow, Russia
Website www.moscow.info/kremlin/index.aspx   **Price** ❶

The first Kremlin was built at Borovinsky Hill during the eleventh and twelfth centuries. It went through a series of reconstructions, including one in 1485 that gave us the redbrick walls and towers that still stand today. At the heart of this mighty edifice is Cathedral Square, home to four cathedrals. Cool in summer, warm in the freeze of winter, the cathedrals are the most beautiful things in the Kremlin.

The oldest of the four is the fifteenth-century Cathedral of the Assumption. Its solemn simplicity and lightness come courtesy of Italian architect Aristotele Fioravanti, who was drafted in from Bologna in 1492, when the structure built by local architects came crashing down. He created a lightness and airiness that is quite distinct from the brooding, gloomy interiors of most orthodox churches. This is Russia's most important church: the place for coronations, burials, and inaugurations of czars.

The Cathedral of the Archangel Michael is the most Italianate of the four, built at the beginning of the sixteenth century by the Italian Aleviz Novyi—it is all gables, whorls, and pilasters. Until Peter the Great, this is where all of Russia's rulers were buried, including Ivan the Terrible. The Church of the Deposition of the Robe is bijou; tiny gilded cupolas grace its roof. Cozy, intimate, and musty, it was the domestic chapel for the czars. Finally, the fifteenth-century Cathedral of the Annunciation sparkles and glows. Here, Ivan the Terrible foresaw his own death when he saw a vision of a cross-shaped comet. Two days later, he died. **LB**

➦ *The dramatic interior of the Church of the Assumption in Cathedral Square, Moscow.*

Stay at the Metropol

Location Moscow, Russia
Website www.metropol-moscow.ru   **Price** ⑤⑤

Were all the famous names that have stayed in this fin de siècle hotel to be listed, the pages of this book would have to extend some distance. There is a reason that the good and the great are drawn toward this triumph of art-nouveau architecture time and again, and that is its simple, timeless elegance and its peerless location. A mere three-minute saunter from Red Square and the Kremlin, and situated opposite the world-famous Bolshoi Theatre, the Metropol could hardly be better located.

The 363 guest rooms are individually furnished, but all have hardwood floors, Asian rugs, Russian floral wallpaper, many works of art, and antiques. The two presidential suites also have private saunas, and the view of Moscow from the upper floors is breathtaking. The sheer size of the hotel means that it takes up an entire block, and the ground floor is home to a host of shops and services, including a fitness center with a small pool and sauna. If you think you have seen the colorful ceiling in the restaurant before, you may well be right. It was featured in David Lean's epic cinematic masterpiece, *Doctor Zhivago*. Mikhail Vrubel's ceramic friezes complement the exterior's spires, colorful tiles, and wrought-iron railings. The skylighted lobby is equally impressive, with gleaming marble, brass and crystal chandeliers, and a famous antique elevator made of cast iron and stained glass.

The Metropol is living proof that although the world may be prone to inexorable change, within these walls, at least, you can narrow your eyes and be transported back to prerevolutionary Russia. **PS**

> *"The ambience is old-style Russian, despite a makeover, with vast, echoey halls and liveried bell boys."*
>
> *Condé Nast Traveler*

↖ *The incredible stained-glass roof of the Metropol's restaurant in Moscow.*

Stay at Hotel Baltschug

Location Moscow, Russia
Website www.kempinski-moscow.com **Price** 🜚🜚🜚

A stone's throw from the Kremlin, Lenin's tomb, and Moscow's Red Square, there is a glamorous hotel with a twist: English royalty designer suites. Viscount David Linley has added his personal touch with bespoke hardwood furniture and a classic cream and navy color scheme, as well as a grand Italian marble bathroom complete with sumptuous chandelier. Her Royal Highness Princess Michael of Kent made over a three-bedroom suite in neutral, relaxing tones with floral designs, bringing a touch of England to Moscow.

The view, though, is as Russian as it comes. One of the Russian capital's most famed landmarks, St. Basil's Cathedral (nicknamed the "ice cream church"), is just

> *"A night at the hotel guarantees all the right amenities . . . along with covetable views of Red Square."*
>
> *Travel+Leisure* magazine

beyond the Moscow River. For a private view of the city skyline, escape to the Bibliothek on the eighth floor, which has a tiny balcony overlooking it all. Below, taste some of Russia's best cuisine, including an excellent champagne risotto with langoustine, turbot with caviar sauce, and praline mille-feuilles for dessert, all washed down with Russia's very own Château Karsov wine.

To have the city to yourself, visit in winter when the temperatures drop dramatically and the streets are deserted. Try your hand at ice-skating on Red Square's outdoor rink, just over the Moskvoretsky Bridge. Bizarre but cool, in every sense of the word. **RCA**

Recharge at Le Meridien

Location Near Moscow, Russia
Website www.lemeridien-mcc.com **Price** 🜚🜚

There are few country hotels that can boast a world-class golf course, but Le Meridien Moscow Country Club goes as far as hosting an event on the main PGA European Tour: the Cadillac Russian Open. It is held on the club's Robert Trent Jones Jr.–designed course, which is suitable for amateurs and aficionados alike. The course is indeed rather elaborate, boasting a computerized golf simulator, mini-golf section, indoor/outdoor driving range, six-person chipping and putting greens, pro shop, and a clubhouse with restaurant, locker rooms, and sauna. All of this is housed in Le Meridien's capacious grounds, which also find room for some major leisure and business facilities. The 131 rooms offer excellent views of a beautiful natural landscape. Looking out onto the evergreen forest, with its birch trees, native wildlife, and scenic lake, it is difficult to believe you are so close to the bustling city of Moscow. However, the Bolshoi Theatre, the Kremlin, and Red Square are all a mere blini throw away—less than 12 miles (20 km).

If you are not a golfing addict and do not feel like going into the city, there is still plenty to do. You can swim in the lake, head to the lakeside bar to try some vodkas, or relax in a private whirlpool tub and sauna in the luxury of your own suite. The resort also offers areas for jogging, beach volleyball, and fishing. Depending on the season, you may try skating, skiing, cross-country skiing, and dogsled riding.

Russia's unique climate is warmer than you might think in the summer, and the balmy evenings are ideal for horseback riding through the picturesque woods around the hotel. It is also possible for families to rent a country house in the complex for as long as they like, with access to all restaurants and bars. **PS**

Ride the Trans-Siberian Railway Past Lake Baikal

Location Siberia, Russia **Website** www.trans-siberian.co.uk
Price $

The Trans-Siberian is the longest, strangest, most epic railway journey on the planet, and a unique way to access Siberia, a region often talked about but rarely visited. You can get to Moscow any way you choose, but for a super–long haul, there are connecting trains from all over Europe. Once in the Russian capital, you head to gray, somber Yaroslavsky station, from which a whole series of trains head east—the Trans-Siberian is the line, not the train.

The shortest trip is to take the 4,735-mile (7,620-km) Trans-Mongolian, which crosses the taiga, Siberian steppe, and Mongolian desert in just six days. The 5,623-mile (9,050-km) Trans-Manchurian trip also takes six days and follows a similar route but loops around Mongolia to enter China through Harbin, famed for its ice sculptures during the winter months. The definitive, wholly Russian trip is the seven-day, 6,152-mile (9,900-km) Moscow to Vladivostok route, which takes you all the way to the Pacific Ocean.

On all routes you will enjoy smoked fish, neat vodka, pot noodles, carriage camaraderie, and broken English and Russian conversations, as well as plenty of time to read, sleep, and take in the bleakly beautiful landscape of silver birch forests. Whichever option you choose, though, make sure you break your journey in Irkutsk, because the real high point of the Trans-Siberian traverse is Lake Baikal, the deepest, coldest, bluest lake imaginable and, with its freshwater seals, salmonlike omul, and remarkable translucent golomyanka fish, a wonderful contrast to Siberia's barren wastes. **CM**

→ *The Trans-Siberian Railway passes along the shore of Lake Baikal, the world's largest freshwater lake.*

Climb Mount Elbrus

Location Caucasus, Russia **Website** www.elbrus.org
Price 💲💲

The tallest mountian in Europe is not Mont Blanc, but rather the little-known Mount Elbrus, a brooding 18,519-foot (5,642-m) colossus set in the remote Caucasus Mountains in the extreme southwest corner of Russia. A twin-cone volcano that has lain dormant for 2,000 years, Elbrus has two peaks, the western being the higher by some 65 feet (20 m).

Reaching either of the summits can be strenuous but is certainly within the capabilities of a climber in reasonably good shape with moderate skills. However, it is crucial to acclimatize yourself properly to the high altitudes, and the specialist climbing tour companies that bring groups here require participants

> "The area is famous for its dramatic glaciers, which feed a handful of rivers in the summer."

Steve Connor, *Independent*

to complete a six-day or more training course, or to provide evidence of having previously acquired the equivalent skills or relevant experience elsewhere.

En route to base camp, winding mountain trails through stunning scenery present ample opportunity to interact with locals at the remote villages. This region is a colorful meeting place of cultures: Russian, Georgian, Azerbaijani, and Turkish. The real thrill, though, is in getting close to the wild. Eagles soar overhead, wild animals roam the forests, and trout swim the mountain streams. The terrain is truly awesome. The accommodation may be basic and the food challenging, but you are at one with nature. **RsP**

See Nalychevo Nature Park

Location Kamchatka, Russia **Website** www.park.kamchatka.ru
Price 💲

Getting back to nature is one thing; exploring the Nalychevo Nature Park in the depths of Siberia is quite another. Remote, silent, and far from anywhere, it's hard to put into words quite how isolated you feel in the far flung inhospitable Kamchatka peninsula in the Russian far east, renowned for its volcanoes (nearly 100 in Kamchatka), bears, and rivers full of salmon.

Nalychevo is the most accessible of Kamchatka's five nature parks. But these things are relative; the Kamchatka peninsula is still 9 hours ahead of Moscow, which is over 4,000 miles (6,400 km) away.

Kamchatka is sparsely populated and is widely recognized as having the world's fastest changing geology, where mountains have grown measurably higher and valleys wider than anywhere else in the course of a single lifetime. Nalychevo itself is dominated by three volcanoes: Koryaksky last erupted in 1956, Zhupanovsky in 1957, and Avacha in 1991. All this volcanic activity gives rise to the formation of tremendous geothermal and cold mineral springs, concentrated near the headwaters of the Nalycheva River. Blueberry bushes, birch trees, flowing rivers, and hot springs fill the landscape, while the valleys are surrounded by snow covered peaks. There are no fences in these parks, enabling the wildlife such as bears, wolves, and Arctic foxes to roam freely.

You can go hiking up one of the active volcanoes, bathe in the hot springs, or fish for salmon. In the winter you can ski or go dogsledding. Whatever the season, breathe in the pure still air, drink the naturally carbonated water, and relish the perfect silence. **HA**

➡ *The park combines stunning mountain scenery with vast expanses of tundra and coastal seascapes.*

In Africa, many organizations now offer exclusive tourist enterprises that aid local communities and help them conserve their environments. There has never been a better time to plan an escape to Africa, which could include anything from a hot-air balloon ride in Egypt, to a luxury spa in Namibia, a safari camp in South Africa, or a walk with nomads in Morocco.

← Shompole Lodge, Kenya

AFRICA

Stay at Dar Roumana

Location Fez, Morocco **Website** www.darroumana.com
Price ⊖ ⊖

It took three years of careful restoration to revive Dar Roumana to its former glory. Step inside "house of the pomegranate" and you will instantly appreciate how well that hard work has paid off. Carved wooden screens, high cedar ceilings, stucco friezes, and tiles were hand-cleaned by local artisans with toothpicks and steel wool; now they are just some of the magnificent details of this spectacular hotel.

Wander past the bubbling courtyard fountain and up the steps to the terrace for incredible views of the sprawling rooftops and minarets of the ancient Medina below. Cozy up on a leather pouffe or comfy sofa with a drink, or sit down to dinner, prepared

> *"The results [of the restoration] are stunning: a gorgeous tiled courtyard and beautiful suites."*
>
> *Harper's Bazaar*

by American owner Jennifer, who is a Cordon Bleu–trained chef. If you are lucky, Jennifer's flamenco-guitarist husband, Sebastian, will serenade you.

Perched on a hillside within the medieval city walls, the hotel is just five minutes from shops and cafés. Follow Jennifer and Sebastian on a guided tour of the Medina and its food markets, or take a trip to the public hammam. Back at the *riad* (house), relax on the rooftop with its sheltered seating, raised crow's nest viewing point, and shade from a huge plane tree. Jennifer also offers cooking lessons so that you can re-create special dishes such as swordfish in spiced pomegranate marinade at home. **AD**

Enjoy Villa Maroc

Location Essaouira, Morocco **Website** www.villamaroc.com
Price ⊖ ⊖

In typical Moroccan fashion the entrance to Villa Maroc gives away little of the delights waiting to be discovered behind its vast blue doors. It hides among the winding lanes of the Medina and souk: Outside all is hustle, bustle, and vibrant color; inside is a peaceful sanctuary within ancient stone walls. Villa Maroc has long been a favorite with the in-crowd of artists, models, and photographers, but it has a relaxed and friendly atmosphere that will appeal to anyone with an eye for style and joie de vivre.

Inside, the beauty of Villa Maroc is startling. All sparkling white and electric blue, the galleried landings, lush with a profusion of plants, overlook the central courtyard. Guests gather here around open fires, chatting and playing chess together well into the night. A cozy conviviality flourishes, and the excellent food and gentle but lively evening scene attracts guests from other *riads* (houses) as well. Topped with a roof terrace and sun loungers for daytime sun soaking, the seductive scene is set with the evocative cries of the muezzin in the background.

The twenty suites, arrayed over three floors, are a delight. Yet more dazzling white walls set off the vibrant colors of the rich cotton fabrics. There is locally carved thuya-wood furniture here, intriguing objects and hidden alcoves there, and the glittering mosaic bathrooms are staggeringly beautiful.

Much of Essaouira's appeal lies in the fact that it is not a sprawling resort but a busy working fishing port. The city was once patronized by Portuguese wood-merchants and Roman dye-traders, and the sense of the past is palpable, yet it bubbles with daily activity. If you are craving an escape, however, you will always find the perfect retreat at Villa Maroc. **SWi**

Relax at Maison M.K.

Location Marrakech, Morocco **Website** www.maisonmk.com
Price 🔇🔇

The Medina in Marrakech is one of the most mesmerizing, bewildering, and seething masses of people, noises, smells, and excitement to be found anywhere in the world. Whether you are experiencing it for the first time or are a frequent visitor, it is practically impossible not to get lost in the winding maze of alleyways that twist and turn and take you farther away from where you actually want to go.

Escape from the madness of the outside world into one of the many *riads* (houses) that have been converted into little hotels. Maison M.K. is the brainchild of fashion photographer Paul Hopkins, who fell in love with Marrakech while on assignments here; the *riad* is more European in its internal touches than some of its more traditional neighbors. The building may look unprepossessing from the dusty alleyway outside, but stepping through the heavy entrance door is like walking into an oasis of calm. Built around a courtyard, there is an ornate, gilt-edged plunge pool that trickles in the background and a relaxing roof terrace where you can surround yourself with cushions on a sun lounger, and look down on the chaos below.

Maison M.K. also has its own spa, and two treatment rooms where guests can indulge themselves in a host of soothing therapies, including a luxurious facial that only uses natural ingredients such as avocado, cucumber, and yogurt. The *riad* is relatively easy to find, situated just yards from one of the main western entrances to the Medina. It is the superlative attention to detail at Maison M.K., as well as its central location, that makes it stand out from the rest. **RS**

↗ *Maison M.K. is a relative newcomer to the Marrakech riad scene, but it offers its own little world of tranquility.*

"Lose yourself in the rhythm [of Marrakech] and breathe in the exotic sights and sounds."

Proprietors, Maison M.K.

Stay at Amanjena

Location Marrakech, Morocco   **Website** www.amanresorts.com
Price ⊖⊖⊖

Aman's chain of resorts have garnered a formidable reputation around the world and rightly so. Amanjena, the company's flagship North African resort, is a perfect example of their smooth and sure approach. A palatial estate set on the outskirts of Morocco's "Pink City," the hotel was designed by American architect Ed Tuttle and melds mellifluously with its surroundings, combining Moorish architectural influences, such as the expansive arches that line the main building, with subtle Asian undertones.

Passing through the grand entrance, the visitor enters an otherworld of terra-cotta villas and ocher pavilions separated by thin reflective rivers and splendidly manicured lawns. Each pavilion boasts a private courtyard complete with gazebo and fountain, and eight of the pavilions have their own swimming pool. The interiors are huge and imaginative: Curving walls vie with bathrooms carved from green Moroccan marble and feature deep-soak tubs for your attention. Should you want extra privacy, try one of the *maisons*, two-story town houses that include fireplaces, guest bedrooms, and personal butler service, plus a private 270-square-foot (25-sq-m) pool and garden.

Amanjena also offers access to a 110-foot (33-m) pool and a health and beauty center with hammams, a spa, and a gym. Breakfast, lunch, and dinner are served in the Thai Restaurant, either indoors or in a garden courtyard next to the pool, and a Moroccan restaurant offers à la carte traditional food in the evenings. Visiting golfers will enjoy the fact that the resort is next door to two courses. **PS**

➔ *The understated luxury of Amanjena is reflected in one of the many turquoise pools around the resort.*

Visit Jardin Majorelle

Location Marrakech, Morocco
Website www.jardinmajorelle.com **Price** 🟢

Tucked away from the traffic noise, hawkers, beggars, and hot, dusty streets of Marrakech is the Jardin Majorelle, an oasis of calm in a city of chaos. These tranquil gardens, just outside the Medina walls, were designed by French expatriate artist Jacques Majorelle in 1924, during the colonial period when Morocco was a protectorate of France. Majorelle's watercolors still survive, but his garden was his real creative masterpiece. It was opened to the public in 1947 and has been welcoming visitors ever since. Since 1980 the garden was owned by designer Yves Saint-Laurent and his friend and patron, Pierre Bergé. Yves Saint-Laurent's ashes were scattered there after his death.

The garden's most characteristic feature is the special shade of cobalt blue that Majorelle used extensively to color the walls of the Museum of Islamic Art, housed in the artist's former home, as well as on flowerpots and other garden features. This brilliant color is now known as "bleu Majorelle."

A variety of birds have been spotted here, including falcons, turtledoves, robins, and storks. A variety of pathways and viewing areas leads you around a series of small pools, in which water lilies, lotus, papyrus, and other aquatic plants grow profusely. This is a welcome respite from the bustle of the city, with only the trickling of water to disturb the peace.

Be sure to pay a visit to the Museum of Islamic Art while you are here. It contains many treasures from the Islamic world, including ceramics, textiles, weapons, pottery and jewelry from Africa and Asia, as well as some paintings by Majorelle himself. **HA**

◄ *The vibrantly colored "bleu Majorelle" walls of the museum contrast with the garden's plants.*

Stay at Dar les Cigognes

Location Marrakech, Morocco
Website www.lescigognes.com **Price** 🟢🟢

For anyone who may wondering, a "cigogne" is a stork. In the case of Dar les Cigognes, it is not just any old stork, but specifically those that sit on the walls of Marrakech's Royal Palace, which is just across the road.

A former merchant's home, located slap-bang in the center of Marrakech's famous Medina, Dar les Cigognes was lovingly restored by architect Charles Boccara and a team of local craftsmen. The traditional techniques are evident throughout the property, from intricate floor mosaics to elegantly carved wooden doors. Enter the building's courtyard to be greeted by fragrant citrus trees and a gently bubbling fountain; seek out the elegant dining room, library, and a

> *"Boccara . . . applied his Midas touch to this seventeenth-century former merchant's home."*
>
> *The Times*

reading/relaxation salon. Although these public areas lean toward classic Asian decor, Dar les Cigognes's eleven rooms are an entirely different matter: beautiful local touches blended with eyeball-popping hipness. The rooms also have enormous, funky beds, creatively carved baths, and luxurious cotton bathrobes.

The overall experience is soothing, luxurious, and attentive. Have your meals made to order and enjoy them at the rooftop café, looking out over the Atlas Mountains. Alternatively, take advantage of the great in-house spa, with its massage room, hammam, and whirlpool tub. The location is also a mere stone's throw from most of the Medina's main sights. **PS**

Unwind at Riad Farnatchi

Location Marrakech, Morocco
Website www.riadfarnatchi.com **Price** 🟢🟢

Riad Farnatchi was originally devised as the home of hotel entrepreneur Jonathan Wix, until he decided to transform it into a boutique hotel—an idea that proved highly successful.

Situated in one of the oldest areas of Marrakech's dusty Medina, the *riad* (house)—actually three *riads* combined—is designed around two courtyards and offers nine deluxe suites. Although the buildings date back as far as 400 years, the decor and amenities are thoroughly modern. Light and airy, each suite is stylishly decked out with every high-tech feature needed as well as elegant desks and traditional rugs and furnishings. Relax in a marble bath or book a daily

> *"A blissful union of traditional and modern. . . . Flowers tumble down the high walls."*

Sophie Lam, *Independent*

appointment at the in-house hammam, which has a superb array of tempting treatments to offer—from traditional Moroccan to the latest fads.

Even when full, the *riad* retains an air of quiet intimacy, an atmosphere engendered by the numerous cozy nooks around the courtyards and a large rooftop terrace with plenty of lounging spots. Romantic candlelit dinners are available (with a menu that changes every night), and the service is effortlessly good, with staff seemingly invisible until the exact moment you need them. In a city that is famed for its chic accommodation spots, Farnatchi works hard to stay well ahead of the pack. **PS**

Experience Caravanserai

Location Marrakech, Morocco
Website www.caravanserai.com **Price** 🟢🟢

Although Caravanserai ranks among Marrakech's top luxury accommodation hot spots, it is easy to mistake it from the outside for a traditional Arabic home. A fifteen-minute drive from the center of Marrakech, this 200-year-old building has been renovated precisely to fit in seamlessly with its surroundings, a tiny Arabic village. Inside is a rather different story.

Designed by local legend Charles Boccara (with his son, Mathieu), Caravanserai is an intimate wonderland of rustic appeal. Ancient techniques have been applied to re-create an authentic kasbah feel, complete with mud walls, old wooden beams, and use of a local material called *tadelakt*. The eleven suites and five standard rooms are arranged around a courtyard and large swimming pool. Two rooms have their own private pools, and most have their own terrace. The bathrooms are breathtaking.

Caravanserai's robe-clad staff seem to mysteriously appear just when you need them and disappear when you do not, and almost all requirements (within reason) are dealt with efficiently and obligingly.

Although not far from the center of the city—taxis and chauffeurs can be arranged—there is a particularly pleasant restaurant/bar on-site with a Moroccan and French menu, plus a serene designer garden and a hammam to coax you to stay. Terraces offer views across the River Tensift, the Atlas Mountains, and the ancient date grove known as the Palmeraie. Sitting there on a clear night, looking out at the dramatic nightscape with a fresh cup of mint tea by your side, is to feel like Moroccan royalty. **PS**

➦ *Caravanserai's central courtyard is dominated by its luxurious heated swimming pool.*

Relax at Riad El Fenn

Location Marrakech, Morocco
Website www.riadelfenn.com **Price** 💲💲

"This . . . is a perfect combination of Asian glamor and pedigreed European-style creature comforts."

Condé Nast Traveler

Hidden in an atmospheric alley close to Marrakech's bustling souks, Riad El Fenn is a haven of tranquility. Behind its formidable 3-foot- (1-m-) thick fortress walls are secreted surprisingly large areas of the most stylish interiors, serene courtyards, and intimate corners. it manages to be a unique mix of grandiose old elegance and cutting-edge contemporary.

The roof terraces offer some of the finest views in Marrakech, looking down onto the Koutoubia Mosque and the bustling Medina. All around the hotel are perfect places to relax. Chill out under flowery pergolas, on sundecks, on one of the huge sofas, or on a mound of cushions. Practice your golf skills, cool down in the plunge pool, or visit the sumptuous spa with its steamy hammam, treatment rooms, and two pools, one lined with Carrara marble, the other with invigorating jets.

The twenty-two guest rooms and suites all have their own individual character, and all are devastatingly alluring. Visitors seeking the most stylish space and cavernous place to sleep may like the idea of Suite 19, with its 16-foot- (5-m-) high ceilings and 645 square feet (60 sq m) of private terrace. Designer Frederic Scholl managed to make this enormous space feel cozy by using hand-sewn camel leather floors, warm-hued furnishings, a roll-top bath, and intriguing art.

Feel at home by choosing to eat wherever you like. If you're feeling sociable, pick a table at the alfresco restaurant; if you're in a mood to enjoy your own company, find a secluded shady corner where you can dine contentedly without being disturbed. **NB**

↖ *One of Riad El Fenn's liberatingly wide open corridors, hidden away in the heart of Marrakech.*

Stay at Kasbah Agafay

Location Near Marrakech, Morocco
Website www.kasbahagafay.com **Price** ⊖⊖⊖

With its panoramic views over ancient olive groves, desert hills, and the Atlas Mountains, Kasbah Agafay has to be seen to be believed. The building was a hilltop fortress 150 years ago, but it was transformed into a luxury retreat by London-based Moroccan designer Abel Damoussi. It took three years just to purchase the Kasbah from its previous thirty-six owners, and the same amount of time again to restore the building to its current status.

The stunning location—forty minutes away from Marrakech—makes this hotel the perfect escape. Kasbah Agafay boasts sixteen main suites, built around five *riad*-style courtyards, all interconnected by a maze of corridors. The suites are individually designed and furnished with a sophisticated blend of Berber and Arabic handcrafts and plenty of contemporary flair. They are luxurious enough to satisfy most mortals, but Agafay also has four Caïdal tents that are fit for kings. Packed with antiques and over-the-top decor (enormous four-poster beds, handwoven rugs, over-sized bathtubs, and even statues), these will certainly suit honeymooners and romantics.

Aside from accommodation, Agafay offers a plethora of in-house facilities, including a large swimming pool, traditional hammams, spa complex (with dedicated yoga pavilion), floodlit tennis court, and a cooking school, all located within the hotel's organic gardens. Staff will also happily arrange hiking and mountain biking, camel treks, or even a game of golf. You do not even have to leave the hotel to find a restaurant: Kasbah Agafay's French-Moroccan kitchen provides world-class cuisine. This is a perfect example of how staying at the right hotel can prove to be an entirely satisfying vacation by itself. **PS**

Stay at Ksar Char-Bagh

Location Palmeraie, Morocco
Website www.ksarcharbagh.com **Price** ⊖⊖⊖

Ksar Char-Bagh may look like a Moorish palace, but it is actually an exceptionally good imitation of one. It was constructed by Patrick and Nicole Levillair, after fruitlessly searching for their dream property. It was created with a painstaking amount of skill and a passion for Moroccan architecture and culture, aided by Nicole's research into Middle Eastern and Moorish art.

After a drive through the slightly surreal area of Palmeraie, Ksar Char-Bagh rises forth like a fairy-tale mirage. The twelve deluxe guest rooms are enormous and decorated with one-off antiques and exclusive objets d'art, as well as modern essentials and creature comforts, and the bathrooms come with silk djellabas.

"At Ksar Char-Bagh . . . you're never far from the soothing sight and sound of running water."

Richard Alleman, *Travel+Leisure* magazine

Outside lies an ornate, manicured landscape of moats, pools, fountains, and gardens, the focus of which is a beautiful black swimming pool.

The gardens, replete with palm trees, olive trees, fruit, vegetables, and herbs, are a delight and provide the raw materials for the hotel's much-lauded kitchen. Other facilities include a billiards room, cigar club, library, wine cellar, gym, luxurious spa, and private golf course. It might not be a genuine fourteenth-century Moorish palace, but the experience of being made to feel like royalty at Ksar Char-Bagh—whose name symbolizes the fundamental link between water and life—is spectacularly authentic. **PS**

Enjoy Palais Rhoul

Location Palmeraie, Morocco
Website www.palaisrhoul.com **Price** 💲💲💲

Legend has it that the eponymous palms of the Palmeraie, a district northwest of Marrakech, were created centuries ago by the date seeds discarded by sweet-toothed Arab warriors. This is a desiccated environment of dusty palms, dry, scrubby ground, and wandering camels, but it is also the Beverly Hills of Marrakech—push open the discreet gates of any high-walled mansion in these parts and you will find a lush green oasis. After leaving a hot, dusty city like Marrakech, it is wonderful to experience such abundant water, lushness, and greenery.

Behind high walls and a fortresslike gate on an unremarkable lane lies one such building, set in romantic, palm-filled gardens. This is the inimitable, eccentric, sexy Palais Rhoul, where beautiful antiques jostle each other for attention and vast candelabras dangle from palm trees. In the vast public atrium, a marble pool takes center stage, filled with rose petals, and columns and palm trees soar upward to a domed ceiling and mezzanine library stacked with books.

Some rooms open onto a large, shallow, colonnaded pool, where floating candles drift at night. Others are Moroccan caidal tents, the kind once used by traveling noblemen. These are found in gardens filled with rosebushes, cacti, oleander shrubs, and olive, pomegranate, and citrus trees.

The hammam is now famous, as is its towering resident masseur. He tosses you about almost viciously: scrubbing, rubbing, slapping, flipping, and roaring with laughter. Afterward, you are dipped in an ice-cold pool, then rubbed with fresh oranges for the ultimate in refreshment. If you do not have the riches to stay in the Palais Rhoul overnight, a visit to the hammam is within reach of more modest pockets. **LB**

Enjoy Jnane

Location Palmeraie, Morocco
Website www.jnanetamsna.com **Price** 💲💲

Brad Pitt and David Bowie are among the high-profile guests who have visited Jnane (formerly Jnane Tamsna), in Palmeraie, not far from Marrakech. Jnane is the creation of Meryanne Loum-Martin, a Senegalese lawyer-turned-designer, and her husband, Gary J. Martin, an ethno-botanist from the United States.

The twenty-four rooms are split between Jnane House, Jnane Salmia, and Maison des Voyageurs-Moussafir. The airy, grand architecture is all stunning adobe walls, Moroccan arches, and lush, bougainvillea-clad patios. Indoors lie handpicked textiles from Senegal, Morocco, and Asia. Rooms are furnished simply but beautifully with generous beds, chaise

"[A] boutique hotel with a coolly contemporary flavour set amid aromatic gardens."

Tessa Boase, *Daily Telegraph*

longues, fireplaces, paintings, and flowers. There are three swimming pools (two are heated in winter), a tennis court, English and French libraries, and a recreation room with CD and DVD collections.

Jnane means "garden" in Arabic, and the gardens here are a huge natural attraction. Ingredients for the restaurant's excellent Med-Moroccan food are grown here. The owners are also dedicated to furthering and exploring Marrakech's cultural life and have devised a series of diversity excursions. Led by friendly, local university-educated guides, these tours take guests off the tourist track to provide unique insights into Moroccan customs, cuisine, and art. **PS**

Relax at Azwou'n Crisaran

Location Rissani, Morocco
Website www.crisaran.com   **Price** $$\$$$$\$$

Perhaps, in the darkest hours of night, you occasionally find yourself dreaming of the ultimate escape. You will throw in that office job, burn your pin-striped suits, and gallop away with the Berbers across the sands of Morocco. Instead, keep the paycheck and satisfy your wanderlust by booking a few nights at Azwou'n Crisaran, where you can wallow in the Berber experience the luxury way: with hammam, haute cuisine, and comfortable four-wheel-drive jeeps.

Azwou'n Crisaran sits at the foot of the Sahara Desert's sand dunes. Accommodation comprises sixteen suites, each with a living room, bedroom, bathroom, and fireplace. The beds feature zebra-striped throws; the floors, Moroccan rugs; and candles and glittering gilt mirrors against sultry terra-cotta walls leave little doubt as to which continent you are in. Daytime activities include excursions to the sand dunes, guided trips to local villages, camel rides, and flights in light aircraft. On Tuesdays, Thursdays, and Sundays, you can follow the nomads to market. You can visit Erfud, famous for dates and fossils; the mighty Merzouga dunes, from where you will see dazzling sunrises and sunsets; and Ksar El Borj, with its panoramas of the Rissani palm groves. At Tafilalet, where the Alauite dynasty was born, you will find palaces and a mausoleum.

Alternatively, lounge by Azwou'n Crisaran's swimming lake, or have a massage in the old adobe hammam. Then, there is dinner. The Jaima restaurant's chefs specialize in Arabic and Berber cuisine. Each day they cook different dishes intended to recall centuries of culinary traditions. Sit back on the low cushions, take a sip of your mint tea, and contemplate: you are far more comfortable than those horsemen. **PE**

Unwind at Dar Ahlam

Location Ouarzazate, Morocco
Website www.maisonsdesreves.com   **Price** $$\$$$$\$$

Getting to Dar Ahlam in the southern Moroccan desert is quite a challenge, but the places that are the hardest to get to are often the most worthwhile, and Dar Ahlam is no exception. A traditional mud-baked kasbah whose name means the "house of dreams," it stands regal like a red fortress in Skoura's green oasis, 25 miles (40 km) from Ouarzazate.

In this Garden of Eden, the birds' intense song is the only noise to break the silence. This last green bastion before the desert is like an enchanted forest, utterly bewitching. It is a blissful parallel world without phones, televisions, or everyday worries: no formality, no rules, no keys, no regulations, just freedom. Inside,

> *"Even the most committed sybarite might be overwhelmed by this 'House of Dreams.'"*
>
> *Harper's Bazaar*

studded wooden doors reveal rooms stuffed with antiques. All nine are unique, with furnishings from Morocco, of course, but also from Bali, Syria, and France. Meals can be had in a variety of locations: breakfast on the roof terrace and lunch beneath the olive trees or by the twinkling pool. For a "1001 Nights" evening, rich red fabrics, decorative spices, and dozens of candles are laid out for the feast.

Escape to one of the terraces scattered with bright turquoise cushions, head to the hypnotic, humid hammam, venture out to the Valley of Roses, or choose a candlelit dinner in the ruins. It is all part of the fairy-tale experience. This is what dreams are made of. **RCA**

Enjoy Kasbah du Toubkal

Location Atlas Mountains, Morocco
Website www.kasbahdutoubkal.com   **Price** ⟐

"The cloud burned off, revealing a sight of such beauty that I had to sit and stare at it for some time."

Anthony Sattin, *Condé Nast Traveler*

Situated at the foot of Mount Toubkal, the highest peak in North Africa, the Kasbah du Toubkal perches on a rocky crag 5,900 feet (1,800 m) up in the Atlas Mountains. The mountains are just 40 miles (64 km) from the city of Marrakech, but their seclusion and relaxed pace of life are a world apart.

The restored fort is reached by a fifteen-minute mule ride from the tiny Berber village of Imlil. The Kasbah does not describe itself as a hotel, it is more an extension of the hospitality of the local Berber villagers, in consultation with whom the Kasbah was originally developed and who run it today. The Kasbah has two huge roof terraces, and although there is no swimming pool—out of respect for local customs—there is a steam room and plunge-pool complex.

Comfortable rather than luxurious, the guest rooms are decorated in traditional Berber style, with carved walnut furniture. They have private bathtubs or showers and stunning mountain vistas. The superior rooms have a balcony or terrace. To the south of the Kasbah is the Garden House, a three-bedroom house for those wanting even more privacy.

What the Kasbah lacks in five-star luxury, it more than makes up for in its magnificent setting, which offers superb treks right from the door. Treks range from short, easy strolls through the surrounding villages to overnight walks, including demanding multiday treks to remote valleys with local mountain guides and mule support. One of the best walking options is the two-day ascent of 13,655-foot (4,160-m) Mount Toubkal itself. **ML**

◩ *Sip traditional mint tea and breathe in the air from the Atlas Mountains on Kasbah du Toubkal's terrace.*

Walk with Nomads

Location High Atlas, Morocco
Website www.epicmorocco.co.uk **Price** 💲💲

Walking with nomads is the perfect way to explore the rugged landscape of the High Atlas in Morocco, following in the footsteps of generations of Ait Atta tribesmen. Camping out in wilderness locations, you and your small tents are dwarfed by giant rock formations in an area where fellow tourists are few and far between. Nonetheless, life is all around you in the shape of hundreds of goats and their kids, dromedaries, sheep, and mules belonging to the Berber family.

After a six-hour journey from Marrakech, you come to the hamlet of Hamdor in the Central High Atlas for the six-day trekking experience. Here you join Zaid, his family, and helpers. After a night at a *gite*, the first

> *"We felt like pioneers, and in a sense we were—this was an exploratory adventure."*
>
> Isabel Choat, *Guardian*

morning of the trek begins with hustle and bustle as the handlers load the mules and dromedaries with provisions and belongings for the trip.

The five-hour daily walks (moderate hiking) along rocky paths are broken with frequent stops for heavily sweetened mint tea. By the time you arrive at the day's camp, the Berber tent and kitchen have already been erected for you and your baggage awaits. In the evenings, after supper of *tagine* (stew) and bread freshly baked on stones, trekkers sit out under the stars around the jasmine-wood campfire, and on one night, Zaid, his nephew, and the mule handlers celebrate a barbecue by singing and dancing in the firelight. **RB**

Stay at La Gazelle D'Or

Location Near Taroudant, Morocco
Website www.gazelledor.com **Price** 💲💲

The bougainvillea tumbles colorfully over the thirty discreet cottage bungalows of La Gazelle D'Or, and the scent of the surrounding 200 acres (80 ha) of organic orange groves wafts across its manicured hedges and perfect lawns.

A mile outside the ancient walled town of Taroudant, in the foothills of the snowcapped Atlas Mountains, this is a quiet, calm version of Morocco. There are no televisions in these elegant stone pavilions, just crackling open log fires in winter and flickering Moroccan lamps after dark. There is quiet luxury in the bare plaster walls, muslin drapes, hand-woven rugs, and fresh flowers in terra-cotta pots standing on antique wooden furniture. La Gazelle is more like a relaxed country house hotel—with a North African flavor. It is renowned as a retreat for celebrities, yet the hotel remains discreet about its famous regulars—and that is probably why they keep coming.

Walk along decorated brick paths between hedges of flowering roses to an 80-foot (24-m) heated outdoor pool carefully hidden by greenery, play tennis on clay courts, or even try a game of croquet on the lawn. Guests can eat privately on their open terrace, or in the grand circular tented dining room, where waiters in floor-length white robes swish between tables balancing silver trays. Dinner is a seven-course gourmet experience. Lunch is usually a magnificent buffet of fresh seafood, meat, and salads with many ingredients fresh from the hotel's organic farm.

The old carved wooden door into the spa reveals a mix of traditional hammam and modern beauty therapies using natural products and essential oils. There is also a gym, and the hotel has its own riding stables, so you can ride straight to the mountains. **SH**

Relax at Dar Dhiafa

Location Djerba, Tunisia **Website** www.hoteldardhiafa.com
Price 💲💲

Dar Dhiafa is hidden away down a narrow lane behind thick walls and studded wooden doors, but entering the bougainvillea-strewn courtyard is like stepping into a different world. Five 600-year-old whitewashed and shuttered houses in Erriadh, the old Jewish quarter of Djerba, have been tastefully converted to offer an exotic but unpretentious retreat. It's a warren of winding passageways, nooks, and crannies, and thick stone arches. There are nine rooms and six suites in all, each built around flower-festooned courtyards, which are linked via a series of shady corridors. The rooms have beamed ceilings, terra-cotta floor tiles strewn with colorful Berber rugs, antiques, traditional

---

"Butterflies flit about a small swimming pool flanked by flower-filled urns and sun loungers."

Condé Nast Traveler

---

lamps, and local pottery. The thick, whitewashed stone walls manage to keep the interiors cool in the fierce summer heat, but there is air-conditioning, too, for when things really start to heat up. There are also two small pools, a hammam, and atmospheric indoor and outdoor dining rooms, that serve delicious traditional and locally inspired food.

A walk into the village of Erriadh feels like you've stepped back in time; old men shuffle around in long robes and sandals, goats roam around freely, and donkeys carrying vast burdens clip-clop around. Be sure to visit the synagogue of El Ghriba, a major Jewish pilgrimage site that dates back to 586 B.C.E. **HA**

Enjoy Pansea Ksar Ghilane

Location Sahara Desert, Tunisia **Website** www.pansea.com
Price 💲💲

Spread between the palm trees in a corner of the northern tip of the Sahara are the sixty linen tents of the Pansea Ksar Ghilane desert camp. Cut off from the rest of the world, this oasis sits in perfect isolation on the site of an old castle. The only way to get here is by four-by-four vehicle; it is a three-hour journey across some of the world's starkest yet most stunning scenery.

Within the traditionally styled romantic tents, you will discover billowing curtains, original local art, and hanging lanterns, as well as beautiful kilims on the floor. There's a nod to modernity in the form of air-conditioning units, which also work as heaters in winter, but there are no televisions or telephones, and there's no cell phone reception at the camp.

Outside the tents, you can lounge by a pool filled with water from a natural spring while you plan your desert adventures. You can take a camel trek to salt pans and dunes, go on a trip to explore Roman ruins, or climb to the top of the restored watchtower for views across the endless sea of sand and dazzling sunsets. Or you could take a four-by-four into the desert to see Chott el Jerid near Douz, where scenes of the movie *The English Patient* were shot, and the old Berber *ghorfas* (ancient podlike granaries) near Tataouine where the early *Star Wars* movies were filmed.

The restaurant is the epitome of Bedouin chic with cushion-covered stone benches and wrought-iron lanterns. Tunisian fare and French cuisine are the highlights of the menu, with specialties including beef stew, simmering lamb casserole, couscous, and brochette. Alternatively, sit in a traditional goat-hair tent and eat dinner cooked in a fire pit in the sand, then finish the night with a puff on a flavored tobacco hookah pipe as you take in the night stars above. **AD**

Unwind at Hotel Dar Said

Location Sidi Bou Said, Tunisia   **Website** www.darsaid.com.tn
Price 🏷️🏷️

One of the most enchanting retreats in Tunisia, the small Dar Said hotel is an exquisite nineteenth-century mansion, formerly a family home. It sits at the top of the pretty blue-and-white cliff-top village of Sidi Bou Said and looks out across the Bay of Tunis.

Surrounded by high, whitewashed walls covered with bougainvillea, the two-story house is set around four courtyards with orange gardens and a pool. The hotel exudes a relaxed, charming atmosphere. You will discover jasmine-scented terraces and sun-shaded tables at which to eat breakfast, as well as sun-dappled tiled courtyards and sparkling fountains to rest beside. Soak up the wonderful interiors, decorated with rich Italian fabrics, tasteful antiques, and silk rugs. High-ceilinged rooms are decorated in pale colors and studded with Moorish furniture. Visit the hammam for a restorative treat, and then stroll through the narrow streets that snake down to the marina.

The village of Sidi Bou Said, 10 miles (16 km) east of Tunis, was founded as a hilltop retreat by a thirteenth-century Sufi mystic, Abu Said. It became a popular summer escape for the Tunisian aristocracy and eventually began to attract artists, including Paul Klee. The small market is a great place to find delicacies and souvenirs, and the galleries and museum-mansions reveal the fascinating local heritage. There are several very nice places to eat in the village, some of which have panoramic views of the Mediterranean. Return to the hotel to sip mint tea in a courtyard beneath a languid night sky, breathing in the scent of local plants. A stay at Dar Said is a feast for the senses. **AD**

↗ *The fantastic view from the terrace at the top of Hotel Dar Said lets you enjoy the sun all day long.*

"The night sky is starry, the silence uninterrupted save for the soft rustle of fragrant eucalytpus trees."

Sean O'Hagan, *Observer*

Balloon over Valley of the Kings

Location Luxor, Egypt **Website** www.egypt.travel
Price 🌐

A predawn balloon flight is designed to catch the sunrise over Thebes, the City of the Dead. There are bird's-eye views of bemused donkeys, and the voyeuristic pleasure of spotting families asleep on mud roofs, or an antlike funeral procession treading across the desert.

Set on the West Bank of the Nile, facing Luxor, Thebes was the counterpart to Luxor's City of the Living. As dawn turns the desert tawny, views across the valley reveal the Nile on one side and mountains on the other. Beside the world's longest river lie mud-brick hovels, harsh limestone cliffs—and the tombs.

"The views across the valley were stupendous, with the Nile on one side and mountains on the other."

Max Davidson, *Daily Telegraph*

The balloon drifts from the Valley of the Kings to the Valley of the Queens, revealing pharaonic honeycomb tombs, including Tutankhamen's resting place and Queen Hatshepsut's tomb, carved from the rock face. The balloon also hovers over the excavations taking place around the Avenue of Sphinxes.

If you visit in October, consider getting married in Karnak Temple; during that month couples can tie the knot in pharaonic style—just as Egyptian kings and queens did more than 5,000 years ago. **LGS**

→ *Watch the sun rise over the Temple of Hatshepsut at Luxor, burning off the last vestiges of the night.*

Stay at Adrere Amellal

Location Siwa Oasis, Egypt
Website www.adrereamellal.net   **Price** $$$

This extraordinary eco-lodge sits in the middle of the Saharan oasis at Siwa, eight long, dusty hours' drive from Cairo. Surrounded by shifting sand dunes and overlooking a shimmering salt lake, the lodge is built from salt rock and mud and is the brainchild of Egypt's most prominent environmentalist, Mounir Neamatalla.

This is an Egypt far from the tourist hordes. There's no electricity, but that doesn't mean forsaking twenty-first-century luxuries. Light is provided by oil lamps and candles, and coal braziers keep the chill of the desert night at bay. There is nothing more relaxing than resting in a bathroom and bedroom lit up solely by dozens of flickering beeswax candles, together

> *"A very special, luxurious sense of the primitive, surrounded by the magic ... of majestic mountains."*
>
> Geordie Greig, *Tatler*

with the blessed absence of telephones, e-mail, television, or even cell phone reception. Primitive pampering doesn't get much better than this.

The lodge's rooms are decorated in traditional Siwan style, strewn artfully with Berber carpets, doors made of palm trees, and beds fashioned from palm fronds. It also has a refreshingly cooling swimming pool, whose water is supplied by an ancient Roman spring. Lie back in the water and soak up the pool's endless horizons, surrounded by olive and palm groves and looking onto the stark and desolate, but beautiful, desert. Enjoy dinner under the inky sky, marveling at the constellations. **HA**

Experience Blue Hole

Location Sinai, Egypt
Website www.allsinai.info/sites/sites/blue_hole   **Price** $

A deep sapphire encircled by a brilliant topaz rim, this Red Sea jewel has garnered a reputation for being the world's most dangerous dive spot, so devastating are its charms. Along the coast from Dahab, past the mountain-cradled desert and sprawling Bedouin camps, you arrive at the cobalt shoal leading to the Blue Hole. Urchins spike the promontory like guardians of the waters, an otherworldly marine adventure considered to be the pearl of the Gulf of Aqaba—the Red Sea's most enchanting stretch.

Enter a world in which psychedelic shoals zigzag, manta rays meander, and ultraviolet jellyfish beckon like sirens of the deep. Coral reefs turn from yellow to red and violet for the foolhardy intent on testing their mettle in exploring the brutal, near-mythic arch, a deceptive rock formation toward the bottom of this submarine pothole. Lying at the bottom of the Blue Hole are the bodies of divers committed to the sea forever—there are thought to be almost a hundred of them—who recklessly pushed themselves too far, and became disorientated under the water.

Waiting up above, for those sensible divers who do not tempt fate with dangerous diving, are Bedouin children dressed in desert cotton. They call out to enchant divers into buying their brightly colored bracelets and trinkets or daring them to a game of sheshbesh—a game they are almost never beaten at.

Beyond the Blue Hole, star-spangled mountain nights or the enchanting hippie villages of Nuweiba and Tarabin beckon. The truly informed may find a native tracker who will lead them to the nearby Rasta Boogaloo—a mountain-hugged cove-cum-Bedouin camp that is accessible only by walking over rocks when the tide is out at night. **VG**

Watch the Sunrise from Mount Sinai

Location Sinai, Egypt
Website www.touregypt.net/parks/stkath.htm **Price** $

Picture the scene: early morning in the desert. The sky and everything around you appears pitch black, illuminated only by the moon and stars. It is time to start the climb to the very top of Mount Sinai, the famed mountain on which Moses is said to have received the Ten Commandments from God.

Mount Sinai stands 7,500 feet (2,882 m) above sea level, and the nighttime climb, often amid flickering flames of candlelight, is something truly special. Although solitude cannot be promised at the peak, the experience of watching the sun rise is a truly spectacular sight. There are two ways to reach the top. The easier track—the one most choose—takes about two and a half hours by foot (although you can opt for a camel ride). There is also a steeper, more direct route—which entails climbing 3,750 steps.

There are buses to Mount Sinai from all of Egypt's major towns and resorts, but it is a long journey just to reach the bottom of the mountain. The popular tourist resort of Sharm el Sheikh is one of the closest, and that still takes two and a half hours by bus. Tour guides like to ensure their groups arrive at the foot of Mount Sinai, and are ready to start climbing, between 1:30 A.M. and 2:30 A.M., so you can forget going to bed that night. On the plus side, you will not be walking to the summit in the heat of the day.

Once the sun has risen and the breathtaking view has been admired, most people make a pilgrimage to see Moses's cave. When you arrive back at the bottom of the mountain, you can also visit the Monastery of St. Catherine and see the famous burning bush. **JA**

↗ *The breathtaking view from the peak of Mount Sinai is a memory that will stay with you for many years.*

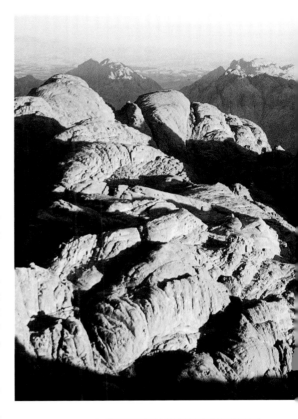

"The air is clean and fresh, the sky a mesmerizing blue, and the land a wind-sculpted dreamscape."

Chris Haslam, *The Times*

See the Nile by Felucca

Location Aswan to Luxor, Egypt **Website** www.egypt.travel
Price

Voyage the thoroughfare of the pharaohs in a classic white-sailed felucca and you will journey from the southernmost tip of Egypt to the Valley of the Kings.

The ancient Egyptians believed the Nile to be a route from life into death and the afterlife. It became the most important trading route in North Africa and the lifeline of their civilization. Egypt's most important temples are based along this route. The mummies of the pharaohs, their wives, their concubines, and even the odd crocodile are all committed to the spectacular sites on the West Bank. Along the route you will be able to soak up the mysterious spirits and legends of the ancient Egyptians, taking in the overbearing

> "When I read [Death on the Nile] I feel myself back on the steamer from Aswan to Wadi Halfa."

Agatha Christie, writer

Nubian rock temples of Abu Simbel and Kom Ombo, Egypt's most perfectly preserved temple at Edfu, beautiful and exotic peasant villages, and the largest religious site in the world, Karnak, which is the project of thirty of the world's most powerful rulers.

If you alight at the magnificent Valley of the Kings, you will discover proud sphinxes lining the causeway and the magisterial statue of Ramses II. Like the temples themselves, a journey along the Nile from Aswan to Luxor withstands the test of time. **VG**

A boat trip along the Nile remains a rite of passage fit for a king—or a pharaoh.

Stay at Mandina Lodges

Location Makasutu, The Gambia
Website www.gambia.co.uk; www.makasutu.com **Price** 💲💲

Imagine a silence disturbed only by the rustle of monkeys hurling themselves through adjacent trees. Makasutu Culture Forest, an hour's drive from the busy coastal resorts of the Gambia, was founded in 1993 by Englishmen Lawrence Williams and James English. Their aim was to establish a cultural center to highlight how local people lived, prevent deforestation, encourage wildlife to return to the area, and create employment for villagers.

Tucked away inside the forest in an idyllic mangrove-lined tributary of the River Gambia is a luxury eco-resort that sleeps a maximum of sixteen. Guests reach Mandina Lodge by elevated walkways or

---

"Mandina Lodge, a gem of a luxury lodge tucked deep in the mangroves."

Kevin Rushby, *Guardian*

---

dug-out canoe. The accommodation is solar-powered with private roof terraces, beautiful views, and carved four-poster beds dressed in white linens. Bathrooms are roofless for bathing under the stars. There is an enormous pool and a relaxing bar. Dinner can be enjoyed alfresco or in your lodge, after a personal talk with the chef. The stillness, heavy with heat all year-round, lulls even the most stressed executive into total relaxation.

Guides will take guests to explore in the forest or on the river. Legend has it that Makasutu (holy forest) is haunted, but you are more likely to spot a baboon or monitor lizard than a supernatural being. **WG**

Bird-watch in the Gambia

Location The Gambia
Website visitthegambia.gm/bird-watching **Price** 💲

Even as the sun is sinking toward the horizon, the birds of the Gambia continue to sing. You will hear this melodic chorus from the moment you wake to well after the stars start shining in the dark African sky. The Gambia is a bird-watcher's paradise. A staggering 540 different species call this tiny country on the west coast of Africa home, probably because of the wide range of habitats found in such a small area: from the shoreline of the Atlantic Ocean, to the inland wetlands, to the dry African bush. The sheer number and variety of birdlife attracts ornithologists from all over the world. However, you do not have to be a serious bird-watcher to appreciate the stunning views.

What you see depends on where you look. Travel the western shoreline of the Atlantic Ocean and you can expect to see kingfishers, seabirds such as egrets and herons, and the curiously named white-faced whistling duck. Head inland and the birds change with the landscape. In the dry dust of the African bush, you will find raptor species, such as goshawks, buzzards, eagles, and vultures. You do not need any particular equipment to enjoy the birdlife, although a pair of binoculars will help you get a better view. It is also a good idea to get a guide who can direct you to the best vantage points and explain the difference between an African fish eagle and a pygmy sunbird.

You can also customize your own bird-watching experience. Paddle a canoe down the mangrove creeks to look for goliath herons, or take a leisurely walk around the wetlands and let the Egyptian plovers and African pygmy geese find you. Spend a few hours at the fishponds of the Gambia River, or an entire day at the Abuko Nature Reserve. You are guaranteed to find the inner bird lover in you. **JP**

Discover Brava

Location Brava, Cape Verde Islands
Website www.archipelagocapeverde.com **Price** ❶

At the southwestern end of the Cape Verde Islands, about 400 miles (640 km) off the West African coast, lies Brava, the archipelago's "island of flowers." The mist-covered mountains rising from the arid, volcanic terrain that dominates the scenery conceal a hidden world. Up to 3,200 feet (976 m) high, these peaks are capable of trapping clouds, and thus create the peculiar humid and temperate microclimate of the country's smallest inhabited island.

Generally undisturbed by tourists because of its lack of outstanding beaches, Brava is the perfect antithesis of the rest of the archipelago and has retained its unspoiled charm. There is no airport, and the irregular

"This tiny island's wet climate produces lush green vegetation and swirling mists."

Janine Kelso, *Travel Weekly*

ferry service from neighboring Fogo makes careful planning imperative. Visitors can walk the ragged coastline, with its steep lava cliffs, or climb the mountains to gaze on deep, flower-filled valleys.

The island's main town is Vila Nova Sintra, at an altitude of 1,700 feet (520 m). It is a colorful town with markets, quaint colonial houses, ubiquitous gardens, and paths offering spectacular views. The true star of the island is the picturesque seaside village of Fajã d'Agua on the west coast, sheltered from the northeast wind by the mountains, with a stunning black-sand beach. Despite the volcanic-colored sand, no volcanic activity has ever been recorded. **DaH**

See the South Omo Valley

Location Near Jinka, Ethiopia
Website www.tour-to-ethiopia.com **Price** ❺❺

Deep in southern Ethiopia is a world largely untouched by modern society. In the South Omo Valley, tribal communities live much as they have done for hundreds of years, with mud huts for homes and goatskins for clothes. A trip here is hard going but unforgettable. This is a total escape from modern civilization as we know it.

The route does demand a four-by-four vehicle, however, to negotiate either the mud or the dust (depending on the time of year) on the bumpy dirt tracks. You will need at least ten days to explore this lush region, plus a driver/guide and a cook, which can all be arranged through socially responsible tour agencies in Addis Ababa or from home.

It is the people rather than the region that you will come here to see. With more than twenty tribes all adhering to ancient traditions and beliefs, the ethnographic diversity is amazing—including the women of the Mursi tribe with clay plates the size of saucers in their bottom lips, the Karo people renowned for their elaborate body scarification and decoration, and the Hamar tribe famous for their rites-of-passage ritual of "jumping the bulls" and their mesmerizing dances in the dark of night. The markets in the Omo Valley are as vibrant as the people, selling animal skins, beads of cowry shells, gourds of all shapes and sizes, sorghum, honey, straw, and wood—all essential items in everyday life here. Do not forget to try a bottle of *tej* while you are at the market—the local mead made with honey is quite an experience.

On the long road back to Addis, you can treat yourself to your first shower in days at the reviving hot springs in Wendo Genet, and wash away the dust—but not the memories—of the Omo Valley. **SWa**

Go Gorilla Tracking

Location Volcanoes National Park, Rwanda
Website www.rwandatourism.com/primate.htm **Price** 🚫🚫

"No one who looks into a gorilla's eyes . . . can remain unchanged, for the gap between ape and human vanishes; we know that the gorilla still lives within us." So wrote Dr. George Schaller, the eminent field biologist, in 1963 on first realizing that mountain gorillas were gentle giants rather than the brutal beasts they were hitherto believed to be.

Once the domain of intrepid scientists like Schaller and Dian Fossey, the opportunity to spend time with these amazing primates is now open to all, provided you pay the $500 permit fee (which is channeled back into their conservation) and are prepared to trek for at least three hours through dense undergrowth and rain forest to find them with the help of expert trackers. Permits are not easy to obtain: Only thirty are issued daily. Gorillas move on every day, too, so the trek does not follow a simple path. Then, once you do find them, you are limited to just one hour in their company to ensure that they do not become too used to humans or catch our harmful germs and diseases.

That single hour, however, will be the most magical and mesmerizing of your life. When you come face-to-face with a silverback and his group of gorillas, you simply forget everything else. As with human families, you will see mothers nurturing their babies or chiding their children; toddlers frolicking and fighting or playing peekaboo; and frisky teenagers flirting with each other or smooching in silence. And the silverback saunters and swaggers around grunting protectively, communicating in a secret language with the trackers who know each individual gorilla by name. **SWa**

➔ *A pair of mountain gorillas cross a log through the thick forest of Rwanda's Volcanoes National Park.*

Go on an Inner Safari

Location Tumaren and Baraka, Kenya
Website www.innersafariyoga.com **Price** 💲💲

The wide, open landscape of East Africa, and the wildlife living on its plains, holds an almost mystical draw for many travelers. A ten-day yoga and meditation retreat in the heart of big-game country would be an irresistible combination to those seeking spiritual sustenance in the arms of the natural world.

Checkie Wood, founder of Inner Safari, has practiced hatha yoga for twenty years, training in a range of disciplines. Wood founded Inner Safari because she struggled to find the right vacation herself: "Yoga was either programmed as a physical workout on its own, or there were silent retreats with no movement. We have married everything together."

> *"Yoga should be practiced with firm determination and perseverance."*
>
> *The Bhagavad Gita*

Inner Safari vacations are held in two Kenyan locations: Tumaren, a ranch in the center of the country, with comfortable private tents, and Baraka House, a villa in a strip of indigenous forest on the coast. Two yoga practices a day are made at sunrise and sunset. Classes are geared toward the abilities of guests, whose ages range from eighteen to sixty-five. There are also meditation workshops, chanting, massages, and tai chi, as well as bike and boat rides, snorkeling, climbing, and hiking. Evenings are spent alfresco, chatting around a campfire, storytelling, perhaps the odd guitar recital—or going straight to bed, to the sounds of the night. **LC**

Discover Lamu Island

Location Lamu Island, Kenya
Website http://ihs-198.magicalkenya.com/ **Price** 🚹

When life in the modern metropolis of Nairobi gets too much, step on a plane to Lamu and step back in time. This laid-back island is the perfect place to chill. Your plane will land on a dirt airstrip on Manda Island, with a reed shelter for an airport, and a dhow will sail you across to Lamu. Dhows and donkeys are the only means of transport here—the streets and alleys are too narrow for cars. Lamu is a UNESCO World Heritage site. Its architecture is typical of rich Swahili culture, with intricately carved wooden doors and lintels dating from the sixteenth century, when the island became an important trading post to the Arab world.

Today, the quiet island exudes such a soporific atmosphere you will not feel like doing much, but the gentle forty-five-minute walk from Lamu Town to Shela Beach becomes a pleasure as you take in more of the ancient culture and meet the elegant residents. Your reward is 8 miles (13 km) of perfect, almost deserted beach with sand like white pepper. Or take a dhow to the beach on nearby Manda Island and sip a cocktail while you sunbathe at Manda Beach Club.

However soporific it feels, do not leave without renting a dhow to glide you around the mangrove forests and some of the other islands in the Lamu archipelago. You should negotiate with the captains who wait on Lamu's harbor for people to take on a day trip. The trip will include your very own freshly caught fish, barbecued on the beach with local avocado and mango. Back in Lamu Town, enjoy some of the best seafood on the East African coast in seafront restaurants overlooking the harbor. **SWa**

▶ *The gentle pace of UNESCO-preserved Lamu will entice you into believing you have gone back in time.*

Stay at Shompole

Location Lake Natron, Kenya **Website** www.shompole.com
Price 💲💲💲

When Shompole opened in 2001, its coolly stylish interiors—free-flowing white concrete, rough-hewn figwood, smooth, round river stones, and plunge pools under thatch—sent shivers up the spines of regular safari goers. Yet the hotel, which clings to southern Kenya's Nguruman escarpment with views over the Rift Valley, is also here to benefit the wildlife and local Maasai people.

Since the conservancy was established, the number of lions on the previously overgrazed, overpoached land has increased tenfold, and elephants have come back down from the Loita Hills—exhilarating night drives also reveal glimpses of civets, bat-eared foxes, and aardwolves. Game drives are a big part of a stay here, as is watching flamingos on Lake Natron.

The community has also used its conservation fee to pay for rangers, teachers, nurses, and secondary school bursaries, and helped to build and run the six-bedroom lodge. This has evolved to include a two-suite annex with a long, thin lap pool (Little Shompole), an intimate, family house with lawns and fountains (Shompole House), and another private unit, 360, practically tumbling down the escarpment, with a dumbbell-shaped pool and a helipad for flying to Ol Donyo Lengai, an active volcano across the Tanzanian border. There is also a shop selling unique pieces of African jewelry and a modest spa, which offers treatments incorporating the muds of Lake Natron.

Even without leaving the lodge, guests can enjoy the astonishing sunsets over Shompole Mountain, and a feeling of utter peace. **LJ**

◄ *Architect Anthony Russell designed the smooth lines and flowing curves of Shompole.*

Relax at Ndali Lodge

Location Fort Portal, Uganda **Website** www.ndalilodge.com
Price 💲💲

Ndali Lodge sits right on the equator—a colonial-style mansion at the center of a farm. It stands on a narrow ridge 5,000 feet (1,524 m) above sea level, at the rim of an extinct volcano that has become a deep circular lake. It offers 360-degree views of the ancient volcanic landscape and the Rwenzori Mountains, known by explorers as the Mountains of the Moon.

The main lodge holds the reception area, sitting room, and restaurant. Guests stay in eight individual stone-built thatched cottages. Ndali feels luxurious, but in a very traditional way. Evenings are spent by candlelight, and all the lodge's water comes from the lake, pumped up by hydraulic technology invented in

> *"[Ndali Lodge] overlooks its own private crater lake and is an immensely relaxing place."*
>
> Jack Barker, *Independent*

the 1770s. The lodge has been owned by the same family since 1920 and is still staffed by local villagers. Ndali provides guides for walks to the Mahoma waterfall, around the crater, as well as a boat for discovering the birds, butterflies, and primates. There are many local walks you can take on your own, a swimming pool, and a sturdy jetty on the lake where guests can swim and lounge in the sun, spotting five different types of kingfishers.

Ndali is a perfect Ugandan base, situated between three national parks. It is just forty-five minutes to Kibale Forest National Park, home of the largest concentration of chimpanzees in Africa. **SH**

Unwind at Chole Mjini

Location Chole, Tanzania   **Website** www.africatravelresource.com   **Price** ⑤⑤

Chole Mjini's tree houses seem to meld into the canopy of the ancient baobab trees that provide them with shelter. Crafted from wood, ropes, and reeds, the rustic hideaways are open on three sides and are set amid verdant jungle, wild orchards, mangrove forests, and age-old Hindu ruins slowly being strangled by the roots of fig trees. The area teems with wildlife, and guests can see fruit bats dangling upside down in the tree branches that surround their rooms, as well as monkeys and a variety of exotic birdlife.

Even though six of the seven rooms are up in a tree, they house four-poster beds lined with fine Egyptian cotton and elegantly swathed in mosquito nets. There are also alfresco showers surrounded by bamboo. If sleeping in a tree bothers you, ask for the ground house suite, complete with sunken Persian bath.

This place is perfect for serious escapism. There is no electricity (although oil lanterns are left on overnight and reading flashlights are provided) on the tiny island of Chole. Which means there is no telephone, television, cars, e-mail, or air-conditioning. Chole is part of the Mafia archipelago and is situated some 60 miles (100 km) south of Tanzania. Scuba diving and snorkeling are big in these parts, with turtles, rays, dolphins, and ray sharks providing the underwater attractions.

At Chole Mjini, meals are usually of fresh fish with plenty of fruit and vegetables, and guests eat with the friendly lodge owners in a number of different locations, the best of which is among the ruins, lit by lanterns hanging from the trees.

A stay here means you are doing your bit for the community, too, because the owners donate $10 per visitor per night to a trust fund that pays toward the local hospital, school, and training programs. **JK**

⬆ *Chole Mjini has luxurious tree houses complete with four-poster beds and wonderful views.*

Stay at Greystoke Mahale

Location Lake Tanganyika, Tanzania   **Website** www.greystoke-mahale.com   **Price** ⊖⊖⊖

Reaching Greystoke Mahale is an adventure. It is set on the remote eastern shores of vast Lake Tanganyika, and getting to the camp involves a four-hour flight on a small plane from Arusha, followed by a ninety-minute dhow trip on the lake. There are no roads within 60 miles (100 km) of this secluded sanctuary, and it is a two-hour boat ride to the nearest town. It is well off the tourist map, so if you are seeking solitude, Greystoke Mahale has plenty.

Accommodation consists of six *bandas* (traditional thatched huts, common in Central Africa). The beach-fronted *bandas* are stylishly designed, with open fronts, spacious decks, and interiors crafted from old dhow timber, giving the camp a look and feel of modest, rustic charm.

At night, gaze at the stars while enjoying a barefoot meal at the water's edge, sip cocktails on a dhow, or head to the bar, which is set picturesquely in the rocky headland. The dining area has four decks that face in every direction, affording fabulous views of the landscape. The hotel also has a library of rare books on the local wildlife.

Behind the lodges are the dense forests of the Mahale Mountains, home to Africa's last remaining wild chimpanzees, mankind's closest relative. Trek through the lush rain forest to spot the endangered primates as they swing noisily and energetically from tree to tree. The rain forest is dotted with waterfalls and giant verdant vines and populated by leopards, monkeys, porcupines, mongooses, butterflies, and birds. There are treasures, too, to be found beneath the lake's transparent water, where 250 species of tropical fish reside, making it ideal for swimming, snorkeling, and kayaking. With no cell phone reception or wireless Internet, this is the perfect hideaway. **JK**

⬆ *Part of Greystoke Mahale's charm lies in its rustic furniture and use of traditional textiles.*

Unwind at Kahawa Shamba

Location Kahawa Shamba, Tanzania
Website www.kahawashamba.co.tz   **Price** ●

Thousands of trekkers flock to Kilimanjaro every year to try to conquer Africa's highest mountain, but not many of them stop long enough to take a breath and look around them at the lives and culture of the local tribes who live in the mountain's shadow.

Kahawa Shamba, which means "coffee farm," is a village where the Swahili people have resided for centuries, farming the land and hunting for game. The coffee farmers who live here struggle with poverty caused by falling prices and rising costs. Thanks to a community project, the local people now host tourists who want to stay at the village, cooking for and taking care of them while earning a salary. Through this program, the finances of the local people have been enriched, and guests are provided with a genuinely meaningful travel experience.

In the village, tourists sleep in traditional-style *chugga* huts, thatched from top to bottom with banana leaves. The accommodation is basic, but there is still luxury—in the warmth of the local people and in the beauty of the surrounding landscape of verdant valleys and gorges, skewered by tall banana trees and small coffee bushes.

If you consider yourself a coffee addict, you can learn more about the origin and journey of your favorite brew by visiting the small Fair Trade coffee farms, eating lunch with the farmers, and being allowed to pick coffee beans and see how they are pulped, roasted, and ground. A guide will explain the process of organic coffee farming and the standards that are expected from Fair Trade farmers. If you're feeling tired after the hard day's sightseeing, you can finish up with a cup of freshly brewed coffee. **JK**

Stay at Ngorongoro Crater Lodge

Location Serengeti, Tanzania
Website www.ngorongorocrater.com   **Price** ●●●

The word "spectacular" does not even begin to encapsulate the experience of staying at Ngorongoro Crater Lodge in northern Tanzania. Perched on the edge of a vast crater in the Serengeti, it feels as though it could be straddling the edge of the world.

The lodge is next to the largest unbroken volcanic caldera in the world, more than 4,970 miles (8,000 km) of pristine African wilderness, a paradise for the wild animals that roam its rich grassland. Most impressive of all is the thundering, dust-raising annual "great migration," when around two million wildebeest and zebra storm across the Serengeti in search of food.

> *"If you could spend one day in Africa, Ngorongoro Crater might be the place to do it."*
>
> Laura Riley, *Nature's Strongholds*

Ngorongoro Crater Lodge was inspired by the Maasai mud and stick *manyatta* (homestead), but with an injection of luxury. Your fireplace is stoked by a personal butler, who will also run rose petal–strewn baths (with a view) between twice-daily game drives, crater picnics, and cocktails. The three intimate, romantic, stilted camps all have stone-and-thatch suites and lavish interiors. This area is known as "Africa's Eden," and it needs to be seen to be believed—preferably from Ngorongoro Crater Lodge. **LP**

➦ *The lavish interiors of Ngorongoro Crater Lodge were inspired by Maasai simplicity.*

Stay at Chumbe Island Coral Park

Location Off Zanzibar, Tanzania
Website www.chumbeisland.com   **Price ❶**

A visit to Chumbe Island Coral Park is an eco-vacation par excellence. The whole island is a nature reserve. No fishing is allowed in the Reef Sanctuary, and the bungalows were designed with solar panels, rainwater, and high-tech filtration and disposal systems to ensure polluted water does not seep into the Reef Sanctuary.

Most people, though, come for the snorkeling. The reef is pristine, and because it is so shallow, snorkelers can see marine life that only divers usually spot. You may not manage to lure out Oscar, the 3-foot (1-m) long potato grouper who lives in one of the caves, but hordes of colorful parrot fish, shoals of barracuda,

---

"Chumbe is now a fully protected area. . . . Revenue from ecotourism is re-invested in conservation."

Sybille Riedmiller, UNESCO

---

hawksbill turtles, lobsters, and stingrays are regularly sighted. Some guests even find themselves swimming among dolphins and the reef's resident batfish.

On land, visitors can hike trails in the Forest Reserve—around 90 percent of Chumbe Island is covered by one of the last remaining "coral rag" forests in Zanzibar. At low tide, you can stroll around the entire island. You may even glimpse the rare robber or coconut crab—the largest land crab in the world, it can crack open coconuts with its claws. **PE**

⬅ *The whole of Chumbe is a nature reserve, and the proprietors run it in an eco-friendly way.*

Experience the Selous Project

Location Selous Game Reserve, Tanzania
Website www.selousproject.com **Price** ⊖⊖⊖⊖

"The power and the waiting in the air . . . the stillness of the glittering water . . . the circle of still trees."

Peter Matthiessen, *Sand Rivers*

Escape the hordes of safari jeep convoys by indulging yourself in 300,000 acres (121,405 ha) of your very own private concession area within the Selous Game Reserve. Named for Frederick Courtney Selous, an English explorer, hunter, and conservationist who died here during World War I, the reserve—the size of Switzerland—is the largest and wildest in Africa.

Parties of up to eight people can experience an area of pure wilderness just for themselves. Formerly the domain of big-game hunters, the Selous Project is now open for photographic safaris with a difference, offering visitors the opportunity to track elephants and buffalo on foot in the bush, to canoe past hippos wallowing in the water and small game drinking at the river's edge, or to watch lions devouring a kill from the shelter of a specially built hide. The emphasis is firmly on conservation and protection, both of wildlife and of the local communities.

The camp itself has been designed to recapture the romance of the traditional safari of Frederick Selous's era. The decor is vintage-style, Edwardian safari, and the furniture in the tents, which is all made from sustainable materials, includes classic campaign wardrobe trunks, writing desks, and luxurious leather easy chairs. The en suite open-air bathrooms are set in gardens of small trees and bamboo.

Each of the four tents has private access to the Luwegu River's shores, where romantic couples can soak in copper bathtubs strategically placed in its shallow waters and share a bottle of champagne in perfect solitude while watching the setting sun. **SWa**

🔳 *The Selous Project allows the opportunity to wallow in privacy amid breathtaking landscape.*

Enjoy Singita Faru Faru

Location Grumeti Reserves, Tanzania
Website www.singita.com   **Price** ❺❺❺

Animal lovers will be spellbound by Singita Faru Faru Lodge, in the heart of the sun-kissed Serengeti, not least because it is in a prime location to view the epic, annual "great migration" of more than a million wildebeest. The lodge is positioned on a rocky slope next to the Grumeti River and a watering hole, a region abundant with magnificent animal life all year-round.

The location—in a private concession on the western corridor of the Serengeti—is not the only thing Faru Faru Lodge has going for it. This hotel is utterly intimate and classically elegant; going on safari has never felt so exclusive. Faru Faru Lodge has just six open-style, air-conditioned tented suites, each with huge picture windows, an outdoor shower or bath, and a deck with a state-of-the-art telescope, from where visitors can enjoy spectacular sunsets and their own private game show. Not to mention the likely chance of seeing herds of elephant meander past while you wallow in the tub.

The colonial, 1940s East Africa–style lodge also comes with a Swahili-inspired "beach," two swimming pools, and a spa. There is a dining room and barbecue area where mouthwatering nouvelle-African cuisine is served, as sometimes exaggerated stories of wild adventures from the day are swapped.

When not on one of the twice-daily four-by-four safari drives, guests can relax in the lounge, although the game action outside is much more entertaining. The lodge can also arrange walking or horseback safaris for you to experience nature in the raw.

The word "Serengeti" comes from the Maasai word "Siringit," which means "endless plains" or "the place where the land stretches to forever." It seems to sum up this natural beauty just perfectly. **LP**

Discover Mnemba Island

Location Mnemba Island, Zanzibar
Website www.mnemba-island.com   **Price** ❺❺❺

When Bill Gates wants respite from the fast-paced business world, he disappears to exclusive Mnemba Island, just off the northeastern tip of Zanzibar. In the bathlike Indian Ocean, Mnemba—Arabic for "octopus head"—offers just ten romantic and understated beachside *bandas* (huts) with thatched palm roofs and wraparound verandas.

Apart from the sweet isolation, one of the biggest draws is the diving. Colorful ocean life flourishes on the protected coral reefs of the Mnemba Atoll; dolphins, whales, bright tropical fish, and giant turtles drift through the lagoons. Nature is omnipresent—guests awake to the song of red-eyed doves in the

---

"Of all the small islands to stay on, Mnemba is one of the most romantic . . . it has everything."

Daily Telegraph

---

forest, where suni antelope and white butterflies also abound, and sidestep ghost crabs on their walk past coconut palms to the main lodge.

The food is equally impressive, with fresh fruit and seafood brought to Mnemba daily. Meals are sumptuous, with candlelit feasts in the dining area, on your private veranda, or on the beach, where eating with the waves lapping at your feet is just sublime.

Tours can be arranged to give visitors a taste of the ancient "Spice Island" of Zanzibar, and guests can enjoy therapeutic massages and deep-sea fishing trips. Or you can just kick off your shoes, lie back, and savor the private sanctuary that is Mnemba. **LP**

Kayak at Mumbo Island

Location Lake Malawi, Malawi **Website** www.kayakafrica.co.za
Price ⓢ

You have to kayak 6 miles (10 km) to reach Mumbo Island from Cape Maclear on the southern shore of Lake Malawi (although the less energetic can take Kayak Africa's boat) but then you have the place to yourself. You will find luxury tents with bathrooms, thatched roofs, and viewing decks, complete with hammocks overlooking the lake. The only other people to break the solitude are the staff who prepare your meals and serve at the bar.

It would be easy to lounge in hammocks all day, watching the sun twinkling on Lake Malawi and spotting the multicolored cichlid fish darting like electric flashes around small islets of granite boulders. If you feel some activity is called for, however, these are among the world's safest waters in which to learn to scuba dive, or you could snorkel from the beach or paddle around the shores of the island in a kayak. Do not be surprised if an otter or two join you for a swim.

For landlubbers, there are five easy nature trails that meander around this tiny paradise full of baobab trees and figs, leading to even more secluded coves and inlets. Spend some time ambling around the island looking for giant fish eagles, colorful kingfishers, or paradise flycatchers. If that all sounds too energetic, simply watch the birds as you chill and sway on your hammock, sipping a glass of wine.

Back in 1861, the renowned explorer David Livingstone named Lake Malawi the "lake of stars" for the way the sun sparkles on its waters. Today, there is no better place to appreciate this romantic epithet than on Mumbo Island. **SWa**

← *You can kayak from the beach at Mumbo Island and take advantage of Lake Malawi's clear waters.*

Stay at Ku Chawe Inn

Location Shire Lowlands, Malawi
Website www.malawi-travel.com **Price** $

Set against the backdrop of the forests of the Zomba Plateau, with spectacular views of the Great Rift Valley and the Shire Lowlands, is Malawi's most upmarket hotel. The landscape is a veritable Garden of Eden. The slopes and ravines are covered with exotic trees, junglelike creepers, wildflowers, orchids, and lichen. Yet despite the beautiful scenery and Lake Chirwa with its white-sand beaches, Malawi is not known as a vacation destination and is unspoiled by tourism.

The Ku Chawe Inn is hidden away in lush vegetation at the end of a long, winding mountain path. Being tucked into this jungle idyll does not mean facilities are primitive. The forty spacious rooms all have their

---

"The beautiful Zomba plateau . . . unrivaled beauty, crystal-clear streams, and numerous species."

Friends of Malawi Association

---

own private bathrooms, telephones, and satellite televisions. Malawians have a very well-deserved reputation for warmth and friendliness, and the staff at Ku Chawe are helpful and attentive. It is wonderful to lunch on the large, shady outdoor veranda watching the resident baboons snacking in the gardens. This is a place to enjoy an evening drink and feast on the spectacular views before dining on delicious food, enjoyed, in cooler winter evenings, around a flickering fire. You could rise early and hire a mountain guide to take you above the clouds to the top of the plateau. Or simply gaze out over the endless views of the lake shimmering in the distance. **SWi**

Unwind at Azura

Location Benguerra Island, Mozambique
Website www.azura-retreats.com **Price** $$$

Azura is not easy to get to: it is a two-hour flight from Johannesburg, followed by a breathtaking helicopter swoop over the myriad hues of the Indian Ocean, but it is worth the effort. Although the lodge itself is a honeymooners' idyll, the real draw is the pristine beauty of the island itself.

The retreat was created in 2007 by British couple Christopher and Stella Bettany, who saw their opportunity when Gabriel Cossa, a Mozambican who ran a backpackers' resort on the site, was told to upgrade or move out. Happily, Cossa is now the Bettanys' business partner, his son Zito has been to hotel school in Durban, and many of the original staff are still working here.

Local techniques and talents are on show in the construction and decoration of the fourteen wooden villas. Driftwood stools and timber floors conjure a mood of laid-back beach chic, whereas tasseled leather stools and Panton chairs add boutique funkiness. Guests can be as private or as sociable as they choose, with firelit dinners à deux on the beach or communal drinks at the Gecko Bar, stargazing in hammocks. The diving and fishing are both exceptional—you can expect unbleached corals, turtles, and sailfish—and humpback whales can be seen between July and October. There are magical excursions to Pansy Island, a sandbar sprinkled with the delicate skeletons of sea urchins at high tide, or a vast dune with the ocean on one side and freshwater pools full of crocodiles and wading birds on the other. Alternatively, just sit by the beach, musing on the moon and the tides. **LJ**

➨ *The shaggy jekka-thatch roofs are an example of local building techniques—and talents.*

Dive at Matemo Island

Location Matemo Island, Mozambique
Website www.matemoresort.com   **Price** 🅢🅢

It may only be 5 miles (8 km) long and 1.8 miles (3 km) wide, but few places on Earth can match Matemo Island for fishing and diving. In the heart of the Quirimbas archipelago off the northern Mozambique coast, Matemo is all white-sand beaches dotted with coconut palms and thatched mud huts. In the deep waters lie the real treasures: kingfish, barracuda, queenfish, dog-tooth tuna, and sailfish, not to mention huge shoals of yellowfin tuna. The abundance of exotic fish is thanks to the fact that the waters are part of a marine sanctuary. This is good news for divers: unspoiled coral reefs and warm waters are alive with a kaleidoscope of marine life, including humpback

> *"Ruins of large Portuguese plantations can still be seen on Quisiva and Matemo."*
>
> Malyn Newitt, *A History of Mozambique*

whales between August and October. Turtles can often be seen as well as, very occasionally, the much-endangered dugong. After a hard day's diving or fishing, take a walk to explore the island's verdant vegetation or take a water taxi to nearby Ibo Island, which has a rich history of piracy and ivory trading.

If you want to stay on Matemo Island, there are twenty-four air-conditioned, thatched chalets situated on the beach just a few short steps from the sea, and a restaurant serves locally caught seafood. **JK**

◁ *Matemo Island is a paradise for anyone who wants to dive, fish, or simply enjoy the beautiful beaches.*

Relax at Ibo Island Lodge

Location Ibo Island, Mozambique
Website www.iboisland.com **Price** 💲💲

For those who have had the pleasure of discovering this Indian Ocean gem, Ibo Island is impossible to forget. The small, forested island lies at the southern end of the beautiful Quirimbas archipelago, a string of thirty-two tropical islands stretching more than 125 miles (200 km) north to the Tanzanian border.

Ibo Island Lodge is housed in historic and stunning buildings that date back to colonial times. The walls are 3 feet (1 m) thick, and high ceilings promote an impression of elegant space. With just fourteen luxury rooms, each individually designed and with views of the waterfront, this is a wonderful retreat in which to escape the world. Antique and handcrafted furniture and the lodge's magnificent wooden doors and shutters evoke the buildings' origins.

Visitors can take a cruise on a dhow around the archipelago and go ashore to visit the historic old town, dating back to the 1600s, and now earmarked as a potential World Heritage site. It was chosen by the Portuguese in 1754 as their main clearinghouse for slaves and ivory, then left deserted for almost a century. It is a mysterious town to wander around, amid forts and ancient buildings, watching silversmiths melt coins to create delicate pieces of silver jewelry.

As well as enjoying the pool and private beach, guests can snorkel or go diving among some of the world's richest coral reefs, or go kayaking through mangroves, with the chance to see turtles, dolphins, and whales in the waters of the Quirimbas national park. Maybe this is the Mozambique that Bob Dylan sang about all those years ago. **AD**

← *Ibo Island Lodge is made up of three beautiful mansions, all of which are over 100 years old.*

Stay at Marlin Lodge

Location Benguerua Island, Mozambique
Website www.marlinlodge.co.za **Price** 💲💲

One of the coolest destinations in southern Africa, Marlin Lodge makes the perfect post-safari stop. Wood and reed-thatched chalets stretch along the sandy, white sands of tranquil Flamingo Bay, connected by walkways on stilts over the vegetation. The freshwater swimming pool is tucked away in a glade of coconut palms. The rooms have glorious sea views from the four-poster beds.

The island is part of a National Marine Park, home to many protected species. Look out for whales, whale sharks, dolphins, dugongs, and manta rays; out on the reef are turtles, stingrays, and moray eels. A tag-and-release program means fishing enthusiasts can still

> *"Guests come here mainly to pad along pristine sand and swim over unspoiled reefs."*

Rhiannon Batten, *Independent*

hunt for marlin and other big-game fish. There is also catamaran sailing, windsurfing, and water skiing, as well as more laid-back cruising in a traditional dhow.

On land, guests can explore the island's grasslands, coastal dunes, freshwater lakes—which are inhabited by Nile crocodiles—and acacia woodland, keeping eyes peeled for colorful parrots.

The lodge charges guests a park fee, which goes into a fund used to benefit the natural environment and the local community, so you can enjoy the surroundings safe in the knowledge that you are doing your part to maintain Benguerua Island as a special slice of paradise for future generations. **AD**

Unwind at Quilalea

Location Quirimbas Archipelago, Mozambique
Website www.quilalea.com **Price** 💲💲💲

From Prince Harry to Leonardo diCaprio, this diamond of the Indian Ocean seduces royalty and A-listers alike, with its awe-inspiring nature and undisturbed intimacy. There are no inhabitants on Quilalea, the pearl of the thirty-two islands dotting the Quirimbas archipelago, whose coastlines are so pristine that it feels as if the shore is untrodden by human feet.

Quilalea was the first member of the Quirimbas archipelago to be designated a protected nature sanctuary. No commercial fishing is allowed. Clear, azure waters, peerless diving in which mesmeric corals flirt with rainbow shoals, 2,000-year-old baobab trees, and mangroves supply the setting. Butterflies flutter

> *"The island of Quilalea is too small for an airstrip. It's too small for much of anything, in fact."*
>
> Douglas Rogers, *Travel+Leisure* magazine

by, turtles rest on the beach, and white-sailed dhows minnow past. In the past, Quilalea was the main rest stop for mariners and merchants. Today it is a rest stop for pleasure-seeking tourists (adults only—children are not allowed here).

On the island are just nine thatched, stone-clad villas, with panoramic views over the sea. Guests can explore nearby Ibo, an electricity-free town that time forgot—the mansions that once marked its riches left to crumble, the inhabitants forever welcoming—or have a desert island picnic on Sencar, rubbing shoulders with the Samango monkeys. Quilalea is a portal to another world, an overlooked world. **VG**

Explore Fish River Canyon

Location Fish River Canyon, Namibia
Website www.nwr.com.na; www.canyonnaturepark.com **Price** 💲

At almost 100 miles (160 km) long, Fish River Canyon is one of the world's most impressive gorges and one of Namibia's national parks. It sweeps through desolate escarpments and steep cliffs, bringing a whole new meaning to the word "remote."

Namibia Wildlife Resorts runs a five-day hiking trail along 50 miles (80 km) of the canyon, but it is not for the fainthearted or the out of shape. Temperatures are gaspingly hot, the terrain underfoot rocky and hard going with a backpack on your back, and there are no quick escape routes or shortcuts should you change your mind. There is, however, a raw beauty in the landscape that somehow makes the hardship worthwhile. Steep ravines with deep orange and pink rocks constantly changing color in the sun, weird-looking, bulbous quiver trees (Namibia's national tree) perched on the edge of precipices, and panoramic views as far as the eye can see all add to a feeling of splendid isolation in its truest sense. The Fish River itself is perfect for skinny-dipping, its cool, clean waters an elixir for parched and exhausted trekkers. In the evening, cook a meal over the fire and watch the flames flickering to sleep as you curl up under the stars, literally miles from anyone and anywhere.

If all this sounds a bit too wild, try the Canyon Nature Park, just north of the national park conservation area where the Löwen and Fish rivers meet. Here, in landscapes equally as stunning and remote, you can opt for guided hikes lasting between two and five days on private trails, complete with food, tents, and even a vehicle to transport your bags. **SWa**

➥ *Fish River Canyon is the second-largest canyon in the world, beaten only by the Grand Canyon.*

Enjoy Le Mirage

Location Sossusvlei, Namibia
Website www.namibweb.com/lem.htm **Price** $ $

Shimmering in the African sand, Le Mirage lives up to its name, rising out of the desert like a fairy-tale castle from *Arabian Nights*. High stone walls with turreted windows wrap around a quiet, central courtyard, its swimming pool surrounded by lush greenery.

Within the walls, cool, shaded rooms with private balconies look out over the Namib Desert. Upstairs, you can sleep under the stars in one of the open-air rooftop tower rooms. The early rays of sun wash across the golden savanna, circled by granite peaks and soaring red dunes. Guests can make the most of the relaxed surroundings with a treatment at the Mystique Spa. Moroccan-inspired treatment rooms are tiled and

> "*Sossusvlei, where the world's largest sand dunes shroud . . . the Earth's oldest desert.*"

Catherine Dunphy, *Toronto Star*

bathed in soft light from glass lanterns. Soak in a salt bath to cleanse and revitalize, or have a massage to soothe the soul and de-stress the mind.

The famous expanse of enormous sand dunes, millions of years old, are most people's reason for coming to Sossusvlei. Hike to the top for views across the soft, rolling peaks or take a hot-air balloon ride to silently drift over the magical surroundings. The more adventurous visitor can try quad biking in the dunes or go on a game-viewing drive, hoping to spot wildlife in the all-encompassing desert. Back at Le Mirage, have a predinner cocktail at the outdoor fire pit, then make time for stargazing under an inky desert sky. **AD**

Stay at The Villa

Location Okonjima, Namibia
Website www.okonjima.com **Price** $ $ $

When Brad Pitt and Angelina Jolie wanted complete privacy, they booked the luxurious Villa at Okonjima. With its own chef, an inviting private infinity pool, and king-size beds that can be wheeled out onto the wide terraces to sleep under the stars, this is indeed accommodation fit for Hollywood royalty.

In a secluded spot in the bush, 6 miles (10 km) away from the main camp, the grand African house has a two-bedroom main house and two separate thatched-hut suites, sleeping a group of up to eight people. A personal host and a chef attend to guests' every need while they have a cooling dip in the specially ozonated pool, which uses ultraviolet light to stay clean instead of chemical detergents, or a nap in the shady Sala overlooking the watering hole.

Inside, there is a wood-burning stove in the lounge, decorated with African artifacts, and bedrooms have concertina-style, glass-paneled doors that fold away to give magnificent, panoramic views of the bush outside. Alternatively, swap them for roll-down canvas partitioning that zip-fastens, tent-style, for a feel of living in the wild. Bathrooms have both an inside shower and a spectacular, outside bush shower, together with a beautiful bathtub-with-a-view.

Okonjima offers an insight into the work of the Africat Foundation, which protects threatened cheetah and leopards. Get up at sunrise with a private guide to track cheetah on foot, go out in a game vehicle to see leopards, or identify some of the hundreds of bird species in the area, including appealing Namibian endemics such as Carp's Black Tit, Hartlaub's Francolin, and the Damara Rock Runner, going no farther than the Villa's shady Sala. No wonder the Villa comes A-list approved. **AD**

Experience Mowani Mountain Camp

Location Twyfelfontein, Namibia
Website www.mowani.com   **Price** 🌓🌓

Nestled between the Ugab and Huab rivers, Mowani Mountain Camp, which means "place of god," sits in the heart of the Twyfelfontein area of western Namibia. From a distance, the elevated collection of domed, thatched rooftops looks like an African village, but this is no ordinary place to stay.

Some of the elegantly decorated tents (complete with bathroom) face west, looking out across the distant valley, whereas others are placed to take in the views east, to see the morning sun rise. Beds in the tents have crisp, white linen, and outside there's a wooden deck area to soak up the Damara landscape.

For a step up in luxury, beautiful, thatched *rondavels* (African round houses), perched among the rocks, have part-canvas walls. The ultimate in chic is the thatched suite, with private butler service catering to your every need. There are indoor and outdoor bathrooms and a shower with a view, the perfect way to wake up.

The pool is lodged between boulders and has a deck area to enjoy the searing African sun. The surroundings of the boulder-strewn valley are reminiscent of a prehistoric age, and the unspoiled wilderness and desert scenery hide geological formations, archaeological sites with ancient rock art, and a unique variety of flora and fauna. Go off on a nature drive in search of elusive herds of desert elephants and hike across the upland scenery.

The amazing 2,500-year-old rock formations at Twyfelfontein are the big draw in this corner of Namibia, along with the engravings and paintings made by bushmen from the same period. **AD**

↗ *The enormous boulders at Twyfelfontein provide a stunning backdrop for photographs.*

"[This] is not your traditional safari. You come here for the landscape as much as for the wildlife."

Lucy Gilmore, *Independent*

Camp at Chiawa

Location Lower Zambezi National Park, Zambia
Website www.chiawa.com **Price** 🅢🅢🅢

When David Livingstone passed through this area on his ill-fated mission to prove the Zambezi River was navigable, there must have been moments when he wished for a camp like Chiawa. This multi-award-winning retreat exudes luxury, yet emphasizes contact with the African bush. Guests sleep in tents—but not as you know them. They have wood paneling, roll-top bathtubs, and showers both indoors and out. The restaurant serves "Afro-Euro fusion" food on the camp's own deck, in the middle of the bush, or even on a boat floating peacefully down the Zambezi River.

Chiawa is particularly known for its canoeing safaris to see hippo, buffalo, and elephant. It is also acclaimed

"Chiawa Camp is the perfect lodge .... Its public areas overlook the Zambezi, and the rooms are huge."

Richard Green, *The Times*

for its fishing, especially of tigerfish and vundu catfish. The camp offers game drives, both in the day and at night, and bush walks, which are slower paced and highlight conservation issues.

If your tent is too luxurious—or you just desire an in-depth exploration of your wild side—Chiawa Camp offers alternative accommodation at Old Mondoro Bushcamp. Accommodating only eight guests, this is a comfortable retreat with an open-air, back-to-nature vibe. Paraffin lanterns provide evening light, and fresh bread is cooked each day in the camp's oven. Activities revolve mainly around nonmotorized safaris, and the surrounding parkland offers excellent walking. **PE**

Canoe the Zambezi

Location Mana Pools, Zimbabwe
Website www.natureways.com **Price** 🅢🅢🅢

The animals of Mana Pools do not see many people. Tucked away in remote northwest Zimbabwe, this pristine national park has no safari lodges and few visitors, so as your canoe glides through the still waters of the river toward a vast elephant standing sentinel in the distance, he watches you with interest, not fear. When you are floating a few feet from the bank, he looks straight into your eyes, making the kind of connection that just does not happen from the back of a safari jeep. It is an experience you will never forget.

Mana Pools, a UNESCO World Heritage site, covers 77 square miles (200 sq km) and is edged by around 50 miles (80 km) of the Zambezi, Africa's fourth-longest river. There are no rapids here and the water is flat and slow, so anyone who is in decent shape can canoe. However, just because this is truly wild Africa, do not think you have to rough it. Natureways Safaris, an excellent owner-operated local company, offers safaris for softies. You do not have to lift a finger. While guests are out on the river, the eco-friendly camp is packed up by staff, leaving no impact on the pristine environment. Everything is transferred to the next site and reassembled, ready to welcome guests to a three-course, candlelit, alfresco dinner.

During the May to October dry season, the area is teeming with birds and game, including impala, waterbuck, hippo, crocodile, buffalo, lion, and leopard. Natureways' professional guides are said to be among Africa's best. After a trip led by owner James Varden, renowned explorer Sir Ranulph Fiennes said he had never learned so much in so short a time. **WG**

▣ *The Zambezi River around Mana Pools is teeming with exotic wildlife—perfect to be viewed by canoe.*

Stay at Abu Camp

Location Okavango Delta, Botswana
Website www.abucamp.com **Price** ⊖⊖⊖⊖

Abu Camp is a luxurious retreat offering three-night stays and elephant-back safaris. Guests arrive and depart together to appreciate, at the same pace, the diversity of flora and fauna found here in the open savannas and island sanctuaries.

Guests stay in custom-made tents set on raised decks adjacent to their own private, natural lagoon. All rooms in the camp are furnished with sleigh or four-poster beds and come complete with full baths and private bathrooms. Each tent has its own private deck, and a separate outdoor layered teak deck and viewing platform is built around matured sycamore and ebony trees that can double as a dining area, with fine wine and gourmet cuisine prepared by Abu Camp's experienced safari chefs. A newly built villa across the lagoon sleeps up to four people and comes with its own chef, guide, butler, and private pool.

Abu Camp is named after former resident celebrity elephant Abu. The camp's present herd of elephants take their human cargo, comfortably seated in large padded saddles, on excursions into the Okavango Delta's wilderness at a sedate pace, accompanied by experienced guides.

The camp's elephants grant unprecedented and unfettered access to resident herds of zebra, antelope, giraffe, and buffalo. Sunrise and sunset rides are offered daily, as well as extended daylong safaris that transplant you into the midst of the wildlife that calls the waters of the delta home, all the while providing a memorable insight into the complex social structures of the African elephant. **BS**

◄ *Abu Camp, on the western side of the Okavanga Delta, stretches over 500,000 acres (202,340 ha).*

Experience Jack's Camp

Location Kalahari Desert, Botswana
Website www.unchartedafrica.co.za **Price** ⊖⊖⊖⊖

Jack's Camp stands on a vast saltpan on Botswana's Kalahari Desert. Ten five-star canvas tents, private bucket showers, flush toilets, and a plunge pool succeed in distracting you from the fact that you have journeyed to the edge of nothingness to sleep over the dried-up bed of an ancient lake.

Established in the 1960s, Jack's Camp is one of the true pioneers of southern Africa's contemporary safari-style retreats and one of the few accommodation options in this remote region of central Botswana. In the Makgadikgadi Saltpans, endless salt flats represent all that is left of what was once the largest inland lake in Africa; the camp's resident archaeologists and

"The silence is so complete you can hear the blood circulating in your ears."

Proprietors, Jack's Camp

geologists will lead you to almost forgotten sites and ancient fossil beds to see the remains of long-extinct hippos and giant ancestors of the modern zebra. Or explore it by yourself on a quad bike.

The arid landscape is transformed in March and April when summer rains swell the Okavango Delta, whose waters flow across the saltpans attracting thousands of wildebeest, zebra, and buffalo and vast numbers of aquatic birds such as pelicans and flamingos. A stay at Jack's Camp will almost guarantee sightings of the extremely rare brown hyena, and the camp's ever-present meerkats will delight even the most seasoned traveler with their presence. **BS**

Explore the Okavango Delta

Location Kalahari, Botswana
Website http://okavango-delta.botswana.co.za   **Price** ⓢ

The *mokoro* (dugout canoe) winds its way through the tangle of lagoons and lakes of Botswana's Okavango Delta, silent and serene apart from the occasional birdcall—or a snort from a hippo that pops out of the water. Hundreds of miles away from the nearest town, there are no televisions, radios, or phones here, so tourists are thrust into the world of nature.

Set amid the stark and arid Kalahari Desert, the delta sprawls across 5,790 square miles (15,000 sq km), an ever-changing wilderness of untamed beauty that alters its appearance depending on the seasons and the subsequent rise and fall of its waters. In winter, rainwater from the Angolan Highlands swells the Okavango River and then spills over into the delta in March. Although much of the water disappears into the desert sands or evaporates in the searing heat, the rest floods plains and swamps, breathing life into the region and transforming it into a lush and green land, a wildlife haven. This happens between July and September, the best time to visit.

The delta's dry lands teem with wildlife and it is easy to spot herds of elephant, zebra, impala, buffalo, and giraffe. Flush with game, the Okavango is also home to predators such as lions, cheetahs, hyenas, and leopards. This is a land of strange and unforgettable sights. You may see palm trees standing proud in a dead-straight line, the result of age-old elephant droppings that contained date seeds. Rich with the scent of wild sage and oozing calm, it is no wonder the region is hailed as the jewel of the Kalahari. **JK**

⬅ *Passing through the still waters of the wildlife-rich Okavango Delta is the ultimate tranquil experience.*

Discover Motlatse Canyon

Location Mpumalanga, South Africa
Website http://kruger2canyons.com/travelguide/blydecanyon.php   **Price ❶**

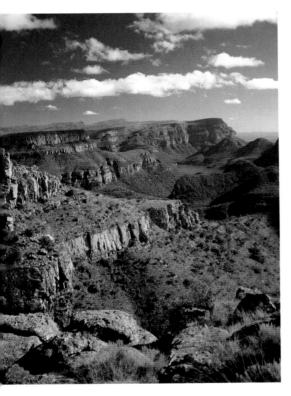

"[This] one of South Africa's lesser known beauty spots was clearly created . . . with lovers in mind."

Alastair Sawday, travel writer

It is not an easy feat to stand out in a country famous for its ancient landscapes and stunning natural wonders, but the Motlatse (formerly Blyde River) Canyon manages to pull it off. Carved over millennia through the soft, red sandstone of the Drakensberg mountain range, the canyon is more than 12 miles (20 km) long. It averages at 2,625 feet (800 m) from riverbed to mountaintop—although at some points it measures 3,280 feet (1,000 m) deep and 3 miles (5 km) wide. It is considered to be the third-biggest canyon in the world, behind the Grand Canyon in the United States and Fish River Canyon in Namibia.

Perhaps the most dramatic sights are the cliff faces that plunge hundreds of feet to sea level. From the peaks, you can gaze across mountain ranges, rivers, lakes, and lush green valleys. It is no wonder that one of the most popular viewing points, a rocky outlook over a sheer drop, is called God's Window.

Another magnificent sight is the Three Rondavels, a trio of cylinder-shaped rock formations rearing up from the canyon floor. Where the Motlatse and the Sefogane rivers meet, the meshing water has created a magnificent geological formation known as Bourke's Luck Potholes, which is also worth seeing. Thousands of years of erosion have drilled holes right into the bedrock, creating a surreal geometric design.

The fauna and flora in the canyon are incredibly rich and diverse, with 335 different types of bird, including the extremely rare and endangered Taita Falcon, and more than 2,000 species of plant. **JP**

◩ *The Motlatse Canyon—one of the largest in the world—wends greenly through the Drakensberg.*

Go Stargazing in Sutherland

Location Northern Cape, South Africa
Website www.saao.ac.za **Price** 💲💲

For most people, particularly those living in cities, getting a clear view of the stars is increasingly difficult. Tall buildings, air pollution, and light pollution distort the image of the sky, obscuring some of its most wondrous sights. None of these problems exist in the small South African town of Sutherland, which is today acknowledged as one of the world's preeminent stargazing sites.

The town's remote, elevated location (4,750 feet [1,458 m] above sea level), complete lack of high-rise development, unpolluted air, and clear, cloudless skies combine to provide almost perfect astronomical vistas. Indeed, so good is the town's setting that it was chosen as the location for the South African Astronomical Observatory, the southern hemisphere's largest optical telescope. Capable of looking billions of light-years back into the past, this powerful machine has produced invaluable information about the history and structure of the universe.

However, it is not just scientists and astronomers who can enjoy the area's enthralling midnight panoramas. At the Olifants Rest Camp in Kruger National Park, visitors can undertake special "Night-Time Experiences." These begin in the afternoon with a game drive on the lookout for the region's other great attraction—its wildlife—and continue as dusk falls with an interesting talk on the stars and local astrological folklore, before ending with a bout of stargazing through the camp's own powerful telescope. Visitors have the chance to see lions, elephants, and giraffes in the heat of the afternoon, and then quietly contemplate the Milky Way and Southern Cross in the coolness of night. **JF**

Enjoy Tswalu Kalahari Reserve

Location Northern Cape, South Africa
Website www.tswalu.com **Price** 💲💲

Simple elegance is the aim of the Tswalu Kalahari Reserve. There are comforts aplenty—indoor and outdoor showers (the latter with views over the Kalahari), personal sundecks, a library, and private dining rooms. Yet there is a rustic feel to Tswalu, in keeping with its African bushveld surroundings. The swimming pool overlooks a wildlife watering hole.

The reserve is always intimate—no more than thirty guests can stay here at once in a choice of two accommodations. The Motse has been modeled on a traditional African community (*Motse* means "village" in the Tswana language). Its cottages have stone walls

---

"While it offers a superb safari experience, its primary aim is conservation."

Good News South Africa website

---

and thatched roofs. Or there is Tarkuni, where wafty white drapes shroud four-poster beds. Sleeping up to twelve, it is perfect for families and small groups.

Tswalu is a family-run operation. Its aim is to "restore the Kalahari to itself." This area was once farmed to devastating effect; dams, houses, and fences drove out the indigenous game. Now cheetah and lions have been reintroduced, and the reserve is also home to leopards, hyenas, jackals, rhinos, zebras, and wild dogs. Should you need a break from lions and leopards, there is a high-powered telescope for stargazing, and there are opportunities for horseback safaris, bird-watching, and visits to meerkat dens. **PE**

Unwind at Garonga Safari Camp

Location Limpopo Province, South Africa
Website www.garonga.com **Price** 💲💲💲

Garonga Safari Camp sleeps just twelve guests, making a stay here a truly private and peaceful escape, ideal for honeymooners. Garonga's tented rooms, which overlook a dry riverbed, encourage guests to relax and connect with the bush. Each has a wooden deck with a hammock, where visitors can relax between game drives, reading or watching the impala graze. Large, draped beds and earthy colors mixed with pure white linens hark back to bygone times.

There is also newly built accommodation at Little Garonga, where three thatched, air-conditioned suites encircle indoor and outdoor lounge areas, a swimming pool, and a barbecue area. The most exclusive of the suites, the Hambleden Suite, has a separate room for children and a private swimming pool. Indian head massage, aromatherapy, and reflexology treatments are available at the massage "sala."

For those who really want to get away from it all, Garonga offers an option for sleeping out on a raised deck overlooking the veldt, a twenty-minute drive from the main camp. Staff will drive you to the deck and leave you with a picnic hamper, a drinks cooler, and hot drinks. You will be given a radio, and a washbasin and toilet are close by. Then you are left all alone with just the laughing hyenas for company, until the vehicle comes back to collect you in the morning.

If that sounds like a walk too far on the wild side, try taking a bath in the bush. Garonga has a freestanding tub that sits within a walled enclosure, decorated with atmospheric candles. Other activities include morning and afternoon game drives and wilderness walks, where you may see lions, leopards, elephants, rhinos, hippos, cheetahs, and spotted hyenas. **PE**

Experience the Clifftop Safari Hideaway

Location Limpopo, South Africa
Website www.clifftoplodge.co.za **Price** 💲💲

Deep in the Welgevonden Private Game Reserve lie eight luxurious suites commanding a splendid view of the Sterkstroom River Valley. From Clifftop's name alone you can glean something of the experience in store. Perched high on a cliff, the lodge was designed by one of South Africa's leading architects to be eco-friendly, both in its aesthetics and in its impact.

Tours of the game reserve in the retreat's open vehicles are the thing here. Welgevonden is well known for its focus on ecological management, in particular the relocation of animals; hence the diversity of the wildlife. Guests can see a myriad of creatures,

---

"The highly attractive terrain is in the rusty-red foothills of the Waterberg (Water mountain)."

Game-reserve.com

---

including lions and leopards, elephants and rhinos, wild dogs, and no fewer than fifteen different species of antelope. In total there are over thirty species of mammal as well as nearly 300 birds. Lodge activities include traditional game viewing in four-by-four safari vehicles and hikes with trained field guides.

Each of the suites enjoys its own private deck and plunge pool. Clifftop's menu offers superb fusion cuisine where African and Western flavors meet and a well-stocked wine cellar. The infinity pool is a focal point, and is the ideal place to have an evening cocktail. The combination of impeccable service and peerless beauty ensures a five-star experience. **PS**

Enjoy Ngala Tented Safari Lodge

Location Kruger National Park, South Africa
Website www.ngala.co.za **Price** 🌍🌍

There are tents, and then there are tents. Although camping may conjure up thoughts of roughing it in damp sleeping bags, the Ngala (meaning "lion" in Shangaan) experience could not be more different. These are the Rolls Royces of tents—just six of them spaced out in the grounds of Ngala Private Game Reserve. The intimate camp is set on the banks of the great Timbavati River, where elephants frequently congregate to take a leisurely drink and families of monkeys scamper around their feet.

There is a contemporary feel throughout, and beautiful timber decks overlook the seasonal riverbed. Tents are romantic, with luxurious bathrooms as well as outdoor showers and cozy electric blankets.

Most important, the game viewing is among the best in the world. There are twice daily drives led by excellent rangers and almost superhumanly skilled trackers in open-top, four-by-four safari vehicles. Sightings of the "big five"—lion, leopard, elephant, rhinoceros, and buffalo—are almost guaranteed. The area, part of the vast Kruger National Park, offers particularly superlative lion and leopard viewing, and buffalo herds numbering more than 300 roam the savanna. It almost goes without saying that wandering around camp at night without a guard is forbidden. The grounds are totally open, and wild animals can occasionally find themselves right on your doorstep.

Above all, the attention to detail at Ngala is endless—poetic notes are left on your pillow at night, bush banquets are laid out in spectacular wilderness settings, and theatrical alfresco candlelit dinners in the dry riverbed are quite stunning. Just be sure to keep an eye out for those roaming lions. **LP**

Stay at Lion Sands River Lodge

Location Kruger National Park, South Africa
Website www.lionsands.com **Price** 🌍🌍🌍

The experience starts early at Lion Sands River Lodge. The first game drive of the day powers off at 5:30 A.M. Rangers and guests regularly spot the "big five"—lion, leopard, elephant, rhinoceros, and buffalo. They stop en route for coffee, then return to the lodge for a robust breakfast at 9:00 A.M., after which the morning activities might include bush walks, lunch, and chill-out time in the spa or on the River Deck, perhaps, until the evening game drive at 4 P.M., followed by drinks and dinner. This resort is devoted to its environment: It has its own ecologist, responsible for ensuring the wilderness is left undamaged by visitors.

"Lion Sands is the only reserve in the Sabi Sand that employs a full-time ecologist."

Proprietors, Lion Sands River Lodge

Eighteen thatched bedrooms have their own deck and indoor and outdoor shower, and are connected to each other by wooden walkways. There are also two swimming pools, a bird hide, and indoor and outdoor bars and dining areas. Plucky guests can spend a night in one of two tree houses that lie fifteen minutes from the main lodge. Jackalberry Treehouse overlooks the dry bed of the Msutu River, and Chalkley Treehouse looks out over open plain, offering breathtaking sunset views of the bushveld. Tree dwellers do not have to rough it: These rooms under the stars have proper mattresses, linen, and mosquito nets. For those who wish, the kitchen will pack a picnic dinner. **PE**

Stay at Earth Lodge

Location Kruger National Park, South Africa
Website www.sabisabi.com/lodges/earthlodge   **Price** ⊖⊖⊖

The Africa World Travel Awards have voted Sabi Sabi Africa's leading safari lodge. *Travel+Leisure* magazine calls it one of the top ten hotels of the world. One of four luxury lodges that lie nestled within the 160,620 acres (65,000 ha) of this private game reserve in the southwestern corner of Kruger National Park, Earth Lodge is a retreat that blends seamlessly with the land around it. From afar, it can scarcely be seen at all.

Earth Lodge has thirteen suites, each with uniquely designed furniture, a private plunge pool, and butler service. Queen of them all is the Amber Presidential Suite, which comes with its own Land Rover, as well as a cocooning, egg-shaped bathtub, private exercise room, steam room, study, and kitchen. The lodge also has an outdoor *boma* (enclosure) and a dining area overlooking a waterhole. The wine cellar holds 6,000 bottles. If that does not leave you feeling woozy, try hanging out in the Zen meditation garden, or taking a trip to the spa, where treatments include hydrotherapy and phytotherapy, which uses plants and seaweed.

Day and night drives in open Land Rovers take guests on and off road, whereas walking safaris encourage visitors to absorb the atmosphere of the African bush. Sabi Sabi is home to lions, leopards, rhinos, buffalo, elephants, cheetahs, wild dogs, and a further 200 indigenous animal species. There are also 350 different species of bird. According to the Sabi Sabi guides, this means that someone visiting from the northern hemisphere may see more bird species on a single summer's day at Sabi Sabi than in an entire lifetime spent back at home. **PE**

➡ *The suites at Earth Lodge combine avant-garde luxury with traditional African tones.*

Experience Londolozi Sabi Sands

Location Kruger National Park, South Africa
Website www.londolozi.com **Price** 💲💲💲💲

More than eighty years ago, Charles Varty and Frank Unger first made camp on the banks of the Sand River. For decades, their families used the land as a hunting camp until, thirty-five years ago, a new generation decided to stop killing the animals. Instead, they turned their land into a revolutionary eco-tourism reserve and renamed it Londolozi, which comes from the Zulu word meaning "to protect."

Londolozi is famous for its remarkable population of leopards. Breeding herds of elephant and buffalo roam here, too, and there are high concentrations of white rhino and lion. Activities include game drives

> *"Londolozi represents a model of the dream I cherish for the future of nature preservation."*
>
> Nelson Mandela, South African statesman

twice-daily, full-moon walks, clay-pigeon shooting, bush running, overnight bush sleepouts, ecology discussions, and fishing on the Sand River.

The reserve offers five different accommodation options. The Granite Suites sleep just six and the decor is created in tones of elephant gray, with slate and silver adornments. Varty Camp has deep-reaching roots: its four *rondavels* (African round houses) date back to this reserve's original hunting camp. There are also riverside chalets at Founders Camp (each with a deck), and three suites and three chalets at Pioneer Camp (with a swimming pool), whereas at Tree Camp guests enjoy private cascading plunge pools. **PE**

Relax at Madikwe Hills Private Game Lodge

Location Madikwe Game Reserve, South Africa
Website www.madikwehills.com **Price** 💲💲💲

With accommodation for just twenty-four guests, Madikwe Hills Private Game Lodge blends intimacy and luxury. Ten glass-fronted suites are situated in the main lodge; each has its own deck and private plunge pool. The decor glows with African tones. White linen at the windows hangs against stone and terra-cotta-painted walls, plump sofas are covered in russet red, and cushions and throws are sprayed with bold geometric designs in black, white, and gold. Facilities include a well-stocked library and a *boma* (enclosure), where copper paraffin lamps create atmospheric lighting. Concertina glass doors bring the outdoors in during the warmer months, whereas in winter, under-floor heating and fires keep the lodge cozy. There are two other suites at Little Madikwe Hills, where a dedicated ranger, butler, and chef are on hand.

As far as game goes, the "big five" are in residence, but Madikwe Hills is also home to rare wild dogs. The 185,300-acre (74,100-ha) reserve was founded in 1991 through cooperation between locals and private enterprise. Its creation involved the relocation of some 8,200 animals. Game drives take place in open four-by-four vehicles in the early morning and evening. On balmy evenings, guests may enjoy their three-course dinner in the heart of the African bush. At the end of their game drive, they will come to a roaring campfire and a fabulous gourmet feast.

There is also a children's club for younger guests. Activities include "animal dung investigation," during which trackers help children learn to identify animals by what they have left behind on the ground. Their parents, meanwhile, may prefer to indulge in a far sweeter-smelling pampering session at the spa. **PE**

Experience Mateya Safari Lodge

Location Madikwe Game Reserve, South Africa
Website www.mateyasafari.com   **Price** 💲💲💲

Forget the "big five"; it is all about the super seven at Mateya Safari Lodge, where guests are promised sightings of lion, leopard, elephant, rhinoceros, and buffalo, as well as cheetah and wild dog. In addition to an abundance of game, the 185,000-acre (74,000-ha) reserve has more than 350 species of bird—all of which can be viewed in a malaria-free environment.

Mateya Safari Lodge can accommodate only ten guests, which promotes a sense of exclusivity. The five thatched suites boast four-poster beds swathed in mosquito nets, striking African art, and a private pool with deck big enough to swing a rhino. The lodge's

---

"From Dogon stools to Yoruba fonts . . . Mateya is home to one of the finest African art collections."

Proprietors, Mateya Safari Lodge

---

high elevation means guests can enjoy a panoramic view of the landscape, including a nearby watering hole where zebras come to drink. A plush free-standing bathtub takes pride of place in the center of the bathroom, and there is also a secluded open-air shower. Guests can lounge on sofas in the living room, crammed with dark, mahogany furnishings, animal sculptures, and hide rugs. Discerning travelers will love the lodge's library and wine cellar, packed with South Africa's finest. After a tough day of spotting game, you can hit the spa for a soak in the hot tub and then eat dinner alfresco around a bonfire, with a fiery sunset providing the stunning backdrop. **JK**

Stay at Hluhluwe River Lodge

Location KwaZulu-Natal, South Africa
Website www.hluhluwe.co.za   **Price** 💲💲

For a down-to-earth safari experience, try the cozy River Lodge in Hluhluwe, just a few miles away from Hluhluwe Imfolozi Park, one of Africa's oldest game reserves. It is famous for being a rhino sanctuary and is even credited with saving the animals from extinction. Overlooking Lake St. Lucia, the lodge offers intimate surroundings for just twenty-four guests.

Go horseback riding in False Bays forest, take a game drive in an open-topped jeep, or go on an eco-walk to experience the best nature has to offer. Join the cultural tour on quad bikes or go mountain biking on the trails. The lodge also has its own private access to Lake St. Lucia, with outings on the lake to see the hippos and Nile crocodiles while sipping a cocktail. It is all terribly civilized. To venture farther afield, take a day trip to Mkuze Game Reserve, a paradise for bird-watchers, or head to Cape Vidal for a day at the beach snorkeling in the warm waters. Divers can easily reach Sodwana Bay, which is said to be one of the top ten diving reefs in the world.

As evening comes, socializing with other guests in the Explorer's Bar and sharing the day's adventures are part of the sociable routine. Dinner is served on the deck or in the *Isibaya*, a traditional Zulu enclosure around a bonfire. With delicacies on offer such as local Kudu and Nyala venison fillet flame grilled, fresh Dorado fish, or spicy African-style curries, every single dish feels more impressive than the next.

Enjoy a drop of local rosé wine or indulge in after-dinner liqueurs around the fire before calling it a night and returning to the thatched chalets. Each comes with a fancy bathroom, a wooden deck, and welcome extras such as air-conditioning. **RCA**

Explore Rocktail Bay

Location KwaZulu-Natal, South Africa
Website www.travel-south-africa.net **Price ◑**

Sat on the northeastern shore of KwaZulu-Natal, Rocktail Bay is one of South Africa's most biologically diverse locations. It offers visitors two main attractions: tranquility and fabulous wildlife-watching. Indeed, the latter is largely the result of the former, with the bay's seclusion and distance from human habitation helping to preserve its ecological integrity.

Part of iSimangaliso Wetland Park, a World Heritage site, the bay is as lush and verdant as the region's other great environment, the bushveld, is dry and sparse. It boasts a range of fascinating, interconnected habitats, both terrestrial and marine—including coastal forests, lakes, wetlands, forested sand dunes, sandy beaches, and coral reefs—that together provide a home to a vast wealth of wildlife.

Starting on land, the forests and wetlands abound with brightly colored tropical birds that flutter and chatter up in the canopy. Farther below them red duiker and reedbeck shyly patrol the forest floor, and hippos wallow muddily in lakes. On the coast, where the beaches stretch for mile after pristine mile, the forested sand dunes welcome the region's most famous visitors: giant loggerhead and leatherback turtles that arrive every year between October and March, clambering clumsily ashore to lay their great clutches of eggs in the sand.

Offshore, protected within the boundaries of the Maputaland Marine Reserve, the balmy Indian Ocean waters swarm with a huge variety of sea creatures— everything from dolphins and whales to small, iridescent fish and multicolored coral. **JF**

→ *The sandy beaches of Rocktail Bay—part of a protected nature reserve—stretch on for miles.*

Enjoy White Elephant Lodge

Location KwaZulu-Natal, South Africa
Website www.whiteelephantlodge.co.za **Price** $ $

For a touch of luxury with your safari, head to White Elephant Lodge in the idyllic Pongola Game Reserve, the first game reserve created in South Africa back in 1874. At the foot of the Lebombo Mountains in the steamy Maputuland plains, the tented camp overlooks the shimmering waters of Lake Jozin.

With a classic feel and all the comforts you could imagine, the luxurious safari-style canvas rooms have everything from fluffy bathrobes to fabulous views over the unspoiled savanna. Originally built in the 1920s, the lodge sleeps just sixteen guests and definitely has a colonial-era romance theme, from the mosquito-netted beds to the Victorian-style, claw-

---

"We want our visitors to feel as though they have arrived at an oasis where time has stood still."

Proprietors, White Elephant Lodge

---

footed bathtubs. For a surreal experience, take a bath out in the plain. Filled with scented bubbles and lit by candles, it is a unique way to experience nature.

Go for game drives, guided walks, and tracking, but you could also try tiger fishing, sunset cruises, and bird-watching. At night, the bush is aflutter. You can lie in bed and be rocked by Mother Nature's lullaby, or take a drive huddled under a warm blanket to see some extraordinary sights: hippos racing past, lionesses and cubs climbing up trees under cover of darkness, or elephants on moonlight patrol. The best time of day is twilight, when it becomes the ideal place to soak up the liberating panorama. **RCA**

Camp at Thanda Reserve

Location KwaZulu-Natal, South Africa
Website www.thanda.com **Price** $ $

Thanda's award-winning five-star safari in northern Zululand is an incomparable experience, despite tough competition in the region. There are more than 400 bird species, not to mention the "big five," to spot in its 14,825-acre (6,000-ha) private game reserve. Guests are invited on two four-by-four game drives a day, with optional guided nightly bush walks to get the best of the animal attractions. Trackers help visitors see the best of the surrounding natural world—whether that be lion, wild dog, buffalo, or giraffe.

In the evening, you can sit around the central lounge and discuss the day's events before retiring to your choice of accommodation: the luxury unfenced and nonelectric tented camp, based on a colonial design, or the main lodge. With four-poster beds and plump mattresses, you are guaranteed a good night's sleep. The lodge is divided into nine private villas with indoor and outdoor showers, plunge pools, and a thatched outdoor game-viewing deck.

One of the greatest things about Thanda is its connection with the community, and staff are happy to share cultural treasures of the region, not to mention the Zulu remedy to help digestion: buchu tea. There is also an exquisite spa wellness center with treatments such as African Queen and Zulu King.

Because of its location near the Indian Ocean, Thanda also offers "bush and beach" packages where you can enjoy a trip to Isimangaliso, formerly St. Lucia, for horseback riding along the beach, turtle-watching, whale-watching, and diving. Luxury fans, spa seekers, and true naturalists will not be disappointed. **LD**

➡ *Thanda brings five-star luxury to the safari-spa experience they offer guests.*

Ride the Rovos Railroad

Location South Africa **Website** www.rovos.co.za
Price ⑤⑤⑤⑤

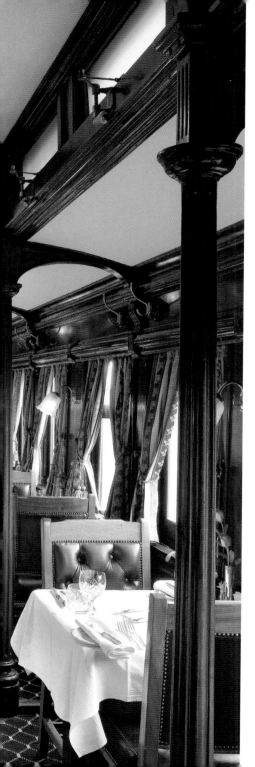

Taking a ride on a Rovos Rail train through South Africa is like returning to a bygone era of elegance and glamour. The carriages of its two trains have been restored to their former Edwardian splendor; in keeping with the old-fashioned style, there are no televisions or radios on board. Although the train is mostly hauled by diesel and electric, part of the journey is pulled by steam, normally on departure or arrival at Pretoria. Each train accommodates seventy-two passengers in thirty-six spacious suites, all of which are decked out with mahogany paneling and period furnishings. Beds are queen sized and the Royal Suites even have Victorian baths.

This is a train with a gourmet reputation; there is one sitting for dinner and the dress code is strictly black tie. Food is top-notch, with South Africa's finest game as a specialty, washed down with the country's best wines. It is all served up with style, using the finest china and the crispest linen.

Recline comfortably in an observation car while watching the ever-changing and vast landscape of southern Africa roll past your window. The train's most popular route runs from Cape Town to Pretoria, a 995-mile (1,600-km) journey that thunders through the lush grasslands of the Highveld, the stark emptiness of Great Karoo, and the mountains and winelands of the Cape. Other itineraries take in Namibia, Durban, Kruger Park, and Victoria Falls.

The train fare includes all food, drink, wine, and excursions, although you will have to cough up a little extra for some champagne. **JK**

◄ *The Rovos train takes in the best sights of South Africa while offering you the best in luxurious travel.*

Visit Shamwari
Eagles Crag Lodge

Location Eastern Cape, South Africa
Website www.shamwari.com   **Price** ⊖⊖

Tucked away in a gorge on South Africa's malaria-free Eastern Cape is Eagles Crag Lodge, one of six lodges in the Shamwari Game Reserve. Each of the nine detached suites has its own plunge pool, deck, and foldaway glass walls that offer great vistas over the cliffs. Shamwari is the vision of one man, Adrian Gardiner, who in 1990 bought a small farm as a weekend retreat. The indigenous fauna and flora of the Eastern Cape had been eradicated by the early twentieth century because of farming, hunting, and drought: lions, buffalo, and rhinos no longer lived here. Gardiner made it his mission to buy more land, to reintroduce the decimated species, and to turn his property into a wildlife reserve. Now Shamwari is one of southern Africa's largest private game reserves.

Game drives take place morning and evening in small vehicles: each ranger takes a maximum of six passengers. Guests are also invited to take part in game walks to visit two big cat sanctuaries, which the reserve operates in partnership with the Born Free Foundation, a British charitable organization that is dedicated to conservation, preventing animal abuse, and keeping wildlife in its natural habitat.

After a busy and productive day, you can then retire for a few peaceful hours to Eagles Crag's dedicated spa. Afterward, head to the upstairs dining room, with the option of outdoor dining, a lounge with fireplace, a library, and a cocktail bar.

If, after all that, you find that you cannot bear to go home, then why not stay a little longer? Shamwari offers a six-week field guide training course, during which you will learn the skills needed to make this little patch of paradise your home forever. **PS**

Experience Samara
Private Game Reserve

Location Karoo, South Africa
Website www.samara.co.za   **Price** ⊖⊖

South of Bloemfontain and southwest of Durban, Samara Private Game Reserve is one of the most exclusive safari experiences in the world. Situated in the Great Karoo, South Africa's arid and malaria-free heartland, the lodge has been a regular feature on the top hotel lists from the likes of *Condé Nast Traveler* and *Tatler*. These discerning magazines rave about the colonial-style lodge and the fantastic food and wine.

Karoo Lodge sleeps six, and the manor sleeps up to eight, so you will not feel crowded. There is a pool for cooling off, and staff are constantly on hand. Dining might be in the lodge or outside underneath the stars.

"The lodge is a stylish interpretation of the original Karoo farmhouse, complemented by gracious service."

Condé Nast Traveler

Wildlife-wise, this is a superlative experience. With none of the traffic or 5 A.M. starts that you would find in Kruger, guests are taken on four-by-four tours of the private reserve, which has rare mountain zebra, white rhino, armadillo, aardvark, kudu, eland, and black wildebeest. The stellar attraction is the cheetahs, however. One in particular steals the spotlight: Sibella. She nearly died at the hands of hunters, but has lived in Samara since 2003. She has had eighteen cubs in that time, thus contributing two percent of the wild cheetah population in South Africa. Visitors can walk in the park in clear sight of cheetahs for stunning photo opportunities with a ranger on hand. **LD**

Enjoy Blaauwbosch Private Game Reserve

Location Karoo, South Africa
Website www.blaauwbosch.co.za **Price** ⑤⑤

In the foothills of the Winterhoek mountain range on South Africa's Eastern Cape are nestled the five-star thatched chalets of Blaauwbosch. Husband and wife owners Craig and Gill Cullingworth firmly believe in luxury amid the lions: Their seven air-conditioned suites each have their own dressing rooms and bathrooms with freestanding tubs that allow you to gaze out over the bush as you soak. Crisp white linen gleams against the polished dark wood of the bedsteads; elegant black-and-white etchings of animals grace the sand-yellow walls. Spacious private decks give onto rolling mountain views.

There is also an exclusive lodge, Kaai's Camp, which is available for use during peak season. Sleeping a maximum of eight people, Kaai's Camp sits between two mountains and enjoys spectacular valley views. Bedrooms featuring the same bare-thatched ceilings as the chalets open onto an extensive veranda that flanks the house.

Whether you stay in chalets or camp, you will rise early for a game drive—lion, buffalo, elephant, leopard, rhino, cheetah, giraffe, zebra, and antelope may all be seen. Cheetah have been introduced to the reserve, and Blaauwbosch offers a "walk and stalk" excursion during which guests can follow a cheetah as it stalks its prey. Afternoons are relaxing times, but even if you intend to read or just to snooze on your deck, you may find yourself distracted by the abundant birdlife that comes to spy. During evening game drives, rangers stop high in the hills so that guests may enjoy the dramatic purple and orange sunsets of the Eastern Cape before returning for a dinner enhanced by fine South African wines. **PE**

Unwind at Grootbos

Location Western Cape, South Africa
Website www.grootbos.com **Price** ⑤⑤

There are more than a handful of nature reserves in the Western Cape but Grootbos is among the best of them. Only two hours down the coast from Cape Town, this is a family-run venture with a dedicated team of award-winning conservationists who together have rescued the area and restored its beauty.

This is a place for nature trails and running wild, for horseback riding on deserted beaches and picnicking among the flowers. Many tourists come to the sandy beach to see the 40-ton southern right whales, and watch spellbound as mothers, calves, and energetic bulls come to within 100 feet (30 m) of the shoreline.

> *"[The Cape Floral Kingdom is] the best example of conservation of biodiversity I have ever seen."*

David Bellamy, botanist

Two lodges of twenty-seven suites nestle in the lush and colorful vegetation. There is the family-oriented Grootbos Garden or the newer Forest Lodge, with its fresh, contemporary design that will appeal to the style conscious. The private decks of the large suites place you amid the beauty of the vegetation while you enjoy all the comforts of a luxury hotel. Through large windows you can gaze out over a vast expanse of unspoiled fynbos heathland or the ever-changing seascape down toward the coast. In the tranquility of the outdoor restaurants, the talented young chef satisfies guests with a five-course dinner menu that would do justice to a gourmet restaurant. **SWi**

Experience Bushman's Kloof Wilderness Reserve

Location Western Cape, South Africa
Website www.bushmanskloof.co.za   **Price** $$$

There is something spiritual about swimming in the rock pools of Bushman's Kloof. Perhaps it comes from the knowledge that they are ancient aspects of this awe-inspiring landscape, or maybe it is because the water is so crystal clear you feel as though you are suspended by air. The reserve in the heart of the Cederberg Mountains, a three-hour drive from Cape Town, overflows with natural wonders. As well as the mystical pools, there are jagged rock formations, indigenous gardens, and mountainous terrain that provide sanctuary for a myriad of wildlife, including the endangered Cape Mountain zebra. Thanks to its seclusion and affinity to nature, Bushman's Kloof is somewhere that encourages reflection, but there is also much to explore.

Bushman's Kloof hosts daily visits to unique rock-art sites that it also guards and conserves. The mountain drawings were produced by the Bushman tribes as long as 120,000 years ago. Nature drives give opportunities to encounter the wildlife and ever-changing landscape, dramatically carpeted in colorful Cape wildflowers each spring. Drinks are served at scenic spots, and "bush breakfasts" are laid on next to cascading waterfalls. Other activities include fishing in the Biedouw River and indulging in spa treatments.

The individually designed rooms have bathrooms, terraces, and in some cases lounges and fireplaces. For the ultimate treat, there is Koro Lodge, a fine villa with a pool, chef, and guide. Meals make use of the retreat's organic garden and local produce. **LP**

← *Bushman's Kloof Reserve is an ecological oasis offering the ultimate wilderness experience.*

Unwind at Kurland Hotel

Location Western Cape, South Africa
Website www.kurland.co.za **Price** ⬡⬡

"The elegant Cape Dutch architecture . . . complements the sumptuous interiors."

Independent

More than fifty years ago, Baron Peter Behr bought himself quite a large patch of paradise near Plettenberg Bay on South Africa's Garden Route. He named his estate Kurland after the Baltic province in which he was born. Two generations later, the baron's grandson and his wife have transformed their idyllic inheritance, which lies between the unspoiled beaches of Nature's Valley and the pristine forest of Tsitsikamma, into a boutique hotel.

The estate covers 1,730 acres (700 ha) but there are only twelve suites, each uniquely furnished with family heirlooms and tasteful objets d'art. A spa, a swimming pool, a veranda, and a library are available for those who wish to relax. For those more energetically inclined, there is a wide choice of activities on hand.

For starters, the place is famous for its polo: Kurland attracts professionals and enthusiasts from December to April each year. The season's highlight is the Kurland International match between South Africa and Australia, which the estate hosts each December. For those who do not know their chaps from their chukkas, there are plenty of other ways to work up an appetite for Kurland's candlelit dinner. Opportunities for canoeing, waterskiing, sailing, and surfing are nearby. Calmer pursuits include dolphin- and whale-watching—the Indian Bottlenose dolphin and the southern right whale both frequent these waters—or, on land, there are bird and elephant sanctuaries and a monkey reserve close by. Mountain biking and guided walks are available, or guests might take a stroll around Kurland's famous rose gardens. **PE**

◸ *The Kurland Hotel combines traditional Cape Dutch style with English country charm.*

Rent Franschhoek Pass Villa

Location Western Cape, South Africa
Website www.franschhoekpassvilla.co.za **Price** 💲💲

Franschhoek Valley may not be at the top of many people's "To See" lists when they visit South Africa, but rest assured, once you have been there it will be well up on the list of places you will want to return to.

It is hard to put into words the sheer jaw-dropping beauty of the Franschhoek Valley. It is as if the best of New Zealand, the Alps, and the American West have been joined together to create one of the most idyllic spots in the world, never mind South Africa.

But there is a lot more to enjoy than just the view. Food and wine are the mainstays of the Franschhoek valley, with some of the oldest and finest vineyards to be found in such a notable winemaking country, vying with what are regarded as some of the best restaurants in South Africa.

Head for the Franschhoek Pass Villa, part of the acclaimed Franschhoek Valley Winery. Perched high on the cool slopes of the Franschhoek Pass, it offers breathtaking views from the privacy of your own luxury private villa, where you can walk or bicycle through the estate's vineyards and nature reserve, or simply kick back and take in the amazing scenery. This self-catering villa sleeps up to four people, and there are many restaurants nearby with mouthwatering menus so you don't have to self-cater the whole time. The villa and winery are both run by Nick Davies. He and his wife made their fortune in interior design and have decorated the villa beautifully.

Golf lovers will also be delighted by the location, and everyone is encouraged to play on what must be one of the most exclusive golf ranges in the world in the valley below. You could also pick up a fishing rod and look for dinner in your own trout-fishing dam before heading back home to Franschhoek. **RS**

Relax at Le Quartier Français

Location Western Cape, South Africa
Website www.lequartier.co.za **Price** 💲💲

Those in the know say this luxurious hidden country inn was the place to launch Franschhoek as the culinary capital of the Western Cape. In the very heart of the Cape Winelands, it has as much charm as the surroundings—once home to the French Huguenots.

The former farm laborers' cottages have been transformed into a seriously chic retreat with a nod to the French style. The rooms are arranged around herb and flower gardens, some with private pools and exclusive butler service. To really get away from it all, book into The Four Quarters, four sumptuous suites with a lounge, dressing room, and outdoor veranda, grouped around a central courtyard with its own pool.

> *"The serious business of fine dining . . . has been set apart and defined by The Tasting Room."*
>
> **Proprietors, Le Quartier Français**

The rooms might be fantastic, but the big draw here is the food. Michelin-starred fine dining restaurant The Tasting Room has been listed as one of the world's fifty best restaurants thanks to the inspired cuisine of chef Margot Janse. Using the very best Cape products and its finest wines, she offers an innovative Cape Provençal menu in this beautiful setting. Choose from a four-, six-, or eight-course dining experience; the eight-course extravaganza also provides a different wine to complement each course. For lighter, less complicated meals, you can always try the café-style iCi, which flows from the street-side terrace to an outdoor fireplace in the garden. **AD**

Explore Kirstenbosch Botanical Gardens

Location Cape Town, Western Cape, South Africa
Website www.sanbi.org/frames/kirstfram.htm   **Price** ◑

Whether you are a full-fledged botanist or simply in need of a tranquil escape from the heat and bustle of Cape Town, the Kirstenbosch Botanical Gardens offer everything from breathtaking views to pastoral oases.

Considered one of the "Seven Magnificent Botanical Gardens of the World," the gardens sprawl effortlessly over the eastern slopes of Table Mountain. The beautiful lawns, softly trickling streams, and winding pathways were created in the early 1900s by a Cambridge botanist, Henry Harold Pearson. However, its origins date back to the 1660s, when its colonial status was confirmed by Jan van Riebeeck, who planted a wild almond hedge around the fledgling settlement that had been established there. Sections of the hedge can still be seen today among the rest of the relatively new 300 acres (121 ha).

There are a variety of themed areas and walks to choose from: The Fynbos Trail is a must if you want to meander through acres of South Africa's indigenous flora, and the magnificent Protea Flower Garden is at its colorful best in winter. One of the trails, up the Skeleton Gorge Ravine, is an easy and popular route for walkers and mountaineers, who pass through the gardens on their way to the summit of Table Mountain. The Dell, the oldest part of the garden, is a soothing place to stop and rest. Clear spring water flows out of Colonel Bird's Bath around stepping-stones to the small pond below, and ferns, impatiens, and gardenias fill the area under large yellowwood trees and provide dappled shade on hot Cape summer days. **SWi**

→ *Tree ferns flourish in the verdant Kirstenbosch Botanical Gardens in Cape Town.*

Stay at Camps Bay Retreat

Location Cape Town, Western Cape, South Africa
Website www.campsbayretreat.com **Price** ⑤⑤

Among some of the world's most expensive real estate is this luxurious and expansive hideaway that sprawls over 4 acres (1.6 ha). Cocooned in a wind-free peaceful glen that runs between Lions Head and Table Mountain, this Cape Town retreat enjoys views of the Atlantic Ocean and the Twelve Apostles mountain range. It might feel utterly secluded, but the handy haven is actually only minutes away from central Cape Town and glitzy Camps Bay with its throng of beautiful people.

In spite of the relatively expansive grounds, this boutique hotel has only fifteen individually decorated rooms, from the historic Earls Dyke Manor to the more contemporary Deck House. Its perfectly preened gardens are awash with waterfalls, mountain streams, nature trails, and pools linked by rope bridges. Dog lovers can take one of the resident pups for a stroll around the grounds, or guests can go for a guided walk with a horticulturalist to learn about the estate's indigenous plants. If in need of rejuvenation, head to the hotel spa, which offers facials and "massages for two." There are three treatment rooms, one of which is outside, ringed by bushes, and within earshot of the ocean's crashing waves.

For top food, visit the on-site restaurant Retreat Kitchen, which serves up meats and fresh fish flavored with herbs from the garden. Guests can enjoy a three-course candlelit dinner on the veranda while watching the sun setting over the ocean. Then quaff back some of the chef's delicious homemade Pinot Noir, available exclusively to guests. The more active guests can also rent mountain bikes, use the ocean-fronted tennis courts (floodlit for night games), or swim in one of the retreat's three pools. **JK**

Relax at Villa Lara

Location Cape Town, Western Cape, South Africa
Website www.villalaracapetown.com **Price** ⑤⑤⑤

With only the hypnotic crashing of the waves and the occasional screeching of the seagulls overhead, Villa Lara looks like something from the pages of a *Vogue* magazine fashion shoot. No surprise then, to learn that the property is owned by an award-winning photographer whose love of shape and light are reflected in this stylish, luxurious beachside retreat.

Suitable for up to eight guests, the villa has three elegant bedrooms, each offering uninterrupted vistas of the Atlantic Ocean and the mountains. There is also a self-contained guest cottage that has an open-plan double bedroom, kitchen, and lounge area. Natural light floods into every room, which enhances the pale

---

"The sound of the sea soothes away any stress; the sweet aromas of frangipani awaken your senses."

Proprietors, Villa Lara

---

minimalist palette of the decor. Rooms are furnished with Asian-style teak furniture, and beds are made up in the crispest white linen.

As you would expect in such a stylish hangout, the technology is entirely state of the art and includes computerized lighting, a home cinema, wireless Internet, and flat-screen televisions. This is the perfect place to relax in considerable style. Take a dip in the pool overlooking the ocean, sit on the deck and doze off to the sound of the waves and the heady scent of frangipani flowers, or cook up something delicious on the barbecue and wash it down with a local vintage. This is beachside living at its very best. **HA**

Enjoy Hotel Anjajavy

Location Majunga, Madagascar
Website www.anjajavy.com **Price**

Recharge at 20°Sud

Location Grand Baie, Mauritius
Website www.20degressud.com **Price** ⊖⊖

Situated on an island so remote that eighty percent of its indigenous wildlife does not exist anywhere else on the planet, the Anjajavy luxury resort on Madagascar's perennially sunny northwest coast takes isolation to a different level. Styled as the "peninsula at the end of the world," the area surrounding the hotel can be reached only by low-altitude airplanes that offer superb views. The Anjajavy is classified as a four-star-plus establishment by Western standards, yet few hotels around the world can rival its location.

Spread along the pure white beaches on the hotel's own bay are twenty-five secluded and air-conditioned rosewood villas with steep-pitched thatched roofs. In addition to the bedroom and bathroom facilities, the villas come with a lounge, a breakfast area, and an upstairs guest room. Satellite telephones are available from the reception, so that utterly exhausted escapers can conceivably spend their entire vacations relaxing in the hammock on the veranda outside their villa.

As well as the pristine beaches, the 2,150-square-foot (200-sq-m) swimming pool, and the restaurant providing excellent cuisine, the surroundings comprise an 1,111-acre (450-ha) nature reserve that is home to 1,800 mostly indigenous floral species and animals such as lemurs, birds-of-paradise, and several types of chameleon. Lemurs also frolic in the hotel's own "oasis," a landscaped garden where vacationers can have some afternoon tea surrounded by Madagascar's famously benign wildlife.

For those who become tired of so much relaxation, the hotel also offers various water-based activities, including sailing, snorkeling, and deep-sea fishing, as well as guided walks in the surrounding jungle or excursions to nearby villages and markets. **DaH**

The pace is relaxed at 20°Sud, Mauritius's only boutique hotel: breakfast is served until 7 P.M. Most guests, however, rise a little before that. Truth be told, there is a lot to get through. Windsurfers and sailors love the huge, sheltered bay with its perpetual light breeze. There is excellent snorkeling around the nearby islands of Coin de Mire, Ile Ronde, and Ile Plate, as well as waterskiing, kayaking, and parasailing.

After lunch (served on the terrace just feet from the sea), you might be ready for a snooze by the pool, followed perhaps by a massage, a Turkish bath, or a gentle paddle in the waters of the hotel's private beach. Maybe when the heat of the day subsides you

> *"The hotel overlooks the huge bay, sheltered from waves and with a light breeze all year-round."*
>
> **Proprietors, 20°Sud**

might take a bicycle out into the surrounding lanes, or to the designer boutiques and chic bars of the buzzing village of Grand Baie. If a bicycle ride is too strenuous, the hotel will shuttle you there in a canoe.

The hotel's twenty-seven rooms and two suites all have views over the ocean and a terrace or balcony. Each has been individually created by Belgian interior designer Flamant, with furnishings that give a historical vibe. On the subject of history, the hotel also owns the oldest motorboat in Mauritius, the MS *Lady Lisbeth*. Lovingly restored under the supervision of Michel Bourgeois, the proprietor, the hotel offers dining cruises to just eight guests at a time. **PE**

Stay at Le Prince Maurice

Location Roches Noires, Mauritius
Website www.princemaurice.com **Price** 🅢🅢

Located on an irregular-shaped, 60-acre (24-ha) sheltered peninsula that includes no less than three unspoiled beaches and its own lagoon, Le Prince Maurice is a tranquil, five-star oasis. In a country that prides itself on the quality of its resorts, this stunning property, with a range of accommodation that includes eight thatched bungalows raised on stilts over their very own fish reserve, is everything you ever imagined a resort in paradise to be.

Le Prince Maurice chose the humble but symbolic nutmeg for its logo, evoking the splendor of centuries past, when Mauritius used to be a key stopover for Portuguese and Dutch traders sailing the fabled spice route around the horn of Africa. Today that splendor lives on in the careful sprinkling of suites and private swimming pools of this exceptional hideaway, which offers guests a degree of seclusion and privacy rarely found in even the finest of five-star resorts.

A recipient of Relais & Chateaux's prestigious "Palace Status" Purple Shield, Le Prince Maurice is the place to go if you like over-the-water living, with its stilted bungalows over the lagoon. For those who prefer dry land, senior suites come complete with heated outdoor swimming pools and direct beach access. Enjoy a romantic candlelit dinner on the resort's very own floating restaurant, Le Barachois.

Free activities include kayaking, windsurfing, excursions on glass-bottomed boats, and waterskiing. Guests can also play golf on one of two eighteen-hole courses, which Le Prince Maurice shares with the neighboring Belle Mare Plage resort. **BS**

⤷ *The open-sided bar and lounge areas of Le Prince Maurice offer glorious views across the lagoon.*

Unwind at Beau Rivage

Location Belle Mare, Mauritius
Website www.naiaderesorts.com **Price**

When twelve brand new thatched villas were opened in 2007 at the Beau Rivage resort on the east coast of Mauritius, it was not just another five-star exercise in self-improvement. The villas, replete with Chinese porcelain and Indian artworks that reflect the peculiar Mauritian mix of cultures, represent the quest for perfection and pure indulgence that is an ongoing challenge at the Beau Rivage resort.

Overlooking an offshore coral lagoon and the powdery-white sands of Belle Mare beach, Beau Rivage is one of the leading resorts in a country that prides itself on having some of the finest tropical hideaways anywhere. Rooms have plush interiors and plantation shutters on the windows; butler service and a 21,500-square-foot (2,000-sq-m) swimming pool ensure you will not be rubbing shoulders with other people unless you want to. For diving enthusiasts, nine dive sites up to 111 feet (34 m) in depth are just a ten-minute boat ride away. Nearly all water sports are complimentary, and there is a dedicated children's pool and club that ensures everyone, regardless of age, is pampered.

The east coast of Mauritius is the least developed region in the country. It offers guaranteed evening breezes through warm Mauritian summers, and can still give you that deserted tropical island atmosphere that is becoming increasingly hard to find elsewhere. The supreme comfort of the guest is what matters here. After all, not too many hotels have a "menu of pillows" to ensure your sleep is every bit as tranquil as your surroundings. **BS**

⬅ *The treatment tents at the Beau Rivage spa are as exotic and exclusive in feel as the resort itself.*

Stay in a Tepee at One&Only

Location Belle Mare, Mauritius
Website www.oneandonlyresorts.com **Price** ⬤⬤

With a hand-sewn, bejeweled, canvas covering and a white and gold gauze interior, camping has never been this glamorous. This is no ordinary tent. Iconic British designer Alice Temperley has styled the tepee at the exclusive Indian Ocean resort with seriously stylish people in mind. Inside, there is an antique glass chandelier from Paris, a natural wood floor, gorgeous cushions and fabrics, and a chest full of champagne.

Guests can book the tepee for private dinners, celebrations, and even indulgent spa treatments. Or try a whole new experience—the Glampfire. Lounge on silk cushions, sipping champagne cocktails served by a butler, then have dinner at a low table set in the

---

"One&Only is about delivering distinctive experiences fueled by imagination and style."

Helen McCabe-Young, One&Only vice president

---

soft sand. Spend the rest of the evening watching fireworks, then dance on the sand into the early hours to the music of local musicians. Alternatively, loved-up couples can have the tepee to themselves, feasting on lobster and caviar, followed by spa treatments.

With restaurants headed by two Michelin-starred chefs—Alain Ducasse and Vineet Bhatia—taste buds are spoiled for choice. There is pampering on hand at the award-winning spa, and activities range from waterskiing, windsurfing, and sailing to tennis and golf. The temptation to lie back on a hammock strung between the palm trees or simply chill out in the decadent tepee is hard to resist. **AD**

Relax at Shanti Andana Maurice Spa

Location St. Felix, Mauritius
Website www.shantiananda.com   **Price** $

Shanti Ananda Maurice is the sister resort to the much lauded Ananda in the Himalayas, and it shares the same philosophy. The resort's holistic approach to well-being is evident at every turn—from the personalized spa program to the extensive yoga and meditation programs, practiced in dedicated pavilions and yoga rooms.

The setting is 35 acres (14 ha) of tropical gardens sporting spectacular views of the coral reef–sprinkled Indian Ocean. The coastal location is integral to the atmosphere and philosophy of Shanti Ananda Maurice; there are views of the turquoise waters at almost every corner, from the spa's Pebbles restaurant, to the junior ocean-view suites. Two of the room types—the luxury villas and luxury suite villas—come with their own swimming pools. The superlative presidential villa goes one step further, with a built-in whirlpool tub and steam room, as well as a pool and verdant landscape gardens.

The 50,000-square-foot (4,645-sq-m) spa makes liberal use of both ayurvedic and Western-style treatments. As well as the ayurvedic panchakarma treatment rooms, there is a couples' spa therapy suite, and there are multipurpose treatment rooms, scrub rooms, and hydrotherapy rooms. It is unusual to find a resort and spa that combines Eastern- and Western-style philosophy and relaxation so seamlessly. Guests begin their stay with a private consultation with a lifestyle assistant, who tailors the programs according to individual needs and wishes. **LC**

↪ *The Shanti Ananda Maurice offers a pampering experience that treats mind, body, and spirit.*

Discover Rodrigues Island

Location Rodrigues Island, Mauritius
Website www.mauritius-seychelles.com **Price**

Rodrigues Island is a simple place. Even in its capital, Port Mathurin, there are no great monuments to visit, no must-see museums. Forget rush hours; this town does not even have a rush minute. There are no traffic jams and no supermarket lines. It is a dawdling, ambling kind of a spot, the perfect escape from the modern urban melee.

Named for a Portuguese navigator who dropped by briefly in 1528, the island of Rodrigues is officially a part of Mauritius, though it has some autonomy over its own affairs. It is less commercial than its big sister island, however. Shoppers are more or less limited to the lively Saturday morning market.

Many visitors head over the water to Ile aux Cocos, a strip of flour-white sand covered with casuarina trees and inhabited by thousands of seabirds, including sooty terns, white terns, and noddies. Others might explore the 85-foot (26-m) deep Caverne Patate, adorned with stalagmites and stalactites, or walk around the coast from Pointe Coton to Gravier over deserted beaches lapped by turquoise waves.

Accommodation options include the Cotton Bay Hotel, which sits on a silent beach on the island's east coast. This is also home to the Cotton Diving Center. Guides lead guests through the island's pristine coral reefs; because Rodrigues's pirogues have always been pole-propelled, the coral has not been damaged. Alternatively the creole-style Mourouk Ebony Hotel faces a turquoise lagoon and backs onto panoramic hills; it also offers water sports. The real point of Rodrigues is that there is not a lot to do here, and that is a good thing. This is an island where one should not aim to be active, but instead take a few deep breaths, kick back, and perfect the art of indolence. **PE**

Enjoy Maia Resort and Spa

Location Anse Louis, Seychelles
Website www.maia.com.sc **Price** ⑤⑤⑤⑤

Lower in profile than some of its more celebrated Indian Ocean neighbors, the Seychelles' unique flora, fauna, and Creole charm are, as a result, better in quality than most. Maia Resort and Spa, built from volcanic stone and bilau wood, comprises thirty villas, situated just above Anse Louis beach on the quiet southwest coast of Mahé.

The luxurious villas are all unique. Think spacious gazebos with thatched roofs, adjacent bars, and oversized daybeds, plus Asian-style bedrooms. The bathrooms have a separate walk-in shower, but there is also an outdoor bath, where you can choose to indulge in a menu of aromatherapy and herbal bath

---

"The island of Mahé is said to be the jewel in the crown of the spectacular Seychelles islands."

Proprietors, Maia Resort and Spa

---

treats beneath a thatched roof. Ocean-front villas are situated on the beach, ocean-view villas are nestled on the slopes of the hill, and the ocean-panoramic villas perched on the hillcrest look out across even more verdant vegetation and sea.

The spa's La Prairie treatments are of the highest standard—therapists are selected for their "touch" and are encouraged to meditate every morning as part of their training. Qigong, yoga, and shiatsu are also available daily on a complimentary basis. The snorkeling and diving are quite simply breathtaking. You can also enjoy eating at Maia's exquisite Asian-Franco-Creole restaurant, Tec Tec. **PS**

Relax at Labriz Aquum Spa

Location Silhouette Island, Seychelles
Website www.aquumspas.com **Price** 💲💲

There is an air of absolute calm at Aquum, a tropical forest spa carved into a mountainside on the beautiful island of Silhouette, in the Seychelles. No sounds of cars or the drum of machinery usually associated with the outside world can disturb the reverie; there is just the soothing song of birds and a gentle breeze blowing through emerald undergrowth.

Treatments, using local ingredients inspired by the lush jungle and turquoise sea, come in many forms, and the caring therapists are only too happy to create bespoke packages for guests. The signature treatment involves being lathered in a warm brown sugar and nutmeg polish, cocooned in a green coffee and coconut wrap, and letting a spiced coconut hair mask infuse your locks—delicious. Local vanilla, cocoa, and cashew are also used in the spa. Other therapies include caviar rejuvenation, a luxurious age-defying facial to peel away the years, and jungle homme, for well-groomed Tarzans in need of spoiling.

Aquum Spa belongs to Labriz, the only resort on Silhouette, located along a mile-long stretch of beach. The name is a Seychelles Creole word derived from the French phrase *la brise*, meaning "the breeze." The contemporary villas and pavilions are tucked inconspicuously among the tropical vegetation and feature back-to-nature outdoor showers.

In addition to endless hours of pampering in the spa, which has an aroma steam room, hydro pool, and hot tub, treks through the tropical jungle can be arranged, plus visits to a giant tortoise sanctuary and excellent diving excursions. **LP**

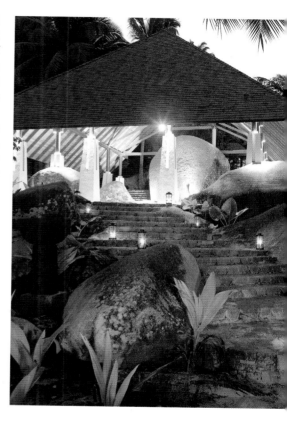

↗ *The setting of Aquum is quite unique—six spa havens set on stilts amid huge granite boulders.*

> *"[The resort stands] on the remains of the ancient southern super-continent of Gondwana."*
>
> Seychelles Nation newspaper

Explore Aldabra Atoll

Location Aldabra, Seychelles **Website** www.aldabra.org
Price $\bigcirc\bigcirc\bigcirc$

Some 152,000 giant tortoises live at Aldabra. It is the world's largest population, and there are five times as many tortoises here as there are in the Galapagos. The atoll has been described by Sir David Attenborough as "one of the wonders of the world" because its isolation in a remote area of the Indian Ocean, combined with an inhospitable terrestrial environment, has helped preserve it in a relatively natural state. It is also home to green turtles and hawksbill turtles, as well as the white-throated rail (the last surviving flightless bird of the Indian Ocean). The atoll is a breeding ground for lesser and great frigate birds, and red-footed boobies inhabit the mangroves on the northern rim of Aldabra's lagoon.

Aldabra Atoll is a naturalist's paradise, but it is not easy for humans to get to. (This, of course, is why the wildlife is doing so well.) The atoll lies more than 700 miles (1,125 km) southwest of Victoria (the capital of the Seychelles), and 250 miles (402 km) north of Madagascar. Inhabited only by scientists and rangers, it has no scheduled flights or ordinary hotels, and if you wish to visit and to stay in the very limited guest accommodation, you will have to seek permission from the Seychelles Island Foundation.

For the persistent—particularly those of scientific bent—the rewards are great. Aldabra provides a perfect natural laboratory for those wishing to study tropical marine ecosystems, seagrass, and mangroves. Those who visit will consider how fortunate it was that the British government did not persist with its plans in the 1960s to build an airstrip on Aldabra, and gave tenure of the island to the Royal Society instead. **PE**

⇥ *Aldabra Atoll consists of four large coral islands and is itself ringed by a coral reef.*

Discover Denis Island

Location Denis Island, Seychelles **Website** www.denisisland.com **Price** ⑤⑤⑤⑤

Denis Island encapsulates every desert island dream rolled into one. A mere dot in the western Indian Ocean, it is the epitome of unpretentious simplicity. The lush island is named after a French explorer, Denis de Trobriant, who first sighted it in 1773. De Trobriant landed on the fertile island and found it to be a haven for a diversity of wildlife, as it remains today. Now visitors will find twenty-five Creole-influenced cottages nestled close to the shore, filled with huge beds and plump armchairs. They have chic, romantic bathrooms with alfresco showers, private verandas, and courtyards dotted between casuarina and coconut trees.

There is little need to do anything but while away sun-drenched days marooned on your very own silky slice of beach, pausing only to cool off in the small pool or stroll around the island's pathways to the old village, chapel, and lighthouse. There are no televisions, radios, or anything else to disturb your peace, except perhaps for the island's endearing inhabitants—some rather large turtles. Active guests can always venture into the turquoise waters and take advantage of the snorkeling and diving—turtles, sharks, and rays abound—and year-round game fishing. Common catches include sailfish, marlin, and tuna, and from September to November, whale sharks and manta rays can be sighted in the area.

Mealtimes are refreshingly casual, incorporating an array of fresh produce from the island's own very well-stocked farm, which includes chickens, pigs, cows, and quail, as well as native vanilla, herbs, and vegetables. Days revolve lazily around long, lavish breakfasts, lunches, and relaxed à la carte dinners, and the hardest decision you might face is whether to dine in the restaurant or on the beach, underneath a starry canopy. Hmm, now that is a tough one. **LP**

⬆ *Set in a secluded natural environment, Denis Island is a favorite among those looking for a romantic escape.*

Stay on Cousine Island

Location Cousine Island, Seychelles **Website** www.cousineisland.com **Price** $$$$

Cousine Island may be tiny, but it is unique, spectacular, and enticingly hidden away. It is also, as an official nature reserve, ecologically important. Measuring only 62 acres (25 ha) in area and 2,625 feet (800 m) in width, the island has been dedicated to the preservation of the Seychelles natural environment since coming under private ownership in 2000. Its pedigree is impressive: the vegetation consists of ninety-five percent endemic plants and is home to more than five species of endemic land birds. The remaining five percent of vegetation is made up of indigenous fruit trees and plants, and hawksbill turtles come here to nest.

Amid this natural splendor, guests can stay in one of four luxury villas, which nestle 100 feet (30 m) from the pristine beach. Each villa aims to be 100 percent in keeping with its surroundings: Architecture is French colonial, materials are locally sourced where possible, and each villa comes with generous floor space, allowing for plenty of relaxation and tranquility. Guests

dine in a single, airy dining room, The Pavilion, overlooking the freshwater swimming pool and the ocean. Headed by South African chef Adriaan van Niekerk, the restaurant produces an array of dishes drawn from Creole and European influences and crafted from fresh, locally sourced ingredients.

The select feel of this island is enhanced by the fact that guests are encouraged to arrive by helicopter, guarding against the introduction of alien species: So far the island's delicate web of endemic bird and supporting flora remains intact. Tourists are also invited to take part in various conservation programs such as tree planting and turtle monitoring. For lazier days, there is always the lure of the spa (the Beach House Wellness Retreat), the beaches, and the simple, gentle lull of the Indian Ocean. **LC**

⊕ *Cousine Island's rare ecological importance attracts visitors with a strong interest in conservation.*

Enjoy Frégate Island Private

Location Frégate Island, Seychelles **Website** www.fregate.com
Price $ $

In years gone by, if you were a visitor to Frégate Island you were quite likely a privateer. These days, pirates are nowhere to be seen on this idyllic Indian Ocean island. From the tropical forests to the white-sand coves, the watchword of the island is privacy—and lots of it.

With no more than forty guests in residence at any one time, this tiny granite island is one of the area's most secluded and desirable destinations. There are sixteen expansive villas, all of which blend in with the surrounding landscape. Fourteen nestle atop the cliffs and afford spectacular views of the Indian Ocean; the remaining two lie in their own private tropical gardens. The interior decor combines colonial and Seychellois design influences and the furniture is reminiscent of artifacts gathered by Indian Ocean traders on their travels. All the villas have their own private swimming pool, whirlpool tub, and dining pavilion, plus sliding glass walls and French doors, which are often left open to place the visitor firmly within the tropical paradise. The paradise can be further explored with the resident ecologist, who leads regular hikes along the coast and into the jungle. The reef-protected lagoon offers safe diving, swimming, and snorkeling, and for experienced divers, boats are available to find dramatic dive sites.

The spectacular Rock Spa—reached through a canyon of waterfalls and freshwater pools—provides holistic treatments, and the Castaway Kids Club takes good care of the children while you work out in the gym, head off to Praslin Island for a round of golf, or just lie back and think about how those lucky pirates must have felt to wash up at a place like this. **SH**

➡ *The thatched-roof villas are built from locally sourced mahogany and teak and all have spectacular views.*

The breadth of experiences available to you in Asia is awe-inspiring. Stay in a temple in the Himalayan mountains or visit an ancient shrine in Cambodia. Alternatively, embrace everything the modern city has to offer by staying in a penthouse in Tokyo or visiting a luxury spa in Hong Kong. If these don't appeal, how about a beachfront lodge in Thailand?

ASIA

← The Sarojin, Thailand

Explore the Farasan Islands

Location Farasan Islands, Saudi Arabia   **Website** www.sauditourism.com.sa   **Price** ◖

The waters of the Red Sea are renowned for their great diversity of animal and plant life, but for a long time only those with ties to the Saudi royal family were allowed to admire the dazzling underwater world around its largest group of islands. Thanks to the kingdom's recent forays into the tourism market, the Farasan Islands—25 miles (40 km) off the southern Saudi Arabian port of Jizan—have become a more accessible divers' paradise that remains (at least for the time being) unaffected by human activity.

These eighty-four low-lying limestone islands and islets were created when sea levels rose after the last ice age, giving rise to vast areas of shallow water around them that have become home to expansive coral "gardens" full of marine life. The area is now a nature reserve. Farasan Kebir, the biggest island, is one of only three that are permanently inhabited, whereas the deserted islands making up the rest of the archipelago are ideal breeding grounds for sea turtles

and birds. The islands are also home to Saudi Arabia's largest population of gazelles, and they are one of the last habitats for the endangered dugong.

The tourist infrastructure here is quite refreshingly unsophisticated. The three-star Farasan Hotel—the only guesthouse on the islands—has limited space as well as some inadequacies, but the staff's genuine excitement about having visitors from faraway places more than makes up for its foibles. When you wander along the empty beaches on the larger islands (where the only traces of life you will encounter are animal tracks and the occasional flock of flamingos curiously looking at you), or when you come face-to-face with dolphins, stingrays, and whale sharks in the warm waters surrounding the islands, you will feel as though you are truly in a different world. **DaH**

⬆ *For many years, only Saudi royalty and their guests were allowed to dive or swim around these islands.*

Stay at Al Bustan Palace Hotel

Location Muscat, Oman   **Website** www.ichotelsgroup.com   **Price** $ $

Imagine a hotel designed by an Arab prince. Then add lashings of gold and a load of jewels, and throw piles of rials at it. The result will not be far off the Al Bustan Palace Hotel. Complete with 250 rooms, the hotel sits against a dramatic mountain backdrop on 200 acres (80 ha) of private beach and lush, verdant gardens. It has recently been refurbished, and some of its worst excesses have been reined in, to be replaced by more elegant, stylish interiors.

However, the foyer of the hotel is anything but subdued; it is still as opulent as befits a property occasionally commandeered for use by none other than HM the Sultan of Oman himself. With bright blue and green mosaic tiles, and a vast lofty atrium, you could be forgiven for thinking you had accidentally stumbled into a mosque instead of an Arabic outpost of the Intercontinental chain. Huge glittering chandeliers hang like stalactites from the ceiling, and richly ornate Asian rugs are scattered over the marble

floor. The rooms are all equally luxurious, with rich colors and fabrics used in abundance to optimum effect. Bathrooms are wall-to-wall marble, with some baths big enough for a football team.

As you would expect from a hotel of this impressive size, there is a well-equipped fitness center with state-of-the-art body conditioning equipment, as well as both a sauna and steam room. However, given the searing temperatures of the typical Omani summer, these latter facilities might be somewhat redundant. Far better to break into a gentle sweat by taking a stroll along the beach, or through the beautifully manicured gardens, and enjoy the space and solitude of your surroundings. If you are looking to live out those Arabian Night fantasies, and you have got princely pockets to match, this is the place for you. **HA**

⤴ *Even more opulent inside than it apears from the outside, this hotel is luxury at its most extreme.*

Drive Through Wadi Adai

Location Muscat to Wadi Shab, Oman
Website www.gulfleisure.com/wadibashing.htm   **Price** Ⓢ

No trip to Oman would be complete without experiencing what is referred to locally as "wadi bashing." A wadi is a dried-up riverbed, and in the blistering heat of this Middle Eastern sultanate, where temperatures have been known to nudge 122°F (50°C), riverbeds are more often found cracked and parched than flowing with life-giving water.

One of the best drives is through Wadi Adai to the village of Mazara, set in an oasis of swaying date palms. This picturesque settlement is almost biblical in appearance, with locals wafting around in crisp white dishdasha and herds of goats skittishly leaping around. Press on through the foothills of the jagged Eastern Hajar mountains through dramatic stark landscapes. You will soon leave the paved road behind and hit the coastal off-road path, lurching across ancient dried-up seabeds and careering along dusty red mountain tracks toward Dihab. You will come upon a huge natural water hole, known as Bait Al Afreet, with clear, emerald water. Farther on, you reach Wadi Shab, which means "gorge between the cliffs." This wadi rarely dries up completely, which makes it the perfect spot for a cooling dip. Situated in a deep ravine, the wadi is a lush oasis of trees, date palms, and grass, and makes a welcome contrast to the rugged terrain.

Make sure you spend some time in the desert, too, to experience some dune bashing; this is how the modern-day Bedouins drive across the soft undulating sand. Ideal for thrill seekers, this involves some hair-raising steep climbs up the vertiginous dunes and stomach-lurching drops over the other side. **HA**

➔ *Drive with a local guide; it is easy to get lost in the various dunes and rocky moonscape of the wadis.*

Discover the Sultan Qaboos Grand Mosque

Location Muscat, Oman
Website www.omanet.om/english/Relegious/grandmosq.asp   **Price** ◐

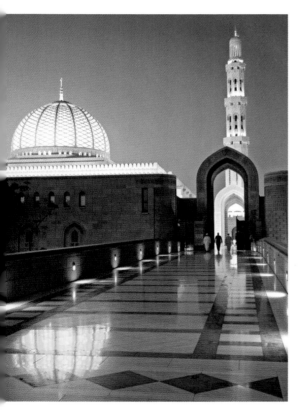

> *"It must be one of the world's most serenely beautiful buildings ... polished marble and smooth."*

Martin Love, *Observer*

In a blistering summer when the mercury can reach 122°F (50°C), where better to find a respite from the blazing sun than in the beautiful Sultan Qaboos Grand Mosque. Walk through the traditional Islamic gardens and enter the dazzling white marble courtyard through a series of symmetrical white stone archways. At midday, it is difficult to see at all because of the harsh glare of the sun reflecting off the marble, but enter into the cool sanctity of the mosque—ensuring you are modestly dressed—and your eyesight will soon adjust to the awe-inspiring spectacle within.

The mosque, which was completed in 2001, is the largest in the world outside Saudi Arabia, with room for up to 20,000 worshippers. The main prayer hall is square with a central dome rising to a heady height of 165 feet (50 m). The dome, main minaret, and four flanking minarets are the mosque's chief architectural features. Women have their own private *musalla* that can accommodate 750 worshippers.

The stunning 230-by-200-foot (70-by-60-m) prayer carpet is the largest single piece of carpet in the world. It was handwoven by 600 Iranian women, took four years to make, weighs over 21 tons and includes more than 28 colors (all vegetable dyes). The mosque also has some of the most stupendous crystal chandeliers you will ever see, dominated by the centerpiece, a truly awesome 600,000-crystal, 1,000-bulb creation by Austrian company Swarovski. It is second in size only to one in Abu Dhabi. Despite the grandeur of the Grand Mosque, and its impressive statistics, it is a place of great calm, peace, and tranquility. **HA**

◰ *The Sultan Qaboos Grand Mosque allows up to 20,000 people to worship together.*

Unwind at Zighy Bay

Location Musandam Peninsula, Oman
Website www.sixsenses.com   **Price** 💲💲💲

For centuries Zighy Bay has been hidden away in the far north of Oman in the Musandam peninsula. Now a resort of the same name has been built and guests have a choice of how they arrive: paraglide; take the winding mountainous drive; or take a scenic fifteen-minute speedboat ride over the water, zipping past traditional fishing dhows and schools of dolphins.

Zighy Bay sits on a bay of golden sand in a dramatic, rugged mountain setting overlooking the Arabian Gulf. The hotel is owned by the luxury Evanson Hideaway brand, and was built in keeping with traditional Omani style. A cluster of dung-colored cubes studded with palm trees does not make for the

> *"Four long, hazy, sunkissed days on Zighy Bay and I have to admit to being . . . utterly smitten."*
>
> Annabelle Thorpe, *Observer*

most aesthetically pleasing of properties, but it does blend in well with the stark beauty of the Hajar mountain range. All the villas have their own private plunge pools, outdoor showers, daybed areas, and terraces, and your own private Jeeves is only a phone call away. If you feel in need of further relaxation, make your way to the Six Senses spa.

It is at night, however, that the resort really comes into its own; then it is transformed by candlelit pathways, and dining tables on the beach are lit up by flaming torches. After dinner, take a stroll along the beach, gaze up at the inky starlit sky, and enjoy the perfect peace of what is still a hidden gem. **HA**

Relax at Al Maha

Location Dubai, United Arab Emirates
Website www.al-maha.com   **Price** 💲💲

Dubai, a flittering, thriving metropolis risen from the sand, is the cosmopolitan hub of the Middle East. Unique and ever changing, it is a feat of modern architecture and cutting-edge design.

Just an hour's drive away from the hustle and bustle of "the city of gold" lies the desert resort of Al Maha. Driving into the desert conservation area feels how it must feel to change planets. After the frenetic chaos of Dubai, Al Maha is still and peaceful, inhabited by smiling camels ambling about. Despite being inspired by Bedouin tented camps, Al Maha is the ultimate in desert opulence.

The intense heat limits activities. Rise early for a spot of falconry or take a walk from your tent and keep an eye out for the oryx, the rare elegant desert antelopes that roam free. Riders should jump in the saddle on the noble-looking pure-blood horses in true Lawrence of Arabia fashion. If it all feels too much, a golf buggy will be available to take you back to your tent.

During the day it is simply too hot to do much aside from relax and take in the beautiful scenery. Rest in the air-conditioned comfort of the decadent suite, with its huge bed, glitzy bathroom, and two-person tub, or relax by your very own dipping pool with a view onto the golden sands. Read that novel you always intended to read, or indulge in the spa. At dusk, join the camel walk. A reward awaits after the trek: a champagne cocktail in the soft, silky dunes. The sand turns a bright orange in the dim light, and couples spread out, adopting their own dune from which to watch the sun disappear in a warm velvety breeze.

There is a pervading sense of isolation here, a feeling that you are really lost in the land of *One Thousand and One Nights*, albeit totally voluntarily. **RCA**

Experience the Burj Al Arab

Location Dubai, United Arab Emirates   **Website** www.burj-al-arab.com   **Price** ❺❺❺❺

"Dubai's most famous hotel is as extravagant and outrageous as you've been led to believe."

Time Out, Dubai

⤒ *The Burj Al Arab was built to resemble a full, billowing sail—the sail of an extremely exclusive yacht.*

⇥ *There are simply not enough synonyms of the word "opulence" to do justice to this hotel.*

There are luxury hotels, and then there is the Burj Al Arab. Taking glitz, bling, glamor, call it what you will, to a whole new level, the iconic sail-shaped Dubai resort is a benchmark of no-holds-barred extravagance that others have tried and failed to emulate since the hotel opened in 1999. Soaring proudly to a height of 1,050 feet (321 m), the hotel is in its element at night when, dramatically and colorfully lit, it stands out on the coastline like a spectacular beacon.

All the suites (the word "room" does not exist here) are arranged over two floors and have a whirlpool tub, living and dining area, and dedicated butler, plus frivolous touches like extensive pillow and bath menus. Lavishly decorated, some suites have spiral staircases, private cocktail bars, dressing rooms, snooker tables . . . the list is endless. Excess is practically a dirty word and the sheer opulence is staggering. There is a helipad on the twenty-eighth floor, and the royal suites have a private elevator and cinema, a marble-and-gold staircase, and even a rotating four-poster canopy bed.

Tempting as it may sound, holing up in your suite would mean missing out on more fun elsewhere. The Assawan Spa and Health Club on the eighteenth floor boasts jaw-dropping views of the gulf, and the immaculate Majles Al Bahar private beach is fit for royalty. There are nine restaurants and bars, including the hotel's underwater restaurant, which contains a shark aquarium. If all that is not enough, guests can charter yachts or get the chance to brandish clubs at world-class golf courses.

A visit to the world's most palatial hotel is certainly eye opening, perhaps as a result of all the sparkly gold with which it is adorned. Just be sure to come with a stuffed wallet—and a head for heights. **LP**

Go on a Camel Safari

Location Dubai, United Arab Emirates
Website www.nettoursdubai.com/camel_trek.htm **Price** 💲💲

Dubai is an ultra-modern vacation destination, with astonishingly opulent six-star hotels and entire new towns seemingly emerging out of the sea on an almost daily basis. However, if you want to get away from the tourists who come to the Emirates just for the air-conditioning, and experience the real Arabia, you need to get on the back of a camel.

Known locally as Allah's gift to the Bedouins, camels can go for weeks without food and water, plodding across the red sands in stately caravans. With their slipperlike feet, armchair saddles, and gently swaying gait, they really do make for a comfortable ride.

A camel safari into the Arabian Desert will take you into a mysterious wilderness, dotted with date palms and acacias and populated by unusual desert animals, such as the sand cat, desert hare, and dune gerbil. Sometimes the sleepy desert fox may put in an appearance, and the plentiful geckos will skitter around the feet of your unfazed and reliable mount. At the end of the day, you can enjoy a traditional Bedouin feast, prepared in front of you as you stretch out on a carpet beside your tent and watch the unforgettable desert sunset, lengthening the shadows of the dunes and shifting the sculpture of the red Arabian sand.

Many people say climbing to the top of a high mountain is the best way to clear your head, gain perspective, and find your own place in the world. But devotees of the desert claim that a wander through the beautiful wilderness of the dunes, where maps and charts and plans are of no real use, is the perfect way in which to discover yourself. **SWi**

▣ *The best way to discover the majesty and silence of the desert is atop a camel.*

Relax at Bab Al Shams

Location Dubai, United Arab Emirates
Website www.jumeirahbabalshams.com **Price** ❺❺❺

It is easy to imagine that you are luxuriously marooned in the desert at this wonderful Arabian fantasy resort, but the incredible Jumeirah Bab Al Shams is actually less than an hour's drive from Dubai. Built to resemble a traditional fortress, there is a real feel of desert adventure about the unique setting. All the rooms are traditionally styled with dark wood and soft rugs, balconies and terraces look out across the dunes, and suites have a separate Majlis-style lounge and large walk-in dressing room connected to the bathroom with separate rain shower.

A great escape for all ages: While the little ones are being entertained at the kids' club, adults can chill out

---

"Inspired by traditional Arabian forts . . . [a] mishmash of styles that fits together seamlessly."

Matthew Lee, *Daily Telegraph*

---

by the infinity pool with glorious views across the dunes or be pampered in the Satori Spa. There are also six restaurants and bars, offering international and Arabian cuisine; the rooftop bar is the place to go for cocktails and watch the sun dip below the sands.

Plan desert adventures with a range of Arabian-inspired activities, from horseback riding and camel treks to falconry displays. Or explore the desert and eat an early breakfast among the rippling sands.

There is only one good thing about leaving Bab Al Shams and that is getting the chance to go shopping for gold, leather, and spices at the bustling souk (marketplace) in Dubai on the way home. **AD**

Enjoy the Royal Mirage

Location Dubai, United Arab Emirates
Website www.oneandonlyresorts.com **Price** ❺❺❺❺

Along Dubai's Jumeirah golden strip, which runs alongside the Arabian Gulf, opulent hotels jostle for space. There is, however, one essential place to escape the city's eternal buzz: the divine hammam at the One and Only Royal Mirage.

The Moorish and Arabian design of the Royal Mirage is pristine. Sand-colored structures are dominated by arches and domes standing out against the azure sky. It is an oasis of lush green palm trees, fountains, secluded pools, gazebos, and exotic Arabian style throughout. In keeping with the spirit of the Orient, the spa has an impressive central towering dome of intricate design and mosaic tiling, and here you will find a beautiful and traditional hammam. The entire experience is extraordinary: ceremonial with a touch of the theatrical. The hammam aims to nurture beauty and well-being within its steamy, wet walls. There is a defined cleansing and bathing ritual. Dressed in a *pestemal*, a traditional soft cotton wrap, a hammam masseur or masseuse will take command and will cleanse, scrub, and pummel your skin until it gleams—and your mind is thoroughly relaxed. You will be led to the alcoves where the air is hot and heavy, a few shafts of light come through the dim light, and lanterns shine off the mosaics.

Continual running water, the gleam of pristine silver bowls, and the rich, heavy heat have an entrancing effect. Being taken care of in such detail is exhausting; spend a little more time relaxing and sipping cardamom tea, sweet with a marked touch of spice. What more could anyone need? **RCA**

➔ *Everything about the One and Only Royal Mirage is designed to relax the body and mind.*

Relax at Sharq Village

Location Doha, Qatar
Website www.sharqvillage.com   **Price** ⑤⑤⑤

This grand hotel offers a wonderful firsthand experience of Qatari culture. Come here to immerse yourself in the lost world of a re-created fishing village: Fishermen and pearl divers once lived with their families on this very spot beside Doha Bay. When the fishing industry changed, the village emptied, but now the land has been given a new lease of life.

Sharq Village is the brainchild of the emir of Qatar and is a living tribute to the country's history. After five years of meticulous planning and two years of careful building, Sharq Village combines a sheik's marble palace with courtyard beits, or villas—like miniature boutique hotels—and a luxury spa.

> "Nudged against white sand coast, this walled enclave . . . intoxicates with sensual detail."
>
> Melissa Rossi, *Luxury Travel Magazine*

Guest bedrooms are furnished with elaborate four-poster beds made from Lebanese cedar wood, and antiques bought from some of the oldest houses in Qatar adorn the reception and public rooms.

Wander the maze of pathways between the old-style houses, through traditional gardens, then buy a shawl or some jewelry in the souk (market). There are several restaurants serving everything from simple Arabian pastries to the finest dining.

Seek out a bespoke smoke, hand-rolled by the in-house *torcedora,* at the cigar bar, or visit the hookah terrace, where butlers glide between canopied booths. Recline on a pillow and stargaze. **AD**

Explore Yazd

Location Yazd, Iran
Website www.iranvisitor.com   **Price** ❶❶

A charming muddle of mud-brick houses and narrow alleyways, Yazd looks as though it has risen out of the desert. Humans have been living here for a remarkable 3,000 years—and given that the city is hot and dry, the people of Yazd came up with an ingenious solution for keeping cool: They built *badgirs*, or wind towers, on top of their buildings. With their vertical slits, these towers are designed to catch the faintest of breezes and to channel cool air to the inhabitants below. Yazd is also known for its *qanat*—ancient water channels that still run beneath the mud-brick houses of the old city. Slip down one of the city's arched brick staircases and you can still see them.

The city's long history is enough, in itself, to impress. One of the oldest continuously inhabited places on Earth, it became a safe haven for artists and intellectuals fleeing Genghis Khan's rampages in the early 1200s. Just over half a century later, in 1272, Marco Polo came here. The fire in the Zoroastrian Fire Temple dates back further still: It is said that this flame has burned, without ever being extinguished, since 470 C.E. There are plenty of sights—one of the most impressive is the Friday Mosque, a fourteenth-century building with exquisite blue mosaic ornamentation and minarets that soar 150 feet (45 m) into the azure sky. But most visitors simply remark on Yazd's delightful atmosphere of laid-back calm.

It is a sizable city—nearly half a million people reside here—yet as you amble the streets, delve into alleyways, and relax in cooling courtyards, sampling the rich Iranian flavors (including the confectionery) for which this city is famous, you will feel yourself slipping back to simpler times, and will allow the hot sands of the desert to embrace you. **PE**

Enjoy Abbasi Hotel

Location Esfahān, Iran
Website www.abbasihotel.com   **Price** 💲💲

Situated in the center of Persia's former capital, the five-star Abbasi Hotel is a throwback to Esfahān's glory days. Built about 300 years ago during the flourishing Safavid dynasty, which ruled Persia for more than two centuries and created its greatest empire since the dawn of Islam, the complex has always provided lodging for travelers, initially as a caravansary and now as one of the most beautiful hotels in the Middle East.

Mindful of preserving the building's original shape and integrity, the architects have turned the formerly dusty courtyard into a quintessentially lush and flower-filled Persian garden that has become the hotel's main attraction. Overlooking the terrace are

> *"The glorious architecture of Iran, like a piece of gem, has been constantly glittering."*

Proprietors, Abbasi Hotel

the tiled blue minarets and Islamic onion dome of the adjacent theological college Madreseh Chahar-Bagh, where Islamic scholars have been teaching since the early eighteenth century.

The buildings that enclose the lovely garden are characterized by a multitude of typical Middle Eastern *iwans* (arched doorways) that lead to the rooms themselves. The rooms number more than 200 and range from comfortable, ocher- and auburn-colored rooms with queen-size beds and a sitting area to sumptuous suites consisting of several rooms adorned with Persian *farsh* (carpets) as well as intricately painted wallpaper and domed ceilings. **DaH**

Stay at Burj Al Salam Hotel

Location Sana'a, Yemen
Website www.burjalsalam.com   **Price** 💲💲

In the heart of the Yemeni highlands, the country's capital city Sana'a—which at an altitude of 7,200 feet (2,200 m)—offers a very pleasant respite from the otherwise stifling temperatures to be experienced on the Arabian peninsula. It is one of the oldest cities in the world, and the architecture and decor of the Burj Al Salam hotel, right in the heart of Sana'a's Old City, is a throwback to ancient times.

After ten years of complete restoration carried out under the guidance of UNESCO, this "tower of peace" (the literal translation of Burj Al Salam) combines Yemeni aesthetics with European sophistication. It is a multistory building with forty-seven rooms and suites and has a beautifully adorned exterior with a huge, arched entrance gate made of wood. It is the only top-end hotel in the historic part of town, as well as the only one that has an elevator. The hotel's restaurant caters to both the Yemeni and Western palates, and organized tours into the surrounding villages are on offer for those who want to explore the country.

The Burj Al Salam's greatest asset is its roof terrace, which offers fantastic views over the Old City, one of the best-preserved medinas in the Middle East with its domes, minarets, multicolored windows, and Sana'a's trademark houses made of clay. It is, in fact, Yemen's architecture that makes it stand out from other countries in the Middle East. Because of the building materials available in its highland climate, Sana'a has an architectural landscape that is altogether different from the coastal plains and deserts to be found farther inland. Its tall, flat-roofed houses look like they might be ancient skyscrapers, with the elaborate friezes and intricately carved frames providing the perfect setting for a truly exotic vacation experience. **DaH**

Experience a Kibbutz

Location Near Eliat, Israel
Website www.kibbutz.org.il/eng/welcome.htm   **Price** ❶

Labor Zionism originated in late-nineteenth-century Imperial Russia, and with it the Kibbutz Movement came into being. The socialist leaders of the movement regarded physical labor in the fields of their ancient homeland of Israel as a means of redemption, as well as a vehicle to free themselves from the social constraints the Diaspora experienced at the time. One of the results of this movement was the establishment of the first kibbutz, at the southern end of the Sea of Galilee, in 1909. By the time the State of Israel was created in 1948, kibbutzim were thriving.

Today, farming is no longer the raison d'être of kibbutzim. Kibbutz Ketura, 31 miles (50 km) north of Eilat, is one of the few remaining Israeli collectives resisting private ownership. Founded in 1973, Ketura distinguishes itself because of its highly educated inhabitants and the resulting prominence of artistic and technological endeavors. The kibbutz's work opportunities range from accounting and algae farming to photography and painting, and, unlike other vacations, a stay at the Ketura will earn you money rather than cost a fortune.

Volunteers are housed in shared two-room apartments, and in addition to free accommodation and three meals a day they receive $65 per month. Staying for two to six months, the volunteers work mostly in the service sector, although some get agricultural work or look after the children of the kibbutz. No matter what you do, the experience of living in a kibbutz will be unlike anything you are likely to encounter in everyday life. **DaH**

⬅ *There are a variety of different tasks that need to be undertaken on a kibbutz, such as picking nectarines.*

Relax at Isrotel Agamim

Location Eilat, Israel
Website www.isrotel.co.il   **Price** ❺❺

Near the shore of the Red Sea and the Eilat promenade, the Agamim—also known as "The Water Garden Hotel"—attracts young, laid-back guests who come here to soak up the relaxing atmosphere. Chilled-out tunes play by the pool, tropical cocktails are mixed at the bar, and hammocks are hung between the palm trees in the lush gardens.

This is a very popular hotel for romantic vacations. Lovesick couples can book to stay in one of the hotel's signature water rooms. The ground-floor rooms open directly onto a private stream that connects with the main lagoon pool. Guests can relax on the private deck or step into the stream under a stone archway.

"[Enjoy] tropical cocktails, cozy hammocks, and the freedom to do absolutely nothing."

Proprietors, Isrotel Agamim

There is no rush to get up early in the morning, with the option of a late breakfast served until noon, and room service is available directly through the swimming pool's On the Water bar. For those who want to venture beyond the hotel, there are jeep safaris into the mountains above Eilat, a wonderful chance to see the breathtaking desert landscape in panoramic detail. This area is teeming with history. South of Eilat is the arrival place of the Queen of Sheba, when she made her historic visit to King Solomon, and farther north, the caves around the Dead Sea are the where the famous Dead Sea Scrolls were discovered in the late 1940s by a young Bedouin shepherd. **AD**

Bathe in the Dead Sea

Location Israel/Jordan **Website** www.deadsea.co.il
Price ◐

The Dead Sea is the lowest place on Earth—and it is fast disappearing because of the local thirst for water. The spiritual nature of the Dead Sea is mesmerizing, as is the privilege of floating in the world's largest natural spa. Biblical references hang heavily in the air, but visit the Dead Sea because it is a beautiful epic in itself, not simply because this is your last chance to see it.

The sea's function as a natural spa is linked to its microclimate, a combination of ozone-rich air, low humidity, high evaporation and atmospheric pressure, and healthy, ultraviolet filtered sunshine. The salty, mineral-rich waters and mud are claimed to help provide soft "Cleopatra skin." For those squeamish

> *"A dip in the Dead Sea is a unique sensation. It is so buoyant . . . you can't even submerge your legs."*
>
> Jacqueline Head, *Daily Mail*

about swimming with fish, the Dead Sea is perfect: Between Jordan and the West Bank, the water contains nothing living but algae.

Slather off the mud and float away toward Jericho, Sodom, or Gomorrah, watching the sun set crimson over Jerusalem. The world's largest natural spa now also has a purpose-built spa, the Ishtar. If your body is your temple, let it be an epic temple. Designed with a passing nod to the Hanging Gardens of Babylon, the Ishtar is a pastiche of Babylonian splendor. **LGS**

→ *The Dead Sea is so thick with salt and other minerals that people can lie on the surface without sinking.*

Stay at Feynan Lodge

Location Wadi Araba, Jordan
Website www.rscn.org.jo   **Price** $

Arriving at Feynan Lodge takes a six-hour hike or a two-and-a-half-hour bumpy ride in a four-wheel-drive vehicle but it is worth the effort. Deep in the remote, arid mountains of Wadi Araba, Feynan Lodge forms the western gateway of the Dana Biosphere Reserve. The Royal Society for the Conservation of Nature (RSCN) constructed this unique, solar-powered eco-lodge to provide a base and accommodation for tourists.

At dusk, the lodge is transformed into a shimmering desert mirage as candles are lit in rooms, on terraces, and around the dining area. It is like stepping back in time to a traditional caravansary. In keeping with the lodge's green credentials, the candles that light it are

---

"The Lodge represents a brave attempt to create a unique tourism experience in Jordan."

The Royal Society for the Conservation of Nature

---

made by local Bedouin women and the restaurant uses fresh local ingredients to make traditional Bedouin vegetarian dishes. The RSCN built the lodge to provide an alternative, sustainable source of income to local Bedouins suffering from the overgrazing of their land. It was built entirely with local materials, and its unique arabesque design incorporates traditional adobe building techniques.

Its wonderful isolation and stunning landscape make this the perfect location for walkers. The region also has fascinating archaeological treasures, including the remains of ancient Roman copper mines and the ruins of a Byzantine settlement. **AD**

Camp at Wadi Rum

Location Wadi Rum, Jordan
Website www.baitali.com; www.visitjordan.com   **Price** $$$

Wadi Rum is a wilderness of more than 270 square miles (700 sq km), and one of Jordan's star attractions. Boulders and cliffs, shaped by millennia of winds and sand, stand like cathedrals. Seminomadic tribes live and herd their goats here as they have for centuries. The dramatic beauty of the mountains (known as *jebels*) can be seen by camel, jeep, or on foot, and mountaineers can try their luck on cliffs that reach 5,740 feet (1,750 m).

Many of the tribespeople will offer adventurous travelers a bed for the night in their goat-hair tents. These desert camps provide a unique experience. The curl of smoke from a hookah pipe slowly perfumes the air as tribesmen entertain the guests with live music, stories, and strong Arabic coffee.

There are also permanent sites, including the luxurious Bait Ali, which has a swimming pool, luxury tents, and hot showers. Guides can also take you into the desert for a private camping experience under the stars, with candles, a barbecue, and a luxury bed, in an ancient riverbed bordered by sandstone mountains. Here, in the Valley of the Moon, legends abound from ancient and more recent history—tales of Lawrence of Arabia, who had his headquarters here during the Arab revolt of World War I, are a common topic.

As the campfire flickers, crags and wind-sculpted rocks are illuminated. Deep in the canyons and caves, rock canvases show ancient etchings from people of the desert dating back 4,000 years. The area inspired Lawrence's *Seven Pillars of Wisdom*, in which he called the scenery "vast, echoing, and God-like." **LD**

➜ *The camp provides a base for exploring the vast, eerie expanse of desert that is the Wadi Rum.*

Stay at Hotel Albergo

Location Beirut, Lebanon   **Website** www.albergobeirut.com
Price ⓢⓢⓢ

Located just outside the city, in the quiet, green area of Achrafiye, the traditional Christian quarter of Beirut, Hotel Albergo is a relaxed and tranquil place. A converted city mansion, it makes the ideal base from which to explore the many treasures of Lebanon's capital city.

The only true boutique hotel in Beirut, Albergo has thirty-three luxurious rooms and suites that are notable for their luxuriant individuality (being a Relais & Châteaux member, the quality is pretty much guaranteed). Themed along various lines, including Asian, colonial, Mediterranean, and European, the rooms boast antiques alongside local curios. Each suite has been separately designed with the absolute comfort of the guest in mind, with such touches as Frette sponges and Dead Sea bath salt adding to Tarfa Salam's exceptional touch as a designer. Lebanon's location has always seen the country draw influences from the Near East, Middle East, and Mediterranean Europe, and this is reflected in the decor of what is essentially a peaceful hotel, with a playful twist. The red velvet bar lifts the lobby to neo–Louis XIV elegance, making it a warming and cozy venue to sip an ice-packed drink or two.

The garden, swimming pool, and whirlpool tub have unparalleled views of the Lebanese mountains. Sit and enjoy the warm, dry air, borne on winds dancing in directly from the African plains.

Albergo also has two restaurants. The Rooftop Restaurant, as its name suggests, provides peerless views, whereas Al Dente is on the ground floor and offers fantastic Italian and Lebanese cuisine. If you feel like a stroll or night out, the clubs, bars, and restaurants of the historic city of Beirut lie literally at your feet. **PS**

Enjoy Beit Al-Mamlouka

Location Damascus, Syria   **Website** www.almamlouka.com
Price ⓢⓢ

Damascus has become an increasingly fashionable destination for Western tourists. Unlike Beirut in the 1960s and present-day Tel Aviv, however, the allure of Syria's capital and largest city does not lie in the decadence of its nightlife or the presence of overpopulated beaches lined with dozens of bars. Instead, it draws people interested in culture and with a penchant for Middle Eastern romance.

Opened in 2005 and situated in a seventeenth-century house in the Christian quarter of Bab Touma—the city's oldest borough—Beit Al Mamlouka is Syria's first boutique hotel. It is inconspicuous from the outside, and only those in the know are able to tell that

> *"In Damascus, your best bet is to simply get lost in the truly ancient Old City."*

Seth Sherwood, *New York Times*

behind the salmon-pink walls there is a dazzling and intimate eight-room establishment centered on a courtyard whose citrus trees and fountain complete the picture of traditional Arabic aestheticism.

Inside, the two single rooms, two doubles, and four suites all have their own character and are furnished with handmade local products. Everywhere in the hotel arched doorways and lavishly painted ceilings abound, whereas the stables of this formerly private home have been turned into a restaurant and bar. Stepping out of the hotel, Damascus's bustling alleyways and its vibrant, atmospheric, covered souk (marketplaces) are only a short walk away. **DaH**

Stay at Four Seasons Hotel

Location Damascus, Syria **Website** www.fourseasons.com
Price ⑤⑤

The world's oldest city has just one five-star hotel and this is it. Sitting outside the old city, the Four Seasons towers above the minarets and domed rooftops of nearby mosques. It is not all modern glitz, however; there are enough touches of traditional style to ensure even the most well-traveled guests get a sense of staying somewhere suitably exotic and with an ancient history. The suites and rooms have all mod cons, but are beautifully decorated with handwoven Syrian textiles and locally made, handcarved furniture.

The hotel has three different restaurants: Al Halabi features the best of the Aleppo cuisine of northern Syria; at Il Circo, savor traditional regional southern Italian dishes in a contemporary setting; and Safran offers alfresco dining with breathtaking views of the city from the terrace.

Pamper yourself with a relaxing or rejuvenating treatment in the elegant surroundings of the Balloran Spa. The hotel's signature massage is the wonderfully calm-inducing Zanobia massage, which was once the favorite of Palmyrian royalty. Heated poultices infused with aromatic oils are used to soothe tired muscles, nourish the skin, and induce relaxation. Alternatively, go for a swim in the outdoor pool, where attentive staff will be waiting to greet you with chilled towels and water spritzes when you reemerge.

Damascus is a living museum—the world's oldest, continually inhabited city. Its mosques, markets, and ruins—including the Roman city wall—entice visitors to imagine themselves in another era, yet the city manages to live to a modern beat with good shopping and acclaimed restaurants. Visit the souk and step back in time to an empire that once stretched all the way from the Atlantic coast to central Asia. **AD**

Relax at Mansouriya Hotel

Location Aleppo, Syria **Website** www.mansouriya.com
Price ⑤⑤⑤⑤

Located in the old part of a very ancient city, Aleppo's Mansouriya Hotel is straight out of *One Thousand and One Nights*. An extensively renovated sixteenth-century building, this tiny boutique hotel pays tribute to the different cultures that have shaped Aleppo, from Hittite and Greco-Roman to Ottoman.

The hotel's alleyway entrance is as inconspicuous as its interior is sumptuous. Unmarked, it is impossible to spot unless you already know where it is. Pass through a small hall and a second arched doorway to enter a stunning courtyard. Everything has been considered with painstaking attention to detail, such as the bathtubs carved from single pieces of marble.

> *"Aleppo stands alone … one of the great lost, thoroughly underrated cities in the world."*
>
> Tariq Elkashef, suite101.com

The hotel has two sitting rooms, the Iwan for balmy summer nights and the impressive, wood-paneled Kaha, complete with cozy sofas and a fountain. There is also a well-stocked and (highly adorned) library, a whirlpool tub, and a hammam.

Two of Aleppo's main attractions—the souks and the citadel—are just around the corner from the hotel. Visit one of the coffeehouses to observe fashionable young Aleppians at dusk, in one of the most enchanting and welcoming cities on the planet. The Mansouriya Hotel's friendly service, delicious food, and gentle care of its guests gives you the impression that your Syrian grandmother is looking after you. **DaH**

Explore Alaçati

Location Izmir, Turkey   **Website** www.tasotel.com
Price $

Alaçati, on Turkey's Aegean coast, is a historic Greek town, set just inland, filled with achingly tasteful boutique hotels and gourmet restaurants—it is also home to a small sandy bay, which has become a popular windsurfing center, complete with very high-end resorts. Just ten years ago none of this existed.

In 2001, Zeynep Ozis, a retired marketing executive, had the idea of turning one of the village's dilapidated old houses into an upmarket hotel. Such was the success of the Alaçati Tas Otel that it spawned a nation of imitators. Now there are thirty-six, and counting. Thankfully, strict planning laws ensure that each respects the architecture and character of the town.

"Whitewashed walls, pale-blue window frames, antique furniture, and an enticing log fire."

The Times

None of these pretenders, however, has managed to improve upon the Tas. The large rooms are charmingly decorated, outside are a peaceful walled garden and a secluded swimming pool, and the delicious food—most of it locally sourced—is served on a leafy terrace. The hotel is quiet and serene, yet it is just a few minutes' walk from the town center, with its lively bars and restaurants that come to life in the evenings, and a short ride from the sunbathing and water sports opportunities offered by the beach. **JF**

⬅ *What makes these bustling streets different is the abundance of opportunities for people-watching.*

Walk the Lycian Way

Location Fethiye to Antalya, Turkey
Website www.lycianway.com **Price** ❶

Lycia is the ancient name for Turkey's Tekke peninsula, which juts into the Mediterranean on the south coast. Mountains rise steeply from tiny bays along the coast, creating beautiful views for walkers on their wooded slopes. The Lycian Way was established ten years ago. It is a 316-mile (509-km) marked path around the coast of Lycia, from Fethiye to Antalya. The route is easier at the start near Fethiye and becomes more difficult as it progresses, with some hefty ascents and descents.

Whether you tackle the whole route or just a small part, it is a spectacular way to spend a few days. You can expect to see the ruins of lost Lycian cities, quaint old houses in remote spots, and the forests, rocks, and blue Mediterranean Sea sparkling beyond. Highlights include the 7-mile (12-km) beach at Patara, views of mountains like Baba Dagi, and gasp-worthy vistas over the coast at Kas and Kalkan.

Along the way, some walkers stay at the lighthouse at Cape Gelidonia; others will tackle the 7,835-foot (2,388-m) Mount Olympos. There will doubtless be some manic splashing in deep cool canyons, jittery but memorable ridge walks, and the thrill of discovering tiny ancient churches far up in the hills. The trail is marked with red-and-white paint every 328 feet (100 m) to the standards of the European Grande Randonnée paths.

The best times to explore this beautiful trail are in the spring or fall. You can stay in one of the many simple pensions or small hotels along much of the trail, but in places it may be easier to stay in a village house or simply camp out in the wild. **SH**

◄ *When walking the Lycian Way, you will pass ancient ruins like these tombs carved into the mountainside.*

Camp at Huzur Vadisi

Location Lycia, Turkey
Website www.huzurvadisi.com **Price** ❷❷

While away a week or two in this Lycian oasis that translates to "peaceful valley." Set among fig and olive groves and based around a restored farmhouse, Huzur Vadisi promises a relaxing stay and holistic activities, such as yoga, in pine-forested mountains. Float away your worries in the natural stone swimming pool, rock yourself to sweet slumber in one of the many hammocks, or relax with an indulgent massage.

You will stay in traditional—albeit fully equipped—yurts. The relaxed, friendly vibe and groups (usually of about twenty) make it a perfect destination for solo travelers, and the array of interesting courses on offer means you are bound to make a new friend or two.

> *"Guests often comment on how visiting Huzur Vadisi is like being welcomed to someone's home."*
> responsibletravel.com

You will sample the vibrant village cooking in serene silence—save for the occasional shepherd's flute in the distance or the tinkling of goat bells from the surrounding hills. The mainly vegetarian menu draws on the spectrum of fresh local produce, including the nuts, cheese, and yogurts the region is famous for.

There are plenty of possible excursions to tempt you to leave for a day. Check out the bars and restaurants in laid-back Gocek, the local village, sail around the islands in a traditional wooden boat, or stop for a swim. Long, sandy beaches are within an hour's drive, as is Dalyan for those keen to visit the ancient ruins, mud baths, and hot sulfur springs. **JS**

Dive at Bodrum

Location Bodrum, Turkey
Website www.divingturkey.com/dive_bodrum.htm   **Price** ❶

The ancient city of Bodrum in Turkey is one of the world's top dive locations thanks to the warm, clear waters of the Aegean Sea. They give reliable conditions and great visibility while avoiding any major problems caused by fierce tides or currents.

The safe bays in the area are perfect for learning to scuba dive or snorkel, yet the rugged volcanic islands offshore appeal to even the most experienced divers. The very diverse locations on these islands include hot springs, caverns, reefs, and spectacular drop-offs. There are even some modern wrecks to explore, and Bodrum offers great diving for those interested in archaeology. Artifacts from the ancient civilizations of

---

"Discover a rich variety of marine life in the crystal clear water surrounding the Bodrum peninsula."

motifdiving.com

---

the area can be seen on almost every dive. Visitors can spot shards of pottery even if the historic vessels themselves are out of bounds. Hundreds of these protected wrecks lie on the seabed, including the oldest-known shipwreck. This was a Bronze Age ship with a cargo of copper and glass ingots and various objects, such as ebony, amber, and elephant teeth.

The Institute of Nautical Archaeology has the largest underwater archaeology library, and Bodrum Museum of Underwater Archaeology houses the world's largest collection of artifacts from underwater excavations. This is housed in the striking fifteenth-century castle of St. Peter that dominates the waterfront. **SH**

Stay at Anatolian Houses

Location Cappadocia, Turkey
Website www.anatolianhouses.com.tr   **Price** ❸❸

If asked to come up with a list of romantic hotel settings, a cave probably would not rank too highly—not unless you had been to Cappadocia, that is. Here, the region's strange, almost lunar landscape is dotted by groups of giant stone pillars, known as "fairy chimneys." Today many are also home to swish, upmarket hotels of which the Anatolian Houses is probably the most swish and upmarket of all.

The complex of suites (no rooms, only suites), which weaves in and out of a group of undulating, Gaudi-esque chimneys, has been created in the traditional style with arched doorways and barrel-vaulted rooms, but to modern specifications. The hotel is well equipped with indoor and outdoor swimming pools, a spa and wellness center, a hammam (Turkish bath), a top-class restaurant, and an extensive wine cellar. Everything has been very tastefully done in a style that could perhaps best be described as designer Ottoman. The beds are draped in muslin, colorful kilims (flat-woven rugs) hang from the walls, and the furniture is a well-chosen mixture of antiques and modern designer pieces. Fourteen of the rooms have private hot tubs. In other words, everything the modern cave dweller could possibly wish for.

To get a better look at the area's unique landscape, which stretches for some 50 square miles (130 sq km), try a hot-air balloon tour, around twenty of which take to the skies every day from May to September. Passengers are often served "Cloud Nine," a mixture of champagne and cherry juice, a suitably bizarre drink for appreciating this alien but beautiful world. **JF**

➡ *The locals have been carving dwellings out of the soft volcanic rock at Cappadocia for centuries.*

Take a Balloon Ride over Cappadocia

Location Cappadocia, Turkey
Website www.cappadociaflights.com   **Price** 💲💲

Hot-air ballooning is one of the greatest ways to travel: floating peacefully with the wind across a landscape. Over Cappadocia, it is truly sublime. This rugged region of central Turkey has some of the most stunning terrain in the world. Soft volcanic rocks have been eroded into strangely shaped pillars and stacks. There are hundreds of these "fairy chimneys" in natural colors ranging from dark pink to yellow, and ballooning is sometimes the only way to see them.

You are collected from your hotel and taken to the launch site just before sunrise. After the balloon is inflated, you climb into the basket. Takeoff is a gentle experience, like rising into the air on an invisible elevator. Then you fly over the valleys and rocks for about ninety minutes. After a gentle landing, passengers usually celebrate with a champagne breakfast.

Cappadocia is in the middle of a landmass with a great difference in night and day temperature. During the night, cold air accumulates in the valleys. Thanks to this reliable flow, which begins around sunrise, balloon pilots can fly almost every day of the year. Passengers can enjoy Cappadocia's great seasonal variety: In spring there is a carpet of miniature poppies, in summer a rush of fruit and flowers, and autumn is the time for grapes. Winter is often beautiful, with a covering of snow. Balloon experts often agree that Cappadocia is the best place in the world to fly. The predictable thermal conditions allow balloons to fly very close to the ground—you can even fly low enough to trees to pick ripe apricots. **SH**

➡ *The steady currents of air in Cappadocia ensure that there is always good ballooning.*

Relax at Yediburunlar

Location Fethiye, Turkey **Website** www.exclusiveescapes.co.uk
Price $

Perched high up in the mountains of Turkey's Lycian coast, lapped by the azure waters of the Aegean Sea, Yediburunlar Lighthouse is a haven of simple stone and wood, draped in colorful kilims (flat-woven rugs). An oasis of calm, with breathtaking views, this is the perfect spot to relax. The air is so pure it feels like being in the Alps. You'll soon feel at one with nature and totally chilled out, with only the occasional tinkling of bells from a passing herd of goats in the far distance to disturb your reverie.

The food at Yediburunlar is one of the main attractions. Dishes are mostly vegetarian or fresh fish, sourced locally and prepared by host Semra, one of

> *"Yediburunlar [covers] the seven bays that make up arguably the country's most stunning coastline."*
>
> exclusiveescapes.co.uk

Turkey's best-known vegetarian chefs. Fresh, seasonal, and mostly organic, this is meze food at its finest. Once a week a fish or goat barbecue is also on offer.

Hiking trips exploring the nearby Lycian Way are organized by co-host Leon. All levels of fitness can be accommodated. Alternatively, find your way down the mountain to a secluded pebble beach, a one- to two-hour walk. Day trips can be arranged to Patara beach and the market at Kalkan. Or enjoy a day's sailing along the coast in a traditional *gulet*, skippered by the mayor of the local village no less. There are also massages available on-site. No need to dress up: simplicity, good food, and relaxation are your only concerns. **JDa**

See Rüstem Pasha Mosque

Location Istanbul, Turkey **Website** www.sinanasaygi.com
Price ❶❶

Istanbul is renowned for its mosques, and rightly so. It seems there are impressive mosques on every corner in this city, competing with each other in their grandeur, the number of minarets they have, the height of their domes, the value of their treasures, and their architectural brilliance.

There is one mosque tucked away in the bustling backstreets by the spice bazaar that goes about its day-to-day business, quietly oblivious to its beauty. Tiny in comparison to its grander cousins, Rüstem Pasha, in Hasircilar Caddesi, is smothered in vibrant blue and white Iznik tiles that make those in the Blue Mosque look faded and tired. It dates back to the mid-sixteenth century, when the famous architect Sinan designed the mosque for Rüstem Pasha, the son-in-law and grand vizier of the great Ottoman Emperor Süleyman I, "The Magnificent."

Its entrance is a small stairway hidden among busy shops selling everything from household goods to cheap T-shirts. It is easy to miss, as if it has been designed to deliberately deter visitors, and it seems to do the trick. There is no constant murmur of visiting voices here, no lingering reminder of visiting crowds, just peace and silence. Walking up the stone stairway to the mosque's main courtyard, you are greeted by a myriad of patterns—every archway and every wall seems to be adorned with different designs of tiles as if you are walking through a giant kaleidoscope.

Daylight streams in through the many honeycomb-patterned windows encircling its dome, highlighting the colors and their vibrancy. It is a stunning exemplar of the adage that small is beautiful, and is the perfect place to escape the noise and mayhem of the city, if you can find your way to the entrance, that is. **SWa**

Stay at Sumahan

Location Istanbul, Turkey **Website** www.sumahan.com
Price $$

Not many hotels can claim to have started life as an Ottoman distillery, but Sumahan on the Water is one such curiosity. During the nineteenth century, its role was to manufacture suma, the grape spirit used in the alcoholic drink raki. In those days, the name for an inn was "han," so when this restoration was completed in 2005, its name was already steeped in legend.

Sumahan is on the Asian side of the Bosphorus, and the view of the iconic European-side skyline is picture-postcard perfect. The hotel is at the forefront of renewed interest in the Asian side of the city, and with its modern extensions and lovingly restored original features, it is an avatar for the city itself. Stone and

> *"Sumahan sits near the soaring Bosphorus Bridge, at the edge of the water."*
>
> *Condé Nast Traveler*

brickwork open out into mezzanine floors of steel, with the twenty rooms boasting open fireplaces, warm carpets, or wooden floors. The bedrooms are light and spacious, with marble bathrooms. Some bathrooms also have a Turkish-style bath or hammam. The terrace garden gives dramatic views of the world going by, mostly on the Bosphorus itself.

The Kordon Restaurant serves fish and seafood, whereas the Waterfront Terrace Restaurant serves Turkish and international food. The hotel also has a wellness center, including a notable Turkish bath. Sumahan on the Water distills all the exciting elements of Istanbul in an inimitable and classy way. **PS**

Enjoy a Cocktail at Mikla

Location Istanbul, Turkey **Website** www.istanbulyi.com
Price $

As the sky turns flaming red, and the sun starts to set, head to Mikla to watch the show from Istanbul's best vantage point. At the heart of Beyoğlu, on the northern side of the Golden Horn, sidewalks are lined with shops, restaurants, and cafés where the sweet, sultry aroma of hookah-pipe smoke hangs thick. The streets are abuzz.

Dive into the elevator to the top floor of the Marmara Pera Hotel to be transported into a completely different world. The location, beautiful decor, and ambience make Mikla one of the world's best rooftop bars. With white soft furnishings, manicured greenery, and a cool DJ spinning mellow tunes, it would put any Manhattan bar to shame. There is even a small dipping pool if things get too hot, and, although it is hip, it is not pretentious.

The truly awesome views make every new arrival's face split into a smile as they burst onto the wooden deck and catch the amazing sight all around. Bathed in the setting sun, the Hagia Sophia and the Topkapi Palace take on another dimension. There is the Bosphorus in the distance, the business district, and thousands of uneven terra-cotta rooftops stretching out like a quilt, glimmering in the last rays of the sun.

Friendly but discreet staff hover close by, always happy to bring a local Efes beer or a cocktail. If you want to stay for dinner, the restaurant is a funky, retro, chrome affair. It also has its own bar, made from stunning wooden rail sleepers, which has been known to accommodate a few dancers during wild nights. The food, created by Istanbul's answer to Jamie Oliver, Mehmet Gurs, is a delicious and sophisticated blend of Mediterranean and Scandinavian cuisine, a direct product of his diverse childhood influences. **RCA**

See Sultanahmet Mosque

Location Istanbul, Turkey
Website www.islamicarchitecture.org **Price** 💲

Amid the hectic bazaars of Istanbul, and the haggling they thrive upon, there is one place where you can be guaranteed some peace and quiet. Take refuge from the heat of the day in Istanbul's Blue Mosque—known to Istanbul residents as Sultanahmet Mosque.

Outside, sharp narrow minarets point to the sky and the great dome dominates this side of the city, overlooking the Bosphorus. The mosque's gardens attract lovers, who sit on the benches and watch the dancing fountains. A great courtyard leads visitors to the inside of the mosque, where low-hung chandeliers illuminate the delicate, intricate blue tiles that earned the mosque its nickname. The sense of awe and reverence provoked in visitors by the cool, hushed interior and atmosphere of serenity is something that everyone should experience.

Sultanahmet Mosque was founded in the early seventeenth century. An early error in translation meant that instead of having a gold minaret, as instructed, the architect built six minarets, confusing the words *alti* (six) and *altin* (gold). Fortunately for the architect, the sultan liked the minarets so much that they—and his head—stayed put. Today, it is the only mosque in Turkey to have six minarets.

One of the most impressive views of Istanbul from the Asian side of the city is still the one that was seen by those entering Istanbul by boat in days gone by. Those travelers would have seen the mosque's grand silhouette on the skyline long before they reached it. It is possible to re-create the experience today on a river cruise along the Bosphorus at sunset. **LD**

← *This historic mosque has become an iconic symbol of Istanbul, immediately recognizable on the skyline.*

Visit Cağaloğlu Hammam

Location Istanbul, Turkey
Website www.cagalogluhamami.com.tr **Price** 💲

The hammam was built in 1741 by Sultan Mahmut I; today, a massage at Cağaloğlu remains the perfect antidote to the stress of city life, for locals and visitors alike, conducted by experts for almost 300 years.

There are separate bathing areas for men and women and you can also opt to bathe yourself instead of being treated by one of the attendants—but most visitors will not want to miss out on the Complete Oriental Luxury Service. After an indulgent hour and a half in the marble *hararet* (steam room) you will be invigorated and left glowing like a firefly. Even gazing around the *hararet* is relaxing: Rays of light cascade down through star-shaped windows in the domed

"Cağaloğlu has soothed the nerves of everyone from Florence Nightingale to Cameron Diaz."

Guardian

roof as you wallow in the steam on the cooling marble benches. Once you have worked up a sweat, a masseur or masseuse (depending on your sex) leads you to the octagonal marble plinth in the middle of the *hararet*. It is time for a full body exfoliation, cleanse, and shampoo and, for the grand finale, a deliciously frothy massage, sometimes soothing and tickling, sometimes vigorous and pummeling, all in the midst of these elegant arches and atmospheric columns. By the end, you will feel as floppy as a rag doll. Take the opportunity to drift off to sleep back in your private cabin or enjoy a glass of apple tea in the pretty outdoor courtyard before returning to normality. **SWa**

Cruise up the Bosphorus Strait

Location Istanbul, Turkey **Website** www.toursistanbul.com
Price $

Istanbul is unique—the only city to straddle two continents, divided between Europe and Asia. Old and new, East and West coexist here, and a cruise along the Bosphorus is the perfect way to experience it.

Instead of jumping on the commuter ferries zigzagging frenetically across the river, or cramming onto one of the many tourist boats, escape the crowds and treat yourself to a private boat. Simply hang around at the ferry terminal at Eminönü for a while and you will soon be approached by eager touts offering their boats for your leisure—then you decide where you want to go, for how long, and when to stop off.

"The sea near the coast freezes over, as does the whole of the Cimmerian Bosporus."

Herodotus, *The Histories*

Passing under Galata Bridge, which arches over the Golden Horn, you will emerge to the sight of the 400-year-old New Mosque, Yeni Camii. Boats of all sizes jostle in the water, somehow avoiding collisions.

The melee of architecture along the waterfront is fascinating. From sultans' palaces, like the nineteenth-century, neoclassical Dolmabahçe Palace, to the wooden waterfront summer residencies (*yalis*) of the former Ottoman aristocracy, and the elegantly simple baroque Mecidiye Mosque, the variety is endless. **SWa**

→ *The architectural medley created by the meeting of Asia and Europe makes the riverbanks unforgettable.*

See the Harem at the Topkapi Palace

Location Istanbul, Turkey **Website** www.topkapisarayi.gov.tr
Price $

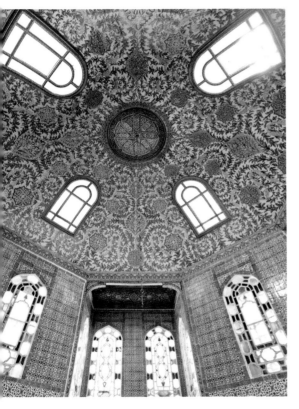

"[At] the main door of the Topkapi harem, the sense of enclosure and secrecy begins to grow."

Nick Trend, *Daily Telegraph*

Escape is not a concept that has always been associated with the imperial harem—harem means "forbidden" in Arabic. Built in the mid-sixteenth century, the harem at Topkapi Palace was the private living quarters of the female members of the Ottoman sultan's rather large family. Its 400-plus rooms provided lavish (and not so lavish) accommodation for the sultan's mother, the sultan's wives, and, most famously, the sultan's numerous concubines (which during the last days of the Ottoman Empire reputedly numbered in excess of 800).

The complex was strictly controlled by a unit of eunuchs, chosen because they would be unable to abuse their position. Contact with the outside world was via one carefully guarded exit, the Carriage Gate. Within, the harem was a hotbed of intrigue, where concubines vied for the sultan's favor, hoping to advance their, and more importantly their sons', fortunes. Indeed, many concubines rose to positions of great power, dominating the royal household, and in some instances saw their sons' rise to the position of sultan, whereupon they would ascend to the coveted rank of sultan's mother, or Valide Sultan.

Today you can tour many of the harem rooms that make up one of the most intriguing sections of the giant Topkapi Palace, the Ottoman Empire's seat of government until the mid-nineteenth century. Ironically, considering the intense history of the place, the harem quarters are today rather serene and quiet—the tour group crowds notwithstanding—and make a welcome escape from downtown Istanbul. **JF**

◹ *Added to and embellished over a four-century period, the palace has many examples of fine craftsmanship.*

Stay at A'jia Hotel

Location Istanbul, Turkey **Website** www.ajiahotel.com
Price 💲💲

This former pasha, a palatial summer mansion of the Ottoman elite, sits on the Asian banks of the Bosphorus and offers commanding views of life on the teeming river. An hour away from the center of the city, the A'jia—which means "Asia" in Japanese—offers the perfect refuge from busy Istanbul.

With only sixteen rooms, the hotel is one of a new breed of boutique hotels fast opening in the city. It has an original, dazzling white facade, but the interior is firmly twenty-first century, with cool contemporary decor and minimalist furnishings. A white-and-beige color palette dominates the rooms, which come complete with every modern convenience you could

---

> *"The striking purity of the hotel's decoration completes the beauty of the Bosphorous."*

Hayallere Visa magazine

---

desire: LCD TVs, DVD players, and wireless Internet. There are king-size beds to snuggle up in, and equally impressive bathrooms, kitted out in creamy marble with vast bathtubs.

The bedrooms offer amazing views of the river and give the impression that you are floating above the Bosphorus. Watch an endless parade of cruise ships, ferries, tankers, and fishing boats glide past on the shipping lanes of the Bosphororus en route from the Marmaris to the Black Sea. Whenever you need to head back into the bustling throng of the city, take the hotel's private boat on a quick but utterly enchanting journey to the European side of Istanbul. **HA**

Relax at Ciragan Palace

Location Istanbul, Turkey **Website** www.kempinski.com
Price 💲💲💲💲

A legendary place straddling two diverse continents, Istanbul is a mythical city that is at once bewitching, exotic and intriguing. A true melting pot of culture and architecture, the city that was once Byzantium and Constantinople comes as an assault to the senses.

The historical sights are all grouped together in Old Istanbul or Eminönü, home to the impressive Topkapi Palace built by Sultan Mehmet II in 1459, the Hagia Sophia, the former Eastern Orthodox church converted to a mosque in 1453 often dubbed the "eighth wonder of the world," as well as the Grand Bazaar, the world's largest indoor market.

Escape the chaos and check into the Ciragan Palace. Once the residence of the last Ottoman Sultans, first built in wood in the sixteenth century, it was rebuilt in marble for Sultan Abdülaziz in 1857. Now a lavish five-star hotel with a guest list boasting Prince Charles, Elizabeth Hurley, Uma Thurman, and Giorgio Armani, it has all the trimmings any A-lister could desire: a gorgeous pool and a boat and helicopter service. To go overboard, book into the Sultan's suite overlooking the Bosphorus, which comes with private butler service, opulent chandeliers, period furniture, and art.

Take an extravagant voyage through Turkish cuisine at the palace's fancy Tugra restaurant. The Ottoman tasting menu ranges from the meze appetizers of spicy hummus and dolma (vine leaf wraps), to steamed shrimp and lamb *börek* pastries. For dessert, there are sticky sweet baklava and *tavuk gögsü*, a creamy dessert made with milk-white chicken-breast meat.

If you can tear yourself away, take a drive to Ortaköy, where the city's famous felines roam, and on to Bebek, a traditional village where luxurious mansions and summer residences sit quietly on the water. **RCA**

Relax at Rakhmanovskie Kluchi Hot Springs

Location Rakhmanovskie Kluchi, Kazakhstan
Website www.kazakhstan.orexca.com **Price** 🕲🕲

As far as escapes from modern life go, it is difficult to find a more remote place than rural Kazakhstan. The biggest landlocked country on the planet—as big as the whole of Western Europe—Kazakhstan has only 15 million inhabitants. However, with its wealth of natural resources, it has prospered since the collapse of the Soviet Union, and is (very slowly) gaining ground as a tourist destination, too.

In the Arasan River Valley in the eastern part of the country—close to the borders of Russia, Mongolia, and China—the waters of the Rakhmanovskie hot springs are said to contain curative radon, a byproduct of the disintegration of radioactive elements. According to legend, a peasant called Rakhmanov discovered the hot springs in the 1760s while chasing a deer he had wounded. The animal allegedly entered the hot waters and left them a short while later having fully recovered. Nowadays, the thermal waters are used to treat joint and back problems, as well as skin diseases. Built on the ruins of a Buddhist sanctuary, the spa of Rakhmanovskie Kluchi is surrounded by cedar forests and alpine meadows, with peaceful mountain passes offering great views over pristine lakes and summits that are up to 14,750 feet (4,500 m) high.

The felt yurts of Kazakh nomads are located on the banks of a mountain stream near the springs. For those who think that breathing the fresh air in one of the most remote corners of this world is not enough, it is possible to spend a few days with the nomads and share their everyday experiences: caring for the horses, milking the fillies, and preparing their traditional meat and dairy dishes—an existence that is far removed from the comforts of home. **DaH**

Explore Dal Lake by Boat

Location Dal Lake, Jammu and Kashmir, India
Website www.kashmir-tourism.net **Price** 🕲

Edged by spiky, snow-glazed Himalayan peaks, the only way to reach the houseboats on Dal Lake is to glide across the crystal waters on a shikara taxi. On this island of tranquility in a region that has seen a troubled past, visitors are now making a welcome return to Dal Lake after a long period of absence.

There are several permanently moored houseboats offering accommodation on the lake, but the Pahktoon Palace comes highly recommended. It sleeps up to eight people and has a large living room and separate dining room, both of which are heated by cozy wood-burning stoves. The interior of the Pahktoon is very

> *"The floating palaces of Kashmir [houseboats] are closely associated with the valley's traditions."*
>
> trekearth.com

ornate; the high ceilings, chandeliers, antique furniture, and intricately carved wood paneling would not look out of place in an English stately home.

Delicious Kashmiri curries are prepared by friendly hosts, who are happy to enlighten guests about the area's history. Sip your morning tea on deck and watch eagles dive for fish that dart among the underwater gardens. Rise early if you want to catch the floating morning market where locals sell okra, lotus flowers, and other produce grown on the lake's islands. **SB**

➡ *Catch the sun setting behind the Himalayan horizon across Dal Lake, one of Kashmir's most magical places.*

Visit the Golden Temple

Location Amritsar, Punjab, India   **Website** www.amritsar.com
Price ⬧

At the end of a causeway in the middle of a man-made lake in the Punjabi city of Amritsar, the Harmandir Sahib (house of God), commonly referred to as the Golden Temple, is the most significant shrine of the Sikh religion. Designed with an entrance on each of its four sides echoing the tent of the Old Testament prophet Abraham, which also had four entrances to welcome travelers, the Golden Temple is a worldwide symbol of equality and tolerance, a serene place of worship whose doors are open to all men and women regardless of faith, race, or caste.

Construction on the site began in 1574 and was completed in 1604 under the reign of Guru Arjan Dev. The interior of the temple is replete with shrines honoring past gurus and is also home to three trees, known as Bers, that are symbolic of significant events in Sikh history. The exquisite gilding and intricate marble work on the temple's exteriors were initiated under Emperor Ranjit Singh and completed in 1830.

The Adi Granth, a collection of prayers and hymns representing the sacred texts of the Sikh religion, can be found inside the sanctuary inscribed on a jewel-studded raised platform. Surrounding the temple is the Pardakshna, a wide pathway that allows you to stroll around the temple and gaze up at its cusped arches and extravagant detailing. The temple's setting, its accessibility, and the profound sense of peace you feel when you approach the temple under the Darshani Deori arch at the beginning of the causeway will leave you in no doubt that this is one of the world's most monumental religious buildings. **BS**

◀ *The Golden Temple draws heavily upon the cultural and artistic traditions of both Islam and Hinduism.*

Stay at Basunti

Location Himachal Pradesh, India   **Website** www.basunti.com
Price ⬧⬧

If you are a keen angler, you may already know that the golden mahseer is India's most prized freshwater fish. What you may not know is that if you decide to spend a couple of nights at Basunti in the mountains of India's Himachal Pradesh, you are likely to catch these 26-pound (10-kg) beauties by the bucket load.

Angling in the man-made wetlands that pass by Basunti's doorstep is by no means the only pursuit afforded in this idyllic retreat. Located in the heart of a wildlife reserve and designed to leave the smallest possible ecological footprint, this boutique six-room retreat also has its own thatched Balinese-style yoga and meditation center. Bathed in tranquility and

> *" . . . a jewel, the kind of magical place that you might spend months looking for . . . and still never find."*
>
> *Sunday Telegraph*

seclusion, Basunti's two guesthouses both have shaded verandas and commanding views of the surrounding wetlands. The area is rich in birdlife, with almost 230 recorded species of bird and more than 50 species of waterfowl. Serious bird-watchers may wish to visit Ranser Island, one of the region's premier bird sanctuaries. In spring, when the waters are at their lowest before the monsoon, the gated temples of the ancient city of Bathu ki Larhi, representing the pinnacle of Hindu art and architecture, eerily reappear above the waterline. The traditional village of Khatiyar is just a thirty-minute walk away, and the area is a lovely mix of quaint rural villages and unspoiled woodlands. **BS**

Explore Shimla in the Foothills of the Himalayas

Location Shimla, Himachal Pradesh, India
Website www.shimlaindia.net   **Price ◑**

For untouched, rugged mountain scenery Himachal Pradesh is the Indian state to visit. Dominated by the mountains that rise steeply from the Punjabi plains, it is formed of several culturally distinct regions, isolated from each other by the mountain ridges.

Shimla is a wonderful place from which to contemplate the foothills of the Himalayas and the faded, melancholy grandeur of the Raj. These days, the town is popular as a honeymoon destination. There is a lot to enjoy, from the lively bazaars on narrow gullies that hug the steep ridges to the extraordinary Viceregal Lodge, a pleasant 3-mile (5-km) walk along pine-shaded roads, where the destiny of the subcontinent was once decided.

Wildflower Hall provides a genuine Himalayan experience without having to sacrifice all the comforts of home. Set in more than 20 acres (8 ha) of pine and cedar forests at an altitude of 8,250 feet (2,500 m), this five-star mountaintop retreat looks out over snowcapped peaks, verdant forests, and deep valleys. Activities at Wildflower Hall represent a departure from the usual choice of hotel pursuits and include archery, white-water rafting on the Sutlej River, horseback riding, and ice-skating. You can even take a day trip to Mount Everest on one of the hotel's two helicopters, or be deposited, with a minimum of fuss, in remote Himalayan valleys. Take in the sunset at the Hanuman Temple, at the highest point of the Shimla ridge. Monkeys appear from nowhere; they might try to divest you of anything not firmly attached to your being. **LB/BS**

➭ *The mountainous terrain can be quite hostile without the experience of a guide and his mule.*

De-stress at Ananda

Location Himalayas, Uttarakhand, India
Website www.anandaspa.com **Price** 🅢🅢🅢

Set in the Himalayan foothills, Ananda aims to restore balance and harmony using a personalized program of yoga and ayurveda that works with mind, body, and spirit in equal measure. Proximity to the holy town of Rishikesh heightens this gentle but deep-seated focus on spirituality. Despite the integral holistic approach, this is far from an ashram experience. Set among 100 acres (40 ha) of virgin forest, Ananda boasts a viceregal palace, acclaimed spa, seventy-five deluxe rooms and suites, and three private villas, housing two double bedrooms, with beautiful views of the Ganges River. The spa is integral to any stay here. The facilities include a Turkish steam bath, Finnish sauna, whirlpool tub, couples' suite, hydro-massage systems, and an outdoor swimming pool.

On arrival, all guests begin their Ananda experience by having a consultation with an ayurvedic expert. A wide-ranging tailor-made program is then devised, which includes nutrition, exercise, stress management, detoxification, and relaxation. Those with a love for yoga will rejoice. So-called "Ananda" yoga embraces a good range of yoga traditions, including hatha, kriya, and raja; beginners and experienced practitioners alike are encouraged to sink into a program that embraces meditation and pranayama (breathing techniques). A dedicated yoga pavilion sets the scene perfectly; an open-air marbled floor shelter nestles by a water pool and expansive lawns.

For a more outgoing experience, guests can take part in a program that includes swimming, squash, golf, nature walks, kayaking, angling, and white-water rafting. A four-hour trek to the Kunjapuri Temple, 9 miles (14 km) north of Ananda, is rewarded with superlative views of the snowcapped Himalayas. **LC**

Unwind at 360° Leti

Location Pithoragarh, Uttarakhand, India
Website www.shaktihimalaya.com **Price** 🅢🅢

For the intrepid traveler prepared to go the extra mile in order to experience something truly unforgettable, 360° Leti will reward tenfold any effort put in to get there—and it has to be said, it is not easy to reach. To get to the Himalayan town of Pithoragarh from the capital, New Delhi, you can either take an overnight train followed by a seven-hour drive, or else a private charter flight for just over an hour followed by a three-and-a-half-hour drive. From there, Sherpa porters will carry your bags on the final one-and-a-half-hour trek to 360° Leti: Himalayan vistas envelop and reinvigorate the senses, and the panoramic views from the 8,000-foot (2,400-m) high plateau are second to none.

> *"Beneath me is the valley floor, a ripple of emerald terraces punctuated by domed hills."*

Sophy Roberts, *Financial Times*

Far from the nearest road, 360° Leti's four cottages were constructed using local stone and timber. Inside there are slate floors, designer bathrooms, the finest linens, and walls of glass. Stone fire pits have been excavated into the ground in your private outdoor terrace so you can comfortably sit outdoors and watch the sun go down.

On a socially responsible note, guests are invited to contribute to a Village Development Fund, which sees 100 percent of any donation going directly to projects in nearby villages. Local people have also been trained in providing guests with an impeccable level of service that ensures 360° Leti will rarely be unoccupied. **BS**

Relax at Haveli Hari Ganga

Location Haridwar, Uttarakhand, India
Website www.havelihariganga.com   **Price** $

The Indian city of Haridwar is one of Hinduism's seven holiest sites and is known to devotees worldwide as the "Gateway to the Gods." Haveli Hari Ganga has been an integral part of the rhythms of its daily life ever since its construction on the banks of the holy River Ganges in 1917.

Once the private residence of the maharajah of Pilibhit, its rooms were built to accommodate guests of equal status, which explains their exceptional size and architectural purity. Arriving in Haridwar, you are met by a hotel representative who will take you the few miles to the hotel in a rickshaw. Haveli Hari Ganga is now a member of the Leisure Hotels group and a listed heritage site; it has been painstakingly restored using rare black-and-white archival photographs as a reference point, yet also provides all the necessary contemporary comforts, such as air-conditioning and luxurious furnishings. Interiors are designed to reflect ancient Hindu mythology, and the hotel has its own private ghat, where guests can safely purify their souls in the clear waters protected from the river's surging currents. If you are Hindu, a one-night stay in Haridwar is equal to gifting 1,000 cows to the gods.

Yoga and spa treatments are held on the outdoor terrace, which is so close to the river that you could almost use it as a diving board, and why not? The waters here are far cleaner than farther downriver along the ghats of Varanasi. Every night, a purifying ceremony, Ganga Arati, is held at the Har ki Pauri gate on the river, where large lamps are held aloft. Hearing the clanging cymbals accompanied by rhythmic chanting is something that should definitely not be missed. Hindus believe that Lord Vishnu himself once left his footprint on its ancient stone walls. **BS**

Stay at the Bagh

Location Bharatpur, Rajasthan, India
Website www.thebagh.com   **Price** $$

With its pleasure gardens based on those at the Taj Mahal, it is no surprise that the Bagh is such a tranquil getaway. The traditional Islamic formal walled garden bisects the 12-acre (5-ha) grounds with channels of water and walkways. There are fruit trees and shady groves, gaily colored flowerbeds, and sweeping spreads of aromatic herbs, but the big attraction here is, of course, the accommodation. The three, low, graceful residences are made of white sandstone with marble interiors. The rooms are furnished with handcrafted furniture and luxurious fabrics, and have pleasant outdoor seating areas. It might have an old-world appearance but this heritage hotel is definitely forward

> *"Works by contemporary Indian women artists are displayed throughout the complex."*

Nature Safari India website

thinking; it uses solar heating, eco-friendly generators, and fresh water drawn from a well in the grounds.

The ancient city of Bharatpur is the eastern gateway to Rajasthan and is a wonderful destination for eco-tourists. Close by is the Keoladeo Ghana National Park and a wildlife sanctuary at Band Baretha. In Agra, apart from the glorious Taj Mahal, there is Agra Fort, a masterpiece of design where the emperor Shah Jahan died in imprisonment looking out across to the Taj, the monument built to his beloved dead wife.

Go shopping in the bustling bazaar, then return to the Bagh for a refreshing dip in the pool to the sounds of gentle birdsong. What could be more heavenly? **AD**

Visit Humayun's Tomb

Location New Delhi, India   **Website** whc.unesco.org/en/list/232
Price $

The urban landscape of Old Delhi is defined by its lost Mughal past: It was the capital of Muslim India between the seventeenth and nineteenth centuries. The legacy of the walled city shows most obviously in its buildings: the vast Red Fort and Jama Masjid mosque, which create a sense of space and beauty within the cramped and labyrinthine streets. Here the alleys and gullies seem stuffed with traffic jams and temples, mosques, beggars, and bazaars. Then there are the wide, well-planned avenues of New Delhi, purpose-built by the British and these days the administrative center of modern India. New Delhi comes as something of a relief after the claustrophobia of the old city, but it lacks the romantic fortresses of Old Delhi. Humayun's Tomb makes up for that.

Built in 1570 by Haji Begum, who is buried there and was the Persia-born wife of Humayun, the second Mughal emperor, the tomb is a beautiful example of early Mughal architecture and displays the elements of its design that worked: The low buildings, high-arched entrances, bulbous dome, and formal gardens—perfect for lolling in—were used as a template for the magnificent Taj Mahal in Agra. Humayun must have been fond of his barber, because he is also buried in the Persian charbagh.

After visiting the tomb, wander around the formal gardens, all green-tended lawns and restored water features. They are full of discreet Indian lovers, holding hands tentatively under the neem, tamarind, and arjuna trees, which provide, incidentally, plenty of shade and the perfect place for an afternoon nap. **LB**

→ *At the first garden-tomb on the Indian subcontinent, visitors enjoy wonderful views from the terraces.*

Relax at Oberoi Amarvilas

Location Rajasthan, India
Website www.lhw.com/amarvilas **Price** 🌓🌓

Agra needs no introduction. It is the home of not only the Taj Mahal, but also the fabulous Red Fort and street upon street of traders selling anything from marble statues to biscuit boxes. Despite the hackneyed image, the Taj Mahal is undoubtedly one of mankind's most glorious achievements. Take the time to enjoy the play of light and colors on the luminous Makara marble: One minute it is pink, the next a warm, pale gold.

At the Oberoi Amarvilas, all the rooms have a view of the Taj Mahal, a mere 1,800 feet (550 m) away. Architecturally the modern hotel is impressive, too. The style of the ground-floor rooms, as well as the formal Indian Garden around the pool, is inspired by

---

"It is amazing that the home of the Taj Mahal should have had to wait so long for a truly first-class hotel."

Condé Nast Traveler

---

the monuments left by the Moghul rulers. The fifth floor is served by a bevy of butlers who bring you cold drinks when you feel the need; you might be excused for imagining you were a Moghul yourself.

The restaurant is a must. The food is stunning, inspired by the "dum" cooking of the Lucknow court. Here you will find gelawat kebabs flavored with cardamom seeds, stuffed potatoes, Thai-style curries (Thai food is very popular in India), lamb curry with a creamy dahl, a spinach dumpling that looks like a French *quenelle*, and gentle lamb biryanis flavored with saffron. The chef admits to an element of Indo-Gallic fusion in his mouthwatering recipes. **GMD**

Enjoy Amanbagh Resort

Location Rajasthan, India
Website www.amanresorts.com/amanbagh **Price** 🌓🌓🌓

Set within a centuries-old walled compound, the luxurious Amanbagh resort is a romantic hideaway. It pays homage to a grand architectural and cultural heritage, with sandstone cupolas, swaths of dark green Udaipur marble, private swimming pools, and soaring, palatial interiors.

A stunning contemporary palace made from pink sandstone in a nod to the famous "Pink City" of Jaipur, Amanbagh emerges almost miragelike, safely ensconced in a small, fertile, wooded valley that protects it from the heat and dust of the Rajasthani desert. The reception, dining room, and lounge are in the main building, but it is the majesty of the suites that will linger in your consciousness. Pink sandstone again dominates, but it is the not-so-little touches such as baths carved from single blocks of marble and the columns required to support the vast ceilings that will impress. Palms and eucalyptus trees are reflected in the waters of Amanbagh's Olympic-sized swimming pool, and a full range of spa packages is available, including yoga, Reiki, and qigong therapies, as well as advanced henna treatments.

The historic setting of Amanbagh makes it special. Within a short drive is the seventeenth-century Ajabgarh Fort, Rajasthan's ancient Narayani Mata Temple (1058 C.E.); the spectacular ruins of Bhangarh, an uninhabited and supposedly cursed city of temples and gardens; and the impressive sixth-century temple town of Neelkanth. Fed by the waters of a nearby lake, Amanbagh is a bright oasis of frangipani trees and manicured lawns, which provides visitors with an ideal base from which to explore the region's rich and colorful history along the lesser traveled roads that wind through the traditional villages of old Alwar. **BS**

Stay at Rambagh Palace

Location Rajasthan, India
Website www.tajhotels.com **Price** $$

Situated in the heart of Rajasthan's capital city Jaipur within 47 lush green acres (19 ha), the extravagant Rambagh Palace was built combining traditional Rajput and Mughal architectural styles. Graceful arches line the majestic building, and ornate turrets rise from either end. Inside, elaborate walkways surround a central courtyard, where guests and peacocks roam in the warm Indian sunshine. Perfectly manicured lawns, gently trickling fountains, and ornamental gardens complete the look.

The Rambagh was originally built in 1835, and in 1925 it was given its palatial overhaul, creating the regal masterpiece that locals named The "Jewel of

---

"Where in the world—but at the Rambagh—will you find a running fountain inside a suite?"

Daily Telegraph

Jaipur." In 1957, it was converted once again to become India's first palace hotel. The rooms were faithfully renovated to retain the glamour and to provide guests with an authentic royal retreat. High ceilings and four-poster beds add an air of grandeur to every room. The look is one of over-the-top opulence.

With a fitness center, golf course, and several bars and restaurants on-site, there is no need to leave your palatial surroundings, although it is worth exploring the picturesque streets of Jaipur. The romantic "Pink City" earned its nickname in 1853, when a state visit by the Prince of Wales prompted residents to celebrate his arrival by painting all the buildings pink. **JP**

Unwind at Neemrana Fort

Location Rajasthan, India
Website www.neemranahotels.com **Price** $

In 1464, before the rise of the Mughal empire, the Maharajah Devi Singh began construction of a fortified palace complex near the city of Alwar. The building first opened as a hotel in 1991, and today the Neemrana Fort is the oldest heritage resort in India and one of the architectural jewels of Rajasthan. It offers guests a rare opportunity to live in medieval splendor and to immerse themselves in the history and traditions of the old Rajputs.

Similar in scale to other monumental forts and palaces of Rajasthan, like Jodhpur's Umaid Bhawan Palace and Mehrangarh Fort, the Neemrana Fort's seventy rooms are individually decorated and themed, with most boasting private balconies. Although overwhelming in its scale, with ten overlapping layers of construction, there are some lovely architectural flourishes, such as the hanging garden that was recently laid along the southern ramparts and an eighteenth-century, eleven-story underground stepwell in the gardens near the palace wall, complete with Roman-style arches and a wraparound staircase. A mere 80 miles (130 km) from New Delhi, the Neemrana Fort Resort is one of the more accessible of India's palace hotels, as well as being the closest Rajasthan palace to the nation's capital.

The hotel is spread over four wings, and its rooms are all beautifully furnished in the traditional Indian style. Within its chiseled walls, there is a swimming pool and fully equipped health spa offering traditional treatments such as ayurvedic rejuvenation. Guided tours of the fort are available every day, but in the unlikely event that you feel the need to get out, camel safaris, trekking, and numerous day excursions can be easily arranged in the surrounding areas. **BS**

Relax at Samode Haveli

Location Rajasthan, India **Website** www.samode.com
Price 🟢🟢

This hidden gem is tucked away down the dusty backstreets of the old walled "Pink City" of frenetic Jaipur, and offers an oasis of calm in a manic hive of noise and activity. Built as a town house for the Samode royal family 150 years ago, this grand old house was converted into a heritage hotel in 1988. It has since been hailed by those in the know as one of the world's hippest hotels.

Surrounded by bougainvillea, this majestic property has a spectacular entrance, with an ornately tiled door, that is reached via an elephant ramp constructed for a wedding ceremony in the 1940s. The lavish decoration continues inside the hotel, which is awash with murals and frescoes. A labyrinth of narrow passages and dark staircases unexpectedly opens out onto endless charming courtyards. The prettiest of these is the central courtyard, studded with pomegranate trees, flowers, and ornamental pools, and frequented by playful monkeys.

Oozing with character, the hotel's twenty-two rooms are all differently shaped and have unique designs. For lovers of jewels, the suites even have floor-to-ceiling mirror mosaics. The huge outdoor pool is stunning, decorated with Moroccan tiles and surrounded by large comfy daybeds, complemented by a whirlpool tub and a wading pool for children. The dining hall is an elaborate affair, richly painted with flowers and dancing girls. If you prefer a more laid-back setting, staff can arrange private lunches or romantic candlelit meals for guests in the hotel's lush garden, alive with flowers and trees. **JK**

← *All the rooms are extremely plush, with old stone arches, Rajasthani antiques, and marble bathrooms.*

Ride Marwari in Rajasthan

Location Rajasthan, India
Website www.thetharmarwarisafari.com   **Price** 🌑🌑

The children gather by the dusty road chattering excitedly. Village women walk alongside the paths balancing huge urns of water on their heads. The men bow their heads and press their palms together in greeting. This is a side of Rajasthan that you will not see in the crowded cities, or on the usual bus tours. This glimpse into everyday Indian life can be seen by horseback riding, quite literally, off the beaten track.

A hundred years ago, Rajputs relied on horses for transport. Even kings and noblemen preferred to travel by trusty steed, sparking the saying: "One cannot separate a Rajput from his horse." For centuries, a particular breed of horse, the Marwari, was the chosen mount of Rajput royalty. Fearless warhorses, found only in Rajasthan, they were also bred for their beauty. They became renowned for their grace and elegance, as well as their distinctive inwardly curved ears. To this day, the majestic Marwari is considered a treasured symbol of strength and wealth in Rajasthan. Trekking on horseback is, therefore, a most fitting way to travel through the region that is still referred to as "the land of kings."

Nothing can beat the romance of riding such beautiful horses, and it is a much more authentic way to experience the "real" Rajasthan, following the same ancient routes the maharajas themselves once rode. View ornate temples and marble castles. Stop in rural villages, untouched by tourism, and drink cups of sweet chai tea. Ride alongside lakes and rivers, and through forests of juniper and jacaranda. Forget the noise and congestion of the bustling cities—the only traffic jam you will need to worry about is a queue of goats being herded slowly home. It is a unique and rewarding way to experience India. **JP**

Enjoy Wilderness Camp

Location Rajasthan, India
Website www.rohetgarh.com   **Price** 🌑

If you are looking for a remote place in India, the Thar desert is as good as it gets. The rolling sands of western Rajasthan are the ultimate backdrop for this luxury camp. Stunning sunrises and sunsets, as well as trekking across the endless dunes, are on offer here.

Wilderness is a seriously impressive tented camp, complete with comfortable beds and tiled bathrooms. Soft rugs underfoot, luxurious fabrics, and beautiful polished teak furniture make the Wilderness Camp a wonderful experience. Eat in the traditional thatch and plaster dining room, then soak up the magic of this desert wonderland. During the day guests can go camel and horseback trekking, visit remote tribes, or

"The elegant tents flutter in the breeze, providing an exotic contrast with the desert wilderness."

Gourmet Travel magazine

take a trip to spot wildlife. The camp is overseen by the Singh family, and they have ensured that special touches give a traditional Rajasthani feel to your stay, from the furnishings to the warm welcome by staff.

The ultimate romantic desert retreat, this is the perfect place to get away from it all with your other half. The candlelit lounge is the ideal location to end a day out on the sea of sand and enjoy a well-earned drink. Most of all, come here to soak up the sense of peace and quiet. The sounds of birdsong and gentle lilting of local voices as shepherds pass by is all you will hear. It also goes without saying that this far out in the desert, the stargazing is second to none. **AD**

Camp at Chhatra Sagar

Location Rajasthan, India
Website www.chhatrasagar.com   **Price** ⊖⊖

In the middle of the frenzied cities of Jaipur and Jodhpur is this luxury encampment that simply oozes tranquility. Originally built as a hunting lodge by the Nimaj family, who have owned the surrounding farmland for more than a century, these eleven richly decorated tents overlook an enormous reservoir teeming with birdlife. This rural haven is set amid verdant fields of wheat, mustard, cotton, chilies, and grazing pastures, where camp guests are free to explore. Aside from a few local villages, the camp is about as remote as you can get in Rajasthan.

All the comforts of a five-star hotel are coupled with the romance of nature, and the hand-stitched tents have private stone bathrooms with hot and cold water, fans, and verandas facing the rolling countryside and the lake where antelopes congregate. Floors are hand-painted with traditional henna designs that look their best when the tents have been newly re-erected after the monsoon season. Arise at dawn to watch the sunrise and have tea brought to your terrace; finish the day with cocktails on a nearby hilltop, followed by an evening of stargazing and a candlelit dinner in the open-air dining tent. Round the night off listening to tales of village folklore around a cozy bonfire.

The camp is run by two charming and hospitable brothers and their wives, and the home-cooked food served up here has been hailed as the best in Rajasthan, incorporating estate-grown produce and tradition. The hosts even offer cooking lessons for guests, as well as jeep safaris, nature walks, and bird-watching. The Nimaj family can arrange sailing trips on the lake and visits to nearby villages to see local crafts, including pottery making. If you get tired of all the rest and relaxation, jogging tracks encircle the reservoir. **JK**

Stay at Deogarh Mahal

Location Rajasthan, India
Website www.deogarhmahal.com   **Price** ⊖⊖

Deogarh Mahal in central Rajasthan is one of the best-kept heritage palaces in India. Surrounded by hills and desert, a short break here is like being transported back in time. Snaking corridors and steep, narrow stairways are haphazardly thrown together, a deliberate ploy by the original architects 350 years ago to make life as difficult as possible for any marauding invaders.

The forts were palatial homes to some of the land's richest families, and many of the rooms have retained all the lavish furnishings of the era. The Queen Suite is covered in decorative mirror tiles, at the time considered as sumptuous an accessory as any precious metal. Original paintings can also be found on the fort's walls.

> *"[Deogarh Mahal] is gorgeous in every way: laid-back but undeniably sexy."*
>
> Tatler

Deogarh Mahal offers its guests all the conveniences of a modern hotel. A pool, spa center, small gym, and excellent restaurant add some contemporary comforts to the heritage experience. Activities such as jeep safaris, desert rambles, and vintage car rides are also available. You can meet Veerbhadra Singh Chundawat (but call him "V. B."), the owner of the hotel, every evening on the roof terrace, enjoying a cocktail under the stars while watching the Rajasthani dancing girls entertain his guests, much as his ancestors would have done. Indeed, for all its impressive opulence and palpable history, the most striking quality of Deogarh Mahal is its warmth and intimacy. **JD**

Relax at Seengh Sagar Fort

Location Rajasthan, India
Website www.deogarhmahal.com **Price** ⊖⊖

One of the best spots in which to spend some quiet time in India can be found in the middle of Rajasthan, the country's colorful desert state, at an old island fortress now converted into a luxury four-room villa. It is a magical, timeless place, where the calls of blue jays and parakeets replace the motorized buzz of daily Indian life. The lake that surrounds the fort during rainy years, making access possible only by boat, enhances the sense of tranquil solitude.

The fort comprises four suites, each uniquely decorated in vibrant Rajasthani colors and fabrics and with its own private balcony looking out over the lake. But do not think Seengh Sagar is a journey back to basics. Each room contains the best in modern hotel furnishings, such as well-stocked minibars, air-conditioning, and a staff ready to tend to your every need. If you get bored of gazing out at the amber sunsets from the open-air terrace, sipping cocktails under the huge neem tree in the central, creeper-strewn courtyard, or indulging in the heavenly ayurvedic massages, you can always book a more energetic activity through Seengh Sagar's sister hotel, Deogarh Mahal, just 3 miles (5 km) away. Activities include desert rambles, horseback riding, jeep safaris, and temple visits. It is also well worth spending some time with Seengh Sagar's owner, Colonel Randhir Singhji, who can recount plenty of stories about the fascinating history of the fort and also about his time in the Indian army (ask him about his bullet wounds).

The fort is small enough to be rented out exclusively by a family or small group of friends, but big enough to accommodate separate couples without anyone's privacy being spoiled. In India in particular, that is a quality that should not be overlooked. **JD**

Unwind at Fateh Prakash

Location Udaipur, Rajasthan, India
Website www.hrhhotels.com **Price** ⊖⊖

The princely state of Rajasthan has no need for palaces and temples to highlight the once immense wealth of the maharajas, yet the city of Udaipur is full of ostentation. At its heart you will find the Fateh Prakash Palace, awash with turrets, balconies, and domes, standing imposingly on the shores of the romantic Lake Pichola, bordered by the Aravali hills.

Built in the early twentieth century during the reign of Maharana Fateh Singh, the palace spent its formative years as an entertainment venue exclusively for royal functions. In postcolonial India, the maharajas found the maintenance of their personal estates untenable without the previous annual stipend from

> *"If the Venetian owned the Pichola [lake] he might say with justice, 'see it and die.'"*
>
> Rudyard Kipling, *Letters of Marque*

the government. Unsurprisingly, they succumbed to the tourist dollar, and threw open their palace doors.

Rooms in the main part of the hotel retain elements of the original decor, such as rare paintings, exquisite chandeliers, and period furniture. Guests also have the opportunity to view the maharani's stunning personal collection of crystal, including crystal chairs, tables, and beds. The real jewel in the crown, however, is the latest addition to the hotel, the Dovecote wing. With a more contemporary feel, the suites have priceless views across the lake toward the ghats and the iconic Lake Palace—a scene best enjoyed from the Sunset Terrace as the desert sun descends behind the hills. **SG**

Relax at Devi Garh

Location Rajasthan, India
Website www.deviresorts.com **Price** 🔾🔾

With its domes, arches, turrets, balconies, and imposing walls, the old fort looks like some peeling relic of imperial India rising up from fields with mountains in the distance. It may be a quiet rural area about a forty-five-minute drive from Udaipur in India's northwest province, but Devi Garh is one of the world's finest hotels.

Once inside the eighteenth-century stronghold, it is like an immediate teleport to the twenty-first century. You cannot fail to notice the clean lines of white marble, glass walls, and chic fabrics. Bedrooms are huge, their private bathrooms opulent displays of marble and glass. The mix of bright silk drapes, bowls of petals, and local art combines seamlessly with air-conditioning, giant plasma TVs, and DVD players. There is even a "pillow menu," and each of the thirty-nine suites is embellished with semiprecious stones set into the walls. It is contemporary luxury with an ancient Indian flavor.

The old and new are combined so well throughout the fourteen-story labyrinth that it seems perfectly natural to use the wireless Internet while lounging on an ancient balcony with views into the Aravali Mountains. If you venture from your sumptuous suite, there are memorable public spaces, too, including five internal courtyards, a candlelit cocktail bar, and a shiny modern gym. Guests may dive into a green marble swimming pool, or do yoga on the roof at sunrise.

If you can bear to leave the hotel, there are camel safaris, spectacular trekking trails, and guided excursions—chauffeur driven, of course. **SH**

🔼 *The Pavilion restaurant has striking mountain panoramas; the food is internationally acclaimed.*

"Devi Garh, a cloud of lavish, urbane minimalism over all, encourages you to stay put."

Condé Nast Traveler

Stay at Fort Chanwa

Location Rajasthan, India   **Website** www.fortchanwa.com   **Price** 💲

Fort Chanwa in Luni is British film star Jeremy Irons's favorite hideaway in Rajasthan. The actor likes to shop in the souk in Jodhpur, where he is enamored of the Marwari bedspreads made of silver and gold cloth recycled from wedding garments.

The fort was built in 1894 by Kaviraj Muraridanji, a poetically inclined prime minister. He had been granted the fiefdom by the Maharajah Jaswant Singh II of Jodhpur. In return, Muraridanji agreed that if his line were to die out, ownership of the castle would pass to the royal family. In the 1940s, Fort Chanwa did, indeed, change hands, and the estate is now run by a son of the maharajah of Jodhpur.

The royal family has turned Chanwa into a delightful boutique hotel. Some of the accommodation is in the outer bailey, where the minister had his manorial court and hall. These rooms are now respectively the restaurant and bar. Some of the rooms here are utterly enchanting, with ogee windows and colored window glass. A small band that serenades guests over dinner has been performing for the local nobility at the castle for many generations.

It is a fascinating experience to wander around the town of Luni and take in its life. Flocks of Marwari nomads in red turbans and white *dhotis* (loincloths) block the roads with their herds of goats, sheep, and camels. In the surrounding streets, local people earn a living by manufacturing pots from cow dung. In the courtyard of one house, a blind bullock turns a mill to make the mustard seed oil that is used popularly in cooking. At times, itinerant smiths arrive in the town to mend pots and pans, dressed entirely in white from their turbans to their breeches. Luni is that rare thing in India: a real oasis of calm, and its lifestyle seems almost untouched by modern times. **GMD**

⬆ *The elegant rooftop terrace complements the majestic Indian architecture of the fort complex.*

Enjoy Taj Lake Palace

Location Rajasthan, India **Website** www.tajhotels.com **Price** ⊝⊝⊝

Taj Lake Palace, in the middle of Lake Pichola in Udaipur, is a gleaming homage to romance and indulgence. This 250-year-old "pleasure palace" of former Maharana Jagat Singh promises luxuries and comforts that, although matched by other hotels around the world, are enhanced by its location. The hotel is surrounded by a lake, which itself is surrounded by mountains, so although the bustling streets of Udaipur are just a two-minute boat ride away, stepping onto the 4-acre (1.6-ha) island transports you into a realm of peaceful contentment that is sure to bring a smile to your face.

Each of the eighty-three rooms is individually themed, with the large suites being especially grand. Particularly arresting is the honeymoon suite, with stained-glass windows dappling the interior with reds, greens, and yellows, and a love swing hanging from the ceiling. The smaller rooms, with the lake's water slapping against the walls just a few feet from the windows, give a sense of being on a luxury yacht bound for the open seas. All the rooms come with a personal twenty-four-hour butler.

The hotel also has a small sculpted garden, three fantastic restaurants, a bar, and a luxury spa, so it would be very easy never to leave the island. For the more adventurous, however, the old king's ceremonial barge floats off over the lake each evening offering food, drinks, and traditional music. Romantic boat rides are also available, replete with lace privacy veil, for those who care to drift over the water leaving all but themselves behind.

To make the Taj experience even more memorable, go in low season and book a basic room (called luxury rooms). Taj has a policy of upgrading guests if better rooms are vacant at the time of check-in. **JD**

⊡ *The white marble and mosaic building almost appears to float on the waters of Lake Pichola.*

Stay at Udai Bilas Palace

Location Rajasthan, India
Website www.udaibilaspalace.com   **Price** ⊜

Pretend you are a maharaja by spending a night or two in an opulent Indian palace. Majestically set on the banks of Lake Gaibsagar, this heritage hotel can be found way off the tourist trail in southern Rajasthan.

Built in the nineteenth century by Maharawal Udai Singhji, the Udai Bilas Palace has always been home to the Rajput family, the maharajas of Dungarpur, and to this day it remains a royal residence. Recently treated to a revamp, the hotel has retained many of its original features—the wallpaper may be fifty years old but it is still in tip-top condition. The miniature paintings, elaborate murals, and carved stones reveal the rich and colorful cultural heritage of the Rajput royal family. The bluish gray building is as grand as you would expect, festooned with sculptured stone pillars and marble-clad arches. At the building's heart are an attractive courtyard, a pool, and an intricately carved pavilion. The lake itself is magical and peaceful, attracting an abundance of birdlife, such as egrets, storks, and night herons, best enjoyed by taking a relaxing boat trip.

Every one of the palace's spacious guest rooms and suites has been decorated in an individual style, but all are kitted out with ornate balconies, mahogany furnishings, and delightful decorations. The grandest suite even has an impressive mirrored floor. An elegant banquet hall provides the dramatic setting for dinner, with lighting provided by crystal chandeliers. The center of the long marble table is inlaid with water, on which float candles and flowers.

If you loathe blood sports, this may not be the pad for you. The family members are respected hunters, and the stuffed trophies of the sport are proudly displayed on the walls of the dining room. **JK**

Enjoy Udaivilas

Location Rajasthan, India
Website www.oberoihotels.com   **Price** ⊜⊜⊜

Inspired by the great palaces of the sixteenth and seventeenth centuries, Udaivilas is a vast assemblage of columns, tiered gardens, decorative arches, and alcoves that immerses its guests in a world of luxury.

This imposing Oberoi property is set against the stark backdrop of the Aravalli Hills and has views across Lake Pichola to Udaipur's famous Jagmandir and Jagniwas palaces. Nothing has been overlooked in this re-creation of the royal Rajasthan palaces of old. Open-air colonnades are set amid hand-carved columns, extensive hand-painted murals, and ornate cupolas finished in gold leaf, with fountains rising from ornamental pools of shimmering white marble.

"This may be one of Rajasthan's best examples of contemporary Indian architecture."

concierge.com

Many of the rooms have private walled courtyards and are furnished with inlaid chairs and tables in the classic Rajput style. Some rooms open onto a semiprivate moated swimming pool that affords views across the lake and back up to the hotel's own 20-acre (8-ha) wildlife conservatory, with its resident wild boars, peacocks, and Indian spotted deer. For the ultimate in indulgence, the Kohinoor Suite is a vast private world of courtyards and pools, and a breathtaking view over Udaipur's City Palace complex.

The hotel's Banyan Tree Spa offers treatments ranging from aromatherapy to ayurveda in rooms that are nothing short of royal in scale. **BS**

Discover Orcha

Location Madhya Pradesh, India
Website www.spiritualjourneys.net/Venues/orcha.htm **Price** ❶

Tucked away off the main road leading to the bustling city of Jhansi, the appropriately named village of Orcha (hidden place) is made up of sixteenth- and seventeenth-century palaces and temples with elaborate ornamental spires. The Bundelas clan that ruled large parts of central India from the early 1500s until the mid-twentieth century chose this island in the picturesque Betwa River as the site for their capital. Nowadays, the palaces are populated only by macaques, but time has been kind to the buildings, which perfectly blend into the peaceful surroundings.

The village's centerpiece is the stunning Jehangir Mahal (palace), which was built in honor of the Mughal ruler Jehangir's visit to Orcha in the early seventeenth century. Standing in the empty, windowless rooms on the top floor of the palace, you have great views over the lush surrounding areas. You can see the locals washing their clothes in the gently cascading river, and bird-watchers will delight in getting a closer look at the many vultures circling in the sky. The Raj Mahal next door has some exquisite murals and is equally isolated from the main part of the village, which is situated on the right bank of the river. The temples in this part of Orcha are still used by the villagers and offer a glimpse into Hindu life outside northern India's overpopulated cities.

With its ancient buildings that complement and enhance the natural beauty of the area, Orcha is well worth a visit simply because of its visual appeal. However, throw in the fact that few tourists have as yet discovered this charming part of India and also that the village is the perfect antithesis to the chaos of the country's towns and cities, and you have a wonderful place in which to get away from it all. **DaH**

Visit Kanha National Park

Location Madhya Pradesh, India
Website www.kanhanationalpark.com **Price** ⓢ

Located in the geographical center of India, the state of Madhya Pradesh is covered by dense forests that are home to 22 percent of the world's tiger population. The best place to spot the animals is Kanha National Park, where the lush bamboo and sal forests, open grasslands, and innumerable streams make for an area of stunning natural beauty—so much so that Rudyard Kipling was inspired to write his novel *The Jungle Book* after visiting the area.

Established in 1955, the wildlife reserve runs several conservation programs to protect its animals, and the number of tigers, bharasinghas (a near-extinct species of deer), gaurs (Indian bison), and leopards roaming

> *"At first sight [the park] looks almost like English parkland designed by Capability Brown."*
>
> Lynn Barber, *Observer*

the park has steadily increased over the years. The period between March and July is the best time to see Kanha's wildlife, because as the temperatures rise, the animals leave their hideaways in the woods to look for water. The local rangers track the tigers down every morning and generally know where to find them. Bird-watchers will also have a field day at Kanha, where the majestic peacocks are probably the pick of the bunch.

One of the largest parks in India and considered to be among the best maintained in the whole of Asia, Kanha provides a unique opportunity to see some of the planet's most fascinating—and sadly most threatened—animals in the wild. **DaH**

Discover the Ganges

Location Varanasi, Uttar Pradesh, India
Website www.varanasicity.com/ganges-ghats.html   **Price ⬤**

The Ganges sustains life. Across the scorching northern plains of India, the river rises up from Gangotri, before twisting and turning for hundreds of miles to empty in the Bay of Bengal. It also sustains faith. It is a sacred river, and the most sacred place on it is the city of Shiva, otherwise known as Varanasi or Benares. Here, Hindu pilgrims come to bathe in the waters of the Ganges, a ritual that washes away sin. The city is also an auspicious place to die, because if you leave earth here, you will attain *moksha*—liberation from the endless cycle of birth and death.

The most intimate rituals of life and death take place here in public. On the ghats—stepped areas that lead down to the river—there are people doing their laundry, praying, practicing yoga, playing cricket, shaving, or just improving their karma by giving money to beggars. Alongside, water buffalo wallow in the shallows, and bodies are burned on funeral pyres. Devout pilgrims and sadhus are cheek by jowl with tourists and dollar-hungry locals; unfortunately, this means that this holiest of places is also popular with fake holy men and rip-off merchants. In the mazelike streets, touts stick to you like glue. To escape all of this, take a boat trip at dawn, before the river is bathed in light. As the boat slips downstream, the mantras from the loudspeakers will fade, lost in the breeze. The only sound will be the swishing of oars as candlelit offerings float by in the dark, like traveling stars. Soon the dawn will come, and the river will be bathed in a magical light. Pilgrims will appear to perform *puja* to the rising sun, and the cycle begins again. **LB**

➡ *The mighty River Ganges is a magical place: the hub of life, both practical and spiritual.*

Visit Glenburn Tea Estate

Location Near Darjeeling, West Bengal, India
Website www.glenburnteaestate.com **Price** 🟢🟢

Established in 1860 by Scottish tea planters, Glenburn is a working tea estate with 1,600 acres (646 ha) of private forest, tea picker villages, and two rivers for you to explore. Wrap yourself up on the romantic colonial-style veranda, sipping a cup of the house tea, and enjoy the glorious views out to the Himalayas and across to Meera's Buddha, an impressive bronze statue on the opposite hill to Glenburn.

A restored tea planter's bungalow sleeps up to twelve guests in four individually designed suites—a favorite is the Planter's Suite, for its fabulous four-poster Spanish mahogany bed and Toile de Jouy furnishings. For more privacy, there is a cottage with a private lounge and veranda, or go rustic and camp out by the River Rungeet at the Glenburn Lodge, which is lit only by kerosene lamp at night. Food is tasty and inventive, from tea leaf pakoras and jackfruit kofta curry to Tibetan *momos* and green-tea ice cream. Herbs and vegetables are grown on-site, and the gardens are filled with sweet peas, jasmine, and roses.

Take a tour of the factory, where the labor-intensive methods are little changed, and enjoy daylong hikes through the estate, which includes an orange orchard and a nearby convent. Darjeeling, Kalimpong, and Mirik are a private jeep ride away, if you can be persuaded to venture farther afield. If not, you will be well looked after by Neena, Glenburn's resident hostess, who has worked on tea plantations all her married life. This is a good place to come to celebrate Christmas and New Year—the estate is 3,000 feet (915 m) lower than Darjeeling Town, so not half as cold. **CSJ**

◄ *Have afternoon tea on the verandah at the Glenburn tea estate where you will see great mountain views.*

Stay at Windamere Hotel

Location Darjeeling, West Bengal, India
Website www.windamerehotel.com **Price** 🟢🟢

More than 7,000 feet (2,133 m) up in the foothills of the Himalayas is one of the last remaining pieces of old-world Britain. Indeed, you might imagine yourself wandering into the set of a 1940s English film.

First you need to get there. Best to fly to Bagdogra, then take the "toy train," a steam locomotive that takes six hours to zigzag up the mountains and tea gardens that make Darjeeling famous. You will arrive shaken in the summer capital of the state of Bengal, but the rest of your stay will pass like a dream. After checking in, you are ushered into afternoon tea: wafer-thin cucumber sandwiches and Darjeeling tea. At 5.30 P.M. a coal fire is lit in your room and a hot-water bottle

> *"The Windamere, with its chintz curtains, afternoon teas, claw-foot baths … was something special."*
>
> Tom Pozzi, *Daily Telegraph*

popped into your bed. Nights are cold at this altitude. Faded photographs and paintings adorn the walls.

In summer, Nepali dancers perform in the walled garden while guests are plied with brandy punch and pies. At the end of the vista is Kangchenjunga—at 28,145 feet (8,578 m) the world's third-highest mountain. After dark, braziers are lit on the terrace to keep you warm on the way to dinner. All meals are included, but you need to observe the times. The candlelit dinner is a treat, especially when the female pianist plays Noel Coward songs. Soup is followed by Anglo-Indian food with Nepali and Tibetan flourishes. Turn in after a Black Dog whiskey in the bar. **GMD**

Explore Calcutta

Location Calcutta, West Bengal, India
Website www.calcutta-tours.com   **Price** $

Calcutta's chaotic streets can be a shock for the novice traveler to India. It is a frenetic city of immense crowds: commuters piled onto rusting ferries crossing the Hooghly River; laborers weighed down with heavy loads toiling across the towering Howrah Bridge; street-dwelling families living by the side of vast traffic intersections. There are vast slums, and the fine colonial buildings are in a state of disrepair that is so advanced one wonders what is keeping them upright. However, it is more of a case of ugliness within the beauty of Calcutta, rather than the other way around.

Unlike ancient Mughal Delhi, Calcutta is a relatively new place, established as a trading post by the British about 300 years ago. Some of the relics from this era are both interesting and somewhat poignant places to explore; they also provide some relief from the relentless urban chaos outside. You can find tranquility on the Maidan, the green expanse that is the lungs of Calcutta, where cows and cricket players roam, and in the dark gloom of the Victoria Memorial, a white marble edifice housing an array of Raj art memorabilia. You can certainly find a sense of peace in the South Park Street cemetery, where the extraordinary tombs, shaded by trees, evoke the past with their epigraphs.

Book into the faded rooms of the Tollgunge Club, another colonial relic, and now a playground for the city's elite. Once a country retreat for Brits, now deep in the metropolis, the Tolly is an immense, verdant oasis of beautiful trees and plants. It is home to the Royal Calcutta Golf Club, the oldest golf club in the world outside Britain. There you can swim in the colonial-style pool, indulge in a spot of croquet, ride the ponies that waddle around the bridleway, or just soak up the lackadaisical atmosphere and space. **LB**

Ride the *Deccan Odyssey*

Location Maharashtra, India
Website www.deccanodyssey.com   **Price** $ $

With more than 60,000 miles (100,000 km) of track, India's rail network is one of the world's largest. Indian Railways owns almost 230,000 wagons and an astonishing 8,300 locomotives, which make more than 19,000 journeys a day. The *Deccan Odyssey* makes the most sought-after journey of them all.

The itinerary takes you through the state of Maharashtra down to neighboring Goa, visiting some of India's most unique destinations such as the World Heritage Ajanta and Ellora caves on the way. It also provides lesser-known delights like sipping high tea at the Pune Turf Club and visiting the tourist-free beaches of Ganpatipule, where the rhythms of Indian

> *"It allows you to see an India most travelers are not afforded the chance to experience."*
>
> Rita Cook, writer

life continue much as they have for hundreds of years. However the real reason you book a ticket on the *Deccan Odyssey* is to experience the train itself.

The carriages are a world of gilded, regal splendor with carved peacocks, sumptuous armchairs, and a personal valet in each car. Traveling is done mostly at night in order to maximize free time during the day. Meals draw heavily on regional cuisine, and all passenger cabins have their own bathrooms and plush wall-to-wall carpets. There are two presidential suites, two restaurant cars, a lounge, a conference coach that transforms into a dance floor at night, a cybercafé, and even a mini-gym and spa car. **BS**

Relax at Panchavatti

Location Goa, India
Website www.islaingoa.com **Price** 💲💲

Set just across a bridge from the mainland, on Goa's island of Corjuem, Panchavatti is the home of Lou Lou Van Damme, a stylish Belgian woman who designed the property herself. Its 24 replenishing acres (10 ha) are a welcome change from Goa's beaches and bustling crowds, and you will find fruit trees, tropical plants, and lawned gardens through which to wander.

The house is built around a grassy courtyard filled with plants, and there is a comfortable, spacious lounge filled with antiques. Put on some Chopin and step out onto the romantic veranda, which enjoys stunning views over paddy fields and the Mapusa River. The four contemporary bedrooms have stone floors and shuttered windows, and are individually decorated with interesting artwork, ornate tables, and luxurious linens. Attractive, giant bowls of fresh flowers are strewn throughout the property. Carefully thought-out, healthful, and delicious meals are exquisitely presented using flowers and vibrant-colored cloths—eat with other guests on the veranda, or at a table in the garden, lit only by candlelight.

You can join Lou Lou in her daily practice of Satyananda yoga, a meditative style of yoga asanas from the Bihar School of Yoga, or ask her to teach you. Therapists can be arranged for indulgent ayurvedic massages or facials using freshly prepared fruit and vegetable concoctions. There are plenty of local walks to enjoy, and bicycles to borrow. If you are hungry for the beaches, some of Goa's best are only a thirty-minute drive away. But really, who needs to venture out? Take your cue from the endearing statue of Ganesh, sunbathing at the end of the lovely pool. Lounge under the trees, sprawl on a hammock, sip tea on the veranda—pretend you own the place. **CSJ**

Unwind at Bhakti Kutir

Location Goa, India
Website www.bhaktikutir.com **Price** 💲

Set 650 feet (200 m) away from Palolem beach in southern Goa, this back-to-nature hippie village is on a mission to connect you with your inner soul. Start with a boat trip to watch dolphins off the headland and visit hard-to-reach beaches, then take a siesta later in the day in a hammock. As evening falls, head to the forest area for a yoga class in the humid open air, with incense and candles burning around you. Sleep in the simple cabanas—but do not forget your mosquito net. This place has no modern conveniences, and there are some things you will need to bring yourself.

If you want to crank up the soul searching, there are yoga classes, run by a yogi who hails from the Ganges,

---

"Come prepared for mosquitoes, dark pathways, and plenty of back-to-nature experiences."

New York Times

---

or intensive three- and six-day meditation courses, called A Journey to Nirvana, which promises to teach you some secret Indian meditation techniques to help you clear your mind and cope better with modern life.

The cabanas are designed around the plans of an old Goan village and are made from local materials. Long before being green was hip, this place was concerned about the environment. It is not just about ecology—although there are compost toilets for each shack. Employees are all local, too, including the women who offer authentic ayurvedic massages. Food is vegetarian and prepared at the central restaurant. Simple pleasures are what this place is all about. **LD**

Stay at Fort Tiracol

Location Goa, India **Website** www.forttiracol.com
Price $ $

Relax at Villa River Cat

Location Goa, India **Website** www.villarivercat.com
Price $

As a former Portuguese colony, Goa has many reminders of its European rulers; among the state's grand whitewashed buildings, Fort Tiracol claims a special place. The heritage hotel is set high on a cliff above the Arabian Sea and the Tiracol River, overlooking dense palm plantations, and is a great example of grandeur within the rain forest.

One of the joys of Fort Tiracol is its size. With just seven rooms, it feels like you have the place to yourself. The colors are regal: gold, white, and black, making the fortress feel imperious and impeccably designed. If you like peace and quiet, Fort Tiracol is sublime. Take the time to unwind with views of untouched beaches,

> *"The sunflower yellow–splashed building with tiled awnings brings to mind Portugal's Algarve."*
>
> *Travel+Leisure* magazine

yoga and massage on tap, and private boats to take you cruising the coast or dolphin spotting. In the evening you can dine alfresco under the stars.

As the sun sets, tourists staying elsewhere in Goa turn up to have a cocktail and watch the sky turn blush pink and the dark night creep in. Once built to repel invaders, the fort now attracts visitors, with its upper ramparts overlooking the sea bordered by eighteenth-century iron railings overgrown with tumbling bougainvillea. Getting here is part of the adventure: You have to navigate bumpy dirt tracks and then take the rickety ferry at Kerim beach. If you are lucky, the ferryman might even let you take the wheel. **LD**

On the beach beside this upscale hippie paradise in north Goa, you are more likely to be disturbed by sea turtles burying their eggs than the touts and hawkers that plague much of the coastline. Run by Rinhoo Sehgal, a creative-minded traveler, Villa River Cat is an idyllic round house deep in the palm trees off a bumpy dirt track in the lost part of north Goa. It is more of a retreat than a hotel: Rinhoo's many cats and dogs mingle in the grounds, where hammocks and daybeds blow gently in the breeze.

The owner's personal touch makes your visit special—and that goes as much for the legions of artists and scriptwriters who head out here time after time as for first-time visitors. Bathrooms are tiled with bright colors—this is India, remember—whereas in the entrance hall, marionettes hang on the wall and statues of Shiva and other gods watch over you.

The food, too, is nothing short of spectacular. Fresh herbs, fruit and spices, delicious organic rice, and homemade curries are all served in the Miau restaurant, with the gentle sound of the river rushing by. If lounging around in the shade is not what you are looking for, Rinhoo will take you to his favorite lagoons for a swim, show you the stars through his telescope, or help you find your way across the country to any number of attractions. One thing is for sure, this side of Goa is not tie-dyed and bursting with glow sticks and deafening techno. It is a tranquil backwater where you can trail your hand in the water, count the coconuts in the trees, and watch the fishermen return with their daily catch in the morning. **LD**

→ *The beach near Villa River Cat is spectacular and there is rarely a single tourist in sight.*

Visit Chowmahalla Palace

Location Andhra Pradesh, India
Website www.chowmahalla.com **Price** $

Chowmahalla Palace takes your breath away. In the heart of Hyderabad's old city, just a stone's throw from the ever-manic Laad bazaar full of glitzy bangle stores and sari shops, the palace is an oasis of serenity. Walk through the huge wooden gates obscuring the beauty of the grounds and you find another world. Once home to the ruling Nizams of Hyderabad, there are in fact four palaces here set in 12 acres (5 ha) of grounds dating back to the late eighteenth century: *Chow* means "four" and *mahalla* means "palaces."

The first thing that strikes visitors is the sweet aroma of frangipani, its white blossoms complementing the columns and archways of the northern courtyard, which in turn are mirrored in the still-water channels alongside. In these tranquil surroundings, the noise of traffic around the Charminar mosque is replaced by birdsong and the soothing sound of running water from the fountains. Walk slowly through the courtyard to savor every moment of peace, and then prepare to be amazed as you enter the grand Khilwat, or Durbar Hall. You need time to take in the grandeur of your surroundings. Here, in this stylish opulence, the Nizams held their religious ceremonies and banquets.

After extensive renovations, the palace opened to the public for the first time in 2005. Glimpses of the Nizam's grand lifestyle are provided in the museums and anterooms full of photographs and portraits. They include an exhibition on the life of the women of the palace—of whom princesses Durru Shehavar and Niloufer were deemed to be among the most beautiful of their generation. **SWa**

◄ *Belgian crystal chandeliers seem to fill the entire space between the high stucco ceiling and cool marble floor.*

Unwind at SwaSwara

Location Karnataka, India
Website www.swaswara.com **Price** $ $

Immersed in coconut groves and paddy fields overlooking the twin coves of Om Beach, SwaSwara invites you to rejuvenate your soul through yoga and meditation and to reconnect to the inner experience of the self. The approach to self-awareness determines everything here, from the daily rituals and preparation of meals to the design of SwaSwara's air-conditioned villas, built in the local Konkan style. Balconies have been created with the pursuit of yoga in mind, and study areas provide privacy for the exercising of the mind. For the more experienced practitioner, a ten-day "Panchakarma" course, applying ancient methods of relaxation, will realign your body, mind, and soul.

"Here is a place oozing peace and isolation ... where you can really remember what you are about."
Tatler

SwaSwara is an environmentally progressive resort. A bio-gas converter turns composted organic matter into gas for cooking, and there is a rainwater treatment plant on-site. Meals are more like diets and are tailored to your individual needs and body type. Meat is avoided in favor of fresh seafood and vegetables sourced from surrounding farms. Time seems to run a little slower here amid the tranquility of the 30 acres (12 ha) and along the walking trails that take you past medicinal shrubs. Only the sound of the rolling waves of Om Beach and SwaSwara's resident long-tailed langurs, geckos, and kingfishers will accompany you on your journey of peaceful self-discovery. **BS**

Explore Hanuman Temple

Location Karnataka, India
Website www.hampi.in/sites/Anjaneya_Hill.htm **Price** ◖

The journey from the hot, sweaty center of Hampi, the medieval capital of the Hindu empire and a UNESCO World Heritage site, to the Hanuman temple on Anjaneya Hill is not easy. Start in the bazaar and wind your way to the river, beside sandstone caves carved with Hindu gods. Pay a boy to take you downstream in a coracle and fix your eyes to the horizon. There, a flash of white on top of a hill will show you your destination: Hampi's Hanuman temple. Of all the temples in the city, it is the one that you will remember.

When you reach the foot of the hill, having walked across fields and along a lane where children greet you with cries for pencils and rupees, you will see what you are in for. A man sells cones of peanuts and, up the hundreds of whitewashed steps that zigzag to the top of the site, monkeys scamper while sadhus, pilgrims, and tourists huff and puff their way up to the top in the burning sun. The journey takes about forty-five minutes—do not forget your water. At the top, the temple is garishly lit inside and smells of incense and bare feet. This is where the god and monkey general is said to have been born—the place has particular significance for followers of Rama.

From the top you can see everything in the area: the vast boulder-strewn plain, the elephant stables, the sunken palace gardens, flocks of white ibis flying across the landscape, and the ruins of the old stone bridge in the river. All the colors of the state spread out before you, and there is almost total peace and quiet, save for the fluttering of the orange flags and the light footsteps of the monkeys. **LD**

← *It is well worth the effort it takes to get to the small whitewashed temple to the monkey god Hanuman.*

Relax in Style at Shreya's

Location Bangalore, Karnataka, India
Website www.shreyasretreat.com   **Price** 🟢🟢

"For the first time in an Indian yoga school, I felt the potential of a merger with cosmic bliss."

Lucy Edge, writer

To stay at Shreya's, an idyllic yoga retreat on the outskirts of the bustling Indian city of Bangalore, is to set off on a journey of self-discovery. Surrounded by more than 25 acres (10 ha) of impeccably landscaped gardens, Shreya's not only offers one of the largest outdoor yoga pavilions in southern India but will also encourage you to get your hands dirty working in the extensive vegetable garden and rice paddy. You can be educated in the principles of sustainable agriculture or even learn to abandon your inhibitions and reconnect with the child within by playing games with the children of an adjacent village before relaxing in one of the strategically placed hammocks.

Shreya's offers an informal mix of canvas tents and stone and garden cottages, sprinkled around an 83-foot (25-m) oxygenated free-form swimming pool. All the accommodation has its own private veranda and is sufficiently remote to ensure absolute privacy. Gourmet vegetarian dining with ingredients from the organic garden is encouraged in the communal dining hall, or enjoyed outdoors on warm nights, and the menus are meticulously crafted to complement Shreya's wellness program and the individual's own body type and personal goals.

Massage treatments include Balinese oil-based therapies, which concentrate on muscle tissue, and traditional Thai techniques focusing on the practice of reflexology and the principles of acupressure. At Shreya's it is the inner journey that matters: the pursuit of tranquility, self-awareness, and an exposure to the layered philosophies of ancient India. **BS**

↖ *Shreya's is for those who like to practice yoga while ensconced in five-star luxury surroundings.*

De-stress at Soukya

Location Bangalore, Karnataka, India
Website www.soukya.com **Price** 😊😊

After the hectic buzz of Bangalore, being welcomed into Soukya's airy reception with a glass of tender coconut juice is like walking into a parallel universe—one full of flagstone pathways, green lawns, fragrant temple trees, and lots of space. It is just you, 24 guests, 116 staff, and 30 acres (12 ha) of peaceful gardens, water features, organic farmland, and orchards.

Soukya is a carefully crafted holistic healing center rather than a spa. The expert care on offer has attracted the rich and famous from all over the world because it gets results. Some guests want to de-stress, others to lose weight or recuperate after an illness or injury. An initial consultation explores where you are,

> ## "To many, this euphoric place might seem a little contrived, but the fact is that it works."
>
> *Society* magazine

from health to relationships, social life to personality traits. After that, you get a personal program that includes a combination of ayurvedic treatments, homeopathic remedies, an organic, vegetarian diet, and a wide range of therapies—whatever your body needs to kick-start it into a better place. Modern, allopathic medicine comes into play, too.

The programs may include more than one hundred treatments and last a month or more, depending on the individual. Although many treatments are luxuriously relaxing, it is not all about pampering. You will like the rewards, though. Weight falls off, skin glows, and you leave a little wiser about yourself. **OM**

Ride the *Golden Chariot*

Location Bangalore, Karnataka, India
Website www.goldenchariot.com **Price** 😊😊

A new chapter in India's increasingly sophisticated tourism market pulled out of Yashwantpur railway station in Bangalore in March 2008. The *Golden Chariot* left on its maiden journey around a circuit that includes the great palace at Mysore and the sun-drenched beaches of Goa. This is luxurious, high-end tourism on a railway that is the rival of any of the great continental train journeys of the world.

The nineteen magenta-colored carriages of the *Golden Chariot* can accommodate up to eighty-eight passengers in sumptuous, air-conditioned chambers, complete with double-glazed windows, decorative wood panels on the walls, and carved reliefs on the ceiling reminiscent of the days of the maharajahs. Western-style breakfasts are served in two dining carriages, as well as fine local and continental cuisine. The menu includes traditional vegetarian dishes and local delicacies such as Neer Dose, a rice dish served with chutney and grated coconut. Meals are accompanied by a fine collection of wines and spirits. The impeccable furnishings of the lounge bar are modeled after the palace at Mysore. There is even a sauna and on-board masseur, with a gym coach and conference coach rounding out the amenities. The only requirement made of the passengers, whose average age is more than fifty years old, is to relax and enjoy the ride.

The journey is not a demanding one, with fewer stops than one might expect. The itinerary is a perfect blend of comfort and extraordinary experiences that will stay with you for a lifetime. Highlights include watching baby elephants washing themselves in the Kabini River in the grounds of the Kabini River Lodge, once the property of the maharaja of Mysore. **BS**

Unwind at Tranquil Resort

Location Kerala, India
Website www.tranquilresort.com   **Price** 🅢🅢

A regular winner of Keralan Tourism's "Best Homestay Award," Tranquil Resort can be found within the boundaries of a privately owned 400-acre (160-ha) coffee and vanilla plantation amid the untainted landscapes of the Indian state of Kerala. With a mere eight rooms, including two extraordinary tree houses, the theme here is exclusivity. On your approach to the main house, you are excused for feeling as though you are entering a privileged, manicured world. Paths and verandas are swept anew twice a day in this retreat, which is in many ways a microcosm of the verdant Wayanad rain forest that surrounds it.

The main house is wrapped in endless, expansive verandas filled with wicker and cane furniture and overhead fans that echo the era of Kipling and Somerset Maugham. There is also a free-form swimming pool set among luxuriant gardens, which provides a perfect setting for a snooze in one of the poolside hammocks. The Tree Villa sprawls over 500 square feet (45 sq m) and is perched 40 feet (12 m) above the ground on four enormous tree trunks. It has 8-foot- (2.4-m-) wide verandas and is safe for children. The nearby Tree House is more than 1,000 square feet (90 sq m) in area and is one of the largest such structures in Kerala. Both have hot water and electricity; they are just a short walk from the main house and are reached via their own inclined walkways.

Guests here are encouraged to take a close-up look at the day-to-day operations and processes of a working coffee plantation, from planting through to harvesting. If you have the time, there is the option of a walk through the 40-acre (16-ha) vanilla plantation to witness the hand pollination of the vanilla pods and the curing process that gives the vanilla its flavor. **BS**

Relax at Kalari Kovilakom

Location Kerala, India
Website www.kalarikovilakom.com   **Price** 🅢🅢

An unusual upmarket ashram in a former maharaja's palace, Kalari Kovilakom offers ayurveda programs in luxurious surroundings. While most people are mooching about on the beaches in the south of Kerala, you can enjoy being off the tourist trail, because this elegant retreat is set inland on the edge of Kollengode, a village in the foothills of the Annamalai mountains.

The minimum stay is two weeks: the time required for ayurveda treatments to have any real effect. Daily programs include gentle yoga and meditation, and you will be guided through a set of expertly devised treatments using this ancient Indian holistic system of health. You can also watch locals train in the martial art

---

"The environs . . . are very beautiful. The high mountains pour down cascades of a prodigous height."

Francis Buchanan, traveler (1762-1829)

---

of Kalaripayattu. Combining body movements with a strong spiritual focus, it is strangely relaxing, and the locals will teach you the technique if you like.

Some rooms are in the original palace, but most are in the interior-designed guest wing, beautifully painted in muted colors with four-poster beds, dark-wood furniture, and cool, tiled floors. Delicious meals are cooked according to ayurvedic principles and served on giant thali dishes at communal tables. Although you will be well looked after, this is not the place to come if you want to live the high life: Red meat and leather shoes are not allowed, and specially prepared beverages take the place of alcohol. **CSJ**

Stay at Coconut Lagoon

Location Kerala, India
Website www.cghearth.com   **Price** 💲💲

The only way to reach Coconut Lagoon is by boat. It sounds like a bit of an adventure and it is—but a very worthwhile one, because you get a glimpse of Kerala's fabulous wildlife and rich tropical vegetation along the way. On reaching Coconut Lagoon, you quickly realize why the resort was thus named. Situated in an abandoned coconut plantation, it lives up to all the glorious resonances of its title.

Accommodation on the resort comes in the shape of traditional Keralan wooden houses known as *tharawads*. Some are traditionally built, others more modern, but all have been constructed to the highest standards by skilled local master craftsmen. The oldest of the residences dates back to the early 1700s, whereas several others are one hundred years old or more. The history of the villas aside, all the residences guarantee a luxurious and thoughtfully designed experience. Bathrooms open out onto private gardens; there are Western-style toilets and beautiful dark-wood furnishings, and a colonial style of decoration adds to the authentic Keralan experience. The grounds are also wonderfully natural. A cow, as opposed to a lawnmower, keeps the grass in check, and butterflies and birds dart freely around the gardens.

Many come to Coconut Lagoon for the ayurvedic treatments, which include physiotherapy, yoga, and a host of alternative therapies, although if you are feeling more active, a wealth of water sports is available, including speedboating, canoeing, and fishing. If you were taken by the scenery on the way in, why not take an hour-long sunset cruise, or rent the resort's traditional wood and straw *Kettuvallom* (houseboat)? Then you can see the mangroves, coconut trees, and paddy fields up close and personal. **PS**

Enjoy Marari Beach Resort

Location Kerala, India
Website www.cghearth.com   **Price** 💲💲

Set in 25 acres (10 ha) of coconut palm groves, Marari Beach Resort boasts a 10-mile (16-km) expanse of coastline. The resort is surrounded by fishing villages that exist today just as they have for centuries—by bringing in the day's catch to make a living.

Marari's cottages are laid out with comfort and elegance in mind, and are resplendent with bamboo, dark woods, and wickerwork that root you firmly in rustic India. The vast bedrooms, each with a veranda, are fully air-conditioned, and the gorgeous bathrooms, part open air, have sloping roofs, ornamental stone rockeries, tropical palms, and part-sheltered showers. This being India, there is a spiritual aura surrounding

> *"A beach is a beach is a beach. Until you seek out its living heart, the culture that calls it home."*

Proprietors, Marari Beach Resort

Marari, the focus of which is the resort's stunning ayurvedic center, which runs beachside yoga classes to boost body, mind, and soul. Once energized, the resort bar, situated in a 200-year-old building, serves local cocktails: Try the Panchamrutam, a drink as psychedelic as the sunset views. Only the best local produce is on the menu in the restaurant, barbecued or cooked to order depending on the day's catch.

Marari is not just a pretty face: It is very eco-friendly, with an organic vegetable garden, solar panels, and a methane gas generator fueled by food waste. You do not often hear the words "luxurious" and "conscientious" in the same sentence—Marari insists on both. **PS**

Explore the Kerala Backwaters

Location Kerala, India
Website www.southernbackwaters.com; www.keralatourism.org   **Price** ⊖

> *"A crystal clear river, which is filtered through the forest ... is great for shaking off the heat."*
>
> Poorna Shetty, *Guardian*

Located close to Kollom, Valiyavila is a Fair Trade and traditional homestay, far away from India's usual hustle and bustle. Arriving at the tranquil lakeside retreat is like stepping back in time. Twice a day ferries transport guests from Kollom to Panamukkam jetty; otherwise negotiate with a local who will row you serenely across the lake in a wooden canoe.

Surrounded by the Ashtamudi Lake on three sides, Valiyavila is the perfect place to relax and plan a tour of the Kerala backwaters. Shady palms, cooling watery breezes, and swinging hammocks adorn the mansion's verandas, and the six spacious guest rooms each have a private sundeck. Unwind to the sound of the swishing water and hear the inimitable language used by the fishermen to communicate with the many *Kettuvallom* houseboats cruising by.

The backwaters comprise 560 miles (900 km) of lakes, lagoons, canals, and estuaries, and the Southern Backwaters Company offers tours around Ashtamudi Lake and the Kallada River from Munroe Island. Mindful of the wildlife and environment, and in a style reminiscent of Venice, a local punter will expertly paddle the canoe around Kerala's tiny canals and waterways. View Keralan life at close quarters as you pass water-bound villages where locals cook and wash their clothes on the riverbanks; sail past luminous hibiscus flowers, water hyacinths, disused canoes sinking in the water, and cashew trees boasting enormous nuts. Back at Valiyavila, you can look forward to some delicious Keralan cuisine, a Kingfisher beer, and a stunning sunset. **SD**

◩ *It is an altogether timeless and calming experience to explore the backwaters of Ashtamudi Lake.*

Enjoy Motty's Homestay

Location Kerala, India
Website www.mottys.uniquehomestays.com **Price** 💲💲

Escape into the depths of southern Indian culture by staying at the delightful home of Motty and Lali Mathew. Their traditional Keralan house is stuffed with intriguing artifacts from the subcontinent: from a Victorian washstand to old framed prints, from ancient walking sticks to displays of antique crockery.

Motty's Homestay boutique guesthouse is in Alleppey, a peaceful town known as "the gateway to the Kerala backwaters." You can walk from the house to the local canals, shops, and temples. Accommodation is basic but comfortable. Guests can stay in the Mathews' home or in one of four fisherman's cottages on the edge of Marari beach, where the palm-fringed

---

"It is like discovering the home of a long-lost uncle in the heart of the Kerala backwaters."

Ellison Roberts travel website

---

sands are littered with fishing boats. Rooms in the main house have private facilities; those in the beach houses have open-air bathrooms.

The cuisine of Kerala is one of the highlights of the area, and the food at Motty's is often highly praised. Guests can even learn how to cook the traditional recipes of southern India. Lali uses only homegrown produce and local ingredients, including the latest catches from the fishermen. You may eat with the family in the candlelit dining room and try traditional rice breads, spicy curries, pickles, and baked bananas. Most guests are so impressed that Lali is compiling a book of recipes that you can take home. **SH**

Experience Kodaikanal

Location Tamil Nadu, India
Website www.kodaikanal.com **Price** 💲

In the south of Tamil Nadu, the town of Kodaikanal offers a welcome respite from the sweltering heat. Located in the Western Ghats mountain range, which stretches from Mumbai all the way down to India's southernmost tip, Kodaikanal is the country's only hill station set up by U.S. missionaries. At 6,900 feet (2,100 m), the temperature—which is not subject to great seasonal variations because of the town's near-equatorial setting—rarely exceeds 68°F (20°C) and hardly ever drops below 46°F (8°C).

Established in the 1840s, the hill station has always been popular with visitors, initially with expatriates who wanted to escape the hot weather of the lowlands and, since the twentieth century, also with affluent Indians. At the periphery of the town center with its more than fifty hotels is the star-shaped, man-made Kodaikanal Lake. Often considered to be the town's landmark, it is beautifully set in the evergreen rolling landscape, and boating is very popular with the many newlyweds who spend their honeymoon in the area. At the southeast end of the lake, the botanical garden Bryant Park is worth a visit before starting on the nearby Coaker's Walk, which offers splendid views of the surrounding peaks and valleys. A couple of miles uphill from Kodaikanal, Kurinji Andava Temple and its surrounding lands are well known as the home of an endemic plant called kurinji shrub. Its color is a mix of purple and blue, although you will have to be very lucky to see it bloom because it flowers only once every twelve years.

Known locally as the "princess of hill stations," Kodaikanal is a scenic retreat that quite literally offers a breath of fresh air after a stay in the more congested and bustling cities on India's plains. **SD**

Discover Mahabalipuram

Location Tamil Nadu, India   **Website** www.mahabalipuram.co.in
Price ◗

Famous for its shore temple, Mahabalipuram was the seaport of the Pallava kings of Kanchipuram, who were at the height of their artistic and political power from the fifth to the eighth century C.E. The beautiful and romantic temple, home to various shrines carved from solid rock and ravaged by wind, salt, sun, and time, was built around the middle of the seventh century.

The wonderful sculptures show scenes of everyday life: women milking buffalos; officious city dignitaries; young girls posing; as well as animals and deities from the Hindu *Panchatantra* stories. Such images are unusual in the state, where other carvings depict divinities, not normal folk. The joy of Mahabalipuram is that the art of stone carving is still very much alive; sculptors and their workshops line the street, chiseling from dawn to dusk. A local sculpture museum contains more than 3,000 works by local artists, some in wood, metal, and brass, as well as granite.

The town is popular with day-trippers from Chennai, but tranquility descends after dusk, when the casual beachside restaurants serve delicious seafood. Along the great expanse of beach, fishermen bring in their catch in the afternoons, and vendors sell chillums and other stone pieces. The shoreline has receded somewhat since the tsunami of 2004, revealing more remains, such as a granite lion. During the tsunami, the waters went back so far that they revealed another temple under the ocean. Those on the beach caught a brief glimpse of its beauty before water covered it again. After the tsunami, a diving expedition confirmed the ruins' existence. **LB**

▣ *The shrines were hidden in the sand until excavated by the British about 200 years ago.*

Stay at Ulpotha

Location Embogama, Sri Lanka
Website www.ulpotha.com **Price** $ $

Tucked away in a corner of the sacred ancient cities region of central Sri Lanka sits Ulpotha, the perfect base to practice yoga and enjoy ayurvedic treatments. It was a pilgrimage site for thousands of years; now it offers peace and tranquility to soothe the pressures of life in the modern world. Most guests call this retreat "paradise on Earth," and you do not need to stretch your imagination to understand why. The village is surrounded by mountains and looks out across lotus-studded lakes and emerald-green paddy fields.

Ulpotha is set in the surroundings of a working organic farm. It is a pioneering experiment in eco-tourism, based around a central pavilion where meals are served and yoga classes take place. There is no five-star luxury, and accommodation is in adobe huts. What you will find, though, is a laid-back house party atmosphere, with delicious homemade vegetarian curries and sambals and a program of ayurvedic treatments. The huts are decorated with locally woven bed linen and colorful cushions, whereas rooms in the main house are furnished with four-poster beds, antiques, and religious deities. The air is perfumed with the scent of burning incense and the aroma of bowls of floating flowers. Oil lamps and torch flames illuminate paths at night to add to that wonderful get-away-from-it-all experience.

Open only for six weeks in June and July and from November through to March, the retreat closes to allow the farmland to be cultivated. Yoga classes are offered daily, as is walking in the surrounding countryside, or you can just lie back and soak up the atmosphere. **AD**

⬅ *For something completely different, stay in the tree hut, the stilted house in the middle of the forest lake.*

Enjoy Ayurveda Pavilions

Location Negombo, Sri Lanka
Website www.ayurvedapavilions.com **Price** $ $

Marigold and frangipani petals float in bowls of water, and the captivating smell of incense scents the humid air. At the Ayurveda Pavilions, the emphasis is on relaxation, which is to be found everywhere, from the meditative tinkling of water features to the curative treatments prescribed by in-house doctors.

The twelve villas are built in the style of a traditional Sri Lankan village, with high-ceilinged bedrooms, indoor and outdoor baths, shaded courtyard gardens, and comfortable verandas furnished with hardwood seating. It is just a short walk to the palm-fringed golden beaches of Sri Lanka's west coast where you can take an invigorating dip in the rolling waves.

> *"Sri Lanka's people have had [2,500 years] to master the ayurvedic tradition of healing."*
>
> *San Francisco Chronicle*

After a consultation with an ayurvedic doctor, soothing hot oils are infused with herbs and gently massaged into aching limbs to the sound of chirping birds or the sweet strains of sitar music played by a local musician in the garden. The health resort uses ancient ayurvedic medicines and practices to treat modern symptoms, from backache and arthritis to migraines and skin problems. This even extends to the restaurant, which has an ayurveda menu packed with fresh fruit and vegetables and locally caught seafood. Yoga, meditation, and music therapy classes are on offer, or you can relax by the pool in the center of the tranquil gardens, surrounded by flowering trees. **AD**

Unwind at Barberyn Reef

Location Beruwala, Sri Lanka
Website www.barberynresorts.com   **Price** 🟢🟢

The 5,000-year-old system of Indian healing named ayurveda (or "science of life" in the ancient Indian language of Sanskrit) is increasingly popular in the West for its ability to rebalance the body and mind.

Barberyn Reef hotel, nestled on the golden southwest coast of Sri Lanka, is one of ayurveda's pioneers. The resort was extensively renovated in the months after the 2004 tsunami and now boasts seventy-five beautiful rooms, some of which lie just in front of the ocean and have a terrace or balcony.

Guests can opt to take an ayurvedic package that includes consultation with a doctor, a special diet, and an individual program. This schedule is likely to include

---

"There's a particular energy that comes from this piece of land. . . . It has a sort of rejuvenating aura."

Nation Newspaper

---

a daily four-handed massage and detox treatments. You will be pampered and rejuvenated in a big way.

Ayurveda aside, one of the hotel's memorable aspects is its location: It is set on a picture-perfect stretch of palm-fringed coral reef and beach, ideal for leisurely swimming or sunbathing. Guests can also take part in a program of events that includes yoga, meditation, and cooking lessons. Alternatively, you can just kick back and relax on one of the most picturesque settings on this coastline. There is a lovely little à la carte beach restaurant, too. It serves tea and drinks and is a magical place to enjoy a relaxing cocktail as the sun sets over the horizon. **LC**

Recharge at Amangalla

Location Galle, Sri Lanka
Website www.amanresorts.com   **Price** 🟢🟢

Part of the Aman chain of hotels, Amangalla is set in the 400-year-old Galle Fort, the mellow old quarter of Galle where you can wander around boutique shops that sell colonial antiques, decorated caftans, and handicrafts. Mostly, however, you will want to stay inside, to sip the house mango Bellini and enjoy the one-to-one attention from an excellent staff.

Amangalla was the colonial base for the Dutch army and then the New Oriental hotel for 140 years, and its historic heritage has been carefully preserved. Pad about on teak floors, sleep in four-poster beds, store your clothes in pettagama chests, and share arrack sours in planter's chairs. Elegant throws and giant vases of fresh flowers dot the twenty-nine individually designed bedrooms—a favorite is Suite 8, at the top of the main staircase, with sweeping views out across the fort and the ocean. Lunches and dinners include inviting European dishes as well as daily changing Sri Lankan rice and curry feasts.

For more intense relaxation, there is a large outdoor pool with shaded *ambalamas* (daybeds), and a wooden-floored pavilion in the pretty gardens offering private sessions in yoga, meditation, and qigong. Where the New Oriental's parade of shops used to be, you will find the Baths, which has a small but calming hydrotherapy pool, cold plunge pool, steam room, and sauna, all softly lit by candles in recesses. Carefully sourced therapists offer luxurious treatments drawing on different cultures. You can even come here for a program of ayurveda, the ancient Indian system of health and personal development. **CSJ**

➡ *A cool and collected white-painted haven, Amangalla has the intimate feel of a much smaller hotel.*

Enjoy River House

Location Balapitiya, Sri Lanka
Website www.taruvillas.com **Price** ⑤⑤

"It is unique in its concept and design and is one of the most beautiful properties in Sri Lanka."

indiatravelite.com

On the southwest coast of Sri Lanka, the fabulous River House sits half a mile up a narrow road, on the outskirts of Bentota. Turn a corner and the house comes into view in all its glory, nestling at the top of a grassy hillside, shaded by palm trees, looking down to the Madhu Ganga River. Set in 7 acres (3 ha) of lush private gardens, this is a serious retreat from the outside world. A haven of style and tranquility, the house is the creation of Nayantha Fonseka, a fashion designer who has turned his talented hand to architecture. Sri Lankan woods such as kitul and jak fruit have been used throughout the accommodation, and carefully chosen antiques blend in with hand-carved reproduction pieces of furniture.

Guests may take it easy on a rattan sofa sitting on an open veranda, surrounded by tapestries, drapes, and luxurious carpets. The five sumptuous suites are named after Sri Lankan astrological signs: Kanya and Singhe have massive beds that are almost as big as some budget hotel rooms; Tulu and Danu are adjoining and perfect for a family group; whereas Makara sits close to the river, just a short distance from the main house. Each suite has a private garden or terrace, with indoor or outdoor plunge tub or pool.

Stay in the enclosed grounds or five minutes away at the private beach house. Take a dip in the infinity pool, head to the private beach, or take out the motorboat. Then come back to the villa to eat in the restaurant or garden, with a choice of mouthwatering dishes. The service is attentive yet discreet, ensuring the ultimate in cocooned privacy. **AD**

⬉ *The River House borders the peaceful Madhu estuary, a haven for bird enthusiasts and fishermen.*

Stay at the Mudhouse

Location Near Anamaduwa, Sri Lanka
Website www.themudhouse.lk **Price** ⊖⊖

The area near the town of Anamaduwa is just a couple of hours north of Colombo, in the western part of Sri Lanka. It is home not only to the imposing Paramakanda Rock Temple, but also to an isolated forest retreat at the sanctuary's foot. Consisting of individually designed huts that are scattered across 60 acres (24 ha) of rain forest, the peacefulness of the Mudhouse befits its remote but beautiful location.

Built from natural materials only, the huts combine modern aesthetics with traditional craftsmanship, and their design ranges from regular Sri Lankan village houses to tree houses. They all come with indoor bathrooms, outdoor showers, a dining area, and an

---

"[There is] a secluded romantic hut on stilts . . . with a curtained four-poster bed and views of the lake."

Guardian

---

area for meditation and yoga. However, this being an eco retreat there is no electricity, meaning that candles and lanterns are used at night, further contributing to the Mudhouse's poetic charm.

Part of the retreat is also an organic farm that provides most of the fruits and vegetables for the dishes served at the Mudhouse. Guests can help pick the fruit, and other activities include bicycle and boat tours, bird-watching at the local bird sanctuary, and trips to the ancient cities of Anradhapura, Yapahuwa, and Pandurasnuwara. The Mudhouse truly is a hidden gem that distinguishes itself by blending in effortlessly with the area's own natural beauty. **DaH**

Unwind at Paradise Farm

Location Kithulgala, Sri Lanka
Website www.paradisesrilanka.com **Price** ⊖⊖

Sri Lanka's tea country has become prime territory for visitors, who pour into the area to enjoy its serenity and to see exactly where the country's fantastic tea is grown. Set in the heart of this tourist region, Paradise Farm stands out. An independent, organic, green-tea farm that gives all its profits back to its workers, the organization is small scale and community focused.

The villa, Paradise Farm itself, is an idyllic retreat with nothing but forest around it. It is popular with artists, writers, and anyone who wants some peace and quiet away from the hectic *tuk-tuks* and potholed roads. There are two double bedrooms in the main villa and two bungalows behind it for guests. The accommodation is not five-star luxury, but it provides a complete back-to-nature retreat. Staying here enables the Worldview International Foundation to train local people in sustainable agriculture and helps to give back to the local community. The owners keep a low profile on-site, allowing guests to do exactly what they wish. Traditional Sri Lankan curries arrive from the kitchen at lunchtime and at dusk, and breakfast is fresh fruit from the forest and delicious pancakes.

From the open-fronted villa's infinity pool, you can look out over the rain forest and see birds soaring high above the ground. Sitting in the swinging cane chair over the pool, you can immerse yourself in a book or just relax among the cushions. On a good day you will be able to take in views of Sri Pada (also known as Adam's Peak), one of Sri Lanka's holy mountains, as well as blue-hazed hillsides and lush plantations. Buffalo graze, monkeys play, and, at night, fireflies drift in the air. Paths from the villa lead you down into the jungle, via spice gardens growing cinnamon, and guides can take you tracking leopards here, too. **LD**

Relax at Helga's Folly

Location Kandy, Sri Lanka
Website www.helgasfolly.com   **Price** $

The Stereophonics were so enamored of Helga's Folly that they wrote a song about the place after spending an unforgettable night here. It is situated atop a hill just outside the frenetic city of Kandy, which is teeming with antiques, jewelry, and trinket-rich shops. However, it is an ideal pad to escape from it all, which might explain its reputation as a celebrity haunt.

Dimly lit by wax-dripping candles and soft lamps, the place has a louche and decadent feel to it. Think nineteenth-century opium den meets Moulin Rouge. Guests can lounge about the many communal rooms, stuffed full of cozy sofas, puffed-up cushions, antique furniture, vases, and dark velvety drapes. The vibrantly colored walls are adorned with pictures of legendary Hollywood movie stars, paintings, drawings, and photographs of the family of owner Helga, a wildly eccentric woman who sports big sunglasses and crazy hats. The sprawling building is musty and dusty, but this adds to the charm. The decor of the bedrooms continues in the same vein, with four-poster beds swathed in black lace and gold sheets.

Outside, the hotel is set in thick unruly jungle, a lush tangle of green. There is a swimming pool surrounded by fairy statues, a paradise for children who love to explore. A sign reads: "Please ensure your windows and doors are firmly closed before leaving your room. The management cannot accept responsibility for the monkeys." The cheeky creatures lurk in the trees and appear in force at breakfast time, so eat outside at your peril. Whatever you make of this eccentric boutique pad, you will be sure never to forget a stay here. **JK**

← *The decor at Helga's Folly is a mix of bohemian and traditional, which makes it stand out.*

Enjoy Tree Tops Lodge

Location Moneragala District, Sri Lanka
Website www.treetopsjunglelodge.com   **Price** $

Tree Tops Jungle Lodge is set within the Sri Lankan Weliara forest, situated between the Yala National Park and the Arahat Kanda Mountains. It is the perfect place to watch and listen to wildlife, in particular some of the jungle's 161 bird species and its wild elephants. Experiences such as sighting an elephant mother and child are truly magical.

The accommodation is pretty basic. Visitors stay in simple huts built from a combination of clay, cow dung, and wood in the local fashion, and they wash in a freshwater well. Guests can go to sleep listening to the murmur of the jungle, after taking a moonlit trek under the stars, and wake up to the chatter of birds.

"An awesome viewpoint into jungle life … the atmosphere is charged with the noise of the wild."

ecohotelsoftheworld.com

Tree Tops is not just a place for animal and plant lovers; staff will also take guests to see some of the nearby Buddhist rock temples that are otherwise off the beaten track for tourists. The vegetarian food is cooked on a wood fire, and the soups and curries are prepared by cooks who know the secrets of ayurvedic plant medicine, often using herbs and spices that grow in the jungle. Wildlife sightings vary according to the time of year and whether it is the rainy or dry season. However, there is always the option to kick back and relax in a hammock and admire the stunning views, as far away from twenty-first-century urban living as it is possible to imagine. **CK**

Experience Baros

Location Baros, Maldives   **Website** www.baros.com
Price 💲💲

This could be the very definition of paradise: tiny hummocks of sandy islands bathed endlessly in golden sun, encircled by turquoise lagoons, soft white shores, and some gently swaying palm trees for good measure. It's a perpetual photo opportunity that will make your vacation pictures look amazing.

From the air, the Maldives are like smudges. They peek out above the water, often by no more than three or four feet (around 1 m), and are inhabited only by the luxury accommodation and spas that cater for the sanctuary-seeker. After touching down at Male airport, the only way to get to your remote and exclusive destination is by private sea-plane or boat. Only 25 minutes after skimming over the still waters, maybe taking in a school of playful dolphins or an occasional flying fish, you'll be marooned in paradise on your very own Robinson Crusoe island.

Baros is one of the most secluded and unspoiled islands in the Northern Atoll. You can snooze all day on your private deck, join the scuba-lovers to explore the crystalline waters, or be pampered to perfection in the Aquum Spa. Or you could book a sunset cruise, a day's deep-sea fishing, or dine on the moonlit sands for a spot of beach-based star-gazing.

First you must find your own portion of Baros bliss by walking barefoot to a private strip of beach. Stretch out on your own portion of powdery sand or indulge in a bit of underwater exploring. You might have a memorable close encounter with a balletic stingray or a darting shoal of tropical fish. And don't forget the Maldivian mantra: no news, no shoes. **SWi**

◄ *With the amazing sunsets and the unspoiled views, Baros is the epitome of a true escape.*

Stay at Hotel Dhonakulhi

Location Haa Alifu Atoll, Maldives
Website www.island-hideaway.com   **Price** 🔴🔴🔴

A thousand Robinson Crusoe islands and lagoons with varying depths and infinite shades of sparkling blue: This is the sublime setting for the Hotel Dhonakulhi, which has bagged the best spot in the whole of the Maldives—the previously uninhabited virgin atoll of Haa Alifu. The resort is surrounded by lush vegetation, and the luxurious villas have the Indian Ocean lapping at their terraces. Graced with private beaches, and some with their own pools, too, the huts have open-air bathrooms that highlight the general feeling of back-to-nature luxury. Visitors may be marooned on an island paradise, but there are first-class restaurants, a rejuvenating spa, and a variety of state-of-the-art media equipment, just in case you need to contact home.

You do not have to be an avid snorkeler to visit the Maldives. Although you could spend a day or two with the dive school, a wade through the aquarium-clear waters will give you just as good a glimpse of the fish in the coral reefs. That is before you stretch out under a coconut tree or relax with a massage in your private open-air treatment room overlooking the ocean.

Dhonakulhi stands out from its Maldivian rivals thanks to its utterly unspoiled setting. Some 95 percent of the island remains undeveloped, so visitors are completely surrounded by the sheer natural beauty of the Maldives. Even the marina, the only one in the entire archipelago, is formed from a channel in the reef, splitting it in two, and thereby making a natural harbor. If you sail over in your private yacht, you will have no trouble docking—otherwise, you can take the speedboat like the rest of us. **SWi**

↤ *Designed to provide the ultimate in seclusion, the airy hut-like residences have their own spacious plots.*

Relax at Dhoni Mighili

Location Ari Atoll, Maldives
Website www.scottdunn.com   **Price** 🔴🔴🔴🔴

The island of Dhoni Mighili, in the Ari atoll southwest of Malé, is something special. It is the only Maldivian island that you can book outright, and it provides a unique luxury experience pairing a secluded island hideaway with boat accommodation. Reached by seaplane, the island itself has just six beach bungalows situated 30 feet (9 m) from the turquoise sea, four of which have private plunge pools. To make your stay even more special, each comes with a Maldivian butler who will be at your beck and call 24/7. They are able to arrange anything you might need, whether that's personalized diving lessons, the perfect martini, or a unique and secluded spot for a marriage proposal.

"The Maldives really do deserve their reputation as the pearls of the Indian Ocean."

Maldives Review website

In this decadent paradise of palm trees, coral-sand beaches, and clear warm sea, you are encouraged to spend the day lazing on your private *dhoni*, a 65-foot (20-m) Maldivian sailboat. As night falls, your butler will organize dinner beneath the stars. You can spend the night in the thatched bungalow or on board the *dhoni* with the hush of the sea lulling you to sleep.

Cruise during the day to unvisited sandbars for a swim, or visit undersea treasure troves to marvel at the reef's brightly colored sea life. There is a chance of spotting gray reef sharks, manta rays, and even enormous whale sharks around the exotic coral. For the lucky few, Dhoni Mighili is paradise found. **LD**

Enjoy Huvafen Fushi Underwater Spa

Location North Malé Atoll, Maldives
Website www.huvafenfushi.com   **Price** ⊖⊖⊖⊖

Set in translucent turquoise seas covering an area of the Indian Ocean the size of Portugal, the otherworldly Maldives are likely to sink in 150 years' time, as global warming continues to make the sea levels rise. Get there while you still can, and when you do, stay at Huvafen Fushi, a sexy and serene resort for dreamers.

Whichever of its forty-three stylish, contemporary, uncluttered water bungalows you choose, you will be guaranteed immaculate luxury. Some bungalows have glass floors so you can watch marine life as you sip a cooling cocktail; others boast giant whirlpool tubs in the bathroom, with only a sheet of glass

---

"The butler feeds the manta rays at sunset, which is a major hit with the children."

Harper's Bazaar

---

between you and expansive private views of the lagoon. Outside, skinny-dip from your deck, sprawl on your daybed, and cool off in your plunge pool.

The spa, built on stilts above the ocean, has underwater treatment rooms, where you can commune with the tropical fish while you have your head massaged. A range of inventive "rituals" using wraps, scrubs, facials, and massages is available; there is private yoga and meditation, and even a resident "wellness mentor." Swim at night in the infinity pool, when it is lit up by colored fiber-optic lights, then dip into the Lonu Veyo, a Malaysian saltwater pool in which it is extremely relaxing to float. **CSJ**

Stay at One&Only Reethi Rah

Location North Malé Atoll, Maldives
Website www.oneandonlyresorts.com   **Price** ⊖⊖⊖

Arriving at One&Only Reethi Rah on a sleek, 55-foot (16-m) yacht, one doubts that there could be anywhere else quite so stunning on the planet. A sparkling lagoon encircles the softest white sand imaginable, and spacious luxury villas are dotted around the beach or hover in the water.

Everything at the resort amounts to one little word: wow! It is a remarkable place to stay, and it is not unusual to bump into glamorous celebrities sipping a cocktail at the Rah Bar. Villas come with mysterious black infinity pools on large decks with cool daybeds. Inside there are plasma televisions, enormous beds, and bathrooms with sunken tubs fit for kings and queens, underneath soaring triple-height ceilings.

There is little to do, which suits most blissed-out visitors down to the ground. Time in the inviting waters is spent swimming, snorkeling, and diving; time above it fishing, enjoying Zen-like spa treatments, and soaking up the sun's rays in one of many secluded spots. In the evenings, a well-dressed clientele savors delectable dishes in the main restaurant, the Japanese tapas fusion restaurant, and the Middle Eastern beach restaurant, described by One&Only as exuding "shipwreck chic." Golf carts and bicycles provide modes of transportation around the island—which is large by Maldivian standards—making discovering its twelve gorgeous beaches that little bit easier.

In case you are wondering what the name means, Reethi Rah is translated as "pretty island"—a serious underestimation if ever there was one. **LP**

➡ *There has been not one iota of skimping in the design of the shamelessly glitzy resort at Reethi Rah.*

Ride an Elephant Through Chitwan National Park

Location Chitwan National Park, Nepal
Website www.chitwannationalpark.org **Price** 💲

"The only sound was the cicadas and the occasional command from the elephant driver."

Lesley Downer, *Daily Telegraph*

Home to the rare Asian one-horned rhinoceros and the Royal Bengal tiger, Chitwan became a national park in 1973. Now a UNESCO World Heritage site, it hosts more than 40 mammals and more than 450 bird species—and the best way to spot them is from the back of an elephant. Private lodges inside the park own elephants trained to carry up to four people on a howdah, a huge wooden saddle, with their driver, the *pahit*, sitting on their necks giving instructions by tickling the elephants' ears with his naked feet. As the elephant lollops through forests or dense grasses, you wobble in rhythm and duck to avoid overhanging branches. Animals are not fazed by their pachyderm neighbors, so it is easy to walk relatively close to a rhino and observe its weird prehistoric form and seemingly armor-plated skin from this perfect vantage point high above. You might also spot sloth bears, leopards, wild boar, or deer—or even one of the park's hundred or so remaining tigers, cleverly camouflaged.

Approaching the Narayani River, keep your eyes peeled for rare Ganges River dolphins popping to the surface to breathe, and for marsh or mugger crocodiles and the severely endangered gharial. Later, in a safer stretch of water, you can help bathe your elephant. Elephants love bath time and, just like children, they love to play. As you sit on their backs in the river, following their pahit's instructions, they will playfully drench you with a trunk full of water or lower themselves underwater, rolling you off their backs. Their final trick is a graceful goodbye, curling up their trunks as the pahit says "Namaste!" **SWa**

The views at sunset are astounding, but you will be awed by the scenery whatever time of day you go.

See the Garden of Dreams

Location Kathmandu, Nepal
Website www.asianart.com/gardenofdreams **Price** $

Kathmandu has a new sanctuary. With its ancient Hindu temples, Buddhist stupas, and Newari palaces slowly crumbling amid congestion and pollution, the aptly named Garden of Dreams is just a stone's throw from the tourist center of Thamel.

Field Marshal Kesher Shumshar Rana initially built the garden in the 1920s, inspired by his love of travel, horticulture, and art. Combining European-influenced pergolas, pathways, and statues with Edwardian pavilions, his garden was his passion and a true work of beauty. Sadly, many years of neglect followed his death in 1964, until 2002 when a Nepali-Austrian project began the restoration of the garden.

"No rock concerts. No weddings. No fashion shows."

Götz Hagmüller, chief architect, Garden of Dreams

Today, the Garden of Dreams is an elegant oasis in the heart of Kathmandu. Wisteria and bougainvillea drape the pergolas. Palm trees and bamboo provide welcome shade, and magnolia, camellia, and azaleas provide brilliant color. Fountains, small moats, and a lotus pond add to the overall serenity of the gardens, and the three remaining pavilions, sensitively restored, add a touch of romantic neoclassical grandeur.

It is easy to while away the time here. Bury yourself in a book lying on the steps of the open-air amphitheater; hide in the secret garden that overlooks the main gardens; or stroll around the pathways admiring the beautiful plants and statues. **SWa**

Balloon over Nepal

Location Kathmandu, Nepal
Website www.adventuresnepal.com **Price** $

A ride in a hot-air balloon must be one of the most incredible experiences you will ever have. The roar of the burners as you rise into the sky is followed by the silence of floating as you continue to gently ascend and drift at the whim of the guiding winds.

Best of all, though, are the views. Suspended almost silently in the skies as the landscape falls away beneath you, you will be as high as a bird or plane, but with no obscuring wing or distracting engine roar to detract from the wonder of the scene below.

There are few more breathtaking views above which to float than those over Nepal. Flights start early as the huge balloons rise with the dawn, rippling and stretching as they expand in readiness for their journey. Setting off above the red roofs of the historic town of Bhaktapur, the flight will head into the Kathmandu Valley. Here the green hills and terraces are dotted with clusters of terra-cotta structures, and gilded temple spires are caught by the rays of the rising sun. However, the most amazing views are still to come. On a clear day this is the serenest and easiest way to climb Mount Everest and view the vast expanse of the Himalayan range. You will be surrounded by uninterrupted views and total hush as you drift slowly and weightlessly between the snowcapped peaks of these stony giants. From such fabled sights as Gosainthan, Phurbi-Gyachu, and Gauri-Sanker to Chhobar-Bhamare, Chomolungma, and Gyanchung Kang, the sheer drama of these ridges is awe-inspiring.

Later, when you return, your wicker cocoon will sink slowly into the terraced paddies in the valley, frequently to be met by an impromptu gathering of onlookers from the nearby villages who look in curiosity at what has fallen from the sky. **SWi**

Stay at Dwarika's Hotel

Location Kathmandu, Nepal
Website www.dwarikas.com   **Price** ⓢⓢ

This peaceful retreat is hidden behind high walls, well away from the dust and chaos of Nepal's capital city, Kathmandu. A cluster of Newari-style buildings separated by cobbled courtyards with carved pillars and traditional windows, Dwarika's Hotel is an inspired hybrid of old and new. It oozes the culture and heritage of a living museum, but with a lush, romantic feel.

Dwarika's is the vision of one man who wanted to preserve Nepali culture for future generations. The late Dwarika Das Sherpa collected ancient carved wooden pieces and terra-cotta from old buildings being demolished in Kathmandu. The carefully preserved pieces of Malla art and architecture are now housed

"It is possible that Dwarika's has no counterpart anywhere in the world."

Taipan magazine

within the courtyards. In recognition of Dwarika's efforts, the iconic hotel has won a PATA Heritage award for its on-site wood-carving workshop and use of traditional carving techniques in the building.

There are seventy-four sumptuous rooms and suites in total, each one with its own character. Furnished with handmade Nepali furniture and hand-printed traditional fabrics, the rooms are immensely luxurious. Attentive staff will see to your every need while you breathe in the air infused with the scent of lemon balm, incense, and the fresh aroma of cut flowers. Relax in the gardens, take a dip in the pool, then look forward to a feast in the Krishnarpan restaurant. **AD**

Visit Kopan Monastery

Location Kathmandu, Nepal
Website www.kopan-monastery.com   **Price** ⓢ

Few places find it necessary to inform their guests as they arrive that there should be "no killing, no lying, and no sexual conduct." It is also rare for any accommodation providers to ask visitors to bring a sleeping bag, flashlight, and insect repellent. However, Kopan is neither a luxury hotel nor an exclusive resort; it is a spiritual retreat with no concessions to physical indulgence. In many ways this lifestyle makes Kopan Monastery one of the most complete "escapes."

The place has certainly got all the ingredients for mental cleansing, de-stressing, and purification. The monastery of Kopan stands high in the Himalayan foothills and is home to 360 monks, mainly from Nepal and Tibet. Nearby is its sister, Khachoe Ghakyil Ling Nunnery, home to 380 nuns. Together they form a tranquil, religious, and philosophical oasis each year for hundreds of visitors from around the world.

Guests come to join courses on meditation or to learn an introduction to Buddhism. The courses last from a week to several years. Some students never leave. The monastic regimen is rigorously applied: male and female accommodation is segregated; alcohol, drugs, and tobacco are completely banned; the daily program starts at 6.30 A.M. and finishes at 9 P.M.; guests are expected to attend all the sessions; and a half-day silence is kept as "a course discipline."

Accommodation is in shared rooms or dormitories; no bedding is provided, and between November and March it can get very cold. And the cuisine? The monastery kitchen serves simple but plentiful vegetarian meals communally three times a day. **SH**

↪ *There are few places in the world as remote and isolated yet spiritually replete as Kopan Monastery.*

Trek to Gokyo Ri

Location Solu Khumbu, Nepal **Website** www.nepaltrailblazer.com
Price ⑤⑤⑤

The summit of Mount Everest must surely be the ultimate escape. The training and risks involved in climbing it are too much for most mortals, so try a twelve-day trek to Gokyo Ri instead and marvel at the sunset reflecting on the world's highest mountain. Here, in the Solu Khumbu region of Nepal, you will encounter the charming Sherpa people, renowned for their climbing skills, and stunning mountain landscapes in the heart of the Himalayas.

The trek itself does not demand technical climbing skills. However, with the summit of Gokyo Ri at 17,500 feet (5,350 m), take your time ascending to avoid altitude sickness. Hire porters to carry your kit and a guide to lead the way, or book the trip through an agency, leaving you free to enjoy the hike without fear of getting lost or exhausted. In the evenings, experience the warm Nepali hospitality in teahouses or lodges—although they are far from luxurious, you can relax in front of the stove and dig in to a hearty meal of *dhal bhat*, the traditional fare of vegetables and rice, washed down with reviving Khukri rum.

The mountain village of Gokyo is on the shores of the glistening Dudh Pokhari, and a two-hour hike above this lake takes you to Gokyo Ri. Here you will see four summits higher than 26,000 feet (8,000 m): Everest, Cho Oyu, Lhotse, and Makalu, sparkling like enormous diamonds in the sky. You will soon forget your shortness of breath and the cold gnawing at your fingertips as you watch the sun casting shades of brilliant gold, turning fiery red and finally baby pink, on the snows of the highest peak in the world. **SWa**

← *From Gokyo Ri, your vantage point reveals an amazing landscape of peaks, high passes, and glaciers.*

Stay at Amankora

Location Paro, Bhutan **Website** www.amanresorts.com
Price ⊖⊖⊖⊖

If trekking in the Himalayas conjures up images of trudging behind Ghurkas and freezing in tented accommodation, then think again. There is another way, thanks to Aman Resorts, which recently opened Amankora, the first luxury hotel and the first foreign venture of its kind in Bhutan.

The resort sits in a quite spectacular setting in the shadow of Jamalhari, Bhutan's highest peak, which overlooks a picturesque village surrounded by thick pine forests. The retreat consists of five separate luxury hideaways. The largest and most impressive lodge successfully combines the rustic with the contemporary, and the twenty-four bedrooms are in six rammed-

> "A cluster of austere buildings whose … exteriors belie interiors of epic scale and opulence."

Mike Carter, *Observer*

earth houses that mirror the shape of a ruined seventeenth-century fort on the hill above. However, there is no getting away from the biggest attraction: those stunning mountain views, which can be best admired from the living room.

The Paro Valley is the starting point for many of Bhutan's treks, which take in spectacular landscapes of soaring mountains, deep valleys, terraced rice paddies, fields of millet, and little hamlets dotting a thickly forested backdrop. It is likely that after a hard day's trekking your aching muscles will be in need of some soothing; luckily, all of the Amankora lodges have spas that offer a variety of relaxing treatments. **HA**

Relax at Uma Paro

Location Paro, Bhutan **Website** www.uma.como.bz
Price ⊖⊖

High in the Himalayan mountain kingdom of Bhutan, Uma Paro is a study in spiritual stillness. The luxury boutique hotel blends the best of Bhutan's exquisite traditions with modern elements to create a retreat as stunning as the scenery. Drawing on the serenity of yoga and meditation practices, a stay here is transcendent.

The hotel consists of a central lodge and nine villas, set in 38 acres (15 ha) of wooded hillsides. Rooms overlook the pine forests and peaks rising in the distance, and the two-bed villas are a highlight, with outdoor hot stone bath tubs and open-air courtyards with fire pits in the center. The rooms are all sleek and modern with brightly colored, hand-painted Bhutanese wall designs and views to die for.

The Buddhist kingdom places much emphasis on yoga and meditation, and with the cool, fresh, unpolluted air here in the mountains, *pranayama* (yogic breathing) has never felt so good. Staff are on hand twenty-four hours a day to make your stay as relaxing as possible. The Shambala spa offers treatments to soothe the soul, with an emphasis again on the spiritual and physical nature of the treatments. Stone bath therapies are just one of many to slow your pulse and help you relax. The Bukhari restaurant serves up Bhutanese-inspired delicacies from yak burgers to chai-infused hot chocolate and local noodle soup.

Bhutan is not the easiest country to visit, and it is to the hotel's credit that it starts the soothing process even before you visit, by helping you to organize all the necessary entry permits, visas, and flights. It is less a hotel stay and more a spiritual experience. **LD**

⤴ *The luxurious setting of Uma Paro means it is the finest place to unwind at the end of a Bhutan hike.*

Enjoy Rongbuk Monastery

Location Rongbuk, Tibet, China
Website www.pbs.org/wgbh/nova/everest/history **Price** $

Elevated in the most revered mountain range in the world, the highest monastery on Earth sits at an altitude of 16,400 feet (5,000 m). A 48-mile (77-km) trek along the dirt road leads past the famous Rongbuk Glacier to the monastery. A destination that imprints upon all who journey here, the building is little more than a century old, and yet the feel is timeless.

Mount Everest appears as a cloudlike apparition on the horizon. Those who climb it must pass by Rongbuk Monastery in order to reach their goal; however, less adventurous travelers may still witness some of the most awe-inspiring panoramas in the world without trekking to the actual summit. The mighty peaks of Shishapangma, Everest, Cho Oyu, and Gyachung Kang guard over Rongbuk like titans of Tibet, their majesty and grandeur protected by clouds and mist.

The hostel at Rongbuk can sleep one hundred guests. There are more beds in the youth hostel than there are monks and nuns—said to total no more than sixty—a dwindling congregation compared with the monastery's heyday, when it housed some 500 members of the devout. The dining room serves delicious vegetarian food while the settling snow turns the courtyards into a wintry wonderland as the nuns and lamas go about their daily prayer. The surrounding valleys and cliffs are full of meditation caves, the palaces of choice for the many hermits who occupied this area for 400 years, the surrounding pathways littered with stone-carved prayers and mantras. Pilgrims—be they Sherpa or backpacker—never forget their stay. **VG**

↩ *Rongbuk Monastery looks out to the north side of Mount Everest, known locally as Chomolungma.*

Ride the Tangula Train

Location Beijing to Lhasa and Beijing to Lijiang, China
Website www.tangulaluxurytrains.com **Price** $$$$

If you want to experience the beauty and exotic landscapes of Tibet and China's western provinces, one of the world's most luxurious and futuristic trains will change the way you see rail travel forever.

The suites on the Tangula Luxury Train are all sumptuous, offering new standards in international rail travel and even your own personal supply of oxygen just in case the astonishing landscapes prove too much for you. Meals are prepared under the watchful eye of the internationally renowned Swiss chef Marco Mazzei and served in elegant dining cars.

Tangula's trains travel the entire length of China on two routes. The northern route achieves a maximum

> *"The name Tangula is inspired by Thang Lha, a powerful grassland deity who protects Tangula Pass."*
>
> *Railway Gazette International*

altitude of 16,640 feet (5,072 m) and will take you from Beijing to Lhasa in Tibet on a five-day journey through the grasslands, deserts, and vistas that once greeted those who traded along the Silk Road. The southern route's four-night odyssey departs Beijing and takes you past the Li River, with its world-famous karst formations and the jagged limestone pinnacles of the otherworldly stone forest of Shilin before arriving in the historic, World Heritage town of Lijiang.

Although the top speed is 100 miles per hour (160 kph), speeds are often reduced to allow for a proper appreciation of the inspiring scenery that will make this trip the most exhilarating rail journey of your life. **BS**

Unwind at Banyan Tree Ringha

Location Ringha, Yunnan, China
Website www.banyantree.com   **Price** ⑤⑤

Once the home of a local Tibetan villager, the Banyan Tree Ringha in Yunnan Province is now a boutique resort with thirty-two palatial villas. Sitting at an elevation of 10,000 feet (3,200 m) on the eastern edge of the Tibetan plateau, it has mountain and river views across a landscape that has been designated the Shangri-la of popular culture by the Chinese government.

The rooms are decorated with Tibetan tapestries and intricate wooden carvings. Rooms have fireplaces, wooden hot tubs with ladles, silk curtains, and private terraces. Then there are the little extras that could exist only in a hotel with a location like this, such as oxygen

---

"In this elevated enclave … lack of oxygen effortlessly coaxes the mind to a dreamlike state."

Guardian

---

canisters for the fainthearted and a pair of comfy yeti slippers. The restaurant serves Yunnan specialties such as hotpots and teriyaki grills, while in the Jakhang Teahouse guests can sample some of the many Chinese and Tibetan teas. The spa offers treatments guaranteed to elevate you to a state of nirvana, and trips to the nearby Songzanlin Monastery and Ringha's own temple provide insight into Tibetan religious life.

Encircled by mustard fields and traditional Tibetan colored flags, the Banyan Tree Ringha blends in so seamlessly with its environment that it becomes difficult to know where the boundaries of the hotel end and the village, of which it is a part, begins. **BS**

Ride a Bicycle Around Yangshuo

Location Yangshuo, Guangxi, China
Website www.bikeasia.com/cycle-tours/china/bcg.html   **Price** ⑤

The town of Yangshuo and its more famous neighbor, the city of Guilin—both situated on the scenic Li River in Guangxi Province—are surrounded by spectacular, conical, karst mountains that have inspired Chinese poets and painters for centuries. Having the region's only airport, Guilin is more popular with tourists, but as the area around Yangshuo is equally stunning, discerning travelers should make this town their base.

Some 40 miles (65 km) south of Guilin, the 1,500-year-old town occupies a small square of flat land between the innumerable eroded limestone mountains that are covered with shrubs and trees. Some of these mountains rise up 2,960 feet (903 m), although most of them are a lot smaller. A boat trip down the Li River (which, like the nearby Yulong River is clean enough to swim in) is virtually obligatory when visiting this part of the world, the snaking waterway providing breathtaking views at every turn. However, in order to avoid the tourist hordes and to gain a closer look at the fruitful landscape that provides the locals with pomelo, sweet orange, and tangerine, it is best to rent a bicycle. Readily available for rent from the shops in Yangshuo's market, they allow you to explore the nearby villages, venture up into the mountains, and journey along the rice paddies that add to the charm of the area, all at your own pace.

The secluded Yangshuo Mountain Retreat, with its traditional Chinese architecture, makes for a tranquil base. Located fifteen minutes outside the town, the twenty-two rooms offer fine views of the mountains and the river passing in front of the hotel, providing an ideal base for those who truly want to savor the peacefulness of the fairy-tale background. **DaH**

Relax at Silk Road Dunhuang Hotel

Location Dunhuang, Gansu, China
Website www.the-silk-road.com **Price** 🟢

Constructed in the style of the old Han and Tang dynasties, the Silk Road Dunhuang Hotel is a remarkable architectural accomplishment, as well as a contemporary reminder of the grandeur of centuries past. It is also conveniently situated just a ten-minute drive from the center of Dunhuang, an oasis town west of Xian on the edge of the Gobi Desert.

Long corridors typical of Han design and Tang dynasty touches, such as large roofs with extensive eaves, all surround a traditionally enclosed courtyard. The hotel is conveniently situated close to some of the most significant religious and historic sites in China,

"[We] provide a relaxing and comfortable environment . . . with a mind-enriching experience."

Proprietors, Silk Road Dunhuang Hotel

including the World Heritage-listed Mogao Grottoes, hundreds of caves carved into a 4,250-foot- (1,600-m-) long cliff face and containing a priceless collection of Buddhist statuary, manuscripts, and murals. The hauntingly beautiful Mingsha sand dunes, famous for the "singing" they produce when graced by Turpan's desert winds, and Crescent Moon Lake, which they surround, are just a short walk from the hotel. The best view of the dunes can be had from the expansive rooftop patio, a perfect vantage point from which to witness the spectacular sunsets while you imagine ancient camel trains heading westward to trade spices and cloth with the nations of Europe. **BS**

Enjoy the Aman Summer Palace

Location Beijing, China
Website www.amanresorts.com **Price** 🟢🟢🟢

The Aman Summer Palace merges seamlessly with some of the original buildings, gardens, and gazebos of Beijing's old imperial residence. It offers a sanctuary in which to take sumptuous refuge from the Beijing bustle, only 9 miles (15 km) from the city center.

The rooms and suites that surround the internal courtyard, formal gardens, and pathways evoke the elegance of the Ming dynasty. There is a sense of mystery throughout: a feeling of looking back to a different, more tranquil time. All the rooms glow with polished clay floors and have cocooning four-poster beds and Ming-style armoires. The soft, muted colors and refined furnishings blend the simplicity of the past with the luxury of the new.

In the world-class spa, imperial Chinese techniques are combined with modern therapies. In the hands of skilled practitioners, you can retreat into a state of pure tranquility. Afterward, a short walk will take you beyond the willow-draped pond to the music pavilion where, on warm evenings, silk-clad musicians strum the *erhu* and *guzheng* to embellish the serenity of the setting. You can dine on delicious Cantonese fare in the Chinese restaurant, whereas succulent Peking duck or more unusual imperial dishes can be enjoyed in one of six small private dining rooms. Explore the courtyard gardens and you will find four more restaurants in which to savor different cuisine.

After dinner, you might like to wander over to the bar. It overlooks the beautiful Chinese pond and garden and is the perfect place to relax. You might also be tempted to step out farther. You are after all, within moments of some of China's most iconic sites: the Summer Palace and the Forbidden City. **SWi**

Stay at the Commune by the Great Wall

Location Beijing, China
Website www.communebythegreatwall.com **Price** $$

It is a commune, but not as you know it. You will not find any straw-sandaled peasants at the Commune by the Great Wall. Rather, this is an escape for the well-heeled crowd. The brainchild of husband and wife team Pan Shiyi and Zhang Xin, the Commune was launched in 2002 with eleven über-chic villas all designed by Asian architects. In 2005, Kempinski came on board and added thirty-one more affordable units. There is also an Anantara spa, tai chi and yoga classes, a swimming pool, and a cinema, as well as a "children's commune" where kids can enjoy their very own adventures while parents stride out for the Great Wall.

> *"I set out through peach and chestnut orchards to the wall, composed of tumble-down steps."*
>
> Susan Spano, *Los Angeles Times*, on the Great Wall

It is the sleek, modern villas themselves that attract attention, however. Take the four-bedroom Suitcase House, for example, designed by Hong Kong architect Gary Chang. Sliding doors allow you to enjoy several separate rooms or to wallow in one big space. There is a private sauna and an elevator to the flat roof, where you can gaze at the Great Wall in all its glory. Furniture House was created by Shigeru Ban from Japan. Based on the traditional siheyuan courtyard houses of Beijing, the four bedrooms, living room, and dining room encircle an open-air terrace. Interior design comes from Serge Mouille, Thierry Hoppe, Von Robinson, and Philippe Starck, among others. **PE**

Relax at Mountain Yoga Fragrant Hills

Location Beijing, China
Website www.mountain-yoga.org **Price** $$

In 2003 an amateur inventor and advertising executive named Gyan Giri drove forty minutes west of Beijing, up into the picturesque Fragrant Hills. There, looking back over his shoulder at the distant lights of the Chinese capital, he thought that he had found the perfect place to build his dream yoga retreat. Today that dream has materialized into two retreats based in the Fragrant Hills, with an additional retreat in a nearby 500-year-old Buddhist temple, and a seasonal tepee-style encampment north of Beijing in a valley by an untouched, crumbling portion of the Great Wall.

Gyan's original retreat west of Beijing—Mountain Yoga Fragrant Hills—is built around an idyllic country chalet and can be found at the end of a dirt road that leads out through ancient magnolia groves from the Dajue Temple, a magnificent Liao dynasty (907 to 1125) temple replete with rare imperial steles. Mountain Yoga now boasts two spacious open courtyards and terraced areas, with many private spaces devoted to the pursuit of oneness under the watchful eyes of the center's yoga masters.

Here guests can participate in art and tai chi workshops, indulge in the ancient therapy of ear candling, learn the art of calligraphy, enjoy an evening of ancient singing and chanting using age-old Sanskrit mantras in the kirtan tradition, or breathe life into their inner actor in the outdoor theater. Mountain Yoga is more than just a yoga retreat. It promises to release you from your own negative energies and introduce you afresh to the myriad possibilities that life has to offer. There are also many hiking trails nearby from which you can relish the fresh mountain air and the beautiful scenery of Fragrant Hills. **BS**

Experience the Red Capital Club

Location Beijing, China
Website www.redcapitalclub.com.cn   **Price** 💲💲

Stay in any one of Beijing's corporate hotels and you would be forgiven for thinking that capitalism had been invented here. They are all as big, as brash, and as anonymous as anywhere else. The Red Capital Club, however, could not be more different.

This former communist party official's residence, a gorgeous Qing dynasty courtyard house that has been transformed into an ironic temple to communist propaganda and paraphernalia, is tiny, with a mere five rooms. It is tucked away in the unassuming residential district of Dongsi. The rooms face a central courtyard and are beautifully appointed; think silk-draped beds and decadent furnishings, just the thing to keep a high-ranking party official happy. If you are feeling louche, stay in one of the two concubine's private courtyards; they are fitted with ornate Qing dynasty beds and are the most romantic rooms in the hotel.

Despite the pervading sense of history, there are some concessions to the twenty-first century: Internet access is available, as is satellite television. There is also an old bomb shelter constructed during 1969, a time of tension with the U.S.S.R., which has been converted into a rather claustrophobic wine bar. You can reach it only via a small underground tunnel, revolution memorabilia covers its walls, and a small adjacent room shows old propaganda films. Dining comes courtesy of the fine, neighboring Red Capital Club restaurant, which serves some of Mao and Deng's favorite dishes. Finish off with a cruise around Beijing in a limo once owned by Madame Mao herself. **HA**

⬈ *The rooms are full of antiques, including a concubine bed that was carried from Myanmar by elephant.*

"The walls and doors gleam in red lacquer; the courtyard oozes the rockeries of a traditional garden."

travelintelligence.com

Visit the Gardens of Suzhou

Location Suzhou, Jiangsu, China
Website www.chinavista.com/suzhou/tour/garden.html **Price** $

Suzhou is a historic gem, filled with canals, bridges, and its famous gardens. The center of silk production in China, Suzhou was for centuries a popular residence for scholars, officials, and merchants. Eager to fill their leisure hours with beauty, they built private gardens in which to escape from the hurly-burly of city life.

There were once 200 private gardens in the city, each designed as a harmonious combination of the elements. Rocks, ponds, trees, and pavilions were meticulously placed so that the view was perfect, wherever one sat. Fewer than half the gardens survive today, but the largest of Suzhou's gardens open to the public, the Humble Administrator's Garden, dates from

> *"A very great and noble city. . . . It has 1,600 stone bridges under which a galley may pass."*

Marco Polo, explorer, on Suzhou

the Ming dynasty. It radiates with bamboo and bonsai, clear, chattering streams, carefully molded rock pools, and pavilions with upturned roofs. More than half of the garden is filled with water, and intricately latticed walkways allow erstwhile scholars to admire the landscapes even in rain and snow. Also worth visiting are the artfully designed Lingering Garden, the long walkway of which is adorned with calligraphy, and the Blue Wave Pavilion, an eleventh-century retreat featuring glorious, mature trees. **PE**

◄ *The Garden of the Master of Nets blends vertical with horizontal, water with land, and yin with yang.*

See Mount Huangshan

Location Mount Huangshan, Anhui, China
Website www.huangshantour.com **Price** ❶

The seventy-two peaks of Mount Huangshan, or Yellow Mountain, have been a tourist attraction for more than a millennium. Painters and poets across the ages have flocked here for inspiration from the granite crags and oddly shaped pine trees.

Anyone with a good level of fitness should avoid the crushing cable car line—Huangshan is a top domestic tourist haunt—and instead walk to the summit via the well-marked paths. The Eastern Steps provide a steep, short, 5-mile (8-km) route. The Western Steps are twice as long, and equally arduous, but reward hikers with outstanding views. On either route, though, you will find yourself almost alone

---

"Huangshan [is] known as 'the loveliest mountain of China.'"

UNESCO World Heritage Committee

---

except for the tough, wiry porters who haul supplies to the mountaintop hotels and restaurants. Away from the preferred package tour routes at the top, it is easy to find solitude. On a clear day, the scenery is spectacular. But it is not for the sunshine that travelers have swarmed here over the centuries; it is for the clouds. In misty weather, there seems at first to be no view at all. Then, the air currents send the brume gently billowing away. Magically, from behind the flurrying alabaster curtain, peaks of rough-hewn rock appear. For a few moments, they seem to hover mystically above a soft sea of white. Then the clouds shift once more, and the heavenly vision vanishes. **PE**

Enjoy Fuchun

Location Shanghai, China
Website www.fuchunresort.com **Price** ❸❸

Surrounded by the surreally beautiful Hangzhou Mountains, mist-swathed lakes, and a working tea plantation, the peacefulness of the Fuchun resort belies its proximity to the bustling modern cities of Hangzhou and Shanghai. This exclusive lakeside hideaway, the first of its kind in China, offers a quiet and luxurious take on rustic rural living. All seventy lakeside and garden rooms and the twelve villas with private pools offer Zen-inspired living quarters. Decked out in soothing neutrals and dark teak furniture, the rooms provide a welcome respite from the heat and humidity of the day.

The resort was originally inspired by a 700-year-old Yuan dynasty painting of the local landscape, and it has successfully captured the dreamlike feel of the art. Total relaxation and revitalization is the philosophy of the resort, where peace and serenity reign supreme. Take time out in the spa for a soothing treatment, such as the Hangzhou-spun silk cocoon package, which is inspired by local traditions, or a jasmine and pearl scrub by the Balinese therapists to buff your body into baby-smooth perfection. Alternatively take a dip in the cool black swimming pool or soak in one of the three outdoor granite whirlpool tubs, and savor the silence and the solitude.

You can indulge your inner hippie with a yoga or tai chi class, both of which are held on the picture-perfect waterside verandas. Golfing enthusiasts will be in seventh heaven because there is an eighteen-hole course within the hotel's grounds, as well as two tennis courts where you can perfect your serve. When hunger strikes, the award-winning T8 restaurant serves up excellent East meets West cuisine, whereas the Asian Corner offers a selection of local specialties. **HA**

Join in Tai Chi at Dawn

Location Shanghai, China
Website www.chenqiang.net **Price** 🌓

Do not stay up too late in the ritzy bars and high-rise restaurants of Shanghai, because you will need to wake up early if you are to enjoy one of the city's more fascinating sights: its residents practicing tai chi at dawn. There is no specific location. Just wander the streets and lanes of the former French Concession and you will see them in groups. Sometimes four or five elderly neighbors slowly undulate their limbs to music played from a tinny old tape recorder.

Head to any one of the city's green spaces and you will find hundreds of people exercising. By the rose beds in Fuxing Park, an old man, totally bald, is wrapped in solitary concentration as he twists his

> *"Tai chi does not mean oriental wisdom or something exotic. It is the wisdom of your own senses. "*
>
> Chungliang Al Huang, tai chi master

hand above his head. Others exercise in groups—and it is not just tai chi. A gathering of about fifty people stands in formation and practices aerobics to loud, tape recorder tones. Women with fancy hairdos dance with fans, while a few feet away a young man is coached by an elder in sword-fighting techniques. Doddering old men walk with birds in cages, which they hang from the trees' branches before sitting on benches and slowly sipping green tea from jam jars.

It is certainly a sociable scene, and one that somehow transcends the modern rush of Shanghai. The traditions still remain in this slick, supercharged city. You just have to get up early enough to see them. **PE**

Stay at Sanya Nanshan

Location Hainan, China
Website www.treehousesofhawaii.com/nanshan.html **Price** 🌓🌓

The island of Hainan is the southernmost of China's provinces and the world's second-largest oceanic island. Bathed in the warm waters of the South China Sea, with a mountainous interior, mild climate, and miles of white-sand beaches, the Chinese refer to it as the "Oriental Hawaii." If you walk back from the beach near the southern city of Sanya on Yalong Bay and gaze up into the forest canopy, you will discover that the hinterland along Hainan's southern shoreline is an excellent place to build a tree house.

Four tree houses, to be precise, all safely ensconced high in the canopies of a small cluster of carefully selected tamarind trees, known for their dense, durable wood and more than capable of keeping aloft your average tree house. The tree houses at Sanya Nanshan are integrated into their living hosts to the point of being camouflaged, and they are linked to one another by rope and plank walkways high above the forest floor. The tree houses do have electricity but a brief walk is required if you need to have a shower. By their very nature they are not spacious, but they are very neat, and all have spectacular views of the ocean beyond. Big Beach in the Sky can sleep up to six people over two levels, or Beach Club Treehouse sleeps two and is just a minute's walk from the beach.

The nearby Sanya Nanshan Buddhist Cultural Theme Park is the largest Buddhist temple built since the establishment of the People's Republic of China in 1959 and is a must-see when in the region. Covering 66 acres (27 ha), it has unrivaled representations of late Tang dynasty (618–907) architecture and also contains the beautiful Golden Jade Kwan-yin statue, a national treasure which is encrusted with more than 221 pounds (100 kg) of gold, silver, and jade. **BS**

Explore Sun Moon Lake

Location Sun Moon Lake, Central Taiwan, China
Website www.sunmoonlake.gov.tw/sun.aspx?Lang=EN   **Price** ◑

Located at an altitude of 2,500 feet (760 m), the emerald and often misty waters of central Taiwan's Sun Moon Lake epitomize Far Eastern serenity and natural beauty. Surrounded by mountains, and consisting of two parts that are crescent-shaped and circular respectively (hence giving the lake its name), Taiwan's largest inland body of water has emerged as one of the island's most popular tourist destinations.

The area is populated by the Thao people, Taiwan's smallest aboriginal tribe, who consider Lalu, the island that divides the two sections of the lake, the home of their ancestral spirits. For just over twenty years a so-called "matchmaker pavilion" that hosted group weddings was situated on the island, but this government institution (along with most other parts of the island) vanished in the lake during the big earthquake of 1999, leaving only a quaint islet behind.

Meanwhile, the scenic shoreline road is interspersed with twentieth-century yet traditional-style temples and parks like the Peacock Garden, where two hundred of the majestic birds roam the grounds. Ita Thao—the local tribe's main settlement—on the other hand, gives a glimpse into Thao culture, with exhibitions and performances providing a stimulating insight into their customs. But a visit to Sun Moon Lake is mostly about the tranquil scenery that is reminiscent of Far Eastern landscape paintings, with Taiwan's tropical location guaranteeing good weather all year-round. The fact that swimming in the lake is prohibited contributes to the region's peacefulness, and renting a rowboat is the perfect way to enjoy some solitude on the water and to appreciate the stunning forests of the surrounding mountains. **DaH**

Visit Big Buddha and Po Lin Monastery

Location Lantau Island, Hong Kong, China
Website www.discoverhongkong.com; www.plm.org.hk   **Price** ◑

Forget the commercial side of Hong Kong for a minute. Visit Lantau Island by ferry and you will see the grand seated statue of the Big Buddha, the world's largest outdoor bronze Buddha, and the most peaceful place to spend an afternoon in the city.

The Buddha is part of Po Lin Monastery, which has been on this mountainous site since 1906. The bus drops you at the bottom of the steps; with the bronze Buddha smiling down on you, it is up to you whether to climb the steps to the top next to the fluttering multicolored flags, browse the trinket stalls, or visit the museum. Inside the monastery are two of the

> *"Three things cannot be long hidden: the sun, the moon, and the truth."*
>
> Buddha

Buddha's relics, which magically appear to change color according to who looks at them. Just looking at the Buddha, you will feel him radiating inner peace—and that is no casual accident. It is all in the design: As he sits in the Lotus pose, his features are wide and calm, signifying serenity. His raised right hand removes all fear, and his left hand on his thigh is placed in the "wish-fulfilling" posture. Take a moment to let it sink in, soaking up his tranquil features and air of peace, before heading back to the hyperactive city. **LD**

⮕ *Big Buddha symbolizes the harmonious relationship between man and nature, and people and religion.*

Unwind at Jia

Location Causeway Bay, Hong Kong, China
Website www.jiahongkong.com **Price** ⑤⑤

> *"The interior focuses on spatial clarity, comfort, and style, with ultra-modern amenities."*

Proprietors, Jia

Jia means "home" in Mandarin, and this Philippe Starck–designed boutique hotel, the first in Asia, certainly offers a welcome respite from the buzzing hustle and bustle of Hong Kong. Situated in the Causeway Bay area of the city, Jia has been styled using nature as its central theme, creating an ultra-chic yet supremely comfortable environment.

With fifty-four rooms in a twenty-five-story former office block, this hotel may look unremarkable from the outside, but once inside, you find yourself in a contemporary oasis: all white walls, teak floors, and tasteful objets d'art. If you are really pushing the boat out, book into one of the one-bedroom suites or two-bedroom penthouses, which offer breathtaking views over the city and outstanding furnishings. If you want to catch some sun, head to the sundeck on the second floor, where you can relax quietly with a complimentary glass of wine at cocktail hour.

Although Hong Kong offers a huge diversity of eating opportunities, from swanky restaurants to stalls in the street, rooms at the Jia come kitted out with well-equipped kitchenettes, so you need not leave your room if you do not want to. That would be a pity, though, because there is so much to see in the local vicinity. Across the road is a traditional Chinese medicine shop that sells birds' nests and more, whereas next door is Jardine's Bazaar with its lovely afternoon vegetable and flower market and its heaving night market. The famous Sogo department store and Causeway Bay subway are just a street away, and Victoria Park is a short stroll to the east. **HA**

↖ *The penthouse living area is simply designed, filled with clean lines, warm lighting, and cozy couches.*

Walk the MacLehose Trail

Location New Territories, Hong Kong, China
Website www.oxfamtrailwalker.org.hk/en/home.html   **Price** 🌓

Those who think that Hong Kong is one big concrete sprawl should think again. Some 40 percent of the territory is protected as country park. The 60-mile (96-km) MacLehose Trail cuts across some of the best parts, traversing the New Territories' lush, snake-infested jungles, immaculate white beaches, turquoise waters, and soaring mountain peaks, including Hong Kong's highest, Tai Mo Shan (Big Hat Mountain), which climbs to more than 3,000 feet (915 m).

Named for a former Hong Kong governor, Crawford Murray MacLehose, who was fond of hiking, the trail was opened in 1979, and two years later the Gurkhas inaugurated the first Trailwalker event—a race that covers the trail's entire length—as a training exercise. In 1986, the race opened to the public and since then almost 50,000 people have taken part, raising funds for international charity Oxfam. The fastest-ever team completed the distance in just under twelve hours.

Meet any of the competitors in the week after the race and they will be sure to tell you about their knees. Those with bad joints, beware: the trail specializes in ups and downs, and there are an awful lot of concrete steps. You do not have to walk the entire distance all at once, however, or in fact more just than a little bit if you want. The route is divided into ten stages, from Pak Tam Chung, on the east coast of the New Territories in Sai Kung Country Park, to Tuen Mun in the west. Most of the sections are around 6 miles (9 km) long, so you can hike just one or two of them, stopping for a dip in the ocean on the way. And, this being Hong Kong, they are all easily accessible from the road, so when you finish, you can hop in a taxi or on a bus and go directly to the nearest noodle restaurant for a much-deserved refuel. **PE**

Stay at Langham Place

Location Mong Kok, Hong Kong, China
Website www.hongkong.langhamplacehotels.com/en   **Price** 💲💲

One of the most exciting things about Hong Kong is its bustle. Set in the middle of Mong Kok, a good distance from any other five-star hotels, Langham Place is technically out on a limb. Yet that is what makes it so special. Just one block away from the humid markets where you can buy anything from durian to goldfish and Nike sneakers, the hotel is the calm in the eye of the storm.

Langham Place was built with the local people in mind; sure, you can see them in clear focus from your hotel window as they hang their laundry out and go about their daily business in the nearby tenements, but just by being in this area, the hotel is giving back

> *"[Langham Place] is a refreshingly elegant and luxurious hotel in the bustling heart of Mong Kok."*
>
> luxurytravel.com

to the local economy. All across the hotel, local art sets the scene, and the stand-out feature, the Chuan spa, is Chinese, too. This offers a sauna, steam room, plenty of Chinese treatments including reflexology, and a rooftop pool, open to all guests.

Service is impeccable, and rooms are wonderfully technologically advanced, from the pillows to the iHome MP3 players. The stand-out room is the Chuan Spa Suite, where breathtaking views of Hong Kong harbor greet you alongside trays of Chinese sweets, herbal teas, soothing music, and an exceptional spa suite. Switch off in your own private steam room, or watch the water overflow in your infinity bath. **LD**

Explore Mai Po Wetlands

Location Mai Po, Hong Kong, China
Website www.wwf.org.hk/eng/maipo   **Price** $

The sky suddenly darkens as a cloud gathers overhead. It is not a storm brewing over the Mai Po wetlands; rather it is a huge flock of birds filling the winter sky. Every year up to 60,000 waterbirds, such as gulls, herons, egrets, and black-faced spoonbills, descend on the marshy wetlands during their annual southerly migration. They travel along the East Asian–Australasian Flyway, which starts in the Arctic Circle and extends through Southeast Asia and on to Australia and New Zealand. Mai Po is a handy midway point—a tropical stopover where the birds can rest and refuel before completing their grueling journey.

More than 350 species of domestic and migratory birds throng to the natural reserve in the northwest corner of Hong Kong, which was designated a Wetland of International Importance in 1995. They flock to the traditional shrimp-breeding ponds, known as *gei wai*, and roost in the trees in their thousands. In spring the weather warms, the winter birds start to make their way back home, and the wetlands enter a new phase of life. The trees bud and blossom; the *gei wai* fill with juicy shrimp, and the shorebirds gorge hungrily before continuing their long flight home. Brightly colored damselflies and dragonflies complete their metamorphosis and begin to emerge from the freshwater ponds.

Summer brings the breeding season. It is at this time that the resident birds shed their dull winter coats and transform into the colorful plumage that they will use to entice mates. In the evening, the night air is filled with the soothing chirrup of the insects and the croaky sound of frogs. You may even see snakes slithering along the paths. In autumn, the annual bird migration begins, and the cycle starts all over again. **JP**

Relax at the Peninsula

Location Kowloon, Hong Kong, China
Website www.peninsula.com   **Price** $$$

A stay at Hong Kong's grand old lady begins at the airport when you are swiftly whisked to the hotel by a chauffeur-driven Rolls-Royce, part of the Peninsula's famous fleet. Or if you are feeling really flash (and flush), you can arrive by helicopter, because the hotel has two rooftop helipads for its super-rich guests.

Opened in 1928, the Pen is the city's oldest hotel. Like the buzzing metropolis of Hong Kong, the hotel's opulent and palatial lobby is a hive of frenzied activity, shimmering with sophistication, but once you step into the elevator to your room, silence and calm prevail.

Right in the heart of Hong Kong's entertainment district, the Peninsula offers dramatic views of Victoria

> *"The service is beyond attentive—it makes you say 'wow' every time."*
>
> concierge.com

Harbour. Choose a top-floor suite to drink in the city's glittering skyline. Rooms are plush, and the devil is in the detail; guests can operate the temperature, curtains, humidity, lights, and television from a bedside panel. Marble bathrooms have mood lighting, and the decor fuses European style with Asian touches; it is all old-world elegance combined with richly colored fabrics, Western furniture, and Asian art, lamps, and porcelain.

On the rooftop is Felix, one of Hong Kong's hippest restaurants, and a Roman-themed pool, festooned with columns, friezes, and statues. If you have not got the cash to splash at this fine hotel, then dress up smart and pay a visit for afternoon tea. **JK**

Camp at Three Camel Lodge

Location Gobi Desert, Mongolia
Website www.threecamellodge.com **Price** $

Nomadic souls can rest their weary heads at this luxury wilderness camp in Mongolia's rugged Gobi Desert. Sitting in the shadows of the beautiful Gobi-Altai Mountains in Gurvansaikhan National Park, Three Camel Lodge blends perfectly with the stunning natural beauty of the surrounding desert.

Sheltered by a 54-million-year-old volcanic outcrop and laid out across the Gobi's floor are the forty-five felt *gers* (nomadic tents) and a striking main lodge. Like the homes of the nomadic herders that inspired them, the handmade gers are rustic, roomy, and comfortable, with wood-burning stoves, hand-painted wooden beds, and indigenous furniture. Each one can accommodate up to four guests and has twenty-four-hour electricity from solar panels. The main lodge has been crafted by local artisans, without using a single nail, in the style of Mongolian Buddhist architecture.

This is a serious eco-retreat; solar and wind power are harnessed to provide evening light and constant hot water, and animal dung fuels the stoves. The remote location in the wild heart of the desert is the perfect place to see ancient stone carvings of wild sheep, ibex, and antelope around the volcanic outcrop. There is also the chance to meet modern-day nomads who pass through the lodge to tend their livestock. Go hiking in the foothills of the Gobi-Altai Mountains, camel trekking through sand dunes, horseback riding in mountain valleys, and digging for dinosaur fossils at the legendary Flaming Cliffs. When the sun sets, simply sit back to watch the spectacular night sky cover the desert. **AD**

↗ *At night take in the views across the desert from the wooden porch and stone terraces of the endless steppe.*

"This is top hospitality in one of the world's most inhospitable regions, the Gobi."

Independent

Discover Lake Khövsgöl

Location Khankh, Mongolia
Website www.mongoliatourism.gov.mn   **Price** ◐

One of the most beautiful and accessible areas of Mongolia, Lake Khövsgöl is surrounded by forest-clad hills and flower-filled meadows. Overlooked by the dramatic Khoridol Saridag Mountains, the crystal-clear waters form the country's largest and deepest lake, and it holds 2 percent of the world's fresh water. Khövsgöl is also one of the most pristine lakes, with water so clean it can be drunk without treatment.

Come here to fish for Siberian grayling or learn how nomad families tend their reindeer herds. Take the ferry between Khatgal and Khankh to explore the reaches of the Khövsgöl National Park, which is bigger than California's Yellowstone Park. The park is home to a variety of wildlife, from ibex and elks to wolves, brown bears, and moose. It is also a stopping-off point for migrating birds from Siberia, which means there is serious bird-watching to be done. For the full-on experience, sleep in a cozy yurt, lined with felt to insulate against the cold and heated with a traditional wood-burning stove.

In an arid land where so many lakes are salty, it is no surprise to learn that Khövsgöl is considered sacred in this Buddhist country. There are few roads in the region, and locals travel on horseback. In winter, when temperatures plummet and the lake freezes over, horse-drawn sleds cross the ice, piled with goods for trading on the Siberian border. The highlight of the season is the Ice Festival, a midwinter celebration held on the frozen lake. Watch nomadic strongmen pit their wits against each other in ice sumo and tug-of-war competitions, then see sled and skating races. **AD**

➡ *One of the world's seventeen ancient lakes, Khövsgöl is more than two million years old.*

See Kamuiwakka-no-taki

Location Hokkaido Island, Japan
Website www.japan-guide.com/e/e6851.html   **Price** 🔴

The thermal waterfalls of Kamuiwakka-no-taki situated in the wild, mountainous peninsula of the Shiretoko National Park on Hokkaido Island make for a unique bathing experience. Translated literally as "water of the gods" in the local Ainu language, the thermal waterfall is one of the world's wonders. It spews out of the depths of the volcanic earth with its faintly sulfurous odor before bubbling past a system of vents and then gushing out into a channel through the woodland, leaving clouds of steam in its wake. The simmering water then splashes through a series of limpid pools offering a choice of bathing opportunities, though the highest pool is the warmest, and probably the most beautiful. As the water is slightly acidic, any minor cuts and grazes will sting when you submerge yourself, but once you get used to the water, it's supremely relaxing, and reputed to have health-giving properties.

The Japanese describe this state of immersion as "boiled octopus," which may not sound particularly enticing, but rest assured, you won't want to leave. You can relax near the trees and listen to the soporific background noise of the rushing water, which is colder at the bottom and swirls and eddies to become warmer nearer the surface. Unlike most hot springs in Japan, you are permitted to wear a bathing suit, though make sure you take some sensible shoes to walk in, as the surrounding rocks can become very slippery. There is a lot to explore in the national park once you have had your fill of the thermal falls, including some spectacular forests of fir, birch, and oak. There are also some great hot springs, including Norboribetsu Onsen, one of the best public baths in Japan, as well as various active volcanoes, including Tarumae-zan, which last erupted in 1982. **HA**

Relax at Aoni Onsen

Location Aomori, Japan
Website www.onsenexpress.com   **Price** 🟢

Oozing rustic charm, the isolated Aoni Onsen offers the most evocative bathing in northern Japan. It is no surprise to hear that it is also known as "lamp no yado" because it has run for decades without electricity. Even today, oil lamps are used to light the hot springs for guests, who are cocooned in peaceful solitude.

Arrive in winter when the *onsen* is surrounded by snow, and the only sound is the gentle tumbling of the mountain stream. The mixed *rotenburo* bath is open to the elements on one side and looks out to a roaring waterfall, whereas inside, segregated baths have soothing views of the nearby river. A favorite of the onsen cognoscenti, Aoni is in a tiny valley deep in

---

"The Japanese have turned onsen, or hot springs, into an art form … the focus on bathing and food."

Independent

---

the idyllic Shirakami mountains close to Hakkoda-san. This traditional *ryokan* has thirty-two rooms and was originally opened in 1931 by a poet, Youga Niwa, in search of the water's curative properties. Today, the ryokan still reflects the artistic and peaceful mind of the poet. The sliding doors of tatami rooms open onto rock gardens and pretty ponds.

This remote getaway offers a return to a forgotten time, and there is a monastic pleasure to be had. Icicles hang from the rooftops, and when the blue winter light of dusk fades on the snow, there is nothing to do but snuggle by a roaring fire. In warmer months, hike in the mountains to see deer, sable, and antelope. **AD**

Unwind at Zao Onsen

Location Yamagata, Japan
Website www.zao-spa.or.jp/english   **Price** 💲

Open-air baths do not come more impressive than this. Nestled at the mouth of the Zao national park, the largest of the steaming pools of purifying waters at the Zao Onsen is big enough to hold 200 people. The highlight of the rustic *dai rotem buro*, a trio of bubbling outdoor pools, is a massive tub built into a ravine with spectacular views of the forest-covered mountains.

Discovered as far back as 110 C.E., the Zao hot springs are the oldest of the three great hot springs of Japan's northeast Tohoku region. According to local legend, a wounded warrior drew an arrow from his body and cleaned the wound at a spring. The injury recovered miraculously, and the healing properties of the waters became famous. The high acidity of the milky white waters, which maintain a constant temperature of nearly 125°F (52°C), is still regarded as a cure for skin conditions and gastrointestinal disorders.

The village has managed to maintain its traditional charm and an almost Zen-like sense of calm. After a soak in the springs, wander through the lantern-filled streets lined with rickety *ryokan* inns. A bus ride away from Yamagata bullet train station, Zao Onsen is as popular with skiers as with hot spring lovers. When snow falls, it is transformed into a winter wonderland with spectacular ice-covered trees, better known as "snow monsters." One of the oldest ski resorts in Japan, the mountain at Zao Onsen reaches an altitude of more than 4,000 feet (1,220 m). For the brave, the Wall is a 1,000-foot (305-m) run with a 30-degree slope. For a more laid-back alternative, lights illuminate the piste for romantic night skiing. **AD**

↗ *The water rushing from the hot springs will ease your joints in all seasons, leaving you completely relaxed.*

"Wash yourself outside the bath. Getting soap in the water is the most heinous of onsen faux pas."

David Atkinson, *Independent*

Discover Nikko

Location Tochigi, Japan   **Website** www.nikko-jp.org/english/index.html
Price 💲

> "Build a small shrine in Nikko and enshrine me as the God. I will be the guardian of peacekeeping."

Shogun Ieyasu Tokugawa, 1542–1616

Packs of chattering monkeys stand between you and the entrance to this atmospheric shrine complex in the mountains of northern Japan. Avoiding the creatures as best you can, pick your way through the woodland up the final stairs, and you will find yourself face to face with the impressive Rinno-ji temple, founded in 766. Its large hall is full of treasures from Edo-period Japan, and there is a beautiful nineteenth-century landscaped garden outside.

Venture farther into the shrine complex and you will find that the temples become increasingly spectacular, with lines of ornate stone lanterns, tombs, treasure towers, and statues showing ancient samurai baring their teeth and fiercely flashing their eyes at visitors. The Taiyuin-byo Shrine, which houses the ashes of shogun Tokugawa Iemitsu (1603–1605), is particularly splendid. It sits at the top of a series of elaborate red and golden gates, in a grove of Japanese cedars.

There is something about the geographic isolation of Nikko, a village set high in the mountains, that makes this complex feel very different from other shrines and temples you may see. The Shinto belief in Kami, the existence of a spiritual being or genius of a particular place, seems particularly poignant here in the silence of the forests, and the sense that something magical lurks nearby is not easily shaken off.

Nearby, the historic, vermillion Shinkyo bridge and Nikko Botanical Gardens are also very beautiful, as is Ganmna-ga-fuchi, a scenic river that runs a pale, mineral blue through the old lava flows of nearby Mount Nantai and has a statue-lined footpath. **CW**

↖ *This five-story pagoda is one of a stunning selection to be found in the shrine complex at Nikko.*

Stay at Seiyo Ginza Hotel

Location Tokyo, Japan **Website** www.seiyo-ginza.com
Price 💲💲

The discreet profile of Seiyo Ginza Hotel is deliberate. Many guests are members of royalty, celebrities, or wealthy chief executives, and the hotel's quietly understated luxury is very welcome. Seiyo is housed in an ultra-modern building between the upscale shopping and lively nightlife of the Ginza area and the bustle of the Nihombashi financial center.

Inside the hotel, exclusive clients are welcomed into a sparse but enormous lobby where check-in happens in comfortable chairs at individual desks amid hushed tranquility. The style is crisp and modern, but as you explore deeper into the hotel, it becomes more cozily opulent. You will find huge displays of fresh flowers on

> ## "The hotel's snob appeal is enhanced by Japan's first 24-hour personalized butler service."
>
> *New York Times*

your way to the traditionally furnished but individually designed bedrooms. The most elaborate rooms have seventeenth-century Japanese screens, four-poster beds, and large dining rooms. The bathrooms are said to be among Japan's biggest; many include a steam bath, shower stall, walk-in closets, luxury toiletries, choice of bathrobes, and a copious use of marble.

Visitors may contemplate where to eat. The hotel has a signature restaurant serving contemporary French cuisine, an award-winning Italian restaurant, and a gourmet Japanese restaurant. If you feel like a snack between meals, a bakery sells pastries, cookies, and chocolates freshly made on the premises. **SH**

Enjoy the Peninsula

Location Tokyo, Japan **Website** http://tokyo.peninsula.com
Price 💲💲💲

In fast-paced, frenetic Tokyo, sometimes visitors crave a place of refinement to escape the crowds, traffic, and flashing neon. Before the Peninsula opened in late 2007, the city's five-star hotels were all located in slightly down-at-heel areas, and the city's designer-clad population was crying out for a hotel in a more chic area. The Peninsula, a block from the city's best luxury shopping area, fits the bill perfectly and is an incredibly upmarket oasis.

In the vast modern lobby underneath a remarkable domed modern chandelier, which drops delicate, hair-fine shards of glass toward the floor, Tokyo's classiest women meet for afternoon tea while the tinkle of a piano plays in the background. The Imperial Palace, home to Japan's royal family, is overlooked by the hotel and had never been seen from this angle before the hotel was constructed. Rooms are vast—impressive, given Tokyo's space crisis—and the hotel has a total of five restaurants. Of these, Peter, at the top, is showing-off at its finest, with sleek modern lines, impressive views of the city, and an ambience that is perfect for aperitifs and cigars. It feels like a scene from a movie set, and members of the Hollywood elite are regular visitors. The cocktails alone will make you feel like you are floating on air.

On level two of the hotel, the Cantonese Hei Fung terrace restaurant offers another special view: a glass-enclosed dining room in the center of the kitchen, called the Chef's Table, as well as three private dining rooms. All this, plus a luxurious spa, chauffeur-driven Rolls-Royce, top-end jewelry stores, and an exquisite patisserie, makes the Peninsula effortlessly glamorous and a place where you can easily convince yourself that you are part of the jet set. **LD**

Visit Hakone National Park

Location Kanagawa, Japan
Website www.japaneseguesthouses.com/db/hakone **Price** $

Hakone National Park is one of five parks that make up Japan's Fuji-Hakone-Izu National Park, centered around Lake Ashinoko, or Ashi as it is affectionately known, a venerated site in Japan with unparalleled views of the majestic Mount Fuji. It is a popular day-trip destination among tourists keen to venture out of Tokyo.

Located within a volcanic region, Hakone is famous for its hot springs, health resorts, spas, and treatment centers. The area has long been thought to possess magical qualities, and people seeking rejuvenation flock here in the thousands. Never fear if you have not booked into one of the treatment hotels; it is still possible to enjoy a sake bath with green tea: Hakone Kowakien Yunessun is a hot springs spa resort and water amusement park open to the public all year-round, a perfect pit stop after trekking the peaks of mounts Komagatake and Kanmurigatake. Those seeking a longer life head to Owakudani, in the Great Boiling Valley, an area with active sulfur vents and hot springs. Here they boil eggs, which turn black and slightly sulfuric, and if you can stand the smell, legend has it that eating one egg adds seven years to your life.

Hakone also boasts the widely celebrated Hakone Botanical Garden of Wetlands and an open-air museum, with masterpieces on display by renowned modern artists, including Picasso, Rodin, and Miro. However, it is Lake Ashi that steals the show. It is set in a dreamlike landscape with snow-covered Fuji as a backdrop and the bright red torii gates of Hakone Jinja shrine to the fore, a Shinto shrine forever marking the entrance to a sacred space, another world. **LM**

→ *At 12,390 feet (3,776 m) high, Mount Fuji dominates the skyline across the waters of Lake Ashi.*

Explore Kamakura

Location Kanagawa, Japan
Website www.asahi-net.or.jp/~qm9t-kndu   **Price** ❶

This sleepy town might be just 31 miles (50 km) from Tokyo, but it feels like a world away. There are no high-rise buildings reaching dizzyingly up into the sky or neon-lit karaoke bars here. Kamakura was the capital of Japan during the shogunate from 1185 to 1333, when it was the fourth-largest city in the world. Steeped in history, it is the antithesis of the modern capital. Day-trippers from Tokyo flock here to enjoy the cooling sea breezes while they visit the Buddhist temples and Shinto shrines. Surrounded to the north, east, and west by mountains and to the south by the waters of Sagami Bay, Kamakura is a natural fortress. The setting is as dramatic today as it was in its heyday all those centuries ago. The landmark is the monumental bronze Buddha, which looks out over the city.

During the thirteenth century, Kamakura was also the cradle of Nichiren Buddhism. Nichiren was not local; he was born in Awa Province, but came to the political center of the country to teach, and the town has been associated with him ever since.

To see Kamakura at its best, follow the three-hour walk from the Tokeiji, up through the forest to the Kotokuin. Go to the Zeniarai Benten shrine to see the money-washing ceremony, which purifies offerings, and stop at temples along the way. The only sound you will hear is the song of nightingales as you pass blooming purple irises and bountiful plum trees.

The city is not all about ancient history. The beach is a big attraction, as well as the *senbei*—crisp rice cakes grilled and sold fresh along the main shopping street. Try one for a taste of the real Japan. **AD**

← *The bamboo forest by the Hokoku-ji Temple is famed for its beauty and Zen-like serenity.*

Unwind at Hoshinoya

Location Nagano, Japan
Website www.hoshinoya.com   **Price** ❺❺

The ritual of bathing has never been more sublime than at the new, stylish Hoshinoya resort. This is no traditional *onsen* (hot spring); Hoshinoya sits firmly in the twenty-first century. Green geothermal energy supplies the underfloor heating, and the surroundings are seriously contemporary. Dark wood and stone floors replace the familiar tatami mats. As well as open-air baths, a maze of low-ceilinged indoor baths leads to a meditation bath lit by underwater spotlights. Soothing music works well with the heat and sulfurous vapors to give a memorable bathing experience.

Outside, lush terraces and waterfalls are a feast for the senses, surrounded by Karuizawa's thick forest of

> *"The most essential elements of an onsen ryokan are its location and quality of onsen water."*

Hiroshi Ebisawa, architect and designer

Japanese maple, which turns glorious shades of gold and crimson in the autumn. Near Nagano, in central Honshu, the resort's cottages are arranged around a small river. No two rooms are the same, although each one has a private bathtub that looks out over the river and luxuriously fills with onsen water at the touch of a button. Walls are the soothing color of green tea, and bedrooms have majestic cathedral ceilings.

Away from the onsen, there are guided eco-tours of the forest and stargazing evenings. Curl up in the library with a good book or join other guests for gentle morning stretching exercises at the Chaya wooden tea house pavilion. Hoshinoya is hot spring heaven. **AD**

Stay in Myoren-ji Temple

Location Kyoto, Japan
Website www.pref.kyoto.jp/visitkyoto/en   **Price** 💲

Although many people who have never been to Japan associate it with *Lost in Translation*–style luxury hotels, those in the know and in search of isolation head for one of the country's many *shukubos*. These are Japanese temples or shrines that provide accommodation for all, even for those who are not spiritually inclined but who would nonetheless like to experience traditional, religious Far Eastern life. Customarily places of worship, these days the *shukubos* welcome people of all denominations, and visitors are able to learn about the Zen Buddhist practice of *zaza* (an exercise aimed at calming both the body and the mind in order to gain insight into the essence of existence).

The thirteenth-century Myoren-ji temple in the former imperial capital of Kyoto is a remarkable sanctuary belonging to the Nichiren Buddhist sect, and it offers basic accommodation in a picturesque setting. Situated in a quiet area and within easy walking distance of Kyoto's city center, the temple's accommodation for visitors consists of rooms with sliding (and often intricately painted) *shoji* partitions and traditional tatami mats. The bathroom has to be shared with fellow travelers and the resident monks, and the only bathing facilities are at the public bathhouse outside the premises. Fundamentally, however, the experience of staying at this temple is not about luxurious indulgence. The stunning rock garden in front of one of the eight smaller temples and the peaceful surroundings more than offset the inconveniences of its limitations.

The elaborate architecture of the old buildings combined with the hands-on introduction to time-honored Japanese traditions make for an experience that is truly worthy of the term "escape." **DaH**

Visit Fushumi Inari Shrine

Location Kyoto, Japan
Website www.japan-guide.com   **Price** 💲💲

The beautiful maple tree–lined woodland trails up Mount Inari in southern Kyoto have been a Japanese pilgrimage destination for the last 1,300 years. Driving a line straight through this natural beauty, however, and somehow managing to create something even more impressive, is the winding pathway of man-made, bright red torii gates that leads from the base of the mountain up to the Fushimi Inari shrine at the top. The 2.5-mile (4-km) passageway passes serene ponds, small waterfalls, beautiful cemeteries, and numerous areas dedicated to private worship. Free to walk around, and open every day at all hours, the walk will take you about two hours, and ends with the same

> *"Wander through the tunnels of torii in the woods . . . it is a magical experience as daylight fades."*
>
> sacred-destinations.com

spectacular view over the entire city of Kyoto, whether you see it in broad daylight or glittering neon at night.

Each season provides the walk with a different backdrop, mesmerizing in its own way. Summer offers a luscious, verdant forest setting, with the torii gates providing much-needed shade, whereas winter offers a snow-covered backdrop, the torii ensuring the steps of the path are clear and safe. Whether it is the bright red on green in the summer, or the more dramatic red on white in the winter, the effect is captivating. **CW**

➜ *Individual torii gates are common in Japan, but at Fushimi more than 10,000 line the way up Mount Inari.*

平成十三年 元旦建之

平成十八年一月吉日建之

平成十七年五月吉日建之

小田原市寿町一二六三二　株式会社　古川美濱

呉市東中央一・六・二　税理士　平松高雄

古川武法

名古屋市熱田区　(株)メイナン

東京都足立区鹿浜　日鈴産業機械(株)　鈴木啓之

京都市　技研トレーディング株式会社

州高岡市上麻生一二〇二　レンゴーロジスティクス(株)

金山月矢　高田良平

大阪近鉄バファローズ　梨田昌孝

愛媛県川之江市上分町　川上寺末口川　加藤絹子

東京都渋谷区渋谷二二五二　株式会社あいち研醸社

(株)奈良オオクワセンター

川庄かず史

株式会社グラディー　佐沢秋一馬

安藤土木建築(株)

昭和建設　山岡宣子　寛治郎

名古屋貴業(株)

高橋剛

Experience Hiiragiya Ryokan

Location Kyoto, Japan
Website www.hiiragiya.co.jp/en **Price** 🟢🟢

> "It is . . . at Hiiragiya that I wistfully recall that sense of tranquility that belonged to old Japan."

Yasunari Kawabata, writer

Should you be given the disturbing news that you are officially dead, do not panic. You have probably just tied your *yukata* (house robe) right over left—kimono speak for "deceased"—and need to retie it.

More than 300 years old, Hiiragiya Ryokan is a historic inn that is widely regarded as the pinnacle of style and traditional hospitality. Look closely and you will see the wooden hitching posts, used by traveling feudal lords who arrived on horseback, on the long clay walls. Such grand arrivals might be a thing of the past, but theater comes with the territory, and thanks to six generations of the same family, service is as sharp as a samurai sword.

After a flurry of bowing on arrival, a personal maid leads guests to their rooms. These are measured in units of tatami mats; the largest sleeps seven. Some come with a delightful cedar tub, which keeps water hot for hours. Rooms are simple but attention to detail is faultless, and to maintain an air of authenticity some do not have televisions. Guests spend far too much time bathing and eating to miss that, though. The traditional *kaiseki* meal (akin to tucking into several major works of art one after the other) is the highlight of a stay here and demands both an empty stomach and a sense of adventure. Ryokans are fertile ground for cultural faux pas, but once you have entered into the spirit and begun to relax, it can be great fun to don the *geta* (wooden clogs) and clip-clop around wearing the *yukata* to the communal bath and to dinner. The maid will fill your tub, roll out your tatami, and—should you need it—assist with tying that robe. **TM**

◩ *Hiiragiya (house of holly) is about as quintessential as the Japanese ryokan experience gets.*

Relax at Nishiyama Ryokan

Location Kyoto, Japan
Website http://nishiyamahotel.blogspot.com **Price** 💲💲

Stay at Benesse House

Location Naoshima Island, Kagawa, Japan
Website www.naoshima-is.co.jp **Price** 💲💲

The old capital city of Kyoto is one of Japan's biggest tourist attractions. It is a maze of alleyways and canals, grand Buddhist temples and tucked-away Shinto shrines, ancient wooden houses and minimalist gardens. In spring it is fragrant with cherry blossoms; in autumn its maples seem afire with color.

Nishiyama Ryokan is in the center of the city, near the City Hall. It stands on a quiet street near the Kamo River and the chic Shinkyogoku shopping area. The building is modern, but this family-run hotel re-creates the traditional atmosphere of a *ryokan*, or inn. With English-speaking staff, Nishiyama makes it easy for visitors to experience some of the culture of old Kyoto.

> *"It has a traditional atmosphere, from the old lantern above the door to the courtyard garden."*

kyotoinside.com

Bathers can gaze at the garden waterfall outside, and bathing is segregated. Japanese culture can intimidate some guests, but here the friendly staff will explain the protocol for public bathing. *Yukata* (light robes) are provided for all guests. Food is authentic, too, and very filling. Breakfast consists of boiled tofu, grilled fish, Japanese omelet, vegetables, miso soup, and rice. The wonderful Kaiseki dinner involves a multicourse ritual of fresh fish and vegetables. Most rooms have tatami mats and low tables that require you to sit Japanese-style on the floor. You are always offered green tea in your room, along with a specialty from Kyoto: delicious yatsuhashi cinnamon cakes. **SH**

The rooms at Benesse House in remote Naoshima Island on Japan's Inland Sea are, quite literally, works of art. A unique hybrid of art museum and boutique hotel, it is the inspiration of Soichiro Fukutake, president of Benesse Corporation, a publisher of books for children and the parent company of Berlitz language schools.

Featuring the work of a dozen internationally recognized names and a handful of rising Japanese artists, the museum takes a revolutionary approach to displaying its collection. The difference between Benesse and other galleries is that here the visitors do not leave—they stay for the night. Benesse also has a very hands-on approach to art. Guests can touch sculptures and get up close to paintings, and they can do it at any time of night or day.

Japanese architect Tadao Ando, best known for his pared-down places of worship, designed Benesse House. Carved out of a rocky headland on the southern tip of the island, it burrows into the earth, then opens out onto vast terraces, sun-filled patios, and sculpture-flecked lawns. The galleries are lit by strategically placed skylights and have massive, sliding glass doors. Roughly hewn marble steps lead directly into native brush, and trees grow out of atriums cut into rooms. The chapel-like central gallery—a concrete riff on a sacred grove—is crowned by a jutting glass pyramid that pierces the lawn above. It is one of the few parts of it that can be seen from the sea.

The beauty of the architecture is seen in the way the gallery space seamlessly blends into the bedrooms. Polished concrete walls and pale wood floors are evident throughout, punctuated by pieces of modern art. Life imitating art, indeed. **AD**

Cruise the Ayeyarwady

Location Ayeyarwady River, Myanmar
Website www.orient-express.com **Price** 🟢🟢🟢

On distant hills, the golden domes of exotic pagodas shimmer through vivid green trees. Along the riverbank, shaven-headed monks in maroon robes walk in single file to collect food and alms from beautiful women with strange gray paste on their cheeks. On the water itself, rickety rowboats stacked with sacks of rice float past shiny buffalo standing knee-deep in the shallows. All the mesmerizing images of an enticingly mysterious land unfold before your eyes as you watch from the top deck of a luxury cruiser drifting along the mighty Ayeyarwady River.

In tourism terms, Myanmar, also known as Burma, is wonderfully undersubscribed. That does not mean backpacking is the only option for visitors. The Orient-Express vessel *The Road to Mandalay* is a five-star, fifty-two-cabin river cruiser that sails between Mandalay and Bagan, and to Bhamo, near the Chinese border, stopping off along the way for sightseeing. The experience can be likened to a Nile cruise in Egypt, although fewer miles are covered and far fewer tourists crowd the best sights, such as Bagan and its 2,000 ornate pagodas and the gold-leafed Buddha in Mandalay's Mahamuni Pagoda. Life aboard is more luxurious, too. The ambience is chic, not stuffy, with lounges and cabins made comfy with local furnishings, furniture, and warm wood. Cuisine is rather special as well, featuring fragrant rice, curried beef and chicken, and spicy fish dishes with extra chili if you wish.

The journey is enriched with on-board cultural insights, from exquisite dancing to relaxed lectures on the country's music, religion, cuisine, and crafts. A beautiful girl also shows guests how to rub their faces with *thanaka*, a sandalwood paste that is used to protect skin from the sun. Mystery solved. **WG**

Relax at Tao Garden

Location Chiang Mai, Thailand
Website www.tao-garden.com **Price** 🟢

Founded by a Taoist meditation and qigong master, this resort in northern Thailand is at once a training camp in the Taoist arts and a relaxing holistic retreat. If you are coming to Chiang Mai from Bangkok—a likely scenario—you will immediately feel awash with relief, especially if you have traveled by sleeper train.

Far, far from the crowds and bustle of Bangkok, Chiang Mai's peaceful vibe is sure to charm, and that is even before you get to the oasis that is Tao Garden. With a holistic health spa and integrative medical clinic on the premises, Tao Garden is a virtual playground for those interested in alternative lifestyles and therapies. Take your pick from tai chi, qigong,

> *"[Chiang Mai] boasts a wealth of spas all geared to treating stressed minds and abused bodies."*
>
> Bob Kimmins, *Nation* magazine

acupuncture, herbal steam baths, saunas, colonic cleansings, and Chi Nei Tsang, a treatment for clearing blocked energy (chi) in the abdomen, which is thought to release toxins and negative emotions.

The retreat's unique fusion of East and West means you will find plenty of modern amenities, including badminton and tennis courts, a swimming pool, and a gym. Naturally, the resort's wellness ethos is at the heart of its restaurant, and the chefs source the majority of produce from the on-site organic gardens. Whether you are visiting the retreat to rev up, relax, or both, you will leave Tao Garden feeling rejuvenated and recharged. New look, new outlook. **JS**

Camp at Four Seasons

Location Chiang Rai, Thailand
Website www.fourseasons.com/goldentriangle **Price** ❺❺❺❺

If your idea of camping is a crawl-in tent, cold showers, and eating hot dogs, the Four Seasons Tented Camp will be something of an eye-opener. Part luxury resort and part wildlife reserve, the camp is located in the mountainous jungle region of the Golden Triangle—where the borders of Thailand, Laos, and Myanmar meet—high above the River Ruak.

The camp is accessible only by riverboat, and the journey itself is quite memorable. Having flown in to Chiang Rai airport, guests are driven to the west point of the camp (which is about a mile long), picked up by a luxury long tail boat, and ferried down the river to the camp's east post, where packhorses and a flurry of hosts bearing welcome drinks await. The entrance to each tent has a miniature shrine dedicated to the spirit Phra Phum, Sanskrit for "guardian of the spirit land," and there is a heart-stopping 260-foot- (80-m-) long suspension bridge over the San Valley leading to the spa. The "tents" at the camp are decked out with Asian antique furniture, king-size beds, a sundeck with two massage beds, and, best of all, enormous hand-hammered, Victorian-style copper bathtubs.

Six Indian elephants, rescued from the streets of Bangkok as part of a rehabilitation program, share the camp, and guests can feed, bathe, and ride them, as well as learn more about them from expert handlers, or *mahouts*. Meals are eaten together, whether it be a barbecue under the stars or a formal five-course meal in the main restaurant, and a party atmosphere soon prevails. You can also choose to dine privately if you wish, but where is the fun in that? **TW**

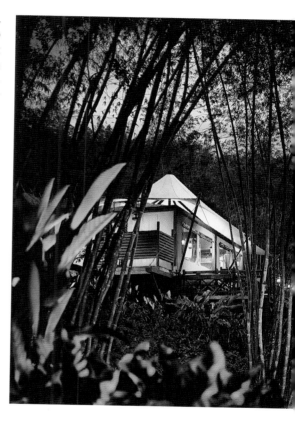

↗ *The intimate luxury camp comprises a collection of fifteen palatial "canopies" on stilts.*

"The magical bamboo-jungle setting is guaranteed to stir all the senses and many emotions."

Condé Nast Traveler

Experience Anantara Elephant Camp

Location Chiang Rai, Thailand
Website www.anantara.com **Price** 💲💲

On the northern border of Thailand, a resort unlike any other has successfully merged luxury and adventure in a place of legends. After a long flight and much driving along the picturesque rice paddies, Anantara feels like forever away. Luckily the reward is soon evident: beautiful exotic gardens and views stretching across the mighty Mekong River to three different countries.

Most of all, though, the resort is famous for its *mahout* (elephant trainer) camp, where guests are taught the art of "ele-driving." The daylong crash course to become a *mahout* is an incomparable experience, and a real privilege. Before you know it,

---

"The relationship with elephants is like a marriage. Trust and respect them—you will be repaid in kind."

Mahout (elephant trainer), Anantara

---

you will be riding elephants bareback and giving your impressive mount Thai commands to follow, then sliding off down its trunk like an old pro.

The entire resort pays homage to elephants: Even the towels in the designer bedrooms are cleverly folded origami style into elephant shapes. After a hard day's ele-driving, reward yourself with a dip in the infinity pool or a visit to the spa to be massaged in style cocooned in an atmosphere of dark woods, orchids, and silk. Excursions to what was once Burma and Laos are also part of the attraction. Once a mysterious no-man's land, the Golden Triangle is now a place to go for something totally different. **RCA**

Ride the Eastern *Orient Express* Train

Location Bangkok, Thailand to Singapore
Website www.orient-express.com **Price** 💲💲

The *Orient Express* has a certain mythical quality borne of its immaculate reputation. Synonymous with glamorous journeys and eccentric travelers voyaging to far-flung places, it is the ultimate in luxury rail travel.

Step aboard the elegant dark green and cream wagon to be transported back in time. The atmosphere is such that you are soon totally engulfed in the experience. The intricate marquetry and the plush soft furnishings are in traditional Thai and Malaysian styles, reminiscent of a time gone by. Originally built for the Silver Star in New Zealand, the train was redecorated by the British Pullman and the Venice Simplon-Orient-Express team, inspired by the 1932 movie *Shanghai Express*.

Televisions, radios, and cell phone ring tones are conspicuously absent, yet entertainment is all around. Set up camp in the observation car, an open-air car that is ideal for socializing with fellow passengers while appreciating the sights, or join in the day trips to the River Kwai or Penang. The restaurant car is another highlight of the trip: A formal dinner is served each evening, and dressing for dinner is de rigueur. The food is worthy of the best awards and is a real treat for the taste buds. Grilled snow-fish steak in peach soy butter or warm goat-cheese soufflé with lobster fricassee is followed by panfried sea bass with lemongrass risotto or even aromatic confit of duck with Szechuan vegetables. Mouthwatering desserts, such as delice of chocolate with cassis sauce or warm mango tart, come with petits fours and coffee before a digestif nightcap in the bar car. **RCA**

➔ *Looking at the view rolling past will keep you busy for hours, from Bangkok's tin shacks to lush jungle terrain.*

Stay at Sukhothai

Location Bangkok, Thailand **Website** www.sukhothai.com
Price 💲💲

Some hotels so cleverly encapsulate the essence of a destination within their hallowed walls that one barely feels the need to step out. Bucking the trend in a region famous for its skyscrapers, the Sukhothai's low-rise architecture, in the midst of lily ponds and lush gardens, offers a hint of what is to come.

Wooing discerning travelers to its fold long before the word "boutique" became fashionable, the Sukhothai wipes the floor with most of its latter-day pretenders. Step in from the maelstrom and you are enveloped in a prevailing ambience of utter calm— some achievement in the heart of Bangkok. Gracious staff, who seem to glide rather than walk about the place, are the icing on the cake in this well-oiled oasis.

In homage to the Thai kingdom's first capital, the eponymous Sukhothai, there is more than a nod to Thailand's golden age in the hotel's decor, which borrows its architectural and interior styling— symmetrical colonnades, reflection pools, and open-air arcades coupled with bronze, teakwood, marble, and fine fabrics—from the palatial salons of the ancient Thai kingdom. Dine alfresco by the lotus pond at the celebrated Celadon and leave time for relaxing by the stunning 80-foot (25-m) infinity pool, where the recently refurbished Spa Botanica brings poolside Thai massages to guests. As an added bonus, the hotel's moderate, seven-story design means the pool is almost entirely free of shade, something of a rarity in Bangkok. Word on the street is—if you want to be seen, you go to the Oriental. If you want to escape all that, check in to the Sukhothai. **TM**

➡ *Hushed, understated, and with a hint of the exotic,
the Sukhothai embodies the best of Thailand.*

Unwind at Leyana Spa

Location Bangkok, Thailand
Website www.leyanaspa.com **Price** ⊖

Amid the mayhem and chaos of Bangkok lies a haven of peace and tranquility, a lush green garden where the Leyana Spa offers original healing treatments that are the perfect antidote to the madness of the Thai capital. Four- and five-star hotels have long dominated the Bangkok spa scene, striving to outdo each other in trendy treatments and exotic preparations, yet too often forgetting the original purpose of a spa: to heal the body and refresh the spirit.

Kae, the young proprietor of Leyana Spa, believes in the healing powers of the touch of a good masseuse, a calm atmosphere, and freshly prepared scrubs and aromatic oils. She offers this in thirteen treatment

> *"All things here must not only be beautiful but super clean because that is what I would like."*

Proprietor, Leyana Spa

rooms (six of them doubles to accommodate couples), with whirlpool tubs and large, petal-filled white baths. Come early and sit in the Zen-like garden before your treatment while a therapist bathes your feet in warm water thick with soft rose petals. Sit back amid the greenery and count the delightful ceramic figures of cartoonlike Thai children peeking from behind the palm trees. Choose the ingredients for your treatments—honey and oatmeal, fresh coconut, juicy lemon, Thai tamarind—or discuss the benefits of an herbal steam bath versus a floral milk bath. Free from the day-to-day stresses at last, you will have the best spa treatment in Bangkok—healing and relaxing. **MN**

Relax at the Eugenia

Location Bangkok, Thailand
Website www.theeugenia.com **Price** ⊖⊖

Tucked away in the heart of downtown Bangkok sits the old-world beauty that is the Eugenia. The late-nineteenth-century, family-owned colonial house is more like a private home than a hotel, charmingly furnished with tasteful antiques and a garage full of vintage sedans and limousines.

Stepping through the door is a bit like taking a trip back in time, but the contemporary touches bring the hotel up to date. The twelve high-ceilinged suites have been lovingly put together with furniture collected from British and French colonial Myanmar, as well as India and Indo-China. Even the bathtubs have a glamorous boudoir feel, made of hand-beaten copper. The crisp white bed linen and soft feather pillows come all the way from Belgium.

Understated elegance is the key here. Guests can sip afternoon tea or a cocktail under swaying palm trees by the courtyard pool, or take a trip around the city in one of the chauffeur-driven Mercedes-Benzes or Jaguars. There is fine dining on offer at the D. B. Bradley dining room, named after a Christian missionary who was a pioneer in the introduction of Western medicine to Siam in 1835. The room is adorned with painted gold wallpaper and delicate china, but the menu has a more contemporary feel and serves truffles and quail eggs as well as crab miso soup and pad thai. The Zheng He lounge is named in honor of the great Chinese voyager Admiral Zheng He; it serves breakfast and an evening tapas menu.

Find a quiet corner during the day in the library to curl up with a good book, or browse the selection of art and design books on the shelves. It is a far cry from Bangkok's high-rise five-star hotels with their hundreds of rooms and full-on bling. **AD**

Stay at Shangri-La Hotel

Location Bangkok, Thailand
Website www.shangrila.com   **Price** 💲💲

In a noisy, humid, and polluted city like Bangkok, a good hotel is absolutely essential, and they do not come much better than the Shangri-La. Its location on the banks of the Chao Phraya River and its relaxing waterside dining terrace mean that cooling breezes counteract the heat of the day. With club rooms of quiet elegance, discreet service, and the famous Chi Spa, the Shangri-La deserves its reputation.

Old Bangkok was built on the river that once was its lifeline. The Shangri-La is right at its center, convenient for private trips on longboats or on the express boat that stops at the Grand Palace, nearby Wat Po, the Temple of Dawn, and Chinatown. Forget the crowds

---

"Your hotel's Tibetan spa massage was a truly exceptional experience —the finest I have ever had."

Jeremy Irons, actor

---

and relax on a riverboat as you enjoy Bangkok from the water, cooled by the breeze as you journey upriver.

Afternoon tea followed by a Chi treatment in the spa before dinner is just perfect. Treatments comprise a blend of Asian techniques, including energizing massage for yang stimulation, and relaxing massage for yin. The essential in the Chi treatment is the Tibetan brass bowl that, when struck, fills the room with waves of sound and has an unbelievable effect. Many people speak of having an out-of-body experience, of being transported to Shangri-La, a legendary land where no one grows old. The Shangri-La Hotel cannot guarantee agelessness, but it certainly offers a peaceful stay. **MN**

Cruise the River of Kings

Location Chao Phraya, Thailand
Website www.manohracruises.com   **Price** 💲💲

Taking a voyage up the Chao Phraya River, Bangkok's lifeline, is a rare and exceptional insight into life in Thailand. The voyage on board a luxuriously converted one-hundred-year-old teak rice barge, the grand *Manohra Song*, is without a doubt the right way to see the River of Kings. The lavishly refurbished, four-cabin, floating hotel is all about classic elegance. The air-conditioned staterooms are decked out in Thai silks with crisp white linens and ethereal white drapes.

On the shore, industrial buildings stand shoulder to shoulder with glittering temples and rickety wooden shacks. The river is busy: Children take running jumps into the murky brown waters for some cool relief as enormous barges heave past, towed by minuscule boats. The journey aboard *Manohra Song* includes several stops. The first is Wat Arun, also known as the Temple of Dawn, with a central Khmer-style tower soaring over four others representing the thirty-three heavens. Later the boat moors up at Wat Nivat, a temple modeled on an English neo-gothic cathedral, where young saffron-robed monks live. Then there is Bang Pa Na, one of the king's summer palaces.

At 4 P.M. a civilized English afternoon tea is served with delicate smoked-salmon finger sandwiches, tiny chocolate fancies, and scones with cream. Surreal but wonderful in these exotic surroundings. Later, delicious classic Thai specialties are served on deck. Traditional Thai soup in a coconut shell is followed by a parade of dishes: everything from fragrant green curry to king prawns with asparagus. In true Thai custom, dessert is deliciously rich and sweet.

The boat's slow rhythmic sway, the gentle breeze, and the mellow pace are mesmerizing, and the sights even more so. It is a truly bewitching experience. **RCA**

Unwind at Chiva-Som

Location Pranburi, Thailand   **Website** www.chivasom.com
Price ❸❸❸

Chiva-Som is a very exclusive hideaway and has a clientele of royalty, celebrities, and VIPs. Located between the world-class beach resorts of Hua Hin and Pranburi in Thailand, Chiva-Som is the crème de la crème of spa resorts. Its policy of no cell phones and no laptops is an inspired one. Anyone who has hankered after total peace and had it disturbed by someone wheeling and dealing on the telephone will understand the thinking.

Nestled on the white-sand beach of the Gulf of Siam are luxurious ocean-fronting rooms and suites with swimming pools; elegant Thai-style pavilions face onto green manicured lawns and lakes reflecting clear, blue skies. The master chefs produce inventive gourmet menus on-site using fresh produce from their own organic garden. (Does herb-encrusted snow fish on a bed of fennel with saffron sauce followed by chocolate cake strike your fancy?)

Guests of the resort can indulge in luxurious massages and beauty treatments, learn to dance, or enjoy aqua aerobics, water sports (including sea kayaking), pilates, yoga, tai chi, and Thai boxing. Try the exclusive Watsu treatment, a passive technique derived from Zen shiatsu and performed in a special warm-water pool in which a sequence of gentle rhythmic movements stretch and manipulate the body, taking relaxation to the next level. If you can tear yourself away from the tranquility of the spa, go shopping in nearby Hua Hin for exquisite Thai silks and carvings, or have something run up by a tailor for the "new" you at a price you will not believe. **MN**

◄ *The name Chiva-Som means "haven of life"*
   —a perfect name for a perfect place.

Stay at the Sarojin

Location Khao Lak, Thailand
Website www.sarojin.com **Price** $$

> *"The open air suites are protected by dunes yet close enough to hear waves washing over the coral."*

Condé Nast Traveler

There is a sense of timelessness surrounding the Sarojin. Its centerpiece, an ancient fig tree, is huge and dominating, towering impressively over a lagoon on one side and the ocean on the other. The fig gazes benevolently upon its reflection in the peaceful lotus pond—another symbol of eternity and nature.

In total, the Sarojin comprises 10 acres (4 ha) of grounds, including a private white-sand beach. The fifty-six residences are blessed with a variety of personalized touches: private gardens, sundecks, two-person baths, and outdoor waterfall showers, plus plunge pools and spa pools. The style is contemporary Asian, and the seven separate two-story buildings are designed to blend seamlessly into the surrounding landscape. The one-bed garden residences have Thai lounges and a private terrace, whereas fourteen pool residences add a plunge pool and a sun garden. The luxurious Sarojin suites, on the upper floor, have an air-conditioned pavilion and outdoor circular relaxation pools. Such luxury is only the beginning, though. The Pathways spa is integrated with the natural surroundings and lulled by the sounds of the Andaman Sea.

Overlooking a deserted coconut grove and the sea, there is a range of activities on offer, from snorkeling, scuba diving, and lagoon fishing to sea-cave canoeing in Phang Nga Bay, renowned for its dramatic limestone islands. You can also visit hot springs, trek on an elephant, or just watch the wildlife. A private charter on the luxury boat *Lady Sarojin* or a Thai cooking class and lunch by the waterfall are particularly magical ways of enjoying the Sarojin and its environs. **PS**

↖ *Dining on the beach with your own personal chef is just one of the perks of staying at the Sarojin.*

Enjoy Veranda Resort

Location Phetchaburi, Thailand
Website www.verandaresortandspa.com **Price** ⊝⊝

The Thai town of Hua Hin lies 124 miles (200 km) south of Bangkok and is the country's oldest beach resort. It first became popular in the 1920s when King Rama VII built a palace there, and members of the Thai royal family still take vacations in Hua Hin. Unsurprisingly, over the years, Hua Hin has acquired a glamorous air as visitors have been drawn to its white-sand beaches, upmarket hotels, and winding streets that are crammed with bars and restaurants, some of which stretch out along jetties into the sea. The town's night market is vast, and you can spend hours wandering through stalls that sell everything from jewelry to cashmere suits and silk dressing gowns; it is a great place to find a bargain and it is always advisable to arrive with an empty suitcase.

The trendy Veranda Resort and Spa lies outside Hua Hin, so you can get away from the town's bustle and relax. Its stunning modern, minimalist architecture houses thirteen pool villa suites and eighty-four rooms. They offer spectacular views out to sea over the Gulf of Thailand, outdoor bathtubs, and whirlpool tubs. Water is a big element at the Veranda: There is a spa where you can take in one of the beauty or massage treatments to really wind down; rooms look out to a central courtyard water feature that is soothingly candlelit at night; and there is an infinity swimming pool with water curtains, surrounded by decking and an artificial beach where you can relax and eat alfresco. As you might expect from a resort like this, the food is superb; the seafood fusion dishes and inventive blend of savory and sour using fresh pineapple and coconut are particularly good. If you are looking for a hip hotel away from the crowds, the Veranda offers the chance to relax in style. **CK**

Relax at Baan Taling Ngam

Location Koh Samui, Thailand
Website www.baan-taling-ngam.com **Price** ⊝⊝

The signature infinity pool at Koh Samui's Baan Taling Ngam Resort & Spa offers unrivaled views of the waters of the Gulf of Thailand and Ang Thong National Marine Park. Sip a cocktail at the swim-up bar and look across the azure sea to limestone islands and jungle-covered hillsides along the southwest coast.

Set in a coconut plantation perched on the side of a hill, rooms at the resort are furnished in traditional Thai style with vaulted ceilings, teak furniture, rich batik silks, and polished hardwood floors. Terraces look out far across the bay, and the gardens are a riot of color, bursting with tropical, scented blooms. Cliff villas, high on the hillside, have the most dramatic views.

> *"The views are stunning—small islands disappear over the horizon into flat, calm seas."*
>
> Caroline Wingfield, *Independent*

Sit at low tables to eat Thai cuisine at Baan Chantra restaurant while musicians play classical Thai music, or have a private dinner in the romantic setting of the covered *sala* next to the infinity pool or on the beach surrounded by flaming torches. After a day on the private white-sand beach or at one of the seven pools, retreat to the spa for a traditional massage, then relax in the herbal steam room or soak in a petal-filled bath.

Beyond the beach, go diving in the marine park, or try windsurfing and kayaking. Or head inland to explore the jungle interior with waterfalls, craggy cliffs, and elephant treks. It is difficult to stay away for long when such tranquility awaits at the resort. **AD**

Recharge at Kamalaya

Location Koh Samui, Thailand   **Website** www.kamalaya.com
Price 🌑🌑

"The idea behind Kamalaya is that by the time you leave, you'll be happy, healthy, and relaxed."

Tiffany Darke, *The Times*

On the tropical island of Koh Samui in the Gulf of Thailand, Kamalaya is a wellness sanctuary and holistic spa. Its name is an amalgamation of *kamal*, meaning "lotus," and *alaya*, an ancient symbol for the growth and unfolding of the human spirit. Everything at Kamalaya is aimed at nurturing the spirit: from the food, to the environment, to the many health programs on offer, such as qigong, tai chi, meditation, yoga, Tibetan singing bowls therapy, and spirit dance. This is a place geared toward finding inner peace.

Guests can relax on a white-sand beach or by a swimming pool set among flowering lotus ponds and waterfalls, or try out the warm and cool plunge pools. The center is elegantly designed with large open spaces that offer breathtaking views and allow guests to feel at one with the surrounding nature. Drawing on holistic medicine and complementary therapies from Eastern and Western traditions, there is a wealth of treatments aimed at detoxification, losing weight, or rejuvenating the tired body and mind. Visitors can choose from Indian head massage, Chi Nei Tsang Taoist abdominal massage, and the traditional Chinese medicinal practices of acupuncture, moxibustion, and cupping. The food is a fusion of Eastern and Western cuisine, and guests can also try out a range of herbal elixirs and medicinal teas.

Whether you are simply taking in the view or exploring the benefits of yoga, the sense of serenity and community spirit at Kamalaya provides an escape, and may perhaps help you hold on to a feeling of peace even when you have left Kamalaya behind. **CK**

↖ *The spa is set on a hilltop among granite rocks and trees with spectacular views out to sea and mountains.*

Stay at Karma Samui

Location Koh Samui, Thailand **Website** www.karmasamui.com
Price ⬡⬡⬡

Most people come back from vacations with a tan, some memories, and perhaps a couple of midnight promises. Karma Samui offers so much more. The Thai cooking classes alone ensure a more memorable vacation than usual because the chefs guide you through the street markets, explain how the authentic elements of this delicate cuisine are put together, help you select the freshest of ingredients, and then teach you to re-create the real flavors of Thailand at the resort.

At Karma Samui, there are the thirty-six pool villas, which sit in five terraces designed to give splendorous sea views to all. Each residence features an open-plan pavilion with that all-important kitchen to test your

> "In short, it's like having your own house surrounded by all the amenities of a five-star hotel."
>
> Susan Kurosawa, *The Australian*

new skills. Part the double doors to find an open-air courtyard and the stunning infinity pool that appears to merge into the magnificent ocean beyond.

The resort is island-famous for its food, which is taken to the highest level at the Thai/Asian restaurant, Padma. Private chefs are also available to prepare barbecues on your terrace for an even more intimate experience. Every month, Ministry of Sound DJs get the moonrise party jumping, after which it is off to the Chakra Spa and Wellness Center for one of a wide selection of treatments. It is hard to believe that it is only a five-minute drive to the island's entertainment and shopping capital, Chaweng Beach. **PS**

Unwind at Napasai

Location Koh Samui, Thailand **Website** www.napasai.com
Price ⬡⬡

A longtime favorite with backpackers, Koh Samui was made internationally famous by the cult Leonardo DiCaprio movie *The Beach*. Despite the influx of visitors, the tiny paradise island in the Gulf of Siam has managed to retain its identity and its soul. Far from embracing mass tourism, the island has tried to keep its natural beauty intact, even ruling that no building be higher than a palm tree. However, there are plenty of cultural sights to visit, such as the Na Phra Larn temple or Big Buddha, the impressive golden figure that sits on the northern tip of the island, and amazing natural resources such as the stunning national marine park renowned for extraordinary diving.

In Maenam, the Napasai is run by the Orient Express hotels group and is a perfect "get away from it all" retreat. Luxury, relaxation, and super-friendly staff are all part of the deal. There is everything you could wish for from a tropical oasis: the infinity pool overlooking Ban Tai beach and the Gulf of Thailand, and the Lai Thai restaurant for amazing local food such as glorious curry and pad thai. The food is presented immaculately with intricately sculpted fruit that says "art" more than "cuisine." For pure indulgence, book into the plush spa for some serious pampering that makes the most of local herbs and Asian philosophies. Try a bracing Thai massage or a holistic treatment using tropical fruits and flowers to balance physical and psychological well-being, or even a Pala energy body massage to encourage energy flow.

Thai-style villas with sea views are spread over 17 acres (7 ha), where coconut palms, cashew, jackfruit, and mango trees abound. All this can be found in a typically friendly Thai atmosphere, with guaranteed sunshine—what more could you wish for? **RCA**

Discover Tongsai Bay

Location Koh Samui, Thailand   **Website** www.tongsaibay.co.th
Price ⑤⑤⑤⑤

Outdoor life is what the Tongsai Bay is all about. The beautifully designed rooms have as much space outside on the open-air terrace as they have inside, which means cooling sea breezes and jaw-dropping ocean views are never far away. The huge teak Grand Villas nestle into the hillside to the right of the bay. Soak in the petal-strewn outdoor bathtub while watching the sunset and sleep under the stars in the gazebo draped with white curtains. Each of the Pool Villas has a private 50-foot (15-m) plunge pool, surrounded by palm-fringed gardens—the perfect place for a cooling dip after soaking up the sun.

Still run by the Hoontrakuls, The Tongsai Bay is the only five-star, family-run resort on the island, with service that is genuinely warm and welcoming. Find a quiet spot to relax on the stretch of beach shelving into the azure sea, or chill by one of the two pools. There is sailing, canoeing, windsurfing, and snorkeling to experience and a chance to meet some of the family at the twice-weekly cocktail party. If you can pull yourself away from the resort, go to nearby Wat Phra Yai to see the mighty Big Buddha statue glittering in the sun. Return in the evening to sample authentic Thai cuisine in chef Chom's à la carte restaurant, or else have an intimate dinner in the Butler's Restaurant, which seats a maximum of twenty guests on the hillside overlooking the crescent-shaped pool.

The place to ease away the stresses of modern life is the Prana Spa, a haven of relaxation on the beachfront, offering soothing treatments and revitalizing massages —plus wonderful open-air floral baths, of course. **AD**

↢ *Overlooking a secluded white-sand beach, the resort sits on the exclusive northeast corner of the coast.*

Stay at the Sanctuary

Location Koh Phangan, Thailand
Website www.thesanctuarythailand.com   **Price** ❺

It takes two speedboats to get to the Sanctuary on Haad Tien beach, but the secluded location merely adds to the allure. With daily yoga, meditation, tai chi, and shamanic journeys, as well as a phenomenal seafood and vegetarian restaurant by the sea, this holistic hideaway feeds body and soul.

Visitors come from around the globe to take part in the on-site fasting and cleansing programs. Led by Moon, a fasting devotee who looks far younger than his years, participants can be spotted popping herbal tablets on schedule, emerging from their daily colonics, and, finally, returning to real food with the restaurant's colorful raw menu. There is also massage

---

"The Sanctuary has grown from a single hut into a full-fledged retreat . . . overlooking the beach."

Time magazine (Asia)

---

within stumbling distance from the shore, and the Sanctuary spa, where you can get scrubbed down with pineapple before you get to work on your tan.

By night the restaurant has an L.A. feel, with a collection of flip-flops by the entrance, twinkling lights strung above hammocks, and a constant soundtrack that never gets boring. The fire circus likes to come out and play after dinner, and every Friday night you can dance until dawn at the beach's renowned parties, a far tamer and more pleasant alternative to the legendary full-moon parties on nearby Haad Rin. A few Westerners came to work here and never left. They look like the happiest people in the world. **JS**

Relax at Amanpuri

Location Phuket, Thailand
Website www.amanpuri.com   **Price** ❺❺❺

At Amanpuri, an austere sanctuary set off a dirt path, hidden walkways, sliding doors, and clever camouflage effects create instant Zen—a perpetual sense of infinity extending from the slate-gray pools peeping out onto the Andaman up to the ocean-view rooms reaching up into the sky. It is the ultimate hideout in which to recuperate from the strains of everyday life, because the sounds of the sea, birds, and leaves act like a salve to the soul, and the slatted *sala* affords glimpses of the trees beneath your feet. Posited high on the jungle knoll, you are king, disturbed by nothing but the silent service laying out refreshments or scuttling geckos come to nose around.

Back at ground zero, the sense of space and consideration continues. Amanpuri lays claim to the only private beach on the island of Phuket: an arcing, golden crescent of coastline flanked by the slate-gray boulders that set the tone for the design.

Amanpuri's restaurant ranks among the best on the island. Like the resort itself, it offers a textbook example in subtlety, well-being, and flair. The Italian menu is crafted from the pearls of the southern hemisphere; its views extend over the inky sea by night. If private beaches, hidden salas, and treetop contemplation are not enough, then Amanpuri's adjoining private residences offer total seclusion and multiple spaces, from swimming pools to games rooms and a variety of bedrooms in which to sleep. Personal staff are ready to minister to your every need. Amanpuri means "place of peace," and the resort certainly lives up to its name. **VG**

→ *A haven of exclusivity, the flagship Aman residence sets a precedent in discretion and design aplomb.*

Relax at Sri Panwa

Location Phuket, Thailand
Website www.sripanwa.com   **Price** ⑤⑤⑤

This tropical island getaway is the ultimate in seclusion for those wanting to get away from it all in style. With panoramic views across Phuket's Cape Panwa, it is the perfect place to go for rest and relaxation that is well away from the crowds.

Villas are perched 130 feet (40 m) up on a cliff, high above the azure waters of the Andaman Sea. Ideally designed for the Thai climate, they offer the very best in indoor and outdoor living, with a sun pavilion and bathtub on the terrace as well as a cooling rain shower. Surrounded on three sides by floor-to-ceiling glass doors, each bedroom opens directly onto an infinity pool with massage jets. You do not even have to get out of bed to take in the jaw-dropping views. Natural materials and sumptuous fabrics have been used in the chic villas at this boutique rain forest resort. They are equipped with high-tech gadgets such as a home cinema system, and every detail has been considered, including an entertainment system that has preprogrammed music channels compiled by a D.J.

Beyond the villas, the extensive grounds boast a stretch of private beach, a gym, and tennis courts, as well as jogging and bicycling trails. The Sai Spa features Thai and Swedish massage treatments and therapy baths. A poolside villa at the top of the hill is home to Baba, Sri Panwa's trendsetting restaurant, which serves an inspired Thai menu packed with fresh fish and seafood. If you want more privacy, you may dine in your own pavilion.

Make sure you venture out of your villa long enough to visit the bar for a relaxing cocktail and to listen to the house and lounge tunes played by the in-house DJ. Then leave the sociable bar area and head back for a private midnight dip under a moonlit sky. **AD**

Discover Bon Island

Location Phuket, Thailand
Website www.sixsenses.com   **Price** ⑤⑤

If you would like to stay on your very own tropical island with all the trimmings of a luxury hotel, try the Evason Phuket's Bon Island. A tiny island set away from the resort, it is a blissful paradise, where space, quiet, and seclusion are guaranteed.

The Evason resort is a master of design work, beautifully laid out in typical Thai style, with shining dark wood and water features. Colorful hanging sofas sway, oversized lanterns glow, and the reception is set against a backdrop of palms and island views. The beach is picture perfect, but the real delight is retreating to your very own island. Bon Island's only suite sits on stilts in the jungle with perfect views onto

"Upon entering, the outside world is left behind. Enter into a realm of nurturing . . . tranquility."

Spa Asia magazine

the Andaman Sea and surrounding islands. With its own terraces for sunbathing and dining, the suite has a luxurious tree house feel to it: all thatched roof and wooden features. An open bathroom means soaking alfresco with a view, whereas indoors a pristine white bed with overhanging mosquito net is utterly romantic. The cabin has all modern conveniences and a phone with the butler on speed dial, too.

Even the short trip out across the emerald sea on the long tail boat with its colorful ribbons flittering in the breeze is special. Nip across for a treat at the impeccable spa, or for dinner at the restaurant where flamingly hot green curries are served beachside. **RCA**

Experience Trisara

Location Phuket, Thailand
Website www.trisara.com **Price** 🅢🅢🅢

Stay at Suan Mokkh

Location Surat Thani, Thailand
Website www.suanmokkh-idh.org **Price** 🅢

Phuket, the country's largest island, has become an increasingly popular tourist destination since the turn of the millennium. While many of the sandy beaches on the western coast have attracted ruthless developers who have contrived to disfigure the area's natural beauty, the exception is the Trisara luxury resort and spa, which is situated on a private bay just fifteen minutes from the island's international airport.

Set in 40 acres (16 ha) of secluded tropical forest and parkland, the resort consists of forty-two sea-facing suites and villas that all have their own private infinity pools. While the suites offer 1,260 square feet (117 sq m) of space, the villas are twice as big. Villas and suites alike come with air conditioning, TVs, DVD players, teak sundecks, broadband Internet connections, vast bathrooms that are complemented by outdoor showers, and huge beds that are styled as "the most comfortable beds you have ever slept in."

Overlooking the beachfront, the resort's main restaurant serves local as well as Western dishes in an outdoor setting, while the Trisara Grill further down the beach is open for dinner and offers grilled seafood and meat both indoors and outdoors. As for entertainment, Trisara's guests have their choice of several motor yachts in order to discover the nearby bays. Two floodlit tennis courts and a library are also part of the hotel, and the spa up in the hills above the villas is famed for the high standard of its treatments, thus completing the perfect vacation experience.

And for those who stay there and wish they never have to leave, the good news is that they do not necessarily have to, as twelve residential villas (featuring between two and five bedrooms) that are part of the resort can be acquired privately. **DaH**

As one of only two Thai meditation centers that offer ten-day retreats for those whose knowledge of Buddhist practices is limited, Suan Mokkh is ideal to gain firsthand knowledge of Far Eastern philosophy. The difficulties many Westerners experience on these shorter retreats should not be underestimated, and dropout rates of up to 70 percent attest to the strenuous path that leads to enlightenment.

The day at Suan Mokkh starts at 4 A.M. Visitors rise from their straw mats, leave the single-sex dormitories, and head for the huge concrete tubs in the vast courtyard. These contain rainwater that the guests splash onto themselves as a substitute for having a

"Meditation takes energy and commitment, determination and discipline . . . it is not easy."

Proprietors, Suan Mokkh

shower. The first reading of the day starts half an hour later. This is followed by a meditation session that precedes almost two hours of yoga. Talks about Buddhist knowledge, more meditation sessions, and chores fill the rest of the day, interrupted only by three basic yet tasty meals. The daily program continues until 9 P.M., and by 10 P.M. the power in the dormitories is switched off. Fortunately, such hardships come at virtually no cost because participants are charged only for the inexpensive food. Throw in the tropical surroundings and the whole thing may seem quite appealing to those who want to experience a culture that is fundamentally different from their own. **DaH**

Discover Angkor

Location Angkor, Cambodia   **Website** www.angkorwhat.net
Price ◑

Abandoned since the fifteenth century, Angkor—once the largest city in the world—is an almost dreamlike archaeological park full of ancient, erstwhile Hindu temples that have been devoured by the relentless rain forest. Located just north of Cambodia's ecological heart, the combined lake and river system Tonle Sap, Angkor was declared a World Heritage site in 1993, and since then the number of tourists visiting the cone-shaped sanctuaries has increased exponentially. In fact, the historically significant hilltop temple Phnom Bakheng—like so many other structures in the park—is threatened by the tourist invasion, as 3,000-plus visitors climb up its steps every evening to watch the sun disappear behind Angkor's centerpiece, the eponymous *wat* (temple).

However, there is more to Angkor than the world's largest religious monument, which has not only become synonymous with the whole site but is also a symbol of modern-day Cambodia and features on the country's national flag. Once you venture beyond the tourist hordes gathering at Angkor's best-preserved temple, you will find more than 1,000 other holy sites of various sizes and, crucially, of various degrees of popularity. Some of them are no more than piles of rubble, whereas others are magnificent ruins with massive trees cracking their walls.

The expanse stretches over 99,000 acres (40,000 ha), and although you can go on organized bus tours, or rent a car or motorbike with a driver, it is best to rent a bicycle to get off the beaten track and find a spot that you do not need to share with strangers. **DaH**

→ *The tree roots that cover the temples' facades provide an eerie atmosphere of timelessness.*

Stay at the Nam Hai

Location Quang Nam, Vietnam
Website www.ghmhotels.com **Price** 💲💲💲

Professional traveler Bill Bryson once wrote that as tourists we expend vast quantities of time and money in a largely futile attempt to re-create the comforts we already have at home. Bill's travels have clearly never allowed him the pleasure of a stay at the Nam Hai.

The resort is a showcase of pure luxury, with one hundred stunning designer villas set in perfect symmetry around manicured lawns and infinity pools that glide seamlessly into the unspoiled white sands of Ha My beach and the aqua-blue waters of the South China Sea, creating an air of peace and tranquility. Inside the opulent villas, there is an abundance of space and light: Split-level platforms contain king-size beds adorned with a mountain of soft cushions; bathrooms boast lengthy, eggshell-lacquered baths opening out onto private gardens for optional alfresco showering; daybeds and giant sofas are located on the terrace for afternoon napping. The forty pool villas have private temperature-controlled swimming pools and the added indulgence of a personal butler.

The five-star quality extends to the two restaurants, which feature an appetizing fusion of traditional Vietnamese fare, international cuisine, and fresh seafood. Rejuvenation can be sought at the eight peaceful spa villas surrounding a lotus pond, where a variety of exquisite treatments will almost certainly bring about an enormous sense of well-being—if not, there is always the comfort of the bar to iron out any last remaining vestiges of stress. Should you begin to suffer from relaxation fatigue, the ancient port city of Hoi An is a mere fifteen-minute car ride away. An intoxicating mix of tailor's shops, markets, riverside cafés, art galleries, and historic buildings, the city is a must-see if you wish to reach inside the real Vietnam. **SG**

Enjoy Résidence Phou Vao

Location Luang Prabang, Laos
Website www.residencephouvao.com **Price** 💲💲

La Résidence Phou Vao sits on top of a hill blanketed in frangipani and palms, and has breathtaking views over Mount Phou Si, Luang Prabang's sacred mountain, and the golden dome of the Vat Chamsi stupa.

The hotel is a sprawling French colonial mansion, with bleached white walls, burnt sienna–tiled roofs, and spacious shuttered verandas—a serious temple to Asian chic. Narrow footpaths wind past crumbling Buddhist stupas and tropical gardens to the spa—local-style pavilions set around a lily pond. Massages and facial treatments use traditional Lao remedies to nurture the body and soul. Relax in the herbal steam room, or float in the infinity pool overlooking the

> *"The ancient city of Luang Prabang, in Laos, is one of the most magical in the world."*
>
> *Evening Standard*

valley. More adventurous guests can rent a bicycle to explore Luang Prabang, the ancient capital and home to the Golden Buddha, or take a cooking class with the hotel chef, who serves French cuisine and traditional Lao dishes in the poolside restaurant.

Rooms are in a traditional style with rich cottons and rosewood furniture. Private terraces look out across the forest canopy to distant mountains dotted with pagodas. There is no noise, apart from the occasional chanting of monks drifting up from the valley. **AD**

➔ *It can be difficult to pull yourself away to explore the World Heritage town nestled in the valley below.*

Unwind at Six Senses Hideaway Ninh Van Bay

Location Khanh Hoa, Vietnam **Website** www.sixsenses.com
Price 💲💲💲

Accessible only by water, the Six Senses Hideaway at Ninh Van Bay is utterly secluded and dazzlingly beautiful. Velvety white sand glistens below towering verdant mountains, and the sea is mesmerizing with its multiple shades of blue.

All the villas at the resort were designed according to Vietnamese architectural traditions and offer the utmost in luxury, with their own gardens, handcrafted wooden bathtubs, wine cellars, and walk-in closets. The Water Villas are easily the most romantic and are accessed by wooden teak boats. Each one has a private teak deck and faces the unparalleled sunsets—perfect for honeymooners. The Spa Suite Villas are for those who want to be pampered; they have their own steam rooms and in-villa spa treatment facilities.

The world-class Six Senses Spa blends into the environment and nestles beside a gentle waterfall to allow the soothing sound of the water and the aroma of essential oils to infuse the air. Expert therapists melt troubles away with traditional Vietnamese and holistic treatments. Such pampering works up an appetite, and thankfully the dining options are impressive. The restaurants are intimate and romantic, but you can also enjoy private barbecues at your villa or on the beach, dinner on the jetty or in the intimate wine cave. By day there are lots of castaway beaches and coves to explore, water sports, and scuba diving. The coastal city of Nha Trang is twenty minutes away by boat. For the ultimate in elusive beach escapes, Six Senses Hideaway Ninh Van Bay is hard to beat. **LP**

→ *There is a range of lavish villas on the beachfront, where pools have been crafted over rock formations.*

Relax at Whale Island Resort

Location Khanh Hoa, Vietnam
Website www.iledelabaleine.com **Price** $

North of Nha Trang, Vietnam's largest seaside resort, tiny Whale Island lies in Van Phong Bay amid the warm waters of the South China Sea. The island is circled by a protective archipelago, and diving is its main attraction. From January to October each year, experienced divers can swim among tropical fish and coral gardens, through labyrinths and caves. They will find sting rays, manta rays, and moray eels, sea horses, clown fish, and giant Spanish dancers. There are dives for beginners, too, and qualified instructors ready to guide novices.

The months between April and July are particularly spectacular around Whale Island. Whales and whale sharks come to Van Phong Bay to feed on the abundant krill and plankton, and, toward the end of March and beginning of April, the locals hold religious ceremonies to welcome these creatures to their waters.

For those who like to keep their head above water, Whale Island also offers catamarans, windsurfing, and canoes. On land, meanwhile, the island features accommodation in twenty-three bamboo bungalows. They are simple thatched constructions—think fan and shower room rather than air-conditioning and whirlpool tub—but simplicity is the joy of this place. Step out of your door and your toes will sink into the island's white sands. Bamboo loungers surrounded by trees and flowers beckon indolent afternoons. The restaurant's menu depends on what the fishermen bring in during the morning: One evening you may be served swordfish and barracuda, another tuna, crab, grouper, and shrimp. The menu is new each day—and the ingredients are sensationally fresh. Robinson Crusoe fans, should look no farther. On Whale Island your desert island dreams could come true. **PE**

Unwind at Evason Ana Mandara Villas Dalat

Location Lam Dong, Vietnam
Website www.sixsenses.com **Price** $$

Evason Ana Mandara Villas Dalat is a sophisticated getaway with a heavenly spa, hidden among woodland in the rural highlands of south central Vietnam. Dalat abounds with vivid green landscape and a plethora of colorful flowers, and has a year-round pleasant climate, giving rise to its affectionate nickname of "the city of eternal spring." It is a strikingly beautiful, seemingly magical land of tumbling waterfalls, pine-scented forests, and lakes such as the majestic Xuan Huong. When mist descends during the rainy season (April to October), the city and forests are swallowed up in it, as if a strange spell has been cast.

> "Striking views . . . abound from all areas of the gently sloping hillside property."
>
> vietnamstay.com

Guests are housed in French colonial villas that were built in the 1920s and 1930s. They are well located to explore the city of Dalat, with its European-inspired architecture, palaces, and flower park. There is much to awaken the senses inside the retreat, too, not least the Six Senses spa. Treatments include traditional Vietnamese massage and therapies incorporating fresh rose petals and Vietnamese green tea.

Romantics will enjoy a visit to Than Tho lake, where a *Romeo and Juliet*–type story is said to have taken place. A woman, who wrongly believed her lover had died, drowned herself in the lake, and the surrounding pine trees are said to have sighed in grief ever since. **LP**

Explore the Mekong by Boat

Location Mekong River, Vietnam
Website www.cruisemekong.com **Price** ⊖⊖

As the sun slowly sinks into the horizon, the entire sky is ablaze with red and orange. The waters of the Mekong River seem to be on fire as the tour boat slowly cruises toward the sunset.

The Mekong River is a huge 2,980 miles (4,800 km) long. Beginning on the Tibetan Plateau, it is fed by myriad lakes and waterways as it stretches through China, Myanmar, Laos, Thailand, Cambodia, and Vietnam before emptying into the South China Sea. Cruising down the river is a unique and picturesque journey. By day you will glide through wide waterways, past wetlands and thick tropical forest. In the evening, nothing beats sitting up on deck with a glass of wine, watching the magnificent sunset. The entire sky burns bright orange, the warm hues lighting up the water. The sun blazes so brightly you almost expect to hear a sizzling noise as it dips below the watery horizon.

The delta is one of the most densely populated places in the world. It gives a fascinating glimpse into the everyday lives of the Vietnamese people who reside and work along its banks. You will see floating schools, markets, and houses, all designed to cope with the annual floods. They may seem like an inconvenience, but the floods that occur every rainy season are actually a vital natural process. They bring millions of fish south to spawn and replace soil worn away through natural erosion. The locals have adapted their lives around the river. Traders chatter noisily at the floating markets, enticing you to buy fresh fish, fruit, and exotic tropical flowers. **JP**

↗ *The locals paddle their wooden boats through the muddy brown waters as tourists watch the sunset.*

"This river has seen the rise and fall of empires and battles between foes of different races and cultures."

mekongboat.com

Hide Away at Amanpulo

Location Pamalican Island, Philippines
Website www.amanresorts.com **Price** 🟢🟢🟢

Escape the world in style on this private island in the Philippines where powder-white sands meet crystal-clear seas and tropical palms sway across bright turquoise skies. Amanpulo means "peaceful island," which could not be a more fitting description. It is part of an archipelago of more than 7,000 tropical islands dotted along the coast southwest of Manila. Fly in on the resort's own nineteen-seater twin-engine plane to the island's airstrip for an unforgettable arrival.

The beach, hillside, and treetop casitas are modeled on authentic *bahay kubo* dwellings, a centuries-old style of family home with steep pitched roofs on timber frames. Hillside casitas offer magical sea views, whereas beach casitas have private overgrown paths leading to the beach. They are all discreetly nestled among the sand-floored tropical foliage, and guests have their own buggy for island exploration. Inside, subtle interiors are warm and sun-dappled, in shades of caramel and bamboo. Bathrooms have raised Cebu marble bathtubs and honey-brown wooden floors.

Laze on the beach, swing in a hammock under a coconut palm, or lie back in one of the open-air *salas* and enjoy a relaxing holistic body treatment. There is a 100-foot (30-m) pool to cool off in, or head out to sea and dive the coral reef, only 1,000 feet (300 m) from the shore. Choose from a European and Asian menu in the restaurant, which spills out onto a terrace that has views to Manamoc Island across the channel. After dinner, take in the star-studded night sky from the terrace of the bar where a telescope looks heavenward and staff offer a guide to the stars for beginners. **AD**

◄ *What could be more romantic than a dinner served to you on the beach as you listen to the waves breaking?*

Visit El Nido Lagen

Location Palawan, Philippines
Website www.elnidoresorts.com **Price** 🟢🟢

The setting for El Nido Lagen Island Resort is surely the definition of seclusion. It overlooks a cove fringed by a white-sand beach and is surrounded by limestone cliffs and rain forest. Part of a marine reserve of more than 600 islands off the most northern tip of Palawan, El Nido is ideal for castaways with a taste for eco-chic. Some cottages are built on stilts over the water; others overlook the 10 acres (4 ha) of tropical grounds. All have verandas, and inside furnishings are crafted from wood from traditional Filipino houses.

This resort is paradise for snorkelers and divers, with its crystal-clear water and reefs teeming with tropical fish. Take a kayak out to get a closer look at limestone

> *"[El Nido] is among the conservation minded places on a mission to protect the local environment."*
>
> *Travel+Leisure* magazine

caves and lagoons; try rock climbing or a hike through the rain forest to see monkeys. The Lagen trail is one of the best sites for bird-watching, to spot flocks of hornbills taking off early in the morning. Guests may also take a boat trip to explore the tiny islands, deserted beaches, and cliffs in the area.

In the evening, an open-air buffet restaurant serves delicious fresh local seafood. After dinner, you can escape to the nearby lagoon where the soaring limestone cliffs provide the perfect acoustics for concerts. A string quartet and tenor appear on a floating platform in the water, under the spotlight of a full moon. A slice of heaven right here on earth. **AD**

Relax at Datai

Location Langkawi, Malaysia
Website www.ghmhotels.com **Price** ⊖⊖⊖

Beautifully cocooned in Langkawi's ancient tropical rain forest, Datai is a true hideaway heaven. Set on the island's less-developed northern coast, the complex fronts onto a sumptuously sandy beach facing the Andaman Sea. Blending comfortably into its verdant jungle setting, the well-designed resort features open-air walkways, pavilions, and hutlike villas on stilts, leaving the lush surroundings intact and alive with wildlife. Chattering monkeys and giant flying squirrels leap from tree to tree while geckos and lizards laze in sun-splashed spots. A resident conservationist leads nature walks through rough tracks in the surrounding virgin rain forest to point out birds and bats.

> "Datai bay has the island's best beaches—white sands and jungle-clad cliffs."

Andrew Catchpole, *Guardian*

Although this is real back-to-nature stuff, a stay at the opulent Datai is a lavish affair. Expect Bose sound systems, Molton Brown products, and staff who remember every guest's name. For top Thai food in an open-air setting, head to the Pavilion, a stilted restaurant raised up in the rain forest canopy. Fancy a dose of pampering? Amble along to the open-air spa where signature treatments range from warm stone massage to an aromatherapy foot polish. The resort's golf course is gloriously set amid the rain forest, flanked by the Andaman Sea and the Mat Cincan mountain range. Active types can rent a bicycle—a great way to explore the mainly traffic-free island. **JK**

Unwind at Pangkor Laut

Location Pangkor, Malaysia
Website www.pangkorlautresort.com **Price** ⊖⊖

Situated off the west coast of Peninsular Malaysia, the resort at Pangkor Laut was opened by Luciano Pavarotti in 1994, who is said to have fallen in love with the island, exclaiming, "How beautiful God has made this paradise." Pangkor Laut's beauty is much more than skin deep, however, and there is substance here alongside style, with an excellent standard of service and top-of-the-range facilities. The accommodation is luxurious, with the most opulent being the Pavarotti Suite. This elegant two-bedroom suite has an open-roofed bathroom and a large balcony overlooking the sea, which affords some of the island's best views from its position high in the rain forest.

Delicious local dishes are served in the elegantly contemporary Fisherman's Cove restaurant, which employs homegrown ingredients, including herbs from the spa village garden, in its fresh seafood dishes. But, for something really special, shun the restaurant in favor of the luxury of private dining, offered either in your own villa or in a romantic setting under the stars on the beach at Emerald Bay.

The languorous pace of life at Pangkor Laut continues in the spa village, where a complete range of treatments inspired by the region's abundance of natural resources and renowned history of healing is on offer. The traditional Malay massage, consisting of long, kneading strokes performed with a unique oil made from local ingredients, including cinnamon and citronella, is a deeply relaxing treat, but the pinnacle of indulgence has to be the ultimate spa experience that takes place in the Belian Spa Pavilion, with its own outdoor whirlpool tub, yoga pavilion, nap gazebo, steam room, and private treatment area—this is one pampering session that is not to be missed. **HO**

Explore Perhentian Islands

Location Perhentian Islands, Malaysia
Website www.perhentian.com.my **Price**

The Perhentian Islands off the east coast of Malaysia are about as near to perfect as a beach retreat can get. There are two islands to choose between. Perhentian Besar is the largest; it is more appropriate for families and those looking for some tranquility. Perhentian Kecil is more often chosen by price-conscious backpackers. Both islands offer several palm-fringed beaches that arc their way past jungle-covered inlands, each of which has a choice of accommodation.

Although most visitors come here to while away a few days under the palm trees, there are a few other things to do. Snorkeling and diving are the major activities, and competition between diving schools

> *"The Perhentian Islands are such a nice place to be. . . . No roads, no mass-market tourism—bliss."*
>
> Jack Barker, *Independent*

makes Perhentian one of the world's cheapest places for a dive. Green turtles and black-tipped reef sharks can often be found around the reefs, and myriad other aquatic species, such as clams, eels, sea snakes, and cuttlefish, are a common sight. Jungle treks can also be arranged with guides, and sea kayaks can be rented if you fancy exploring the water on your own.

Inevitably the islands have, in some places, lost their untouched quality, with Long Beach on Perhentian Kecil being particularly built up. Many other beaches contain just a single resort, and some are completely free of man-made intrusions. During peak season, February to October, it can get quite busy. **JD**

Recharge at the Aryani

Location Terengganu, Malaysia
Website www.thearyani.com **Price** ⊝

Inspired by an ancient sultan's palace, the Aryani was built in the style of a traditional fortress and draws on classical Malay architecture throughout. Situated on the east coast of Malaysia, which has one of the longest coastlines in the country and offers white-sand beaches, marine parks, and top-class snorkeling and diving, the Aryani sits at the edge of the warm South China Sea, in the fishing village of Kuala Terengganu.

This is a gorgeous hideaway where it is easy to relax and instantly feel at one with nature. Succumb to an incredible massage or float away under the relaxing ministrations of one of the facialists. If you are a bit of a spa princess who likes her treatments in pristine white surroundings, you might be better off elsewhere. Set amid coconut fronds, banana trees, and tropical flowers, and reconstructed from original timber to provide an authentic sense of an old Malay building, the Aryani's Heritage Spa is a wooden hut on stilts. The tiny gaps in the wooden walls allow fresh flower-scented air to flow inside, and the lack of cold, tiled treatment rooms gives the exquisite sense of being pampered inside a luxurious tree house. There is no need for oxygen facials here, because the fresh ocean breeze and exotic scents wafting through the windows do the job naturally.

Surrender to a floor cushion and be massaged, scrubbed, and invigorated with herbs, spices, fruits, and flowers. Then soak in the outdoor tub with fragrant jasmine, tropical magnolia blooms, and rose petals while the waves crash on the shore beyond shady frangipani leaves. Afterward, sip a chilled lemongrass tea, the Aryani's signature drink, at the Pulau Beach Club. The Aryani's rich and royal ambience soon has guests feeling every bit the sultan or sultana. **SD**

Relax at Tanjong Jara

Location Terengganu, Malaysia
Website www.tanjongjararesort.com **Price**

Soaking up the history of Malaysia at Tanjong Jara Resort is a very hands-on experience. The ancient philosophy of Sucimurni practices purity of spirit, health, and well-being. Nowhere is it more relevant than in the award-winning, sumptuous Spa Village.

Generations-old treatments dating back to the days of the Malacca sultanate have been revived to treat modern-day needs. The Asam Roselle experience uses the healing power of the hibiscus plant's red flowers in a relaxing massage, creamy scrub, and rejuvenating tea drink to improve the complexion and benefit the kidneys. Traditional Malay massage, floral baths, and scented steam rooms ease tensions away.

On the east coast of Malaysia, Tanjong Jara sits amid 42 acres (17 ha) facing the sea. Rooms, surrounded by palms, have been inspired by the seventeenth-century palaces once made for Malay kings. Handcrafted by local craftsmen, the teak floors and high ceilings offer a cooling escape from the tropical heat. A ringing bell at noon announces the arrival of the day's fresh catch from the sea. Sample local delicacies at the Di Atas Sungei restaurant, which sits above the river, or the Nelayan fish restaurant, where guests can dine by torchlight on the beach.

There is plenty to discover in the natural surroundings. Take a fishing trip on the river, bicycle to local villages, trek through the jungle to the highest waterfall in the region, or take a Malay cooking class with the resort's chef. Endangered giant leatherback turtles come ashore nearby to nest, and unspoiled islands offshore are a paradise for beach lovers. **AD**

↵ *The spa is housed in seven magnificent treatment pavilions surrounded by tranquil gardens and pools.*

Discover Gunung Mulu

Location Gunung Mulu, Malaysia
Website www.mulupark.com/index.htm **Price**

About two hours' flight from the coastal city of Miri in the Malayan part of northern Borneo, the UNESCO World Heritage site Gunung Mulu National Park boasts exceptional scenery both above and below ground. Covered by rain forest, the park is home to some of Earth's most breathtaking caves, including the world's largest underground chamber: Sarawak Chamber is 2,300 feet (700 m) long and over 230 feet (70 m) high.

Scientists have mapped over 185 miles (300 km) of the park's underground passages, but visitors can only explore four of the caves on guided tours. They are categorized according to their difficulty level, with the Sarawak Chamber being considered the most

---

"A remarkable series of caverns, dripping with stalactites . . . exploration is worth the effort."

Ben Davies, *Daily Telegraph*

---

treacherous. Evidence of previous caving experience is required in order to join this tour, but the completion of one of Mulu's easier tours is also regarded as a sufficient qualification to undertake a descent into the park's main attraction.

While the limestone mountains that make up the area have been eroded by water below the surface, they rise and drop steeply above ground. Several different guided forest tours are offered at the park's headquarters, some highlights being the Mulu Canopy Skywalk, the longest tree-based walkway on the planet, and the spectacular Pinnacles, with razor-sharp karst formations that rise near Gunung Api. **DaH**

Dive at Lankayan Island

Location Lankayan Island, Sabah, Malaysia
Website www.lankayan-island.com   **Price** 🜚🜚

You'll experience a real get-away-from-it-all feel as you approach Lankayan Island Dive Resort, a tiny dot in the Sulu Sea off the coast of Malaysian Borneo. A ninety-minute speedboat ride cuts across the azure water, bouncing off waves until the paradise island comes into view. Covering 10 acres (4 ha) at high tide, it is fringed with palms, and the shores are dusted with shell-blown white sand. The island is so small it takes only fifteen minutes to walk around the coast.

Rooms are teak, thatched huts with wide balconies to enjoy the views. Hardwood chairs are sunk into the sand for a lazy afternoon on the beach, and hammocks swing from the trees in front of every room for laid-

---

"The dive sites boast unbelievably colorful macrofauna . . . and regular sightings of whale sharks."

diveborneo.com

---

back living. Head out from the gently shelving beach to swim in the warm sea. Then walk out along the jetty and look below at the water teeming with hundreds of tropical fish, from clown fish to baby sharks and giant starfish. The island is within the protected area of a marine conservation area, which means no jet skis, power boat racing, or fishing is allowed. Instead, it is perfect for divers. Explore the coral reef and underwater wrecks, and keep an eye out for stingrays, manatees, and barracudas. In season, green and hawksbill turtles come onto the island to nest. End your day by having dinner on the open-air terrace, as small black-tip sharks swim in the water below. **AD**

See Tabin Wildlife Reserve

Location Sabah, Malaysia
Website www.tabinwildlife.com   **Price** 🜚

Situated in the Malaysian state of Sabah on the island of Borneo, the dipterocarp forest of Tabin Wildlife Reserve is among the most biologically diverse areas on Earth. Home to orangutans and eight other species of primate, as well as the region's three largest mammals—the Sumatran rhinoceros, the Asian elephant, and the tembadau (an indigenous type of wild cattle)—the park plays a truly vital role in the preservation of its wildlife.

The 298,000-acre (120,500-ha) expanse of protected land comprises seven mud volcanoes and several saltwater springs, whose high mineral content attracts the many species of animal inhabiting the park. Likewise, the mud volcanoes are ideal spots from which to observe the local fauna, because both mammals and birds frequent them. In fact, bird-watchers will have a field day at Tabin's, with 220 different species of birds to look out for.

Despite its relative remoteness, the park is easily accessible (from Sabah's capital, Kota Kinabalu, which has an international airport) and provides comfortable accommodation with modern facilities. A total of twenty hotels—half of them located at the river and the other ten in the hills—ensure that a stay in the wilderness does not necessarily have to be synonymous with hardship. The impeccably clean timber bungalows are furnished with double beds and have private bathrooms with hot-water showers as well as secluded balconies that allow you to observe the surrounding primeval forest without having to get up-close and personal. The Tabin Wildlife Reserve is the perfect place for those who would like to experience raw nature without sacrificing their twenty-first-century amenities. **DaH**

Explore Kinabalu National Park

Location Sabah, Malaysia
Website www.sabahparks.org.my **Price** ◑

At 13,435 feet (4,095 m), it is the tallest peak in Malaysia and proudly overlooks Kinabalu National Park. What makes this park unique is its range of climates, from subalpine flora at the summit of the mountain to tropical hardwood forest on the lowlands. This diversity has allowed more than 6,000 plant species to thrive, many of which can only be found within Kinabalu. For this reason, the park was designated a World Heritage site in 2000.

Perhaps the most famous park resident is the rafflesia, the state flower of Sabah. It blooms just once every nine months, and only for a few days, but it is a sight worth waiting for. The rafflesia is the world's largest flower, and its spotty orange-red blooms can measure nearly 3 feet (1 m) across. Although the sight is quite remarkable, the smell is not so pleasant—it is also known as the corpse plant, and emits an odor of rotting meat to attract flies.

The summit trail up the granite slopes of the mountain is both a challenging and popular climb for hikers. It is recommended to tackle the slope over two days, pausing overnight at a rest house near the peak. Beginning in a forest of chestnut and oak trees, the trail is lined with brightly colored rhododendron and exotic orchid plants. As the altitude thins, so does the tree canopy. You will see an abundance of pitcher plants, the unusual bowl-shaped flowers that also feed on insects and bugs. Near the summit, few trees can tolerate the climate. Instead you will find mosses and hardy grasses covering the rocky slopes, and at the very top, possibly the best views in Borneo. **JP**

↗ *Mount Kinabalu dominates the skyline of Sabah, its jagged domed summit shrouded with clouds.*

"[Kinabalu] is said to contain 1,000 species of orchid as well as hot springs, a butterfly farm and turtles."

Lesley Reader, *Daily Telegraph*

Unwind at Fullerton Hotel

Location Singapore
Website www.fullertonhotel.com   **Price** ⊖⊖

There are worse ways to feel you have "arrived" in Singapore than swirling a lychee Martini in the uber-glam Post Bar of the Fullerton Hotel. Both the iconic Merlion statue and the silvery slick of the Singapore River that snakes past the hotel's front door lend the Fullerton a sense of place, but it is the Post Bar's signature Martini that makes the biggest impression. This relatively new contender has pole-vaulted to the top of the Asia's list of hotels, where it remains.

The 1920s Fullerton building—peppered as it is with distinguished Doric columns, cornices, and coffered ceilings—has scrubbed up rather well. Classic

---

"The hotel's infinity pool overlooks the Singapore River and offers striking views of the urban skyline."

Condé Nast Traveler

---

architecture aside, where the Fullerton truly scores is on its superb facilities and personal service. When Asia does high-tech, it does it well, and the Fullerton is no exception—right down to the gadgets in the Philippe Starck-designed bathrooms. Couch potatoes will drool over the sophistication of the bedside control panel and, should you feel homesick, an I.T. concierge can deliver a multimedia trolley and install a web cam so you can communicate with the rest of the world. There is even an in-safe power outlet for laptop recharging.

Everyone should stay in a hotel like the Fullerton once in their life—if only for a night. Rumor has it the presidential suite is fit for a queen. **TM**

Explore Bunaken National Marine Park

Location Sulawesi Island, Sunda, Indonesia
Website www.divetheworldindonesia.com   **Price** ⊖

With some of the planet's highest levels of aquatic biodiversity, Bunaken National Marine Park, in the waters north of Sulawesi Island, is a divers' paradise. The 220,000-acre (89,000-ha) expanse comprises the small islands of Nain, Siladen, Mantehage, Manado Tua, and Bunaken. The surrounding waters are inhabited by at least the same number of fish species as can be found in the whole of the Philippines, where 70 percent of the Indo-Western Pacific marine life is at home.

Within the park are barracudas, dolphins, reef sharks, stingrays, turtles, and even whales and dugongs. The area is also home to seventy genera of coral, compared to Hawaii's ten, and the steep coral walls off Bunaken island teem with marine wildlife. These reefs are even more impressive at night, when numerous animals rarely seen during the day suddenly appear.

Around 20,000 people live on the park's five islands, many of whom are professional fishermen who often use unsubtle means such as explosives to catch fish. The Indonesian government created the park in 1991 to prevent these damaging practices and overfishing, and the entrance fee that visitors pay constitutes an alternative source of income for the locals, and helps to preserve this exceptional ecosystem. The North Sulawesi Watersports Association (NSWA) not only strives to protect the marine life, but also passes on the financial benefits of tourism to the villagers. Travelers should only consider dive operators that are members of NSWA in order to ensure that the area continues to remain unspoiled. **DaH**

→ *The pristine tropical waters are up to 5,150 feet (1,570 m) deep and attract divers from across the globe.*

Trek Through Gunung Leuser National Park

Location Sumatra, Indonesia
Website www.geocities.com/rainforest/4466/leuser1.htm **Price** Ⓢ

Gunung Leuser National Park in Sumatra—the largest island belonging entirely to Indonesia—consists of several different nature reserves covering a 62-mile (100-km) stretch of the volcanic Bukit Barisan mountain range. Named after its highest peak, 11,100-foot (3,381-m) Gunung Leuser, the park comprises many steep areas that are inaccessible to humans and hence constitute a refuge for threatened animals such as the Sumatran orangutan, the smaller and rarer of the two species of orangutan. Estimates put their number at 5,000, and at the Orangutan Rehabilitation Center in Bukit Lawang—the park's main access point—visitors can get a closer look at these great apes.

The region also distinguishes itself as the only place where orangutans, crocodiles, rhinoceroses, elephants, and tigers all share the same habitat. The great differences in altitude mean the park also boasts an eclectic mix of plant species, exemplified by the various types of forest that cover the terrain, ranging from rain forest in the lowlands to beech and swamp forests as well as subalpine forest higher up the mountains.

In order to explore this vast expanse, it is best to go on an organized trekking tour. These tours can last from a few hours to two weeks, with accommodation provided in tents that are pitched in caves, or in basic bungalows by the river. Given the park's extraordinary biodiversity—with more than 700 animal species—an extended stay is advisable to fully appreciate the contrast between this unspoiled natural habitat and the man-made world we know as home. **DaH**

→ *One of the three national parks within the Tropical Rainforest of Heritage of Sumatra World Heritage site.*

Stay at Amanjiwo

Location Java, Indonesia **Website** www.amanresorts.com
Price 💲💲💲💲

"Amanjiwo's architecture renders it the perfect complement to Borobudur's timeworn grandeur."

Daily Telegraph

The world's largest Buddhist sanctuary, the eighth-century Borobudur temple stands opposite a breathtaking circular limestone monolith; the Menoreh Hills rise behind, and volcanos smoke gently in the distance. A deep sense of serenity pervades throughout. This is Amanjiwo; perhaps the world's most spiritual escape.

Do not be surprised to see fellow guests meditating in quiet spots or discussing the meaning of life. Amanjiwo, set in the verdant countryside of central Java, provokes serious contemplation thanks to its awe-inspiring setting amid ancient monuments. A box of watercolors is even provided in each suite for those who feel moved to capture their resplendent surroundings on canvas. However, there is no monklike abstinence here. Guests stay in one of thirty-four domed suites with beds surrounded by majestic pillars and hand-carved furniture. Many have private pools and all have views of sacred mountains, hills, or the Borobudur temple. Then there is the colonnaded pool club, with a 130-foot (40-m) infinity pool stretching into paddy fields, serene dining room and bar, and the spa area, where guests can sample the royal treat of Mandi Lulur, a traditional Javanese preparation of a princess on the eve of her wedding.

It is the less tangible things at Amanjiwo that leave a lasting impression, such as being showered with rose petals by local sarong-clad girls upon arrival and exploring Dagi Hill on the back of a Sumatran elephant. Guests return home from Amanjiwo feeling, quite literally, blessed. **LP**

⬉ *Amanjiwo has a grand temple-like appearance with soaring stone columns and a mystical aura.*

Relax at Waka Gangga

Location Bali, Indonesia **Website** www.wakagangga.com
Price 💲💲

Perched on rolling rice terraces overlooking the Indian Ocean, Waka Gangga's blend of elegance, luxury, and seclusion is as magical as it is seductive. These ten exclusive natural bungalows and six private villas are built from local materials, and the resort's eco-credentials are solid enough to have earned it an environmental tourism award. On one side are the slick rice fields and on the other a black-sand beach slips into the sea, although swimming in the sea in trickier weather is discouraged due to some often harsh undercurrents. Horses from the local stables can take you the short journey down the sand toward the famous rock-cleaved Tanah Lot temple, one of South Bali's most sacred places.

Waka Gangga is purely about relaxation. The rooms, shorn of some of the ultra-slick modern gadgets you might find elsewhere, almost demand that you forget your worries and learn how to relax. Unpainted woods, local fabrics, alang-alang grass roofs, and stone villas with their dressed slate and copious flowers all flow harmoniously with the surrounding area. Despite the rustic nature of the resort, basic amenities such as air-conditioning are provided, and all rooms have deluxe king-size beds, open fireplaces, large sofas, sunken bathtubs, garden showers, and an outside sundeck. The resort's shared areas are also comprehensive, and include an art gallery, library, and spa and yoga area—all perfect ways to help you unwind even further. Cocktails are served at sunset in the bar before you dive into the delightful Balinese food served in the restaurant, which comes with a camera-grabbing ocean view thanks to its cliff-edge location. That spectacular vista is a reminder as to why Bali's nickname is, deservedly, "island of the gods." **PS**

De-stress at Alila Ubud

Location Bali, Indonesia **Website** www.alilahotels.com/Ubud
Price 💲💲

Ten minutes from the Balinese cultural capital Ubud lies an oasis of sheer beauty that cannot fail to alleviate stress. The real world seems light years away when you alight at the tranquil and secluded hill resort of Alila Ubud, a place designed specifically to complement its gorgeous surroundings as well as emulate a traditional Balinese hill village.

With fifty-six rooms and eight villas, a stay here is about waving the wider world good-bye and entering an idealistic inner state of peace and tranquility. There are lots of ways to de-stress, starting with the rooms themselves. Those on the ground floor boast their own garden terraces, plus invigorating and refreshing

> *"The emerald infinity pool . . . has been called one of the most beautiful pools in the world."*
>
> *Daily Telegraph*

open-air showers and bathrooms that let you commune as closely with nature as you like. The views from the wraparound private balconies of the rooms above are nothing short of stunning.

Massages, needless to say, are magnificent at Spa Alila, and the resort's library and 24-hour, in-room dining service help promote the relaxed vibe. Tours of the mountain village of Kintamani and the nearby rice terraces at Tegalalang are available; the volcanic surroundings provide not only a sense of eternal majesty but are also a reminder of the harsh forces that created this place millions of years ago. All in all, Alila Ubud is the perfect place to be at one with yourself. **PS**

Stay at Gajah Mina

Location Bali, Indonesia
Website www.gajahminaresort.com   **Price** 🟢

This simple little hideaway stands in a lonely spot on the picturesque southwest coast of the island, among rice paddy fields and local temples, miles from tourist resorts. There are only nine Mediterranean-style villas forming an intimate boutique beach hotel. They stand in a garden of fragrant flowers and enormous butterflies, overlooking Gajah Mina's private black-sand beach and jagged volcanic rocks, riddled with caves and ancient stone carvings. Guests explore grassy cliff tops, rice paddies, coconut groves, and empty sandy beaches that stretch for 19 miles (30 km). Energetic visitors take mountain bike trails through cocoa plantations to a nearby volcano; others surf the powerful, pounding waves.

Back at your villa, it is peaceful and private within individual walled gardens with terraces looking out across the rugged coast and rice fields. Inside the bungalows you will find the same simple atmosphere —natural materials like volcanic stone, coconut wood, and teak, a few Indonesian antiques, a big, comfortable bed, a bit of stained glass, and a lounge chair under your private veranda to slump in and stare at the waves. You can slump still further under the influence of a traditional Balinese massage in a thatched pavilion alongside the palm-fringed swimming pool or with a yoga session among the bird songs and fragrant flowers. Food is another relaxed highlight at Gajah Mina. The restaurant menu, with lots of organic vegetables and fresh seafood, is a unique blend of local Balinese cuisine and the owner's French influence. Specialties include banana flower curry or mahi mahi fish in green pepper sauce. And that is it. Gajah Mina is just a quiet and beautiful spot—a place to be romantic and a place to relax. **SH**

Experience Tembok Bali

Location Bali, Indonesia
Website www.spavillage.com/tembokbali   **Price** 🟢🟢

Set among a striking landscape of soaring peaks, black volcanic beaches, and the twinkling sapphire Indian Ocean, Spa Villa Resort Tembok Bali is a mecca for spa aficionados. Balinese spas are not only about hedonistic pampering but are also infused with a heritage of ancient healing remedies. Visiting a spa is about cleansing the mind and soul as well as the body, and that is exactly what the Spa Villa Resort, in the unspoiled north of the island, is all about.

The resort provides each visitor with a tailored program, which begins upon arrival. Guests are welcomed with a foot massage and are invited to select a "discovery path": balance, creativity, or vigor.

"Tembok Bali's only neighbors are small fishing settlements and the odd roadside shop."

Independent

Everything from wood carving and basket weaving to guided meditation and scuba diving can be incorporated into a program.

Despite the focus on spirituality, life's simple pleasures are not denied. Guests may enjoy cocktails beside the large infinity pool, and a spectacle of seafood and organic seasonal fare is served daily in the Wantilan restaurant. The suites and villas both provide flawlessly luxurious accommodation. There are also many activities offered, such as a sunset cruise on a traditional Balinese boat to admire the towering Gunung Agung mountain. Above all, the resort delights in celebrating ancient Balinese culture, and is all the better for it. **LP**

Relax at Panchoran Retreat

Location Bali, Indonesia
Website www.lindagarland.com **Price** §§

What do you do when you have a beautiful home in an idyllic location and you feel inclined to share your good fortune with others? Well, in Linda Garland's case, you turn your home into an incredible hotel. Garland's unique and peaceful 25-acre (10-ha) haven, Panchoran Retreat, located along a river gorge close to Bali's cultural capital of Ubud, was transformed in 2003 from her own private hideaway into a blissful ecological sanctuary for worldwide visitors.

Panchoran—meaning "water spring" in Balinese—blends in effortlessly with its surroundings. Throughout the Main House, Waterfall House, and River House, the style is shabby-chic. The large thatched villas embody effortless cool, with lots of scented flowers, Javanese carvings, hammocks, open-air showers, and beds draped in mosquito nets. Waterfall House has a natural spring-fed pool and outdoor whirlpool tub. It overlooks the waterfalls, which provide a perpetual soothing soundtrack. River House is larger and has a pool and a generous deck overlooking rice fields and a bamboo forest.

Delicious Indonesian meals are whipped up using ingredients from the estate's organic garden, and a masseuse trained in traditional Balinese techniques is at hand to help ease away any nagging stress. The estate seems to cast a spell over artists and romantics seeking absolute solitude. Only a short walk through the Monkey Forest from the bohemian town of Ubud with its ancient temples, hip cafés, and thriving cultural scene, the retreat offers a different kind of magic just waiting to be discovered. **LP**

↗ *Panchoran was built and decorated using recycled ironwood, bamboo, and other natural materials.*

"I wanted to promote the use of bamboo as an alternative to wood in decoration and architecture."

Linda Garland, designer, Panchoran Retreat

Enjoy Villa Balquisse

Location Bali, Indonesia
Website www.balquisse.com **Price** 🟢🟢

Step through the carved stone doorway into Villa Balquisse and you will find glorious Indian fabric draped across an old Moroccan sofa and old metal lamps hanging from wooden roof beams. An antique Indonesian carved wooden elephant stares out across the worn stone floor. Welcome to one of Bali's most glamorous boutique hotels.

The hotel and its restored Balinese villas are set in tropical gardens between a mangrove swamp and a coconut grove in the popular village of Jimbaran. The beach is a few hundred yards away. The owner is a Moroccan-born interior designer, hence the stunning eclectic atmosphere. Among the traditional Balinese

"Chairs and tables stretch down toward the water attracting visitors eager to dine under the stars."

Jo Adetunji, *Guardian*

architecture there are chandeliers, French baroque chairs, enamel standalone baths, and Arabic screens.

The villas have private pools, and guests in the main hotel have an emerald swimming pool surrounded by bamboo, palms, and bougainvillea. Dinner is a fine mix of local ingredients with culinary inspiration from India, Indonesia, South-East Asia, the Middle East, and Europe. Enjoy a Moroccan couscous by candlelight, followed by a wonderful five spice crème brûlée. The open-air, thatched spa is as unique as the hotel, and traditional Balinese massages are a specialty. Many glossy magazines have published photographs taken at Villa Balquisse—but it is even better in real life. **SH**

Cruise Lesser Sunda

Location Lombok Strait, Indonesia
Website www.lomboksailing.com **Price** 🟢🟢🟢

Traveling on a boat that blends in with the stunning scenery is the best way to enjoy the turquoise waters surrounding Indonesia's Lesser Sunda islands. A few hours' sail west of Bali in the Lombok Strait—the biogeographical boundary between the Indo-Malayan animal kingdom and its distinctively different Australasian counterpart—the small island of Gili Trawangan is home to an 82-foot (25-m) hand-built wooden vessel whose elegance is reminiscent of the ships used by European explorers in centuries gone by. Staffed with four crew members and a captain, the *Bulan Purnama* has a maximum capacity of nine passengers and ensures high standards of comfort. A lack of air-conditioning and hot showers prevents it from being classified as a luxury boat, but its nostalgic flair and the spectacular tropical surroundings make for an unforgettable and relaxing experience that is far removed from the daily grind.

The company that owns the boat can recommend several itineraries, but passengers are welcome to plan their own route according to the length of their cruise. However, one place that should not be missed is the 55,700-acre (22,540-ha) nature reserve Moyo Island Hunting Park on the island of the same name just north of Sumbawa. Covering most of the island, the park teems with wildlife such as deer, wild cattle, and numerous species of bird. The local marine park's coral reefs are popular with divers and snorkelers. Farther east, the World Heritage site of Komodo National Park is worth a visit, too. It is home to the world's largest lizard, the Komodo dragon: a 10-foot (3-m) carnivorous animal that looks like a relic from prehistoric times. A cruise on the *Bulan Purnama* is an experience that is unlike anything you will find back home. **DaH**

Stay at the Oberoi

Location Lombok, Indonesia
Website www.oberoilombok.com **Price** 💲💲💲💲

The hotel is encircled by thick jungle, stands on a remote peninsula miles from any settlement, and is on a small, poor, and undeveloped island. But when guests step into the Oberoi's open-air reception area, immaculate uniformed staff descend from all directions —just as they would at the Ritz in Piccadilly, London.

Half the accommodations are villas surrounded by high stone walls, each with an individual gatehouse. Inside this personal perimeter, there is a pool, patio, thatched dining pavilion, fishponds, and lush gardens. The villa itself is a thatched stone bungalow with a giant canopied bed overlooking the sea and has a marvelous marble bathroom with private garden.

> *"A self-contained temple of pleasure complete with swimming pool and ornamental ponds."*
>
> Richard Madden, *Daily Telegraph*

Evening passes amid a spectacular amphitheater of bars and gourmet restaurants around a series of pools leading down to the beach. Everyone waits for the sun to set behind a distant volcano on Bali. By day, local craftsmen squat by the reception hall carving wonderful mahogany animals. Later local musicians play simple Indonesian music accompanied by a chorus of frogs and insects. The sea is calm, clear, and warm. Hotel boats will whisk you away for fishing, snorkeling, diving, or sightseeing trips to reefs and islands. Guests who opt for a sunset cruise will arrive at the jetty to find four staff members—one to steer the boat and three to mix the cocktails. **SH**

Unwind at Amanwana

Location Moyo Island, Indonesia
Website www.amanresorts.com **Price** 💲💲💲

Most of us have never heard of the island of Moyo, probably because it is one of the world's few remaining, totally unspoiled paradise islands—and it deserves protecting all the more so for it. A 135-square-mile (350-sq-km) drop in the ocean off the coast of Sumbawa, to the east of Bali, Moyo is remote, wild, and definitely not somewhere you are likely to bump into neighbors.

Reached by motor boat, turboprop floatplane, or even helicopter, Amanwana is set in one of Moyo's secluded coves and caressed by the bath-like waters of the Flores Sea. Twenty luxury tents—either jungle or ocean-front—provide stylish accommodation while macaque monkeys swing in the surrounding trees and sea eagles soar above in the aquamarine sky. Although covered in canvas, you can banish all thoughts of the boy-scout school of camping. These tents have solid wall foundations, king-size beds draped romantically in netting, large bathrooms, and elegant, polished wood interiors. Delicious Asian meals are served in an open-air pavilion with a soaring bamboo roof, and Borneo body scrubs take place beneath shady tamarind trees at the Jungle Cove spa.

There is plenty to do on the castaway island: Observe turtles mingling with pygmy seahorses on a scuba trip and wild boar foraging the land deeper into the nature reserve. The more adventurous guests can book the Komodo expedition, which combines time at the resort with a boat trip that takes you to two nearby islands inhabited by Komodo dragons.

How to round off a day in paradise? At Amanwana, which aptly means "peaceful forest," a campfire dinner on the beach with a dazzling sunset as a backdrop provides the perfect epilogue. **LP**

See Kelimutu Mountain

Location Flores, Indonesia
Website www.bali-travel-online.com **Price** ◗

The island of Flores, east of Java and part of Indonesia's Lesser Sunda islands, has many claims to fame. For one, it is the home of indigenous giant rats and dwarf elephants. For another, archaeologists recently unearthed the remains of "real-life hobbits," a race of people that only averaged a height of 3 feet (1 m) and a possible predecessor of the pygmy.

Kelimutu Mountain is one of the best places in the world to watch the sun rise. Three volcanic crater lakes sit at its peak, and, because of the unusual geochemical conditions, the water in the lakes changes color. At the far west, the Lake of Old People has blue water; next to it, the Lake of Young Men and Maidens has green water, and sitting beside that is the red water of the Bewitched or Enchanted Lake on the southeast side of the volcano. Over time, the water changes color due to the fluctuating acidity levels— what was green one day might be black, coffee-colored, or bright blue on another day. Streaks of mineral deposits leak into the lake and provide yet more colors, confirming the theory that things on Flores do not operate according to the usual rules.

Visitors have to get up in the very early hours of the morning to drive up the mountain and walk the final steps to the top, but it is worth it. Watching the sun rise over an ethereal scene in the barren volcanic moonscape, with the painted pools of water behind, is an extraordinary experience. Some people have called the lakes "god's paint pots"; others say that they should be on the list of the Wonders of the World. You can certainly sit for hours and enjoy the view. **LD**

← *The different colors of the lakes at the top of Kelimutu are a source of intrigue for geologists and tourists alike.*

Discover Nihiwatu

Location Sumba, Indonesia
Website www.nihiwatu.com **Price** ◗◗

Sumba was once regarded by foreign traders as an island of fierce warriors where head-hunting expeditions were common. After battles with enemies and between clans, heads were considered to be trophies and were displayed on "skull trees" in the villages. Although this particular gory practice has— thankfully—died out, much of the small eastern Indonesian island's fascinating culture remains and the Sumbanese people still cherish their traditional way of life and tribal unity.

At Nihiwatu resort, which has been applauded for its dedication to helping local communities, visitors get an insight into the islanders' history from the Stone

---

"The resort is famous among surfers for the fat left-hander that breaks off its beach."

Condé Nast Traveler

Age sites and villages that have remained unchanged for centuries. Nihiwatu is an exclusive tropical retreat where guests enjoy simple luxury unknown to the ancient Sumbanese. There are just seven spacious air-conditioned bungalows and three two-bedroom villas with thatched roofs, built by Indonesian craftsman using local materials. The style is contemporary, with glass walls and doors magnifying the stunning views.

In addition to exploring the island, visitors can indulge in more contemporary pleasures like surfing, diving, and game fishing. A rustic open living area and clifftop bar complete the laid-back island vibe. There is also a pool, jungle spa, and water sports center. **LP**

Whether it's a visit to the earthly paradises of Bora Bora or the Cook Islands, a journey through the mesmerizing Australian outback, or a stay at a luxurious mountain lodge in New Zealand, Oceania offers a range of seductive destinations. Why not enjoy the best of both worlds by relaxing on a quiet beach one week and exploring inland jungles the next?

OCEANIA

← Le Taha'a, French Polynesia

Ride the *Indian Pacific* Train

Location Perth to Sydney, Australia
Website www.trainways.com.au **Price** ⊖⊖

Packs of wild kangaroos, never-ending stark desert plains, and mountains swirling in blue mists—these are all just part of the view when you grab a seat on the world's last remaining transcontinental train journey. Chugging along from coast to coast, the *Indian Pacific* takes sixty-five hours—that is three days and three nights—to travel a distance of 2,702 miles (4,352 km), making it one of the world's longest train rides. After leaving Sydney's Central Station, the train rattles through the suburbs before winding its way up through the dramatic Blue Mountains, so-called because of the eerie blue mist that rises up from the eucalyptus trees. There is a short stop at the outback town of Broken Hill, a small and remote mining town home to numerous artists who love the inspiring landscape. Further along, the train passes through the stark, desert-like Nullarbor Plain, where the train bolts through the longest straight stretch of track: a cool 297 miles (478 km).

There is plenty of wildlife to spot along the way, such as wild camels, emus, kangaroos, wombats, and parrots. Keep an eye out for the Australian wedge-tailed eagle, with a wingspan of 6.5 feet (2 m), as it is the train's striking emblem. Accommodations are comfortable and divided into two classes: sleeper cabins or airline-style seats.

Although 65 hours is a long time to travel from one side of Australia to the other when you can fly from Sydney to Perth in five hours, if you take the *Indian Pacific* you can do your bit for global warming and treat yourself to a once-in-a-lifetime scenic feast. **JK**

🡐 *The* Indian Pacific *passes a historic viaduct on its journey across the vast continent of Australia.*

Snorkel in Ningaloo

Location Ningaloo Marine Park, Western Australia, Australia
Website www.environment.gov.au **Price** ⊖

If you are an enthusiastic snorkeler, you should head directly to Ningaloo Marine Park on the coast of Western Australia. Here you can swim with the largest fish in the world—the whale shark. This giant of the sea measures in at up to 40 feet (12 m) and can weigh 14 tons, yet has a pleasing tendency toward not eating the divers. It is a filter feeder whose diet consists of plankton and krill.

The Ningaloo Reef—most of which remains pristine thanks to low levels of pollution—is one of only two places on Earth where whale sharks regularly congregate, and they are here from March until June. The reef is also home to humpback whales and manta

---

"Ningaloo Reef . . . is at the heart of the region's outstanding natural heritage significance."

UNESCO World Heritage Committee

---

rays, and hawksbill, green, and loggerhead turtles all breed in the area. Ningaloo Reef is about 200 miles (322 km) long. The marine park that was created in 1987 to protect it covers 600 acres (243 ha). In all, there are 500 species of fish and more than 200 species of coral at Ningaloo—and the reef's marine life is remarkably accessible to visitors. Close to the shore, it encircles shallow lagoons that are suitable for family snorkeling and less confident swimmers. Here you can see vividly colored clown fish, tiger fish, and sea anemones. For those who do not want to get their feet wet, there are also whale-watching trips, glass-bottomed boat tours, and scenic flights. **LD**

Enjoy the Kimberley Region

Location Kimberley Region, Western Australia, Australia
Website www.elquestrohomestead.com.au **Price** 🌑

Western Australia's rugged Kimberley region boasts some of the most spectacularly remote and rugged landscapes in the world. The area, roughly the size of California and three times larger than the United Kingdom, contains breathtaking natural attractions such as Purnululu, (a World Heritage site), the flowing Mitchell Falls, and the fabulous 410-mile (660-km) Gibb River Road.

El Questro Wilderness Park occupies one million acres (404,685 ha) of the Kimberley expanse, set across the top of the Chamberlain Gorge above a river that is home to fish, turtles, and crocodiles. Surrounded by lush tropical gardens that cascade down to a pool and tennis court, the homestead offers seven individually themed guest rooms, all of which were given a contemporary makeover by Sydney interior architect Pike Withers in 2007. Rustic Australian artifacts nestle next to Zanotta sofas, modern Italian ottomans, and woven cane chairs. The Chamberlain Suite is simply to die for, with a bathtub on the outdoor balcony and panoramic views from a wraparound veranda.

Yet the real highlight of El Questro is the dizzying range of excursions. You can boat on the Chamberlain Gorge, relax at nearby thermal pools (Zebedee Springs), horseback ride, or take a scenic helicopter flight through the Kimberley's canyons and gorges. Many trips are included in the room fee, although adventurers can book many more. In the mood for a gourmet picnic at Mirimiri Falls or a heli-fishing tour? El Questro will organize it in a heartbeat. When you are back from admiring the Kimberley terrain, the homestead's chef will titillate you with delicious food. You can even dine beneath the palms that grace the clifftop ledge—just do not feed the crocs below. **PS**

Explore Purnululu

Location Purnululu National Park, Western Australia, Australia
Website www.westernaustralia.com **Price** 🌑

The World Heritage-listed Purnululu National Park (also known as Bungle Bungle) is often considered to be Australia's equivalent of the Grand Canyon. Situated between the Western Australian towns of Kununurra and Halls Creek, the 593,000-acre (240,000 ha) expanse is characterized by a multitude of beehive-shaped karst mountains that rise up to 1,000 feet (300 m). The flat land that is home to these eroded sandstone peaks is located at another 1,000 feet above sea level. The plains are covered by woodland and grass, whereas the western area is distinguished by steep rocks. The rugged territory became a national park in 1987, when it was unknown to most foreign travelers.

"[Bungle Bungle] is not only totally unique . . . it's also breathtakingly weird and completely inexplicable."

Mark Moxon, travel writer

Two camp sites provide basic accommodation in the park: Kurrajong Campground is 4 miles (7 km) north of the visitor center, and Walardi Campground is 7.5 miles (12 km) to its south. The park possesses a number of captivating stone formations including the Echidna Chasm, Piccaninny, Frog Hole, and Cathedral Gorges. Still relatively inaccessible and largely unknown outside Australia, this extraordinary scenery provides the perfect setting for those in need of a break from their own hectic surroundings. **DaH**

➡ *The beehive-like domes of Purnululu, with their distinctive stripes, are an unusual sight.*

Enjoy Bamurru Plains

Location Bamurru Plains, Northern Territory, Australia
Website www.bamurruplains.com   **Price** ⊛⊛⊛

Within the boundaries of Swim Creek Station, not far from the western edge of Kakadu National Park, is the exquisitely isolated retreat of Bamurru Plains. Just a twenty-five minute flight from the Northern Territory capital of Darwin, Bamurru Plains offers guests the ultimate Australian outback experience.

Bungalows of timber and corrugated iron are a mix of undiluted rustic charm and unpretentious luxury, raised above the red earth on timber platforms high enough to deter the herds of buffalo that amble past at dusk. Nights relaxing on your private balcony are accompanied by the sounds of barking owls, raptors, black flying foxes, frogs, and cicadas. From December

> *"Bamurru Plains has taken the quintessential safari experience and made it Australian."*
>
> *The Australian*

to March, the annual monsoon rolls in from the Timor Sea and brings with it egrets, blue-winged kookaburras, geese, and an abundance of bird life, all of which can be seen from the comfort of your own personal airboat or on organized safaris.

Mouthwatering meals are prepared by your own five-star chef. They will likely include Bamurru staples such as oysters, barramundi, and buffalo fillets. Each of Bamurru's nine bungalows is sufficiently isolated from the next to ensure a private sense of discovery. **BS**

➥ *The outback experience offered here is markedly different to those of drier, rockier regions.*

Explore Arnhem Land

Location Arnhem Land, Northern Territory, Australia
Website www.australianexplorer.com/arnhem_land.htm   **Price** ⊖

"Another special place to experience the Aboriginal culture of the Top End is Arnhem Land."

Lesley Parker, *Daily Telegraph*

Stretching out over 36,300 square miles (94,000 sq km), Arnhem Land in the northeastern part of Australia's Northern Territory is one of the few remaining refuges for the country's indigenous population. In order to protect the Aborigines' ancient habitat only a limited number of travelers are allowed to visit the handful of designated tourist areas in Arnhem Land.

From May to October, visitors who have obtained the necessary permits can explore parts of the virtually uninhabited Cobourg Peninsula (also known as Garig Gunak Barlu National Park). It is a two-day trip east of the state capital, Darwin, and has dramatic coastlines and virginal sandy beaches that are a walkers' paradise. Protected from commercial fishing, the peninsula's lagoons and coral reefs teem with marine life, and along the coast there are many spots that are suitable for recreational fishing with or without a boat. Further east, the lush tropical forests and pristine beaches of the Gove Peninsula are equally scenic.

Meanwhile, the subtropical savannah just south of the Cobourg Peninsula is home to more than 200 species of bird, as well as wallabies, dingoes, turtles, tree snakes, and the world's largest reptile, the saltwater crocodile.

Ancient rock paintings can be found in this area too, with those near Mount Borradaile dating back some 50,000 years. Visitor centers all over Arnhem Land provide travelers with information about the cultural achievements of the local people, who are known all over the world for having invented the Aborigines' most famous instrument, the didgeridoo. **DaH**

⬉ *This area has one of the highest concentrations of Aboriginal rock art sites in the world.*

Camp at Longitude 131°

Location Uluru-Kata Tjuta National Park, Northern Territory, Australia
Website www.longitude131.com.au   **Price** ❺❺❺❺

Think eco-tourism, and it is all too easy to envisage images of compost toilets. Come to Longitude 131°, and any such lingering preconceptions will soon be vanquished for good.

This award-winning luxury wilderness camp in Australia's Red Centre is not only eco-friendly, but it is also a wildly romantic escape, set atop an isolated sand dune close to the border of the Uluru-Kata Tjuta National Park and only 6 miles (10 km) from the iconic Uluru (Ayers rock) itself. Accommodation consists of fifteen luxurious air-conditioned tents, which feature expansive stone floors, neutral, earthy decor, and state-of-the-art bathrooms for an indulgent touch.

> "From your luxury tented room you have uninterrupted views of this icon of Australia's Red Centre."
>
> Paul Miles, *Daily Telegraph*

Unlike the early explorers, guests at Longitude are cosseted in five-star luxury. The flick of a bedside switch is all it takes to raise the blinds and watch the spectacular views of Uluru at sunrise and sunset. Meticulously designed to remain cool in the summer and warm in winter, the tents have reverse-cycle air-conditioning for complete control. There is also a restaurant, that serves up the best of contemporary Australian cuisine, with the emphasis on fresh produce. Total immersion in the wilderness and Aboriginal culture can be achieved through eco-walks with experienced guides, visits to artists' communities, and outdoor evening dining hosted by an astronomer. **HA**

Enjoy Bedarra Beach House

Location Bedarra, Queensland, Australia
Website www.bedarrabeachhouse.com.au   **Price** ❺❺❺

There are no shops or restaurants, no television, limited cell phone coverage, and few residents. Welcome to the tropical island of Bedarra, in Australia's Great Barrier Reef, the perfect hideaway for people who do not want to be found. Accessible only by a twenty-minute boat ride from Dunk Island, Bedarra offers true escapism, privacy, and indulgence.

Alongside its pristine coastline, the island's slopes blossom with the delightful scent of hibiscus and frangipani flowers, creating a riot of color along winding paths that lead the way to Bedarra Beach House. Situated high among the trees in the island's lush rain forest, it is an exceptionally romantic retreat. Children are strictly banned from this adult-only refuge—an architect-designed pavilion that makes dazzling use of its location, blending comfortably into the natural surroundings with its timber decks and large granite boulders. The decor fuses Queensland style with Asian influences. The luxury is in the detail: the master bedroom has a king-sized bed with feather pillows, whereas the bathroom has a plunge pool that opens out onto the rain forest. The house is a stone's throw from two private beaches, the palm-fringed, crescent-shaped Doorila Bay and the sheltered Coomool Bay with its sweep of powdery sand.

Before their stay begins, guests are asked to create their own shopping list and, upon arrival, the cupboards and fridge are stocked with everything they need—from fresh seafood to tropical fruits plus wine and champagne. While away the afternoons reading and lazing in one of the beach house hammocks and, if you tire of that, use paddle skis to explore the island. For tranquility in natural surroundings, make a beeline for this calm retreat. **JK**

Relax at Daintree Ecolodge and Spa

Location Daintree Rain Forest, Queensland, Australia
Website www.daintree-ecolodge.com.au **Price** ⊖⊖

Hollywood A-listers love this rain forest spa, ninety minutes' drive north of Cairns in Queensland, and they are not the only ones. The small lodge and spa, which offers rain forest walks, an introduction to Aboriginal art, and fifteen stylish tree house villas, has won awards for just about everything.

What makes the lodge so special? Well, there is the location for starters. It is in the heart of Daintree Rain Forest, the world's oldest living rain forest at around 135 million years old, the home of thirteen species not found anywhere else in the world, not to mention tropical birds, tree frogs, and reptiles. The lodge is set on 30 acres (12 ha) of land and has a commitment to keeping its surroundings in pristine condition, as well as protecting its Aboriginal heritage. Guided interpretative walks show you the local bugs and trees with medicinal properties. There is also a waterfall that has a special meditation and yoga deck, and is often used for Aboriginal-style wedding ceremonies and Aboriginal art classes.

Back in the lodge, the spa is a key attraction. It is inspired by the Aboriginal people, and takes note of their philosophy of Wawa-Kawba, the healing of the spirit. Treatments use rain forest berries, and Daintree Essentials products are available for purchase. The villas themselves are a perfect combination of eco and modern with Internet connections, cable television, and all the modern conveniences you would expect, as well as whirlpool tubs, luxury screened beds with bamboo canopies, and Aboriginal art. **LD**

→ *The eco-lodge has a stylish restaurant, Julaymba, that serves local food and overlooks a freshwater lagoon.*

Ride the Kuranda Scenic Railway

Location Cairns to Kuranda, Queensland, Australia
Website www.kurandascenicrailway.com.au **Price** 🌀

Conceived in 1882 and built nine years later, the Kuranda Scenic Railway was originally intended to connect Cairns and Kuranda in northern Queensland, and so help local tin miners deprived of food and essential supplies.

The thick jungle and steep rocks, up to 1,000 feet (300 m) high, were the main barriers to construction. Workers, mainly Irish and Italian, had to build fifteen tunnels and dozens of bridges in order to complete the 47 miles (75 km) of rail tracks. Many workers lost their lives achieving this dangerous engineering feat, but today's visitors have a far more leisurely experience

> "The historic Kuranda Scenic Railway climbs the mountain past waterfalls and ravines."

Jay Canning, *Daily Telegraph*

of the journey, enjoying dramatic views of Cairns and the Stoney Creek Falls as the train makes its way along the track to Kuranda.

The village of Kuranda occupies an area of rain forest that has been inhabited by indigenous people for more than 10,000 years. These days Kuranda is most famous for its picturesque train station (built in 1915) and the Skyrail Rainforest Cableway, which provides splendid aerial views of the World Heritage-listed tropical rain forest and the spectacular Barron Falls. Various packages are available to allow tourists to discover some of the world's oldest rain forest in the comfort of a train or gondola. **DaH**

Stay at Dunk Island

Location Dunk Island, Queensland, Australia
Website www.dunk-island.com **Price** 🌀🌀

The Bandjin and Djiru people who have lived on this island for thousands of years call it "Coonaglebah"— isle of peace and plenty. Renamed Dunk Island by Captain Cook, it lies off the northern Queensland coast by the Great Barrier Reef and is Australia's most beautiful resort island complete with perfect, white-sand beaches, tropical gardens, and virgin rain forests.

The resort is just a forty-minute flight from Cairns, but devotees approach it by ferry from Mission Beach. On the journey, they trail their hands in the water, watching out for dolphins, sea turtles, dugongs, and migrating whales. Dunk is designated a national park for its outstanding natural attractions, which include Mount Kootaloo, standing at 889 feet (271 m) high. From the look-out point at the top, you can see the turquoise sea studded with dark islands, with coral reefs strung around them like necklaces. Up here in the rain forest, you will see the Ulysses butterfly, also called the Blue Mountain Butterfly, a beautiful iridescent blue creature with a wingspan of 5.5 inches (14 cm), a key draw for nature lovers.

The resort is run by Voyages, with all the modern conveniences you could wish for; boats to take you snorkeling or diving on the Great Barrier Reef, tennis courts, visits to the artists' colony, or sailing trips. The Spa of Peace and Plenty offers Elemis treatments near a water lily pond, where you can watch dragonflies hum as your cares are soothed away. The service is first class—no wonder so many honeymooners choose the resort as an idyllic island getaway. **LD**

> ➔ *Beachfront properties don't come much more heavenly than this resort at Dunk Island.*

Stay at Qualia

Location Whitsunday Islands, Queensland, Australia
Website www.qualia.com.au **Price** ⊖⊖⊖

Qualia is the epitome of Australian laid-back style. The retreat harmoniously makes use of local timber and stone and takes pride of place on the Great Barrier Reef. Guests stay in private hideaways, either Leeward Pavilions or Windward Pavilions, dotted among the native eucalyptus with picture-postcard views from spacious wooden decks and infinity plunge pools.

The word "qualia" derives from Latin and refers to a collection of sensory experiences, thus it was deemed by the resort's creators to "fit the essence" of their handiwork. And the senses come alive at Qualia— sight is stimulated by panoramic views of turquoise waters and the lush green Queensland coastline, while the sound of the sea rushing over the pebble shore and the scent of eucalyptus leaves permeates the air.

Visitors can take a closer look at the extraordinary underwater life to be found here on a snorkeling or scuba trip. They can also savor an array of taste sensations rustled up daily; for example, gourmet treats overlooking the Coral Sea at Long Pavilion or informal Australian fare waterside at Pebble Beach.

The world-class spa at the resort is also very much a part of the sensory experience. Guests can be pummeled into blissful submission, or indulge in Roman baths and an invigorating Swiss shower, or make use of the steam room and an open-air yoga and meditation pavilion. The overwhelming sense is one of peace and harmony, enhanced no doubt by the adults-only rule. For those willing and able to splash out a bit of extra money, chartering a private yacht or a helicopter trip is the icing on the cake. **LP**

⬅ *The views from the infinity pool are wonderful. You will feel as though you are in a different world.*

Enjoy Paradise Bay

Location Whitsunday Islands, Queensland, Australia
Website www.paradisebay.com.au **Price** ⊖⊖⊖

Zipping across the calm waters of the Coral Sea to the aptly named Paradise Bay, the lush green mountain peaks rise dramatically from the azure depths and incredible white-sand beaches resemble scenes that most people only experience in their dreams. Perched on the edge of South Long Island, on Australia's Queensland coast, is Paradise Bay Island Eco Escape, the most exclusive, sustainable resort on all seventy-four islands of the Whitsunday Island chain.

Hosting only sixteen guests at any one time, the owners of this eco-tourism development are keen to provide all the luxury trimmings of an island retreat, while at the same time considering the environmental

> *"This utopia sits in sublime isolation on the northernmost tip of Hamilton Island."*
>
> *Condé Nast Traveler*

cost. Built using locally sourced materials, the resort uses 100 percent alternative energy and everything that can be, is recycled. Waterside guest bungalows are simple but elegantly decorated; each has a king-size bed, bathroom, and solar lighting.

Guests are free to roam the dense bushlands of the surrounding national park, take a trip on the resort's own yacht which sails daily to nearby deserted bays and coves, or go snorkeling in the warm waters of the Great Barrier Reef which is just in front of the resort. Dinner is served outdoors beneath the stars along with fine wines and the company of kindred spirits happy to abandon the hustle of everyday life. **LM**

Experience Hayman Island

Location Whitsunday Islands, Queensland, Australia
Website www.hayman.com.au   **Price** ⚅⚅⚅⚅

As your boat cruises toward Hayman, the Great Barrier Reef's most feted island retreat, you witness the stark natural beauty of this captivating archipelago rising out from the deep blue sea. Here, every care and whim is catered to by the ever-ready, unobtrusive service. There are eight restaurants, including convivial weekly sittings at the chef's table where guests are joined by expert food and wine specialists. Meals of a more intimate nature can be savored via a candlelit supper from your balcony or veranda, or a gourmet hamper on a secluded beach.

Total pampering and relaxation is on offer at Spa Chakra, with luxury treatments carried out in idyllic settings. Meditation and dedicated wet treatment rooms sit alongside a restorative itinerary of health and fitness regimes. Afterward, relax in the serenity of your room, suite, villa, or penthouse.

Natural fauna can be found in the Retreat Wing, which is set within delightful tropical gardens. Other enclaves offer access to Hayman's dreamily iconic swimming pool, ash-blond sandy beaches, cerulean lagoon, or a bird's-eye view from high across the Coral Sea and islands, each with their own soothing, beautifully considered, classic designs.

The reason most visitors travel to Hayman is to experience its gateway to one of the greatest natural wonders of the world: the mesmerizing Great Barrier Reef. Sea kayaking, sailing, whale watching, and game fishing are also on the menu. In fact, the options are endless: golf, tennis, and trips to the purest beach in the world, Whitehaven, are all available, too. **VG**

⮕   *Hayman offers a lush, tropical island paradise at the end of the world, with activities to fit every mood.*

Stay at Seabreeze House

Location Town of 1770, Queensland, Australia
Website www.seabreeze1770.com   **Price** ⊜⊜⊜⊜

The explorer Captain James Cook first stepped ashore here as a lieutenant on May 23, 1770. It was his second landing in Australia, and today the Town of 1770 represents the birthplace of the state of Queensland. The great English navigator would almost certainly recognize this unspoiled mix of rivers, reefs, and lagoons even today, thanks in no small part to the careful development of the region with ecologically sensitive hideaways such as Seabreeze House.

Set within 1,600 acres (647 ha) of pristine nature reserve, Seabreeze House is part of a handful of beach houses at Agnes Waters, just minutes from Bustard Bay where Cook and his small landing party first came

---

"Nature lovers will enjoy walking the Red Rock trail . . . to view loggerhead turtles."

Proprietors, Seabreeze House

---

ashore. A gated compound surrounds this carefully designed home, which blends seamlessly into the surrounding flora. Bedrooms have king-size beds draped in Egyptian cotton sheets and massive sunken baths. A glorious 40-foot (12-m) lap pool looks out over the azure waters of the Coral Sea and the lagoons and reefs of the Great Barrier Reef.

Don't miss the chance to swim in the Fitzroy Reef lagoon, rated one of the top snorkeling sites in the world. Just an eighty-minute boat ride from 1770, it boasts 2,500 species of marine life. Or you could spend the night on the lagoon's calm waters aboard Seabreeze's very own 75-foot (23-m) superyacht. **BS**

Visit Fraser Island

Location Fraser Island, Queensland, Australia
Website www.fraserisland.net   **Price** ⓫

Some 78 miles (126 km) long, and 9 miles (15 km) wide, Fraser Island, the largest sand island in the world, is an ecological paradise of wild horses, where multitudes of dingoes howl by night, and countless humpbacks pass by from August to October, making the 5,000-mile (8,050-km) round trip from Antarctica. There is so much sand here; one beach is 75 miles (120 km) long. It is not for swimming though—these waters are pulled about by currents and owned by the menacing tiger sharks, even the shallows. If you go up to India Head, you can see them gliding around in the surf.

The usual mode of transport for the visitor is simply to hop in a four-by-four vehicle and drive over the hard-packed sand; if you see a plane descending to land on the beach, it is up to you to give way. In the interior, as well as hushed, virgin rain forest, the island has deep-green, pristine lakes of pure water—more than one hundred of them—some surrounded by sand dunes. The Aboriginal name for Fraser is *K'Gari*, which means "beautiful woman," and a myth maintains that the spirit who created the island was so awed by its beauty that she stayed there alone, inviting the wildlife to help stave off her loneliness.

The waters of these beautiful lakes are exceptionally cleansing. The beach sand of Lake McKenzie is nearly pure silica, and it is possible to wash hair, teeth, jewelry, and exfoliate one's skin. Watch out for the dingoes, though; they will eat anything that is not nailed down once the darkness descends. These are some of the last remaining pure dingoes in Eastern Australia, so whatever you do, do not feed them. **LB**

➔ *The wonderful long beaches of Fraser Island stretch for miles, with barely a tourist to be seen.*

Enjoy Secrets on the Lake

Location Sunshine Coast, Queensland, Australia
Website www.secretsonthelake.com.au   **Price** 💲💲

The cabins have names such as Dragonfly, Two Frogs, and Lizard's Lair, but do not let that put you off. If you ever dreamed of spending the night in your own tree house, accessed by a network of elevated walkways and surrounded by rain forest, you need look no further. Overlooking the placid waters of Lake Baroon in the Sunshine Coast hinterland north of Brisbane, the 45 acres (18 ha) that comprise Secrets On The Lake contain ten superbly detailed and crafted cabins and one 100-year-old federation-style cabin.

With individually carved front doors, handcrafted king-size beds, log fires, and solid timber representations of Australian native animals and flora, each cabin is designed to create the sense of being in your own personal tropical environment. Barbecues on the veranda allow you to enjoy meals in the company of some of the forest's more permanent residents, including kookaburras, possums, bower birds, and tree frogs.

To call them cabins is almost a misnomer. Designed with high ceilings and galley kitchens, the buildings have expansively glazed exteriors that bring the deep greens of the forest indoors and flood every corner with day-long dappled light. Although they may be sumptuous in scale, the little things that make you feel like you are at home have not been forgotten, such as granite hearths, stained glass windows, oil lamps, and handmade pottery crafted by local artists.

Guests are welcomed with baskets filled with complimentary champagne, breakfast cereals, and fruit. Fresh breads are delivered to your door daily and baskets of delicious barbecued food can be supplied for lunch and dinner, which can be enjoyed in the privacy of your own cedar porch swing. **BS**

Relax at Gaia Retreat & Spa

Location Byron Shire, New South Wales, Australia
Website www.gaiaretreat.com.au   **Price** 💲💲

A cocooning, uncluttered retreat created by Olivia Newton-John and her friend Gregg Cave, Gaia Retreat & Spa strikes just the right balance between luxury and simplicity. Set in the rural hinterland a fifteen-minute drive from beach and surf hangout Byron Bay, it is a world away from the town's partying tourists. Visitors can kick back in peaceful grounds strewn with jacaranda trees, hammocks, and hand-carved Tibetan stone urns. Meditation benches and canopied day beds offer inspirational views of green hills and valleys, and there is an elegant pool, hot tub, and sauna. The Amala Day Spa employs some of the best therapists in the area, with naturopathy, iridology, acupuncture,

"Deliciously long, three-hour body treatments (scrubs, steams, and oil wraps) leave you dreamy-headed."

Tatler

and hypnotherapy on the menu alongside beauty treatments and every type of massage you could want. Attend a class or two from the daily-changing rota of subjects, which can include yoga, sound meditation, pilates, art, cooking, and tai chi. The yoga studio itself is large and lovely. There are also tennis courts and bicycles for you to use.

The accommodation is in wooden lodges set around a central Samoan longhouse. The Sura Terrace rooms have their own courtyards, day beds, and baths, and the Acala Suites are even more spacious. The cuisine is modern Australian by design. If you are a fan, Olivia herself visits about four times a year. **CSJ**

Discover Lord Howe Island

Location Lord Howe Island, New South Wales, Australia
Website www.lordhoweisland.info **Price** 🛇🛇

Lord Howe Island is a tiny island set 430 miles (690 km) off the coast of New South Wales in the Pacific Ocean. It is a very remote but gorgeous place that was discovered in 1788 by a British lieutenant on his way to Norfolk Island where he intended to establish a second colony. The island was not settled permanently until 1833, and since then its main claim to fame has been as the native home of the Kentia palm, a type of houseplant that was ubiquitous in the 1970s. Nothing much has happened since.

Just 7 miles (11 km) long and 2 miles (3.2 km) wide, the island allows only 400 visitors at any one time and remains beautifully innocent. There is a 25 mile per hour (40 kph) speed limit, free piles of wood next to public barbecues for anyone to use, everybody gets around by bike, and nobody locks their hotel room door. Two-thirds of the island is natural forest, so there are some inspiring treks to be had—the steep climb to Goat House Cave is worth it for the views out to the Dalí-esque Ball's Pyramid. There is a more tranquil walk along the Max Nicholls Memorial Track to Ned's Beach, where giant kingfish swim in the shallows.

The place to stay is the nautically styled Capella Lodge, the only hotel on the island with views out to sea and to the island's two imposing and mysterious mountains, Mount Lidgbird and Mount Gower. Guests can kick back with champagne and gourmet canapés on the decked terrace, or brave the cold plunge pool. There is also a hot tub to soothe tired bodies and a tiny spa offering treatments including rubs for walkers' feet and a traditional Kodo massage. If you want to sample some ayurveda treatments, a bike ride away you will find Arajilla, which has an ayurveda spa in a hand-built wooden yurt surrounded by banyan trees. **CSJ**

Stay at Rae's On Watego's

Location Byron Bay, New South Wales, Australia
Website www.raes.com.au **Price** 🛇🛇

Many hotels claim to offer unparalleled levels of privacy. One look at the guest list of Rae's on Watego's, which includes security conscious stars such as Russell Crowe, Tom Cruise, and Meg Ryan, underlines how seriously this resort takes its claims. A luxurious boutique hotel located on Watego's Beach on Australia's most easterly point, it sits in the shadow of Cape Byron lighthouse. Owner Vincent Rae has created a part-Mediterranean, part-Moorish retreat that is one of Australia's most exclusive destinations.

Hand-painted Javanese tiles, handmade furniture, Italian marble, and Moroccan mosaics are just some of the stylish elements found in this exquisite mansion

"If ever a hotel was a beautiful dreamer [Rae's on Watego's] is the one."

GC Magazine

by the sea, and with just seven sumptuous suites, you will never have to bother with crowds. The natural bushland that comprises Cape Byron Headland Nature Reserve has more than 2.5 miles (4 km) of walking trails, and coastal rain forests virtually surround the property, providing a calming buffer between Rae's and the crowds of tourists that flock to the nearby hip township of Byron Bay.

The opulent suites and penthouses open onto either palm-fringed courtyards or expansive terraces. Offering a rare combination of privacy, luxury, and fine cuisine, Rae's was voted one of the twenty-five best hotels in the world by *Condé Nast Traveler*. **BS**

Visit the Blue Mountains

Location Blue Mountains, New South Wales, Australia
Website www.bluemts.com.au **Price** ◗

The romantically named Blue Mountains sound like something from a fairy tale and almost beg to be visited. Luckily, they more than live up to the promise of their name. The blue haze that is visible as you look out over the valley is created by the ninety-one species of eucalyptus that thrive in this UNESCO World Heritage site. The area covers more than 3,860 square miles (10,000 sq km) and includes seven national parks and the Jenolan caves. Although more than 3 million people visit yearly, the Blue Mountains are so vast, it is easy for urbanites to escape into nature here.

The diversity of the region, taking in as it does ancient rain forest, heath land, dramatic canyons, and tall forests, makes it a natural paradise. Adrenalin fiends will be thrilled to go exploring in the huge cave system, rock climbing, rapelling, mountain biking, horseback riding, and more. Those who prefer a more sedate activity can choose from one of the 87 miles (140 km) of scenic walking treks. The less intrepid tourists may prefer to visit one of the many look-out points to view perhaps one of Australia's most impressive waterfalls at Kanangra Falls, or the panoramic vantage spot at Echo Point looking over the iconic Three Sisters at sunset.

The Wollemi Pine, the world's oldest tree and a true "living fossil," flourished here undetected until it was discovered in 1994. As well as being rich in flora, this area is also home to hundreds of species of endangered animals, including long-nosed potoroos and, of course, koalas. The Blue Mountains offer visitors an escape into nature that is also easily accessible. **EP**

→ *It took European settlers fifteen years of exploratory trips to find a definite way across the mountains.*

Enjoy Old Leura Dairy

Location Blue Mountains, New South Wales, Australia
Website www.oldleuradairy.com **Price** 🟢🟢

The Old Leura Dairy is a collection of lovingly restored, typical bush structures that has grown into one of Australia's most eclectic and unique escapes. The grounds and associated buildings that were once a working dairy farm have been given an invigorating new lease on life. What was once a modest 1920s weatherboard building is now the Workers Cottage, a three-bedroom home with typically irreverent Australian flourishes, such as walls made from fence palings and furniture fashioned from old lining boards. The Milking Shed is a Dali-esque building with crooked walls and angled floors, as well as clever internal uses of wrought iron and tin. The owners have also maintained the shed's hayloft and original barn doors that can still be melodramatically flung open should the mood be right.

A recent addition is the eco-friendly, solar-powered Straw Bale House, with its thick walls packed with straw to provide insulation throughout Leura's bone-tingling winter months. Inside you will find recycled timbers from an old jetty on Sydney's Parramatta River, and the doors and windows were sequestered from the city's famous old Queen Victoria Hospital.

Paddock grass has been transformed into an extensive native garden, and drought-resistant shrubs have been planted throughout to stabilize the soil and attract native birds. Instead of succumbing to the wrecking ball, this dairy farm and some fine examples of Australia's pioneer heritage have been preserved, set within the boundaries of the majestic, World Heritage-listed Blue Mountains. **BS**

← *The Old Leura Dairy is the culmination of eight years of painstaking and loving restoration.*

Explore Barrington Tops

Location Barrington Tops, New South Wales, Australia
Website www.barringtons.com.au **Price** 🟠

A two-and-a-half-hour drive north of Sydney, the rolling subtropical forest of the World Heritage area of Barrington Tops is an easily accessible region of unadulterated natural wilderness. Benefiting from a climate that supports both southern Australian and tropical flora and fauna, this plateau connecting two extinct volcanic peaks within the Mount Royal Range is home to more than fifty uncommon plant and animal species.

Often shrouded in mist, the peaks rise up to just over 5,000 feet (1,500 m) and offer splendid views of the lush meadows and endless forests. The Antarctic beech forests that thrive above 3,000 feet (900 m)

> *"Barrington Tops is a world of streams, waterfalls, forests, and soaring cliffs."*
>
> visitnsw.com

are a reminder of the Triassic southern hemisphere supercontinent Gondwana, and the granite boulders scattered across the park are thought to considerably predate Australia's separation from that landmass 167 million years ago. The ubiquitous rivers—fed by mist as well as melting snow and large quantities of rain—often turn into spectacular waterfalls.

Although it is possible to find accommodation in the forest itself, another option is to stay in nearby towns such as Gloucester and Dungog. European settlers arrived in the area in the early 1800s, and local history museums offer a fascinating insight into the challenges faced by those pioneers. **DaH**

Stay at Tower Lodge

Location Hunter Valley, New South Wales, Australia
Website www.towerlodge.com.au   **Price** ⊜⊜⊜

Set in the heart of Hunter Valley within the grounds of Tower Estate winery, Tower Lodge is an exclusive haven of unrivaled comfort and intimacy. The impeccable rooms complement the gastronomic delights of Roberts Restaurant, one of the valley's most iconic eateries. The meals are accompanied by an extensive award-winning wine list and are served in the historic ambience of an early settler's slab cottage.

From a distance, the lodge has the appearance of a classic European manor house, characterized by rendered external walls and a formidable facade, all dominated by a square bell tower and set around a delightful cloistered courtyard. All the rooms are filled

> "Should you want to venture out for a spot of wine tourism, there's no shortage of wineries."

John Stimpfig, *Observer*

to overflowing with antiques and furniture crafted from recycled local timbers. A number of the rooms have a fountain, whereas others have a private courtyard or plunge pool. Throughout the lodge there are tiny eccentricities that are typical of the attention to detail brought to every corner of this grand hideaway, such as the 300-year-old Rajasthani bed and Louis VXI writing desk that are yours if you book the opulent Chairman's Suite.

Memorable events in this popular region include jazz and opera festivals, hot-air ballooning, walking the convict trail, wine-tasting excursions, and visiting historic towns such as Wollombi and Morpeth. **BS**

Relax at St. Killians

Location Hunter Valley, New South Wales, Australia
Website www.stkillians.com.au   **Price** ⊜⊜

Built in 1879 to be the religious focus of the then-tiny farming community of Brookfield in the Hunter Valley north of Sydney, the sandstock church of St. Killians has been lovingly transformed into a romantic getaway with a mix of old world charm and contemporary luxury.

At St. Killians you can do as much or as little as you like. Beneath its aging cedar cathedral ceilings, there are two cozy lounge areas where St. Killians's masseurs can provide a private massage in front of one of two open fireplaces. Or, should you choose to venture outside, you can picnic down by the nearby Williams River, go bargain hunting in the local antique shops, or indulge in an afternoon of wine tasting in some of the eighty-plus wineries for which the region is famous.

There are two bedrooms, one in the choir loft and one in the old vestry, which has superb views from the comfort of its antique, queen-size brass bed. A gourmet kitchen allows you the choice of cooking for yourself and dining alfresco in the sun-drenched courtyard, or you can call on the expertise of St. Killians's chef, who will happily prepare breakfast, lunch, or dinner using the freshest of locally sourced ingredients. Prawn and salmon cakes with saffron dressing, Mediterranean lamb tagine, lime and almond friands, and toasted banana bread bagels give you an idea of some of the cuisine provided by the European-trained chef Stephen Kennedy.

At St. Killians, elaborate Persian rugs are spread over polished timber floorboards, and white internal walls combine with dark cedar ceilings and stained-glass windows to provide a visual feast of elegance and spaciousness. This is a relaxing setting guaranteed to slow pulse rates and recalibrate the soul. **BS**

Enjoy Eagle View Escape

Location Lake Lyell, New South Wales, Australia
Website www.eagleview.com.au **Price** 💲💲

If an underground passageway to your room appeals to your sense of the dramatic, then the spa suites of Eagle View Escape are waiting for you. Overlooking Lake Lyell, a man-made lake created by the damming of the Coxs River and stocked with enough bass and rainbow trout to tempt even the most jaded of anglers, Eagle View Escape is a romantic, couples-only resort for those looking for complete privacy.

Five "wilderness cabins" come with corrugated iron bathrooms and outdoor verandas complete with sunken tubs overlooking untouched native bush land. Picnic baskets are available, leaving you free to walk the impressive network of bush trails, where you are

> *"Our Wilderness Cabins have private verandas looking out through trees towards Lake Lyell."*
>
> Proprietors, Eagle View Escape

almost guaranteed to meet some of the other residents, including wombats, kangaroos, echidnas, and wallabies. Lake Lyell's sprinkling of sand beaches makes swimming its pristine waters a delight, and its five boat ramps allow for easy access to this meandering lake's many inlets and hidden coves.

The 110 acres (45 ha) that comprise Eagle View Escape will provide you with panoramic views of the Australian bush and a true sense of isolation. The resort is only a half-hour drive from the towns and antique-filled hamlets of the World Heritage-listed Blue Mountains, and a short drive from the splendor of the subterranean world of the Jenolan caves. **BS**

Walk Mrs. Macquarie's Road

Location Sydney, New South Wales, Australia
Website www.discoversydney.com.au/parks/mmc.html **Price** 🍴

Much of the great beauty of Sydney is in its harbor, and walking to the top of Mrs. Macquarie's Road is one of the loveliest ways to appreciate the city's character.

More than 150 years ago, the wife of the first governor of Australia, Mrs. Macquarie, liked to sit in this particular spot. From her vantage point, directly east of the Opera House, on the eastern edge of the Royal Botanic Gardens, she enjoyed unrivaled views of the natural harbor. Today, you look west from here to Harbor Bridge and Circular Quay—the iconic heart of Sydney—where the First Fleet arrived in 1788. On a clear day, you can spy the Blue Mountains in the far distance. Looking north and east you can see Kirribilli House, Pinchgut Island, and the navy dockyards at Wooloomooloo. Watch the green and cream ferries chug past and the people of Sydney go about their business: workers on their cell phones, joggers going for a run, tourists taking photographs, and romantic couples posing for wedding shots (countless Japanese and Korean couples marry in the gardens).

This spot is in the heart of the city, yet you can still find a patch of grass to drink your coffee and shoot the breeze with a friend under a blue sky. The Royal Botanic Gardens next door are a wonderland of Australian native and European trees, bathed in sunlight and shade by turn, and home to more than a million specimens. There are wild creatures here, too: shrieking parakeets, enormous bats hanging upside down in the trees, ibises and cockatoos, melodious mynah birds, and ducks. This is where the first Europeans tried their hand—albeit fruitlessly—at agriculture. Since then, a couple of hundred years of composting have made this a paradise of tropical foliage: the green heart of the city. **LB**

Walk From Bondi to Bronte

Location Sydney, New South Wales, Australia
Website www.bondivillage.com **Price** ◖❶

"Bondi beach is iconic … a crescent of golden sand lapped by an ocean the perfect shade of blue."

Peter Moore, *Guardian*

World-famous Bondi Beach, where Australia's first surf club was founded in 1906, was conceived as a kind of Coney Island for Sydney when surfing was a new sport. These days, Bondi is a rag-tag mix of boutique cafés, restaurants, hotels, burger joints, juice bars, and cheap clothing stores. The walk from Bondi Beach to Bronte Beach is a rite of passage, a simple, free-of-charge pleasure for new visitors and locals alike, and it is the best way to imbibe the windswept spirit of the relaxed eastern beach suburbs.

Set out from North Bondi and walk the length of the beach, past the bustling surf club, baking tourists, and lifeguards until you reach the south end of the beach and the rockpool, where you will find a stunning, glass-fronted bar that hangs over the rocks. Ascend to the coastal walk there and tread the path that hugs the cliffs toward Bronte Beach. You will pass jogging moms with strollers, bronzed hunks bench pressing, and, if the time of year is right, you might spot breaching humpback whales. The area also hosts the Sculpture by the Sea exhibition, and you might witness an informal wedding (many Australians like to get married outdoors when possible). The route takes you through Tamarama, a thin wedge of yellow sand book-ended by cliffs, and also goes through the most romantic graveyard in the world, its Celtic crosses and Victorian headstones blasted by salty sea air and sun. When you arrive in Bronte, where a perfectly sized beach awaits, backed by a nature reserve and a lawn where people grill burgers on the public barbecues, you may wonder why you do not live here. **LB**

◤ *The beach was opened to the public in 1882; its name is an Aboriginal word for "water breaking over rocks."*

Stay at the Shangri-La

Location Sydney, New South Wales, Australia
Website www.shangri-la.com **Price** 💲💲

Sydney's five-star Shangri-La Hotel rises up from the fringes of the city's business district and casts a long shadow across the blue waters of Sydney Cove. It is as though the phrase "location, location, location" was coined by the real estate industry and applied specifically to this Sydney landmark, where everything you could possibly want to see in the city is only an invigorating stroll away.

The hotel rooms provide jaw-dropping panoramas that take in all the iconic images of this vibrant city. Look down on Sydney Harbor Bridge, the Sydney Opera House, Botanical Gardens, the former harbor island prison of Fort Denison, and the comings and goings of the city's fleet of ferries at Circular Quay. Enjoy views of the tree-lined suburbs of North Sydney all the way to the Pacific Ocean beyond.

The Shangri-La is the largest hotel in a sassy city where size still matters. Its 563 rooms and suites are some of the largest in Sydney, and the hotel towers above the city streets, topping out at the thirty-sixth floor where guests can enjoy bird's-eye views of the city courtesy of the massive floor-to-ceiling windows. Here you may dine in the award-winning and aptly named Altitude Restaurant, followed by a cocktail in the Manhattan-inspired Blu Horizon Bar, which was awarded Sydney's best hotel bar by *Forbes Magazine*. A mouth-watering selection of pastries and breads is available daily, fresh from the hotel's own bakery. Hart's Pub, a traditional Australian pub restored to reflect its colonial heritage and housed in an original private residence, is open day and night for pizzas, light snacks, ales, and wines, after which you can return to your room and gaze at the array of lights laid out across the city beneath you. **BS**

Enjoy Paperbark Camp

Location Jervis Bay, New South Wales, Australia
Website www.paperbarkcamp.com.au **Price** 💲💲

For owners Irena and Jeremy Hutchings, the vision to bring sustainable safari-style camping to Australia started in Africa. On their return, they happened upon pristine Jervis Bay and set up camp in a protected bush wetland. The rest, as they say, is history.

With twelve "tents" floating on timber platforms underneath a canopy of spotted gums and peeling paperbark trees, Paperbark Camp is the perfect foil for those who like roughing it, without actually roughing it. Wafts of eucalyptus and pine tickle your senses at every turn, and eco-tourism is taken very seriously.

Paperbark is near one of the world's best beaches (Hyams), and you can rent a canoe for paddling along

"Ideal for those who love being close to nature, but equally appreciate the finer things in life."

Travelling in Australia magazine

Currambene Creek, or a bicycle for forays into the eucalyptus forest, woodland, or nearby town of Jervis Bay. Locals come from miles around for gourmet treetop dining at the Gunyah restaurant. Aboriginal for "meeting place," the Gunyah doubles as the camp's nerve center—a place to chill with a book by day and chat by the fire at night. The eclectic menu might include kangaroo kebabs with lemon and myrtle yogurt, salmon baked in paperbark, and kaffir lime and ginger sorbet with lychees and rum. Pesky possums have been known to poke their noses into unzipped tents and, come morning, you will wake to a dawn chorus that is second to none. **TM**

Visit Rawnsley Park Station

Location Wilpena Pound, South Australia, Australia
Website www.rawnsleypark.com.au **Price** ⊖⊖

This working sheep station sits in Wilpena Pound: a natural amphitheater of ancient, eroded mountains in the midst of the mighty Flinders Ranges, 270 miles (435 km) north of Adelaide in the Australian outback. The 7,410-acre (3,000-ha) park represents the ultimate in solitude, a place where you can do as much or as little as you like. Scenic flights, horseback riding, or hiking along the graded network of unspoiled bush tracks that spread out in all directions will provide an unforgettable introduction to the landscape and flora and fauna of the world's driest continent.

Today Rawnsley Park is a vital pastoral property that runs heavily fleeced South Australian Merino sheep of exceptional quality. Sheep-shearing shows for visiting guests began in 1968, and nowadays tourism has overtaken farming as the station's principal source of income. Accommodation ranges from caravans and basic vacation units to a series of superb eco-lodges that represent the pinnacle of Flinders Ranges's hospitality. Privately situated with breathtaking views over Wilpena Pound, the lodges are naturally insulated with rendered straw bale walls that minimize the region's extreme temperature fluctuations. Large verandas with overhanging eaves provide plenty of shade; inside, polished timber floors, cathedral ceilings, and huge beds provide all the comforts of home. There is even a sliding canopy above your bed which can be easily opened for the nighttime viewing of star-filled skies. It is no surprise that more than 20,000 people a year come here to experience the Australia of the early pioneers. **BS**

← *Rawnsley Park Station, set in the Australian outback, offers a rugged pioneering experience to its visitors.*

Recharge at Poltalloch Station

Location Lake Alexandrina, South Australia, Australia
Website www.poltalloch.com **Price** 🌓🌓

"Founded in 1839 and owned by successive generations ... Poltalloch is virtually a self-contained village."

Mark Chipperfield, *Daily Telegraph*

In 1829 the explorer Charles Sturt sailed down the Murray River for forty-seven days looking for Australia's mythical inland sea. When he arrived at the shores of Lake Alexandrina in South Australia, he must have thought he had found it. Today the same view that greeted Sturt can be had by anyone lucky enough to spend a night at the historic Poltalloch Station.

The excitement of staying at Poltalloch begins long before you arrive. Descending eastward from the lush greenery of the Adelaide Hills, the land flattens into an expanse of grassland and tiny saltpans. Towns are scarce, and the endless fence lines that mark the boundaries of cattle stations are your only companions.

Poltalloch Station straddles the waters of Lake Alexandrina, and the various outbuildings and workers cottages have been transformed into quaint accommodation. Boundary Rider's Cottage, Station Hand's Cottage, and Overseer's Cottage constitute an all-too-rare assemblage of Australia's social and architectural heritage, preserved in refreshing detail due, in no small part, to Poltalloch's relative isolation and the owner's commitment to preservation.

Poltalloch's carpenter and blacksmith workshops contain enough historic oddities to fill a museum. Scythes, wood-block vices, old medicine bottles, and thousands of other artifacts secured behind an aging padlock, vividly bring into the present the pioneering days of the past. The huge, double-arched shearing shed, the only one of its kind in Australia, helps make this one of Australia's most unique hideaways. **BS**

◩ *At Pontalloch Station you will experience Australia's trailblazing past, not to mention some lovely views.*

Unwind at
Moonlight Head Lodge

Location Otway National Park, Victoria, Australia
Website www.moonlighthead.com   **Price** ⊖⊖⊖⊖

Moonlight Head Lodge in Victoria is a deluxe hideaway overlooking Otway National Park, Victoria's largest national park, with over one million acres (400,000 ha) of coastal bush. Surrounded by eucalyptus bush and farmland (and plenty of Australian wildlife), the modernist lodges offer privacy and tranquility in an exclusive setting. They have been built using materials specially chosen for their recyclable qualities.

The interiors of Moonlight Lodge have been lovingly embellished with an array of sophisticated furnishings and worldly decor. There is a unique mix of original artworks, antique Persian rugs, and modern,

> *"The building is a discreet creature, a minimalist masterpiece that slowly reveals its hand."*
>
> Frances Hibbard, *Harper's Bazaar*

Italian Artemide lighting. The wonderful bluestone bathrooms contain Olympic-sized bathtubs in which you can soak and admire the stars through a glass roof.

The service is as sophisticated as the surroundings: Want a special meal? No problem for the chef. In the mood for a fishing trip, helicopter ride, or a dive for some wrecks? Done. Thanks to the resort's impeccable list of adventure partners, you may spend an evening viewing the Milky Way with professional astronomers or watch an intensive storm blow in from the Great Southern Ocean. All this is set in delightfully natural surroundings—it is not unusual to spot kangaroos and kookaburras while you have breakfast. **PS**

Ride Through
the Victoria Vineyards

Location Mornington Peninsula, Victoria, Australia
Website www.onedge.com.au   **Price** ⊖

The Mornington Peninsula is popular with people from nearby Melbourne because of its scenic views, sheltered beaches on Port Phillip bay, and the open sea to the south. Much of the rolling landscape is used for agriculture, and oenophiles in particular will appreciate this fact, because wine tours abound. However, it is advisable not to get too drunk, because the tours across these fertile hills are done on horseback. Saying that, the equestrian center and organizer of the tour, Spring Creek Farm—located near the charming vineyards surrounding the sleepy towns of Red Hill and Shoreham—provides horses that are safe for both experienced riders and novices, and you will be in very good hands.

The area is home to a large number of Australia's best wineries, and the rides take in at least two of them. There are tours of different lengths to choose from. The shorter tour's first port of call is Manton's Creek Vineyard, a small, pleasant estate that produces eight different varieties of wine. After sampling these vintages, the riders saddle up again and trot off to T'Gallant winery up the road. This vineyard produces high-quality Pinot Grigio, the region's signature varietal. This is also the second stop of the longer trip, after a wine tasting and lunch at the Red Hill Estate.

More tasting is on offer at some of the other local wineries, such as Montalto and Tucks Ridge. Although children are naturally not allowed to share in the bacchanalian delights, they are nevertheless welcome to join the picturesque horseback tour. Regardless of whether you indulge your palate or not, riding through the vineyards on this beautiful peninsula makes for a fun and relaxing day out. **DaH**

Stay on Kangaroo Island

Location Kangaroo Island, South Australia, Australia
Website www.southernoceanlodge.com.au   **Price** ❺❺❺

There is nothing between wild, untouched Kangaroo Island and Antarctica. As soon as you arrive, you inhale the fresh smell of eucalyptus and a sense of remoteness. This is Australia's answer to the Galapagos.

The island has twenty-one conservation and national parks and a panoply of different plants and animal species. The beaches are rugged and banked by dunes and sheer cliffs. Some are dominated by wild colonies of sea lions or tiny penguins; others are overlooked by granite outcrops sculpted by the wind and saltwater into extraordinary shapes; many are pounded by vicious waves. It is a place of endless bush broken by the occasional paddock or the path of a bush fire, creeping with kangaroos, wallabies, possums, echidnas, and koalas. At night, kangaroos and wallabies shoot across the road with no warning; trying to drive is like playing bumper cars.

The locals are unhurried; no one on the island has personal space issues—there are only 3,000 residents on this 1,737-square mile (4,500-sq km) island. It is unlikely that Aborigines were here: When Flinders circumnavigated in 1802, he realized there were no bush burn-offs and that the kangaroos were not perturbed by human presence. So they clubbed some, had a feast, and named the place Kangaroo Island.

Southern Ocean Lodge is a low-rise palace that snakes down the cliffs at lonely Hanson Bay, in a remote southerly corner of the island. Its public spaces are so vast that they give the sensation of being in a very cool airport terminal. It is a marvelous place to stay when exploring the wildness of the island. **LB**

← *Perched on rugged cliffs, Southern Ocean Lodge has a beautiful view out to the sea.*

Hike Around Bay of Fires

Location Bay of Fires, Tasmania, Australia
Website www.bayoffires.com.au   **Price** $$

The Bay of Fires is an untamed landscape. Along parts of its coastline, stretching some 20 miles (32 km) from Binalong Bay to Eddystone Point, there are more extraordinary white-sand beaches than houses.

The four-day, fully guided Bay of Fires walk serves up some of Tasmania's best attributes: fine local foods, cool-climate wines, and breathtaking landscapes. With a maximum of ten walkers and at least two guides on every tour, guests are guaranteed individual attention. Besides eating, drinking, and walking (a maximum of about 8 miles [13 km] is walked on any one day), time is also allowed for guests to relax, snorkel in the beautiful Tasman Sea, and kayak on Ansons River.

> *"From far away to up close, the sea offers up a myriad of delight, both intricate and wild."*

Anthology Travelers' Collection website

The walk begins at Boulder Point where secluded beaches and rocky headlands dress the landscape. At the end of day one, a standing camp melds into one of the dunes and yet is so close to the water you could just about fish from your bed. Typically the sleeping "tents" have canvas roofs but they also have timber floors. Two nights are spent at the Bay of Fires Lodge— something of a benchmark for stylish and sustainable accommodation. Sitting low among the sand dunes, the lodge has a light carbon footprint. Rainwater is collected and used on-site; solar panels provide power for all lighting. This helps not only the house, but also the guests to blend into the environment. **GC**

Relax at Islington Hotel

Location Hobart, Tasmania, Australia
Website www.islingtonhotel.com   **Price** $$

A basic audit of the Islington Hotel may prove disturbing to accountants, because each of the hotel's rooms has something near the value of a Lamborghini attached to its refurbishment. It will doubtless pay off. It is not too hard to imagine guests spending the better part of a week here soaking up the numerous features and the personable service.

The Islington Hotel opened in January 2006 in an 1847 Regency-style mansion that was once home to the Tasmanian premier Sir James Milne Wilson. The transformation from private home to eleven-room luxury hotel has been helped in no small part by an eclectic collection of antiques: Louis XV chairs, a Biedermeier table, Chinese cabinets, and Austrian beds in the Grand House Room. There are also works by Picasso, Brett Whiteley, and Ju Ming, fabrics from Jim Thompson, and a well-stocked library.

Although king-size beds, private bathrooms, back-lit marble panels, wonderfully deep baths, and heated granite floors are standard in all of the rooms, each one has its own character. Indeed, the owners have helped meld an extraordinary bespoke hotel. The Islington has a striking conservatory. It opens out onto a terrace where there is a reflecting pond and, beyond that, formal gardens. There are views to forested Mount Wellington from the rear of the property. Guests are offered complimentary drinks and canapés on the terrace at sunset. In the mornings, sumptuous breakfasts using fresh Tasmanian produce are prepared in the stylish and visible kitchen, which has a French farmhouse theme. The Islington chef will even prepare bespoke dinners on request. Allow some time to choose an accompanying wine though, because the hotel's cellar runs to 1,000 bottles. **GC**

Unwind at Cradle Mountain Lodge

Location Cradle Mountain, Tasmania, Australia
Website www.cradlemountainlodge.com.au **Price** ⊝⊝

With an alpine spa retreat and comfortable cabins on the edge of a World Heritage location, living the green life at Cradle Mountain Lodge has never been so luxurious. It is certainly no hardship to be at one with nature at this eco-certified wilderness retreat on the Australian island state of Tasmania, surrounded by misty, mirror lakes and craggy peaks.

Some of the cozy cabins have a hot tub out on the deck and a wood-burning fire in the lounge to keep evening mountain chills at bay. If you can pull yourself away from the views, there is even more inspiring scenery on offer from the Waldheim spa. Treatment rooms have floor-to-ceiling windows to let the outside in, and the adjoining Sanctuary relaxation area has an open-air hot tub with panoramic views of the forest.

In keeping with the lodge's green credentials, the menu features the best of local produce, and helpful staff offer recommendations on Australian wines from the extensive cellar. A delight for food and wine lovers is the annual three-day "Tastings at the Top" gourmet extravaganza, a showcase for boutique winemakers, growers, and handmade cheese makers.

The site attracts hikers of all abilities. Take a picnic and follow self-guided walking trails to find a peaceful spot to enjoy the solitude of Cradle Mountain and Dove Lake. Go canoeing on the lake or rent mountain bikes to get off the beaten track. Local guides offer tours to get a closer look at native animals such as wallabies, possums, and maybe even a Tasmanian Devil. Or look out over the forest to spot them while enjoying a relaxing massage in the spa. **AD**

↗ The secluded but luxurious cabins are tucked away in the fairy tale setting of an ancient forest.

"The cradle in question is more literally a crater, spectacularly fenced with rocky peaks."

Daily Telegraph

Enjoy Meadowbank Estate

Location Meadowbank, Tasmania, Australia
Website www.meadowbankwines.com.au   **Price** $

Meadowbank Estate is way more than a vineyard. It has an award-winning restaurant, a cellar-door food and wine shop, an art gallery, and a concert program—all just a fifteen-minute drive from Hobart's waterfront.

The location is sensational. The restaurant's massive windows look out over the vineyards of the Coal River Valley and the estuaries of Barilla Bay. There is an appreciation of history here, too: For example, the restaurant's timber pillars were once used as ballast for Tasmanian ships. The restaurant's concept is small-dish and local—think smoked eel with potato pancakes, Dunalley oysters, and kingfish seviche—with wines, all available by the glass, to match. A large proportion

> *"The hilltop view over the vineyards and some 11,000 fine-wool merinos soothes the soul."*
>
> John Bell, *Daily Telegraph*

of the produce used by the kitchen is sourced in the vicinity of the Coal River Valley, and the menu changes almost daily. The cellar-door shop, meanwhile, offers free tastings of up to six of Meadowbank's standard wines. The art gallery holds exhibitions of local artists' work, and Meadowbank hosts regular concerts of, for example, Tasmanian chamber music and Tasmanian jazz guitarists—Tasmania itself is a distinct theme.

It is the wine that started it all, though. The first vines were planted here in 1974. The idea was to create a few bottles for personal enjoyment, but the results exceeded expectation, and the vineyards grew. Now Meadowbank produces an enviable range. **PE**

Discover Wineglass Bay

Location Freycinet National Park, Tasmania, Australia
Website www.wineglassbay.com   **Price** ◑

Wineglass Bay is perhaps Tasmania's most curvaceous figure. This natural beauty's prized feature is a stretch of white sand that replicates the shape of a wine glass rim. Wonderfully, however, there is not a hint of exploitation here, not a building or even a sniff of commercial enterprise about the mile-long beach.

Wineglass Bay is on Tasmania's east coast, on a peninsula known as Freycinet National Park. Dutchman Abel Tasman may have been the first European in these parts, but it was the French in the early nineteenth century who named the peninsula. An imposing granite range, known as the Hazards, watches over the park. It is a bodyguard of sorts because it has made road building fortuitously problematic. There is no vehicular access to Wineglass.

At the beginning of the trail there is no clue to a beach. Rather, a cleverly honed trail is sculpted through the pervasive granite and forest. The trail rises steeply to a saddle wedged between some of the Hazard's highest peaks. Indigenous green rosellas, fan-tailed cuckoos, and wallabies are often encountered on this part of the journey. The first views of the bay come from the lookout in the saddle. From this elevated position, a mile or so away, the waves lap at the curve of sand as though on a quest to reach into the nearby forest. The eucalyptus gives off a bluish hue and contrast with the shimmering turquoise water. In short, the view is a pinup for beaches the world over, but many visitors, satisfied with the view, return to their cars from the lookout. How could you come this far and not put footprints in the sand? **GC**

➡ *The sand appears white enough to suggest somebody has taken to manicuring it regularly.*

Relax at Eagles Nest

Location Bay of Islands, North Island, New Zealand
Website www.eaglesnest.co.nz **Price** ⊝⊝⊝

Located within strolling distance of the historic town of Russell on New Zealand's Bay of Islands, Eagles Nest can be found perched on the edge of a private peninsula. Surrounded by a largely secluded 75-acre (30-ha) estate, this luxury resort has only five self-contained villas to rent—but they are all exclusive.

The resort has been designed in resolutely contemporary style, although the owners have ensured all gardens and lodgings blend seamlessly into the natural environment. Each villa is uniquely appointed, with a mix of modern and antique furnishings, original local artwork, and all the modern conveniences you will ever need. The villas vary in size: The smallest sleeps two, the largest eight, but all have generous dimensions and are filled with oodles of natural light. Although Eyrie and Eagle Spirit rooms have their own 60-foot (18-m) infinity pools, First Light Temple offers a more romantic ambience that is perfect for a honeymoon vacation. The two-story Sacred Space serves as the resort's showpiece, with three suites, a living area, and private cinema, plus butlers and personal trainers on request. Gleaming chrome and marble bathrooms featuring glass-encased showers and heated floor tiles are just some of the attention-grabbing details within the villas.

Accommodation aside, the scenery is breathtaking. The Bay of Islands is world renowned and contains more than 144 islands to explore. With everything from big-game fishing, sailing, diving, mountain biking, hiking, and helicopter flights on offer, there is little chance of getting bored. Eagles Nest has it all. **PS**

⮕ *The design is simple—glass walls, expansive decks, private pools—but the effect is nothing short of majestic.*

Stay at Orongo Bay

Location Bay of Islands, North Island, New Zealand
Website www.thehomestead.co.nz   **Price** 💲💲

Orongo Bay Homestead enjoys an unparalleled location with breathtaking views over the clear, green waters of the subtropical Orongo Bay in the Bay of Islands. The two-story wooden homestead, which dates back to the 1860s, has been fully restored to its former glory with the assistance of the Historic Places Trust. The result is a hotel that has historic gravitas and attention to detail throughout, from the vintage Austrian grand piano and the handcarved Victorian chaise longue to the private bathrooms with their robes, fluffy towels, and native plant skincare creams at hand. Co-owners Chris Wharehinga Swannell and Michael Hooper both have backgrounds in wine and food, which is evident

> "A unique combination of home and hotel with a healthy regard for organic gourmet luxury."

Proprietors, Orongo Bay

with one glance at the superb gourmet menus. Imagine organic bananas, guavas, papayas, kiwis, and numerous locally grown vegetables, plus an excellent New Zealand wine menu.

Available activities include swimming with dolphins in their natural habitat, cruises on tall sailing ships, and games of croquet and boules on the lawn. The Finnish sauna and plunge tub are a great extra touch, and massages are available on request. Russell—New Zealand's first capital—is close by, and Chris, who is part Maori, is an affable source of information about the history of his people. History, culture, nature, and creature comforts all rolled into one. **PS**

See the Kauri Forests

Location Kauri Forests, North Island, New Zealand
Website www.doc.govt.nz   **Price** 💲

The kauri trees of New Zealand's North Island are not just large, they are truly enormous. They are so huge, in fact, that in the 1880s an enterprising family—two parents and their thirteen children—set up home inside the rotting trunk of one. They lived in their "tree house" for fourteen years.

Fourteen years is a mere blink of an eye to a kauri tree. These giants of the forest can live for millennia. The tallest tree in the Waipoua Forest on Northland's west coast is thought to be between 1,250 and 2,500 years old. It was growing peacefully in this corner of New Zealand when the Romans were building their empire, and it is still there now. Tane Mahuta, or Lord of the Forest as this tree is known, is more than 160 feet (48 m) tall. Its phenomenal trunk—which has a girth of 45 feet (14 m)—soars high and straight, towering above the canopy until, near the top, its branches spray. They are gnarled and full of character, betraying their venerable status. Even for those who think that they are not very interested in trees, this is a humbling sight.

A little farther along, Te Matua Ngahere—Father of the Forest—has planted its extensive roots. Te Matua Ngahere is not as tall as Tane Mahuta, but it has an extraordinary girth. This tree's trunk has a 16-foot (4.8-m) diameter and is also very impressive.

There used to be even larger trees than these in the north of New Zealand. Sadly, they fell victim to the logging industry and the gum trade of the nineteenth and early twentieth centuries. However, anyone passing through New Zealand's Northland should stop their car and stroll along the easy paths and boardwalks to visit the mighty, magnificent kauri trees that remain. They are, quite simply, breathtaking. **PE**

Enjoy Delamore Lodge

Location Waiheke Island, Hauraki Gulf, New Zealand
Website www.delamorelodge.com **Price** ❸❸❸

A picturesque blend of farmland, forest, beaches, vineyards, and olive groves, Waiheke Island is one of the Hauraki Gulf's larger destinations. Trace your eyes along the undulating coastline and you will discover Delamore Lodge, an exclusive retreat molded into the hillside at Owhanake Bay. Local architect Ron Stevenson and owner Roselyn Barnet-Storey have blended Mediterranean architecture with Maori symbolism, building the lodge in the shape of the *matsu* (the traditional bone fishhook of the Maori people).

Each of the four suites enjoys panoramic views of the bay. Sip a cocktail on the patio or slip into a luxurious bubble bath and admire the ever-changing blue of

> "[Delamore Lodge] is beautiful and intimate with one of the most stunning sea views."
>
> *Vogue Travel*

the Hauraki Gulf. Glide down a sweeping staircase to find the spacious lounge and dining room, where chef Aaron Smith serves dishes using produce from the hotel's garden. Waiheke Island's world-renowned vineyards and olive groves are celebrated with an annual food and wine festival. Ask Aaron kindly, and he will select a special vintage from the wine cellar and even cook up a catch caught with your own *matsu*, should you have had a lucky day. Activities include sailing, diving, kayaking, and fishing; simply inhaling the fresh island air creates a sense of inner calm. Any remaining stress is banished with a trip to the hotel's private spa and grotto-style whirlpool tub. **PS**

Unwind at Cotter House

Location Auckland, North Island, New Zealand
Website www.cotterhouse.com **Price** ❸❸

Cotter House was built by English immigrant Joseph Newman in 1847. Ironically and tragically, the teetotaler Newman met his end in 1892 when he was struck on the head by a falling billboard advertising whiskey. These days, the regency-style heritage building functions as a wonderful hotel in which you can find a host of exceptional antiques juxtaposed with a collection of modern art.

The lovely gardens are a showcase for young Auckland and New Zealand artists, and many of the pieces are for sale. After a day of impromptu art collecting, it is worth spending some time in the rooms themselves, where the lavish decor is equally astounding: largely classic French with fantastic antiques offsetting eye-catching window treatments. The 1892 ballroom is still used mostly for formal gatherings and the occasional wedding. Current owner Gloria Poupard-Wallbridge's French breakfasts are becoming as famous as the mansion itself, which now boasts a great cellar.

Cotter House offers all the business services you would expect, plus a host of more personal amenities such as a babysitting service and an on-call dentist and doctor. Life simply does not get more convenient. The staff speak a range of different languages from French, Spanish, and Portuguese to Mandarin and Korean, so there is no danger of your requests being misunderstood. In such wonderfully relaxed and elegant surroundings, it is a pleasure to soak in the heated outdoor pool or whirlpool tub, to energize with Pilates and kickboxing, or to relax, try a few yoga poses before a day's golfing. For the ultimate lunch date, you might want to try a helicopter flight to one of the intimate Gulf islands close by. **PS**

Stay at Mollies

Location Auckland, North Island, New Zealand
Website www.mollies.co.nz **Price** 💲💲💲

Mollies is an impressive building that was built in the 1870s. It has been fully renovated recently by Frances Wilson, a singing teacher, and opera set designer Stephen Fitzgerald. The pair are justifiably proud of their masterful restoration of what is now the city center's best five-star boutique hotel.

There are thirteen luxury suites and apartments within this outstanding building. The upstairs suites have elegant balconies whereas downstairs the rooms open onto a beautifully maintained garden. Dotted with antiques and contemporary touches, the rooms are large by Auckland standards, and even the smaller studio rooms include private bathrooms and their own view of the courtyard's garden. Guests can dine among the sea of flowers in the conservatory, or simply at leisure in their own suites. The cunningly named restaurant, the Dining Room, is renowned throughout New Zealand for its gourmet cuisine and, of course, a range of excellent local wines. Mollies has won several awards, and the Dining Room itself was recently named one of the top Auckland restaurants, such is the quality of the fare.

To burn it all off, the hotel's East Day Spa offers a range of ayurvedic treatments including facials, massage, and many holistic treatments. The level of service at this St. Mary's Bay gem is second to none, and the library, although on the bijou side, is impeccably stocked. The sense of relaxation when you close the door of your suite is enhanced by the knowledge that attentive staff are only a call away, a reassurance that resonates throughout your stay. **PS**

◀ *The atmosphere of grandeur is partly due to the fact that it was once the home of Auckland's first mayor.*

Unwind at Puka Park

Location Coromandel, North Island, New Zealand
Website www.pukapark.co.nz **Price** 💲💲

Guests at Puka Park are shown to their rooms via a creaking wooden pathway through the misty rain forest. There you will find a luxurious tree house with living plants incorporated into its structure. In the morning, step out onto your wooden balcony and gaze out through the foliage. It is quite a spectacle: the long, empty, sandy beach and the Pacific surf curving away toward more trees and hills to the north. Puka Park sits on a steep green mountainside above Pauanui Beach on the wild and beautiful Coromandel Peninsula. It is only a two-hour drive from Auckland, but secluded in its 25 acres (10 ha) of lush and verdant bush, the city seems like a world away.

"Amid New Zealand's beautiful native bush, you will find an idyllic and very special hideaway."

escapenewzealand.com

The resort has an award-winning restaurant—eat in by the open fire or out on the deck overlooking the ocean. Guests collapse into incredibly soft sofas in the cocktail bar enjoying views through every window. Some sit and gaze out from their private balconies among the trees, hypnotized by the panoramas. Others are inspired to visit Puka's gym, pool, or spa. Daring guests can try the purpose-built, high-ropes course through the tree tops, including the "sky plunge"—a 755-foot (230-m) rope ride across the valley. There are boat trips to nearby islands and walking trails up the 1,310 foot (400-m) Pauanui Mountain for more spectacular views. **SH**

Enjoy Hot Water Beach

Location Coromandel, North Island, New Zealand
Website http://mercurybay.co.nz/index.php **Price** 🌓

Digging yourself into a big hole is not usually recommended—unless you are on Hot Water Beach located on the east coast of Coromandel Peninsula.

New Zealand is crisscrossed by fault lines. Centuries of shifting tectonic plates and volcanic activity have created a geothermal wonderland of steaming mineral lakes and bubbling mud pools. Hot Water Beach is a picturesque sweep of flat golden sands. It is fringed on one side by scarlet-flowered Pohutukawa trees and on the other by frothy aquamarine seas.

The entire Coromandel coastline is stunning. What sets this beach apart is the fact that it sits over a superheated underground lake. Two conveniently placed natural fissures allow rivers of boiling water to bubble upward through the cracks. When they reach the cooling waters of the Pacific Ocean, you can actually see plumes of steam rising from the water, except for the two hours either side of low tide when these volcanic vents empty onto the golden sands of Hot Water Beach. During these times, if you burrow just beneath the sand, you will hit a spring of water rich in salt, calcium, and magnesium. Dig deeper and the water rushes to fill the sandy pit, so you can literally carve out your own private spa pool. Although now drastically cooled, the mineral water still reaches temperatures up to 147°F (64°C). Add some cooling seawater if necessary, and sit back and enjoy a muscle-relaxing soak. Always keep an eye on the incoming tide, because Hot Water Beach has strong currents and rip tides that can cause problems.

The springs bubble up throughout the year. For a unique experience, visit the beach at nighttime. Dig out your hot pool, then lie back and watch the shooting stars as they streak across the dark night sky. **JP**

Relax at Polynesian Spa

Location Rotorua, North Island, New Zealand
Website www.polynesianspa.co.nz **Price** 🌓

According to Maori legend, the high priest Ngatoroirangi felt cold as he prayed on the summit of Mount Tongariro. The gods in the mythical Maori homeland of Hawaiki responded by sending jets of fire deep underground. More recent scientific research counters that Rotorua's frenzy of geothermal activity is caused by shifting tectonic plates.

The bubbling mud, scalding geysers, and lurid mineral pools have kept Rotorua high on the tourist agenda for more than a hundred years, and the Polynesian Spa has transformed these natural assets into an oasis of relaxation. It has no fewer than twenty-six hot mineral pools, many of which overlook Lake

> *"The steam rising off the water creates a dreamy state and is the perfect prep for a . . . mud wrap."*
>
> *Ranch & Coast* magazine

Rotorua. The Priest Spa pools—named for Father Mahoney who hiked 50 miles (80 km) from Tauranga in 1878 to bathe in a hand-dug pool and thus alleviate his arthritis—feature slightly acidic water, which is famous for soothing tired muscles, aches and pains, arthritis, and rheumatism.

The other pools are slightly alkaline. Among them are the deluxe Lake Spa, where you can laze in warm waters beside two waterfalls; a family spa; an adults-only spa; and private spas for those who want to bathe with just their nearest and dearest. Treatments include the use of New Zealand manuka honey, New Zealand kiwis, and Rotorua thermal mud, of course. **PE**

Unwind at Huka Lodge

Location Taupo, North Island, New Zealand
Website www.hukalodge.com **Price** ⊖⊖

The low-rise, postwar building looks innocuous from a distance. A big family summerhouse, perhaps, nestled in the woods near a river? The sleepy-looking lodge between the trees is actually one of the world's finest luxury hotels. Huka has won numerous global awards and accommodated many famous guests, but one is definitely worth a mention: H.R.H. Queen Elizabeth II has chosen to stay here five times.

Not surprising then that the hotel is exquisitely designed, equipped, and decorated. Food, service and attention to detail are superb. A stay here is fantastically expensive, too. All twenty rooms open out toward the river just a few yards away. Many guests sleep with the huge glass doors open, listening to the Waikato River, New Zealand's longest, rushing through the rain forest toward the Huka Falls nearby (*huka* is a Maori word meaning "falling water").

The relaxed hunting lodge theme includes touches such as antelope heads above roaring fireplaces, tartan rugs, leather sofas, and timber paneling. Dine fabulously in the formal dining room or at a private table by the river, watching ducks waddle across the lawns under overhanging ferns.

Huka's position in the middle of New Zealand's North Island is close to Lake Taupo, whose clear blue waters are surrounded by forested mountains. Guests are offered private trips to Taupo or the erupting White Island off-shore volcano—both by helicopter, of course. Only in New Zealand would guests at this category of hotel be offered a 150-foot (45-m) bungee jump above the Waikato or a hair-raising jet-boat ride under the Huka Falls. Nobody seems to be letting on as to whether Her Majesty decided to try any of these activities—but one suspects not. **SH**

Stay at Treetops Lodge

Location Bay Of Plenty, North Island, New Zealand
Website www.treetops.co.nz **Price** ⊖⊖⊖

Treetops Lodge and Wilderness Experience is in one of the most unspoiled natural landscapes on Earth. Set within 2,500 acres (1,012 ha) of private wilderness and surrounded by 800-year-old trees that make up the local native virgin forest, this eco-lodge sits within a carefully managed game and wildlife habitat where fly fishermen make the most of the wild trout in the seven spring-streams.

The lifelong dream of owner John Sax, the lodge took eight careful years to build. It is located in the Maori heartland and trout fishing capital of the world, Rotorua, and the ecology-inspired architectural style was derived from the country's pioneering past.

> *"Treetops was . . . a place of calm, beauty, and intimate connection with a sublime landscape."'*

Victoria Homewood, *Daily Telegraph*

Fine cuisine is an integral part of Treetops, with flavorful and healthy dishes created by talented chefs using the finest game and local produce. Dining is complemented by premium New Zealand wines. Among the wilderness experiences at Treetops are on-site trout fishing, four lakes, and more than 44 miles (70 km) of adventure trails. Other activities include photography safaris, helicopter tours, luxury treks to spectacular waterfalls, and a four-wheel-drive experience. You can, of course, choose to lay back and give in to the sedative sounds of nature all around you. You may even hear the distant voices of fishermen on the breeze, discussing the "ones that got away." **PS**

Visit Karamea

Location Karamea, South Island, New Zealand
Website www.karameainfo.co.nz   **Price** ●

Karamea is where the road runs out. After this, there is just bush. It is for the bush that most people come, because Karamea sits at the end of the Heaphy Track, which runs for 50 picturesque miles (80 km) through the Kahurangi National Park and along the white-sand beaches of the coast.

If preferred, you could skip the hiking and drive here. Even the road up to Karamea is glorious. A verdant canopy of green reigns facing a long beach often strewn with driftwood, where the waves shimmer silver. For lodging, try the Last Resort or the Karamea Village Hotel, where the landlord will serve you a whitebait patty and a pint of local beer.

"Karamea serves as the beginning (or the end) of the famed Heaphy Track—a gorgeous, rugged trail."

viewpoints.com

Karamea is a tiny, sleepy little place, but there is plenty to keep the active crowd occupied, such as kayaking and bird-watching in the estuaries that are home to pied stilts, black swans, oyster catchers, and blue herons. Even if you do not want to hike very far, walk at least a little of the wonderful Heaphy Track. At the Karamea end, groves of princely nikau palms soar overhead before the path leads onto a coastline replete with flashing spuming waters, weaving bays, and boulder-strewn beaches. **PE**

← *Although the landscape can vary around Karamea, you will always find unspoiled stretches of beach.*

Enjoy Hidden Valley Lodge

Location Lake Poerua, South Island, New Zealand
Website www.hiddenvalleylodge.co.nz **Price** $

In 1923 a small wooden lodge was built at the back of New Zealand's Grey Valley. In 1953 it was relocated a few miles from Lake Poerua, where it served a small Catholic community for the next forty-three years. In 1996 the small church was put up for tender, purchased by its present owners, and now sits nestled in a small grove of native New Zealand ferns overlooking the trout-filled waters of Lake Poerua.

After an extensive internal renovation using native timbers and ensuring the preservation of its original detailing, such as its many stained-glass windows, Hidden Valley Lodge can now accommodate up to seven guests. Visitors enjoy perfect isolation by the

---

"There are wild red deer in the bush and mountains around the lodge along with chamois on the tops."

Proprietors, Hidden Valley Lodge

---

shores of Lake Poerua. One side of the lake is under private ownership, and the other is managed by the Department of Conservation.

Anglers come here for the bounty of brown trout that inhabits the lake and surrounding streams. You can also take to the water on one of the lodge's kayaks, a popular activity affording the chance to view some of the area's abundant birdlife, including wild geese, keas, swans, and the elusive white heron. Hidden Valley Lodge provides an excellent base for exploring the rugged beauty of New Zealand's west coast. The drive from Christchurch will take you along precipitous gorges and beneath towering snow-clad peaks. **BS**

Stay at Wilderness Lodge

Location Arthur's Pass, South Island, New Zealand
Website www.wildernesslodge.co.nz **Price** $

The snowcapped peaks of the Southern Alps soar majestically across the horizon. At their base, the Waimakariri River winds like a silvery ribbon. Such views make the Wilderness Lodge at Arthur's Pass the ultimate eco-retreat.

Built in 1996, the elegant timber and corrugated iron building was designed to complement and blend into the natural forest clearing. The twenty Mountain View rooms are modestly decorated. Extravagant decor is an unnecessary distraction when you have such a spectacular landscape on your doorstep. The four Alpine Lodges provide more luxurious accommodation. Nestled within a beech forest, all the rooms have gas fires and spa baths that look out over the mountains. With no television or Internet, the real attractions lie outside. The lodge is set in a 6,000-acre (2,400-ha) nature reserve and is also a working sheep farm. Owners Ann and Gerry are passionate conservationists, who also own the original Wilderness Lodge further south at Lake Moeraki.

The lodge is nirvana for hikers, with a myriad of surrounding tracks to explore. Take in the fresh air and unspoiled forest, and keep an eye out for the native bellbirds and keas. Guests can choose from any number of other excursions, from canoeing on nearby Lake Pearson to discovering the Southern Cross during a night sky stargazing trip.

Alternatively you can explore the nearby Arthur's Pass National Park. From trout fishing in the crystal-clear lakes to mountaintop picnics among the alpine flowers, such is the unique and diverse landscape of New Zealand that you can be relaxing on a beach in the morning, trekking through a rain forest in the afternoon, and scaling an ice cave the next day. **JP**

Ride the TranzAlpine Train

Location From Christchurch to Greymouth, South Island, New Zealand
Website www.tranzscenic.co.nz   **Price** Ⓢ

Voted one of the top-ten short train journeys in the world, the TranzAlpine service runs daily between Christchurch on the east coast across the Southern Alps to Greymouth on the west coast. The trip may take just four hours, but in that time you will see some of the grandest scenery New Zealand has to offer.

The TranzAlpine is hauled by two locomotives and has nine passenger carriages and a buffet carriage that serves light snacks and drinks. At the rear, an open-air carriage provides an ideal platform for photography. The spectacular route takes travelers along the broad, flat Canterbury Plains and alongside the Waimakariri River. After passing over five viaducts, affectionately known as the Staircase, the TranzAlpine arrives at the small village of Arthur's Pass before beginning its steep descent to the west coast and passing through the 5-mile (8.5-km) Otira Tunnel (1923), an epic feat of engineering through some of the world's hardest rock that took sixteen years to construct. It is only one of sixteen tunnels that the TranzAlpine enters on its 140-mile (224-km) journey. If you are hiking in Arthur's Pass National Park, it is also possible to board the train from there. Progress slows considerably on Mount Philistine because of the steep gradient.

The descent down the western slopes of the Southern Alps passes through lush forests heavy with clouds and provides a stark contrast to the plains and vast scree slopes on the eastern side of the divide. Naturally such an array of scenery can make you hungry, so in Greymouth try the meat pies in Blanchfield's Bakery before boarding for the return trip. **BS**

↗ *The beauty of the scenery takes your breath away as the train climbs into the Torlesse Mountain Range.*

"The varied scenery takes in a labyrinth of gorges . . . and valleys encircled by dense beech forest."

Guardian

Relax at Hapuku Lodge

Location Kaikoura, South Island, New Zealand
Website www.hapukulodge.com   **Price** ⊜⊜

The stunning Hapuku Lodge on the east coast of New Zealand's South Island is a real family affair. In 1982, fresh from designing residences in the bay area of San Francisco, Tony Wilson and his brother Michael joined with their younger brother Peter and sister Sara to create Wilson Associates, which in turn gave birth to this state-of-the-art country lodge nestled in the midst of the family's 120-acre (48-ha) deer farm overlooking the waters of Mangamanu Bay.

Every aspect of Hapuku Lodge, from the planting of its 1,000-plus olive trees to the creation of its superb menu, has been the responsibility of the Wilson family. There are six guest rooms in the main lodge and five

---

"The overall effect is playful and natural … perfect for living out those shipwreck fantasies."

Urbis magazine

---

luxury tree houses, elevated on steel girders and with exteriors of copper shingles and native cladding built over a Manuka grove. Sweeping views include the snowcapped peaks of the Kaikoura Seaward mountain range and a pounding Pacific Ocean surf.

The tree houses are far from rustic. Beds are king size and draped in the finest linens, and the furniture is handcrafted from local timbers. Toilets are hidden behind massive sheets of green frosted glass, and showers with walls of glass open directly onto private decks that provide panoramic ocean views. The Wilson family plants one native tree for every guest night booked. Some 11,000 so far, and counting. **BS**

Walk the Fox Glacier

Location Westland National Park, South Island, New Zealand
Website www.foxguides.co.nz   **Price** ⊜

Named after the nineteenth-century New Zealand prime minister Sir William Fox and hosting more than 1,000 visitors a day during the summer months, Fox Glacier on New Zealand's South Island is one of the most accessible glaciers in the world. From its genesis in the Southern Alps, the longest glacier on the west coast descends 8 miles (13 km) to its terminus at the Fox River. Unlike many other glaciers across the world that are retreating in the face of global warming, the Fox Glacier has been advancing at the rate of about 3 feet (1 m) a day since the mid-1980s, due mainly to its peculiar funnel-like shape. It has a neve (upper part) the size of the city of Christchurch, which tapers substantially as it descends on its journey to the coast.

There are many options for walking on Fox Glacier, and all of them are exhilarating. You can approach it at lower elevations via regenerated bush land left from previous glacial advances, or access remote higher sections via helicopter. After being equipped with instep crampons, you will be led through spectacular ice caves, tunnels, and seracs where experienced guides will cut ice steps to help you navigate your way across this frozen world. They will even assist you in climbing its walls of ice using ice tools and the front points of your crampons. Ice-climbing adventures have a ratio of four clients per guide, and the adrenalin flows freely as you scale near-vertical walls, held securely in place by a rope and harness. Guided tours are also available to take you along the Fox River Valley floor to the face of the glacier.

Part of the Westland National Park and a designated UNESCO World Heritage area, when you walk on Fox Glacier you continue a tradition that began in 1928 with the establishment of the Fox Hotel. **BS**

Explore Stewart Island

Location Stewart Island, Foveaux Strait, New Zealand
Website www.stewartisland.co.nz   **Price** ◑

There are two ways of getting to Stewart Island, the locals say: an hour of seasickness or twenty minutes of sheer terror. The Foveaux Strait, which divides this charmingly remote outpost from South Island, is notoriously choppy but the flight from Invercargill can be too exciting for comfort, as well.

Stewart Island is worth a little bravery. Only about 400 people live on the island, and most of those are in the town of Oban. There are 450 miles (725 km) of coastline, but only 12 miles (19 km) of roads. The Rakiura National Park covers 85 percent of the island and has more trails than most enthusiastic hikers could ever hope to cover. The 80-mile (128-km) northwest

---

"The island is the likeliest place in New Zealand for you to spot the elusive kiwi."

Kathy Marks, *Independent*

---

circuit takes ten to twelve days to complete. Lesser mortals can opt for the Raikura track, which is completed in a mere two or three days.

Whether you opt for a multiday marathon or a few hours' guided stroll, on Stewart Island you will walk along virgin beaches and through native forests of rimu and kamahi where lush ferns and delicate orchids grow. Stewart Island is also renowned for its birdlife, and there are fewer predators here than on the mainland. Kaka, parakeets, tui, and bellbirds all flourish and perform a rousing dawn chorus. Offshore, you will see albatross, cormorants, and blue penguins; the rarer yellow-eyed penguin is also regularly seen. **PE**

Visit Madang Province

Location Madang, Papua New Guinea
Website www.pacificislandtravel.com   **Price** ◑

Almost totally destroyed during World War II, the picturesque coastal town of Madang was later rebuilt and has since become one of Papua New Guinea's major points of interest for overseas tourists. Often called the prettiest town in the South Pacific, it overlooks several islands, many of which are active volcanoes. These boast black sand beaches as opposed to the mostly untouched pristine white ones that line the mainland, where tropical rain forests cover the rugged mountains.

The region is famous for its underwater world, which is considered to be as beautiful as the waters of the Red Sea and the Great Barrier Reef. The dazzling coral gardens are teeming with wildlife, and the spectacular drop-offs in the clear waters attract divers from around the world, while those with a penchant for decaying man-made structures revel in the sight of the thirty-four ships that sank just off Bogia (in the north of Madang Province) during World War II. Small numbers of sunken ships and airplanes can still be found all along the coast, while further inland wetlands and Alpine meadows dominate the scenery. Just beyond the beaches, vanilla as well as coconut and cocoa plantations abound, while Madang Harbor, set against the backdrop of steep cliffs, is probably the most stunning port in the entire South Pacific.

Despite its natural beauty and decent infrastructure (and several charming resorts by the ocean), Papua New Guinea has not yet fully established itself as a tourist destination. The goods on display at the bustling street market are still aimed at the locals rather than any foreign visitors, and this refreshing innocence combined with the beautiful scenery make for a perfect place to get away from it all. **DaH**

Discover Vatulele Island

Location Vatulele Island, Fiji
Website www.sixsenses.com **Price** 🌑🌑🌑

Newly arrived guests emerge tentatively from their private thatched Fijian house or *bure* (pronounced "boo-ray") hidden in the beachside jungle. Shaking off their jet lag, they decide to test Vatulele Island Resort's internal communications. If they want anything—and that means anything—they simply have to raise a flag on their personal flagpole on the white-sand beach. A uniformed, barefoot waiter will promptly appear scurrying across the sand to take the order. With anything from chilled French champagne to fresh local seafood snacks available, flags are soon whizzing up and down the poles.

There is acclaimed diving and snorkeling along the reef, but it is the laid-back hours that characterize this resort. Egos dissolve in the easy warmth as barefoot bankers and off-duty celebrities foresake candlelit dining in their villas and choose to eat communally in the central open-sided *bure*. There is a cooperative, sustainable aura across the small island. The architecture is locally inspired, the kitchen uses seafood caught offshore and fresh produce from its own organic garden, and, unlike other luxury resorts, Vatulele staff do not call guests "Sir" or "Madam." Everyone is addressed by their first name.

Smiling villagers assemble to sing a welcome to guests at the airstrip, where tiny planes land on a path cut into the vegetation after a spectacular twenty-five-minute flight from Fiji airport. Cynical visitors who ask whether villagers are paid to deliver this welcome are always met with puzzled expressions. "We do it to welcome you to our island," they explain. **SH**

◄ *The combination of top-end luxury and beachcomber's informality makes Vatulele a top destination.*

Canoe at Kosrae Island

Location Kosrae Island, Micronesia
Website www.kosraevillage.com **Price** 🌑

Kosrae Island is one of Micronesia's least-developed islands. Lying southeast of Guam, it is the most easterly of the Caroline islands and has an impressive seagoing history—when you take to the waters here, know that you are doing it in the shadow of many, many others.

For a start, the island is supposed to have been settled in the first millennium by the seafaring people from the Marshall Islands of Vanuatu. These were the area's first and bravest explorers. Skip forward several hundred years, and the island was regularly visited by whaling parties, traders, and pirates. The infamous nineteenth-century pirate of the South Seas, Bully Hayes, supposedly left buried treasure on the island.

> *"Dive for a coral-monitoring project, learn to weave … and dine on coconut-smoked wahoo."*
>
> *National Geographic*

Naturally, a great way to explore is by boat. There are numerous diving and snorkeling trips to take out to the reefs, but the real delight is the Utwe-Walung Marine Park in the very south of the island. This protected area of mangrove channels offers a unique look at the forests and the ecosystem as you travel around them by traditional canoe. You can see the ancient stone ruins in the rain forest from the water, reach isolated beaches, and even come upon the site of Bully Hayes's famous shipwreck. Slow paddling takes you to parts of the island that are unreachable by foot and out to areas where you can snorkel in clear water and see the healthy coral beneath. **LD**

Unwind at Etu Moana

Location Aitutaki, Cook Islands
Website www.etumoana.com **Price** 💲💲

As you enter Aitutaki's rustic airport, you may have a sneaking suspicion that you have stumbled across paradise. Untouched by the modern world, this simple structure is filled with melodic local music and the heady aroma of handmade leis. A short ride away is Etu Moana: a boutique resort on one of the largest atolls in the Cook Islands.

With just eight villas, this exclusive hideaway is tucked away in a perfect location framed by a long, white, sugary beach and the warm crystal waters of a Pacific lagoon. Each of the Polynesian-style villas has an authentic thatched roof and exposed timbers, and

---

"Etu Moana does great foliage. In fact, the gardens are drop-dead gorgeous."

Yvonne van Dongen, *Listener* magazine

---

is filled with teak furniture and fresh linens. There is also a private garden and a spacious shaded veranda decorated with luxurious outdoor furnishings. The owners and staff at Etu Moana are delightful—nothing is too much trouble. Delicious breakfasts are served by a private pool surrounded by volcanic rocks and colorful gardens and there is also an honesty bar. The resort is also just a short stroll away from some of the island's best restaurants, which serve delicious eclectic local cuisine in candlelit settings. Choose whether to relax in your own romantic abode or to discover island life and explore the diverse culture above and below the waters of this charming paradise. **JH**

Relax at Bora Bora Lagoon Resort and Spa

Location Motu Toopua, Bora Bora
Website www.boraboralagoon.com **Price** 💲💲💲

Adam and Eve would feel at home in this small enclave of paradise where the air is heavy with the rich scent of hibiscus and the pristine beaches are fringed with palms. Bora Bora Lagoon Resort and Spa is set on the secluded island of Motu Toopua, a fragment of an ancient volcano on a shimmering turquoise lagoon.

The tiny island has no roads, no villages, and no nightlife, so visitors have no choice but to plunge headfirst into a world of laid-back luxury. The resort's accommodation can be found in Polynesian-style bungalows, thatched with pandanus leaves and decked out with polished wood interiors. There are forty-four over-water stilted bungalows, each one of which has a glass-topped coffee table from where guests can watch or feed the sea life.

Discover further serenity in the resort's beachfront spa, ringed by exotic basins, waterfalls, and lilies. Bathe in coconut milk and fresh flowers before receiving a massage in one of the treatment rooms, dramatically positioned in wooden cabins in the canopy of two large Banyan trees. Therapists use Polynesian products that incorporate local plants, flowers, and fruits, renowned for their benefits to the skin and hair. Honeymooners can choose to have treatments side by side in double massage rooms, followed by an exotic rain shower. If you tire of gazing dreamily into each other's eyes, the resort has a good, freshwater swimming pool, deep enough to practice scuba diving. Other activities include snorkeling, kayaking, shark-feeding excursions, and sunset cruises. **JK**

➡ *This view of the extinct volcanic peaks of Bora Bora must surely be one of the finest our planet has to offer.*

Relax at Le Taha'a

Location Taha'a, French Polynesia **Website** www.letahaa.com
Price $$$

Hot honeymoon destinations do not come any more exclusive than this. The ultimate hideaway, Le Taha'a Private Island & Spa is tucked away in the sparkling waters of French Polynesia. The flower-shaped island is located 143 miles (230 km) west of Tahiti and sits on its own coral atoll. Spread out at the foot of soft mountains, where farmers grow watermelons, vanilla, and copra, the resort is surrounded by tiny *motu*, or islets, with sandy beaches.

There are twelve cool and spacious beach villas, all with private pools, which are decorated in traditional Polynesian style and have wooden floors and thatched roofs. Or for something really special, stay in one of the over-water suites. Spend your day snorkeling in the coral gardens, relaxing on the white-sand beach, taking in the sweeping views of the lagoon and Bora Bora, or being pampered in the magnificent Manea Spa. Nestled in the shade of coconut groves between the meandering waters of a small lake and the lagoon, the spa has been built from natural materials to ensure that it merges perfectly with the environment. Try a Polynesian massage or treatment using pure natural oils and essences.

Whatever you do, it is impossible to escape the rich aroma of vanilla lingering in the air, the scent of traditional Tahitian life. This might only be a tiny island in the middle of the Pacific but there is no shortage of excellent cuisine. Indulge in an exquisite meal at Ohiri, the fine-dining restaurant hidden away among the trees in the middle of the island and watch Tahitian dancers perform while you eat. Bliss. **AD**

→ *The beach villas have their own private pool and tropical gardens, and are surrounded by rock walls.*

Fly into Space with Virgin Galactic

Location Space   **Website** www.virgingalactic.com   **Price** ⑨⑨⑨⑨

"[We make] the 'Final Frontier' a reality for tens of thousands of pioneering space tourists."

Will Whitehorn, Virgin Galactic President

⬆ *This shows White Knight and Spaceship One, the space vessel and its "mother ship" transport.*

➡ *A view like this is difficult to put into words. Imagine staring out at it from your passenger window.*

Imagine careering through that most enigmatic, mystifying terrain, the black space that is seen every night yet touched by so few. Imagine undertaking a journey past the stars on virgin odysseys said to leave an indelible mark. Imagine the ultimate escape, where so few people have gone before. This is a Kubrick-esque fantasy where budding astronauts will have the chance to venture into extra-terrestrial climes.

In a world where so little remains unexplored, Richard Branson's flagship spacecrafts are at the head of the new, commercial space race. Disembarking from the New Mexico spaceport close to Roswell, designed by the chief architect of otherworldly genius, Philippe Starck, your companions will comprise a two-man crew at the helm and five fellow space adventurers. Experience the sensation of weightlessness in this gravity- and belief-defying adventure as you are propelled over the sky, past the stars, and out into space. This trip will take up only two and a half hours of your life, but those hours will change you forever.

After three days' training, in which every care is taken to prepare you for an experience for which nothing can fundamentally prepare you, you will follow in the path of previous space-buccaneers and adventurers as the sky morphs from blue to mauve to indigo to black. Eerie, startling silence engulfs as Mother Earth is left behind you, as you ascend gently and smoothly into the galaxy.

It is a privilege that has been reserved for a very few—and at $200,000 it will remain so—representing the future, the past, and all the mysteries of human existence. Forthcoming expeditions include a plan to fly through the Aurora Borealis. Who knows? Maybe, one day, we will all have our chance to fly through the stars and experience the ultimate escape. **VG**

General Index

Contributors

(AD) Angela Dewar is a travel writer and photographer who travels extensively. She is a specialist on India and the Far East, contributing to travel guides and consumer and trade magazines in the U.K. and U.S.

(AM) Andy Moss is a travel writer based in the U.K.

(BS) Barry Stone is a travel writer based in Sydney, Australia. A compulsive traveler, he has co-authored books on geography, history, and architecture. Stories of his wanderings have appeared in some of Australia's leading newspapers, including Sydney's *Sun-Herald* and *The Canberra Times*.

(CD) Christabelle Dilks chose Argentina as her place of escape twenty years after leaving dramatically during the Falklands War. In 1982, she was living with her family on the edge of the Pampas, and was in love with an Argentine man. In 2002, she returned to fall in love all over again, this time with the wild landscapes and wonderful people. Argentina remains her place of dreams.

(CK) Carol King is a freelance writer based in London, England and a small town in Sicily, Italy. She has lived in Madrid, Spain and Buenos Aires, Argentina, and her appetite for travel has seen her track gorillas in Uganda, climb Adam's Peak in Sri Lanka, visit salt mines in Poland, and puff cigars in Cuba.

(CM) Chris Moss lived in Argentina for 10 years. He is the author of *Patagonia: A Cultural History*, published in 2008.

(CFM) Caroline Mills has been a magazine editor for twelve years and a freelance writer for two years. She specializes in travel throughout Europe, particularly lesser-known places and gardens. She has written for many U.K. publications, including *French Magazine*, *The Times*, *Practical Motorhome*, *France Magazine*, and *Great British Food* and is currently working on another travel book.

(CR) Claire Rigby is a British writer and editor who has lived in many countries, including Hong Kong, Kuwait, Brazil, and the U.S. She is currently based in Argentina, where she is editor of *Time Out*'s *Buenos Aires for Visitors* magazine.

(CSJ) Caroline Sylger-Jones is a spa and retreat specialist and the author of *Body & Soul Escapes* and *Body & Soul escapes: Britain and Ireland*. She writes regular reviews and features for newspapers and magazines, which include *The National* in the UAE, and the *Daily Telegraph*, *The Times*, *Guardian*, *Condé Nast Traveler*, *Wanderlust*, *Red*, and *Psychologies* in the U.K. Based in Devon, she's at her happiest when walking the southwest coastal path. *www.carolinesylgerjones.co.uk*

(CW) Chrissy Williams is half-English, half-Italian, and has traveled extensively worldwide. She has written for a variety of British travel publications and organizations, including *Italian Magazine*, *Red Guide Florida*, *Weddings and Honeymoons*, and the Portuguese Chamber of Commerce.

(DA) David Atkinson is a travel writer based in Chester, England. He writes for U.K. newspapers the *Observer*, *Sunday Telegraph*, and *Daily Express*. He is the author of *Bolivia: The Bradt Travel Guide* and his Bolivia feature

for *Wanderlust* magazine was named Latin America Travel Association (LATA) Article of the Year in 2008. *www.atkinsondavid.co.uk*

(DaH) David Hutter was born in Germany and briefly lived in both England and France during his teens. After finishing high school he moved to Italy for a lackluster and ultimately futile attempt at studying economics. Two years later, he moved to England to study creative writing and religious studies at Middlesex University. Having travelled extensively in Europe, the Middle East, Asia, and Australasia, he now works as a freelance writer and editor and is based in London.

(DN) Daniel Neilson is a freelance journalist and guidebook editor. He has contributed words and pictures to *Four Four Two*, *CNN Traveler*, and *The Wire* among many others, and has edited five guides for *Time Out*.

(EP) Eleanor Parkman has written about her travel experiences for U.K. newspaper the *Observer* among other publications. She met her husband while living in Turin, and they now live in London with their two daughters.

(GC) Greg Clarke is an Australian writer who contributes regularly to magazines in Australia and Asia. He once lived in London's East End, which proved handy while he was at the *Sunday Times*. When he's not traveling or writing, his daughters take him on trips in search of the fairies that live around their house.

(GMD) Giles MacDonogh A former Paris resident, Giles MacDonogh wrote about luxurious destinations for the *Financial Times* for fifteen years. He is also an authority on food and drink, and is Chairman of the juries for Germany and Austria at the World Wine Awards. MacDonogh has written for many publications, including *The Times*, *Guardian*, *Specator*, *New Statesman*, and, more recently, *Standpoint*. He received a Glenfiddich Special Award in 1988 and is the author of thirteen books, many of them about Germany.

(HA) Helen Arnold is a travel and food and drink journalist with over 17 years' experience. She has contributed to a wide range of newspapers and magazines, including the *Observer*, *High Life*, *Scotland on Sunday*, *Travel Weekly*, *Woman & Home*, *Family Circle*, *Harpers Wine & Spirits*, *Zest*, and *Eve*. She has also written for corporate clients, including the Orient Express Group, Easy Jet, and Thomas Cook. First bitten by the travel bug after a year-long, around-the-world trip in 1992, she has lived in Oman in the Middle East and has since settled in London, where she lives with her husband and children.

(HO) Helen Ochyra is a freelance travel writer. She has lived in California and is now based in north London. She currently contributes to many publications, including the *Guardian*, *Observer*, and *Time Out*.

(IA) Ismay Atkins is a travel writer and editor based in the wild western reaches of Cornwall, England. She writes about travel for a range of publications, including the *Independent*, *Rough Guide*, and *Time Out*, and regularly edits books for *Time Out* guides. Thanks to a long-standing fascination with Latin America, Ismay has lived in Havana, rural Mexico, and Buenos Aires.

(JA) Jane Archer is a freelance travel journalist and one of the U.K.'s leading cruise writers. She has a weekly column on the *Telegraph* online and has contributed to the *Daily Telegraph*, *House and Garden*, and *Condé Nast Traveler*, among a host of other titles.

(JC) Joe Cawley is an award-winning travel writer based in Tenerife, Canary Islands. He has written for many publications, including the *Sunday Times*, *New York Post*, and *Condé Nast Traveler*. His first book, *More Ketchup than Salsa*, was voted Best Travel Narrative 2007 by the British Guild of Travel Writers.

(JD) James Durston has written for numerous publications, which include *Travel Weekly*, the *Independent*, and the *Express*. He spent his formative years in East Africa, one developmental year in Japan, and has spent the last two years trying not to fall in love with India. It hasn't worked, so he currently lives in the middle of Mumbai, India.

(JED) Judy Darley is a U.K. travel writer who has contributed extensively to *Portugal Magazine*, *Greece Magazine*, and *The Italian Magazine*. Before becoming a freelance writer, she was the Features Editor for *Spanish Homes Magazine*. She recently completed her first novel.

(JDA) Jess Darby is a former BBC Magazines journalist (writing for *Eve* and *Vegetarian Good Food*) turned freelance feature writer. She spent her formative years in places as diverse as Ibiza, Zimbabwe, and Ireland before settling in southwest London, England with the three men in her life and Digby the dog.

(JF) Joe Fullman has been a travel writer for over ten years, during which time he has written for many of the major international guidebook publishers, including Rough Guides, Lonely Planet, A.A., and Cadogan. He is the author of guides to Costa Rica, Belize, London, England, Paris, Berlin, Venice, and Las Vegas, and has also contributed to guides to Italy, Turkey, Central America, and the Caribbean. He is currently based in London, England.

(JH) Jane Hannon had her first short story published in the 2007 travel anthology *More Sand in My Bra* and has also written for *Psychologies* magazine. A freelance writer based in Essex, she's had 24 jobs, explored 34 countries, and has lived and worked in New York and Australia.

(JK) Janine Kelso is based in London, England, and has written for *Travel Weekly* and numerous women's magazines. She has a special passion for Latin America after spending nine months traveling there. Her other specialist areas include the Caribbean and Poland. While at university, she spent two summers living and working in the United States, in New York, Colorado, and Maryland. Her trips often include an extreme sports element, such as rock climbing, surfing, skiing, or skydiving.

(JP) Jacqui Paterson is a travel and features journalist, with 15 years' experience writing for newspapers and magazines in New Zealand, Australia, and the United Kingdom. Her travels have included parachuting onto a beach in northern Queensland, bungy jumping over the Zambesi River in Zambia, and swimming among the icebergs in the Arctic Circle.

(JS) Jessica Stone grew up a Cuban American in Miami before studying journalism in New York. She has contributed to a variety of international publications, including the *New York Times*, *The Times*, *Guardian*, and *Men's Health*. *Ripelondon.com* is a website that chronicles her dining and dating journeys in her adoptive home in London, England.

(JW) James Williams is a U.K., London-based travel journalist specializing in Greece, and writes for a host of U.K. magazines. His travels have taken him everywhere across the world, from far-flung tropical islands to hidden corners of Athens, Greece.

(KF) Kathryn Farmer worked in legal publishing for fifteen years and, following a career break when her children were very young, now works as a freelance writer and has written for many U.K. publications.

(LB) Lydia Bell currently lives in London, England and was the deputy travel editor of *Harper's Bazaar*. She has lived in (or spent months hanging out in) Scotland, Spain, Greece, India, and Australia.

(LC) Lucia Cockcroft traveled around Spain for Rough Guides and is the Spanish writer for *Luxury Travel Magazine*. She recently contributed to *Body & Soul*, and also writes for *EasyJet Inflight* and *Overseas Living Magazine*.

(LD) Laura Dixon writes about style, travel, and trends for fashion magazines and travel publications. She reviews boutique hotels for I-escape.com, and has been featured in *Sunday Times Travel Magazine*, *Sunday Express*, *Business Life*, and many more. She is a member of the British Guild of Travel Writers.

(LGS) Lisa Gerard-Sharp is an award-winning journalist and travel writer who has lived in Paris, Brussels, Rome, and Tuscany. Although currently based in London, England, she spends much of her time traveling and researching features for *Vogue*,

for whom she is correspondent, as well as contributing to national newspapers and magazines in the U.K. and abroad.

(LJ) Lisa Johnson was an arts writer at *The Bulletin* in Brussels, Belgium for three years before switching to travel to continue using her languages (French, German, and Spanish). Now based in London, England, she has written for a number of publications including *Condé Nast Traveler*, *House and Garden*, *Red*, *Evening Standard*, *Guardian*, *Spectator*, and the *Daily Mail*.

(LM) Linda McCormick is the senior writer and editor for news website *Environmental Graffiti* and content editor of *EcoTravelLogue.com*. She has traveled extensively, having put down roots for a while in Australia, but now lives in London, England; although she continually threatens to move to Barcelona, Spain.

(LP) Lisa Pollen is an experienced U.K. London-based journalist, specializing in the luxury travel and celebrity market. Formerly the Features Editor at *Star* and *OK!* (Hot Stars), she contributes to publications including the *Daily Express*, *Now*, *Closer*, *She*, and various in-flight magazines.

(ML) Martin Li has a passion for exploring the adventure and culture of the world's great mountain regions. He is the author of *Inca Trails*, the story of a journey across the Andes tracing the rise and fall of the Inca empire, and *Adventure Guide to Scotland*.

(MN) Mari Nicholson is an award-winning travel writer based in the Isle of Wight. Published by major outlets including *Guardian*, *The Times*, *BBC History*, *Wanderlust*, and the major inflight magazines, she is the feature

writer for east Asia on the online travel magazine of *www.suite101.com*.

(NB) Nick Bruno is an Anglo-Italian journalist who divides his time between Scotland and Italy, writing and taking photographs for various publications. His latest book, *Naples and Amalfi Coast*, is published by Footprint.

(NS) Nicola Smith is a freelance journalist based in Cornwall, England. She has written travel features for a number of different titles, including *The Times*, New Zealand's *World*, *Coast*, and *Cornwall Today*.

(OM) Olivia Mackinder is a travel and lifestyle writer, for print, online, and television. An N.L.P. Practitioner, she is also now in the process of setting up her own retreat center in the U.K.

(PE) Polly Evans is a London-based award-winning travel journalist who writes for publications that include the *Independent on Sunday*, *Wanderlust*, *Condé Nast Traveler*, and *Food and Wine*. She has also written five travel books, including *It's Not About the Tapas* and *Mad Dogs and an Englishwoman*.

(PS) Paul Sullivan is a Berlin-based writer/photographer specializing in travel and music. His articles have appeared in many publications, including the *Independent*, *Observer Music Monthly*, *Fly Europe*, *National Geographic Music*, BBC magazines, and others. His previous travel books include *A Hedonist's Guide To Berlin*, *Marrakech & Prague*, *Time Out Italy*, and *Cool Camping France* and *Cool Camping Europe*.

(RB) Rory Brogan is a U.K. journalist who has traveled extensively in South America.

(RCA) Rowena Carr-Allinson has been published in everything from the *Toronto Star* to London's *Metro*, *Elle*, *Harper's Bazaar*, *OK!*, and many more. She has traveled from Buenos Aires to Bankgok via Maui and Moscow, and can't decide if home is in France or the U.K. *www.carrallinson.com*

(RS) Richard Siddle is an award-winning U.K. business journalist. A former editor of *Travel Weekly*, he currently travels the world as editor of *Harpers Wine & Spirits* magazine.

(RsP) Roger St. Pierre has visited 125 countries and counting during his long and illustrious career as a travel writer and broadcaster. He is the author of 33 published books including a number of bestselling travel guides, as well as works on cycling and music.

(SB) Sam Baldwin specializes in Japan, adventure, and winter sports writing, especially off-the-beaten-path locations. He is the editor of *SnowSphere.com* and has also contributed to the *Guardian*, the *Scotsman*, and Footprint books, and is also a columnist for several ski and snowboard magazines.

(SD) Sally Dowling is a freelance travel writer based in the U.K. She is a regular contributor to *Take a Break* magazine and associated titles and was the winner of the 2006 Visit U.S.A. Media Travel Award. She specializes in finding memorable hotels and unique resorts. *www.sallydowling.co.uk*

(SG) Si Gray began his writing career as editor for Itchy U.K. city guides. He has visited over fifty countries, compiling his observations on the popular food and travel blog featured on *jamieoliver.com*, which is being published in extended form.

(SH) Simon Heptinstall is a U.K. author, journalist, and broadcaster who visited 23 countries in his first year as a travel writer and once even held the world record for the most countries visited in one day (12). His ultimate escape, however, remains his quiet family house on the edge of a village in rural Wiltshire, England.

(SM) Shona Main, a Shetlander, started out as Pop Editor of *Jackie* and pursued lackluster careers in law and politics before settling back into journalism. She splits her time between Scotland and Italy, and her latest book is the *Footprint Guide to Venice and the Veneto*.

(SoH) Solange Hando is a professional travel writer. She has won a number of awards and contributes to a broad range of publications worldwide. She is a member of the British Guild of Travel Writers and Travel Writers U.K.

(SP) Sudi Pigott is passionately committed to good food and travels widely in pursuit of new gastronomic experiences. Sudi writes on food, restaurants, and travel for a wide range of international publications, including *TIME* magazine, *FT How to Spend It*, *High Life*, *Centurion*, *Delicious*, and *The Good Food Guide*.

(SWa) Sue Watt is a freelance travel writer based in London. She mainly specializes in Africa, inspired by her belated gap year traveling across the continent. Sue contributes regularly to *Travel Africa Magazine* and is also published in British publications such as the *Guardian*, and *Italy Magazine*.

(SWi) Stephanie Wilson made the most of her long vacations as a teacher to travel extensively in Europe and Turkey, before giving up the profession to focus on travel writing.

(TL) Tim Locke's writing spans many subjects, from national parks, walks, and numerous regions of Britain; rail travel in Europe; and guides to New England and Thailand. He is also a consultant in sustainable travel and an editor of the *Good Pub Guide*. He lives in Lewes in southeast England.

(TM) Teresa Machan sees life as one big adventure where she can go pearl-diving in Panama or get tips from a gondolier in Venice. She has been published in more than 20 worldwide travel publications, including national newspapers, guidebooks, and magazines. Lucky enough to have lived in Hong Kong, she returns regularly to Asia while continuing her globe-trotting.

(TW) Tina Walsh is a freelance journalist specializing in travel and lifestyle. She has written for the *Guardian*, *Sunday Times*, and *Daily Mail*, among many others, and is a contributor to the Dorling Kindersley *Eyewitness Guide* series.

(VG) Victoria Gill is an author, broadcaster, and journalist for U.K. Channel Five, *Mr. and Mrs. Smith*, and the *Sunday Times*, among others. A bonafide globetrotter living in Highgate, London, she is the author of *Cityspots Fez*, published in 2009.

(WG) Wendy Gomersall spent ten years on staff at the *Daily Mail*, and went freelance in 2000. She is now a freelance travel writer, writing for many newspapers, magazines and websites, including the *Mail on Sunday*, *TravelMail.co.uk*, *ABTA magazine*, and the *Scotsman* magazine. She has also written for the *Daily Mail*, *Zest*, the *Guardian*, and many other local newspapers and international magazines.

2 Johnny Stockshooter / Photolibrary.com **20** Little Good Harbour **22** Pep Roig / Alamy **24** Inn on the Lake **25** Stefan Wackerhagen **26** AlaskaStock / Photolibrary.com **27** Buddy Mays / Alamy **29** Clayoquot Wilderness Resort **30** Poets Cove **31** Mowgli Frere / Frere Images **32** All Canada Photos / Alamy **34** Fairmont Chateau **36** Baker Creek Chalets **38** AndrC Kedl **39** AndrC Kedl **41** All Canada Photos / Photoshot **45** John Shaw / Photoshot **47** Michael S. Lewis/Corbis **48** Sundance **51** The Point **54** Wave Hill Gardens **55** Gramercy Park Hotel **56** Waldorf-Astoria and Waldorf Towers **58** Della Huff / Alamy **60** East Brother Light Station **62** Calistoga Ranch **63** Spa Vitale **64** Philip Lee Harvey / Getty **68** Radius Images / Photolibrary.com **71** All Canada Photos / Photoshot **73** Cody Duncan / Alamy **75** Mii Amo **76** Mowgli Frere / Frere Images **77** Ml Sinibaldi / Photolibrary.com **80** The Setai **85** Rod McLean / Alamy **86** Kevin Spreekmeester / Photolibrary.com **88** David Muench/Corbis **89** Peter French / Photolibrary.com **90** nik wheeler / Alamy **92** Esperanza Resort **93** Las Ventanas Al Paraiso **94** Blaine Harrington III / Alamy **96** One&Only Palmilla **98** Cuixmala **102** Hemis / Alamy **103** M. Timothy O'Keefe / Alamy **104** Esencia **107** La Lancha **108** Nitun Reserve **111** Blancaneaux **112** Stephen Frink Collection / Alamy **115** Mowgli Frere / Frere Images **116** Christabelle Dilks **118** Bob Stefko / Getty **122** IML Image Group Ltd / Alamy **125** Musha Cay **126** Parrot Cay **128** Danita Delimont / Alamy **130** Alex Bartel / Photoshot **133** Rolf Nussbaumer / Alamy **134** The Caves **137** Biras Creek **138** Jean-Marc Lecerf (Ocean Images) / Photoshot **140** Rodger Klein / Photolibrary.com **143** La Samanna **144** Tom Bean/Corbis **147** Tim Larsen-Collinge / Photoshot **148** Rock Cottage **150** Jade Mountain **153** Jean-Marc Lecerf (Ocean Images) / Photoshot **154** Charlie Knight / Alamy **156** Palm Island **157** L'Anse aux Epines **161** Pies Specifics / Alamy **162** Jose Enrique Molina / Photolibrary.com **164** Arco Digital Images / Tips **165** Rosemary Calvert / Photolibrary.com **167** Andoni Canela / Photolibrary.com **169** Vidler Vidler / Photolibrary.com **170** Hotel Monasterio **173** Jason Rothe / Alamy **176** Image Brokers / Photoshot **178** De Agostini / Photoshot **179** Worldwide Picture Library / Alamy **180** Interfoto / Alamy **185** Villas de Trancoso **186** Fasano Hotel **188** Robert Harding Picture Library Ltd / Alamy **190** Frédéric Soreau / Photononstop / Tips **193** Ponta dos Ganchos **194** Frédéric Soreau / Photononstop / Tips **197** Sunset / Tips **198** Elqui Domos **200** Secret Ranchito **201** Hemis / Photoshot **203** Cephas Picture Library / Alamy **205** Christabelle Dilks **207** Martin Harvey / Photoshot **209** Javier Etcheverry / Alamy **210** Eduardo Longoni/Corbis **212** Christabelle Dilks **214** Estancia El Colibrí **219** Faena Hotel **221** Christabelle Dilks **223** Christabelle Dilks **225** Christabelle Dilks **227** Ismay Atkins **229** David Tipling / Photoshot **230** Castello di Vicarello **233** blickwinkel / Alamy **235** StockPile Collection / Alamy **236** Gregory Gerault / Photolibrary.com **238** Danita Delimont / Alamy **240** Blue Lagoon **243** Chad Ehlers / Tips **244** Hotel Kakslauttanen **246** Snow Castle **248** Finland Tourist Board **250** Arctic-Images/Corbis **251** Hans Strand/Corbis **252** Nordic Light Hotel **255** Yasuragi **256** Frank Chmura / Alamy **261** OJPhotos / Alamy **262** Park Hotel Kenmare **264** Temple County retreat **267** John Warburton-Lee Photography / Alamy **268** Ard Nahoo **269** O fabulous **271** Belle Isle Castle **272** Radius Images / Alamy **275** Derek Croucher / Alamy **276** Rua Reidh Lighthouse **278** Paul Glendell / Alamy **281** Alistair Petrie / Alamy **285** Hebridean Princess **286** The Witchery **289** james jagger / Alamy **291** Steve Peake, St. Curig's Church **292** Eco Retreat **295** Mint Photography / Alamy **296** Les Gibbon / Alamy **299** Roger Coulam / Alamy **303** Le Manoir **304** Oxford Picture Library / Alamy **307** The Victoria **311** james kerr / Alamy **313** Ellen Rooney / Photolibrary.com **314** Terry Williams / Getty **316** Alamy **319** SenSpa **322** Royal Crescent Hotel **325** Lundy Island Tourism **328** ImagesEurope / Alamy **331** Marc Hill / Alamy **332** way out west photography / Alamy **334** Arco Digital Images / Tips **338** Liz Garnett / Alamy **341** Island of Rugen **342** Carsten Koall/Stringer / Getty **345** 68images 68images / Photolibrary.com **348** Bildagentur RM / Tips **351** Martin Rugner / Photolibrary.com **353** imagebroker / Alamy **356** Camille Moirenc / Photononstop / Tips **358** Yann Guichaoua / Tips **359** Arco Digital Images / Tips **361** Steve Vidler / Photolibrary.com **365** S.Nicolas / Photolibrary.com **367** TTL Images / Alamy **368** Bateau Simpatico **371** Roy Rainford / Photolibrary.com **375** Picture Contact / Alamy **376** Tristan Deschamps / Tips **379** Hemis / Photoshot **380** Robert Harding Picture Library Ltd / Alamy **383** Yann Guichaoua / Tips **384** A. Demotes / Tips **387** Jupiter Images / Agence Images / Alamy **389** Les Fermes de Marie **392** Marion Bull / Alamy **397** Emmanuel Lattes / Alamy **399** Papilio / Alamy **400** Abbaye de Sainte Croix **402** tbkmedia.de / Alamy **405** Hemis / Photolibrary.com **406** Le Couvent des Minimes Spa **408** Horse and Ventures **412** Arco Digital Images / Tips **417** Piotr & Irena Kolasa / Alamy **419** Dumrath Dumrath / Photolibrary.com **421** imagebroker / Alamy **422** Liebes Rot-Fluh Hotel **425** Corbis / Photolibrary.com **426** Bella Tola **427** The Lodge **428** Riffelalp Resort **431** Lisa Pollen **433** Daniele Comoglio / Alamy **434** CuboImages srl / Alamy **437** Brian Lawrence / Photolibrary.com **438** L'Albereta **441** Vigilius **442** Roy Rainford / Photolibrary.com **444** Bauer Palladio **446** David Noton Photography / Alamy **449** Mark Bolton / Photolibrary.com **453** Silwen Randebrock / Photolibrary.com **457** Arco Digital Images / Tips **459** The Travel Library Limited / Photolibrary.com **460** Todi Castle **463** La Posta